HUMAN SEXUALITY 81/82

Ollie Pocs, *Editor*
Illinois State University

ANNUAL EDITIONS

The Dushkin Publishing Group, Inc. Sluice Dock, Guilford, Ct. 06437

Volumes in the Annual Editions Series

- Abnormal Psychology
- ● Aging
- ● American Government
- ● American History, Pre-Civil War
- ● American History, Post-Civil War
- ● Anthropology
- Astronomy
- ● Biology
- ● Business
- Comparative Government
- ● Criminal Justice
- Death and Dying
- ● Deviance
- ● Early Childhood Education
- Earth Science
- ● Economics
- ● Educating Exceptional Children
- ● Education
- Educational Psychology
- Energy
- ● Environment
- Ethnic Studies
- Foreign Policy
- Geography
- Geology
- ● Health
- ● Human Development
- ● Human Sexuality
- ● Management
- ● Marketing
- ● Marriage and Family
- ● Personal Growth and Adjustment
- Philosophy
- Political Science
- ● Psychology
- Religion
- ● Social Problems
- ● Sociology
- ● Urban Society
- ● Western Civilization, Pre-history – Reformation
- ● Western Civilization, Early Modern – 20th-Century
- Women's Studies
- World History
- ● World Politics

● Indicates currently available

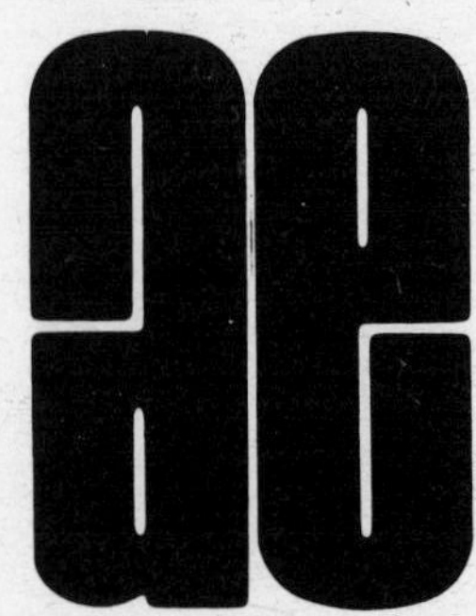

Sixth Edition

Manufactured by George Banta Company, Menasha, Wisconsin, 54952

ADVISORY BOARD

Members of the Advisory Board are instrumental in the final selection of articles for each year's edition of *Annual Editions.* Their review of articles for content, level, and appropriateness provides critical direction to the editor and staff. We think you'll find their careful consideration well reflected in this volume.

Colin Box
University of Missouri at Columbia

Iris Praeger-Decker
George Mason University

Thomas Eckle
Modesto Junior College

Annette G. Godow
The College of Charleston

Narendra Kalia
SUNY College
Buffalo

Frances O'Keefe
Tidewater Community College
Virginia Beach

Mina Robbins
California State University
Sacramento

Helene Sloan
CUNY, Brooklyn College

Doris Sands
University of Maryland
College Park

David R. York
Seminole Community College

AND STAFF

Rick Connelly, Publisher
Ian A. Nielsen, Program Manager
Celeste Borg, Editor
Addie Kawula, Acquisitions Editor
Brenda Filley, Production Manager
Cheryl Kinne, Permissions Coordinator
Charles Vitelli, Designer
Sharon M. Canning, Graphics Coordinator
Libra VonOgden, Typesetter

CONTENTS

1 Sexuality and Society

2 Sexual Biology and Health

3 Interpersonal Relationships

4 Sexuality Through the Life Cycle

5 Continuing Sexual Concerns

B. SEXUAL HARASSMENT AND VIOLENCE

C. SEXUAL ORIENTATION: BISEXUALITY AND HOMOSEXUALITY

D. SEX IN SPECIAL SITUATIONS

TOPIC GUIDE

This topic guide can be used to correlate each of the articles in *Annual Editions: Human Sexuality 81/82* to one or more of the topics normally covered by human sexuality books. Each article corresponds to a given topic area according to whether it deals with the subject in a primary or secondary fashion. These correlations are intended for use as a general study guide and do not necessarily define the total coverage of any given article.

TOPIC AREA	TREATED AS A PRIMARY ISSUE IN:	TREATED AS A SECONDARY ISSUE IN:
Abortion	22. 80% of Americans Believe Abortion Should Be Legal 23. The Abortion Repeaters 24. The Husband's Rights in Abortion	18. Fetal Adoption
Adolescent Sexuality	8. Reflections of a Dean Who Is "Into Sex" 37. A Major Problem for Minors 38. A Pregnant Pause in the Sexual Revolution	14. Young, Single and Pregnant 28. The Games Teen-Agers Play
Aging and Sex	43. Is There Sex After 40? 44. The New Sex Education and the Aging	13. The Male Orgasm 47. Menopause Counseling
Birth Control	20. Rating the Latest Methods of Birth Control 21. Birth Control Methods 22. 80% of Americans Believe Abortion Should Be Legal	37. A Major Problem for Minors
Bisexuality	54. Bisexuality	2. Alfred C. Kinsey 25. The Friendship Bond 55. The Meaning of Gay
Childhood Sexuality	35. Kids and Sex	6. What You Tell Your Child About Sex 7. Putting Sex Education Back in the Home 9. The Battle over Sex Education in New Jersey
Communication	6. What You Tell Your Child About Sex 30. The Semantics of Sex	28. The Games Teen-Agers Play 32. New Rules in the Mating Game
Cultural Values	3. Learning to Talk About Sex 4. Sexuality and College Life	8. Reflections of a Dean Who Is "Into Sex" 9. The Battle over Sex Education in New Jersey 19. Margaret Sanger
Equality and Sex	49. Sexual Harassment on the Job	24. The Husband's Rights in Abortion 33. The Perfect Lover 36. Adolescent Sexuality
Extramarital Relations	41. Infidelity and Extramarital Relations 42. Swingers	
Family Planning	14. Young, Single and Pregnant 15. Warning: Cigarette Smoking Is Dangerous to Reproductive Health 17. Barren Couples	16. Genetic Counseling: Is It Right for You?
Gender Roles	29. First Night Disasters 32. New Rules in the Mating Game	6. What You Tell Your Child About Sex 26. Intimacy Is Not for Amateurs 28. The Games Teen-Agers Play 36. Adolescent Sexuality
Handicapped and Sex	57. Love, Sex and Marriage 58. How the Handicapped Make Love	48. Sex and Heart Disease 59. Enjoying Sex During Pregnancy
Health	15. Warning: Cigarette Smoking Is Dangerous to Reproductive Health 16. Genetic Counseling 17. Barren Couples 29. First Night Disasters 48. Sex and Heart Disease	47. Menopause Counseling
Homosexuality	55. The Meaning of Gay 56. A Message to Parents of Gays 60. Prison Sexology	1. The Pleasure Bond 2. Alfred C. Kinsey
Infertility	17. Barren Couples 18. Fetal Adoption	
Intimate Relations	25. The Friendship Bond 26. Intimacy Is Not for Amateurs 27. Sex: The 3 Levels of Intimacy	1. The Pleasure Bond 32. New Rules in the Mating Game
Interpersonal Sexuality	4. Sexuality and College Life 29. First Night Disasters 31. What Is Your Sexual Respon-sibility to Your Mate?	27. Sex: The 3 Levels of Intimacy 36. Adolescent Sexuality 39. Marital Relations
Love and Attraction	25. The Friendship Bond 26. Intimacy Is Not for Amateurs 28. The Games Teen-Agers Play	32. New Rules in the Mating Game
Marital Sexuality	39. Marital Relations 40. Is There Sex After Marriage? 43. Is There Sex After 40?	17. Barren Couples 41. Infidelity and Extramarital Relations 42. Swingers
Masturbation	60. Prison Sexology	11. All About the Clitoris 13. The Male Orgasm
Menopause	47. Menopause Counseling	44. The New Sex Education and the Aging

TOPIC AREA	TREATED AS A PRIMARY ISSUE IN:	TREATED AS A SECONDARY ISSUE IN:
Myths and Stereotypes		13. The Male Orgasm 44. The New Sex Education and the Aging 47. Menopause Counseling
Orgasm, Female	11. All About the Clitoris	13. The Male Orgasm
Orgasm, Male	13. The Male Orgasm	
Physiology	11. All About the Clitoris 12. Women's Most Versatile Muscle	47. Menopause Counseling
Pornography	53. Erotica and Pornography	
Pregnancy/ Childbearing	15. Warning: Cigarette Smoking is Dangerous to Reproductive Health 16. Genetic Counseling 17. Barren Couples	59. Enjoying Sex During Pregnancy
Psychosexual Health	10. The Most Erotic Part of Your Body	27. Sex: The 3 Levels of Intimacy 34. The 10 Common Sexual Spoilers for Women
Quality Sexual Relations	33. The Perfect Lover 34. The 10 Common Sexual Spoilers for Women	4. Sexuality and College Life 31. What Is Your Sexual Responsibility to Your Mate?
Rape	51. Rape 52. The Marital Rape Exemption	30. The Semantics of Sex 60. Prison Sexology

TOPIC AREA	TREATED AS A PRIMARY ISSUE IN:	TREATED AS A SECONDARY ISSUE IN:
Sex Education	6. What You Tell Your Child About Sex 7. Putting Sex Education Back in the Home 8. Reflections of a Dean Who Is "Into Sex" 9. The Battle over Sex Education in New Jersey	28. The Games Teen-Agers Play 35. Kids and Sex 37. A Major Problem for Minors
Sexual Dysfunction, Female		11. All About the Clitoris 29. First Night Disasters
Sexual Dysfunction, Male	13. The Male Orgasm 29. First Night Disasters	40. Is There Sex After Marriage?
Sexual Research/ Study	2. Alfred C. Kinsey: Man and Method	1. The Pleasure Bond 3. Learning to Talk About Sex
Sociosexual Attitudes/Change	1. The Pleasure Bond 2. Alfred C. Kinsey 3. Learning to Talk About Sex 4. Sexuality and College Life	13. The Male Orgasm 30. The Semantics of Sex 53. Erotica and Pornography
Teenage Pregnancy	14. Young, Single and Pregnant 38. A Pregnant Pause in the Sexual Revolution	37. A Major Problem for Minors
V.D.	29. First Night Disasters	38. A Pregnant Pause in the Sexual Revolution
Virginity		28. The Games Teen-Agers Play 36. Adolescent Sexuality

PREFACE

> Sex lies at the root of life, and we can never learn to reverence life until we know how to understand sex.
>
> —Havelock Ellis

The above quote by one of the first sexologists highlights the objective of this book. Learning about sex is a life-long process that can occur informally or formally. With knowledge comes the understanding that we are all born sexual, and that sex, per se, is neither good nor bad, beautiful nor ugly, moral nor immoral.

While we are all born with basic sexual interests, drives, and desires, human sexuality is a dynamic and complex force that involves psychological and socio-cultural dimensions in addition to the physiological. That is, sexuality includes an individual's whole body and personality. We are not born with a fully developed body or mind, but instead grow and learn; so it is with respect to our sexuality. Sexuality is learned. We learn what "appropriate" sexual behavior is, how to express it, when to do so, and under what circumstances. We also learn sexual feelings: in some cases positive feelings accepting our sexuality; in others, negative and repressive feelings such as guilt.

This rich subject, sexuality, which effects human life so basically and powerfully, has, until recently, received little attention in scientific research and even less attention within communities of higher education. Yet our contemporary social environment is undoubtedly expanding its sexual horizons toward greater freedom for the individual. Without proper understanding, this expansion in sexual freedom can lead to new forms of sexual bondage as easily as to increased joy and pleasure. The celebration of sexuality today is most likely found somewhere between the traditional, rigid, repressive morality that is our socio/sexual heritage, and a new performance oriented, irresponsible, self-seeking mentality. Our goal in seeking to understand sexuality is not concerned with knowing how to "do it the right way," with specific acts or "supertechniques." Rather, we seek a joyful acceptance of being sexual and expressing this awareness in the most considerate way for ourselves and our sexual partners. There is no substitute for learning to understand the sexuality of each person individually.

The articles selected for this edition cover a wide range of important topics and are written primarily by well-known professionals for the non-professional audience. Health educators, psychologists, sexologists, sociologists, and sex therapists present their views on how and why sexual attitudes are developed, maintained, and changed. Various types of sexual activity are examined and described. This edition of *Annual Editions: Human Sexuality 81/82* is organized into five major sections. Sexuality and Society discusses the changing society and sexuality, and sex education. Sexual Biology and Health, the second section, covers such topics as the human body and its sexual responses, healthy reproduction, and reproductive control. The third section, Interpersonal Relationships, deals with friendships, establishing sexual intimacy, and the responsibility and quality of sexual relationships. Sexuality Through the Life Cycle looks at what happens sexually throughout the individual's lifetime from childhood to the later years. Finally, Continuing Sexual Concerns covers sexually transmitted diseases, sexual functioning, sexual orientation, violence, sex and the handicapped, and sex and prison populations.

The articles have been reviewed for quality, currency, and interest by the Annual Editions staff and the members of the Advisory Board listed at the beginning of this anthology. I also wish to express appreciation for the help and support provided by my colleagues Robert H. Walsh and Stephen C. Sievers.

We think *Annual Editions: Human Sexuality 81/82* is one of the most useful, up-to-date books available but we would like to know what you think. Please fill out and return the article rating form on the last page of this book. You are welcome to include other suggestions for our consideration. Any book can be improved. This one will continue to be—annually.

Ollie Pocs
Editor

Sexuality and Society

People of different civilizations, in different historical periods have engaged in a variety of different modes of sexual expression and behavior. Despite this cultural and historical diversity, one important principle should be borne in mind: sexual awareness, attitudes, and behaviors are learned within sociocultural contexts that define appropriate sexuality for society's members. That is, our sexual attitudes and behavior are in large measure social and cultural phenomena.

For several centuries, Western Civilization has been characterized by an "antisex ethic" which has normatively limited sexual behavior to the confines of monogamous pair bonds (marriage) for the sole purpose of procreation. Today, changes in our social environment—the widespread availability of effective contraception, the liberation of women from the home, the reconsideration of democratic values of "individual freedom" and "pursuit of happiness"—are strengthening our concept of ourselves as sexual beings and posing a challenge to the "antisex ethic" that has traditionally served to orient sexuality.

Are we in the midst of a sexual revolution? The past few decades have witnessed a massive increase of social awareness with regard to such topics as cohabitation, sex for pleasure, homosexuality, premarital and extramarital sex, sexual equality, and pornography. But these issues and dimensions of human sexuality have always been present throughout history. So what's new? What is of paramount interest in our contemporary situation is the magnitude of the public awareness that surrounds these facets of sexuality. Sexologists along with many individuals in society share a vital interest in the translation of this emergent social consciousness into meaningful and rewarding sexual awareness and expression.

Of equally vital interest is the matter of sex education. As noted earlier, human sexuality is primarily learned behavior. This can be both a blessing and a curse. The learning process enables humans to achieve a range of sexual expression and meaning that far exceeds their biological programming. Unfortunately, however, our lingering "antisex ethic" tends to foreclose constructive learning experiences and contexts. Often prevailing socio/cultural myths and misconceptions are learned instead. Anachronistic morality and educational opposition drive the learning process underground. Quality sex education programs are desperately needed to counteract the locker-room and trial by error contexts in which most individuals in our society gain misinformation as opposed to knowledge.

In the articles of this section you are invited to explore the socio/cultural nature of sexuality. In addition to underscoring the environmental nature of human sexuality, these articles address contemporary currents of change that are a part of the society in which we live and, therefore, an important aspect of our own sexual awareness, growth, and expression.

Looking Ahead: Challenge Questions

How do social institutions shape our concepts of sexuality?

What does our society's sexual behavior reveal about its basic underlying values?

Does college life have a major influence on an individual's sexual life? How and why?

Why is formal sex education of importance to all? Why is it controversial?

Should schools and colleges be the primary sex education sources?

The Pleasure Bond: Reversing The Antisex Ethic

Western society is on the verge of developing a new sexual ethic based on pleasure, caring, and mutual growth, say two experts on marriage and sex. They predict that, despite antiquated laws and mores which uphold monogamy and fidelity, a "pleasure bond" ethic of non-reproductive sexual relationships outside of marriage will fundamentally alter society, the family, and values in the future.

Robert T. Francoeur

and Anna K. Francoeur

Robert T. Francoeur, a professor of human sexuality and embryology at Fairleigh Dickinson University, has authored and edited eight books and over 140 articles on marriage, alternative lifestyles, theology, and evolution. His most recent books are *Hot and Cool Sex* and *The Future of Sexual Relations*, which he coauthored with his wife, Anna K. Francoeur.

Anna Francoeur, a member of the Groves Conference on Marriage and the Family, is researching the history of sexual customs in America.

For 3,000 years, people in western society have been nervous about most things sexual.

In the early Christian era we denied sex in our religious traditions by extolling female virginity and recommending celibacy for all. We have ignored sex by claiming only married people should do it, and then only to conceive children.

We've put down sex by talking about "private" body parts, by our uncomfortableness with nudity, and by our constant attempts to hide sex behind bedroom doors and the dark of night.

Much of this antisex mentality started when the Hebrews were influenced by the Persian cult of Mithra during the Babylonian captivity. That religion, a type of gnostic dualism, said the body was evil, a prison for the divine soul. The world was split into black and white, and sex was definitely black.

In early Christianity, a similar antisex influence came into the new religion from the disciples of the Greek philosopher Plato. Again dualism divided humans into a good soul and a not-so-nice body.

Christians fought this heresy, but like the Hebrews, they were often unconsciously influenced by it. In the third century, Augustine joined a gnostic group, the Manicheans, and kept a mistress. Later he converted, became a bishop and a great Christian saint. When many were denying sex and labeling it evil, Augustine argued that sexual pleasure was permissible if it were used as God intended, as an inducement for a husband and wife to go through the trials and tribulations of parenthood. Progeny redeemed sex.

The Three R's of Sex

Nine hundred years later, as the battle to segregate sex from life continued, medieval theologians finally spelled out our basic sexual ethic, the Three R's of Sex. Sex with the Right person, your spouse; Sex for the Right reason, children; and Sex in the Right position,—male prone—female supine (the "missionary position").

A hundred years ago the medical profession endorsed this commonly held view and introduced physical education programs into our public schools. If we were going to keep our kids in school instead of letting them work in the fields, mines, or factories, we should keep their minds and hands off sex. "Idle minds and hands are the devil's workshop," was a commonly held view. A fatigued boy or girl has little time or energy for playing around.

In America, the western frontier was built on this philosophy. The best remedy for concupiscence and lust is good hard work, and plenty of it. Instead of playing with himself, a young man was urged to chop down an oak. If he masturbated anyway, what better way to work off his guilt and get out of his childish fixation on play and pleasure than to cut down two more oaks?

Cornflakes Reduce Lust

Graham crackers and cornflakes came out of this tradition of denying sex in the same era. Sylvester Graham, an advocate of dietary reform, believed that Americans in 1850 were going the way of Rome—down, and fast. Spicy cooking, too much meat, and hot foods, he said, promoted excessive sexual indulgence. The remedy, besides hard manual labor, was an organic, nutritious and bland diet of Graham bread or crackers three times a day. Stimulants, coffee, tea, alcohol, spices, meats, and all animal products were discouraged. For variety, there was always Dr. Kellogg's cornflakes without benefit of milk or sugar.

This antisex philosophy continued well into this century. Doctors often recommended removal of the clitoris to suppress unwanted sexual drives in women and spiked penile rings to discourage males from masturbating. Marital intercourse was recommended only for males over 30 and then never during pregnancy, nursing, which lasted 18 months, or during the mother's six to eight month recovery period after weaning.

Antisex Ethic Lingers On

In 1976 this history of our sexual values sounds either pathetic or ridiculous, or both. But our parents and grandparents lived like that, and so do we in a less obvious and extreme way. The antisex tradition is still with us.

Our laws still make criminals of millions of Americans who engage in non-marital and non-reproductive sex. Oral sex is punishable by a year in jail or $1,000 fine in New York, in New Jersey by 20 years or $50,000! Same-sex relations are outlawed because homosexuality is unnatural, meaning non-reproductive. Heterosexual relations before or outside marriage are unnatural because they are non-marital and should be non-reproductive. But if no contraceptive is used, they are immoral because of the risk of illegitimacy.

So do we really have a sexual revolution?

The real meaning of the sexual revolution, we believe, is the fact that despite our antiquated laws and changing mores, we are really tossing overboard the marital-reproductive-female property ethic. In its place we are beginning to develop a new ethic, or new aesthetic, based on communication, pleasure, relationship, and recreation.

The revolution began when Freud challenged the Victorian belief that women and children were somehow entirely innocent of any sexual desire or enjoyment. And it really caught hold in the 1960s when the birth control pill and the socioeconomic liberation of women became a part of our lives.

We can't turn back without reversing all our technological, social, and economic advances. But going ahead is not easy either. A lot of us get nervous, even frightened, just thinking about what life would be like if we honestly decided to stop trying to segregate sex from everyday life. We get uncomfortable thinking about what life and society might be like if we become truly comfortable with our sexuality. What would life in South Dakota be like if we eroticized our businesses and politics?

Lack of Rules Marks New Sex Ethic

The old life-styles and antisex mentality had a nice, neat compartment for sex, with very clear licenses, precise rules, and definite penalities for infractions. The new world is not so well defined. In fact, a lack of rules and guidelines seems to be the only rule in a society that is comfortable with sex. Durkheim, the sociologist, called this condition *anomie*, "normlessness."

The new values we are finding in sexual relations and behavior are varied. Sex alone or with others is for self-knowledge, for pleasure, for friendship, for enjoyment, for variety, for learning, and for mutual growth and support.

There are several specific areas in which this shift in values has concrete meaning for us as individuals and for our society.

Sexual Experience Among Youth

The most obvious form of non-reproductive and non-marital sex today is found among youth. College cohabitation and its off-campus parallel are common and becoming more so. On many campuses one-quarter or one-third of the students are living with an opposite sex partner at any one time.

A White House survey taken in 1973 revealed that over 50% of America's 19-year-old single women were sexually experienced. In 1969, 66% of Americans polled said premarital sex was wrong; by 1973 disapproval was down to a minority of 48%. Among those under 30, disapproval was only 29%. Eight percent more Catholics approved of premarital sex than Protestants. Other surveys indicate that single women are much more sexually active than the same-aged single male, an interesting inversion of the old "double standard."

For many adults, especially parents, this is an uncomfortable reality. The young are marrying later and later in life and reaching sexual maturity earlier and earlier—four months earlier for girls with each passing decade. We recognize this, often reluctantly, but we continually try to ignore it. Instead of creating relaxed, positive settings for our youngsters' first sexual experiences, we shove them backhanded into a cheap motel, the back seat of a car, the hypocrisy of a college dorm, or the anxiety of home before a parent returns.

Middle-aged Singles Sexually Active

Non-marital cohabitation is also common among middle-aged Americans. Over half of Americans between ages 18 and 39 are single, divorced, separated, or widowed. How many of these are sexually active? A good number, no doubt.

For Americans over 50 or 60, non-marital cohabitation is encouraged by social security and pension laws. Many retirees on fixed income know that marriage will cut their income in half. So Grandma lives with her boyfriend, and their kids blush.

In the year 2000, just 25 years from now, the first of the post-war "baby boom" generation will be retiring. Our birth rate has dropped like lead from 2.7 children per fertile woman 10 years ago to under 1.7 today. If this continues to drop, or even stays constant, we will soon reach the time when the average American is over 50. Unless our pension laws and social security change, non-marital living together may become more common than marriage!

Sex and the Mentally Retarded

Several million Americans live in institutions—the mentally and physically handicapped, the aged, the law-breaker. What kind of sex does our society allow these persons?

The mentally retarded of all ages are commonly segregated according to sex. Until recently very little was done to deal with their sexual needs and rights. They can, are, and perhaps should be, protected from the responsibilities of parenthood they cannot handle. But we can protect them from unwanted pregnancies without denying them the psychological and emotional support normal non-reproductive sexual relationships could give them. Why do we limit them to secretive masturbation or a closet homosexual experience? Allowing these persons free expression in loving sexual relationships that are non-reproductive could make their lives much richer, more fulfilling, and probably better adjusted.

Aged and Handicapped Have Sexual Needs

The same can be said about the sexual needs and rights of the physically handicapped and aged—the stroke victim, the paralyzed victim of automobile and other accidents, the 120,000 quadriplegics and paraplegics, those suffering from neurological and muscular disorders like muscular dystrophy and multiple sclerosis, and the aged. In one home for the aged, inmates lose their privileges for five days if they are caught in the room of another inmate of the same sex. The penalty is 10 days if the person is of the other sex!

Criminals Denied Normal Sexual Outlets

We claim to rehabilitate the criminal, but in this rehabilitation we deny them the emotional and psychological support of sexual relations with their spouses. We even expect the mate to be there waiting patiently and faithfully to resume normal marital life five, 10, or more years later. Our penal system is carefully designed to cut the criminal off from all sexual relations and expression, save masturbation and homosexuality.

Masturbation Shapes Sexual Self-image

Masturbation is the most common and least acknowledged form of sexual expression. It can and does occur within hours of birth. It is common in early-childhood, preadolescence, adolescence, young adulthood, middle, and old age. Kinsey reported that 98% of husbands do it, at least occasionally, and many married couples do it together. Engaged or dating couples who want to "save themselves for marriage" do it. Still we deny its existence and practice, especially for women.

"Know thyself," Socrates urged us. Masturbation—self-exploration, self-learning, self-pleasure, self-knowing—can play an important role in the image we develop of ourselves as sexual persons. How can you tell another person what to do to turn you on unless you have gained some knowledge of yourself? Many women's consciousness-raising groups highly recommend self-examination and self-pleasuring for women. Sometimes this is a negative expression towards men, but more often it is a healthy development designed to put the woman in touch with herself and help her communicate better with her man. Masturbation, both alone and with a partner, is an important exercise in many sexual therapies.

Homosexuality Slowly Gains Acceptance

Between five and 10% of the U.S. population is exclusively homosexual in orientation, most studies indicate. And many researchers believe that a much larger percentage, 70 or 80%, is potentially, if not actually, bisexual or ambisexual in their enjoyment of sex. If this is true and we are indeed shifting from a marital-reproductive-property ethic to an aesthetics based on communication, pleasure, friendship, enjoyment, variety, and mutual growth, then why are we still so uptight about the logical application of these values to sexual relations between two or more males, two or more females, or any combination thereof?

Ten states are in varying stages of adopting "consenting adult laws" which hold that any sexual activity between two or more consenting adults is legal, provided it is not a public nuisance or disturbance. Even the Vatican recently authorized publication of a book by a noted Jesuit theologian which reinterprets the morality of homosexual relations in terms of "loving concern" or its lack in the relationship, rather than on the basis of unnatural acts of sodomy, anal or oral sex, or any other form of non-reproductive behavior.

Americans Teach Young Guilt About Sex

For well over 100 years, Americans have tried to protect their children from the primal scene of mating. The result has been generations of youngsters totally puzzled by a basic aspect of life. Sex becomes a mystery and a problem, instead of a joyful, wonderful part of their lives.

In most cultures today, sex is not a great taboo secret. Children are raised with a natural comfortableness with nudity and sexual behavior of all kinds. In many cultures, children are encouraged and even taught to explore their bodies. When they discover what turns them on, their elders rejoice. Children are often allowed, even encouraged in playful explorations of love-making and intercourse. Playfully they prepare for their adult life.

In America we show our children every form of violent behavior on television. But God help the kid who accidentally walks in on his parents making love. We drive our children's natural curiosity underground. We load their natural explorations with taboos and our own guilt and shame. We do everything we can to create a negative, "forbidden-fruit" image of sex. Many children never overcome this negative learning. They end up gutted adults, incapable of appreciating one of the richest sources of pleasure and communication we have.

Removing Taboos from Sex

Why can't we have a ritual to celebrate a girl's first menstrual flow, or a boy's first wet dream? Why can't we parents share with our children the anxieties, insecurities, and joys we find in sex? Why shouldn't a son or daughter feel free to discuss his or her hesitant explorations of sexuality with a parent?

We toss our children into one of the most important areas of human communications with a few words about sexual plumbing and a few abstract instructions about good and bad. We refuse to admit sexuality to our children until they marry and can have kids, instead of seeing their natural sexuality as a process which may or may not lead to marriage and/or parenthood.

Monogamy vs. Sexually Open Marriage

A final issue is raised by the value shift to sex for communication, pleasure, friendship, enjoyment, variety, learning, and mutual growth: the question of monogamy.

Several noted theologians and a fair number of marriage counselors, sociologists, and psychologists are suggesting today that we have gone far enough down the devastating path of trying to save monogamy with no-fault divorces.

Divorce today is far more socially and religiously acceptable as a modification of the "until death do us part" vow than is a sexually non-exclusive marriage which maintains the commitment of a lifelong bond but modifies the "forsaking all others" to include others. It is about time we ask ourselves which of the two values is more important in a good marriage, and whether modifying one or both will lead to a fuller, more human life.

Three Concepts of the Family

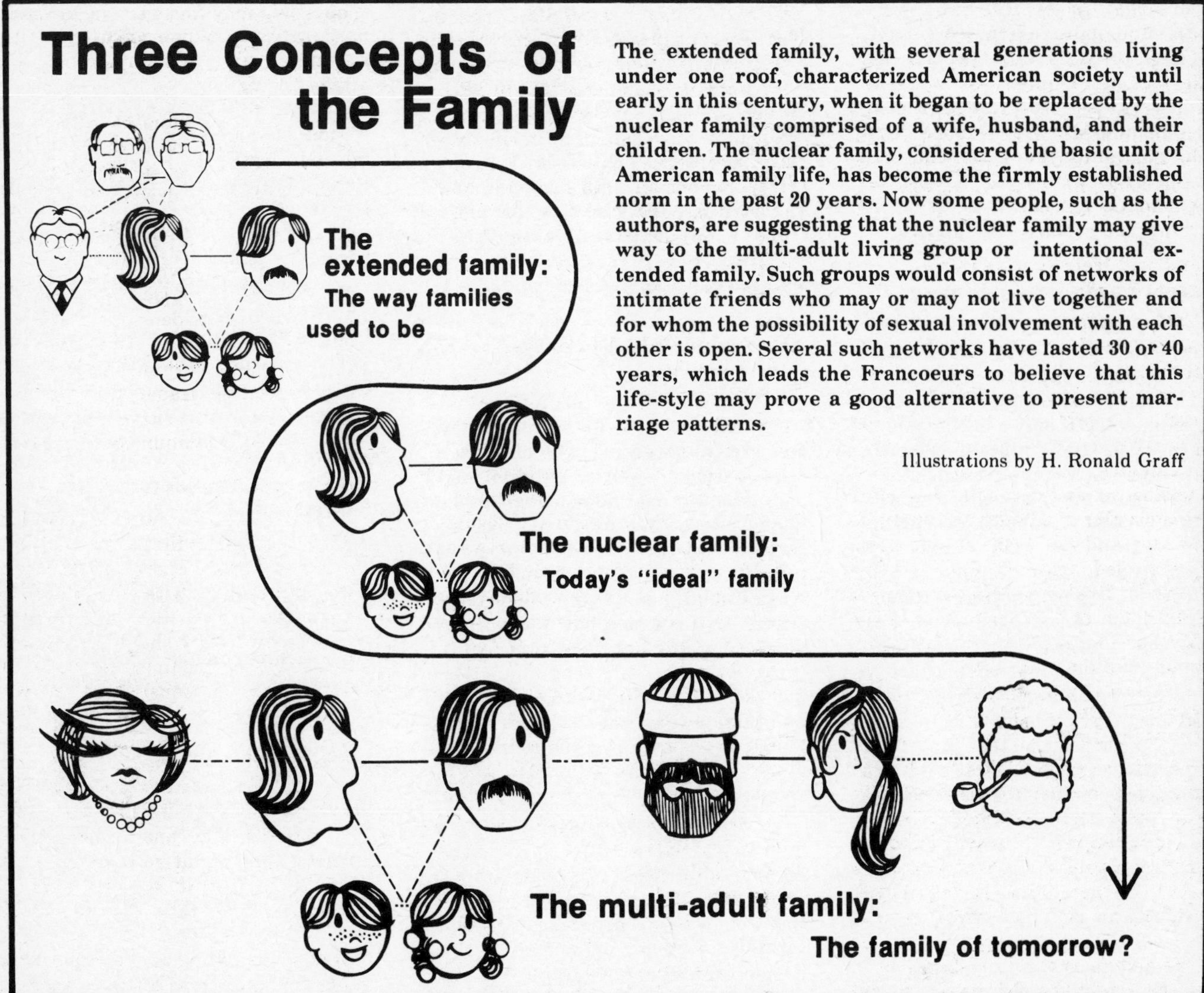

The extended family, with several generations living under one roof, characterized American society until early in this century, when it began to be replaced by the nuclear family comprised of a wife, husband, and their children. The nuclear family, considered the basic unit of American family life, has become the firmly established norm in the past 20 years. Now some people, such as the authors, are suggesting that the nuclear family may give way to the multi-adult living group or intentional extended family. Such groups would consist of networks of intimate friends who may or may not live together and for whom the possibility of sexual involvement with each other is open. Several such networks have lasted 30 or 40 years, which leads the Francoeurs to believe that this life-style may prove a good alternative to present marriage patterns.

Illustrations by H. Ronald Graff

In this perspective some theologians are suggesting that maintaining the long-term commitment while expanding the circle of love to include others may be a viable Christian option.

Can a man and woman have a lifelong, healthy, growth-oriented, open and trusting marriage that allows each to have supporting friendships, even when these are sexually and genitally involved? Can a good marriage be enriched and strengthened by satellite or comarital relations? Does all extramarital sex have to be destructive forbidden fruit?

Alternatives to Monogamy

There are many ways a couple can modify traditional sexual monogamy. These include couple-front swinging, group marriages, and intimate networks based on the acceptance of the possibilitv of any friendship involving the sexual and erotic. Another alternative is a sexually open marriage, where the amount of information about the satellite or comarital relationship that comes back to the other spouse can vary from simple knowledge it will happen sometime, to the name of the person and some brief details about him or her, to mutual friendships developing between the satellite and the other spouse. This variety has been carefully documented in several recent books: Francoeur's *Eve's New Rib*; the Francoeurs' *Hot and Cool Sex*; Rogers' *Becoming Partners*; Bartell's *Group Marriage*; Myers' *Adultery and Other Private Matters*; Clanton and Downing's *Face to Face to Face*; the Lobells' *John and Mimi*; and Ramey's *Intimate Friendships*.

James Ramey's research is perhaps the most interesting in our context here. Director of the Center for the Study of Innovative Life Styles, Ramey has examined the "intimate networks" that develop when happily married couples and contented singles accept the legitimacy of sexual expression as part of traditional friendship. Some of these networks have been in existence for 30 or 40 years. The existence of such intimate networks and their durability suggest that this form of marriage may prove a good alternative for some to the serial polygamy, divorce, and remarriage that is now our most common pattern. (See Ramey's articles, "Intimate Networks," THE FUTURIST, August 1975, and "The Multi-Adult Household: Living Group of the Future?," THE FUTURIST, April 1976.)

The environmental situation we face today in America is quite different from what existed 100 years ago. What worked then in terms of marriage patterns, sex roles, and sexual values is obviously no longer working today. Yet we still have some basic human needs: for intimacy, support, growth, communication, and pleasure.

The old pattern of the extended multi-generation family still survives in some rural areas. But in our vast urban-suburban regions we have millions of isolated, fragmented nuclear families, often single-parent families. The psychological, emotional and economic support we once drew from our aunts, uncles, cousins, grandparents who lived nearby or next door no longer exists. What, if anything, can replace this support?

Opening Up the Pleasure Bond

Sex researchers Masters and Johnson in their latest best seller, *The Pleasure Bond*, say that there is no need to replace this support network. They argue that if only a husband and wife work at their mutual commitment and recognize the growing erotic pleasure bond between them, they will not need outside support or enrichment. In their Victorian, reactionary conservativism, they argue that a healthy, committed marriage cannot exist without sexual exclusivity. For them, the suggestion that we might develop a new definition for fidelity and commitment in marriage not based on sexual exclusivity is, in their words, "to encourage the dangerous and self-serving malady of megalomania" and "the most seductive of rationalizations."

Actually, our sexual ethics have been constantly evolving over the centuries. Our marriage patterns have also evolved, because behavior patterns and values that worked well in one era may not work at all when the environment changes. Of 185 cultures in today's world studied by Beach and Ford, America from 1930 to 1960 had one of the most restrictive and anti-sexual.

Given the overall pattern of marriage in western civilization and our current trends in both behavior and values, it may be wise to allow more freedom of expression to what William Masters and Virginia Johnson call the pleasure bond.

New Sexual Values to Shape Future Society

It seems likely in the future that American society will be more concerned with parenting. The laws have always tried to protect children and assure their proper upbringing. Maybe in the future, the laws will focus on this aspect and leave the non-reproductive sexual relations of consenting adults alone, in the private sphere. In this event, our laws will ignore the whole realm of premarital, comarital, postmarital, nonmarital, homosexual, bisexual, adolescent, and infantile sexual behavior, provided the behavior is non-reproductive.

In a zero-growth society where children are rare, where blood relatives are few and scattered, where mobility, contraceptives, and the economic liberation of women are accepted realities, our needs for intellectual, emotional, psychological, and sexual support may no longer have to be met exclusively by one person, our spouse. We may find that the old intimate network of blood kinships with its incest and adultery taboos is already being replaced by the pleasure bond of non- or comarital, non-reproductive relationships. This new intimate network, a kind of intentional family without incest and adultery taboos, may be even more supportive and creative than blood kinship because it is not determined by birth, but rather is open to creative spontaneity and new additions as we encounter new persons and new needs.

The pleasure bond will very likely be the foundation of our future society, marriage and family, but it will be with a whole new set of values and life-styles which we are still struggling to develop and articulate. The central issue we will have to face in developing these new values and life-styles is two-fold. On the philosophical and religious plane, there is our need for a whole new philosophy and theology of play, pleasure and non-goal-oriented human activity including non-reproductive and non-marital sexual behavior of all types. On the social and economic plane, we will have to deal with the impact of this new aesthetic on our American capitalistic (property-oriented), consumerist (competitive) Puritan work ethic. In simple words, can our present society survive the shift to a person-oriented, non-competitive value system that accepts play and pleasure as prominent realities in life, equal to—or superior to—work?

Alfred C. Kinsey Man & Method

by Wardell B. Pomeroy

An intimate memoir by his closest associate— Excerpts from *Dr. Kinsey and the Institute for Sex Research*, published by Harper & Row.

When I walked into Alfred C. Kinsey's office at Indiana University on my first day of work in 1943, I had a somewhat let-down feeling. I had seen it before, but not as a place where my life would be centered. It was a typically drab office in a typical gray-stone Middle-Western university building left over from the last century. The office was large, but it was designed for utility, not comfort, about which Kinsey cared little. It had a musty, institutional air, and it was still cluttered with the remains of his gall-wasp collection.

I was impressed from the beginning with Kinsey's supreme dedication. He was fired-up with a driving resolution that he communicated to me and to the other staff members. He spent most of the first day talking to me about future research, and how he would train me in two-hour sessions every day.

My job was to be chiefly interviewing, and he was extremely careful about those he chose for that work. There were only nine interviewers over the years, and three stayed only a short time. Kinsey and I took about 85 percent of the ultimate 18,000 histories, dividing them almost equally between us. This was of course a vital part of the project, and Kinsey was never more arbitrary than when he was hiring interviewers.

Demands. He sought in each instance an interviewer who embodied three paradoxes: he must be happily married, but be able to travel about half the time; he should have an M.D. or a Ph.D. in some related science, yet he must like and get along with people from low social levels; and he must have been born and raised in this country and exposed to our mores and customs, yet must never evaluate what others did sexually. That third point was the largest stumbling block, and Kinsey was ruthless about it.

He had sound reasons for his paradoxical demands. He wanted interviewers who were happily married because people who had never been married were suspect to a good many Americans. It was necessary for them, obviously, to be able to work with lower socioeconomic groups, and he wanted to avoid ivory-tower academic types who could not do so. Finally, it was important for an interviewer to be familiar with our culture, but not prone to moral evaluations, as far as humanly possible, because there were few areas of research where the investigator's own system of morals was so challenged and so crucial as in the study of human sexual behavior.

It was suggested to us at various times that he ought to have women interviewers to interview women, and black interviewers for blacks. But by that logic, Kinsey pointed out, he would have to have prostitutes for prostitutes, drug addicts for drug addicts and so on.

Joke. In hiring me, the objections were my lack of a doctorate, which Kinsey insisted I remedy as soon as possible, and my age (29), about which nothing could be done. For a while, considerable attention was given to ways of "making Pomeroy look older," until Kinsey saw that it did not help. In any case he was overjoyed to get a qualified full-time staff member, now that he could afford one. He turned to me in one of his infrequent outpourings of feeling and said, like a boy, "Gee, I'm glad you're going to be on

From *Psychology Today,* March 1972. Abridged and adapted from Chapter VII, "Interviewing" in DR. KINSEY AND THE INSTITUTE FOR SEX RESEARCH by Wardell B. Pomeroy.

"He came to believe that people would tell him anything about themselves if the circumstances were right."

the staff." He always treated me as a colleague, never as an inferior.

More and more as I began to work with him, I came to esteem his total dedication. We rarely talked about anything but sex research in general and the project in particular. Like many scientists, he was largely incapable of dealing with the commonplace preoccupations and amusements of other people. I could never forget how one day as we lunched together at the Oliver Hotel in South Bend, just before I joined the staff, he announced he had heard a sexy joke he wanted to tell me. I waited with some anticipation, wondering what kind of smoking-car story the authority on sex would produce. He told it straightforwardly, without a hint of humor. It was a terrible joke, badly related. I tried to laugh, but my polite appreciation was as grim as the joke. Kinsey didn't appear to notice, and laughed at his own humor with the heartiness that always sounded so convincingly Midwestern, even though it came from a former New Jersey boy. It was the only time that I heard him try to tell such a story—mercifully, I might add.

Space. Kinsey found an office across the hall from his own and divided it into three parts, for me, for Clyde Martin, who also was doing interviews, and for a secretary who would work for both of us. So that we could take histories in them, our offices, like his, were soundproofed, and that had not been easy to accomplish, but Kinsey was adamant. His insistence was characteristic; he was a perfectionist.

I may have had a little anxiety at first about doing interviews. At least two psychology departments had dismissed researchers in the early 1930s because the administrators were not yet ready to look at sex objectively. Before 1940, only five psychologists had published anything approaching good statistical data on sexual behavior, and consequently, in spite of my tremendous confidence in Kinsey, I ventured into the deep water with some initial, and concealed, reservation. It was only momentary.

Kinsey was concerned that I be drawn into the project gradually. The first history I took was that of a male college student. Kinsey called these "baby histories," because the young men were like lambs jumping after each other and their histories were innocuous by comparison with, say, those of inmates he had interviewed in prisons. Consequently this first history made little impression on me.

Before I could begin, of course, he had to teach me the code. I was so anxious to get started that I learned it in a little less than two months—a phenomenal time, and possible only because I worked at it night and day. This was the code used in taking the histories. There was another code, involving a rearrangement of the symbols, that was the key to identifying histories in the files. I was so wrapped up in my work that I cracked this second code by myself, and soon, examining the files, to which of course I had access, I was able to identify Kinsey's own history, that of his wife and his daughter and those of about six other persons

I told him at once what I had done. At first he appeared irritated, but then, quickly, he was pleased because I had shown myself so anxious to absorb everything as rapidly as possible. Nevertheless, he prudently changed the coding of the names so that no new person coming to the project could crack the code so easily. He took every conceivable precaution to protect the identities of the persons who had given histories. The codes were not on paper; they were taught by rote, verbally, to those few who had to know them.

Secrets. Since so many of the interviews at first had come from the campus itself, a primary consideration from the beginning was the necessity to keep the identity of the people and the facts related to them absolutely secret. No one was more insistent on this point than Kinsey himself, who recognized that it was his guarantee of absolute confidence to those who gave histories that made the research possible. He drilled it into everyone who came to work for him.

I believe there was something more to this than Kinsey's basic rocklike integrity. I think he liked secrets, that their possession gave him a sense of power. And there was no question that the histories did give him a unique potential power. They included political, social and business leaders of the first rank, and with his intimate knowledge of their lives Kinsey figuratively could have blown up the United States. On the Indiana campus alone, as would be true of any campus, there were at least 20 professors with homosexual histories unknown to anyone else, not to mention the professors whose numerous extramarital experiences were recorded.

Acts. Martin thought that Kinsey never ceased to be amazed that people, especially in high places, would tell him the things they did. At the beginning Kinsey was so naive that everything was a revelation to him. He came to believe, however, that people would tell him anything about themselves if the circumstances were right, and the way the research was conducted gave them the proper circumstances. Nevertheless, at the start, he was constantly astonished by the difference between public behavior and private acts.

I wondered how he could have taken his own history, but he told me that he had given it to himself just as Freud had analyzed himself. After I joined the project, I took his history about every two years, and he took mine. This was good practice at the beginning, to perfect techniques and discover possible inadequacies, and it helped to measure error in recall.

Code. The staff discovered that we could converse with each other in the same shorthand we used in taking histories. We did it in ordinary conversation in private, and of course it permitted us to speak much more openly in public. I might say to Kinsey while we were going up in a public elevator, "My last history liked Z better than Cm, although Go in Cx made him very er." Translated: "My last history liked intercourse with animals better than with his wife, but mouth-genital contact with an extramarital partner was very arousing."

There was, I am sure, a tremendous

"We never asked *whether* a subject had ever engaged in a particular activity; we assumed that everyone had engaged in everything."

amount of public curiosity about exactly what questions we asked in taking a history. People viewed the idea sometimes with horror, sometimes with fear or distaste, often with anticipation of various kinds. But in reality there was nothing mysterious or frightening about the interview, as nearly all of our 18,000 subjects discovered. In that number we found only six persons who were visibly upset in the course of history-taking. Three of them were psychiatrists, one of whom was asked to rate himself on the zero-to-six homosexual scale. On the basis of the history he had given, he was obviously a four, and when he was compelled to face this fact, he rushed to the bathroom to vomit.

But time after time people would say, "This has been one of the most therapeutic experiences I've ever had," or, "We should be *paying* you," or commonly, "I've told you things I never thought I'd tell anybody." One psychiatrist told us, "I've been in therapy for three years, and this is the first time I've ever put it all together."

Explorers. The interview was, of course, at the core of the project, and Kinsey's success must be attributed in large part to his complete mastery of the interviewing art, applied to this most difficult of topics. For *Sexual Behavior in the Human Male* he wrote a truly extraordinary chapter describing the techniques we used. It remains, in my opinion, one of the best accounts in the literature of how to interview.

In each history, there was systematic coverage of a basic minimum of about 350 items. A maximum history covered 521 items. However, whenever there was any indication of sexual activity beyond what the questions covered, we would go as far beyond the basic interview as we thought necessary to get the additional material. "As scientific explorers," Kinsey wrote, "we . . . have been unlimited in our search to find out what people do sexually."

If a subject found it hard to estimate the frequency with which he had engaged in some activity, we were careful not to give him any idea of what the frequencies might be in the general population, or what he himself could be expected to have. Instead we suggested that his activity might average once a week, three or four times a week, three times a day, or once a year—indicating the widest possible range. We were also on guard against people who were obviously very suggestible; we took care to avoid implying an answer and to check the answers for consistency.

Touch. We asked our questions directly, without hesitance or apology. Kinsey correctly pointed out that if we were uncertain or embarrassed in our questioning we could not expect to get anything but a corresponding response. Unlike previous researchers, we did not say "touching yourself" when we meant masturbation, or "relations with other persons" when we meant "sexual intercourse." We also never asked *whether* a subject had ever engaged in a particular activity; we assumed that everyone had engaged in everything, and so we began by asking *when* he had first done it. Thus the subject who might want to deny an experience had a heavier burden placed on him, and since he knew from the way we asked the question that it would not surprise us if he had done it, there seemed little reason to deny it.

Since there were so many questions to be asked, the questioning went as rapidly as the subject could comprehend. But there was a better reason for doing this. Under the rapid fire, the subject was much more likely to answer spontaneously, and so it would be virtually impossible for him to fabricate answers. We looked our subjects squarely in the eye and fired the questions at them as fast as we could. These were two of our best guarantees against falsifying.

In making cross-checks on accuracy, we used interlocking questions. Before we ever asked direct questions about homosexuality, for instance, there were 12 preliminary inquiries, whose significance only a psychiatrist would have recognized; and it would have been hard for anyone with more than incidental homosexual experience to deny it after he had answered them.

If we thought a subject's answer was wrong or incomplete, we tried to rephrase the question so that he would have to prove his answer or expose its falsity. If a subject was of low mentality we might pretend that we had misunderstood his negative reply, and ask another question as though he had answered affirmatively. To make it as easy as possible for subjects to correct their answers, we ignored contradictions, accepting the correction as though it were a first reply. On a few occasions, as Kinsey recalled in the *Male* volume, we took a complete history even though we were convinced from the outset that it was going to be a fraud, then put it aside and told the subject, "Now give it to us straight." Naturally, we had to be sure of our ground in such cases. Kinsey pointed out that the false record, viewed against the corrected record, gave us valuable insights into an individual's public admissions compared with his actual behavior.

There were times, too, when we did not recognize the falsity of an interview until after it had been given, and in each of those cases we went back to the subject and demanded that he correct the record. These cases included feeble-minded subjects, prison inmates and even clergymen. We did not lose a single history by taking such action. It was Kinsey's firm belief that giving a history was voluntary, but once the commitment was made, the subject assumed responsibility for its accuracy.

Names. A way of reassuring our subjects was to make it clear that we had no desire to have the names of persons with whom they had been involved sexually. If names were given anyway, we let the subject know that they were not being recorded. Even so, it was obviously impossible to avoid identifications in many instances, and that was why we found it hard to get histories from some married persons, or from those who had had sexual relations with relatives or persons prominent in their communities. It was also difficult with those who were involved in deeply emotional love affairs and

"It was particularly important that we know the sexual viewpoint of the cultures from which our subjects came."

consequently might find it hard to avoid identifications.

Pimp. It was particularly important that we know the sexual viewpoint of the cultures from which our subjects came. Kinsey illustrated this point with the case of an older black male who at first was wary and evasive in his answers. From the fact that he listed a number of minor jobs when asked about his occupation and seemed reluctant to go into any of them, Kinsey deduced that he might have been active in the underworld, so he began to follow up by asking the man whether he had ever been married. He denied it, at which Kinsey resorted to the vernacular and inquired if he had ever "lived common law." The man admitted he had, and that it had first happened when he was 14.

"How old was the woman?" Kinsey asked.

"Thirty-five," he admitted, smiling.

Kinsey showed no surprise. "She was a hustler, wasn't she," he said flatly.

At this the subject's eyes opened wide. Then he smiled in a friendly way for the first time, and said, "Well, sir, since you appear to know something about these things, I'll tell you straight."

After that, Kinsey got an extraordinary record of this man's history as a pimp, which would not have been possible without his understanding that Kinsey knew all about his world.

Again, we would ask a prostitute when she "turned her first trick," not "how old were you when you were first paid as a prostitute." Then we might ask her how many of her tricks returned after their first contact, and much later in the interview we would inquire how often she "rolled her tricks," that is, robbed them. If she had reported that few of the men ever returned, and then later said that she never robbed any of the men, we would tell her that we knew it didn't work that way. If she didn't roll them, why didn't they return? Very often that question would produce a smile and the admission that, since we seemed to know how the business operated, she would tell us the whole story—and it was usually that she robbed every time she thought she could get away with it.

Tour. If, at this point, there is any further curiosity about the questions we actually asked, let me give you a guided tour through the interview, which has been so much debated and discussed.

When the subject arrived, we began with some general conversation, thanking him for coming, perhaps explaining the value of the contribution he was making if we had not discussed that before. There would even be desultory chat about the weather.

Then we asked, "Do you have any questions?" Usually the subject did not, but occasionally there were casual inquiries, and sometimes he would ask a question about his sexual problems. We had a standard answer for that contingency: "Well, we need to get your history first. When I have more information about you, we'll come back to that."

There were routine questions about age, birthplace, place of residence. We were establishing bench marks with the early questions. For example, a subject might say he had lived in Connecticut until he was 14, then had moved to California. Then later, when we asked such questions as "How old were you when you first masturbated?" if the subject said "Fourteen," we could say, "Oh, that was after you went to California?" to which he might respond, "No, it was before," and thus we could tell whether he was older or younger than 14 when he first masturbated.

Stops. Next we took a religious history, both the subject's present status and his relationships with religion from his early days onward. That would give us some idea of what his particular frustrations might be and where blocks might occur. Then came his health, his hobbies and his interests. Obviously all of this was nonthreatening material. People concentrated so much on answering these questions that they began to forget they were giving a sex history at all.

We moved on to the subject's nonsexual activities in high school or college, if he had attended, and went on from that point chronologically to his marriage; how long the marriage had lasted, how long he had known his wife, and so on. From that series we went to family background—the relationships with brothers and sisters, occupations of father and mother, and similar questions.

It took about 15 or 20 minutes to answer all these, and not one of them had been about sex. Thus usually it was easy at that juncture to go on to early sex education. Again the subjects did not feel threatened, because these things had happened when they were little children and they did not feel responsible for them. Here, too, we began using sexual terms for the first time, asking questions about how and where the subject got his first knowledge of sexual matters. We asked, for instance, how old he was when he first learned that babies grow inside mothers, how old he was when he first learned there was such a thing as intercourse, how he acquired a knowledge of such things as condoms and how he found out about homosexuality. We asked males when they first ejaculated, females when they first menstruated. That led naturally to questions about when pubic hair developed, when the voice changed in males, how quickly or how slowly growth occurred. When this series had been answered, our bench marks were firmly established.

Habits. Now we could go directly to early sex experiences. It was still fairly easy going for the subject, because again it had all happened when he was small and he was not responsible.

From this point, the order of the questions varied. For example, with upper-level males we could go next to masturbation, a natural consequence of the question about first ejaculation, and then we got a history of the subject's masturbation, the fantasies accompanying it and his reaction to it. This would be followed by questions about nocturnal emissions, the subject's petting experience and his premarital intercourse, if any, his extramarital intercourse, and his use of contraceptives.

In the questions about masturbation,

"We were quick to explore any lead the subject gave us into any rare or unusual masturbatory activity."

we would ask about his use of the basic techniques. If we found a man who had used all or most of them, this would open the way to pursue with other questions what further techniques he might have used, and the frequency as well. Specifically, we asked male subjects about techniques, including manual masturbation, making coital movements against a bed or some other object, self-fellation (possible for only a few men, but attempted by most), insertion of various objects in the urethra and anus, and the use of melons or similar objects to masturbate in. We asked about any unusual position that the subject might have employed, the use of ropes to tie up the penis, or the use of toilet paper tubes, bottles and condoms as aids. We were quick to explore any lead the subject gave us into any rare or unusual masturbatory activity, because the purpose was to record the whole range of human sexual behavior.

Clues. If the subject were a female, the masturbation questions naturally were a little different. Routinely we asked about the subject's use of clitoral friction, about bed masturbation (that is, lying on her stomach and making coital movements), crossing the legs and using thigh pressure, stimulation of breasts and insertion of objects into the vagina. If it became obvious that she was using a wide variety of techniques, that would open the way to such questions as whether she used a vibrator, or whether she practiced anal stimulation.

With both men and women, we routinely asked about erotic fantasies during masturbation, and if these were elaborate we might spend several minutes eliciting further details. In this as in other types of behavior, answers to questions about one kind of activity would tell us whether nothing more was to be learned, or whether we could further explore a subject with additional questioning.

We asked how subjects responded sexually to reading about sex, or seeing it, or hearing music that might excite them, or whether they were excited sexually by traveling in vehicles. From such questions we could get clues to the homosexual content of a subject's history. His erotic response to dreams, for example, might be greater, he would say, if he dreamed about masculine figures, and that might be supplemented with similar images when he masturbated. It was possible, then, to build up a picture of the relative components of the individual's sex life. Another clue to homosexuality might be a subject's desire to look at his penis while masturbating.

S-M. Now we were at the core of perhaps the deepest and strongest of the taboos—that against homosexuality—in persons who had no idea they had such feelings, or who were aware of them and had tried to suppress them. If there was any resistance to be encountered, this was where we would find it.

There followed the details, if any, of the subject's sadomasochistic feelings. Did he bite when he was having intercourse? Did he enjoy being bitten? Similar questions completed this aspect, if it existed. We asked if the subject was aroused by seeing animals copulating, and this would lead to queries relating to his own sexual activity with animals, if any. We asked about the individual's anatomy—the size of his penis, whether he was circumcised and the angle of the penis in erection.

With lower-level males, we could go directly from here to intercourse, then back to masturbation, petting, wet dreams and homosexuality. It was the same with lower-level females. If an individual had an extensive homosexual history, from the point at which we discovered it we could go into 250 more questions. The two major extensions from the questions were in homosexuality and prostitution.

Truth. Though the average interview ran from an hour and a half to two hours, college students did it usually in an hour, partly because they were so quick and precise in their answers, having more rapid mental reflexes and less to remember. Older persons might take three hours to work their way through. Those with multiple marriages quite naturally took more time. The 350 questions, which had to be memorized, were in one order for females and in another for males, and there were other variations.

How do you know people are telling you the truth? I am confident that those who hated the whole idea of the research, or were skeptical of it for other reasons, would never believe any answer Kinsey or I or anyone else might give to that question. Yet the answer is a simple one. There are only three possible ways of not telling the truth: by denying or covering up, by exaggerating, or by remembering incorrectly. Exaggeration was almost impossible with the system we used for asking questions rapidly and in detail. Persons who later told us they had tried deliberately to exaggerate reported little success. Not remembering accurately could be dealt with statistically; the errors one person might make were offset by errors another one made in the opposite direction.

Retakes. Covering up was the most serious problem, since there were so many taboo items in most histories. But there were numerous cross-checks, so that an answer at one point actually gave us a clue to an answer elsewhere. We took histories of husbands and wives and could cross-check certain parts of their backgrounds. We made some retakes after a minimum interval of two years, and an average interval of four years, to see how well people could reproduce the same material. In most cases, the cover-up factor was very slight, although some leeway had to be made for it.

We added questions as the project developed. For example, it was not until 1948 that we started asking about extramarital petting. We were late in getting to this area primarily because Kinsey was still a little naive on the subject and because he resisted changing the interview questions. The later histories, then, were better and more productive. Yet there were few changes. Of the 350 questions in the basic interview, only about 10 were changed.

It was possible to get the equivalent

"He was determined to get sex information from people, and he intended to get it no matter what obstacle might intervene."

of 25 typewritten pages on one page by using our code.

Tone. The recording of a history was a sensitive process because we were taking down not only the answer but also the tonal inflection. The answer might be "YES," "*Yes!*" or simply "Yes," or perhaps a very hesitant "Ye-e-e-s." We would record these answers four different ways. To be sure that we were setting down the inflections in the same way, it was necessary sometimes for Kinsey and me (or any other combination of interviewers) to record simultaneously, which also gave us an opportunity to criticize each other's techniques.

Understandably, it was an anxiety-producing situation the first time "the master" sat in while I took a history, but I got used to this, as did the others. When we observed Kinsey taking a history, we tended to be a little deferential, partly for the obvious reason and partly because he was quite defensive; he had an explanation for everything he did. We found that we were able to record an individual's history simultaneously with about 98 percent accuracy.

Case. The longest history we ever took was done jointly by Kinsey and me. We had heard of a man who had kept an accurate record of a lifetime's sexual behavior. When we got the record after a long drive to take his history, it astounded even us, who had heard everything. This man had had homosexual relations with 600 preadolescent males, heterosexual relations with 200 preadolescent females, and intercourse with countless adults of both sexes and animals of many species; he also had used elaborate techniques of masturbation. He had set down a family tree going back to his grandparents; of 33 family members, he had had sexual contact with 17. His grandmother introduced him to heterosexual intercourse, and his first homosexual experience was with his father. If that sounds like *God's Little Acre*, I will add that he was a college graduate who held a responsible government job. We traveled from Indiana to the Southwest to get this single extraordinary history, and felt that it had been worth every mile. At the time we saw him, this man was 63 years old, quiet, soft-spoken, self-effacing—a rather unobtrusive fellow. It took us 17 hours to get his history, which was the basis for a fair part of Chapter Five in the *Male* volume, concerning child sexuality. Because of these elaborate records, we were able to get data on the behavior of many children, as well as of our subject.

At one point in his history-taking, he said he was able to masturbate to ejaculation in 10 seconds from a flaccid start. Kinsey and I, knowing how much longer it took everyone else, expressed our disbelief, whereupon our subject calmly demonstrated it to us. I might add, in case this story confirms the worst fears of any surviving critics, that it was the only sexual demonstration among the 18,000 subjects who gave their histories.

Weight. Few interviews were anything more than routine—or seemed so, after the first few thousand—but some responses were memorable. Early in the interviewing we learned that the most embarrassing question we asked, particularly for women, was "How much do you weigh?" I remember, too, the female psychiatrist, quick and sharp in her answers, who said, when I asked how she found out about masturbation: "I invented it, and if I could have patented it, I'd have made a million dollars." Memorable, too, was the female gynecologist, an inhibited old maid, who told us she thought masturbation was normal unless it was excessive. When we asked her what "excessive" meant, she said, "Anything over once a month." Not surprisingly, her own masturbation occurred once a month.

Always in the interviewing we had the example of Kinsey before us, and it was inspiring, to say the least. He was never the rigid, academic college professor, but a scientist whose pragmatism and willingness, even urge, to experiment at any time gave him the flexibility to handle any kind of problem that arose.

He was inflexible about one thing, though. He was determined to get sex information from people, and he intended to get it no matter what obstacle might intervene. If he went into a house and found every room occupied, so that it seemed impossible to find a place for confidential interviewing, Kinsey would nevertheless find one. Sometimes it was a bathroom, more than once an attic. If there was no room inside, he would take a history sitting out on a lawn under a tree. Often he used his car, if nothing else was available.

Boasts. For Martin, as he recalled later, interviewing meant shedding some cherished preconceptions. He found, for example, that there was no relationship between the sexy appearance of a girl and her actual sexual experience.

As soon as Martin had learned the code and was ready to interview, he was able to read the earlier histories that Kinsey had taken, including those of students who had been in classes with him, and whom he had heard boasting about their sexual exploits in dormitory bull sessions. Their records disclosed the truth, and Martin was astonished by the discrepancies.

Problem. In April 1943 we went with Kinsey to Nicodemus, a tiny hamlet in the northwest corner of Kansas, near Hill City. It had been an exclusively black community since its founding in 1877. Nicodemus could boast only two stores and three houses, so it was not difficult to get the histories of three quarters of the township's people over 15. Not difficult, that is, given Kinsey's powerful ability to knock on a door and persuade persons whom others would surely have thought unpersuadable.

It was in Nicodemus that I encountered my first real interviewing problem, a 35-year-old man who lived in Hill City. I met him one night at a farm where he was visiting. There was nowhere in the crowded little farmhouse where we could get any privacy, so I suggested we get into my car and do the job there.

We drove out a little way into the country. I stopped and turned on the dome light, then began to take his his-

"It was hardly surprising that we encountered a few sexual approaches. The men were usually more direct about it than the women."

tory. By this time it was near midnight, but I gave no thought to any possible difficulty until I discovered that my subject was homosexual—the first one I had encountered since I began interviewing. We had switched seats so that he sat behind the steering wheel, leaving me free to write. Fortunately that gave me freedom in both directions, since I found myself able to fend him off with my left hand and write with the other.

In the course of taking so many sexual histories over the years, it was hardly surprising that we encountered a few sexual approaches, both male and female. The men were usually more direct about it than the women. Kinsey taught us that the best way to handle this situation was to remain completely impassive, neither making any motion forward in an interested way, nor backing off in obvious disinterest. Nothing cools sexual ardor more than impassivity, he told us, and he was right.

Challenge. Perhaps the most difficult part of the technique for me to learn was how to control the interview. As I have said, we asked about a dozen questions indirectly related to a person's homosexual history before we came to the direct question: "How old were you the first time you had sexual contact with another person of your own sex?" By this time we would be fairly certain whether or not he had extensive homosexual experience. If at this point he denied an overt history of homosexuality but there were enough indicators in a positive direction to make us reasonably certain he was covering up, we learned to challenge his denials.

Then it became necessary to say, with firmness, even vehemence, and yet always with kindness, "Look, I don't give a damn what you've done, but if you don't tell me the straight of it, it's better that we stop this history right here. Now, how old were you the first time this happened?" Surprisingly, in not a single case did a person refuse to continue. In all of the histories we took, fewer than 10 persons refused to complete one once they started.

I remember taking the history of an Armenian scientist who spoke broken English, so that I had some trouble understanding him.

"How old were you the first time you ever ejaculated?" I asked him at one point.

"Fourteen," he answered.

"How?" I asked.

"With a horse," I thought I heard him say.

My mind went into high gear. This subject was telling me voluntarily about animal intercourse, and my instinct was to jump far ahead in the questioning and pursue the subject.

"How often were you having intercourse with animals at 14?" I inquired.

He appeared confused and taken aback, regarding me amazedly.

"Well, yes," he said, "it is true I had intercourse with a pony at 14."

Later in the interview it developed that what he had said was "whores," not "horse." He thought I was a genius to have known somehow that he had had intercourse with animals.

Since we never knew what we would get in an interview, it was necessary to ask all the questions, even when some of them did not seem applicable to the subject. Interviewing an upper-upper-level woman with an advanced degree, for example, we would nevertheless ask her, "Have you ever been paid for intercourse?" and sometimes the answers to this question were surprising. A Chicago social worker of whom I asked this question answered affirmatively and gave me a long history of prostitution before she got her job. She had had no intention of giving me this information until I asked the question.

Road. The interviews were numbered at the time they were taken, and then renumbered in Bloomington when they were filed. Paul Gebhard, the anthropologist who joined the staff in 1946 and now heads the Institute, was once taking histories in a famous music school where we knew there were a great many homosexuals. As one subject sat down, he saw Paul write "69" on the sheet, and looked up at him in amazement, thinking his sexual behavior had been categorized before he had even begun to talk.

While we encountered relatively few difficulties with the interviewing itself, there were endless problems on the road, as one might imagine from the constant traveling we did from one end of the country to the other. It tried our constitutions as much as it did our endurance. Still vivid in my mind is a trip to Miami with Kinsey and Gebhard, during which Kinsey went through one of his periodic obsessions with a certain kind of food. This time his passion was tropical fruit, and as he did when he was in this frame of mind, he saturated himself with it. We joined him on this fruit binge, and as a result I got a severe case of diarrhea.

Our suite at the hotel consisted of two bedrooms with a connecting bath. One morning I was taking histories in one of these rooms, while Paul worked in the other. About noon, having finished with his morning appointments, Paul speculated as to whether I was through or not, and whether he should wait for me to go to lunch. To see how far along I was, he tiptoed into the connecting hall and put his ear to the keyhole of my room; he would be able to tell from the questions I was asking how near I was to the end of the interview.

I was taking the history of a married woman who had been living a difficult, painful sex life, which she was trying to tell me about as best she could. Suddenly I felt a wave of diarrhea sweeping over me. Much as I hated to interrupt, I knew I must reach the bathroom with the greatest possible speed. With a muttered excuse, I rose and almost ran to the door, pulled it open and exposed Paul in the process of straightening up. When I returned, I tried to explain to the lady what had happened, but I'm sure she must have thought he was listening to her answers, not my questions.

Worlds. The interviewing trips were a grand tour through America. From Miami or Philadelphia, we might be plunged into the life of minuscule communities like Nicodemus, Kansas. Suburban matrons would be followed

" 'I am Dr. Kinsey, from Indiana University, and I'm making a study of sex behavior. Can I buy you a drink?' "

by prostitutes in prisons, highly placed executives by underworld characters. Often, in our explorations, we would plunge into a subculture that was unknown to people not only in the city where it existed, but to 90 percent of the public in general. I am thinking of the world of homosexual prostitution in the New York Times-Square area.

As early as 1942 Kinsey had heard something of this world from inmates of the Indiana State Penal Farm, and decided to explore it. He went to Times Square with no contacts whatever, and hung around the bars on Eighth Avenue that he recognized as gay. Observing for hours at a time on different occasions, he noticed a man who also seemed to be constantly hanging around. Going over to him, he said, "I am Dr. Kinsey, from Indiana University, and I'm making a study of sex behavior. Can I buy you a drink?"

That the man accepted is a testimonial to Kinsey's personality and the persuasion he could put into the simplest statement. I suppose, too, that such an invitation coming from someone who looked like the squarest of the square to a Times-Square denizen had the ring of authenticity. No one would be likely to make it up. Still, the man was skeptical until he was having his drink and listening to Kinsey, who had turned on the full power of his persuasion. It was impossible, one must believe, to doubt this clear-eyed, earnest, friendly man from the Midwest. In the end, the pickup agreed to give his history, which proved to be filled with drugs, prostitution, and prison terms. From then on, he became a valued contact and persuaded other male prostitutes to cooperate.

Room. On one Times-Square trip we used the Lincoln Hotel as our interviewing place. The manager and his staff knew what we were doing, but apparently the parade of prostitutes, drug addicts and other members of the Times-Square underworld through the lobby and in the elevators unsettled them. They told us we would have to leave. We remonstrated that we were doing nothing illegal or immoral. The manager was adamant. "Nobody's going to undress in our hotel rooms," he said. We protested that this was not what we were doing. "Yes, but you're undressing their minds," he insisted. We had to go.

Critics. We had much help from fellow professionals, though there was often a problem, understandably, with other professional people, particularly psychiatrists, some of whom found it hard to accept what we were doing. The outstanding example of this was at the Menninger Clinic. In 1943 Kinsey was invited to speak there, and the letter indicated that they had heard of our research and wanted to know more about it. Kinsey was quite willing to lecture to this or any other professional audience, because close behind Kinsey the researcher came Kinsey the teacher. At the time we had decided that we needed a good many more histories of psychiatrists, so we resolved to combine the lecture with history taking, as we usually did. But Kinsey accepted without telling his hosts about his plan, fearing that they might put him off.

The lecture was held in the large board room of the Clinic. To our surprise, there were more than 30 psychiatrists sitting around the large boardroom table. Plainly this was not intended on their part to be a simple lecture about the research. Later we learned that at least some members of the Clinic were opposed to everything they had heard about the research, and they had set a trap for Kinsey, confronting him with a board of professional inquisitors whose intention was to show him up. The questions were biting, snide and hypercritical, and there was little warmth in the room.

But that was exactly the kind of arena in which Kinsey excelled. He fielded every question deftly, often even counterattacking. By the end of the session, respect if nothing else had been achieved. As the meeting came to an end, Kinsey said, "Just a moment, gentlemen. We are here to get your histories, and of course I expect all of you to contribute." They were set back a little by this announcement, but they had no rebuttal. As scientists they felt compelled to cooperate. We spent 10 days there collecting histories, and went away with a 100 percent sample. (Kinsey was lax about sampling techniques in the early research. But he soon developed more rigid criteria, particularly his 100 percent sampling.)

Sailor. What I remember most, I think, from thousands of hours of interviewing, is the driving, driving, driving under the lash of Kinsey's determination to get more and more histories. On one field trip to Chicago we were taking histories of schoolchildren and faculty members in a private school during the day, and homosexual histories from the Near North Side in the evening. Because of the hours the homosexuals kept, we often worked late into the night, but the next morning we had to start in early with the school histories. Kinsey always wanted to take "just one more."

In this homosexual community one evening, Kinsey encountered a sailor from the Great Lakes Naval Training Station, and after a brief conversation, decided it was imperative to get his history. We took him back to our hotel room, which we shared. There was no place for me to stay while Kinsey took the history, so we decided to do it jointly.

It was a long and complicated history. At 4 a.m. we were still at it, and by this time Kinsey for once was completely exhausted. There was a long pause in the questioning and I looked up to see that he had fallen asleep in the middle of a query. I went on with the questioning until Kinsey could rouse himself and take over once more. The sailor was startled at first, but he smiled and indicated he understood.

Kinsey, in fact, once fell asleep while he was lecturing at the University after a strenuous night of interviewing. I was often just as exhausted, but like Kinsey I kept going through sheer willpower. Like him, too, I could see the goal shining clearly before us in the distance—not so much the remote figure of 100,000 histories, but the opportunity to correlate everything we were taking down and to produce a book that would make a truly significant contribution to sex research.

"Quiet, Determined, Undegenerate"—A sketch of Alfred C. Kinsey

In *Beyond Freedom and Dignity*, B.F. Skinner contends that "Man has not changed because we look at him, talk about him, and analyze him scientifically." I don't agree. Alfred C. Kinsey's research did change man—and woman, too. The first Kinsey Report, *Sexual Behavior in the Human Male*, came out nearly a quarter of a century ago, at the beginning of a sexual revolution, and it dispelled the superstitions that could have held the revolution back. Before Kinsey we may have had no less sex, but after Kinsey we were free to enjoy it more.

Probably because I grew up in Bloomington, Indiana, where Kinsey lived and worked, I took an early and prurient interest in what he was doing. "Sex" was the dirtiest three-letter word in the language in those days, and before I was in my teens I had learned the dirtiest six-letter word—"Kinsey."

Kinsey didn't publish his first Report in time to save me from a sexually flustered adolescence—and god knows that period takes years of living to get over. But by the time I enrolled there, Indiana University had an unmistakable Kinsey aura that helped pull me through the worst tensions of the college days. Kinsey already had gathered an ample supply of sexual histories from college men—"baby histories," as he called them—so I never got to contribute. But I used to walk almost daily past the old building that housed Kinsey's Institute for Sex Research, and often saw Kinsey himself with his shock of hair blowing in the wind, a quiet, determined and reassuringly undegenerate presence. This combination of circumstances made me consciously—and happily—aware that I was a member of the first post-Kinsey generation.

It was thanks to my predecessors, the sexually bewildered I.U. students of the late 1930s, that Kinsey had become a sex researcher. He was a respectably successful zoologist, teacher, collector of gall wasps, and author of a widely used high-school biology text when, in 1938, he was chosen to coordinate a new course on marriage. He threw himself wholeheartedly into the project, prompted principally by students who went to him demanding frank answers to their questions about sex. He quickly realized that he couldn't answer the questions himself and that, in fact, there were few scientific answers to be had.

Kinsey turned the tables on his students. If he couldn't tell them what other people did sexually, at least he could ask them what *they* did. Within a year, he had taken some 350 sexual histories of his students, and before long he was traveling back and forth across the country to get the histories of all kinds of people. His gall-wasp collection took a permanent back seat. At 45 he was fully launched on a second career.

"How do I love thee? Let me count the ways," Elizabeth Barrett Browning had written in the Victorian era. Kinsey took her words literally, and counted. The figures he came up with played havoc with our Judaeo-Christian tradition and our archaic sex laws, and the persons who supported them. Kinsey's noncondemnatory attitude was too much for them, and so were his statistics, which showed that many sex acts, far from being "perversions," were commonplace. They were especially disturbed by his concept of "outlets"—masturbation, nocturnal emissions, heterosexual petting, premarital intercourse, marital intercourse, extramarital intercourse, homosexual relations, animal contacts—in which each carried equal weight and validity and none was labeled right or wrong, since each was a part of human sexual response.

Wide World Photo

Kinsey's opponents fought bitterly to retain their self-proclaimed status as arbiters of the bedroom which they weren't about to yield to mere scientific researchers. In a way, of course, they were tilting at a windmill, for Kinsey never set himself up as an arbiter. He was first and last a taxonomist—a namer, describer, and classifier of behavior. His great scientific contribution was his audacious decision to use the modern taxonomic approach, which he had helped develop by studying gall wasps, in a field so controversial as human sex behavior.

We members of the post-Kinsey generation were more than happy to change arbiters, however. Kinsey's statistics, cold as they may have appeared in his countless tables and graphs, accorded much more accurately with the world as we knew it than did the never-never-land dogma of his opponents.

The furies were lying in wait when the second Kinsey Report, *Sexual Behavior in the Human Female*, appeared in 1953. One opponent, Henry Van Dusen, president of the Union Theological Seminary, wrote that Kinsey's facts, "if trustworthy," revealed "a prevailing degradation in American morality approximating the worst decadence of Roman era," and a Presbyterian minister, caught up in the spirit of the McCarthy days, called the Report Communistic. Worse, Dean Rusk, the new and fainthearted president of the Rockefeller Foundation, which had supported Kinsey's research for several years, cut off his funds in 1954 to forestall a threatened Congressional investigation.

The few times I passed Kinsey on campus after that, he looked anxious and tired. I was away from Bloomington for a year, then returned in the summer of 1956 to take a reporting job on the local newspaper. I had been there only a few weeks when I got the saddest assignment of my life: to write Alfred Kinsey's obituary. The whole newsroom was solemn as I phoned and talked to the persons who had been closest to Kinsey. All of us—associates, friends, passers-by—felt a personal loss.

Nearly 16 years later, it is good to have Kinsey with us again, in the memoir of Wardell Pomeroy.

—Kenneth Goodall

LEARNING TO TALK ABOUT SEX

Paul H. Cashman, PhD
Professor, Department of Speech-Communication
University of Minnesota, Minneapolis, Minnesota

In our society there appears to be a noticeable "conspiracy of silence" around the subject of sex. Professionals not specifically trained in sexuality may approach the topic with clients and patients gingerly or not at all. Couples may never talk about sexual intercourse before, during, or after the act. Children may hear little or nothing about sex from their parents directly. Radio and television usually permit discussion of sex only within rules carefully worked out well in advance.

Some of the silence may be the result of the personal anxieties of the persons involved. Some may be the result of cultural factors. It seems likely, however, that much of the lack of open communication about sexuality in our personal and professional lives comes from the lack of a sexual language and from the problems that occur whenever language developed for use in one situation is used in another. It seems equally likely that our lack of an adequate sexual language may lie behind many of the sexual issues that create misunderstanding between client and therapist, parent and child, between sexual partners, and between professionals in the field of human sexuality and the public at large. It is the purpose of this article to explore these issues, as well as to make some recommendations regarding the use of sexual language.

We communicate with others in three ways. Part is *verbal*—conveying meaning through the words we choose to use. Part is *vocal*—the pitch, volume, rate of delivery, and quality of our voices carry important information. Finally, we convey messages through our *nonverbal* behavior, in many ways that the observer can *see* and interpret as part of the message.

Serious problems may arise when people who do not share the same communication system use different verbal comments, vocal styles, or nonverbal behavior; or when one or both persons appear to be inconsistent, that is, the verbal, vocal, or nonverbal languages do not add up, giving mixed messages to the other. Unfortunately, both situations can easily arise when the communication is sexual. The basis for this is the lack of a precise sexual language. There are at least four other language systems developed for other purposes that are used, at least in part, to communicate about sex. The difficulties in deciding which language system to use, as well as the uncertainties associated with the use of any combination of language systems, can make human sexual communication especially troublesome and can result in misunderstanding in both personal and professional situations. Each language system has specific advantages and disadvantages and each is useful for some purposes, but none is entirely suitable for communication in all professional and personal circumstances. As a result, misunderstandings and problems occur.

Child language. When we are very young, we learn that there are certain terms our parents prefer to use with us. There are terms of endearment *(baby doll, snooky, sweetie, itsy bitsy baby,* etc.), terms that refer to certain organs of the body *(wienie, bottom, tushy,* etc.), and other terms that refer to functions of some of those organs that have nothing to do with sex but suggest a negative or evasive feeling toward the functions and organs involved *(number 1 and number 2, tinkle, poo-poo, grunt, etc.).* The purposes of this language seem clear enough. It allows a parent or other adult to express affection, describe parts of the body, and get the child to conform to certain standards while carrying out necessary bodily functions. Not all parents use such terms, of course, but many do. Children also hear them used by other adults or on radio or television. But the fact is that rarely does a child grow up knowing all of the correct terms for all of the sexual parts and functions. Certainly at least some of these childhood terms become part of our available vocabulary.

Street language. As we are growing up, we usually learn that, in discussing sex-related matters, there is a language used by our peers or by those somewhat older that seems to have as its intent a demonstration that we are part of the "in" group and that we have some knowledge about sex. It is often the language of graffiti. For the most part, the words used seem to be power-laden terms that show that we are among those who have power. By using this bold and suggestive vocabulary (e.g., *ass, screw, make out*), we often impress one another, but we learn if we use it with parents or other adults that these older people appear to disapprove (although we may overhear them using the identical terms when they don't know we are listening). Even so, we now have available another language which we may continue to use in some personal and professional settings if we wish to do so.

Euphemisms. By the time we have entered the adult world, we have been exposed to still another language intended to make it possible to avoid using explicit terms while carrying on any necessary conversation about matters related to sex. We discuss *making love, sleeping together, that time of the month* —in other words, we camouflage the message with terminology more comfortable to use.

Medical-scientific language. Finally, in school and from books, we learn that there is a concrete, technical language of sexual terms. It may be then that we first hear terms such as *penis, vagina, defecate,* and *coitus.* Such language may even be presented by professionals or parents as the "correct" language.

What seems clear is that no one of these four languages is sufficient to provide for all of the circumstances in which we may wish to communicate about sex. No one language conveys accurate messages to everyone with whom we talk about sexuality, and each system has its own special problems. For example, child language tends to confuse words that deal with elimination with sexual terms, and street language can be so offensive to a hearer that the real message may be lost. Moreover, few people are comfortable with all four languages. A professional person who uses medical-scientific language relatively easily may find it difficult to use the street or child languages to which his client is accustomed. Each may be uncomfortable when the other uses a language with which he/she is unfamiliar or for which he/she has unpleasant associations. A spouse who finds the language choice of the partner offensive may be reluctant or afraid to discuss this reaction, but the resentment could eventually harm the relationship.

These difficulties are compounded when we consider the vocal and nonverbal aspects of communication. Our four vocabularies are accompanied by vocal and behavioral patterns characteristic of the language selected. Child language, for example, especially in the form of "baby talk," has a distinct pitch, volume, rate, and quality. Street language, too, has a recognizably rough vocal style, and euphemistic and medical-scientific languages have a relatively bland vocal approach. When a person mixes verbal language, he/she may also mix vocal styles, and the result is a puzzling lack of clarity. For instance, when a mother snatches a baby's hand from its genitals and says, in firm, controlled tones, "No, no. Baby doll mustn't touch her little peepee," the message styles are clearly in conflict.

Because the range of nonverbal behavior is greater, it becomes more difficult to identify it with the four languages. Child-like, playful behavior does not harmonize with the more reserved and distant medical-scientific language, and when we compare other aspects of nonverbal behavior, we find that cultural and individual variables are so important that they make it difficult to relate nonverbal behavior to the four language choices.

Because so many are not yet comfortable discussing sex at all, the tendency is to talk as little as possible about it. But if we must talk about sex, we tend to use a language with which *we* are comfortable whether or not that language suits the situation or the person with whom we are communicating. In responding to a youngster's questions about "where babies come from," a parent may use medical-scientific language and be unaware that it lies far beyond the child's comprehension.

When others communicate with us using a language system of which we disapprove, we may simply suffer through it, leave, or express discomfort directly or indirectly. If people use "baby talk" at a party we are giving, we may wish silently that they would "grow up." If someone else's child uses street talk in our home, we may exclaim that we do not allow that kind of talk in our presence. If a spouse, while relating sexually, uses language that makes the partner uncomfortable, the latter may suffer in silence or may demand that a certain term be avoided in the future.

It is apparent that lack of an adequate, broadly accepted sexual language interferes with the effectiveness of interpersonal communication. To obviate this, certain guidelines might be considered:

1. Develop a wide tolerance for language choice. Language is used to communicate. Yet words carry value judgments that can result in conclusions being made about the person who uses them. Whenever possible, use language that will not offend the listener and thus create barriers to communication. But, in turn, it is also important when you are a listener not to overreact to the use of vocabulary you disapprove of. Don't let the choice of a word get in the way of what the person is trying to say. It is well to remember that "people, not words, have meaning."

2. Determine what languages the other person can use. If you are communicating with another person, you should learn as much as possible about his/her sexual language choices. If you are a parent, be alert to the language choices the child is making, but also be aware of what you are modeling about sexual language by your own choices. Within a relationship, observe the language choices of your partner. To do so is to cut down on the unexpected responses you will receive from violating the preferred language choice of the other.

3. Whenever appropriate, talk in the language system of the other person. Your goal is good communication, so if, in your professional work, your client uses street language, be prepared to use some key street terms yourself. You will both be more comfortable.

4. Negotiate language choice. While you may in the short run choose to use the language system of another person, you may, in the long run, have some educational, personal, or other reasons to prefer a compromise. You can negotiate a language choice with your son or daughter, your partner, or a client. If a particular term makes you feel more comfortable than another, express this preference. There are some limits, of course. The other person may find your preference unattractive or you may belong to a profession in which a particular term is the one that will be used whether you wish it or not. Within the limits, much can be done to negotiate language which is both meaningful, accurate, and comfortable.

5. Change your language choice when desirable. Be flexible. Recognize the need to adapt to changing concepts and contexts. Many couples in therapy with problems in relating sexually have found that a simple change in sexual vocabulary and communication patterns can significantly improve their relationship.

6. Above all, keep your sense of humor about sexual language. Since there is no specific set of rules governing sexual language, uncertainty about it exists and surprise responses abound. "What the heck does that mean?" may be an excellent response to a puzzling word that you think has a sexual meaning but aren't quite sure about. Expressing your puzzlement in good humor will get you over the rough spots and you may learn some new language into the bargain.

The word *sex* itself can produce blushes, leers, smiles, frowns, coughing, tittering, apprehension, bravado, pursed mouths, moist lips, open ears, closed minds, guilt, or pure joy. But the more appropriately and freely we use it and all the other words in the sexual vocabulary, slim as it still is, the sooner we will reach the time when communicating about sex will be as comfortable and natural as communication about other very important aspects of life, and far more rewarding than many of them.

Sexuality and College Life

Joseph Katz and Denise M. Cronin

JOSEPH KATZ, professor of human development at the State University of New York at Stony Brook, is writing a book on German university students. He has written several books on academic life and is a coauthor of Faculty Development in a Time of Retrenchment (Change Magazine Press). DENISE M. CRONIN teaches sociology at Queens College, City University of New York.

In the early 1960s a woman student at a distinguished university in Massachusetts fell sick in her boyfriend's apartment and stayed there overnight instead of returning to her dormitory; she was subject to disciplinary procedures even though she had slept in a separate bed. About the same time a young Stanford woman was summarily dismissed when the dean of women discovered that she had had sexual relations with a married man. Sometime later there was much publicity about a Barnard student who had shared an apartment with her boyfriend while officially occupying a dormitory room. She too was punished for her offense. All three cases are from the most liberal institutions in the nation. Everywhere penalties for sexual improprieties were severe; even legitimate pregnancies were considered embarrassing if the women continued to attend classes. A vast army of housemothers and other residential staff were hired expressly to watch over the sexual conduct of students. Elaborate security measures were devised to keep the sexes divided. Male and female dormitories often were built far apart to underline the separation of the sexes.

The students of the early 1960s began to protest these restrictions on their personal lives. In 1961 students at Harvard and elsewhere asked for liberalization of visiting rights. Controversy ensued as to whether doors should stay open when men and women students were together. It was decreed that doors be left open at least the width of a book; enterprising students responded by defining the distance as matchbook-wide. Things really got moving in 1966 when Stanford students asked the university to allow one experimental residence in which men and women students would live together. Such housing arrangements had already been practiced on Stanford's European campuses, but they had escaped notice here because there was a certain moral extraterritoriality about what happened abroad. Now students asked why coresidential housing was not suitable on the home campus. Stanford's first coresidential house was a great success; it was followed the next year by four such units, then by eleven, and then by the majority of Stanford residences. The experiment caught on and soon over half of American campuses offered coresidential living.

From the beginning one of us (Joseph Katz) watched the rise of coresidential houses on the Stanford campus and as soon as funds could be obtained for a study we and a group of researchers* started to collect data to find out what new relationships and attitudes were developing between men and women. We were supported by the Grant Foundation for the first two years. From a base, first at Stanford and later at Stony Brook, we undertook 7 surveys between 1970 and 1977, collecting data from 6,098 men and women residential students at 13 colleges and universities that differed in size, location, and academic status. Three universities were surveyed continuously; the others participated once or twice. In addition, we interviewed over 100 students at three universities.

One of the great surprises was that coresidential living met with little resistance from the public, including the parents of the students. Shortly before its first coresidential experiment Stanford had liberalized the rules about on-campus drinking and that move had met with some resistance in the press. But very favorable reports and picture essays about men and women living together in college residences soon began to appear in national magazines and local Sunday supplements. In our early interviews we found that parents, and mothers in particular, were supporting their daughters' new living styles. This was true even of mothers whose strict religious upbringing might have produced more negative responses. Some parents even acquiesced when their sons and daughters brought friends of the opposite sex home for vacation and asked to share a bed. Other parents allowed a protective mythology to ease acceptance of the new arrangements: Coresidential living was said to encourage brother-sister kinds of relationships. It was clear from the beginning that sexual relation-

*In addition to the authors, researchers who have participated in the study at various times are Alfred Bochner, M.D., Enid Hunkeler, Marjorie Lozoff, and Ronald Starr.

Reprinted with permission from *Change* Magazine, Vol. 12, No. 2 (February-March 1980). Copyrighted by the Council on Learning, 271 North Avenue, New Rochelle, New York 10801.

ships among people living in the same dorm were by no means uncommon. Yet the comforting if misleading notion of an "incest taboo" helped parents who were uneasy about premarital sex to go along with the new mores.

It is not difficult to assign reasons for this rapid transformation. The sixties was a time of protests—political, racial, and sexual—and students were in the vanguard. Women began to resent double standards both in their work for political movements and in bed. At least two other factors furthered greater sexual freedom and equality: Various psychological movements of the sixties preached openness in expressing one's feelings and this often included a special emphasis on sensuality; and the pill, whose side effects were still unbroadcast, made possible an easy avoidance of the pregnancies that had frightened so many previous generations.

The events and behaviors examined in this article bespeak more than greater sexual freedom. They arise from an altered regard for authority among today's young people. Interventions on the part of college authorities that a decade ago were accepted unquestioningly have become intolerable to students even at relatively conservative institutions. The decline of authority in many areas of life has coincided with a reduced sense of responsibility and a lessened commitment to sustained work on the part of many students. But where relations between the sexes are concerned, our data suggest that the effects on the whole have been beneficial.

The data we have collected over the years attest to a considerable liberalization of the sexual behavior of most students and some surprising changes in the attitudes of the public. To begin with, there have been great changes in the attitudes of college students toward premarital sex. Near the beginning of our study in 1970, when we asked undergraduates whether they believed that "full sexual relations are permissible before marriage," slightly more than half approved; a somewhat lower proportion approved of premarital sex for women than for men. By 1975, 90 percent of students surveyed thought that premarital intercourse was permissible for both sexes.

These attitudinal changes go hand in hand with altered behavior. Today's students have sex more often and their first sexual experiences take place at an earlier age. In 1970 about half of the men and women students reported having had sexual intercourse. Seven years later the figures were much higher: nearly four fifths (78 percent) of the men and three quarters (72 percent) of the women. (These figures are for all four college years combined.) The incidence of intercourse is lower for freshmen, but sophomores are not greatly different from seniors. In 1970 students on the average reported that their first sexual experience had taken place at age 18. This average has dropped a whole year to age 17.

These changes in sexual behavior appear even more dramatic when compared with student behavior of a few decades earlier. Though surveys of sexual behavior undertaken before 1950 have produced different results, they all report figures considerably lower than those we obtained in the seventies. Pre-1950 surveys report the incidence of sexual intercourse for college women in a range between 13 percent and 33 percent; for college men, between 52 percent and 58 percent. The difference in the reported behavior of men and women is striking. At present nearly as many college women as men are nonvirgins. The double standard has clearly become a thing of the past. (There is some possibility that the considerably expanded public permissiveness about sex in the 1970s may make it easier for college women to report sexual activities. The incidence of intercourse in the past may thus have been higher than self-reports indicated. But we know of no study that gives evidence for this occasionally expressed surmise.)

Our data contain a still greater surprise. The women engage in sexual activities much more frequently than the men. In 1977, 52 percent of women vs. 40 percent of men reported having intercourse 5 times a month or more. In addition, many more women than men consistently reported participating in a sexual relationship at the time they responded to our questionnaire. For instance, in 1977 nearly three fourths of the women (73 percent) as against somewhat more than half of the men (57 percent) said they were *currently* engaged in a sexual relationship. But the difference between men and women is not only quantitative. Over the last few years more women than men have described themselves as enjoying their sexual experiences highly. In our last survey 66 percent of the women, as against half of the men, described their current sexual relationships as very satisfying. Considering these results, it is astonishing to reflect that not long ago women were thought not to enjoy sex; they were believed to tolerate it only for the sake of their husbands and for procreation.

Figures can reveal only the quantity of sexual experience. Our interviews and observations, however, indicate important changes in the quality of relationships. With greater sexual liberality come increased expectations of mutual openness and responsiveness. In many instances the women are asking the men to awaken dormant capacities for affection and caring. Women no longer so readily subordinate their desires to the male power trip or to their own security needs. One of our interviewees told us:

> I have had an enjoyable sex life. Part of it is luck and part of it is taking a close look at your partners. It takes courage when you are sitting in a dark room and someone makes aggressive moves to say: 'Wait a minute, let's talk about it and find out if we both feel the same way about the situation.' It takes a lot of courage to say, if our attitudes differ, that we should not go out any more. You have to be honest with people even if it involves a tense confrontation, but it pays off.

Another student, sounding a bit like a pop psychology book, reported the joint search she and her boyfriend undertook about his sexual problems:

> To me it was perfectly understandable; there were so many things going on in our lives that it was an effort to keep up the relationship. But he got very ego-involved because of his difficulties. He had never had trouble before. He thought we were in a sexual rut. It was not my fault that I wanted him when he was busy or tired. But when he wanted me, I had to be in his room. The role orientation was very much on his terms. I could understand his having to take it out on me but there was a point where I could no longer stand it. How much do I have to surrender of my self-respect and my concept of our relationship? We were very honest about it and things are better now.

For the men, responding with greater depth of emotion and empathy for their partners has not always been easy. Not only has it strained those relationships that would have been psychologically inadequate anyway, but in some instances it has led to depression and sexual dysfunction. The positive side of the situation is an awareness of new possibilities. One male student said that it struck him as "unfair that men in our society must always give an appearance of being tough and hard to crack"; that they should have to hide their "need to be sensitive." Once the men are started on that road, they gain a new sense of self, a liberation of what used to be called their "feminine" side. Their relations with women become more tender, mutually supportive, conducive to growth. Over half of the women and nearly half of the men say they have made conscious efforts toward role reversal, with women playing a more aggressive role and men a more passive one.

It should be clear from what precedes that male-female relations on campus go much beyond "fun" and that students approach each other with some seriousness. Contrary to occasional insinuations and fears our data do not show any great degree of promiscuity. Throughout the years of our surveys half of the sexually active people reported having had no more than two or three partners over the entire course of their sexual history. An additional 30 percent reported up to 10 partners. For 1976-77 three fourths of the women and a slightly smaller proportion of the men said they had only one partner; most of the rest had two relationships.

Frequently, however, sex was accepted within a relatively short relationship. In fact, one male interviewee, who at first said sex was satisfying only as part of an important relationship, went on to describe a brief encounter with a friend of his sister:

> She was here for only four days and that pretty much defines the level of commitment. We talked a lot about what she was doing and what I was doing—she was leaving to go to see her boyfriend whom she is living with. We just enjoyed each other and it was a really nice thing to do with her. I do not think your body is something that is reserved entirely for one person. I do not idealize sex to the extent that it is purely an expression of love. It can be an expression of friendship.

He also described a relationship with another young woman who was temporarily concerned that she might be pregnant. The woman told him that if she were pregnant she would never tell him because she would not want to "lay this on him." The student was annoyed about her attitude. But it illustrates a tendency we find in many students not to use sex for the ulterior purpose of binding people to each other against their wills, but to make it something freely given and part of a mutual discovery.

Brief sexual encounters can serve as more than a momentary physical release. They can be explorations on the way to a firmer sexual identity and they are consistent with the respect of the two partners for each other. One striking change we have noted is that sex is less often considered dirty or associated with guilt. Instead it tends to be regarded as only one of many facets in achieving closeness and mutual understanding. Nevertheless, our data continue to show differences between men and women in another regard: the tendency to link sex with affection. In our last survey many more women (67 percent) than men (42 percent) described a relationship with a current sexual partner as one of great mutual affection. Similarly, far fewer women than men said that they would have sexual intercourse if they were only physically attracted to their partner.

Reference should be made to the incidence of more unconventional sexual practices on campus. In our last two surveys we asked the respondents whether they had ever engaged in any form of group sex. About 15 percent said they had done so, though about double this number claimed their friends had *told* them they had engaged in group sex. And less than 15 percent reported that other people had ever been present during intercourse. These data, together with what we have reported about promiscuity, disprove lurid notions of sex on the campus.

There is, however, one area of special concern. It appears that a considerable proportion of couples never use contraceptives and others do not always use them. The principal reasons students give are that contraceptives interfere with sexual activity and that they have possible medical side effects. Thus it is not surprising that in 1977 16 percent of all sexually active women reported having undergone an abortion at some time. Given the psychological pain that can accompany an unwanted pregnancy and an abortion, there seems to be a need for further education to reduce resistance to easily available contraceptives. Those of us who observed the mental and physical suffering of college women who underwent abortions during the 1960s, when the practice was clandestine and dangerous, find the present a considerable improvement. But we still have far to go to reduce unwanted pregnancies. The Yale Sex Counseling Service has demonstrated the capacity of a good service to reduce unwanted pregnancies to a minimum. (See *Sexual Unfolding: Sexual Development and Sexual*

Therapies in Late Adolescence by Lorna J. Sarrel and Philip M. Sarrel of the Yale Sex Counseling Service. Boston: Little, Brown, 1979.)

Changed ideas of male and female roles and relationships go together with changed attitudes toward career, marriage, and child rearing. Our data, like those of other researchers, show a greatly increased desire on the part of college women for a career as a means of self-fulfillment. In fact, in our last survey more women (87 percent) than men (82 percent) declared that a career was crucial. A considerable proportion of women put career above marriage and having children.

In light of these untraditional views one wonders about the attitudes of men. The college men we interviewed show willingness to face some of the possible consequences of women's greater participation in the labor force. They are overwhelmingly in favor of equal job opportunities for women even if it means fewer jobs for men. They also are willing to share household tasks. Over two thirds of the men expect to spend as much time as their spouses in bringing up their children and a devoted additional 6 percent expect to spend more time. Most of the men plan to share cooking and other domestic chores equally. Increased participation of women in the labor force calls for male cooperation and apparently that support may be forthcoming. But it also calls for institutional arrangements, such as flexible work time, to aid women in the tasks of childbearing and child rearing, and in these areas very insufficient progress has been made.

In a recent article in the *New York Times Magazine* (November 18, 1979) Betty Friedan pointed out the burden for many women who take up professional careers without domestic help; once more they have been cast in the role of superwomen. She suggests a redefinition of the family that would increase the sharing of domestic tasks. Our data show that the current generation of college men are largely in tune with Friedan's proposal, at least in words. Friedan goes on to suggest that when a man's "wife is also earning money and his identity and standard of living do not depend entirely on his paycheck, a husband is something more than just a company man. Such a man has more freedom and opportunity to develop human values and to share the reality and responsibility of parenting." The college men we surveyed showed themselves aware of the opportunity that rests on the new financial base. Two thirds said they would like their future mates to contribute equally to the family income. In contrast to the traditional ego-boosting image of the male as exclusive provider our respondents declared themselves open to the idea that, for at least part of their adult lives, their mates would provide *total* financial support.

In a few years we have obviously traveled some distance from traditional notions of male and female roles. As late as 1964 psychologist Jerome Kagan summed up the prevailing definition of gender roles in American society as follows: Women are supposed to inhibit aggression and open display of sexual urges, focus energies on marriage and children, be passive with men, be nurturant, cultivate attractiveness, and maintain an effective, socially poised, friendly posture with others. In contrast, males are supposed to be initiators, sexually aggressive, independent in problem situations; they are supposed to focus energies on their careers and be suppressive of strong emotions, especially anxiety. Nearly everything expressed in these definitions is at variance with the data we have collected.

Changes in male-female behavior and attitudes during the last 10 years have been dramatic. But, as one would expect, traditional attitudes also persist and both men and women are ambivalent, drawn first in one direction and then in the other. This is borne out by a 1978 study done at Brown University and five other northeastern institutions in which we participated. Women students at those institutions reported intellectual put-downs and sexual slights by male professors and students. In our own studies we have interviewed women who felt very insecure about men and who showed a strong tendency to be submissive. Such realities help to explain why—despite their strong commitment to careers that we have mentioned—a great many more women (52 percent) than men (8 percent) think it likely that they will postpone their professional lives for the sake of raising children. Other data we have collected indicate that on a deeper, less conscious level many students still cling to traditional conceptions and stereotypes of male and female roles that are at variance with consciously expressed ideas.

For several years we have given the students who participated in our surveys a list of adjectives and asked them to check those that applied to themselves. A majority of women have consistently described themselves as less aggressive than men but more sensitive, outwardly emotional, and capable of giving love. The men feel they share some of these qualities but they do not regard themselves as less sensitive or less capable of giving love. A majority consider themselves more ambitious, independent, and rational than the women.

These persistent perceptions of male-female differences reflect long-established patterns of gender roles, different experiences, and the differential education of women. Perhaps in the future non-discriminatory definitions of gender differences may emerge. But the responses to our checklist indicate that we are in a transitional period. There is a further implication: Our observations and interviews of the past two years suggest that in the immediate future college women may veer somewhat more toward traditional conceptions of female roles. We may soon witness some slowing down of the movement toward greater female autonomy. Such a period would not represent a "backlash" but rather a time to absorb the changes that have been made, to consolidate and take stock.

Recent gains in women's autonomy and changes in women's self-concepts make it highly unlikely that traditional male-female patterns will ever return.

In the early sixties, when the students first began to protest the old custodial arrangements, some administrators and faculty worried that greater freedom would lead to licentious behavior. As we have seen, the movement toward greater sexual freedom was only one manifestation of something far more serious: It reflected new ways in which students viewed their needs and rights; it provided an outlet for feelings; it redefined the psychological and social roles of men and women. In fact, greater sexual freedom has led to a de-emphasis of sex. Many students in the past were preoccupied with sex. Marriages often took place because of unfulfilled, obsessive fantasies influenced by sexual inexperience. The elimination of barriers between the sexes has made possible expanded opportunities for acquaintance, friendship, and work between men and women, quite apart from direct sexual expression. Sex has been de-emphasized as a test of prowess or popularity and has become a form of self-expression and caring. There has been an enhancement of nonsexual relationships between members of the same sex and opposite sexes. Women feel greater freedom to expect a deeper emotional response from men. For many men this has been a cause of anxiety, but it has also stimulated previously underdeveloped capacities for feeling. There is the promise of more egalitarian, mutually respectful, and giving relationships as college students mature into full adulthood; future marriages may be based more on knowledge than on romantic idealization, with both partners able to work at overcoming the problems that inevitably emerge in close relationships.

While the emphasis of this article has been on heterosexual relationships, changes in attitudes toward homosexuality are also occurring. Ten years ago who would have anticipated that homosexual men and women would openly declare their orientation on campus and would organize into groups that would offer companionship and represent their interests? Those of us who watched students closely were aware of the agonies that many young people with a homosexual orientation felt. Not only did they fear external reprisals; they suffered uncertainties and pain inflicted by those who stamped homosexuality sick or even criminal. It must be remembered that until a few years ago the American Psychiatric Association officially labeled homosexuality an illness. Of course, anyone acquainted with the college scene knows that homosexuality is not nearly so widely accepted among students as premarital intercourse. Ugly antigay graffiti still appear on college walls. In a recent survey at Stony Brook we found that while very few students (7 percent) disapproved of premarital sex, nearly half (47 percent) disapproved of open homosexuality.

As one might expect, greater sexual freedom has brought its own problems and challenges. Difficulties that formerly manifested themselves only in marriage now appear earlier in life, as college students tangle with intense and intimate relationships. There is an advantage to working things through before long-term commitments have been made, but coping is difficult because the guidelines or norms of behavior are less clear than in the past.

What has the response of institutions been? After some initial wariness, or perhaps shock, universities breathed a sigh of relief that much of the custodial apparatus could be dispensed with. In times of budgetary restraints this was particularly welcome. In loco parentis has been replaced by laissez faire. Students today would not easily brook the interference with their autonomy that was common in the very recent past. Many feel that the experiences of their elders, particularly in the areas of social and sexual behavior, are of little help in understanding the situations they confront with their peers. For some students there has even been a curious reversal: The student himself becomes the parent vis-a-vis his own parents, trying to help them understand the younger generation's situation and feelings.

Nevertheless, our encounters and observations tell us that, more than ever, students need guidance and instruction. Precisely because relationships are more intense, anxieties have come to the surface full-blown. This should not be viewed as necessarily negative. It provides an unprecedented opportunity for colleges to deploy their resources in the service of young people while they are still within the institution and therefore within reach. Once a student is married and on his or her own, higher education is far more helpless. But the opportunity carries with it the charge: the continuing need for counseling in all its forms. It is deplorable that during the current retrenchment such services are first cut in the mistaken belief that education is limited to the classroom.

To respond effectively to the intricacies of the new relations between college men and women, however, one would have to do more than individual and group counseling. A systematic replanning of educational opportunities is called for. The curriculum should expose students to human relationships in many different settings. Margaret Mead's proposal for "internships" in families other than one's own was one response to that need. Much more could also be done in the classroom. Over the last few years courses in human sexuality have been highly popular. They have done their share to dispel the shocking ignorance of many students about human anatomy, health-related sex issues, the nature and use of contraceptives, and the different physical and emotional responses of men and women to sex. Here and there one finds courses on aspects of human relationships or on psychological growth that push beyond the conventional curriculum without sacrificing intellectual sophistication. Almost any discipline from biology to the study of literature has something to say that bears vitally on human relationships. In order to realize the potential of such contributions, a more flexible concept of the curriculum is required. Moreover, the courses we have in mind would need to be entrusted to faculty who are more than intellectually competent. They would require a gift for understanding the emotional side of life so that they could respond to the spoken and unspoken feelings of their students. They would also need to be willing to enhance their capacities through seminars with peers and through further training.

It is intriguing to note that the changes described here were almost entirely due to the initiative of students, in the face of initial administrative and faculty resistance. This is a telling comment on the comparative wisdom of youth and adults. We urge a much fuller response on the part of institutions to help students cope with their changed situation. We plead for educational institutions to take seriously their mission to education in areas that are essential for well-being. For while male-female relationships show a net gain, this same cannot be said for some other aspects of campus life. Students frequently display an invidious and damaging competitiveness. Their sense of responsibility for one another and for the larger society in which they live is underdeveloped. Much in the attitudes of young people toward each other cries out for redress. But in higher education a response is largely wanting. Faculty go on modifying the established curriculum and pay not nearly enough attention to the rich and painful lives their students live, as they struggle to cope, insufficiently illuminated by the classroom.

What Every Woman Should Know About Men

Alan Alda

Alan Alda is an actor, writer, director, and a member of the National Commission on the Observance of International Women's Year.

Everyone knows that testosterone, the so-called male hormone, is found in both men and women. What is not so well known is that men have an overdose.

Until now it has been thought that the level of testosterone in men is normal simply because they have it. But if you consider how abnormal their *behavior* is, then you are led to the hypothesis that almost all men are suffering from *testosterone poisoning.*

The symptoms are easy to spot. Sufferers are reported to show an early preference (while still in the crib) for geometric shapes. Later, they become obsessed with machinery and objects to the exclusion of human values. They have an intense need to rank everything, and are obsessed with size. (At some point in his life, nearly every male measures his penis.)

It is well known that men don't look like other people. They have chicken legs. This is symptomatic of the disease, as is the fact that those men with the most aviary underpinnings will rank women according to the shapeliness of *their* legs.

The pathological violence of most men hardly needs to be mentioned. They are responsible for more wars than any other leading sex.

Testosterone poisoning is particularly cruel because its sufferers usually don't know they have it. In fact, when they are most under its sway they believe that they are at their healthiest and most attractive. They even give each other medals for exhibiting the most advanced symptoms of the illness.

But there is hope.

Sufferers can change (even though it is harder than learning to walk again). They must first realize, however, that they are sick. The fact that this condition is inherited in the same way that dimples are does not make it cute.

Eventually, of course, telethons and articles in the *Reader's Digest* will dramatize the tragedy of testosterone poisoning. In the meantime, it is imperative for your friends and loved ones to become familiar with the danger signs.

Have the men you know take this simple test for—

THE SEVEN WARNING SIGNS OF TESTOSTERONE POISONING

1. *Do you have an intense need to win?* When having sex, do you take pride in always finishing before your partner? Do you always ask if this time was "the best"—and gnaw on the bedpost if you get an ambiguous answer?

2. *Does violence play a big part in your life?* Before you answer, count up how many hours you watched football, ice hockey, and children's cartoons this year on television. When someone crosses you, do you wish you could stuff his face full of your fist? Do you ever poke people in your fantasies or throw them to and fro at all? When someone cuts you off in traffic, do violent, angry curses come bubbling out of your mouth before you know it? If so, you're in big trouble, fella, and this is only question number two.

3. *Are you "thing" oriented?* Do you value the parts of a woman's body more than the woman herself? Are you turned on by things that even *remind* you of those parts? Have you ever fallen in love with a really great doorknob?

4. *Do you have an intense need to reduce every difficult situation to charts and figures?* If you were present at a riot, would you tend to count the crowd? If your wife is despondent over a deeply felt setback that has left her feeling helpless, do you take her temperature?

5. *Do you tend to measure things that are really qualitative?* Are you more impressed with how high a male ballet dancer can leap than with what he does while he's up there? Are you more concerned with how long you can spend in bed, and with how many orgasms you can have, than you are with how you or your partner feels while you're there?

6. *Are you a little too mechanically minded?* Would you like to watch a sunset with a friend and feel at one with nature and each other, or would you rather take apart a clock?

7. *Are you easily triggered into competition?* When someone tries to pass you on the highway, do you speed up a little? Do you find yourself getting into contests of crushing beer cans—with the beer still in them?

If you've answered yes to three or fewer of the above questions, you may be learning to deal with your condition. A man answering yes to more than three is considered sick and not someone you'd want to have around in a crisis—such as raising children or growing old together. Anyone answering yes to all seven of the questions should seek help immediately before he kills himself in a high-wire act.

WHAT TO DO IF YOU SUFFER FROM TESTOSTERONE POISONING

1. *Don't panic.* Your first reaction may be that you are sicker than anyone else—or that you are the one man in the world able to fight it off—or, knowing that you are a sufferer, that you are the one man ordained to lead others to health (such as by writing articles about it). These are all symptoms of the disease. Just relax. First, sit back and enjoy yourself. Then find out how to enjoy somebody else.

2. *Try to feel something.* (Not with your hands, you oaf.) Look at a baby and see if you can appreciate it. (Not how *big* it's getting, just how nice she or he is.) See if you can get yourself to cry by some means other than getting hit in the eye or losing a lot of money.

3. *See if you can listen while someone is talking.* Were you the one talking? Perhaps you haven't got the idea yet.

4. *Practice this sentence:* "You know, I think you're right and I'm wrong." (Hint: it is useful to know what the other person thinks before you say this.)

FOR WOMEN ONLY: WHAT TO DO IF YOU ARE LIVING WITH A SUFFERER

1. Remember that a little sympathy is a dangerous thing. The sufferer will be inclined to interpret any concern for him as appropriate submissiveness.

2. Let him know that you expect him to fight his way back to health and behave like a normal person—for his own sake, not for yours.

3. Only after he begins to get his condition under control and has actually begun to enjoy life should you let him know that there is no such thing as testosterone poisoning.

What You Tell Your Child About Sex (Without Saying A Word)

Anne Bernstein

Anne Bernstein, Ph.D., is a California-based family therapist and the author of "The Flight of the Stork," a book about how to discuss sex and birth with children.

"I am going to do a better job talking to my kids about sex than my parents did with me" is a frequent vow in today's households, but a difficult one to put into practice. Even without saying a word about sex, though, we teach volumes, by the example of our lives. Children learn by observation; they are acute receivers of nonverbal messages. For them, as for us, actions speak louder than words.

Sometimes we actually teach what we want to teach. Often, we do not. For instance, parents who tell a child that it is all right to masturbate, their voices flat and controlled, are giving her a double message. Their words say one thing, but their intonation tells her that on a deeper level they believe just the opposite. Children then are left with ideas and feelings about sex that they can neither question nor explain.

Babies and sex education.

Teaching about sexuality begins at birth. The touching and handling and caressing loving parents provide teach infants to relate warmly to others, while touch deprivation leads to emotional and physical problems. From their parents, children learn either "I am a lovable person whom others will care for " or "I am unlovable and must protect myself from caring too much for anyone."

To like oneself one must like one's body. How others respond to one's body is an important part of how we feel about ourselves. Spoken and unspoken messages set the tone for who and what can be touched and what conditions exist to see, show, or ask questions about bodies. Is it okay to touch Mother? Father? Her breast? His penis? Until the child is how old? Can he still look after he can't touch? And how will he be stopped when the line is drawn? The way parents touch children as well as family and cultural attitudes toward nudity and modesty, bodily pleasure, or physiological development all affect a child's sexual development, leading to positive or negative attitudes toward the body.

Toilet training provides an important arena for transmitting attitudes about body parts and processes. The young child values his waste products as part of his body. If he is made to feel that his bowel movement or urine is bad, he may internalize these attitudes and start to feel that he himself is bad. Dr. Warren Gadpaille, in *Cycles of Sex*, decries calling the sex organs by "nursery or babytalk words which, in their initial application, refer to excretory functions," because they foster "the association between sexuality and dirtiness." Similarly, Selma Fraiberg points out that children who discover that the genitals that give them pleasure disgust their parents will often feel that their genitals are bad, their feelings are wrong, and that they are unworthy as people.

"I enjoy being a girl (or boy)."

Feeling good about being a girl or a boy is another important source of self-esteem. To like the fact of one's own sex one must feel good about one's genitals. It is hard for a child to feel good about himself if his parents would have preferred him to have been put together differently.

In learning about sex differences, children learn both facts and values. But until they see evidence to the contrary, both sexes assume that everybody is "just like me." Seeing the body of a naked child of the other sex will stimulate questions about why there's a difference. Boys may ask, "Where's her penis?" or "Why doesn't she have one, too?" From girls, the questions may be "What is that?" or "What happened to mine?"

Unless complicated by negative attitudes toward the little girl's sexuality, penis envy is common but harmless. Teaching more about other sex differences is often useful when children first begin to ask questions about genitals, so that each sex is defined by what it has rather than what it lacks. Both sexes need to understand that they are specially designed, "on purpose," to be different so that they can make babies together when they are grown up.

Masturbation is one way that children explore their bodies' potential for pleasure, and while most children do masturbate, some 40 percent of their parents think that it's "not all right" for them to do so, according to a Cleveland-based study in *Family Life and Sexual Learning*. There is, however, evidence that masturbation is a sign of healthy normality.

As early as 1905, Freud wrote that the sexual instinct is aroused by maternal affection as well as by direct excitation of the genitals. Later research supported this connection. Child-development researcher René Spitz, M.D., who observed infants throughout the first year of life, found that babies who received virtually no nurturance did not masturbate, even though they received all the usual stimulation involved in ordinary diapering and bathing. Those whose mothers had personal problems that hindered the quality of the care they offered showed some self-stimulation, but no genital masturbation. The babies given the best maternal care all began to masturbate by their first birthdays. The study concludes that infantile sexuality develops spontaneously with quality nurturance, clearly demonstrating that it is both normal and healthy.

This does not mean that parents cannot or should not put limits on their children's masturbation or other sexual activity. Preschool children, even toddlers, have already learned that there are appropriate times and places for many of their activities: eating is done at the table, sleeping in the bedroom, elimination in the toilet. Masturbation need not be treated differently. A parent may say: "I know it feels good to play with your penis (or clitoris or vagina), and it's okay, but it makes me uncomfortable when you do it here in the kitchen where I have to work. I would feel much better if you would go to another room, where you can have privacy." This parent acknowledges that the child's good feeling is appropriate and respected, but she also takes care of her own discomfort, without leading him to confuse her needs with his own.

What about family nudity?

Parents' attitudes toward their own bodies have an important impact on their children's sexuality. If parents hide their bodies and are embarrassed upon being discovered unclothed, children will learn that there is something shameful about the human body. In appropriate settings, casual and unaffected parental nudity conveys the message that parents are "at home" in their bodies.

Parental nudity is sometimes thought to be overstimulating to children. I think it is the attitude of the adults—how they feel when they are undressed—and not the nudity itself that can be distressing.

Seductiveness, not nudity, is what overstimulates children. Parents can be seductive without being nude and nude without being seductive. A look at other cultures shows us that nudity is not necessarily damaging to children. It is the emotional messages the parent is broadcasting, not how many clothes he or she is wearing, that influence how children will feel. If parents are self-conscious about being undressed, they will transmit anxiety and doubt rather than comfortable self-assurance. If this is the case, parents can quietly request privacy, avoiding a show of distress.

Uproar during the teen years.

Puberty is a critical time for youngsters' evolving sense of themselves as sexual beings. Parents' responses to the physical changes in their children go a long way in shaping their sexual self-esteem. Often criticism of the child's sexual development is veiled in comments about clothing and makeup, rules for getting home, and choice of acceptable companions. A father who feels aroused by his adolescent daughter's womanhood may react with anxiety and denial. In so doing, though, he may lead his daughter to blame herself for the change in him, which she sees as rejection. She is left feeling that she has done something wrong by becoming sexual.

Typically, parents who have sexual feelings toward their children—and these feelings are quite normal—will do something to put more distance between themselves and the children. Picking a fight with the child reassures the parent that his feared and shameful thoughts will stay just thoughts. While this way of retreating from sexual feelings may reduce the possibility of acting them out, there are less destructive ways of assuring the same result. Even when children are their most seductive, adults can set limits without either rejecting them or mystifying the issues to produce distance. Adults often overestimate what their children's sexual goals in flirting actually are. The child is likely to want the feelings of closeness and "being special," not a more adult approach to sexuality.

Sugar and spice versus snips and snails.

Learning about sexual identity involves more than just physiological differences and physical development, however. Parents' beliefs about male and female roles in the family and in society affect the way children are treated from birth, when the first fact told about the newborn is what it has between its legs. Expecting them to be "tougher," baby boys are bounced and thrown into the air more; little girls are fondled more than their brothers. In *Family Life and Sexual Learning*, educators Elizabeth J. Roberts, David Kline, and John Gagnon report that while girls kiss, hug, and take care of others more, boys are discouraged from being gentle and physically affectionate or from asking for help or comfort. Boys are still rewarded for controlling emotions, and much of their play occurs in large groups, avoiding one-to-one closeness. Girls, on the other hand, are encouraged to be affectionate and to express vulnerability and get more of a chance to practice intimacy, focusing their affection on a best friend or two.

Whatever parents say about sex roles, how they themselves live is a more powerful lesson. When children see who cooks, works, nurtures, and punishes, they receive important messages about what men and women can and cannot do. Roberts, Kline, and Gagnon point out that because women are mothers, providing most of the tender and intimate care of children, children learn that affection, love, and emotional intimacy are women's special province. If the only place their father is affectionate is in the bedroom, children may deduce that the only way for sexually mature people to be held, touched, or comforted is to engage in erotic behavior.

Children need to know that sex includes emotional intimacy as well as sexual intercourse and making babies. By watching their parents' marriage, they learn how sexual intimates relate. Is the love between a woman and a man mutually supportive, caring, tender, responsive, and responsible? Or is it exploitative, critical, barren, and debasing? What they see at home as children will influence their expectations of what is possible for them when they become sexually active adults.

In our culture, experts agree that this does not include making love in front of the children. Witnessing adult sex can be both overstimulating and evocative of scary misconceptions. Of course, children sometimes wander into their parents' bedrooms at inopportune times. These occasions are best handled without panic or guilt about wounded young psyches. Telling the child you want to be left alone and will be available in a short time is usually sufficient for the time being. Later you can explain what you were doing and ask if the child has any questions. Hearing you speak of the love and pleasure of sex will help counteract any impression of violence. Clear, simple, and forthright answers to questions can give children the information they seek without compromising your own intimacy and comfort or overstimulating the children.

What parents need to know.

Clearly we cannot avoid communicating about sex to children. The way we relate to one another and how we talk about sexual differences, reproduction, and relationships all form a part of their sex education. But how can we guide them in their efforts to integrate their sexuality into their lives as whole people when this is a task very much in progress for most of us? In order to help the children we love, we must first explore our own feelings about sexuality and become comfortable with them. To be clear with children we must first be clear with ourselves, recognizing our abilities and limits and acknowledging our true values.

There will be mistakes. But mistakes can be remedied. Elizabeth Canfield, a prominent sex-education counselor at the University of Southern California at Los Angeles, suggests: "It's a marvelous experience to walk up to a child and be able to say: 'You know, I've done some more thinking about our discussion the other day and I've decided what I said didn't make sense, so let's talk some more.' A child (or friend, neighbor, student, employee, lover) will be so delighted with this admission . . . that a whole new world of communication will have opened up!"

By keeping the communication channels open about sex, parents who establish themselves early in their children's lives as receptive in dealing with sexuality will find that when their children have questions or worries to be cleared up, they will turn to their parents.

For information does not equal permission. Socially inappropriate behavior is more often the result of ignorance than of knowledge. None of us, child or adult, does everything we know to be possible. Nor do we want to. But when we know the score, we can choose which tune to sing, fitting the song to the scene and to the characters with whom we share the platform.

Putting Sex Education Back in the Home

Sol Gordon

Parents are expected to be the primary sex educators of their own children. Yet in survey after survey, it has been found that fewer than 20% of young people today feel that their parents gave them a satisfactory sex education. In fact, some parents who report that they did educate their children about sex might be surprised to learn that their adult sons and daughters scarcely agree.

"My parents?" some laugh. "You must be kidding!"

"I learned more from my friends," others explain, "only to discover in college that most of what I learned was not true."

Let me first try to put to rest the two most prevalent and noxious sex myths which I see as largely responsible for the ever increasing incidence of irresponsible sexual behavior, particularly among young people.

Myth One: Today's Youth Already Know Everything There Is To Know About Sex.

Some do, of course, but research reveals shocking ignorance about critical issues. Young people are having sex earlier, beginning at 12, 13, or 14 years of age. And the earlier a child has sexual intercourse, the less, repeat *less,* he or she usually knows about it. Worse, sexually experienced young people will often feel compelled to exaggerate their knowledge, to pretend they understand as much as their experience suggests. In an important 1976 Johns Hopkins study of adolescent girls, for example, only 41% knew when in the menstrual cycle the risk of conception was greatest.

Don't believe the stories that all young people knowingly take risks, or that girls from disadvantaged homes deliberately try to get pregnant. Remember that research on teenage pregnancy usually involves asking pregnant girls if they had originally wanted to conceive. In one such study of 300 teenagers (in *a single* high school), we asked why the girls hadn't practiced birth control. "Oh, but we did," was the general response, but their specific answers revealed that quite the opposite was true.

"I used one of my mother's pills."

"I didn't think I could get pregnant standing up."

"He said he'd pull out in time."

"I didn't think I could get pregnant the first time."

"I used foam." (Careful questioning subsequently confirmed that many had used contraceptive foam, but as a douche *after* intercourse.)

When we asked 300 sexually active girls if they wanted to become pregnant, a resounding 95% said they did not.

"What?" many asked in disbelief. "Do you think I'm stupid? I'm only 14!"

At this point, some readers may already be thinking that surely their own children are not involved in sexual experimentation. It should be remembered that whether anyone likes it or not (including the teenagers themselves) more than half of all high school students will have had sexual intercourse before graduation.

In surveys of high school students, more than 90% did not know that the original symptoms of venereal disease disappear after a while. Most assumed that the disappearance of symptoms meant the disease had been cured. A majority of the same students did not know that females are generally asymptomatic with respect to gonorrhea.

Each year our Institute receives hundreds of poignant letters from teenagers. A large number begin something like this:

"I'm 15, pregnant and I can't tell my folks (they'll kill me). What should I do?"

More typical are those like this one from a Nebraska girl.

> Dear Mr. Sol Gordon,
>
> I come from a family where I have learned sex from my friends. My mother don't mention it to me. And I still don't know what most of sex and love is all about. So I would like to know because I'm only 14 years of age. And I've seen my friends get pregnant. I'd like to know what it's all about. Thank you.

"Putting Sex Education Back in the Home," by Dr. Sol Gordon, *Community Sex Education Programs for Parents, Training Manual for Organizers, Institute for Family Research & Education,* 1977. Reprinted by permission of the author.

The one million adolescent pregnancies in 1976, the three million new cases of venereal disease in the same year (two-thirds of which were among young people under 25), and the plainly destructive consequences of misinformation about masturbation, homosexuality, and, in general, the nature of normal and abnormal sexual behavior emphatically contradict the myth that young people know everything there is to know about sex.

Myth Two: Knowledge Is Harmful.

Virtually all opposition to sex education is based on the assumption that knowledge is harmful, that children who know about sex will practice it. It's not even uncommon for editors of metropolitan newspapers to blame sex education for the rise of illegitimacy and venereal disease. Critics of the Scandinavian countries have long held sex education in the schools partly responsible for moral and social deterioration, as reflected in high rates of sex crime, suicide, and out-of-wedlock pregnancies. The truth of the matter, however, is that compulsory sex education in the public schools of Denmark, Sweden and Norway is a recent development, and the best available statistics reveal sharp reductions in teenage birth rates and in serious sex crimes since that advent.

As for the United States, I couldn't name a dozen public schools which have what I consider an adequate sex education program. I'd be hard-pressed to identify even one program that could be called a model in this regard. In fewer than 50% of the schools with any sex education program at all, the course usually consists primarily of a few lectures about plumbing, often a relentless pursuit of the fallopian tubes. For the vast majority of American students, sex education is simply absent from the curriculum.

To the question whether our communications media contribute to the responsible sex education of young people, we must give an emphatic no. Certainly, we do find out about rape, violence, sado-masochism, and various forms of sexual titillation from newspapers, magazines and especially television, but what have these to do with sex education? These are anti-sex messages. In television sex education has been largely deemed inappropriate for family viewing!

Our research tells us that ignorance, not knowledge, leads to irresponsible behavior. In fact, knowledgeable young people are more likely to postpone sexual experiences until after the teen years, and then to use effective contraception. In the whole world, literate and well-informed women usually take measures to control their fertility and limit the number of children they have to two or three.

A dangerously convoluted logic has prompted some to claim that the pill is leading young women to promiscuity. The fact is that no more than 30% of sexually active teenagers regularly use any reliable contraception whatsoever. If only they would use birth control, society wouldn't be in so much trouble.

Roadblocks to Effective Sex Education in the Home

Most parents, after all, want to educate their children about sex. They realize that schools, churches, community organizations and the mass media can only offer supplementary sex education at best and, in any case, cannot be expected to mirror their personal values. Unfortunately, however, many parents also fear that too much information too soon will have the negative consequence of overstimulating their children.

Contrary to a *few* experts in this field, I've never been able to discover a documented case of a child's having been overstimulated by facts alone. Indeed, when was the last time you tried to tell your child too much about *anything?* Should parents err in the direction of too much information, children will simply get bored, turn them off, or cut it short with an irrelevant question. This is not to say that overstimulation is not a problem. It is, and it derives from fears, unresolved curiosity and ignorance. Our campaign against ignorance has led opponents of sex education to tell jokes about us. A popular example is about the child who asks where she came from and whose mother responds with an elaborate explanation of the seed and the egg. At the end, the child explains that she only wanted to know if she came from Philadelphia. To this, my response is very simple. "So what? Now the child knows not only where she was born but also how she got there." The moral of this and similar stories is that most children would learn very little if education was restricted to what they themselves chose to learn.

Quite understandably, many parents who did not receive sex education in their own homes feel uncomfortable talking about sex with their children. There is no instant remedy for such feelings, but it may be helpful to point out that no one is really comfortable about anything these days. When is the last time someone told you not to worry and you stopped? Contrary to much modern theory, it simply is not necessary to feel totally comfortable about your own, or anybody else's, sexuality in order to be an effective sex educator for your children.

As the primary force in your child's life, you are providing sex education in one form or another no matter what you do. The question is not whether you will teach your children about sex, but how well. Silence teaches no less eloquently than speech. Interestingly enough, if you convey to a young child, or even a teenager, the impression that you feel a bit awkward discussing love and sex, the chances are good that *you'll score.* Your child might well respond to your honesty with genuine affection and appreciation, with a hug and a kiss and with verbal assurances that your discomfort is perfectly understood. Many a parent has been happily surprised to hear a child say, "Don't worry, Mom! It's all right."

Parents who worry that they don't know enough about the subject to be effective teachers ought to pause and consider a question. How much is it really necessary to know? How much really is there to know? To a particularly technical or baffling question, a parent can always respond with the truth. "I don't know, but I'll look it up for you and I'll tell you tomorrow." Or, better still, "Let's look it up together."

If you think about it, what do you really have to know that you don't know already in order to answer a small child's questions? Older children are more likely to ask questions about values than anatomy. And with hundreds of good books no more distant than your local library, what excuse do you really have?

Some parents are concerned about the possibility of traumatizing their children by making honest mistakes, by giving wrong answers. Remember that the resilience of children is legendary, and for good reasons. Parents should realize that they can make mistakes without harming their children. A few examples may be illustrative.

A child wanders into the bedroom while his parents are having sexual intercourse. What to do? Tell the child to leave. In the morning you can apologize for not having said please. And then you can explain what you were doing. If your child asks to watch the next time, tell him he cannot. Kindly and firmly explain that sex is private. A child may not understand the prohibition, but later in life he will grow to appreciate the concept of privacy, not only for his parents but for himself as well. Most important, learn to laugh at the outrageous proposition that a child who has witnessed the "primal scene" will need five years of analysis to get over it. A more likely candidate for analysis is the person who, as a child, never once saw his parents being naturally and openly affectionate.

Some parents worry about the neighbors. What if your child tells the truth about sex to some little friends whose parents hear about it and inform you, in no uncertain terms, of their horror and indignation? Let's take this one from the opposite point of view. What about parents who tell their children that babies grow in cabbage patches? Do you suppose they care about your feelings when your children come home with such news? Your responsibility is to tell your own children the truth, and without instructions to keep it confidential. If your neighbors don't like it, that's their problem. It's about time that the well-educated children—your children—became an important neighborhood resource with respect to sex education. No matter what parents do, children will share whatever information they might have about sex. Isn't it better that they share truth and fact?

Some parents believe that sex education belongs exclusively in the home, but it is grossly unrealistic to try to protect children from all external influences and viewpoints. No parents can have exclusive control over the sex education of their children unless they are prepared to rear them in virtual isolation—no friends, no books, no magazines, no television, and no school.

Of course, even the best-intentioned parents have questions to which the best qualified professionals cannot give satisfactory answers. Of the thousands of questions I get from parents, the following are the most common. To be sure, some of the responses reflect my personal values, but if any of them conflict with yours, stick to your own. It is important to stress and respect the fact of individual differences. Perhaps we might have some differences which do not threaten a more fundamental agreement. In any case, it is you who must decide where you stand on specific issues. I make a special point of this because the subject of sex education often attracts extremists who try, often in the guise of "morality," to impose their personal views on everybody else.

The key question for all of us should be, "Am I an askable parent?" or, put somewhat differently, "When should I tell?" The answer is simple. It is time to tell whenever the child asks. And if you are an askable parent, your child may begin to ask about sex from the time he is two. With young children, the questions are sometimes nonverbal. For example, a child may constantly follow you into the bathroom. Some shy children might ask no questions at all, even of the most askable parents. If your child hasn't raised sexual questions by the age of five, then you should start the conversation. Read a book with him. Tell him about a neighbor or a relative who is going to have a baby. While it's fine, on occasion, to refer to animals, do not concentrate on them in your explanations. People and animals have very different habits.

Askable parents should feel generally responsive to the suggested answers given in the series of questions which follow. Parents who are not askable may find themselves feeling somewhat provoked and perhaps indignant. (This might be a good time to ask yourself whether you are an askable parent. If so, you can test yourself by turning to the quiz on A/E p. 37.)

1. How much should I tell?

You should tell your child a *bit* more than you feel he can understand.

2. How explicit should I be?

In the first place, always make it a point to use the correct terminology. Avoid such infantile euphemisms as "pee pee" or "wee wee". Say directly that when a man and a woman love each other and want to have a baby, the man's penis is placed into the woman's vagina. If the sperm from the man's body joins with the egg inside the woman's body at the right time, a baby gets started. Depending on the child's age and other factors, you might say more. "Sometimes it takes a year or more before a baby is conceived." Or, "Your father (or mother) and I enjoy loving each other in this way. Right now we are using birth control because our family isn't ready for a new baby just yet."

The main idea is that parents can be explicit without overstating the case or feeling compelled to describe sexual techniques to a child who hasn't yet grasped much more basic ideas. It is also wiser to say at the start that a baby has its beginning in the mother's uterus, not the stomach.

3. What about nudity in the home?

Many parents are relaxed about undressing in front of young children or about bathing with them. These are good opportunities for children to ask important questions. "How come you have one and I don't?" "How come yours is bigger than mine?" "How come you have two and I don't have any?" Parents should respond directly to these and similar questions.

A question also arises when a child wants to touch a parent's genitals or breasts. There are several perfectly acceptable responses, one of which is simply that you don't want him to do this. Even if a child protests against that familiar double standard—"but you touch me"—you can explain that that is because you have to bathe him and keep him clean. For parents who do not object to their children's requests to touch, it is important to remain casual about it. Generally speaking, a child's own growing sense of modesty will tell you when to start undressing in private. When a child wants to go to the bathroom alone or to undress without an audience, you will have indications that he is developing a sense of privacy that you need to respect.

4. Is too much masturbation harmful?

Masturbation is a normal expression of sexuality at any age. The only thing wrong with it is the guilt that people are made to feel, and it is this guilt that creates the energy for impulsive and involuntary masturbation. All children old enough to understand should be taught that masturbation should be done in private. As they get older, they will sense that masturbation is a normal enjoyable substitute for sexual intercourse, and they will realize that as long as it gives them pleasure, there is no such thing as too much.

5. What about the use of obscenities?

Children invariably use vulgar language to get a rise out of their parents, to test a new and powerful weapon. If a child uses an obscenity, the parent should quickly and calmly explain its meaning, perhaps using the word itself in the explanation. Even the most common four-letter word can be handled in this way, provided the parent explains its gross intent as well as the fact that it's a crude synonym for sexual intercourse.

6. What about the child who likes to look at his father's "girlie" magazines?

There is no harm in this. In fact, it may provide a teachable moment. You might point out that ordinary people don't look like that, or that people sometimes like to look at unusual photographs of the nude, or that women sometimes enjoy looking at pictures of nude men. It's not a big deal. Generally speaking, frontal nudity is becoming more common in established magazines.

Pornography, however, is something else again. True, it has not been proven harmful, but it is clearly not educational, and many parents would understandably prefer to keep their children away from it. While it may not always be possible to shield a child from pornographic material, parents can take some comfort in the fact that people who have received responsible sex education show a marked tendency to grow quickly bored with pornography.

7. What about embarrassing questions in public?

Children have a great knack for asking the most delicate questions in the supermarket or when special guests have come to dinner. The best approach, no matter how embarrassed you are, is to tell the child that he has asked a very good question and, if you still have your wits about you, proceed to answer it then and there. In most cases, your guests will silently applaud. If you feel you can't answer the question right away, it is very important to praise the child for asking and to tell him specifically when you will discuss it with him. Generally speaking, it is better to risk shocking a few grown-ups than to embarrass your own child.

8. What should I do if my husband thinks it's my job to tell?

Sex education is properly the responsibility of both parents, as it is reflected in their behavior with each other and in communication with children. If your husband stubbornly refuses to have any part of it, you must take it upon yourself to explain love and sex to all the children in your family. Incidentally, it has never been established that girls are best educated by their mothers or boys by their fathers. Single parents, relax.

9. What can I do to keep my child from becoming homosexual?

Some parents have rather strange notions of what would constitute protection against homosexuality. Some fathers are not affectionate with school age sons for fear of encouraging homosexuality, despite the absence of any compelling evidence linking a father's love with a son's homosexuality. There are cases where fathers have rejected sons and the sons are homosexual, but even here it is very difficult to establish a connection between the rejection and the homosexuality. With as much research as we have on this subject, we still do not know why any one person, male or female, becomes homosexual. There is certainly no evidence that girls who are tomboys and boys who prefer books to footballs are more likely to become homosexual adults. Nor can we say that a child with a strong mother and a weak father has a greater chance of becoming homosexual. What we do know is that about 4% of the population will develop a homosexual orientation, no matter what parents try to do about it. While it is perfectly all right not to want your children to become homosexual, it is important to understand that good mental health is not exclusively or necessarily a function of sexual orientation. Just as homosexual adults can be happy and creative people, heterosexual adults can turn to drugs, crime, and generally lead unhappy lives.

In dealing with homosexuality, parents should convey an attitude of consideration for people who have different orientations. At the same time they should make it abundantly clear that their children are to reject any sexual overtures made by adults. Moreover, they must emphasize that such overtures do not in any way suggest that a child was somehow to blame. A child must never be allowed to think that he himself must be homosexual simply because he was approached by someone.

10. What if my children think I'm old-fashioned?

They will be right! All parents are old-fashioned. The best thing to do is acknowledge it and continue expressing your views without worrying which label your child might attach to them.

11. How can I talk to my teenage daughter about birth control without giving her the message that it's all right for her to have sexual intercourse?

Some parents erroneously believe that teenagers equate information with consent. Your teenage children know very well what your values are. It's one thing to tell a daughter that you will disown her if she becomes pregnant. It's quite another to explain your feelings something like this:

"We really think you're much too young to have sex, but if you're not going to listen to us we urge you to practice birth control. In any case, you *should* know something about birth control and, more important, we don't ever want you to feel that there's *anything* you can't talk to us about.

12. I worry about my children being molested. How can I talk about this without frightening them?

A little known fact is that as many as 70% of all child molestation cases involve someone the child knows, such as a stepparent or babysitter. As part of a family's general discussions about sexuality, children should be taught never to go off with strangers and never to allow anyone to touch their genitals. Some individuals force children to submit to sexual activities and make them promise never to tell anyone what happened. Should you suspect that your child has been abused in this way, it is essential to make him understand that such promises should never be kept. The fact that most people are decent and kind must be balanced with the reality that some people take advantage of children. The critical point is never to let a child who has been molested feel any guilt or blame whatsoever. (Some parents unthinkingly ask, "Why did you let him do this?") Such crimes are *always* and *entirely* the responsibility of the adult.

13. We've never talked about sex. Now I want to, but my teenage son absolutely refuses. What should I do?

This is a common situation and it is appropriate for a parent to begin the conversation something like this: "I really made a mistake by waiting this long and I wish we had talked when you were younger. Now I can understand why you might feel embarrassed to talk with me." Plan ahead for such discussions; have a book ready. Tell your son that you think he might be interested in it. Explain that some of the material might embarrass him, but that you're going to leave the book around just the same. The main thing is for him to understand that you are available to talk anytime he is ready. Another technique is to "hide" a book like the one I've written entitled "YOU" (a consciousness-raising guide for teenagers). Most teenagers are very adept at finding such "hidden" material.

14. What do you mean by normal or responsible sexuality?

Normal sexuality is voluntary, generally pleasurable, and inclined to enhance the personalities of the people involved. Abnormal, or immature, sexuality tends to be involuntary. People engage in it not because they want to but because they can't help it. Immature sexuality is exploitative, rarely enjoyable, and often degrading. Responsible sexuality, by contrast, is always characterized by respect for oneself and by genuine caring for another human being.

15. What is your opinion on premarital sex?

First let me say that I'm opposed to teenagers having sexual intercourse. Teenagers are too young, too vulnerable. They do not have ready access to contraception. They tend to be impulsive. The double standard is still, alas, very much with us. Boys still use lines as, "If you really love me, you'll have sex with me." Girls rarely reply with, "If you really loved me, you wouldn't put this pressure on me." In addition, teenage pregnancy is definitely unsound from the medical, moral, and psychological points of view.

While I am opposed to sex for teenagers, I also must say that in my 25 years as a clinical psychologist, no teenager has ever asked for my consent. It is unrealistic for parents to assume their teenagers will not have sexual relationships in the absence of parental permission or consent. Thus, parents must face the possibility that however clear they have made their own values, their teenagers may just as clearly reject them. Should this occur, however, parents can *still* exert a positive influence. Without anger and without recriminations, they can simply say, "We do not want you to have sex, but if your mind is already made up, at least be sure to use birth control." Young adults who are working or in college should receive similar parental messages. The decision must be up to them, but if they do choose to have sexual relationships it is their duty, to themselves and to their partners, to act responsibly.

One of the most encouraging signs on campuses across the nation today is that women (and men) influenced by the women's liberation movement have become extremely sensitive to exploitation. More and more, young people of both sexes are coming to insist upon what they call egalitarian relationships in which the partners do not take advantage of one another.

There is absolutely no evidence that people who are virgins at marriage have better marriages than people who are not. Let those who counsel against premarital sex refrain from the absurd argument that if people have sex before marriage they'll have nothing to look forward to after the wedding. My own view is that if sex is the only thing one looks forward to in a marriage, it's better not to marry, for marital sex takes on preeminent importance only if the partners are hung up on it or dysfunctional in it.

If I were to develop a 10-point scale of the most important things in a marriage, number one would be mutual love and caring. Second would be the ability to have interesting conversations. Third would be a good sense of humor. Ninth would be a satisfying sexual relationship. Last would be discovering how to clean the house together.

16. What should be the role of the public schools in sex education?

Sex education should be part of the regular curriculum. It is currently excluded because of censorship and because of extremist pressures exerted against school boards and administrations.

17. My 14-year-old son worries about having lustful thoughts. Are these harmful?

One of the key concepts in the whole area of sexuality is that *all thoughts, desires and dreams are normal.* Anyone with the slightest imagination or creativity has occasional thoughts of lust, sado-masochism, incest, and rape. Behavior can be abnormal, but never thoughts by themselves.

Guilt is the energy for the repetition of unacceptable thoughts. For example, if a boy has homosexual fantasies and feels guilty about them, he'll have these thoughts over and over again until they become part of a self-fulfilling prophecy. If, however, he recognizes that all thoughts are normal, nothing will happen and most of his thoughts will be voluntary; the remainder will be involuntary but of negligible duration.

18. How can I bring up my children to respect the values of other people?

This depends largely on the kind of life you lead and the kinds of values you translate into your behavior with others. For it is as a model for your children (which, of course, does not imply perfection), that you have the best opportunity to foster a true respect and appreciation for individual differences.

A Final Comment

Sex education is a family affair. It is related to how you feel about yourself and your ability to communicate with your husband or wife. Askable parents talk to each other. They also have a sense of humor. Not everything is a trauma. Children with askable parents tend to talk to them. While their developing sense of privacy prevents them from telling parents everything as they grow older, most want very much for their parents to respect that privacy. Askable parents have a lot of common sense. If you feel you've made mistakes, you can smile and say, "I've made some mistakes. My child will understand when I explain that I don't know everything." And then you'll feel more askable than ever.

QUIZ
ARE YOU AN ASKABLE PARENT?

Parents wishing to take the major responsibility for their children's sex education will almost certainly have to deal with a variety of questions and behavior, some of which may catch them by surprise or come at inopportune moments. Conscientious parents are concerned about doing the "right" thing when, for example, a child asks a specific question about birth, or finds a magazine with photographs of naked people, or "plays doctor" with other children. But most people are somewhat uncomfortable about these and other aspects of sexual curiosity, in large measure because their own parents did not provide them with effective models for dealing with such things.

Following are some typical situations which a majority of parents will face at one time or another. Several alternative responses are suggested for each. Consider the situations, and circle the number next to the response that *most closely coincides* with your own. The given responses are necessarily abbreviated; real-life exchanges are naturally more complex. In choosing your answers, it might help to think of each one as the way you would *begin* to respond to the particular situation described. There are, of course, no objectively right or wrong answers. The right answer is simply the response which comes closest to your own. When you complete the quiz, add up all the numbers you have circled. For your askability quotient, see A/E p. 39 .

1. Your 4-year-old comes up to you and asks, "Where do babies come from?" What do you say?
   1) "When you get older, I'll tell you about that."
   2) "When a Mommy and a Daddy want a baby, and they love each other, they'll have a baby."
   3) "Babies come from a special place in a Mommy's body."
   4) "When a man puts his penis into a woman's vagina, the woman may become pregnant, and a baby will begin to grow in her body in a place called the uterus."

2. Ten-year-old Doug comes home from the playground and asks his father what a rubber is. What should Doug's father say?
   1) "It's nothing that need concern you at this time."
   2) "Why do you want to know? Where did you find out about it?"
   3) "A rubber is something a man uses in sex, as a birth control."
   4) "A rubber is something a man can use to keep a woman from getting pregnant. He puts it on his penis and it keeps the sperm from coming out. It helps prevent venereal disease as well."

3. Your six-year-old asks, "Why do you and Daddy close the door when you go to sleep?" What do you answer?
   1) "That's not really your business, dear."
   2) "We don't want to be disturbed."
   3) "We do personal things that you shouldn't see."
   4) "Sometimes we want to make love and we want to do it in private."

4. Nine-year-old Ted asks his mother, "What are homosexuals?" What should his mother say?
   1) "They're sick people, and you'll become one if you play with girls as much as you do."
   2) "They're people who are different from the rest of us."
   3) "They're people who are attracted to their same sex."
   4) "They're people who have and prefer sexual experiences with people of their same sex."

5. You are buying toys for your nieces and nephews and have to choose between "sexless" dolls and dolls with penises and vaginas. What do you do?
   1) You decide on the sexless ones because your sister and brother-in-law would never understand and it would make you look like a sex fiend.
   2) You decide on the sexless dolls because that's what you had and you turned out okay.
   3) You choose the new dolls because they're the latest model and you like to keep up with things like that.
   4) You decide on the dolls with sexual components because they're the most accurate.

6. Your 13-year-old daughter asks if a male could ever urinate in the vagina during intercourse. What do you do?
   1) You laugh at her silly question and say, "That's ridiculous."
   2) You try to hide your embarrassment and quickly change the subject.
   3) You tell her you don't really know, and tell her to ask her health teacher.
   4) You say you are not sure, but offer to find out the correct answer. If you know, you'll say the answer is no, because sexual function inhibits the urinary one.

7. Eight-year-old Kenny says, "I saw Tom and Sue kissing with their mouths open. Why is that called yukky kissing?" What do you answer?
   1) "That's disgusting."
   2) "It's something naughty that I don't ever want you to do."
   3) "It's a kind of kissing for grownups."
   4) "One name for it is french kissing. It's not 'yukky', but it is one of the ways in which people usually show that they like each other."

8. Your nine-year-old comes home from school and asks you the meaning of a couple of obscene words he saw painted on the schoolyard wall. What do you say?
   1) "I don't know what they mean."
   2) "They're bad words for sex and I don't ever want you to say them."
   3) "They are not polite words, and we don't use them in our house."
   4) You say the words yourself and explain that they're expressions that people use in anger

and sometimes to describe sex between a man and a woman.

9. Your four-year-old comes to you and asks, "What's the difference between boys and girls?" What do you say?
   1) "You know."
   2) "Girls cook and clean and boys go to work when they grow up."
   3) "Girls can have babies when they grow up and boys can't."
   4) "Girls' breasts get larger when they grow up. They have vaginas and can have babies. Boys have penises and can become fathers."

10. Your 8-year-old daughter asks whether it hurts to have a baby. What do you say?
    1) "Just wait till you have one. You'll find out."
    2) "No, it doesn't hurt."
    3) Yes, it hurts for a while, but the doctor shows you special exercises and ways to breathe, and can give you medicine for the hurt."
    4) "I'll answer that question, but I wonder if there is another question about all this that you are curious about."

11. Johnny is 6 and his brother Ed is 4. They fight a lot. (It's called sibling rivalry.) Johnny has punched Ed, and their mother has seen it. What should she do?
    1) Slap Johnny and say, "Don't you ever do that again."
    2) Comfort Ed and say to Johnny, "He's your brother and you're supposed to love him."
    3) Say, "I think we ought to try and get to the bottom of this," as she comforts both children.
    4) Take a sympathetic approach to both, but say to Johnny, "You don't have to like your brother, but I still don't want you to hit him."

12. Susan comes home from school and says her teacher is an idiot. What should her mother say?
    1) "Don't you ever say things like that. It's very disrespectful."
    2) "Aren't you exaggerating? Isn't there something nice about her?"
    3) "You seem really unhappy. I wonder what that's all about."
    4) "I'm sorry to hear that. It's bad enough to have a teacher you don't like. I hope you don't punish yourself twice by not doing the work, anyway."

13. You discover your 4-year-old and a neighbor's 5-year-old without any clothes, playing doctor. What do you do?
    1) Send the other child home with an "are you going to get it!" and then scold your own child.
    2) Say to both children, "This is not a very nice thing to do. If you do it again, I won't let you play together."
    3) Say, "This is not something we do in our house, so get dressed and play some other games."
    4) Say, "I know it's enjoyable, but it's not polite to take off your clothes. I'd appreciate it if you'd play in other ways."

14. Your small son asks, "How come I have a penis and you don't?" What do you answer?
    1) "Go ask your father."
    2) "Because God made us different."
    3) "Because you're a boy and I'm a girl."
    4) "Because I have a vagina instead."

15. What do you tell a child who wants to know "how babies get inside the mother's stomach?"
    1) "You're too young to know that."
    2) "By love."
    3) "Babies don't grow in the stomach. They grow in the uterus, a special place in the mother's body."
    4) "A man's body produces sperm; a woman's body produces eggs or ovum. When men and women feel like having sex, the man puts his penis in the woman's vagina and sperm comes out the penis. If the sperm joins an ovum in the mother's body, a baby starts to grow in a special place called the uterus."

The maximum score is 60. If you scored between:

55-60: You are unhesitatingly askable (which doesn't mean that you'll always be asked or always be successful).

45-54: You are askable. (You'll still make mistakes and that's okay.)

25-44: Your askability needs improving. (Try reading a current self-improvement book.)

0-24: You are not askable. (Check out your sense of humor first, and then rethink whether you want to be a parent or a supervisor.

Reflections of a Dean Who Is "Into Sex"

Fred Dobens, M.A.
Associate Dean of Students
Colgate University
Hamilton, New York

During one of our summer orientation weekends a few years ago, the mother of a student told me she had been referred to me by her discussion-group leader because she had raised a question relative to sexuality and was told "See Dean Dobens. He's into sex on the campus." Before I could answer the woman's specific question, I had to explain what being "into sex on campus" really meant.

Sexuality, as I am sure we all agree, is a topic which has always been "on campus" but it has not really come out of the closet for open and honest discussion until recent years.

I can recall working in another institution during the early 1960s which had a separate men's and women's college within the same university. The dean at the women's college suspended a student because she was pregnant and not married and, upon receiving the name of the male student involved, her counterpart at my institution asked the male student to come in to see him for counseling, but no further action was taken. An interesting but sad commentary on the "double standard."

Also, the dean at the men's college saw no reason to include a ladies room in a new residence hall being planned, because "ladies" did not visit men in a residence hall.

The same deans, now no longer deaning, were also strongly opposed to permitting visitation hours in the residence halls, for they felt that such permissiveness would definitely lead to a significant number of additional unwanted pregnancies.

Those of us who survived the 1960s on college campuses have learned to live with "open 24-hour visitations" and, in general, without any significant increase in unwanted pregnancies. I believe this has been in part because we accepted a responsibility for providing programs in the area of human sexuality with all the problems inherent in attempting to approach this particularly sensitive topic.

One of the basic problems in attempting to establish a broadly based program in human sexuality on a small private campus, without the facilities of a teaching hospital or medical school for support, is the lack of awareness, acceptance, and support from all levels that there is, in fact, a need for programming of this nature.

In order to determine the extent of need on my particular campus, I applied for and received support for a Faculty Research Council grant to administer the Sex Knowledge and Attitude Test (SKAT) to a sample of our student body. (Although the SKAT was initially developed for use with graduate students, enough undergraduate institutions have used it that comparative scales are available.) The results of my study demonstrated a need for additional educational programming in the area of human sexuality.

During this period, my institution was moving from an all-male to a male/female institution, and the process of convincing people of the need for programming in this area was enhanced somewhat by the presence of young women on the campus. Previously, with an all-male institution, programming dealing with sexuality just wasn't necessary in the eyes of many people. This type of logic obviously did a significant amount of harm, in my opinion, to a number of men who graduated from our institution, for I feel I could present as strong an argument for programs in sexuality for a single-sex institution as I could for a coeducational institution.

In order to administer the SKAT to one class, I agreed to provide a lecture to the class on "Human Sexuality on the College Campus." As a result of that presentation, a group of students came forward expressing an interest in establishing a "hot line" to provide an opportunity for information on sexuality for our students. Initially this group was recognized as the "Birth Control Information Center" but presently is more aptly titled "The Sexuality Counseling and Information Center."

Representatives of this group became part of a student membership of a committee to select a new director of our college infirmary. This led to the selection of a physician who had a supportive interest in providing a "preventative medicine" approach to sexuality, both in the infirmary and on the campus. The director was also interested in providing his expertise in the classroom on the topic of sexuality, and was led to believe during the interview process that this could be an option open to him.

The director and I attempted on two occasions to obtain

approval for a credit-bearing course in human sexuality, but to no avail. We felt it important to offer the course for credit for two major reasons: it officially identifies human sexuality as an area worthy of study, and it provides the opportunity for both students and faculty to prepare and participate fully within the normal academic schedule without acting as the additional burden on time and commitments which a noncredit course can too easily become.

Our proposals for such a course were made in great detail, and on the second presentation we even included the concept of a team of academicians to preview the audiovisuals we planned to use in an attempt to insure that they were "acceptable to the mores of our community." The second denial was one of the reasons that the director of the infirmary resigned his position.

Fortunately, the present infirmary staff, again selected with input from the Sexuality Counseling and Information Center, have continued to provide the same type of services and, in fact, spend a significant amount of time educating students at the infirmary about their bodies and not simply dispensing pills. They continue to work closely with the Sexuality Counseling and Information Center which, in conjunction with the infirmary, has begun to offer for sale nonprescription contraceptives.

As the Sexuality Counseling and Information Center grew in scope, a more extensive training process for the peers who served as volunteers was established, in conjunction with the infirmary and other key personnel on campus. Also, because it was recognized that students frequently turn to the resident advisors in their residence halls for counsel on this subject, and in addition to providing each resident advisor with copies of *Our Bodies, Ourselves,* and McCary's *Human Sexuality,* sessions were added to the resident advisor in-service training program on the topic of sexuality. An outgrowth of that experience was a January independent study experience in the area of sexuality which I offered, as well as a series of lectures on sexuality jointly sponsored by my office and the Sexuality and Counseling Information Center, as well as a noncredit course.

(Because of my previous experiences, I have not attempted again to obtain approval for a credit course in human sexuality. And, indeed, the additional demands on my time made by the noncredit course were such that until some present responsibilities are reassigned, it will be unlikely that I will be able to find time to offer another noncredit course again in the near future.)

One caveat in establishing any kind of human sexuality course on campus pertains to finding the teaching faculty. Without the resources of a teaching hospital or medical school, there may be difficulty in finding qualified personnel either to participate in an actual course or to provide lectures on the subject of sexuality. One obviously must be very cautious about simply turning to a physician or a local minister, recognizing that it has been only within the last decade or so that courses in sexuality have been provided to them in their formal training. Fortunately, a number of good films are presently available covering a wide variety of topics, and, of course, there are always qualified people from Planned Parenthood, if one seeks them out. There have been campuses similar to mine where successful programming in sexuality has been achieved. Hamilton and Kirkland Colleges, in Clinton, New York, for example, have had an excellent series on masculinity. Hobart and William Smith Colleges are presently planning a similar program for the forthcoming academic year.

Although growth in programming in this area on campuses such as mine has been gradual, a number of my colleagues have found impossible roadblocks. At one institution, for example, the college physician, who is retired and in his late seventies, happens to be a member of the college Board of Trustees and is chairman of the trustee Committee on Student Life. Because of his attitude, the trustees have become involved in an area usually delegated to the on-campus governance system, for they have established a policy prohibiting the issuance of contraceptives of any type in the infirmary, and in addition, they do not permit any services related to sexuality at all on the campus. As a result, students have been forced to use the local Planned Parenthood, which, because of the institution's geographical location, is presently overburdened with cases from within the regular community. Consequently, the college was informed that, beginning with the fall term 1977, the Planned Parenthood group would no longer be able to offer services to students.

At another college which has a physical education requirement based on the philosophy of the need for "a sound body to match a sound mind" through the concept of carryover sports, a parent approached the dean of students at Commencement, with a concern: "If you can justify your physical education requirement, a philosophy which I support, how can you not offer a course in human sexuality? In addition to having a need for a carryover sport to keep her body in good physical condition, my daughter will also have a need for greater information than you have provided relative to her body in the area of sexuality."

At another institution, during a reception for Phi Beta Kappa seniors a student approached the speaker, a key administrator known to be against the concept of course credit for courses in human sexuality on that campus. During his presentation, the administrator had asked the initiates the question, "Have you received an adequate liberal arts education during your four years here?" The student responded that he had been shortchanged, he felt, for, although he knew how to disect a frog, he knew practically nothing about his own body let alone that of the woman he was engaged to. The student explained further that in order for one to reach the nearly impossible goal of being truly educated, each person must understand himself, including one's physical makeup, at least in the area of sexuality. The response from the administrator was that sexuality courses were not appropriate within the liberal arts curriculum for "sex was something one learns by rubbing elbows."

On one campus, the president of the university, who had a very conservative attitude on sexuality programming, purposely overlooked promoting one of his staff to a key administrative position because that staff member had differed with him over the need for services and programming in this area.

Some people have thought it paradoxical that I, as a college dean, am "into sex," for when they were in college it was the dean who always seemed to be so much against permitting social relationships to develop to that point.

Fortunately, many of my colleagues are becoming sensitive to the needs for programming in this area, and as a result, participation and attendance at various national and regional conferences on presentations relative to sexuality programming and counseling on college campuses continues to rise.

In my own professional life, I have found that the presence of my AASECT certification as a sex educator, hanging on my office wall near the shelf of books dealing with sexuality, has frequently been used by students and parents to raise questions on sexuality by simply referring to the certification document, and has served for many as an opener to a number of discussions which have proved helpful to all concerned. Also, students with a concern of a sexual nature, including same-sex relationships, have either been referred to me by faculty or by other students, in an attempt to discuss and work through some of their concerns about their own sexuality.

Although somewhat frustrated in my attempts to provide a more formalized experience within the classroom through a credit course in human sexuality, I have found that one simply does not give up but continues to use the various other resources open on a small campus. The experience of one-to-one contacts in my office; advising the Sexuality Counseling and Information Center; periodic lectures in classes; in-service training with the resident advisors—all have been avenues by which I, and similar members of my profession on campuses across the country, have begun to make a dent in providing students with those sexuality programs and services which we as educators know that they need and deserve.

The Battle Over Sex Education In New Jersey

A mandatory kindergarten-to-graduation sex education program is raising important political and ethical issues for the public of New Jersey and elsewhere.

Robert T. Francoeur, Ph.D. and Linda Hendrixson

Robert T. Francoeur, Ph.D. is Director of the Institute for Human Sexuality, Health Care, and Education at Fairleigh Dickenson University. Linda Hendrixson is a New Jersey health educator and AASECT certified sex educator.

EDITOR'S NOTE: *As we go to press, the New Jersey State Board of Education has bowed to strong pressure from the Legislature and vocal community groups and has backed down from its order mandating specific sex education courses from kindergarten to grade five. Sex education will still be mandatory from the sixth grade on. The revised curriculum will eliminate certain topics as well as the requirements that sex education be taught in every grammar school grade. The State board will now permit local school boards to develop the curriculum and to decide at which elementary level the courses would begin.*

The proposed new rules are expected to be put into effect by 1983.

The following article recounts the thirteen-year controversy over sex education in New Jersey leading to the proposal for and the subsequent modification of the mandatory family-life curriculum.

The 1980s may hold in store a new version of the famous Scopes "monkey trial" that took place in Dayton, Tennessee in 1925. This time, however, instead of the teaching of evolution, the controversy is over the teaching of family life and sex education in schools. The scene has also shifted, from the rural Bible belt of Tennessee to urban, industrial New Jersey, the most populated state in the union. Fortunately, although it is often heated and emotional, the new controversy is devoid of the circus atmosphere and hysteria that were generated by the debates between fundamentalist William Jennings Bryant and agnostic lawyer Clarence Darrow.

The Background

The controversy over teaching sex education in the New Jersey schools has been brewing since January 1967, when the New Jersey State Board of Education adopted a policy *recommending* "that each local Board of Education make provisions in its curriculum for sex education programs." The state board noted that "sex education is a responsibility which should be shared by the home, church and school" and that "schools are important agencies in the development of healthy habits of living and moral values."

For ten years the idea of a comprehensive mandated family-life education program in the schools went unexplored as the local school boards avoided getting into this area of education. Meanwhile, teenage pregnancy and VD rates continued to rise. Teenagers started having sexual experiences earlier and did much more than their parents had done before leaving high school, but their sexual ignorance was often just as great as that of their conservative parents.

Between 1967 and 1979 the controversy surfaced several times in newspaper headlines, which reported court cases testing the rights of parents to exempt their children from such voluntary or recommended programs and local debates over what should be included in them.

How did the mandated policy come about? The effects of the sexual revolution among teenagers in the late 1960s and 1970s caused much concern among New Jersey parents and educators. Dr. Margaret Gregory, Supervisor of Maternal and Child Health Services for the New Jersey State Department of Health Services for the New Jersey State Department of Health, spoke for many people when she wondered out loud how well the New Jersey schools were dealing with the skyrocketing incidences of adolescent pregnancy, abortion and sexually transmitted diseases. She felt that neither the parents, the churches, nor the schools were meeting the challenge of the times through voluntary programs and that the only solution might be to establish a required family-life education curriculum with very specific topics appropriate for all levels from kindergarten to senior high.

By January 1979 the evidence of sexual activity and the problems resulting from such activity among teenagers were undeniable. Susan Wilson, a State Board of Education member, was appointed to head a committee to find out what, if any, family-life education was being conducted in New Jersey schools and to recommend some action. On the committee were state school board members from all areas of the state and a student representative.

In August 1979 the committee's "Family-Life Education Report" was issued. It found a disastrous lack of knowledge and motivation regarding sexual matters among teenagers. Consequently, in accordance with Dr. Gregory's original recommendation, it called for *mandatory* family-life education in all public schools from kindergarten through senior high.

The controversy then began in earnest. It is still going on today.

The Program

Two southern states had already mandated family-life education: Maryland in 1973 and Kentucky in 1979. New Jersey is the first northern state to do so, and its attempt to suggest specific subjects for the curriculum is unique.

A code was worked out in early 1980 that defines the family-life education program as "instruction to develop an understanding of the physical, mental, emotional, social, economic and psychological effects of interpersonal relations between persons of various ages." The last phrase, "persons of various ages," obviously upset many people because, by implication, it recognized the fact that sexual relations were increasingly common among unmarried teenagers.

The program, furthermore, is intended to explore the "physiological and psychological basis of human development, sexuality and reproduction" in a way that will give pupils an opportunity to develop attitudes and practices which will strengthen family life in the present, aid in establishing strong families of their own and contribute to the improvement of the community." The curriculum will be designed on the local level by concerned teachers, parents, curriculum designers and other concerned parties, including students in the ninth to twelfth grades. The mandate prescribes certain basic subjects as part of the curriculum, but local programs in the individual schools can add to and build on this base.

The projected outcome of the program is as follows. By the end of the eighth grade a pupil will have explored such basic topics as the importance of the family unit, communications and responsibilities within the family, family roles and duties, parenting, reproduction of plants and animals as well as of the human male and female, human heredity, social and emotional growth, responsibilities of adolescence, dating, interpersonal relations, child abuse and neglect, sexual assault, incest, VD prevention and prenatal care.

In high school, the basic subjects include parenting and child rearing, psychosocial development, sexuality, personality and the physical changes of adolescence, marriage preparation, family planning and childbirth. High school students will build on what they have already learned in the elementary school program, will review and expand their insights into dating, human reproduction, heredity, child abuse, sexual assault, incest and interpersonal relationships.

As might be expected, the mandatory nature of the program is stirring much fear and many emotional reactions across the state among many parents who are still now aware of—or prefer to ignore or deny—the world their children live in. It was this real world that convinced Susan Wilson's committee that, despite all the problems it would face, a required program was necessary.

The situation, country-wide, is abysmal. In 1978 only a third of the nation's high schools offered sex-education courses. There is also evidence that only a third of modern mothers tell their daughters anything about menstruation, one of the basic aspects of a woman's sexual development. And even among those schools that deal with menstrual education for girls, no comparable sex information is provided for the fifth and sixth-grade boys. In New Jersey the situation is very similar. Less than half of the 1.4 million New Jersey students are offered the opportunity of taking a family-life course, and most of the schools that do offer such a course never mention six sensitive areas: masturbation, contraception, VD, homosexuality, abortion and sexual intercourse.

So, although 84 percent of New Jersey adults favor providing sex education in the schools, including information about contraceptives, three quarters of today's teenagers continue to get their sex education from friends and "the street." Only fifteen percent learn about sex from actual school courses and another 10 to 15 percent find out the facts of life from their parents—usually their mothers.

If it were up to the students, the schools would be the main source of sex education.

A nationwide Gallup poll found that 95 percent of high school students favor getting their sex education in school because they know they do not get it at home.

Studies in recent years indicate that well over half of the 21 million American adolescents in the age range of fifteen to nineteen years of age are sexually active. This means there are 4.5 million sexually active women in this age group and over a million pregnancies every year. In 1977 *The New York Times* estimated that in New Jersey this activity resulted in 33,000 pregnancies and 18,000 abortions! Altogether, we now have calculated that one in ten American girls between the ages of fifteen and nineteen was pregnant last year and that one in twenty girls between the ages of eleven and fifteen was in the same situation.

Obviously, the limited, often narrow sex education offered by our churches, schools and parents is not meeting the needs of today's teenagers. Many critics of the New Jersey mandate say that the sex education currently provided in the schools is ineffective in curbing the epidemic of pregnancies and VD, so why make the situation worse? "Sex education only promotes promiscuity!" is the rallying cry of these critics. However, one could just as easily, and probably more safely, conclude from the facts that the current high incidence of unwanted pregnancies and VD would be much higher than it is today if we did not have the few sex education programs we do have in the schools. Over half of the students we have talked with in colleges feel the need for more extensive programs. They say that their high school sex education was "too little, too late," "too Mickey Mouse," and, for these reasons, "a waste." Only a few students feel that they got what they needed from their schools and parents.

The Battle: The Public Hearings

A preliminary skirmish occurred in 1976 and 1977 when a family took the Dumont, N.J., Board of Education to court in order to have their daughter excused from taking the board's mandated family-living course in the school she was attending. One important outcome of that case was a suggestion from the state attorney general's office that the state board of education should do more than just "recommend" that parents have the right to exempt their sons and daughters from sex education courses. An excusal policy, the assistant attorney general said, should be clearly spelled out. In the current debate this issue has become a central concern.

In the public hearings of 1980 the controversy and issues have become quite sharply focused.

On the educational level, objections have focused on the old issue of local school board home rule versus state control. Some opponents feel the state board assumed too much authority in setting up the mandate that it did. This action of the board comes on the heels of its instituting a school classification system, which would rate schools according to the performance of the students and minimum standards for high school graduates, both set by the State Board. Understandably, the home-rule advocates are not happy with the trend that this activity of the board indicates.

The New Jersey Education Association, which represents the teachers, argues that the mandate puts the local schools in a "very explosive" situation, and the New Jersey School Boards Association, representing the local boards, not wanting interference from the state level, claims that it is a "radical departure" from the public school tradition of home rule.

Religious opposition has come from fundamental ministers and groups, from the Right to Life people, and from CURE (Citizens United for Responsible Education). CURE is ferociously against the Sex Information and Education Council of the United States (SIECUS), headed by Mary Calderone, which supports school sex education. Also vehemently antihumanist, CURE tends to quickly label any person or group in favor of the mandate as humanistic and atheistic.

At one hearing in Trenton, Jean Belsante, an area coordinator for CURE from Passaic, quoted *The Siecus Circle: A Humanist Revolution,* the antimandate handbook:

> Secular humanism . . . is an aggressive atheism which denies God, denies life after death and shuns all moral absolutes . . . Humanism defies free enterprise and all organized religion, as this movement's leaders seek to establish a one-world collectivist order that rejects God's laws and most civil laws . . . The humanist code of ethics heartily endorses abortion, euthanasia, suicide, premarital sex, homosexuality, pornography and drug usuage . . . in short, family life education is the major transmission belt for the humanist revolution.

At a second hearing a very organized vocal opposition made itself heard in a nine-hour marathon session. Charges of "secular humanism" and "godless atheism" were hurled at the board members and proponents of the mandate.

A grandmother yelled, "How are you going to teach my grandchildren masturbation—tell me? How are you going to teach them homosexuality?"

"God forgive you: In the end, it is your souls that will go to hell for eternity!" one parent warned. A Baptist minister argued, "Normal kids don't think about things like this," and another fundamentalist minister denounced the code as "vile and pornographic."

Endorsements of the family-life mandated curriculum have come from many different sources: The New Jersey Catholic Conference; the Junior League; the state and several local medical societies; the New Jersey Parenting Council, and large newspapers like *The New York Times, The Philadelphia Inquirer* and the *Bergen Record,* as well as from local papers like the *Asbury Park Press* and *Red Bank Register.*

At the hearings, educators, physicians, students, parents and some local board members have cited the increasing rates of teenage pregnancy, abortion and VD, and have urged the board to pass the code after clarifying the provisions for teacher training and funding. One woman brought a petition in favor of the mandate that had been signed by 32 high school seniors.

Robert Bierman, M.D., who heads the Rutgers University Student Health Center, said of the program: It is "solid and middle-of-the-road . . . it will foster the ability [of young people] to make decisions on the basis of knowledge rather than myths and peer pressure . . . the individuals encouraging the passage of this regulation are not smut dealers or individuals hoping an entire new industry in pornography can be built . . . "

In spite of Dr. Bierman's attempt to quell people's fears, the mandate is still being linked with the onslaught of many terrible evils. A one-page flier circulated around the state and entitled "New Jersey Schools Pushing Sex Perversion!" reads:

> Do you know that when your child enters school in New Jersey from kindergarten to 12th grade, he or she will be 1) attending classes in pornography 2) given homework assignments to practice masturbation in front of a mirror 3) given demonstrations of contraceptive techniques featuring red and blue condoms, and their use graphically illustrated 4) viewing simulations of sexual intercourse 5) reading comic books with heroes such as Wanda Lust and Captain Vee-Dee-O. The real goal of this program is to turn your sons and daughters into mindless perverts who can easily be manipulated by anyone who offers him or her sexual gratification. Your children will be turned against you. They will be urged to interrogate their parents on their sexual attitudes and behavior to prove the arbitrariness of their parents' values. These were techniques of the Hitler youth. This is part of a larger Aquarian Conspiracy to destroy the United States and turn it into a fascist state in which zombified citizens will accept rule by decree, slave labor, and austerity. The first step in the Conspiracy is to capture America's youth by drugs and perversion. This can only be accomplished by weakening the moral authority of their parents. To accomplish their overall purpose, the Aquarians are subjecting the population to a planned series of national disasters which both legitimize rule by decree and allow the fascistic Federal Emergency Management Agency to take direct control, while crushing the population's will to resist.

In supporting the mandate, coauthor Linda Hendrixson urged that the content of the program be expanded to include education in "love." "Students," she pointed out, "are anxious to explore the relationship between love and sex, and the place of love in personal relationships."

As chairperson of the committee responsible for the mandate, Susan Wilson brought the lengthy hearings to a close with the following statement:

> I've spoken with many students. They want and need this education so badly—they need somewhere to turn. None of us are comfortable in forcing the schools to offer this sort of instruction. But to oppose the use of the schools, while not offering alternatives, is to leave the question unanswered. The school is the one social organization through which all children pass. Should the New Jersey public schools accept conditions as they presently exist, or should they seek to improve these conditions?

In April the state board again passed the mandated code, in a revised form, by a vote of 9 to 1. The major revision had to do with a provision for an annual *review* by the parents, which was now termed "parental examination." According to this provision, final approval of the course contents would remain with the local boards of education.

The state board of education is preparing guidelines for parental exemption procedures, for teacher training and certification, and for expansion of the program content. Funding is still an issue. Training qualified teachers who can comfortably cope with this demanding curriculum is going to be costly, and the question of who is going to foot the bill for the training has not been resolved.

With all these matters still to be worked out, the final successful outcome of mandated sex education in New Jersey schools is far from ensured.

In the past some programs and proposals for sex education have been unsuccessful because their advocates failed to initiate or continue communications with the parents and teachers. At times this communication is difficult to maintain. Many parents are concerned that when their children, stimulated by the contents of the courses, ask them questions, they will not be able to handle or discuss them. Parental embarrassment is a real concern. The fears of fascistic, humanistic and atheistic "plots" are also hard to dispel.

No matter how vocal and negative, opposition to sex education in the schools is not necessarily constructive and usually it does not present viable effective alternatives. Instead, it tends to restrict itself to the use of such measures as harassment, confrontation, labeling, demonstrations, book-burning and scare tactics like the charge that "New Jersey schools (are) pushing sex perversions."

Constructive resistance to sex education, on the other hand, can be a very important element in developing an effective, quality sex-education program that meets the needs of the students without overly threatening the more conservative, the anxious or the less knowledgeable parents. We hope that constructive resistance will help to clarify the issues of parental and student rights, teacher qualifications and training, course contents, and, most of all, the way teachers can best handle questions relating to attitudes and values.

For example, a valuable point was highlighted by the resistance of James Kimple, superintendent of the South Brunswick school system. "Mere facts aren't enough," he remarked. "We know what works and doesn't work. We know that information about drugs, smoking, alcohol and VD do not stop students from using these substances or acquiring these diseases. We know that attitudes and behaviors of instructors towards students and the subject are more important than content."

Speaking as a member of the board, Susan Wilson pointed out that totally value-free sex education in Sweden only resulted in an increased incidence of unwed parents. In its mandate, the board echoed this concern and asked that teaching values be included in the family-life program. The continuing debate over the controversial mandate is thus likely to produce a mandated family-life program with emphasis on education for values and responsibility that will become an important model for other state and local school systems.

In New Jersey, at least, educators and parents are becoming aware that we have a moral obligation to do something positive about a situation in which misinformation or the lack of information prevails. Furthermore, it is recognized that the "how-to" approach to sex education needs to be replaced with an effective education program that respects the whole person. This approach must be concerned with student values and the future, and options of students in a culture that offers so many choices but does not, as yet, teach our young people how to make reasoned decisions.

Whether this awareness will survive vociferous opposition, whether it will spread to other parts of the country or spring up elsewhere independently, only time and the events of the 1980s will tell.

Sexual Biology and Health

Changing attitudes on sexuality are instrumental in opening avenues toward more humanistic sexual relations. Indeed, freeing the mind for awareness and acceptance of bodily sensations is an important measure for maximizing sexual expression. But this is only half the story. Of parallel importance is developing a clear understanding and appreciation for the workings of the human body. This section directs its attention toward this end.

Males and females have a great number of misconceptions and a general lack of knowledge concerning the bodily responses of the opposite sex. This less than optimal situation is further denigrated by the fact that many individuals have less than a working knowledge of their own bodily responses and functioning sexual activity. In an effort to develop an understanding of and appreciation for a healthy sexual awareness, potential quality physiological information is desperately needed and sought after by females and males alike. Several articles in this section focus on the physical sexual response of females and males, laying to rest many of the fallacies that individuals have grown-up with. Such issues as fears and fantasies surrounding the vagina, what the clitoris is and its role in sexual functioning, female and male orgasm, and "masculine adequacy" and penis size are discussed.

The physiological dimension of sexuality also includes reproduction. Surprisingly, some individuals in the height of their passion fail to correlate "having sex" with becoming pregnant, yet nine months later the full implications may become strikingly apparent. This issue is addressed as are some health concerns related to pregnancy and reproduction. Additionally, for those individuals who wish to but cannot conceive, psychological and physiological health concerns and solutions are discussed and examined.

Finally, this section addresses the issue of birth control. In light of the attitudinal change toward sex for pleasure, birth control is becoming a matter of prime importance. Before sex can become safe as well as enjoyable, people must receive thorough and accurate information. Despite the relative simplicity of this assertion, birth control has been and remains today an emotionally charged and fervently contested issue in society. One of the most controversial aspects of the birth-control issue is abortion. As evidenced by opinion surveys, the public is largely supportive of the legalization and public funding of abortion. Yet, individuals who seek abortions (especially repeated) often face and bear the brunt of negative stigmatization. Despite recent Supreme Court rulings toward greater permissiveness, many wrinkles need to be ironed out on the abortion issue. The power of the state still weighs heavily upon the personal and familial decision making process and the rights of those concerned.

Looking Ahead: Challenge Questions

Why is quality information about the human body important to sexuality?

What are some of the similarities and differences in sexual responses between men and women?

How can teenagers be made more aware of the implications of early parenthood?

What factors should one consider in choosing a birth control method? What are some of the bases for the abortion controversy?

Is correct information about reproduction and its control sufficient for proper decision making?

The Most Erotic Part of Your Body

Judith E. Steinhart, D.A.

Judith Steinhart has a doctoral degree in human sexuality. She is on the faculty in the Department of Health Science at Brooklyn College and is a clinical assistant professor at the State University of New York at Stony Brook.

What is the most sensitive, most erotic and most powerful sex organ in the human body? Now think for a moment before you answer. No, it's even more sensual than the genitals or the skin. It's the mind, of course. The mind is the most erotic part of the body. The mind is amazingly powerful. The mind can make fair sex good and good sex great. The mind can enhance physical sensations, create relaxed environments and can visualize images of techniques and modes of sexual expression that people might like to try.

We get hints of how powerful the mind is in several ways. For example, if we are with the perfect partner, who is touching us in our sexiest, favorite ways, and we are thinking of any or all of the following, "This is wonderful, but what if the phone rings, or if the neighbors hear, or if the baby cries, or if I/he comes too soon, or what if I/she doesn't come, I wonder if he/she loves me?" then the sensations get lost in the fog, and we hardly even realize that we are being touched, stroked, stimulated or caressed. Our mind has taken charge and has changed the focus from pleasure to tension, blocking the feelings.

Since we are (or should be) in control of our minds and our thoughts, we have the power to change both, to add to rather than detract from our pleasure. When people are tense from work or from the responsibilities of daily life, they can use their minds to control and alleviate the amount of tension that they feel by changing the visual pictures in their minds. When people recognize that worrying about work problems or wondering when the laundry will get done work against them they can change their thoughts to those that promote relaxation and warm feelings.

Someone might say to him/herself, "Just for the time being, I am going to pretend that I am on vacation. The only thing that is important to me is being here at this moment with my lover, enjoying the warmth of our touch." One can visualize that instead of being in the bedroom, or wherever one is usually sexual, that one is on a deserted beach and can feel the penetrating, healing rays of the sun, while with one's lover. Rather than distracting from the immediate experience, these visual images can provide the atmosphere that will allow one to appreciate the sexual experience happening at the same time the fantasy is allowing greater relaxation.

In the mind we can explore the smorgasboard of sexual expression. We can survey all of the items and possibilities and then can taste those that look appealing. After that we can decide how we liked it, if it is something that we would like to try in our mind again, or if the thought looked better than it tasted. For example, if a woman knows that her husband would like her to go down on him, she can try out the idea in her mind. Perhaps at first all she can think of is, "What if he comes in my mouth? I'll throw up!" But as she turns the idea around in her mind, she might think about what could possibly be appealing to him about it, perhaps the warmth of her mouth, the saliva making the sensation easy and not irritating, the movement of her mouth and tongue on the sensitive parts of his penis. Then she could think about what could possibly be appealing to her, perhaps knowing that she is giving him pleasure, the excitement of trying something new, the feeling of her lover's velvety smooth penis on her cheeks and lips. She can think about the good feelings until she is comfortable with the idea, and then after having successfully practiced in her mind, she could try it with her lover in real life.

The mind also remembers. I know a woman who is so taken with the scent of Old Spice after shave, that she melts when she smells it, regardless of who is wearing it. The scent's memory has been with her for years, probably since she first remembers her father shaving and throwing on Old Spice afterwards as an astringent.

Just think for a moment about your own personal preferences, including colors, tastes, scents, looks, and try to remember their associations. Then, see if you can incorporate any of those pleasant sensations or preferences into your sex life, either in fantasy or reality.

Masters and Johnson have developed the term "sensate focus" to describe the sex therapy technique of placing your awareness completely in the sensations of physical feelings. For example, when someone is stroking your arm, sensate focus means concentrating on nothing but the sensations of what you are feeling, the lightness, the pressure, the warmth, whatever you are subjectively feeling. By focusing on those sensations, you are actually augmenting the sensations, rather than overlooking them or taking them for granted.

We have learned from spinal-cord-injured patients, who are unable to experience a physiologic response to sexual stimuli, that many are able to train themselves to experience orgasm. The sensation may be different from the orgasm that they had when they were able-bodied, but they now describe increased body tension, building toward a release and accompanied by pleasure. They, too, focus on sensations and use visual images to increase their pleasure.

Kinsey also reported that two percent of women could reach orgasm through fantasy alone. Men, too, have been able to separate the process of orgasm and ejaculation and have learned to experience orgasm without ejaculating. Karezza, as this is called, was practiced in ancient times in certain cultures, as well as in the Oneida Community in the United States in the nineteenth century.

The mind, indeed, has amazing potential, and we have barely begun to tap its resources. It is important to remember that we are in control of the mind and we can choose our thoughts carefully so that we experience as much pleasure as we think we deserve, and even more.

All About THE CLITORIS

Well-known and little-known facts about the source of female sexual pleasure.

Howard R. and Martha E. Lewis

Howard R. and Martha E. Lewis are medical writers who frequently write about sexual health. They are the co-authors of The Parent's Guide to Teenage Sex and Pregnancy, *to be published in the spring by St. Martin's Press.*

Many otherwise well-informed adults don't know what the clitoris is for, how it works or even where it is.

Small wonder. Little girls are told they have a vagina. But they're likely to remain ignorant for many years about their clitoris. Little boys—and the grown men they become—are rarely more knowledgeable.

What every woman needs to know: The clitoris is a small knob of tissue located above the opening of the urethra, the passage to the urinary bladder (see illustration). It is surrounded by a fold of tissue, the clitoral hood. The hood is attached to the labia minora, the liplike structures at the entrance to the vagina.

While in the embryo stage, a group of specialized cells became the clitoris. Had the embryo been a male, the same tissue would have become part of a penis. Unlike the penis the clitoris has only one known purpose—as a focus of erotic sensitivity in women. In the entire human anatomy, it is the only structure whose sole function is sexual pleasure. The clitoris is much smaller than the penis but has an equal number of sensory nerve endings. Hence it is potentially far more sensitive than the penis.

Normal clitorises vary tremendously in size, shape and position. Such factors have no bearing on sexual responsiveness.

Clitoris and orgasm. It is clitoral rather than vaginal stimulation that produces an orgasm. The clitoris is an organ with a dense concentration of nerve endings that transmit erotic sensations. By contrast, the vaginal walls are largely devoid of such nerves.

Therefore, women commonly masturbate by stroking the clitoris with a finger or vibrator. At any time in lovemaking—before insertion (or instead of it), during intercourse or after the man has ejaculated—many couples stimulate the clitoris manually (with hands and fingers) or orally (with lips, mouth and tongue).

Or the clitoris can be stimulated by manipulating the partner's penis against it. The texture and size of the penis can produce an unusually pleasurable sensation, shared by the man.

Most women evidently prefer clitoral to vaginal stimulation. Psychologist Seymour Fisher of the State University of New York's Upstate Medical Center asked a sampling of women which they would choose, clitoral or vaginal stimulation. About two-thirds of the women opted for clitoral stimulation.

During excitation, the first stage of sexual response, the clitoris swells because of increased blood flow. But clitoral erection is not a good indicator of adequate stimulation. For about half the women studied by Masters and Johnson, the enlargement was not sufficient to be noted by the naked eye.

These clitoral changes may be caused by direct stimulation of the genitals or of another sexually sensitive part of the body, such as the breasts. Erotic fantasies, too, may cause the clitoris to swell.

During the second (plateau) phase of sexual response, the clitoris retracts. It draws away from the vaginal entrance and is covered by the clitoral hood. This retraction is functional, concludes gynecologist Harry A. Croft of the University of Texas. Further stimulation of the clitoris would be uncomfortable because of the organ's markedly increased sensitivity.

When the clitoris retracts under its hood, the man may have trouble finding it. He may interrupt his lovemaking to go in search of it. This can be distracting and frustrating. Actually, it is rarely necessary for the man to relocate the clitoris. Stimulation of the hood or the general area is usually sufficient, indeed preferred.

At this stage, the clitoris continues to respond to direct stimulation, as by a finger. Intercourse generally provides only indirect stimulation.

The shaft of the penis generally does not remain in contact with the clitoris. Rather, the thrusting of the penis exerts pressure on the labia minora. This rhythmic pulling may be transmitted to the clitoral hood, and then the clitoris itself.

For a minority of women—estimated at as few as 30 percent—this indirect stimulation can bring orgasm. Most women require more direct stimulation than the penis alone provides.

Often this can be achieved during intercourse if the women or the man stimulates the clitoral area. A woman may regard this as masturbation and have negative feelings about it. Psychiatrist George J. Langmyhr of the University of Pennsylvania School of Medicine Division of Family Study counsels women to "understand and accept that any form of clitoral stimulation is acceptable."

During intercourse, a woman may find that her partner's penis can bring her to orgasm more readily if she is on top of him. In this position, the rhythm, angle and amount of friction may be found that best brings his penis in contact with the clitoris. The woman-above position also allows greater freedom of movement for the woman and permits her or her partner to manually stimulate the clitoris. Rear-entry positions similarly promote clitoral massage.

Physiologically, orgasm—the third stage of sexual response—is a release of the muscular spasm and engorgement of blood vessels built up by sexual stimulation. It is accompanied by many physical changes other than clitoral.

The clitoris returns to its normal position five to ten seconds after the orgasmic contractions stop. Its swelling subsides during the final (resolution) phase of sexual response. This can take from five to thirty minutes.

Stimulating the clitoris. With clitoral stimulation, there's a very fine line between pleasure and pain. Pressure that's too hard or lasts too long can cause an irritation, ending sexual pleasure.

Women differ widely in the stimulation they prefer. Some may like it firm and vigorous; others gentle and delicate. Some may enjoy a steady rhythm; others, stop-start teasing. A woman may wish a light touch at the outset, with increasing pressure as orgasm approaches. And preferences may vary from minute to minute.

The head of the clitoris (the glans) is particularly sensitive, and many women prefer that it be avoided. "The majority of women experience discomfort on direct stimulation of the glans," reports gynecologist Mona Devanesan of the New Jersey College of Medicine and Dentistry. A few women in Dr. Devanesan's practice prefer firm "rolling" of the shaft. Most prefer gentler manual stimulation of the tissues adjoining the clitoris and labia minora.

Rough hands may be irritating. If so, make liberal use of hand lotion. You're likely to find manual stimulation of the clitoris pleasurable only when you have adequate lubrication—saliva, vaginal secretions or moisteners such as K-Y jelly or cold cream.

Clitoral pain is unusual. Although the clitoris is richly supplied with nerve endings and is sensitive to touch, it is rarely a source of pain. Any irritation from sexual activity usually soon passes. Consult a physician for any persistent clitoral discomfort.

Clitoral pain may be experienced because of an allergic reaction to a medication applied to the area, such as an anesthetic or antibiotic ointment. Some women have allergic reactions to clothes, deodorant sprays or detergents (including bubble bath products). The clitoris may become irritated by a build-up of dirt and sweat.

Almost all dermatological conditions can affect the clitoral area. The clitoris is subject to ulcers, abscesses and tumors. Clitoral pain may result from vaginal infections. Urological conditions such as urethritis can cause pain to the clitoris.

Some venereal diseases, such as chancroid and granuloma venereum, can cause painful ulcers, sometimes on or around the clitoris. Venereal warts, transmitted through intercourse, are sometimes painful.

Conversely, the clitoris may develop a lack of sensation. This may result from such physiological conditions as nerve injury, diabetes or multiple sclerosis. Alcoholism and vitamin deficiency also may dull clitoral feeling. Lack of sensation may be psychological; if so, psychotherapy may be required.

The clitoris can be damaged by objects used in masturbation. Gynecologist Herbert W. Horne of the Harvard Medical School tells of a young girl who was treated for a painfully enlarged clitoris—caused by a hair she had tightly wrapped around it. Another patient as a child would rub her clitoris on the branches of trees she climbed. This damaged the nerve endings beyond recovery.

Some woman are born with, or acquire, clitoral abnormalities, most frequently clitoral enlargement. Pathological enlargement may be due to endocrine disorders, infections or tumors. Treating the cause can often reverse the enlargement.

Clitoral surgery. Female circumcision is the clitoral counterpart of the procedure for the penis. It consists of retracting and removing the foreskin, the tissue surrounding the clitoris. Normally, it's an outpatient procedure performed under local anesthesia.

Circumcision may enhance sexual stimulation for women who are dissatisfied with their present responsiveness—and who feel distinctly greater sensations when the foreskin is retracted. Gynecologist Takey Crist, director of the Crist Clinic for Women, in Jacksonville, North Carolina, comments: "The procedure should never be considered routine, but clitoral circumcision may have its place in certain select women. We do not consider it appropriate for nonorgasmic women."

Surgical removal of the clitoris (clitoridectomy) is rarely necessary. When it is done, as in cases of cancer or congenital deformity, the surgery does not seem to impair sexual functioning, erotic sensations or orgasm. Evidently the nerve supply for sexual sensations is so lavish that a woman can lose large amounts of tissue without destroying her sexual gratification.

Clitoral versus vaginal orgasm. Is there a difference between clitoral and vaginal orgasm? Do women who require clitoral stimulation have "less real" orgasms than women who achieve orgasm without it? Are such women, indeed, "less sexually mature"?

Unfortunately, these are still concerns of women and their sex partners. This dilemma is a legacy of the theories of Sigmund Freud in the early 1930s. Little was known then of female sexual anatomy or response. Freud arrived at the erroneous conclusion that there was a difference between the type of orgasms achieved by women. He theorized that clitoral orgasm was on an infantile, prepuberty level, but that vaginal orgasm was a mark of "maturity."

According to Freud's "vaginal transfer" theory, the mature woman transfers the primary site of erotic excitation from the clitoris to the vagina. Thus the truly sexually mature women would achieve orgasm during vaginal penetration. He deemed anything different a sign of incomplete psychosexual development.

Wrong as Freud's theory was, it became dogma. A woman would consult a psychiatrist with the complaint that she was unable to achieve orgasm during intercourse. She would be told that she suffered from an arrest of psychosexual development. She was usually depressed and anxious to begin with, and on hearing this pronouncement her symptoms often would worsen.

Some psychotherapists challenged Freud's theory from the outset, but to little avail. It took Masters and Johnson's pioneering physiological measurement to prove objectively that an orgasm is an orgasm is an orgasm. Their laboratory work clearly showed that there is not one kind of orgasm involving the vagina, another involving the clitoris.

A woman's experience of orgasm may vary according to mood, state of health, feelings about the partner and herself and where she's stimulated. Women may find some orgasms more satisfying, others less.

But physiologically an orgasm is the same, no matter how it is produced.

Women's Most Versatile Muscle: The PC

Exercising the PC should be a life-long habit for women of all ages. It can ensure a safer childbirth, increased sexual response and proper urinary function.

Jan Dailey

What's the most important muscle in your body? You can't see it. If it didn't work right, sex would be pretty much of a bust. About a third of all women suffer because it is weak and do not even know they have any control over it.

It's the PC (pubococcygeus) muscle and its strength and tone are pivotal in safe, successful childbirth, increased sexual response and proper urinary function. Broad, slinglike, attached to the pubic bone in front (tailbone) and the (coccyx) tailbone in back, the PC is the pivotal structure of the pelvic-floor musculature. It incorporates the sphincters (muscles surrounding and pinching off the opening) of the rectum and urethra in men, and, additionally, the vagina in women, and is largely responsible for keeping the internal organs functioning in place.

Unfortunately, relatively few people have even heard the word pubococcygeus, although in the last thirty years millions of women have learned to exercise with Kegel exercises (see box for description of exercises). The exercises were named after Dr. Arnold Kegel who did pioneering work at USC curing urinary stress incontinence in women. The problem, which usually appears after childbirth, manifests itself in embarrassing loss of urine on sudden laughing, bending and the like. Kegel discovered in 1952 that strengthening the PC also improved sexual response, often bringing about orgasm for the first time.

The story goes that Kegel, on a trip around the world to learn as much as he could about the PC, found that until the missionaries came Tahitian mothers had always taught their virgin daughters how to control the vaginal muscle in order to give the most pleasure to both partners in their future lovemaking. It was also the custom of the grandmother to see that her daughter after childbirth got her "love muscle" back in shape quickly by exercising it.

PC exercise is also recommended to women in childbirth classes—although a majority of women do not attend such classes. The exercise is valuable because a strong, elastic PC will retract out of the way of the emerging baby's head without being damaged; a thin, sagging one can get crushed between the head and the mother's pelvic bone and be permanently damaged. After pregnancy, women may have areas on their vaginal walls that do not respond to stimulation because of PC scarring, extreme stretching or gaps in the muscle, usually due to childbirth or other causes.

Happily, once the vaginal muscle is strengthened, it generally remains so with normal sexual activity. Marilyn Fithian, Co-director of the Center for Marital and Sexual Studies in Long Beach, California, says it would be very unusual for a woman who has sex three or more times a week with orgasm to be found to have a deficient PC. This fact illustrates that it doesn't take that much to keep the muscle in proper tone. PC contractions at orgasm average only six or eight, but through having regular sex, the muscle's tone can remain excellent into older age and can be improved at any age.

Another important benefit of a healthy PC is that stimulation of it during intercourse may be another possible mechanism for triggering female orgasm. Georgia Kline-Graber and Benjamin Graber, in *Handbook of Sex Therapy,* suggest that the PC may be both *trigger* and responder in female coital orgasm: "Women who were totally incapable of achieving orgasm . . . had the worst PC muscles; those able to achieve only non-coital orgasm (as with clitoral stimulation) had somewhat better muscles; and women able to achieve both noncoital and coital orgasm had the muscles that were anatomically and physiologically in the best condition."

The vaginal muscle can be brought into play in intercourse as a trigger if the man uses relatively gentle, slow side-to-side motions of his penis to move the walls of the vagina. Using deep or rapid thrusts may cause discomfort and actually desensitize the woman and make orgasm difficult or impossible for her. During thrusting, the woman should squeeze the PC to bring on orgasm. The most sensitive spots on the vaginal wall are to the lower right and left, and the greatest source of

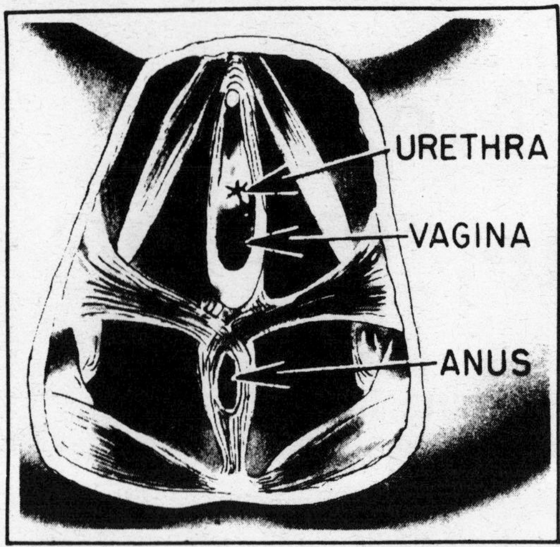

The patterning of pelvic muscles which support the internal organs, illustrated above, is called the PC (pubococcygeus) group.

sensation is only about two inches inside the entrance to the vagina.

As already suggested, a weak PC muscle has been related to a number of ailments. In her prize-winning paper "Rehabilitation Principles in the Care of Gynecologic and Obstetric Patients" (Archives of Physical Medicine Rehabilitation, Feb. 1980), Betty Joan Maly, M.D. says: "Laxity of pelvic floor tissues [chiefly the PC] results in problems such as urinary stress incontinence, prolapse [sinking] of the pelvic organs, retroversion [bending back] of the uterus, and decreased or absent sexual satisfaction . . . Disabilities . . . are associated with decreased venous [blood] return from the lower half of the body, postural changes, lax abdomen, back strain, lax perineum [area between anus and genitals], and sexual dysfunction." Of course, these conditions may be due in part to a sedentary life style and lack of exercise in general, as well as to a poorly functioning PC.

In view of the importance of keeping the PC muscle in tone, it is amazing how few women are taught to exercise it. A survey showed that a majority of pregnant women who attend childbirth classes do not get these until they are about seven months along in their pregnancy, and, of those, only one out of five has been given pelvic exercises to do by her doctor. "A majority of medical schools devote little time to . . . the development of clinical skills in prescribing exercise," Maly says.

According to additional research on stress incontinence, 30 percent of an average adult population of women and up to 63 percent of postmenopausal women have the problem. Among two-thirds of the second group, the condition is due to alteration of pelvic-floor anatomy, along with other factors; such an alteration is no doubt related to a decreased capillary blood flow in the pelvic floor after menopause, and, we might venture to say, indicates a greater need for PC exercises in older women.

As to the relation of the PC muscle and sexual responses, Kegel found that *thrity percent of women studied . . . were unaware of voluntary control over the PC.* Of 123 women who had lacked gratifying sexual response, 78 became orgasmic after they learned to exercise awareness and control. He further noted that vaginismus [too tight vagina] is a reflex that may be associated with protection of a tender PC. Muscle education and exercise was successful in curing 16 of 24 patients with dyspareunia [painful intercourse]."

The Kegel Exercises

Learning to contract the PC by concentrating on tightening urinary, rectal or vaginal sphincter muscles is at least as easy as learning to wiggle your nose. To learn to do the exercise, sit on the toilet with your legs spread and simply hold back the flow of urine with your legs spread and simply let out urine one teaspoonful at a time, then hold back. You have discovered the working of the PC muscle.

At first, three times a day, lie flat on your back on a hard surface, with knees bent, legs spread. Work up to a total of 200 Kegels (PC contractions) a day until you have achieved as much progress as you can; then work fewer than this sum to maintain a good tone. Vary the contractions: You can make them slow, counting to three, then fast, like a flutter. (You can see the contractions in a mirror, or feel them by inserting two fingers in the vagina.)

Later, you can establish an automatic lifelong health habit by doing the exercise during any routine daily activity that does not require moving about, such as watching TV, talking on the phone or lying in bed.

For the treatment of patients with conditions due to a malfunctioning PC, a recent new method has been the use of electrostimulation.

Inventor Will DuVall, who holds over thirty patents, first worked with Kegel in 1960 in setting up a means of stimulating the PC electrically in a woman patient who for years had never been able to identify her PC. DuVall describes the scene when Kegel felt her PC contract suddenly: "He jumped up and down delightedly shouting, 'It works! It works!' The patient said, 'So *that's* what I'm supposed to be doing.' "

This instrument was the prototype for today's Vagette, a hand-held, battery-operated device that a woman inserts into her vagina. Two ring electrodes, about a quarter of an inch apart, contact a very small area of the vagina with a weak electric stimulus at the level of the PC and set off the contraction of the whole muscle. The Vagette automatically turns on for two

Electronic Aid

Along with the Kegel exercises, some physicians are recommending home use of the Vagette, a hand-held battery-operated vaginal stimulator designed to aid strengthening of the PC in women. The Vagette, held in the vagina, contracts and relaxes the PC at a slow, controlled rate—two seconds on, two off. (It is not a vibrator and not for orgasm.)

Dr. Robert S. Scott, Asst. Clinical Professor of OB/GYN at the University of Southern California and Director of Southern California Women's Medical Group, says that his patients have indicated quicker, more profound PC strengthening with addition of electronic stimulation to Voluntary Muscle Control (VMC).

He believes his method is far more efficient than VMC alone, making the exercises easier to do. Many women have such weak PC muscles that they have great difficulty identifying them. Some people also find the Kegel exercises a chore and forget to do them. There have been no unpleasant side affects with the Vagette, Scott says. However, some scientists say that not enough research has been done for adverse side effects to show up.

For further information on the Vagette, write to Myodynamics, Inc., 1129-F E. Dominquez Street, Carson, Ca. 90746.

seconds, off for two seconds, alternately. The woman should reinforce each induced contraction by her own contraction, and do the exercise two or three times a day for 15 to 20 minutes.

Sex therapists Dr. William Hartman and Marilyn Fithian call the Vagette an "ingenious device" in helping some women with sexual dysfunctions, especially if they cannot have an orgasm because of a good deal of vaginal muscle relaxation or stretching due to childbirth. "Sometimes the PC is like a loose, relaxed rubber band," Hartman says. He adds, "Virtually all preorgasmic women (women who have not yet had orgasm) can profit by the additional contraction from electronic stimulation when combined with the woman's own efforts."

The Vagette is definitely not for everybody, however, as some women report that it is uncomfortable or even painful to use. In such cases the exercises alone are advised.

Whether PC muscle tone is regained by exercises alone or through a program incorporating the use of the Vagette, the benefits are likely to be great. These include not only improved specific functions—better urinary control, safer childbirth, more satisfying orgasms—but increased awareness and control of the body itself and its sexual potential. Fortunately, stereotyped sex roles are changing and women are becoming more aware of their bodies and are asserting more authority over their surroundings. As many women who have successfully strengthened this vital muscle report, control over the PC brings with it a larger sense of a women's control over her own body and the healthy sexuality that is her natural right.

The Male Orgasm: What Every Girl Should Know

Dr. Wardell Pomeroy

□ Women often complain, correctly, that men can't get inside their heads to understand how they feel about sex. Since, for the same reason, the male experience is inaccessible to women, I'm writing here, from a man's point of view, about orgasm and ejaculation. The more fully each sex understands the other's sexuality, the easier it becomes for two people to manage the adjustments that make relationships between men and women work.

Orgasm and ejaculation, like other physiological mechanisms, are more complicated than would appear. Many of the questions concern *technique,* and I would like to stress, as I do repeatedly in my speaking and writing, that sex involves much more than that. As any intelligent, experienced person knows, two people who really "have it on" are influenced by factors far more profound than technique.

Here, then, are the questions women ask about ejaculation and orgasm, and answers that I hope will prove helpful.

Can a man have an orgasm without ejaculating, or are the two the same? Though ejaculation ordinarily implies orgasm, the converse is not true, and a man *can* climax without any ejaculate being released. Until recently, it was not generally understood that in both men and women sexual response has two phases. In the male, there is a period of excitement, erection, and orgasm, followed by ejaculation, but as Dr. Helen Kaplan points out in her book, *The New Sex Therapy,* these two components are separate and both erection and orgasm can take place without ejaculation.

In young boys, as we commonly observe, orgasm without ejaculation occurs simply because they are not yet old enough physiologically to ejaculate. Some men who have had prostate operations ejaculate into the bladder, a condition known as retrograde ejaculation. Among adult males, those who have multiple ejaculations to the point where the liquid content of the prostate gland and the seminal vesicles are exhausted are nevertheless still capable of orgasm, but without ejaculation. Otherwise, in these males, ejaculation normally follows orgasm.

Can a man be called "frigid" if, like some women, it takes him a very long time to have an orgasm, or if he can't have one during intercourse? No, but first let's abandon that word "frigid." It's one of the most misused words in our sexual vocabulary, and is not a good term to describe the lack of responsiveness in either women or men. There is a clinical state of unresponsiveness, for which new therapies have now been developed; then there are times when a man (or a woman) is simply not interested in sex. Men may erroneously call a woman "frigid" at such a time, but the word is less often applied to men, since they are assumed, again incorrectly, to be always interested.

If a woman is totally or quite unresponsive, a better description than "frigid" would be "generally sexually unresponsive." If she is unable to have an orgasm, we call that "orgasmic dysfunction."

A man who fails to have an orgasm, even though he has an erection, is known as a retarded ejaculator, which sounds more derogatory than it is. Some men fail to have an orgasm and an ejaculation even though they are in a state of erection for a long time, a condition which may please some of their partners but often requires therapy. (This therapy is usually effective.) In any case, such a person is certainly not "frigid" in the sense of being uninterested in sex. However, it is possible to have a simple reflex erection without any real interest in sex.

Is it possible for a man to "fake" an orgasm? A man can fake orgasm, of course, but it is more difficult to fool a woman into believing ejaculation has also taken place. If, however, the man is wearing a condom, or if the woman is too naïve to be able to tell the difference between the man's ejaculate and her own lubrications, or if the amount of ejaculate the man releases is very *small,* then a man could possibly convince a woman ejaculation had taken place when it hadn't. Given the proper circumstances it's quite possible that a woman would be unable to tell if a man had had orgasm. Just as with women, there's great individual variation in the man's response. In some males (and females) orgasm is scarcely more than a sigh. In others, at the opposite extreme, it is more like an epileptic seizure.

Is it more difficult for a man to reach orgasm as he gets older—say, after forty-five? Yes. As the Kinsey studies established, men begin to age sexually after eighteen or so, and present a profile of aging long before they are forty-five. Orgasms tend to be slower in coming, and the penis is less turgid. Retarded ejaculation also increases with age. On the other hand, there is no physiological reason why men cannot continue to have erections and orgasms all their lives; such sexual activity has even been recorded in centenarians. If it takes older men longer to reach orgasm, well, that is not necessarily a bad thing for their partners.

Why can some men have repeated ejaculations during one act of intercourse, while others are "through" after just one? The only explanation for this difference is the variation among individuals. It would be as hard to say why such differences exist as it would be to explain why some men are five feet, two inches, and others are over six feet. We do know that the experience of multiple orgasm in men, that is, repeated climaxes accompanied by ejaculations during a continuous act of intercourse, is largely limited to young adolescents, and to only about 20 percent of these. The percentage of men having multiple orgasms declines rapidly with the years, so that among men in their fifties, only 3 or 4 percent can still have them.

Also, a man's experience of multiple orgasm is somewhat different from a woman's. In the male, each orgasm is distinct; after ejaculation the penis again grows turgid, excitement builds, and another climax is achieved. With women, however, multiple orgasm is often experienced as waves of more and more intense climaxes, each blending into the other, without marked detumescence or build-up of excitement. The man's experience might be compared to the up-and-down levels of a graph, the woman's to widening concentric circles.

Does a man's orgasm *feel* to him the same way a woman's does to her? I've heard that it's more "local," and is less pervasive of the entire body than the female's. The male orgasm probably does feel different to a man than a woman's does to her. Although being a male, I have some difficulty in understanding what a woman feels like when she is having an orgasm. Judging from studies that have been made, the female orgasm *is* less localized, but Masters and Johnson have cast some doubt on this idea. They have shown that the muscles surrounding the female vagina and the male urethra cause them to contract at about the same rate—that is, once every eight-tenths of a second. The number of contractions in orgasm, a total of three to five, is also about the same. It is safe to say, then, that the similarities between the sexes during orgasm are much greater than the differences.

Studies show that it's often easier for a woman to get to orgasm through masturbation than through intercourse. Is this ever true also for men? Yes, but with a difference. It could be argued theoretically that this would be true for both, but in practical terms, I think, the difference is evident. For women, intercourse is a poor technique for achieving orgasm because there is less clitoral stimulation than there is in masturbation. For men, however, there is much more specific penile stimulation during intercourse, and the action is not much different than in masturbation. Another difference involves the way both sexes experience manual stimulation: The male thinks in terms of penetration and can experience an approximation of that sensation through the caress of a woman's hand. This, of course, is not true in the female.

Does the strength or firmness of a man's erection have anything to do with the intensity of his orgasm? No, the intensity of an orgasm is more related to psychological factors than to firmness of erection. The emotion the man feels at the moment of climax is the main determinant of his pleasure.

Is there any certain way most men feel after an orgasm? For example, do they feel energetic, tired, empty, loving, or what? Most men feel tired, and often want to go to sleep. As the French put it, "After intercourse, all animals are sad." That may be a sexist aphorism, however, because women, on the contrary, want to be held and to feel a closeness with the male. Inhibited males often get up and wash or smoke or walk around the room because they have a vague feeling of being ill-at-ease. Males who have multiple orgasms and those who have powerful psychosexual drives toward their partners will probably want to continue love-making or resume it after an interval.

What determines a man's capacity for having a good orgasm? Is it having orgasm frequently, an individual's background, the lack of inhibitions, sufficient stimulation, past experiences, or what? That's a hard question to answer simply because of the variation in individuals. It would be safe to say, however, that some or all of the conditions mentioned, and no doubt a good many others, may be related to the capacity for having a good orgasm. But certainly the absence of guilt and fear, and the lack of inhibition, play a major part, if by a "good" orgasm we mean a joyful, uninhibited experience.

Do men really enjoy "holding back," or is it only a favor to women? Neither. A major difference between male and female sexual behavior is that men tend to be goal oriented, while women are more likely to be process oriented; that is, the male drives directly toward the orgasm, but the female enjoys as much, or more, the process that leads to her climax. To men who are really at ease with their sexuality, it is not a matter either of "holding back" or of having their orgasm quickly, but rather the enjoyment of giving and receiving pleasure with a woman.

How long does it usually take a man to reach orgasm if he isn't worried about pleasuring the female? That depends on the male. A goal-oriented man can reach orgasm in less than a minute after erection if he cares nothing about his partner, a sexual style long known in our language as "slam, bam, 'thank you ma'am.' " "Pleasuring," on the other hand, and delay of orgasm, may go on indefinitely. For most men, however, climax is reached from two to five minutes after intercourse begins.

Why do some men seem to experience the orgasm so much more intensely than others do? Are they simply more theatrical in their reactions, or do some really feel more powerful physical sensations than others? Yes, some men *do* receive more powerful sensations than others—as does the same man at different *times*. There are not only individual physiological differences here but also varying psychosexual elements. A man's experience of orgasm when he is having intercourse with a girl he loves will differ greatly, for example, from a climax reached with a prostitute.

Is a man's orgasm basically the same sensation with every woman he goes to bed with, or does it vary? It varies. The first time with any woman is often more intense, because the experience is with someone new and desire is likely to be heightened. Intensity also varies with different women simply because each responds differently. Often the male's excitement and resulting intensity of feeling is brought on by the woman's excitement. For both, the newness of the situation may heighten intensity, and sometimes feelings of guilt (childhood memories, for example, of doing something "naughty") can elevate excitement.

Then there is the old and undisputed truth that some women turn some men on, and there is no way to explain this except for the "chemistry" that suddenly exists between them. Describing such a turn-on, men often say a woman just "smells good" to them. They don't mean that she wears a particular perfume, but that the total odor she exudes, wrapped in the aura of her personality, produces that mysterious "chemistry" that creates strong attractions between people. The male response to this is sometimes so unconscious that it could be called subliminal; at other times he is acutely conscious of the assault on his five senses, in which appearance, the sound of a woman's voice, the feminine odor she gives off, the touch of her skin, and the taste of her mouth are all blended. There is, too, turn-on by association, when any of these sensual attributes in a woman may recall a sexual stimulation remembered from childhood.

Is it true that smoking and/or alcohol inhibit a man's ability to have orgasm? No and yes. There's no reliable data to indicate a relationship between smoking and orgasm. As for alcohol, it is a depressant and everyone knows how depressants act. A small amount of alcohol lowers the level of inhibition so that men (or women) grow more relaxed and calm, and are likely to experience *more* intense orgasms as a result. But a larger amount, more than two ounces, depresses the lower nervous centers so that males may have more difficulty in reaching orgasm, and sometimes even in attaining erection.

Does a male really suffer physical discomfort if he gets an erection and finds no release, or is this just something men say to make women feel sorry for them? It's true that many men do experience physical discomfort if they are aroused for a long period of time without having orgasm. The sensation is similar to a muscle cramp, and in many cases the discomfort is great enough to make it difficult, if not impossible, for the man to ejaculate, even through masturbation.

If a woman wears a diaphragm or an IUD, can the male feel it during intercourse, and if so does it affect or diminish his pleasure? Yes to both questions, but with some qualifications. Though a man shouldn't feel the IUD, pleasure may occasionally be diminished if he feels the "threads" of the device protruding into the vagina from the uterus. Sometimes too, he will rub up against the diaphragm, especially if it happens to be poorly fitted. Even if it is properly adjusted, a few males report they can feel a diaphragm, and a few men do say it is distracting and diminishes their pleasure.

Many people say that the size of a man's penis doesn't affect his or his partner's pleasure—unless he's really got a problem, one way or the other. But how about the size of a woman's vagina? Does a "tight" vagina yield the greatest pleasure, and does "loose" mean the man doesn't get enjoyment? Yes, "tightness" may produce a better feeling for the male, but "looseness" doesn't *necessarily* mean he will enjoy intercourse less, since so many other factors are involved, including psychological ones. The vagina is like an uninflated balloon. As the penis is inserted, the vaginal walls expand far enough to accommodate it. If the walls have good muscle tone, the penis will be held firmly inside. There are muscle exercises a woman can use to build up muscle tone, tightening the muscles around the vagina with only a few minutes of exercise several times a day. In a few weeks, the muscle tone will be built up to a satisfactory level.

Age makes a difference in muscle tone, of course; it diminishes as we grow older. Having children also affects the muscles around the vagina, stretching them and eventually causing them to lose some of their original elasticity. If there is too much perineal repair (scarring of the area between the vagina and the anus) as the result of childbirth, further loss of elasticity may result.

Does circumcision reduce the sensitivity in a man's penis? No. There are no studies indicating any significant change as a result of circumcision. Men who have been circumcised and those who have not respond in the same way.

Why do men vary in their ability to maintain an erection? How wide is the range? The range is very wide indeed, including as extremes the man who can never really get an erection and the one who is able to maintain one for several hours. There is no satisfactory explanation for this variance. Psychosexual factors are certainly involved, and though the extent of these has not been determined, it seems likely they are predominant since the physiological mechanism is the same for all men, except those with some kind of physical abnormality or deficiency.

Why do men like to have orgasms early in the morning? More men than women like to have orgasms early in the morning because then they are well rested and their male hormone level is at its highest. Since there is a definite difference between the sexes in this respect, both men and women should try to understand and accept it, adapting their needs to the other's feelings at particular times. Perhaps you can plan to get up a bit earlier now and then; have your coffee and a shower before engaging in sex.

Most men, athletes and creative people particularly, seem to feel that an orgasm saps their strength. Is this true? No, but there appears to be no way to kill this myth. We still find coaches sequestering athletes from wives and girlfriends before athletic events, and sex is still blamed for a star's poor performance. Yet there is not the slightest shred of scientific evidence to support this notion. In fact, during my years with Dr. Kinsey [Dr. Pomeroy was Director of Field Research for the Kinsey studies and interviewed more than 40 percent of the 18,000 histories taken], we interviewed one noted athlete who broke a national track record only an hour after he had masturbated to relieve his pre-meet tension. The idea that vital quantities of energy are lost during climax isn't based on fact. Actually, the energy expended in an orgasm is about the equivalent of that used by walking up a flight of stairs or jogging a block.

Do studies indicate that men prefer to have their orgasms before, with, or after their partners? None of these three options are necessarily preferred. Here we are dealing with the relationship between sex and selfishness. In the first stage of intercourse, there is usually a good deal of foreplay or petting in which both partners need to be unselfish. They play to the reactions of the other person. Then follows the build-up to orgasm, a completely selfish phase of intercourse since each person is tuned in primarily to his own response, no matter how considerate he may be of the other person. At the same time, and paradoxically, it is unselfish because of the pleasure each partner takes in the other's excitement. In the third and final phase there is a letdown from the preceding cumulative tension and climax, and in this there is a return to unselfishness.

For years the myth has been perpetuated, derived from early marriage manuals, that the best and most satisfying intercourse occurs when the partners have a simultaneous orgasm. While such mutuality can, indeed, be an extremely satisfying experience, it is not necessarily better than having the orgasm at different times. For example, men often like to enjoy the female orgasm and try to help her attain it without attempting to have their own at the same time. Since most males lose their erection shortly after orgasm, it is actually better for the woman to have hers first. The excitement of the male's later coming to climax may induce subsequent orgasms in females who otherwise might not think themselves multiorgasmic.

Why do some men have such plentiful ejaculations while others seem relatively sparse? Does this depend on age? Not necessarily. Plentiful or sparse ejaculations depend on individual variation, for which there seems to be no specific reason. Age *is* one factor, however, since as men grow older, the volume of their ejaculate diminishes.

I've heard that the longer a man has been celibate, the faster he's likely to come to climax—true or false? True, in general. A man who has had no sex for a long time is bound to exhibit urgency when with a woman. The excitement is psychological, however, rather than physiological. Women similarly deprived demonstrate the same urgency, probably for the same reason.

How long after ejaculation does it take to build up a sperm count sufficient for fertilization? It takes from twenty-four to forty-eight hours.

Does the female's orgasm during intercourse precipitate or retard the male's? It usually has a tendency to precipitate the male's climax because the intensity of her experience is communicated to him and excites him beyond any restraints. However, there are so many other factors involved that it would be difficult to set this down as anything approaching a norm. Some men, as I noted earlier, deliberately postpone their own orgasm for as long as possible, no matter what is happening to the woman. Sometimes, too, an early orgasm in the woman may dampen or even remove some of her partner's urgency, particularly if she then becomes relatively passive. Complicated psychological factors can make a difference as well, adding to the virtually infinite variations in human sexual behavior.

As I've already said, the questions asked here, while they certainly express a keen curiosity about male orgasm, are largely concerned with technique. Let me stress once more, however, that while understanding technique is definitely important if both partners are to experience the greatest enjoyment, it ought never to take precedence over emotion and feeling—over love, if you will—unless the people involved acknowledge that their sexual activity is going to be only on the genital level, as in prostitution, or very often in group sex. Honest emotion, honestly expressed, is still the best guarantee of a satisfying sexual relationship.

This is especially true if people are having trouble in achieving orgasm. In such cases, the couples who are able to communicate with each other on a nongenital level are able to relax and talk out the problem honestly. If that fails, therapy, undeveloped until only a few years ago, is now available, and has a high rate of effectiveness. People with serious problems should seek professional help.

Perhaps the most encouraging aspect of the whole sexual process that leads up to orgasm in both males and females, is that couples can remain turned on to each other over long periods of time. The divorce rate may be high and climbing, but there are many cases on record of men and women who are capable of producing orgasmic response in each other even after fifty years. And that possibility, at least, exists for everyone.

FOUR TEENS TELL WHY THEY'RE YOUNG, SINGLE AND PREGNANT

Mort Weiser

The figures are alarming. There are ten million young women between 15 and 19 years of age in the United States. Four million of them (40 percent) are sexually active. The bottom line: *one million pregnancies a year.*

Little comfort can be taken from the statistics for 13- and 14-year-olds, either—a category in which sexual activity is accelerating rapidly. There are 3.8 million girls in this age bracket, and 420,000 of them (14 percent) have had intercourse. The end result: *30,000 pregnancies a year.*

Why so many pregnancies? Why do teenagers fail to use contraceptives? Do they regard abortion as a birth-control method? Are they ignorant about birth-control measures? Or, are they simply careless and irresponsible?

To find answers to these puzzling questions, I interviewed four girls who were, or had recently been, pregnant. While broad conclusions can't possibly be drawn from so small a sampling, I gained a certain amount of insight into this extraordinary problem, and I think you will, too. I chose girls from middle-class families to emphasize the fact that it's not only the poor and disadvantaged who get into trouble. It could be anyone's daughter. (The girls' names, as well as some unimportant details, have been changed to protect their identities.)

***Holly Andrews** is a slight, attractive brunette. She presents an odd, appealing mixture of innocence and maturity.*

Holly was interviewed five days after giving birth to a child she surrendered for adoption. The interview took place in a Birthright home. (Birthright is an organization offering "an alternative to abortion," and its services include, when needed, the house of a volunteer couple in which a girl can live during her pregnancy.)

With four brothers and two sisters, Holly is the oldest child in a large family. Both her parents attended college, her father graduating from a major university. A night club manager, he's earned a good living most of his life.

Because of marital problems, Holly's parents separated for a short time. It was during this period that she became pregnant. She was 16.

Holly talks: "In the sixth grade we had a movie about our menstrual cycle. That's when I first learned about sex. And my parents talked to me about sex. You know, not that sex is bad, but that it's not right to have it before marriage. I don't really know where I learned about contraceptives, though. I think I always knew about them. I just didn't use them. You see, I had sex once, and I got pregnant. I mean, it's not my lifestyle. I never engaged in sex as an everyday thing. It was once, and I got pregnant. I'm not a lucky person. If I do something wrong, I never get away with it. It wasn't something I planned. I didn't go out and say, 'I'm going to have sex tonight.' It just happened.

"And the possibility of becoming pregnant didn't occur to me. It was a guy I knew very well, someone I thought I loved. I hadn't seen him in a long time because I had been living in California. I went to visit him, and it happened in his house. His mother was home, but she was sleeping. When it was over, I told myself I couldn't get pregnant having sex just once.

"I know one thing now; I'll never have sex again until I'm married. There's somebody else to think about. There's a third person involved, a perfectly innocent third person—the baby.

"I don't think anybody ever correlates having sex with becoming pregnant. I know it sounds foolish, but it's true. It's funny, but I've lived in New York and California, and things are different in the two states. In New York, a lot of my friends are having sex, and none of them is on anything. In California everybody's on the Pill.

"My parents were very hurt. I contemplated having an abortion—though not very seriously—to keep them from knowing about it all.

"I never told the boy who made me pregnant. I think he probably knows now because some kids in his town were aware of it. But I never told him. I felt it was my problem. I got myself into it. I felt dumb, you know, being pregnant. I felt it was my fault."

•

***Betty Michaels**, a dark-haired young woman, appears angry. She speaks brusquely, authoritatively.*

Betty became pregnant at 18 and was interviewed eight months after having an abortion. An only child, she lives with her mother in a large, comfortable apartment in New York City. Her parents were divorced when she was five.

Each parent has a master's degree. Betty's father, who owns a fashionable antique shop, has an income of more than $100,000 a year. Her mother is a college instructor.

Betty: "I was fourteen when I started having sexual relations. There have been two other boys since then—a total of three. I became pregnant with my current boyfriend, Rick. The first guy was twenty-four and had his own apartment. Contraceptives weren't necessary. He'd had a vasectomy. I was sixteen when I started seeing Rick, and I began taking the Pill about a month before I met him. I didn't know about the diaphragm at first, but I did know about the Pill and IUDs. Nowadays, girls know all about birth-control measures. You can get answers at home, school, from older sisters, friends, baby-sitters—just about everywhere. My mother told me about my menstrual cycle when I was young. But we never talked about birth control because I told her I was taking the Pill and she said, 'Fine.' I told her then that I wasn't a virgin.

"Later, I went off the Pill because I gained forty pounds on it, and I began having other side effects. I decided to switch to the IUD, but I had to wait two weeks. It was during that two-week period that I became pregnant. I was having sex once a day, maybe twice a day.

"Maybe the decision to go off the Pill and switch contraceptives was just an excuse; maybe I wanted to get pregnant. A lot of my girl friends get pregnant because they have nothing better to do. It gives them something to care about, a purpose in life. Of course, they have the babies. I didn't. Some girls get pregnant to hold on to their boyfriends.

"I went through with the abortion but I don't want to go through one ever again. I'm using an IUD now. They should stress birth control more in school and scare you away from thinking abortion is easy. I thought an abortion would be like pulling a tooth out, but it's really not. I'm not talking about the physical side of it; I'm talking about the emotional part. It's hard to describe. It's your baby and, no matter what anybody says, it's being flushed down the toilet. It's a big thing in your life, and a girl should be spared that if possible. And another thing: Clinics shouldn't have abortion centers right next to where girls that are having their babies are being examined. They share the same waiting room. It's not fair to the girls who are having abortions; it makes them miserable."

•

***Faith Lockwood** is a tall, blond-haired girl. She answers questions easily, with an air of confidence.*

Faith became pregnant at the age of 17. Five months later she married the young man with whom she'd had sexual relations. She was interviewed a month before she was due to give birth.

Faith's father is a salesman, her mother an elementary school teacher. Together, they earn about $50,000. Faith quit high school when she became pregnant, but intends to earn an equivalency diploma.

Faith: "I was sixteen when I started having sex and it was with Tommy, my husband. He was the only one. I had been going with him about a year before we had intercourse. After that we had sex frequently. About once a week. We weren't using contraceptives the first four or five months. Then I started using the Pill. I went to a clinic for it. My mother didn't know, but then she found a letter in my coat pocket. A letter Tommy had written to me. Then she knew, but she was very cool about everything. She said it was my decision. She knew she couldn't stop me. It was a shock; I wasn't her little virgin daughter anymore. My mother didn't tell my father—I asked her not to. My father is very strict, so we decided it was best not to tell him.

"We first had sex at Tommy's house, in his room. His parents had gone out to dinner. He had asked me once before when they were out, and I'd said no. Then he didn't ask; it just happened, and afterward I got a little nervous about becoming pregnant. But then I had this feeling it couldn't happen to me, that it wasn't likely—not the first time. I had two scares later on, before I started taking the Pill. Once I was ten days late and I went for a pregnancy test, but it turned out negative. Even then I figured I was overreacting. I said, 'All these months have gone by and nothing's happened; there's nothing to worry about.' Tommy and I discussed the condom, but I wouldn't let him use it. I didn't want him to touch me with one of those things. I wouldn't have enjoyed sex, just knowing he was using it. Then I got the Pill but the clinic only gave me a three-month supply. I was supposed to go back, but I didn't. I was too lazy. The clinic was only about twenty minutes away but I had no car, and that was a problem.

"I learned I was pregnant after I had broken off with Tommy. I had gone out with him so long, and I wanted to see what it was like not to be with him. Right after that, I began to get sick in the mornings. My parents sent me to the family doctor and he kept giving me medicine to calm my stomach. Then, the doctor scheduled me for a pregnancy test, and I made the mistake of mentioning that to Tommy's sister. She must have told him because he raced over to my house to tell my parents he loved me and wanted to marry me. Without even knowing for certain I was pregnant! This really got me mad because I hadn't told my father anything. My father felt like a jackass. He was really angry at my mother, because she hadn't told him anything.

"My father then walked to town to get a pregnancy test from a drugstore. When the test result was positive, he was very understanding. I decided to keep the baby even if I didn't marry Tommy. I wanted to have the baby and raise it. But we did get married, and we are happy.

"My close friends had said they would stick by me, but that was just hogwash. I haven't heard from any of them. The only friend I have is Laura, and she was in the same condition as me so she knows what it's like to go through it.

"If I'd had an abortion, it would have been acceptable because lots of girls have them. I think a lot of girls still don't know where they can go to get protection. They think they have to ask their family doctors or that their parents have to know, and that's the last thing they want. They don't know there are plenty of clinics that can help them."

•

***Connie Decker** is a beautiful, full-bodied girl. She could be a Hollywood starlet or a bathing-suit model. She remained poised, though initially reticent, throughout the interview.*

Connie's parents were divorced when she was five, and her mother later remarried. Her stepfather heads a small construction company in Florida, while her mother has worked as a wait-

ress in a cocktail lounge. Connie describes her background as "middle-income," observing, however, that the family once had to go on welfare when the construction business in Florida turned sour.

Connie became pregnant at 16 and had an abortion. She is now 17 and living in New Jersey with Bob, the boy who made her pregnant in Florida. She was interviewed in a Planned Parenthood office, where she had gone when she feared she was pregnant again. The test turned out negative.

Connie: "I started having sex with a boy named Owen. He was sixteen. I was fifteen. We had been going out for two years so I figured it was going to last. My mom had put me on the Pill when I was thirteen. I was still a virgin, but she said it was a precaution. One of her friend's daughters had gotten pregnant, and the girl was my best friend, so she was afraid. I think my mother knew when I did have sex two years later. But I never discussed it with her. I was still fifteen and I had just broken up with Owen when I met Bob." (*Slight hesitation, embarrassed laugh*) "One week later, we started having sex. At that point, my doctor had advised me to get off the Pill for three months to give my body time to get back to its natural functioning. He suggested a diaphragm, but I didn't get one. And it's kind of hard to ask someone to use a rubber—I was afraid of Bob's reaction.

"I had sexual relations with Bob for three months before I became pregnant. Eventually I started using foam and he used a rubber. Sometimes I didn't use the foam, though, and that's when I became pregnant. He used a rubber, but there was a hole in it, and some of it went through.

"I was having bad pains in my back, so my mom took me to a doctor. That's when we found out. She was going to kill me, but my little brother, Stephen, who was only five, wouldn't let her. Suddenly, for some reason, we were all laughing. Bob, outside in the waiting room, could see us, but he didn't know why we were laughing. My mom said she was laughing because if she didn't laugh, she'd kill me. Then the doctor said sixteen was pretty young to have a baby, and he suggested an abortion.

"We told Bob's mother only after I had the abortion. His father still doesn't know. They would have helped if they knew, but we were both too scared to tell them. I had been totally against abortions. But my mom, Bob and I had several long discussions about it. I would have had the baby, but we were on welfare and Bob had only one job, and there just wasn't enough money.

"After I graduated from high school, I moved to New Jersey to live with Bob. I'm not back on the Pill because of all I've heard about the side effects, so lately we've been using a rubber, but no foam. Sometimes we use nothing. That's why I'm here today. I'm going to get a diaphragm from Planned Parenthood now. You know, if I had been pregnant this time, I don't think I could have gone through with another abortion. I read somewhere that once you have an abortion you may not be able to have children, and I do want children eventually.

"I can't really set an age limit for having sexual relations." (*Laughing*) "I would say under thirteen is kind of young. But I think if a girl wants to, she should."

When my interviews were finished, I turned back to the questions with which I began. Had I found answers? Perhaps a few. None of these girls was ignorant about birth control, and only one thought it was likely that other girls were. Only one had regarded abortion as a logical method of birth control. Intellectually, the girls were well-informed; socially, they were capable of acting on their information: going to a clinic and making appropriate use of contraceptives.

How about my final question: Are these girls simply careless and irresponsible? The answer apparently is yes—with qualifications. These are not grown-up young women who are fully aware of the potential consequences of their acts and wantonly choose to go ahead anyway, confident that other people, or society in general, will pick up the pieces. They are children who don't really recognize that there will be pieces to pick up. On some very deep level they remain untouched by what they are taught by parents and teachers, even by what they see happening to their friends. *They just don't believe that what has not happened to them in the past can happen to them in the future.*

The girls I spoke to grew up very fast when that assumption proved false. Betty almost choked on her rage and anguish as she spoke of the reality of abortion as compared to her fantasy of it, and insisted that other girls ought to know what it's really like. Holly accepted her pregnancy as her own fault, for being "dumb," and decided not to have sex again until she was married because she now knew that "there's a third person involved—the baby." Faith, deeply disillusioned about friends who deserted her, nonetheless wanted other girls to know that their parents might well stick by them—as hers had—even if they gave their pregnant daughter a hard time for a while. Connie, though she continued to be careless about contraception, had decided never to have a second abortion lest it interfere with her ability to have the children she knew she wanted in the future.

For all these girls, getting pregnant was a deeply troubling experience. In each case, greater tragedy was averted only because the girls were able to cope and even mature through the experience. I have no way of knowing if, in this, they are typical. Even so, unplanned pregnancies can hardly be viewed as acceptable "learning experiences" in life; some better way to instruct our children should be found.

Warning: Cigarette Smoking Is Dangerous To Reproductive Health

By Sadja Goldsmith Greenwood

Sadja Goldsmith Greenwood is a physician in practice in San Francisco, is a clinical instructor in the Department of Obstetrics, Gynecology and Reproductive Sciences of the University of California, San Francisco, and is a member of the National Medical Committee of the Planned Parenthood Federation of America.

Summary

Smoking presents particular dangers to women of childbearing age. With other smokers, they face the well-known hazards of lung cancer and other malignancy, respiratory illnesses such as emphysema, and cardiovascular disease. In addition, they run special risks connected with contraception and childbirth. Recent studies indicate that older women who take the pill and smoke heavily have as much as 39 times the risk of myocardial infarction of women who do neither. Smoking and pill use together have also been shown to be associated with increased rates of subarachnoid hemorrhage. Smoking during pregnancy is associated with lower-birth-weight babies, fetal deaths and congenital anomalies. Children of smokers suffer greater risks of respiratory illness than the infants of nonsmoking parents.

Against the background of these and other dangers of smoking for women of reproductive age, 252 Planned Parenthood clinics were surveyed in 1978 to determine whether educational campaigns about smoking were in progress, and what the clinics' smoking policies for patients and staff were. Responses from 197 clinics indicated that there was a strong interest in informing patients about the risks of smoking. Half the clinics had banned smoking among patients. Only about one-fifth, however, had banned smoking in the clinic by staff (although another fifth had restricted staff smoking to certain areas). Banning or restricting staff smoking was seen as a thorny issue involving individual rights and job efficiency. The issue is being worked out in different ways, depending on the balance of opinion at individual clinics. Six out of 10 respondents said no visual materials on the hazards of smoking were used, although more than eight out of 10 said they saw a need for such materials. Almost nine out of 10 clinics provided patients with written material on smoking hazards, and almost all dealt with the subject in counseling sessions.

Introduction

Smoking is a health hazard which should be of particular concern to family planning agencies. More than four million women attend family planning clinics in the United States each year;[1] for many of them, the clinic may be their only contact with the health care system. The family planning clinic sometimes serves as the primary health care facility for teenagers and poor women, much as the private gynecologist is often the primary physician for middle-class women. About one million of the women who come to family planning clinics each year smoke; for many of them, the family planning agency may be the only source of accurate medical information on the potential dangers of smoking.

It is particularly important to reach teenage patients of family planning clinics. They represent about 30 percent of all patients, and smoking among teenagers is a serious and growing problem. Teenage girls have taken up smoking with a vengeance in the last decade. The proportion of 15- and 16-year-old girls who are regular smokers grew from 10 percent in 1968 to 20 percent in 1974. Among 17- and 18-year-olds, the rise in the same period was from 19 to 26 percent. Since 75 percent of smokers take up the habit before the age of 21,[2] and because the sooner one begins to consider the dangers of smoking, the easier it is to quit, teenagers and young adults at family planning agencies are a particularly critical target for a vigorous educational campaign about the hazards of smoking.

Hazards of Smoking for Women of Reproductive Age and Their Children

Among all the information on the hazards of smoking for women of childbearing age, data on smoking and oral contraceptives provide the most compelling reason for family planners to initiate educational programs about smoking. A recent study of women in the northeastern United States examined the relationship between smoking, pill use and myocardial infarction (heart attack).[3] Among women not taking the pill, smoking alone seriously increased the number of heart attacks. For women who were light smokers (1-24 cigarettes a day), the risk of heart attack was 3.4 times that of nonsmokers. For women who were heavy smokers (25 or more cigarettes), the risk was seven times that of nonsmokers.

Use of the pill alone also increased a woman's chance of having a heart attack, the study showed. There were 4.5 times as many heart attacks among women who took the pill but did not smoke as there were among women who did neither. All of the increased risk for the nonsmokers, however, was concentrated among women aged 40 and older.

But it was among women who were heavy smokers and pill users that the most dramatic increases in the risk of heart attack appeared. Women who both smoked heavily and took the pill had a risk of myocardial infarction that was 39 times as high as the risk among women who neither took the pill nor smoked. The largest increase in risk appeared to be among the older women who were heavy smokers.

These results confirm previous British and American studies showing that women who take the pill run increased risks of death from all cardiovascular diseases, and that these risks are sharply increased by a woman's age and by cigarette smoking.[4]

The results of these studies have led the U.S. Food and Drug Administration to require that a warning be printed in the insert which accompanies each package of oral contraceptives: "Women who use oral contraceptives should not smoke." The data have also led many family planning agencies to consider smoking a contraindication to pill use among women over 30 or 35 years of age.

A recent study has linked smoking, pill use and subarachnoid hemorrhage (a type of brain hemorrhage), showing that the risk of this disorder is multiplied when women over age 35 smoke and take the pill.[5]

The adverse effects of smoking during pregnancy have recently been summarized in the medical literature.[6] Smoking is associated with lower-birth-weight babies, shortened gestation, spontaneous abortions, fetal deaths, congenital anomalies, premature rupture of the membranes and bleeding episodes during late pregnancy, including those caused by premature separation of the placenta and a low-lying placenta. Babies born to smoking mothers have a higher neonatal death rate.

Infants who inhale tobacco smoke from their parents' cigarettes have a greater risk of respiratory illness than the infants of nonsmoking parents. The risk to the infant of an attack of pneumonia or bronchitis in the first year of life is almost double that of infants of nonsmoking parents. Such respiratory illness can result in infant death or in damage to the respiratory tract that persists into adult life.[7]

The effect of parental and sibling smoking on children and teenagers is striking. In homes where one or both parents smoke, boys and girls are more likely to take up the habit if their mothers smoke than if their fathers do. Older siblings who smoke also play a role in encouraging the adoption of smoking by teenagers. If at least one parent and one older sibling smokes, a teenager is four times more likely to smoke than if no parent or older sibling smokes.[8]

A recent study indicates that women who smoke have an earlier natural menopause than nonsmokers, with a relationship between number of cigarettes smoked and age at menopause.[9]

The association between smoking and cancer of the respiratory tract is well known. Lung cancer among women is rising; a doubling of age-adjusted death rates for lung cancer in women was seen between 1965 and 1974, and was correlated with the increased use of cigarettes among women that began around the time of World War II. Less well known are a relationship between smoking and cancer of the bladder[10] and a possible association with cancers of the ovary[11] and cervix.[12]

Smoking is one of the causes of increased blood pressure in many people. Nicotine stimulates epinephrine and norepinephrine release from the adrenals, causing constriction of blood vessels and an immediate rise in both systolic and diastolic blood pressures.[13]

Smoking is thought to be associated with vascular changes in the skin which lead to earlier onset of wrinkles and decreased skin color.[14]

Clinic Survey

Because of the special hazards of smoking for women of reproductive age, it is of interest to know what the current policies and practices of family planning clinics are with regard to smoking. To this end, a survey of 252 Planned Parenthood chapters and affiliates was made in 1978. The questionnaire included questions on current smoking policies and on the kind of smoking education carried out at the clinics. The clinics' interest in and awareness of the issue is indicated by the fact that 197, or 78 percent, replied. Their diverse responses are summarized in Table 1.

Forty-nine percent of the clinics did not allow patients to smoke, 41 percent permitted smoking anywhere on the premises and 10 percent allowed smoking only in restricted areas. Of clinics where smoking was not allowed, 50 percent had banned it before 1977, the rest, since 1977. Sixty-four percent of clinics said the response from patients to the no-smoking policy was positive, 29 percent said it was mixed and seven percent said it was negative. Several respondents wrote that nonsmokers "loved" the ban while smokers disliked it. Many affiliates indicated that smokers had to leave the premises or stand out of doors to smoke. Some clinics which still permitted smoking indicated that they discouraged the practice by posting antismoking signs and by not providing ashtrays. Many replies indicated that the ban had been well received: Patients had understood that Planned Parenthood was a health care facility. Many respondents also said that the questionnaire had made them realize that they wanted to mount a more vigorous educational program on the hazards of smoking for women, and they asked for relevant visual materials on smoking and the pill.

Table 1. Smoking policies in 197 Planned Parenthood Affiliates, 1978

Question	% answering		
Is smoking allowed in your agency?	**Yes**	**No**	**In certain areas**
By patients?	41	49	10
By staff?	58	22	20
If you have a no smoking policy, what has been the response?	**Pos.**	**Neg.**	**Mixed**
By patients?	64	7	29
By staff?	60	10	30
Are you using posters or wall displays to explain the risks of smoking?	**Yes**	**No**	—
And the pill?	34	66	—
And pregnancy?	39	61	—
Are you developing such posters?	**Yes** 16	**No** 84	— —
Do you see a need for such visuals?	**Yes** 85	**No** 15	— —
Have you included information on the risks of smoking in handouts and educational/counseling sessions?	**Yes**	**No**	—
In handouts?	86	14	—
During counseling	94	6	—

Two respondents indicated why they opposed a ban on patient smoking. One wrote that it is difficult to restrict smoking during counseling sessions, when women are often upset: "Sometimes it seems more appropriate to light their cigarette than to enforce the rules." The other said that out of 35,000 patients who turned in an evaluation form on the medical services provided, only one had asked for a ban on smoking. This respondent went on to say that she or he was "pro-choice—for abortion—for smoking—against having someone else's life-style imposed on me or trying to impose mine on others. Planned Parenthood has plenty of work to do without getting involved in the smokers vs. nonsmokers battle."

When asked if staff were allowed to smoke in their facility, 58 percent said yes, 20 percent said only in certain areas when not in contact with patients, and 22 percent said no. In clinics where a ban or partial restriction on staff smoking had been instituted, the response was described as positive by 60 percent of the respondents, negative by 10 percent and mixed by 30 percent. Not surprisingly, nonsmokers were elated by the restriction, while smokers were angry. Many accompanying notes indicated that such bans had caused great difficulties: Staff smokers were openly rebellious, or would sneak away from their desks to smoke, thus becoming less productive. A note from an executive director said: "We permitted brief cigarette breaks for addicts on our staff—our doorways started to look like red-light districts—women lurking about, puffing on cigarettes in all kinds of weather—nonsmokers started to get very jealous of the smoking breaks—mutinous feelings were aroused—about three months after the ban was instituted I was forced to lift it—since the ban was lifted I have resumed smoking with a vengeance, and personally would welcome an absolute prohibition."

From an opposite viewpoint, one respondent wrote: "Banning smoking in our affiliate was carefully planned and has been successful and meaningful. As a health facility it was important; we cannot ask our patients to stop smoking without showing our own willingness to live without cigarettes."

Posters or other wall displays on the risks of smoking and pill use were used by 34 percent of respondents, and visual displays on smoking and pregnancy, by 39 percent. A few respondents mentioned that they were making their own displays with messages such as "Women who take the pill should not smoke." Others used posters on the dangers of smoking during pregnancy from the American Cancer Society or the American Lung Association. Eighty-five percent of the respondents said they saw a need for visual materials on smoking, the pill and pregnancy. Many respondents wrote that they would use such materials immediately if they were available, while others specified that posters should be attractive, nonthreatening and factual.

A large majority of respondents had already included information on the risks of smoking and the pill in patient education handouts (86 percent) or in counseling sessions (94 percent).

Strategies for Informing Family Planning Patients

How can family planning clinics inform women most effectively about the risks of smoking, reinforcing their motivation not to start or helping them to quit? Important target groups are teenagers, who may be making the decision to start smoking; women over 30 on the pill, who run the highest risk of pill/smoking complications; and women who are pregnant or contemplating pregnancy.

A recent DHEW survey found that 90 percent of teenagers believe smoking is harmful to their health, and 85 percent of smoking teenagers say they definitely or probably will not be smokers five years from now.[15]

It appears that teenagers know about the harmful effects of smoking, but do not feel that the remote risk of lung cancer in middle age outweighs the current advantages of the habit. Messages should therefore emphasize the disadvantages of smoking in the present—increased length and severity of colds and coughs, decreased athletic ability, decreased energy and bad breath—rather than warning of cancer and emphysema 20 years hence.

Teenage smokers in the DHEW survey rejected the concept that they had started smoking to attract the opposite sex. However, most advertisements for cigarettes (like other products) suggest that one's sexual attractiveness will be enhanced by the use of this or that brand. Antismoking messages should also take up this theme, pointing out that *not* smoking is attractive. The attractiveness theme is being developed in a poster. Similar posters could be developed showing popular rock stars, models, actors and athletes talking about why they *don't* smoke.

The desire for autonomy in young adults can also be addressed in messages about smoking risks by emphasizing personal ability to control life and health, the desirability of not becoming dependent on nicotine and the idea that advertising and tobacco interests are manipulating them into buying an addictive and unnecessary product.

Teenagers can be encouraged to develop their own ideas. Clinics can provide incentives or contests for developing posters, photographs, buttons and slogans emphasizing the negative aspects of smoking. The Door, an adolescent health center in New York, has mounted a campaign against smoking and has a graffiti board for antismoking slogans, as well as smoking withdrawal programs run by young members.

The National Interagency Council on Smoking and Health is currently funding pilot projects for the prevention of smoking in teenagers.*

*The address of the Council is 419 Park Avenue South, New York, N.Y. 10016. Youth must be directly involved in the planning and implementation of the projects.

The information on the combined effects of smoking and the pill in multiplying the risk of cardiovascular disease is summarized in the patient and physician package inserts of oral contraceptives. This information may be interpreted and presented to patients in educational and counseling sessions, in simple handouts and in wall displays and audiovisual materials for people who do not read easily.

It is important that this kind of educational material be factual, and that it emphasize the dangers of smoking rather than the dangers of the pill so that the woman is motivated to stop smoking rather than to abandon her birth control method. It is essential, however, to provide older women who prefer to continue to smoke with alternative birth control methods that they will use.

Family planning clinics serve large numbers of women before they become pregnant with a wanted pregnancy. Many of these women will want to become parents at some future date, which makes information on the adverse effects of smoking on pregnancy important in such a setting.

Some clinics provide prenatal as well as contraceptive care. Pregnant women are highly receptive to health messages and can often be persuaded to give up smoking during a pregnancy if the facts about its adverse effects are made known to them in a vivid way.[16] The Massachusetts Department of Public Health has recommended that a carboxyhemoglobin level be obtained for every patient at her first prenatal visit.[17] Women can then be shown abnormal laboratory results and told that the high level of carbon monoxide, which poses a threat to the fetus, can be lowered to the normal range only if they stop smoking. The use of such an assessment among nonpregnant patients would also help give them an immediate personal appraisal of the effects of smoking on their individual physiology.

Doctors, midwives and nurses, aware of the hazards of smoking and pregnancy, can urge pregnant women to quit by personal persuasion, written explanatory material and visual and audiovisual materials which outline the risks to mother and baby.

A message that would reach the public with every package of cigarettes has been proposed by the Massachusetts Department of Public Health, which has petitioned the Federal Trade Commission to revise the warning on cigarette packages to read as follows: "Cigarette smoking is hazardous to your health and can cause fatal cancer, heart disease and lung disease. Smoking during pregnancy increases the risk of death to the unborn baby or newborn infant."[18]

Many people are asking whether family planning agencies should broaden their scope to include various kinds of health care. One logical area of expansion is other types of reproductive health care. Another is broader health education for young women and their partners. An educational campaign about the hazards of smoking is consistent with both these directions because of its relevance to women on the pill and to women who may be pregnant or contemplating pregnancy. The millions of women of childbearing age who attend family planning clinics deserve the best we can offer in preventive health care, including a clear and factual informational campaign about the risks of smoking and pill-taking, and smoking and pregnancy.

References

1. The Alan Guttmacher Institute, *Data and Analyses for 1977 Revision of DHEW Five-Year Plan for Family Planning Services*, New York, 1978.

2. National Institutes of Health, DHEW (NIH), *Teenage Smoking: National Patterns of Cigarette Smoking, Ages 12 Through 18, in 1972 and 1974*, DHEW Publication No. (NIH) 76-931, 1976, Table A.

3. S. Shapiro, D. Slone, L. Rosenberg, D. W. Kaufman, P. D. Stolley and O. S. Miettinen, "Oral Contraceptive Use in Relation to Myocardial Infarction," *The Lancet*, **I**: 743, 1979.

4. J. I. Mann and W. H. W. Inman, "Oral Contraceptives and Death from Myocardial Infarction," *British Medical Journal*, **2**:245, 1975; J. I. Mann, M. P. Vessey, M. Thorogood and R. Doll, "Myocardial Infarction in Young Women, with Special Reference to Oral Contraceptive Practice," *British Medical Journal*, **2**:241, 1975; J. I. Mann, W. H. W. Inman and M. Thorogood, "Oral Contraceptive Use in Older Women and Fatal Myocardial Infarction," *British Medical Journal*, **2**:445, 1976; A. K. Jain, "Mortality Risk Associated with the Use of Oral Contraceptives," *Studies in Family Planning*, **8**:50, 1977; and H. W. Ory, "Association Between Oral Contraceptives and Myocardial Infarction, A Review," *Journal of the American Medical Association*, **237**:2619, 1977.

5. D. B. Petitti and J. Wingerd, "Use of Oral Contraceptives, Cigarette Smoking and Risk of Subarachnoid Haemorrhage," *The Lancet*, **II**:234, 1978.

6. M. B. Meyer and J. A. Tonascia, "Maternal Smoking, Pregnancy Complications, and Perinatal Mortality," *American Journal of Obstetrics and Gynecology*, **128**: 494, 1977; B. B. K. Pirani, "Smoking During Pregnancy," *Obstetrical and Gynecological Survey*, **33**: 1, 1978; and R. L. Naeye, "Relationship of Cigarette Smoking to Congenital Anomalies and Perinatal Death," *American Journal of Pathology*, **90**:289, 1978.

7. J. R. T. Colley, "Influence of Passive Smoking and Parental Phlegm on Pneumonia and Bronchitis in Early Childhood," *The Lancet*, **I**:529, 1974; and S. Harlap and A. M. Davies, "Infant Admissions to Hospitals and Maternal Smoking," *The Lancet*, **I**: 529, 1974.

8. NIH, 1976, op. cit.

9. H. Jick, J. Porter and A. S. Morrison, "Relationship Between Smoking and Age of Natural Menopause," *The Lancet*, **I**:1354, 1977.

10. Center for Disease Control, DHEW, *The Health Consequences of Smoking—1975*, DHEW Publication No. (CDC) 76-8704, 1977.

11. D. R. Mattison and S. S. Thorgeirsson, "Smoking and Industrial Pollution, and Their Effects on Menopause and Ovarian Cancer," *The Lancet*, **I**:187, 1978.

12. D. B. Thomas, "An Epidemiologic Study of Carcinoma in Situ and Squamous Dysplasia of the Uterine Cervix," *American Journal of Epidemiology*, **98**:10, 1973; and R. Cederlof, I. Friberg and Z. Hrubec, "The Relationship of Smoking and Some Social Covariables to Mortality and Cancer Morbidity," Department of Environmental Hygiene, The Karolinska Institute, Stockholm, 1975.

13. B. B. K. Pirani, 1978, op. cit.

14. H. W. Daniell, "Smoker's Wrinkles: A Study in the Epidemiology of 'Crow's Feet'," *Annals of Internal Medicine*, **75**:873, 1971.

15. NIH, 1976, op. cit.

16. E. B. Hook, "Changes in Tobacco and Caffeinated Beverages During Early Pregnancy," paper presented at the fifth annual Birth Defects Institute Symposium, Albany, N.Y., Oct. 1974; and NIH, *Cigarette Smoking Among Teenagers and Young Women*, DHEW Publication No. (NIH) 77-1203, 1977.

17. J. E. Fielding, "Smoking and Pregnancy," *New England Journal of Medicine*, **298**: 337, 1978.

18. Ibid.

GENETIC COUNSELING

IS IT RIGHT FOR YOU?

Marcia Kamien

• Antonia is thirty-six and has two children. She's decided to have another baby before it's too late. Is genetic counseling for her?
• Hal and Barbara are second cousins. They scoff at the "old-fashioned" notion that cousins shouldn't marry, and are planning their wedding. Is genetic counseling for them?
• George is a twenty-eight-year-old with no health problems. However, he realizes that many members of his family have deteriorated physically and died quite young. Now he's engaged and doesn't know what to tell his fiancée. Is genetic counseling for him?
• Marianne comes from a family in which only males are afflicted with a terrible form of dystrophy. Girls never have this problem. Since she obviously doesn't have the disease, she feels it's perfectly safe to have a baby. Is genetic counseling for her?

Some 250,000 American babies are born each year with defects. Just two decades ago, there was nothing to do about such tragedies. This is no longer true: Now we have genetic counseling, the modern medical study of human heredity and congenital disease. Begun only twenty-three years ago, it has since proven that over two thousand diseases and disorders are passed on from parents to their children through chromosomes and genes.

All of us have forty-six chromosomes—half from Mom and half from Dad—made up of millions of genes. Our genes program us for everything from our eye color to the way our hearts and nervous systems work.

It's now possible to see our chromosomes—photographed, enlarged, cut out and arranged in twenty-three matched pairs. The twenty-third pair are the sex chromosomes: two of the same (called X's) for normal females, and two different ones (called X and Y) for normal males. By studying this chromosome lineup (called a karyotype), genetics experts are able to spot genetic disorders associated with too many or too few chromosomes, or with arrangements of the genetic material.

Down syndrome Only 13 percent of all pregnant women in this country at any time are over the age of thirty-five (although this number seems to be growing lately). Yet, about half of all babies born with Down syndrome (or mongolism, as it used to be called) are born to mothers in this age group. Women under thirty have only one chance in 1,500 of having such a child, but if you're between the ages of forty and forty-four, the odds soar to one in a hundred. What's more, recent research into the cause of Down syndrome indicates that the age of the father may also be a factor.

The child with Down syndrome has slanted eyes set widely apart, and flat facial features. This child also has a 40 percent chance of congenital heart disease and suffers from mild to moderate mental retardation. Twenty years ago, it was found that the child with Down syndrome also has extra chromosomal material.

This is why more and more pregnant women over thirty-five are seeking genetic counseling. The counselor will explain to them that Down syndrome (more technically known as Trisomy 21) is a genetic accident—that is, it can happen to anyone—and that it certainly seems to be age-related. Most important, it *can* be detected before the baby is born. Between the sixteenth and twentieth weeks of pregnancy, the expectant mother can have amniocentesis. During the procedure, a small amount of amniotic fluid is withdrawn from the intrauterine sac surrounding the fetus. Fetal cells floating in the fluid are cultured, stained, photographed and analyzed. If the fetus does have Down syndrome, an extra number twenty-one chromosome will appear. Under these circumstances, many women opt to terminate the pregnancy and try again for a normal child. The decision is rarely an easy one but, with genetic counseling, there is plenty of opportunity to discuss the alternatives and to get important, ongoing psychological support.

Niecee Singer, genetic counselor at Westchester County Medical Center's medical genetics unit, points out to her patients that, 95 percent of the time, amniocentesis reveals normal chromosome makeup. "A good deal of the time," she says, "we can reassure patients that what they are at an increased risk of—Down syndrome—is not going to come to pass."

Unfortunately, that's not how a lot of people see it. "I wish everyone would realize that genetics does not equal abortion!" emphasizes Jessica Davis, M.D., who directs the genetic counseling unit at North Shore University Hospital in suburban Long Island. "But of course, the availability of legal abortion is at the core of realistic genetic counseling—what would be the sense of prenatal diagnosis without the choice?" She points out, however, that as a matter of fact, abortion is the exception—not the rule.

In all cases, genetic counseling really begins with a careful, thorough, painstaking, time-consuming family history. Your family tree—a pedigree, as it's technically called—is an intricate piece of detective work that covers you and your family as far back as you can go—every member, living or dead, their illnesses, their pregnancies and miscarriages, their general health, hospitalizations—everything that was ever recorded or can be recalled. Once this is all charted, generation by generation, you have a family tree of your heredity, which an expert in the field can evaluate. Any problem showing up over and over again might very well be a genetic, inherited problem. (It's important to find out, because lots of problems with other causes mimic the symptoms of genetic diseases.) If called for, the pedigree is followed by blood or urine tests, perhaps a chromosome analysis, or other tests. But, most of the time, what the pedigree shows is a nice normal ancestry with no more than its fair share of health difficulties.

"People so often worry needlessly," says Dr. Davis. "Genetics is not always bad news." Many who could use it refuse to go for counseling because they're afraid to find they have "bad blood."

As a result, the vast majority of couples will call for genetic help only after they have had a child born with a defect. Every once in a while, even the most exhaustive detective work can only conclude that both parents are carriers of a recessive gene as yet unknown to genetic science.

Yet all defects do have a cause and, very often, that cause can be discovered. It could be a recognized genetic accident, such as Down syndrome. It could be environmental: the mother's effect on the growing fetus through drugs, alcohol, disease, infection, radiation and so forth. It could be "multifactorial," a word used to cover those defects caused by a combination of what happens to the fetus in the womb, genes, and other unknown influences occurring at a critical time in gestation.

Or, the reason could lie within the genes of one or both parents. These genetic traits are passed on in three ways. *Recessive traits* don't affect anyone unless both parents possess them. Over one thousand such traits are recognized. A *dominant trait* is one that runs rampant through a family, of which 1,500 are now confirmed or suspected. *X-linked* (or sex-linked) diseases are carried by females but only males are affected, and we now know there are at least two hundred of them.

But how about some of the specific problems we mentioned earlier?

Second cousins It's not just an old-wives' tale that cousins should think carefully before marrying. First cousins share identical traits in a fraction of their genes and the spread of many diseases, deformities and defects can be traced back to marriages between blood relations. Cousins also share an ethnic as well as a familial background, which creates even higher risks. There are many diseases besides Tay-Sachs, a disease that affects Jewish people, that hit specific ethnic groups hardest—among them, Cooleys anemia (people from Mediterranean backgrounds) and sickle-cell anemia (American blacks).

But if you're not dealing with a marriage between close relatives, it can be centuries before two individuals with identical recessive traits meet and mate, making it difficult (if not impossible) for a genetic counselor to track the gene through family histories. It's entirely different, however, with a dominant trait.

George realizes that many of his relatives die young A few years ago, newspapers all over the country front-paged the story of a West Coast family, numbering over one hundred members, that had suffered for generations from a rare, fatal, dominant genetic disease. The first signs showed up at about the age of thirty—stumbling and slurred speech—and the disease progressed rapidly to further deterioration and early death. There was no name for this disease, partly because it was a closely guarded secret. One ancestor had passed it on to three of his children before his symptoms began; those three had children, many of whom inherited the faulty gene; and thus dozens of grandchildren and ever-growing numbers of descendants were at risk to contract the disease.

Different stories were made up to hide the fact that the disease was inherited. And—in spite of all the siblings, parents, cousins, aunts and uncles who exhibited identical symptoms and died in the prime of life—each generation swallowed all of the myths and believed them!

Genetic counselor Judith Weinblatt, of the National Genetics Foundation (N.G.F.), says that this is typical. "There's a great deal of stigma attached to a family disease," she explains. "Members are ashamed of it and it's not easily discussed—if it's discussed at *all*." The haze of mystery surrounding it only adds to the fear; and any explanation, however far-fetched, is likely to be eagerly accepted.

It was the staff at the N.G.F. that first learned of this particular family disease, because one member, a forty-three-year-old woman (who did not have it) read about another family whose skeleton-in-the-closet affliction had been uncovered with the help of N.G.F. Already skeptical of family myths that the disease was dying out, that it had been syphilis or alcoholism, she asked the Foundation if a giant genetic counseling session could be arranged for the entire extended family. About one hundred relatives were located and invited; even so, many refused to come to hear the "frightening truth."

Marianne comes from a family where only males are afflicted. Of all inherited disorders, the most difficult to understand are the X-linked (or sex-linked) ones, the cause of color-blindness as well as hemophilia, among others. Here's how a disease can be passed on or "carried" on: Genes work in pairs. The female (with her two X chromosomes) has one X with a normal gene while her other X chromosome carries its abnormal partner gene. Her male partner has an X chromosome with the normal gene and a normal Y. During conception, if the child is to be male, the father will give his Y chromosome and the mother will give one of her X chromosomes. So, in each pregnancy there is a 50-50 chance that a male fetus will get the chromosome with the abnormal gene and be born with the disease.

This means that, in any family where just the boys are born with a particular problem, the females should be warned that they may be carriers of the disorder. This sounds simple, but it often isn't. This kind of disease, too, is often hidden away.

For instance, genetic counselor Marjorie Williams, of North Shore Hospital, has been doing genetic detective work for two years with just one Long Island family. A teenaged boy was discovered who had actually been hidden by his mother in the house his whole life. His disease was obvious: he was mentally retarded, and had enlarged joints and coarse facial features. "We just had to decide whether he had Hurlers disease or Hunters disease because one is X-linked and the other is not," explains Mrs. Williams. The boy's mother had died and his father knew nothing of her family history. "It didn't really make much difference to the boy; but if it *was* X-linked, it was very important that all the females in the family come in for genetic counseling."

"A genetic disorder is the concern of everyone in the family, especially if it's a disease that could affect many members!" asserts Judith Weinblatt of the N.G.F. "Why should a couple have a child with a birth defect because they don't know they're at risk?"

The N.G.F. is a clearing house for medical geneticists and genetics centers all over the country. They help collect histories and records, make referrals and send out "Family Health History Scans" on request. The Scan is a questionnaire designed to help the individual plot her or his own family tree. Staff members will then review this history and make pertinent suggestions—where to go, if necessary, whom to see—and an evaluation of that history.

So far, we seem to have been talking only about bad news. But what may seem to be negative really isn't: It's far better to be prepared than to get a nasty surprise. And remember that every one of the known chromosomal abnormalities and more than seventy metabolic genetic disorders can be detected *before* the baby is born. Also, carriers of nearly sixty different diseases can be identified *before the baby is even conceived.* Nowadays, couples can decide together what is best for them. Twenty years ago, none of this was true.

But the question still remains: Is genetic counseling for you? Well, you should think seriously about it if:

- You have had a child with a genetic problem or birth defect and would like more children.
- There is a disease that runs in your family or ethnic group, or you were born with a disorder that may be inherited.
- You have taken prescribed medication or street drugs (LSD, marijuana, etc.) over a long period of time, have had a lot of X-rays, or been exposed to radiation.
- You (or women in your family) have had many miscarriages or stillbirths.
- You are older than thirty-five.

Above all, never make up your own mind about whether you are at risk. Human heredity is complicated and needs an expert in the field to trace histories, find causes and make diagnoses. If you think you want to see a genetic counselor, your physician can probably refer you to one. The National Genetics Foundation can also offer information. You can contact them at 555 W. 57 St., New York NY 10019 or by calling 212-586-5800.

BARREN COUPLES

More and more Americans are marrying late and postponing their childbearing years until the 30s, increasing the risk of infertility or damage to the reproductive system. When they discover—too late, in some cases—that they have problems in conceiving, the psychological consequences for both the man and the woman can be devastating.

Miriam D. Mazor

Although exact figures are almost impossible to obtain, evidence suggests there has been an increase in the number of people in the United States who find they are unable to conceive children. One reason is that both men and women are maximally fertile in their mid-20s. The present phenomenon of postponing marriage and childbearing into one's 30s and 40s for a variety of personal, social, and economic reasons contributes to the number of people who have or who will have a fertility problem. The longer the decision to conceive is delayed, moreover, the greater the risk of some physical impairment may be to the reproductive system (see box, page 73).

Approximately one out of every six married couples of childbearing age, or 3.5 million couples, are believed to have some difficulty conceiving or carrying a pregnancy to term. (The American Fertility Society defines an infertile couple as one that has not achieved a successful pregnancy after a year of having sexual relations without using contraception.)

Today, there is far less pressure on young adults who cannot—or choose not to—conceive. Indeed, for many in this generation, raising a family has a fairly low priority. But if the social pressures for parenthood have dwindled, I believe there are still important pressures from within. For most people, parenthood remains an integral part of their development as adults. For infertile couples, the frustrations and difficulties in attaining that goal have an impact on many aspects of their lives, both on their relationships with others, and on their sense of self-esteem.

The powerful attraction of parenthood for such people is best dramatized by the recent birth of Louise Brown in England, an infant who was conceived outside the womb but carried to term by her previously infertile mother. This event, acclaimed as a medical breakthrough of major proportions, aroused hope in thousands of women who may be able to benefit from this particular procedure. (Although the technique is new and enormously difficult to accomplish, more than 500 women have already applied to undergo the procedure at a fertility clinic in Norfolk, Virginia, that plans to try to repeat the test-tube birth.)

My interest in the problem of infertility grew out of personal experience. Several years ago, as my residency training in psychiatry was drawing to a close, the time seemed right to start a family. But for several months, nothing happened. Although my husband and I knew that we were supposed to wait a year before declaring it "a problem," we were sufficiently distressed after six months to seek medical attention. Later on, we learned that many couples, especially those in their 30s, find that they are ready for some kind of help at the six-month point, and do not find it particularly reassuring when a doctor tells them to go home and "relax" for another six months.

Fortunately, our doctor listened to our concerns, and we began to study our infertility problem, with all the emotional turmoil that that involves. Suddenly, my getting pregnant became the major focus of our lives. We learned what it felt like to chart my basal body temperature each morning, have sexual relations on schedule, plan vacations and time off around medical and surgical procedures.

An infertility investigation may include some or all of the following procedures: for the woman, a daily temperature measure to determine whether and when she ovulates; biopsies of the uterine lining during the phases of the menstrual cycle to determine its responsiveness to hormones; introduction of gas or dye into the uterus and tubes to check for blockage; direct visual examination of the tubes with an optic instrument (laparoscope) inserted through the abdomen; blood hormone assays, immunologic and chromosome studies; cultures to detect any infections that may prevent conception. The man may undergo sperm count and evaluation, various tests to explore circulation and spot abnormal tissue in the testicles, and other procedures to detect genetic flaws or trouble with the prostate gland, hormones, or the immunological system.

Treatments may include trials of various drugs that can permit or induce ovulation in the woman (medical efforts to increase sperm production have been less successful); surgery to repair blocked tubes, cervical and uterine problems, or (in the male) to repair a varicose vein in the testicle that may be blocking or harming the sperm passage. None of the treatments can guarantee a successful pregnancy, and all carry some degree of risk for the patient—including the risk that they will make the condition worse, rather than better.

Our story ended happily; after five years and three corrective surgical procedures on my fallopian tubes, we became the parents of a little girl and, later on, a boy. But the infertility experience left its mark, and made us keenly aware of what a real and agonizing crisis it is for so many people. It also made us aware of how different our lives might have been had we never become parents, or had the process been something that we could have taken simply for granted.

Because of my experience, colleagues began referring patients to me for psychotherapy who were in the midst of, or emerging from, an infertility investigation. I also became more attuned to those of my patients who had entered therapy for other reasons but for whom infertility remained an old and often unhealed wound. I soon became a psychiatric consultant to an organization called Resolve that provides support groups, counseling, and referral services to infertile people. Thus, during the past five years, I have had the opportunity to listen to a large number of people facing the problem of infertility.

By the time a couple seeks medical attention for an infertility problem, they may have spent months or even years trying to conceive. They are already in a state of crisis, having slowly become aware that something may be wrong with their procreative powers. Once the initial shock or sense of disbelief has worn off, the patient goes through three phases that vary in length and may overlap, to some extent.

The first phase revolves around the injury to the self implicit in the situation. Patients are preoccupied with the infertility study and with formulating theories about why it is happening to them, what they have done wrong, why they are so defective and bad that they are denied something the rest of the world appears to take for granted. The second phase occurs when treatment is unsuccessful; it involves mourning the loss of the children the partners will never bear, and an intense examination of what parenthood means to them as individuals, as a couple, and as members of families and of society. Finally, in the third phase, they must come to terms with the outcome of the study: they must make some kind of decision about their future, whether to pursue plans for adoption or for donor insemination or to adjust to childlessness and go on with life.

For every individual and every couple, the experience is unique. Old psychological conflicts are reactivated, and much of what people feel and do depends on their characteristic way of dealing with other disappointments and losses in their lives. Those who are aggressive and optimistic tend to approach the infertility crisis that way; those who view life as an insurmountable struggle and themselves as failures will tend to see infertility as confirmation of that.

Initially, there is a kind of denial or disbelief and an underlying feeling that a dreaded fear has come true. Despite the common presumption that everyone is fertile, fears about infertility are almost universal. Single women and married women who are not planning to become pregnant sometimes do so "accidentally" in order to test out their own fertility. Teenage girls and women in their 30s are often most articulate in expressing their concern and their need to know "if I could get pregnant." Teenage boys, too, sometimes worry about the efficacy of their semen.

Another important aspect of the initial reaction to infertility is the sense of helplessness at losing control over one's life plans. We place a high premium on freedom of choice—choice of careers, partners, living styles—in the pursuit of happiness. It comes as a rude shock that, although we can be fairly efficient about preventing unwanted pregnancies, we cannot always produce children on demand. One woman I interviewed was dismayed when she did not conceive the month after she stopped using a diaphragm; she explained that, like many people in the academic world, she wanted to give birth in June, after school was over.

Compounding the sense of helplessness is the intrusive, sometimes even assaultive nature of the infertility study itself. Patients must expose their bodies for tests and procedures; they must also expose the intimate details of their sexual lives and their motivations for pregnancy to their doctors. A useful defense against the sense of helplessness is information. Patients often become experts in their areas of special concern, and that enables them to feel like active participants in the process. Unfortunately, some doctors seem to feel threatened by that attitude, or else believe that they are genuinely reassuring patients by telling them "not to worry."

Regardless of the cause of the infertility, a man or woman feels damaged and defective, concerned about his or her bodily integrity. Women describe themselves as feeling "hollow" or "empty." One woman described her insides, which were full of adhesions, as "looking like Hiroshima after the bomb." Men will describe feeling like castrates, or talk about intercourse as "shooting blanks." The sense of defectiveness spreads to the individual's overall sense of self-worth and body image, as well as to his or her productivity and performance in almost every area of life. Patients talk about feeling "ugly," even though the defect is invisible to others. They describe general feelings of incompetence, of not being able to do anything right. One woman was unable to work on her doctoral dissertation, complaining that her mind was sterile, too; another called herself "The Sterile Cuckoo."

Infertile people worry about their sexual desirability and performance. During the first few months of trying to conceive, before medical help was sought, one man said: "I was sure I was doing something wrong; maybe there was something about sex I didn't know." (That is rarely the problem.) Infertile people also may feel that their partners could not possibly want them because they are so damaged, or that they do not deserve to enjoy sex, since they cannot produce a baby. (That may reflect a residual belief that sex is justifiable only for procreation.) During the infertility investigation, most people experience some temporary loss of sexual desire or capacity for orgasm, which compounds the sense of undesirability. Episodes of impotence are common, regardless of which partner has the infertility problem. In part, that is related to the couple's general sense of stress and depression; in part, it is a consequence of the necessity for sex on schedule. Almost everyone has a story about rushing home from a business meeting in order to have intercourse at ovulation time. One young woman described how she "raped" her husband in the housestaff quarters of the hospital where he was an intern on call, and how humiliating the experience was for both of them. Some women confess that they "cheated" on their temperature charts when they turned them in to their doctors; they marked little *x*'s on days they were supposed to have sex but were too worn out to try.

HUMAN REPRODUCTION: WHAT CAN GO WRONG

Modern improvements in diagnostic techniques and in our understanding of the reproductive process itself have removed much of the mystery from infertility. A diagnosis can be established for about 80 percent of the couples who complain about the problem and have been thoroughly investigated: about 50 percent of those can be helped to achieve a pregnancy. In about half the couples diagnosed the problem resides in the female partner, and in about 30 percent, the male partner. The rest have a problem that is partly attributable to both partners.

In women, blockage of the fallopian tubes that guide the egg from ovary to womb may account for 30 to 35 percent of all infertility. Hence, the current interest in the in-vitro (test-tube) fertilization procedure developed by Patrick Steptoe and Robert Edwards in England. Another important cause of female infertility is endocrine disorders that affect the delicate balance of hormones required for normal ovulation, implantation of the egg, or maintaining pregnancy early on.

In males, sperm production may be inadequate, perhaps as a result of fevers, exposure to chemicals, or elevated temperatures in the genital region. The motility of the sperm and its chances of reaching and fertilizing an ovum may be affected by genetic or hormonal factors, prostate disease, scarring, or problems with ejaculation.

Small problems in each partner may combine to prevent conception: for instance, a man with a marginal sperm count and a woman with some tubal blockage each may be able to conceive with a different partner, but not easily with each other. And some couples simply don't know enough about optimal timing of intercourse.

Other developments may contribute to infertility. As the prevalence of venereal disease rises, for instance, so does the incidence of reproductive-tract scarring—in both men and women. Certain contraceptive methods—the IUD, for example—may cause infection and scarring of the fallopian tubes; pills may lead to problems in ovulation later.

Abortions may cause damage to the cervix and an inability to carry a later, desired pregnancy to term. Other problems include exposure to various drugs, chemicals, and radiation, whose effects may not be evident until years after exposure.

In the absence of a diagnosis, too many couples go home with the idea—explicit or implied—that it's "all in their heads." As recently as the 1950s, doctors attributed roughly 30 to 40 percent of all infertility to psychological causes. Psychological factors may be at work in some cases of impotence or failure to ovulate. But the diagnosis of what was then called "functional" or "psychogenic" infertility was made largely by a process of elimination, after no organic pathology could be demonstrated. Many elaborate theories were formulated but not substantiated, blaming infertility on conflicts about sexuality or on rejection of the maternal role (and occasionally, the paternal role.) But such conflicts occur in fertile as well as in infertile adults. It may be better, in the future, to use the term "unexplained infertility" when no physical cause can be identified; at least, the expression honestly admits that there are still limitations in our diagnostic procedures.

Finally, there may appear to be more cases of infertility now because the subject itself is less taboo than it used to be. The traditional association of sex and reproduction made the subject seem shameful and embarrassing. Now that sexual matters are discussed more frankly, it has become easier for couples who are victims of this very distressing disability, giving them a real reason to pursue treatment.

—M.D.M.

There is an enormous buildup of tension toward the end of the woman's cycle, as the couples await the onset of the next menstrual period. The woman is acutely aware of the changes in her body, and may become preoccupied with searching for signs of pregnancy. Physiologic changes during the latter part of the cycle may intensify her anxiety and emotional volatility, but not all of the tension can be attributed to her hormonal changes; many husbands also report great anxiety at that time. Drugs used to stimulate ovulation, such as Clomid, may delay the menstrual period and increase the patient's hope that she is pregnant. When the flow actually begins, many women are plunged into a depression verging on despair—one woman called it the "cataclysm." The intensity of the disappointment may diminish with time, but many women continue to feel that their menses are a personal reproach; that may reintensify in times of stress.

Some people may seek to restore their feeling of sexual adequacy and self-worth by having extramarital affairs or by becoming promiscuous or inappropriately seductive. But, in my experience, that kind of acting-out is relatively uncommon. Although my sample may not be typical, most of the patients I see are trying extra hard to be extra good, to atone for whatever real or imagined sins they feel may have caused their infertility.

For, associated with the narcissistic injury, there is also a great deal of guilt and anger entailed. The guilt may be focused on a past event that, rightly or wrongly, the patient believes to be responsible for his or her infertility. It may be an extramarital affair, a history of venereal disease, a past pregnancy or abortion; sometimes the event has been kept secret from the spouse and only emerges during the infertility workup. Often, the guilt is more general—guilt about fantasies, masturbation, incestuous wishes, homosexual longings, or anything the patient believes to be "bad." Patients describe feeling that they will "do anything" in order to get pregnant. They may bargain magically with God, offering to suffer in return for a baby. (Some of the procedures involved in the infertility workup are physically and emotionally painful enough to serve as a form of expiation for some patients.)

Anger is often directed at physicians and at other members of the medical team for the indignities and physical discomforts involved in the workup. Many complaints are quite legitimate, but patients may become disproportionately enraged when their doctor is five minutes late, or they may misinterpret a casual remark as an insult. The medical jargon often adds to the confusion. One patient blew up at the doctor who informed her that she had a "hostile vagina," an unfortunate term sometimes used to describe secretions unfavorable to the survival of sperm.

Family members may become the target of anger, especially if the couple's parents are pressuring them to produce a grandchild or seem indifferent to their plight. At times, patients feel anger at the "betrayal" of an implied promise from their parents that they would have the power to make babies when they grew up. One woman recalled the fantasy she had had at the age of 12: her mother did not approve of her growing up and had arranged to have the doctor remove her reproductive organs during an appendectomy. Even as an adult, she felt that her infertility was somehow the product of her mother's revenge. That kind of feeling is reminiscent of folklore in which witches cause women to become barren, and goddesses or saints make them fertile.

Men may recall with vivid intensity experiences of being belittled or humiliated by their fathers, and may associate those memories with their current situation. Old rivalries with parents and siblings take on a new intensity, especially if the siblings have children.

Sometimes the anger is directed at the spouse, especially if he or she seems less interested—or overly interested—in achieving a pregnancy. But even when husband and wife are equally concerned, the woman may resent the fact that it is usually she who must undergo most of the procedures for diagnosis and correction. Most fertility specialists appear to "suspect" the woman's physiology first, in part because the odds are somewhat greater that the problem is hers, in part because the science of investigating male infertility is less advanced. But doctors may also be more concerned about protecting the husband's ego. One Resolve member told the group's director, Barbara Menning: "After a month of testing me, my doctor thought my husband should also be tested. He urged me to handle that with utmost care. His message was clear: go easy on his self-esteem and sense of masculinity. It was clear he felt my husband's feelings were more important than my own. I had to shoulder the burden of responsibility—and protect my husband from threatened feelings. My feelings were not considered. I felt alone, and even guilty that my husband had to have tests done."

A common fear among infertility patients is that the fertile partner will abandon them—or, even worse, remain in the relationship resentfully. Some make open offers of divorce; others take to testing and provoking their partners with remarks like "If you had married someone else, you'd have a family by now." The fertile partner may feel an obligation to maintain a front of unswerving loyalty and disavow any anger or disappointment instead of dealing honestly with his or her feelings. Single people who know that they are infertile often retreat from relationships with members of the opposite sex or strive to keep them at a very superficial level, anticipating that they will be abandoned or rejected once the dreadful secret is out.

The second phase in the adjustment to infertility—in which the couple come to reevaluate their feelings about parenthood and begin the process of mourning—is in some ways more painful but less intense than the first. It usually comes when the couple is ready to stop trying to conceive, ready to call a halt to the investigation. It may be an agonizingly difficult decision, especially for those couples whose infertility remains unexplained or for those who have a small, lingering chance to achieve a pregnancy.

In some respects, the entire developmental process, from infancy onward, is a preparation for parenthood. In her discussion of women and midlife, psychiatrist Malkah Notman says that the phases of a woman's life—even these days—tend to be marked by events related to her reproductive function: the experience of pregnancy, childbirth, and the launching of her children into the adult world. Childless women, even if their childlessness has been voluntary, often go through a period of depression and mourning at some point in their 30s, grieving for a part of themselves never to be realized.

At its best, the wish to have children represents a desire to share and experience love in a new way, to discover the parent within ourselves, to actualize an identity as a generator and nurturer. There are, of course, narcissistic aspects to the desire for children—fantasies of being reborn, of creating an extension or better version of oneself, a desire to insure oneself against loneliness and to experience all that life offers. For women, the wish to experience pregnancy, childbirth, and breast-feeding may be important. For many people, parenthood is a credential of full adult status—for many women, the only one. Some patients feel their infertility marks them as too immature for parenthood; they may doubt their right to own a house or make important adult moves. Many people feel compelled to tell the world about their infertility, for fear that their childlessness will be seen as selfish and irresponsible. The view of a man's character is also colored by his achievement as a "family man."

Infertile people must find their own place in the flow of generations. Some express their feelings about being the end of the genetic line: a number of patients in my practice who are the children of Holocaust survivors feel that very acutely—as if they must reproduce not only for themselves, but for the sake of extended families annihilated during World War II.

The birth of a first child is a major turning point for many people; it allows men and women to look at their own fathers and mothers as individuals very like themselves, with strengths and vulnerabilities. Until then, the parents may have been idealized or devalued, but viewed primarily in relation to their function as parents. The infertile person must work harder than others to renegotiate his or her relationship with the actual parents of adult life, and must struggle to set aside the child's view of parents as omnipotent creatures, good or evil.

Together, the couple must come to terms with the loss of their reproductive function and mourn the loss of the biologic children they could not have together. It is a difficult task, because the loss is so vague—more a loss of potential—and because there are no formal rituals, like funerals, to assist the bereaved. The loss is "invisible" to the outside world, and the couple feels isolated in their grief.

Many couples report that the period of mourning has in many ways brought them closer together, confirming the strength of the bond of love between them. In some ways, they must complete at an earlier time a task that many couples postpone until their children are grown and gone. The loss may be remourned periodically, for the world is full of reminders that other people go on having babies, but the pain becomes less acute with time. In a way, learning to live with infertility is like learning to live with the idea of death: one can't quite forget about it, but one can't think about it all the time.

At some point, the partners must reassess their own inner resources and decide how best to realize their own creative, generative, and nurturant potentials in the absence of biologic children. Then, the couple must come to a joint decision acceptable to both of them—if their relationship is to last without chronic unhappiness. That represents the third and final stage of adapting to infertility.

Some couples choose adoption, fully aware of how difficult a process that may be, because they feel that parenthood matters enough to them. They are willing to undergo the rigors of an adoption agency's home study, or the expense of a private lawyer's fee; to wait as long as five years for a healthy newborn baby of any race; they may agree to handle the problems and expenses involved in adopting a child from abroad, or a child with a physical or mental handicap, or an older child who may come from a background of serious emotional deprivation or physical abuse.

It should be noted that adoption has never cured infertility. Although pregnancy occasionally follows adoption, the fact is that couples who do and do not adopt conceive at about the same rate. The idea seems tied to the notion that the causes of infertility are psychological—which is largely unsubstantiated. As one patient told me, "When the doctor suggested I was too neurotic to get pregnant, I blew up. I told him that if he thought I was uptight, he should meet my mother! My grandmother was even worse, and she had eight children. I come from a long line of uptight fertile women!"

For those couples in which the woman is presumably fertile, there may be the option of artificial insemination by donor (AID). Though often cloaked in secrecy, the procedure is done far more frequently than the public may realize. The legal status of the procedure itself, and of a child conceived by AID, is extremely complicated, and inconsistent from one state to another. The emotional issues are also very complex, and require a separate discussion in their own right. In my experience, those people who have conceived a child by AID appear happy enough about the procedure; their major concern seems to be whether, when, and how to tell the child about the circumstances under which he or she was conceived.

But, for some couples, the exhausting efforts of the infertility workup, of adoption procedures, or of AID are too much to handle; they may choose to direct their energies elsewhere—into their professions, hobbies, or their other activities. The resolution of the infertility problem is a very personal matter, contingent on past experience in coping with disappointment and loss. Each individual must prepare himself or herself to assume a comfortable identity as a middle-aged and older adult, whether or not parenthood is ever achieved.

Miriam D. Mazor, M.D. is clinical instructor in the Department of Psychiatry at the Harvard Medical School, and associate at the Beth Israel Hospital in Boston. An expanded version of this article will appear in *Medical and Psychiatric Aspects of Infertility*, to be published by Human Sciences Press.

For further information, read:

Mazor, Miriam. "The Problem of Infertility," in *The Woman Patient*, Malkah T. Notman and Carol C. Nadelson, eds., Plenum, 1978, $19.95.

Menning, Barbara E. *Infertility: A Guide for the Childless Couple*, Prentice Hall, 1977, $9.95, paper, $3.45.

Notman, Malkah T. "Women and Mid-Life: A Different Perspective," *Psychiatric Opinion* 15 (1978): 15-25.

Fetal Adoption
A Technological Solution to the Problem of Abortion Ethics

A new technology may make anachronisms of adoption agencies and abortion clinics.

Robert A. Freitas, Jr.

Robert A. Freitas, Jr., has degrees in law, physics, and psychology. His book Lobbying for Space *(1978) is a political-action handbook. He is readying a book on the ethics of interspecies contact. His articles and research papers have appeared in* Omni, Mercury, Analog, Spaceflight, *and the* Journal of the British Planetary Society.

The ethical problem of abortion has been the subject of heated debate for many years, especially since the controversial *Roe v. Wade* (1973) Supreme Court ruling and the recent flap over federally funded abortions. The conflict is rich in content and charged with emotion, including themes of "us versus them," a war of verbal propaganda ("pro-choice" or "anti-life"?), legal questions and social-policy issues, political posturing, and timeless philosophical inquiries ("What is Man?").

There is, however, a technological solution to the problem of abortion ethics which has received insufficient attention in the literature: fetal adoption.

The birth of the world's first "test tube" baby in Oldham, England in 1978 demonstrates that medical science already has the ability to bring safely through pregnancy a human ovum fertilized *in vitro* (outside the body). Fertilized ovum transplants into female host animals have been utilized commercially for many years, and the modern practice of human surrogate mothers (*in vitro* fertilization) is well-known. Progress at the forefront of current medical research suggests that human fetal transplantation and full-term *in vitro* gestation may become technologically feasible by the end of the 1980s.

Assuming these techniques are available, unwillingly pregnant women have an alternative to feticide or unwanted childbirth. The reluctant prospective mother simply visits the local Fetal Adoption Center, undergoes surgery for removal of her viable fetus, signs legal documents, and exits a free woman. At the same time, the developing embryo is preserved. Fetuses removed during the first trimester are transplanted into the uterus of a surrogate or infertile adoptive mother and carried to term in the usual manner. Second trimester fetuses are nurtured in warm, organic artificial wombs until the third trimester, when conventional modern incubation techniques can be brought into play. Fetuses taken during the third trimester are transferred directly to the incubator, an existing medical technology often used to save the lives of infants born up to three months premature.

The elegance of this scheme is evident in its ability to placate both proponents and opponents of abortion. Pro-choicers under a system of fetal adoption would never be forced unwillingly to suffer pregnancy or to bear an unwanted child. A woman must retain full legal control of her own body and should be free to surrender her fetus for adoption at any time during gestation. On the other hand, pro-lifers would be satisfied because no "human being" (here defined *arguendo* as a "fertilized or developing human embryo") is ever put to death. Healthy newborn babies placed for adoption are in very short supply, so there would be no problem finding an adequate number of adoptive or surrogate parents to absorb the surplus nonaborted infant population.

Fetal Adoption Centers would offer free educational programs on contraception and human reproduction, pregnancy and childbirth, parenting, and child psychology. These public centers will also distribute a wide variety of free materials and services, including birth control devices, annual pelvic examinations, and pregnancy tests furnished with no questions asked. Centers would become guardians of life, in stark contrast to modern abortion clinics, emotionally characterized by pro-life advocates as "death factories." Furthermore, a global program of family planning plus fetal transplan-

This article first appeared in *THE HUMANIST* July/August 1980 and is reprinted by permission.

tation is unlikely to aggravate the world population problem. Experience has shown that people given both the knowledge and the means of birth control usually choose voluntarily to reduce the number of offspring to near the replacement level.

Funding for a national network of Fetal Adoption Centers would come partly from sources which today support adoption agencies and abortion clinics (anachronisms in an era of fetal transplantation technology) and partly from new federal and state "Feticare" programs designed primarily to assist indigent women. Additional funding will issue from numerous pro-life church, community, and fraternal organizations that today lobby and protest against abortion but would be willing to help "pay for life," and from various pro-choice and feminist groups able to divert their abortion-support monies to "pay for liberty." Humanitarian funding may also come from private and international sources. A few may object to fetal transplantation and adoption on the religious or moral grounds that such programs may encourage promiscuity and premarital sex among the young. However, it is often these same individuals who are heard to assert that inescapable pregnancy is the proper "punishment" for illicit sexual activity, a moral position that overlooks three important factors: (1) A ban on fetal adoption denies the technological option to unwillingly pregnant married couples, forcing them to choose between two equally unwelcome alternatives—feticide or unwanted childbirth; (2) The incidence of teenage pregnancy is high in all jurisdictions regardless of whether legal abortions are easy or difficult to obtain, suggesting that the expression of sexuality among the young is predominantly a *sociocultural* phenonmenon little affected by the withholding of available medical technology; and (3) The birth of an unwanted child to unwilling or irresponsible parents is a calamity for the parents but a catastrophe for society, which decades later must deal with the products of parental ignorance, neglect, and abuse.

MARGARET SANGER

Rebel in the Midst of Victorian Moralism

TOBY A. CLINCH

September 14, 1979 is the 100th Anniversary of the birth of Margaret Higgins Sanger. Who was Margaret Sanger? The question was recently asked of 23 people attending a local community art center exhibition. Two individuals knew her as the founder of Planned Parenthood. The other 21 either made wild guesses, or had no idea.

Amazingly, in spite of the tremendous influence this woman has had on the life of almost every individual living today, Margaret Sanger is relatively unknown to many. Perhaps because information on, and practice of, birth control is so accepted and established, it is difficult to imagine that at one time, one individual spent 50 years fighting to secure this basic human right for every woman, and lived to see the battle won.

In the process of the campaign she waged, Mrs. Sanger was constantly harassed by Federal authorities, police raids, numerous indictments and lawsuits; she led and took part in hundreds of street rallies and went to jail nine times. No doubt this sounds as if it comes from the pages of history documenting the demonstrations of the 1960s. Actually, Mrs. Sanger's "notoriety" began in March, 1914 with her publication of the first issues of *Woman Rebel* in which she announced (among other then-radical ideas) that the newspaper advocated the prevention of conception and "would impart such knowledge in the columns of this newspaper." Although contraceptive practices were not detailed, what she had written was apparently enough for the Post Office Department to declare the publication to be in violation of Section 211 of the Criminal Code of the United States — a group of obscenity statutes drafted and hastily pushed through Congress in 1873 at the insistence of Anthony Comstock, founder and lifelong Secretary of the New York Society for the Suppression of Vice.

The Comstock Law, as it was to be popularly known, prohibited the mailing, transporting or importing of "obscene, lewd, or lascivious" materials, including information and devices concerned with "preventing conception." Congress unfortunately offered no guidelines or definitions to determine what was to be considered obscene; this judgment was left to the discretion of individual postal authorities, including the Post Master General's Special Agent, Anthony Comstock. Soon, twenty-two states had instituted their own Comstock-type statutes; the most stringent were those in Massachusetts and Connecticut.

Later issues of *Woman Rebel* (May, July, August, September and October) also were declared unmailable. The June issue was the first to use the phrase "birth control", a term Margaret Sanger and a few friends had devised. Ironically, this was the only edition the Post Office did not censor!

In August, 1914 Margaret Sanger was indicted on nine counts for violating the Comstock Law. Mrs. Sanger failed to appear for her trial. With the flair for the dramatic that was to characterize her career, she fled the country, leaving behind her architect husband, William Sanger and their three children.

Woman Rebel never gave contraceptive information. However, her secretly-printed pamphlet, "Family Limitation," did describe contraceptive techniques which included the use of douches, condoms, suppositories and cervical caps. She had planned to break and challenge the law banning the dissemination of contraceptive information and articles by distributing this pamphlet, but her court indictment was not based on the provisions of the Comstock Law that she had planned to challenge. Deeming it not advantageous to her cause, Mrs. Sanger left for Montreal and there, under the assumed name of Bertha Watson, sailed for England. After three days at sea, using a pre-arranged code, she cabled word to release the 100,000 copies of "Family Limitation" which were strategically hidden in key cities around the U.S. They were distributed primarily through locals of the Industrial Workers of the World.

In England, Mrs. Sanger met, among others, H. G. Wells, the Drysdales (leaders of the Malthusian League), and the renowned sexual psychologist Havelock Ellis. Under the tutelage and guidance of Ellis and the Drysdales, Margaret Sanger learned to focus her ideas and energies, develop an ideological structure, philosophy and justification for the cause she was to pursue for the rest of her active life.

Two months after her arrival in England, Mrs. Sanger went to Holland to see the government-supported birth control clinic in operation. There she learned of the superior diaphragm developed by Dr. Wilhelm Mensinga in the 1880s and, most significantly, she learned that each woman wanting birth control must be medically examined and specially fitted with the appropriate type and size of diaphragm. In "Family Limitation" she advocated that women learn from pamphlets or teach each other. This cost her, at that

"Margaret Sanger: Rebel in the Midst of Victorian Moralism," Toby A. Clinch, *Impact: Journal of National Family Sex Education Week,* 1978. Reprinted by permission.

time, the support and respect of the medical profession.

By then, Margaret Sanger had decided to spend the rest of her life promoting family planning. Why she came to this decision is really not known. What was it that motivated Margaret Sanger to champion the cause of birth control with such fervor and such exclusivity that it was to take precedence over everything — even her marriage and her children?

It could have been her poor beginnings on the banks of the Chemung River in Corning, New York, where she was the sixth-born child of a frail, submissive mother who died at the age of 48 after giving birth to 11 children. Her father, described by Mrs. Sanger as a "philosopher, a rebel and an artist," lived to the disparate age of 80.

Irish-born Michael Higgins, carver of graveyard tombstones, a freethinking, iconoclastic man who lived his socialist beliefs, was himself the champion of many then-radical causes. Throughout her childhood, Higgins fought and argued for socialism, women's suffrage, the single tax, free libraries, free education, free books in public schools, and freedom of the mind from dogma. In fact, his open resistance and dispute of the dogma of the Catholic Church in their predominantly Roman Catholic community caused his family extreme social and economic hardship. Poor as they were, though, Higgins provided his family with significant books — books Higgins believed would stimulate the imagination and promote thought. His credo, espoused to each of his children as they left home, was to leave the world better than they had found it.

Margaret Sanger may have gained other insights growing up in Corning. She could not help but notice and reflect on the disparity of the lives of the well-to-do people who lived up on the hill; they all had less children than the poorer families down near the river.

If not from her insights in Corning, Margaret Sanger's dedication could have come as a result of the suffering and death she witnessed when she worked as a nurse in the teeming tenements on New York's Lower East Side, where desperate women who didn't have the $5 to go to an abortionist punctured themselves with, among other things, knitting needles, to keep from having another baby. It was estimated at that time that 25,000 women died from abortions each year.

Amboy Street in the Brownsville section of Brooklyn where Margaret Sanger opened the first birth control clinic in 1916.

Undoubtedly, Margaret Sanger witnessed many deaths in the course of her work on the Lower East Side, but the one that seems to have had the most traumatic effect on her, the one incident that immediately preceded her resolve to discontinue her nursing profession and search for the truth about contraception, concerned Sadie Sachs. Mrs. Sachs was a woman whose life Mrs. Sanger and a doctor had worked laboriously to save after a self-induced abortion in the spring of 1912. Afterward, Mrs. Sachs pleaded with the doctor to tell her the "secret" of how to prevent another pregnancy. The only advice the doctor gave was a suggestion to have her husband Jake sleep on the roof. Margaret Sanger couldn't help Mrs. Sachs, any more than she was able to help the countless other women who had pleaded for the same information, because she didn't know the "secret" either. Three months later, in the fall of 1912, Sadie Sachs died from another attempted abortion. Margaret Sanger was the nurse in attendance. Afterward, Mrs. Sanger began her pursuit of the "secret."

For almost a year after the death of Sadie Sachs, Margaret Sanger visited dozens of libraries, including the Academy of Medicine and the Library of Congress to "ascertain something about the subject which was so mysterious and so unaccountably forbidden." She found, she claimed, "no information more reliable than that exchanged by back-fence gossips in any small town." At the suggestions of Bill Haywood, leader of the International Workers of the World and one of the coterie of well-known radicals, artists and intellectuals befriended by the Sangers soon after their move to New York City, Margaret decided to go to France, where family planning had been in practice since the Revolution, to learn about contraception. Going to Paris seemed to suit Bill Sanger, too. He had been talking about giving up building suburban houses in order to paint. To finance the trip, they sold their house in Hastings, where they had lived before moving to New York City, gave away some furniture, put the rest in storage, and sailed for Europe on a small, crowded, cabin boat.

Actually, there was a great deal of information on contraception available in America at that time. Casual research would have revealed the oldest recorded contraceptive information translated from ancient Egyptian documents dating back to 1850 B.C. More lucid and detailed accounts of contraceptive methods also appeared in the 2nd Century, A.D. in the writings of the Greek gynecologist Soranus of Ephesus. Robert Dale Owens, a social reformer who was later to become a U.S. Congressman, offered in his 1830 *Moral Physiology* fairly crude but effective prescriptions to prevent pregnancy. The next truly comprehensive publicaton on contraceptive techniques, *The Fruits of Philosophy: or The Private Companion of Young Married People* by Dr. Charles Knowlton, a respected Boston physician, appeared in 1832, 47 years before Margaret Sanger was born!

In addition, the road to birth control was well paved by: Moses Harmon and his daughter Lillian, who edited and published the midwestern journal of sex radicalism, *Lucifer, the Light Bearer* from 1883-1907; Ezra and Angela Heywood who, in 1873, began publishing *The Word,* a journal dedicated to the abolition of woman's slavery; Dr. Edward Bliss Foote, and later his son, Dr. Edward Bond "Ned" Foote, who wrote and published, in 1858, the best seller *Medical Common Sense* which contained two essays on pregnancy preventions and explanations of various contraceptives (two for men and two for women). One pamphlet, "Words in Pearl," published in 1873, described contraceptive techniques and devices, and told how to obtain them.

In 1898, the *Index Catalogue of the Library of the Surgeon-General's Office* contained two pages listing the articles and books available on pregnancy prevention. And, interestingly, in 1912, the same year Margaret Sanger researched information on pregnancy prevention, Dr. Abraham Jacobi, founder of the *American Journal of Obstetrics and Diseases of Children,* and the man who made pediatrics a specialty in this country, openly espoused family planning in his presidential address to the American Medical Association.

Sanger in court with her sister, Mrs. Ethel Byrne (right) in 1917.

Was Margaret Sanger denied access to all this material? Or did she choose to suppress or ignore it? The answer can only be left to conjecture. Some who have known Margaret Sanger, and some who have written about her, contend that her dedication to the birth control movement was a result of her vanity, her need to be the central figure, a rebel demanding attention to her exploits and to be recognized as the sole leader of the birth control movement.

In January, 1914, Margaret Sanger did, indeed, return to the U.S. and dramatically made preparations to introduce her collection of formulas, techniques and devices she had learned about from Parisian doctors, midwives, druggists and women. It was this information that was contained in her pamphlet "Family Limitation," which before long had been translated into 13 languages, reaching a circulation of over 10 million. While berated by some for her techniques, it must be recognized that her actions did have impact; they made many aware that compared to France, America still lived in the Dark Ages, and it made many women cognizant of the birth control movement as well as the existence of birth control methods.

Though dramatic and unorthodoxed techniques were to characterize Mrs. Sanger's career, she was hardly the typical firebrandishing, foot-stomping, harrassing, blustering female reformer. Most people who met her were rather surprised by her conservative dress, her soft-spoken voice and her personal charm. New York University Professor, and social scientist, Henry Pratt Fairchild, in the *Nation,* described her as "a rather slight woman, very beautiful, with wide-apart gray eyes and a crown of auburn hair, combining a radiant feminine appeal with an impression of serenity, calm, and graciousness of voice and manner . . . [but with] tremendous fighting spirit . . . self-generating energy, and . . . relentless drive . . ." It was her charisma and her intelligence that made a great many converts to the birth control movement.

Even her husband, Bill Sanger, who had returned to America just before Mrs. Sanger fled to England, was converted to the cause. While Mrs. Sanger was in England, Anthony Comstock, posing as an impoverished father seeking means of preventing pregnancy, visited Bill Sanger who gave him a copy of "Family Limitation." Sanger was arrested and convicted on obscenity charges. Instead of paying the fine, however, he chose to go to jail for 30 days. This was the test case Margaret Sanger had wanted; her exile was over. Risking a prison sentence on her own criminal charges, she returned home.

The climate for Mrs. Sanger's trial was right. Bill Sanger had become a hero and a martyr to the cause, and the magazine headline that greeted Mrs. Sanger when she arrived in New York harbor read, "What Shall We Do About Birth Control?" And, in New York City, the first American birth control organization, the National

Birth Control League, had formed under the direction of Mary Ware Dennett. But less than four weeks after her arrival, before her case was reopened, tragedy struck — a personal tragedy from which Margaret Sanger never quite recovered — the death of her youngest child and only daughter, Peggy, from pneumonia. Shattered and suffering a nervous breakdown, Mrs. Sanger nevertheless was determined to face the indictments against her, even though they dealt not with contraception, but with articles in ***Woman Rebel*** concerning assassination, feminine hygiene and marriage. Her lawyers all advised compromise; if she pleaded guilty, she would get off with a suspended sentence, or if she wrote a letter saying she would not break the law again, she would not even have to go to court. Margaret Sanger would not compromise.

Disgusted with her lawyers, Mrs. Sanger decided to appear in court without counsel. Meanwhile, public opinion had begun to swing toward her. The judge and district attorney were besieged by petitions and letters. President Woodrow Wilson had received scores of letters, some from England's most prominent people, including H. G. Wells, who pleaded in behalf of free speech. With all this public concern, the government suddenly seemed reluctant to prosecute, and without any explanation, and after several postponements, dismissed the case.

Margaret Sanger had won a moral victory, but the law had not been tested. Her next move was to dramatize and focus attention on the obsolete laws. To do this, she set out on a speaking tour, criss-crossing the country. Her tour served several purposes — it attracted a devoted group of followers, inspired opposition, and caused possibly millions of people to talk about her.

Returning to New York, Mrs. Sanger put another of her plans into action. This she did with her sister, Mrs. Ethel Byrne, also a registered nurse, and another woman, Fania Mindell. On October, 16, 1916, to implement all she had learned in Holland she opened America's first birth control clinic at 46 Amboy Street in the poor, heavily populated Brownsville section of Brooklyn. After distributing flyers (in Italian, Yiddish and English), advertising the services offered, the clinic opened for business. At 7 a.m., the line of women stretched around the block; they saw 140 women that first day. Newspapers carried the story, and dozens of women came from as far away as Pennsylvania, Massachusetts and Connecticut.

Ten days after they opened their doors, the three clinic operators were arrested. Released on bail, the women reopened the clinic. Again they were arrested, and this time the clinic closed for good. The arrests were made under Section 1142 of the New York State Penal Code, which made it a misdemeanor for anyone to "sell, lend or give away" contraceptive devices. Section 1145 of the code made exception to Section 1142 in the cases of physicians, who *were* permitted to advise and prescribe articles "for the care and prevention of disease." Most physicians interpreted this to apply only to venereal disease. However, there was no physician in attendance at the clinic.

Margaret Sanger and her sister each were sentenced to 30 days in jail for "maintaining a public nuisance." Mrs. Sanger chose to spend that time teaching the women she met about contraception, and issuing statements to the press about the deplorable prison conditions. Mrs. Byrne, on the other hand, went on a hunger strike and accounts of her "forced feeding" through a tube inserted in her esophagus made front-page headlines, alongside news of the war in Europe. The publicity enhanced Mrs. Sanger's cause tremendously and paved the way for the appeal of her conviction in the N.Y. Supreme Court. Although her conviction was upheld, Judge J. Crane did broaden the interpretation of Section 1145, allowing physicians to legally prescribe contraceptive devices and give advice to married people in N.Y. state for health reasons, not only to prevent venereal disease.

Public education, Mrs. Sanger reasoned, was the next logical step in furthering the birth control cause. Along with speaking engagements, she launched, with the help of Frederick A. Blossom, a leader in the Ohio Birth Control League, the *Birth Control Review* to keep the movement apprised of various birth control activities. Much of her time was spent in fund-raising activities, and promoting the *Birth Control Review,* which she personally hawked on N.Y. street corners.

1920 was a noteworthy year for Margaret Sanger. Her marriage to Bill Sanger ended in divorce; they had been separated for seven years. And, the first of two books she had been working on, *Women and the New Race* was published, selling over 200,000 copies. Her other book, *The Pivot of Civilization* appeared two years later. Both books, which contained every conceivable rationale for birth control, were read all over the world and lent an air of respectability to the movement. They also served to establish Margaret Sanger as the unofficial leader of the birth control movement.

Margaret Sanger died on Sept. 6, 1966, eight days before her 87th birthday. She was one of the few crusaders in the world who lived long enough to see her dreams become a reality. Ironically, after over 60 years of efforts, the Comstock Law, the statutes Margaret Sanger worked so tirelessly to nullify, are still Federal Law, though all of the birth control and most of the other restrictions they imposed have been modified by judicial interpretation. It is as the brilliant civil rights attorney, Morris Ernst, has said, "In the United States we almost never repeal outmoded legislation in the field of morals. We either allow it to fall into disuse by ignoring it . . . or we bring persuasive cases to the courts and get the obsolete laws modified by judicial interpretation." And such is the situation concerning the Comstock Law in 1979, 100 years after the birth of Margaret Sanger.

RATING THE LATEST METHODS OF BIRTH CONTROL

Judith Greenwald

The majority of single women 18 to 45 years of age are sexually active and most utilize a method of birth control. While it is most important to use the method that you feel is most comfortable and most natural, some methods give more complete protection than others. But it is a highly individual matter. The choice of methods depends on many factors—upon religious attitudes; frequency of intercourse; on the available methods; on relations between the couple if they are already established; the question of who can most happily and efficiently accept the responsibility for avoiding pregnancy; on feelings of modesty; on the effects of various methods on physical safety and psychological fulfillment; and, perhaps, upon cost.

Many options are available—birth control pill; intrauterine device; condom; diaphragm with jelly or cream; vaginal foam, cream or jelly used alone; rhythm; coitus interruptus (withdrawal); abstinence; abortion as a backup if pregnancy occurs; and voluntary sterilization.

The pill remains the dominant method of birth control used by single women, by a five to one margin. Among single women, the pill and IUD appear to be the methods of choice for long term use, while the condom, diaphragm and foam are used primarily as interim methods. These results are reported in the 1974 second Annual Birth Control Study Among Unmarried Women compiled by National Family Opinion, Inc. They also note that most women using the pill and IUD have employed the method for more than a year, and most don't anticipate changing in the near future. This year, single women reported a generally less favorable attitude toward the various methods of birth control. And much of this is caused by increased anxiety over side effects.

ORAL CONTRACEPTIVES

"The pill" is currently used by some 50 million women throughout the world, including 12 to 14 million women in the United States. It is the most effective method of contraception, and the only method that is essentially 100 per cent effective when the pills are taken as directed. Certainly the late Dr. Alan Guttmacher, past President of the Planned Parenthood Federation of America, was correct in 1958 when he predicted: "We are on the threshold of a new era in birth control." Since then the pill has probably become the best known contraceptive in the world.

Combination pills containing both estrogen and a progestogen are the most widely used oral contraceptive. They are taken for three weeks, followed by a week with no pills or a week of placebo (dummy) pills, during which time menstruation takes place. By the 1970's, combination pills were judged superior to so-called sequential preparations, which were designed to mimic more closely the normal female hormonal pattern. Unfortunately they are less effective than combination pills in preventing pregnancy.

The combined oral contraceptives add a small daily dose of estrogen and a progesterone-like compound to the body's own production of these hormones. These added hormones prevent conception since no ovulation occurs and no egg is released. This is similar to what occurs during a normal pregnancy, except that menstruation continues.

Most women are healthy and can take the pill, after a good physical examination by a doctor, without any problems. There are, however, certain medical problems which make it undesirable for some women to take the pill. The FDA lists five absolute contraindications—(1) tumors that are estrogen dependent in the breast or uterus; (2) serious liver disease which would interfere with metabolism of the hormones contained in the pills; (3) a past history of thrombophlebitis or thromboembolism; (4) abnormal uterine bleeding of unknown cause; and (5) pregnancy. To the above list, Dr. Daniel Mishell of the University of Southern California School of Medicine, adds patients with gestational diabetes, and those with congenital hyperlipidemia (presence of excess lipids in the blood from birth).

In addition many physicians would not prescribe the pill for you if you have the following problems; a history of epilepsy, depression, migraine headaches, high blood pressure, uterine tumors, a history of abnormally infrequent menstruation or absence of menstruation (amenorrhea). Women with the latter two symptoms may have a high incidence of amenorrhea after stopping pills and difficulty conceiving if they eventually choose to get pregnant.

The next decision the doctor and patient must make is which pill to choose. The FDA recommends that the practicing physician use the contraceptive with the least amount of estrogen, with the lowest effective dosage and minimal side effects. At the present time a pill containing 50 micrograms of estrogen prevents a pregnancy and pills with higher dosages may not be necessary. Two studies in England have shown that pills with 50 micrograms of an estrogen are indeed associated with a lower incidence of thromboembolism than those with a higher dose. In some cases the pills containing 20 or 30 micrograms of estrogen may cause a higher incidence of abnormal early and late cycle bleeding during the time the pills are being taken, and then a missed period during the week that no pills are taken. Also the lower dosage pills may be only 95-98 percent effective in preventing conception.

Many pill users experience side effects, which often decrease as the body becomes adjusted to them. Others may be eliminated by switching to a different pill. Or, the doctor may decide it's not necessary to go off the pill at all since the problem may be transient. Some side effects women experience are: nausea (if that bothers you, try taking the pill in the evening); weight gain, fluid retention, breast fullness or tenderness; headaches; spotting of blood; decreased menstrual flow; missed periods; more trouble with vaginal infections; depression, anxiety, fatigue and mood changes; skin darkening on upper lip and under the eyes, which the sun may make worse; decreased sex drive; and acne (though some pills with high estrogen content help acne patients).

The pill rarely causes drastic side effects. About one pill user in more than two thousand a year is hospitalized for blood clotting disorders (thromboembolic disease). Hardly anybody just keels over and dies from pill complications since the body usually warns of impending catastrophe. The signs to watch for are severe headache, sudden blurring or loss of vision with a sensation of flashing lights, severe leg pains, chest pains or shortness of breath. If you should experience any of these symptoms, call your doctor immediately. Don't wait to see if these symptoms will go away.

Women often experience benefits other than effective contraception from oral contraceptives. Pills minimize menstrual cramps, decrease the number of days of bleeding and amount of blood lost, and produce regular menstrual periods in most instances. Also premenstrual tension, anxiety or depression may be diminished. Probably because of diminished fear of pregnancy, women and men often experience an increased enjoyment of sexual intercourse. Some women even have an increased sex drive while on the pill. And some are pleased with their increased breast size. There is decreased incidence of functional ovarian cysts in pill users and no proof of pills causing breast cancer.

Says Dr. Mishell, "Patients with a family history of carcinoma of the breast are most concerned about the effect of the pill and its relation to breast cancer and benign breast disease. There is absolutely no evidence in the human to implicate the use of estrogens from pills in the development of breast cancer, although after cancer is present, the use of the pill is contraindicated."

If the pill is properly introduced to the patient, the likelihood of discontinuance and bad reactions is very small. Spotting of blood is common in the first two cycles of the pill. But if it continues into the third cycle, you should consult your doctor. Also, if after three cycles you have not gotten your period at all, contact your doctor.

When normal healthy patients are given medicine to control their fertility some definite risks are involved. Although the risk is infinitely small, death may occur in one per 100,000 users a year. Yet this is a very small risk compared to other risks. In the United States, driving a car has a risk of death of 27 per 100,000 a year; becoming pregnant and carrying a pregnancy to term has a risk of 1.7 per 10,000, and there are other risks of pregnancy, too. If a woman gets pregnant and the pregnancy is unwanted and she decides to terminate it, the risk of death is five or six per 100,000 per year. In addition there are psychological risks to the young woman having the abortion, as well as the danger of trauma to the uterus.

If you miss a pill and discover it the next day, the risks are not very high. Just take the missed pill immediately and also be certain to take the pill that pertains to the present day as scheduled. But if you miss two or three pills, you must use additional contraception, such as a condom or foam for the completion of the cycle. If you've missed a few pills and don't get your period, take a pregnancy test.

Mini-pills that are taken once a day and contain progestogens alone are not as effective as the combined oral contraceptives and have a much higher pregnancy rate, especially in the first six months of use. They also produce more irregular bleeding. Some women switch from combined pills to mini-pills because of estrogen-related problems such as high blood pressure, breast tenderness, headaches, premenstrual tension or anxiety, excess weight gain. As an initial method of treatment, mini-pills might be given to the woman with migraine headaches or hypertension.

Estrogens alone, as a contraceptive, are given in the postcoital "morning after" pills. Diethylstilbestrol (DES) is a synthetic estrogen recently approved by the FDA for women who've had unprotected sexual intercourse mid-cycle. It probably prevents implantation of a fertilized egg. Warning: DES should be used as an emergency measure only. It should not be considered for continuous or frequent use in birth control since it may be harmful to the fetus if conception has already occurred. It often causes nausea and vomiting. If DES fails, the FDA recommends a therapeutic abortion.

INTRAUTERINE DEVICES (IUD)

Although intrauterine contraception has been known for hundreds of years, only a decade ago, when IUDs became popular, many experts began viewing them theoretically as a first-class method of birth control. They come in assorted sizes and shapes, and most require insertion only once. In contrast to oral contraceptives which have a systemic effect because they inhibit ovulation, IUDs act locally on the genital tract. In addition, their low cost—as little as $25 for the one-time insertion, compared with about $2.25 per month for the pill—and easy reversibility, appealed to both physicians and women, many of whom were reluctantly giving up the pill because of its reported side effects. The IUD was the only method that gained significantly greater usage among single women during 1974, and most are satisfied with the method.

In practice, however, the early IUDs proved far from perfect, with drawbacks such as bleeding, pain, perforation, pelvic infection, bowel obstruction, expulsion of the device, and accidental pregnancy. For women wearing an IUD, they can safely be left in place, since normally the risk of infection is not that high. But if you get pregnant with the device in place see your physician immediately. It is now considered dangerous to continue the pregnancy with the device in place. "Most pregnancies that occur with an IUD in the uterus may result from the downward displacement of the device so that its contraceptive properties are not where implantation of the egg is occurring," suggests Dr. Howard J. Tatum, associate director of the biomedical division of the Population Council. All IUDs have an average first-year pregnancy rate of 2.5 per cent.

More than 30 million IUDs have been inserted in women of all nationalities and in the US alone, the FDA estimates that six million American women have opted for the IUD instead of the pill.

IUDS are usually plastic foreign bodies which are placed by the physician into the uterine cavity (if necessary with local anesthesia) and have a tail or string which protrudes from the cervix. Two new devices, one shaped like a "T" the other shaped like a "7," have copper wire wrapped around them and seem to give better protection against pregnancy without producing any toxic effects from the copper. Both are small and especially well accepted by the woman who has never borne a child.

IUDs do have a fairly high discontinuation rate, with 20-30 per cent of women either expelling it or having it removed within the first year of use. Aside from expulsions, many removals are due to pain and bleeding. If these early problems are overcome, most women tolerate the IUD very well.

Insertion of the device is usually carried out during menstruation since the slight bleeding accompanying the insertion is unnoticed, discomfort is reduced and insertion is easier since the cervix is softer and more open. Proper, careful insertion is needed to avoid the serious complication of uterine perforation which occurs in one of every 2,500 women.

Before you leave the clinic or office after IUD insertion, learn how to feel the strings which protude an inch or so into the vagina. You are not truly protected by your IUD unless you can feel the strings after each menstrual period. If you can feel the plastic tip of the device, it means that downward displacement has taken place, and see your doctor immediately to have a new one inserted.

Nuisance side effects of the IUD most commonly reported are increased menstrual flow, menstrual cramping and spotting. If it turns out that you can't tolerate the IUD, you can always have it removed. And heavier menstrual bleeding may be serious if you are anemic. If at any time after getting an IUD you have fever, pelvic pain or tenderness, severe cramping or unusual vaginal bleeding, contact your doctor immediately. These may be signs of infection and you should consult your doctor about the possibility of removing the IUD. Never remove it yourself.

No doctor should insert an IUD if a woman is already pregnant or has active pelvic infection. Other women who may be unable to have an IUD inserted are those with distortion of the uterine cavity due to a tumor, congenital malformation, recent history of undiagnosed vaginal bleeding, cardiac disease, anemia, painful menstruation, excessive uterine bleeding, intermenstrual bleeding, or a history of fibroids.

For 100 per cent protection against pregnancy, some women use foam or a condom with the IUD for seven to ten days at mid-cycle. Many Planned Parenthood Clinics advise women to use a supplemental birth control method for the first three months while using an IUD, since that is the time when conception seems to take place most often. The IUD's contraceptive effect is reversible, and after removal the chances of becoming pregnant are the same as before using the IUD.

CONDOM

The condom (rubber) is an excellent and popular method of birth control, and is the only one that plays a major role in the prevention of gonorrhea and syphilis if properly used. That's why many couples use a condom along with other methods of birth control. Its use has sharply decreased in the single population. Many of the younger users of condoms may be doing so because of the ease of obtaining them rather than satisfaction with the method.

Condoms are usually made of rubber and serve as a sheath that fits over the erect penis, working as a barrier to sperm transmission into the vagina. In constant users, or those who use the condom exactly as directed and with each act of intercourse, the failure rate is three pregnancies for every 100 women using it a year. In actual use, however, the failure rate rises to 15 to 20 pregnancies per year, due to errors by the users. These failure rates can be greatly improved if both foam and condoms are used with each act of intercourse. Most people consider it a short term method of birth control compared with the pill or IUD.

The major complaint that users of condoms have is the reduction of sensitivity at the tip of the penis. Others claim that interrupting the act of intercourse to put the condom on is an annoyance. A very small number of people are allergic to the rubber used in making condoms. Switching to natural skin condoms may be a solution.

Don't keep condoms more than two years before using them, and keep them away from heat. Remember, the condom must always be put on the penis before it touches the vagina. If you put the condom on the man, make sure to leave about one half inch of empty un-air-filled space at the tip, or use condoms with nipple tips to hold the ejaculate. Lubricated condoms minimize the risk of tearing, facilitate entry, and increase sensitivity. After ejaculation, the condom should be held on to as the man withdraws the still erect penis, taking care not to spill any semen on the woman's genitals. If the condom should tear or come off in the vagina, contraceptive foam or jelly should be immediately inserted. Foam also protects against sperm which may leak out around the edges of the condom after intercourse, or from fluid leakage containing sperm before ejaculation.

No side effects are caused by condoms, and the only contraindication may be the rare allergy.

THE DIAPHRAGM AND JELLY/CREAM

The diaphragm, which must always be used with spermicidal cream or jelly, is a dome-shaped soft rubber cup ranging from two to four inches in diameter, depending on the size of your upper vagina. The jelly or cream is first placed within the rubber dome and around the rim of the diaphragm in order to keep as much of the sperm killing agent as possible near the opening of the cervix to keep the sperm out of the cervical canal. The sperm that swim up around the rim of the diaphragm, run into the cream or jelly which kills them.

When the diaphragm is used properly, it is 90-98 per cent effective—depending on the effectiveness of the cream or jelly, proper fit, and consistent and careful use. Yet failures occur 2 per cent of the time even when the diaphragm is properly used.

Diaphragms are now used by about 4% of single women. However, with the possible complications of other methods and increased activism on the part of health consumers, the diaphragm may again become more widely used due to its high effectiveness and absence of any serious side effects, except possible allergic reaction to the rubber or spermicidal agent, or growth of bacteria if left in place too long.

You can insert your diaphragm with the jelly or cream up to six hours before you have intercourse. But if you've had it in for more than two hours, insert an extra applicator of cream without removing the diaphragm, before you have sex. When you insert the diaphragm always check to make certain you can feel the cervix through it. That's the only sure way to know that it's in correctly. Each time you have sex subsequently, insert another applicator of cream, but don't remove the diaphragm to do this. If things start to get messy after several acts of intercourse, leave the diaphragm in but switch to a condom. The jelly or cream needs six to eight hours to do the job of killing the sperm, so leave the diaphragm in for at least that long after your last lovemaking. To remove the diaphragm, hook a finger under the rim and pull. Wash it with soap and water, dry it, and then dust it with cornstarch, not talcum powder.

One unsettling thought about the diaphragm is that it's more likely to become dislodged during lovemaking when the woman is in a superior position. Apart from that, it's a highly effective method when used conscientiously. One additional plus with diaphragms is that they hold back about 24 hours of menstrual flow, and may allow more sexual spontaneity during menstruation.

A woman with a severely displaced or prolapsed uterus cannot use a diaphragm. Yet if the uterus is tipped slightly the doctor can still prescribe a properly fitting diaphragm. Be sure to practice putting it in when you are in the doctor's office so you will know if you're inserting it correctly. The first time may be awkward but it becomes easier and quicker with each insertion.

The close relation of the diaphragm to the sex act, may be considered a disadvantage by some women. If either you or your partner feel that sex must be absolutely spontaneous with no interruptions, or you are self-conscious about touching your own genitals, putting the diaphragm in may seem like a messy hassle, but remember, its effectiveness approaches that of the IUD. Today with more positive feelings about your sexuality, and your increasing ability to communicate more openly with the men you sleep with, you may be more able to use the diaphragm happily.

FOAM OR CREAMS ALONE

Spermicidal foams and creams should not be ignored as a means of contraception, although they are not considered a primary method. The effectiveness rate, as with all secondary methods, greatly depends on the woman's motivation. Its usage among single women is quite low—falling from five per cent in 1973 to three per cent in 1974. It's used most often as a temporary method, without great satisfaction. Still, the contra-indications are almost nil. At worst there may be an occasional incidence of irritation.

The creams and foams stop sperm from reaching the egg by setting up a chemical roadblock at the opening of the uterus. The woman can use foam, cream, or jelly. Of the three, foam is the easiest to use, the least messy, and the most effective—even so it's only rated fair to good as solo protection. It is not as effective as a condom used alone, or a diaphragm used with jelly or cream. All three spermicides come with special applicators that measure the right amount and help you get it into the right place. Your job is to put it in at the right time—30 minutes or less before each act of intercourse, and left there for six to eight hours after. All three can be purchased at any drugstore without a prescription, and are harmless except to sperm.

If you have an allergic reaction to one brand, try another. Creams and jellies are not usually as effective as foam, so unless foam irritates your vaginal tissues, use it. If you must use cream or jelly alone, get your partner to use a condom. The stronger, more effective creams and jellies tend to be more irritating to the vagina and the penis than the others.

RHYTHM

Rhythm can be effective when faithfully practiced, with willpower playing a major role in its effectiveness. When using rhythm, abstinence must be practiced during the period when viable sperm can come into contact with a viable egg—during the fertile ovulation period. The calendar method for calculating the fertile period is not very good if your cycle lengths tend to be irregular. More accurate for the couple choosing rhythm is the concurrent use of basal body temperature to identify time of ovulation. To use this method you have to keep an accurate daily record of your basal body temperature which is best done just after waking and before any activity. When the temperature is elevated for three to four days as a result of elevated progesterone levels, ovulation is past, and the chances of conception small.

Consult your doctor if you wish to use rhythm as your birth control method. Charts used for recording and interpreting basal body temperatures are often confusing in the first few months when most contraceptive errors occur. Since during days 10 to 17 of the cycle (unless you use other methods of birth control) you must refrain from having intercourse, you might try to take advantage of the days during menstruation.

With the rhythm method, use-effectiveness rates vary widely from couple to couple due to the fact that only eight per cent of women of childbearing age have regular menstrual cycles. In constant users of the rhythm method failure rates of as low as 15 pregnancies per 100 women using it a year, have been obtained. Among total users of the method, however, rates as high as 25 to 40 pregnancies have occurred.

The only known side effect to rhythm is the frustration due to long periods of abstinence. Also the method may not work well in a woman who has irregular intervals between her menses.

Rhythm is not recommended as a highly effective or easily practiced technique. Unfortunately the basal body temperature method cannot predict in advance when ovulation will occur. In some cases there is an abrupt temperature rise, but sometimes it takes as long as four or five days to stabilize.

COITUS INTERRUPTUS (WITHDRAWAL)

Withdrawal works sometimes, but you are always taking a chance. The man must always get his penis out in time before he ejaculates so the semen containing the sperm is not deposited in or near the vagina. This can be done but it takes perfect timing. There is luck and danger involved since a few drops of fluid from the glands lining the man's genital tract may be released into the vagina even before ejaculation. And many sperm are in the few drops.

Many couples have used withdrawal for years and find it perfectly acceptable—but less than 100 per cent effective. Although it introduces a certain amount of tension into the sex act—since the man must be alert to the first signs of orgasm and prepared to terminate intercourse abruptly—for most couples it does not appear to have any ill effects. To many men who have practiced the technique over long periods, the act of withdrawal becomes almost second nature and they do it automatically.

Withdrawal should only be used as an emergency measure, since it results in more pregnancies than other methods. Sperm have been known to swim all the way from the vaginal lips into the fallopian tubes. So ejaculation must take place completely away from the vagina.

When using withdrawal, the woman must be completely dependent on the man's control over his ejaculation and must trust him greatly in order to be free of anxiety. When used over a long period of time, it can lead to premature ejaculation. Withdrawal might also be hard on the woman since the man might have to withdraw before you reach orgasm, causing a complete interruption of the flow of your sexual response. And multiple acts of intercourse in a short period of time increase the likelihood of failure of this method.

The only advantage to coitus interruptus is it requires no devices or chemicals, and is available under all circumstances at no cost.

PREGNANCY TESTING

Early pregnancy testing allows the opportunity for

adequate counseling and an early abortion if the pregnancy is unwanted. The standard urine test can be done quickly with a high degree of accuracy, but cannot positively determine if you're pregnant until 35 to 40 days after your last menstrual period. A new, very early pregnancy test has been developed which can detect a pregnancy as early as six days after intercourse, and certainly before the first missed period. The test uses the woman's serum, and "is three to 400 times more sensitive than other tests," says its developer Dr. Robert Landesman, Clinical Professor of Obstetrics and Gynecology at Cornell University Medical College. He reports "at least 99 per cent accuracy in the first 1,000 women I've tested since November 1973. The results are known in 1½ hours and cost $12." This test is not widely available yet, but is also being used at the University of Louisville School of Medicine in Kentucky. "The test detects a pregnancy even before an abortion could be performed," he says. "And it will be most helpful in detecting ectopic pregnancies in the tube before the doctor can even see it." The test does have one drawback—since it is a radio-receptor assay test it needs very sophisticated equipment and a trained nurse or doctor to run it. The equipment is usually available in big medical centers and hospitals, not in the private physician's office. A spokesman at Planned Parenthood in NYC noted that the test would probably not be used by them, but would be confined to the large medical centers.

STERILIZATION

Only one method of birth control is final and irreversible—sterilization. Both men and women can choose it, and get a vasectomy or tubal ligation, respectively. After the first few months, there is no more worry about pregnancy or birth control after you are sterilized, since the egg or sperm cells are simply absorbed by the body. The hormones secreted by the body do remain the same, and sexual ability and pleasure doesn't change. Although you don't have to be any special age nor have had any children to be sterilized, you do have to be absolutely certain that no matter what, you'll never choose to have children of your own in the future. (Although, in an infinitely small number of cases, vasectomies can be reversed.) You have to be comfortable with the knowledge that you can't. If not, there are many other alternatives.

BIRTH CONTROL METHODS

	RHYTHM	CONDOM	FOAM
What is it?	A plan not to have sexual intercourse during a woman's most fertile period — the 11th through the 17th days of an average (28-day) cycle. Most women release an egg cell once a month — usually 14 days before the next menstrual period.	A sheath of thin rubber or animal tissue (shaped like the finger of a glove) which is worn over the man's penis during intercourse.	A foam containing a chemical that immobilizes sperm. It is placed in the vagina before intercourse to cover the cervix (entrance to the uterus).
How does it work?	Since the couple abstains from intercourse during the woman's most fertile time, there are no sperm present during the time just before, during, and after ovulation. But because the date of ovulation may vary from month to month, it is impossible to know exactly when to abstain from intercourse.	It catches the man's semen so that sperm cannot enter the woman's vagina and continue through the woman's reproductive system to fertilize an egg.	The foam spreads evenly and forms a barrier to block sperm from entering the uterus. At the same time, contact with the chemical ingredient immobilizes the sperm.
How do I use it?	The three major methods of rhythm are the calendar system, basal body temperature system, and the vaginal mucus system. Consult a doctor or family planning clinic for help in determining your fertile period. You will need to record dates of menstrual periods for several months, and perhaps keep a record of early morning temperature for several months.	Leaving about ½ inch of space at the tip, the condom is unrolled over the erect penis before there has been any contact between the penis and the vagina. The extra space at the tip holds the semen. After ejaculation, and before the man loses his erection, the man should remove his penis from the woman's vagina, holding the condom firmly against the base of the penis to avoid spilling any semen into the vagina. Condoms should be used only once.	Insertion is similar to a tampon. Shake the container well. Fill the applicator. Lying down, insert the applicator into the vagina and push the plunger to release the foam. Insert the foam as short a time before intercourse as possible (preferably within half an hour). More foam must be inserted if more than half an hour passes before sex relations, and again each time intercourse is repeated.
How reliable is it?	Method failures: 15 per 100 women in a year. User failures: 25-40 per 100 women in a year.*	Method failures: 3 per 100 women in a year. User failures: 15-20 per 100 women in a year. If the woman uses contraceptive foam as additional protection, only 5 women in 100 per year will probably become pregnant.*	Method failures: 3 per 100 women in a year. User failures: 30 per 100 women in a year.*
What are the advantages?	It is accepted by many religious groups which prohibit other methods of birth control. There are no physical side effects.	Condoms are easy to purchase, easy to use, inexpensive (25-30¢ each for plain ones, $1.00 or more each for animal tissue, shaped or tinted ones), do not require a doctor's prescription, and offer protection against venereal disease.	Foam is easy to obtain, easy to use, no medical examination or precription needed.
What are the disadvantages?	Many women have periods which are too irregular to use this method. The rhythm method requires expert instruction for successful use. It often inhibits spontaneity. Many couples find it difficult to abstain from sexual intercourse for the time required.	Care is needed to prevent the condom from tearing or slipping off. It is necessary to interrupt foreplay in order to put the condom on. Some men feel that the condom dulls sensation. A small percentage of men and women are allergic to rubber. This problem can be solved by switching to animal tissue condoms.	Must be inserted immediately before intercourse. More foam must be inserted each time intercourse is repeated.
How much does it cost?	Basal body temperature kits are available in drug stores for $3.00-$5.00.	25¢ to $1.25 each in a drug store. Lower cost or no cost at Planned Parenthood or other family planning clinic.	It ranges from $3.85 to $4.50 for the whole kit in a drug store. Lower cost or no cost at Planned Parenthood or other family planning clinic.
Where can I get it?	Instruction in the rhythm method and charts for recording menstrual dates can be obtained from a clinician, Planned Parenthood or other family planning clinic.	Any drug store, Planned Parenthood or other family planning clinic.	Any drug store, Planned Parenthood or other family planning clinic.

*Reliability figures obtained from: Hatcher, Robert A. M.D. *et al*, Contraceptive Technology 1976-1977, Irvington Publishers, Inc., New York, 1976.

DIAPHRAGM	INTRAUTERINE DEVICE ("IUD")	"THE PILL"	STERILIZATION
A flexible rubber cup which is inserted into the vagina so that it fits snugly over the cervix (entrance to the uterus).	A small object made of plastic with a nylon thread attached to the bottom.	A series of pills containing one or both of two synthetic hormones similar to the ones that naturally regulate a woman's menstrual cycle. Pills come in packages sufficient for one month.	An operation that permanently blocks the tubes in males or females, and prevents sperm or eggs from moving into their reproductive systems and causing a pregnancy. In the male, the operation is called a vasectomy ; in the female, a tubal ligation.
It is used with a spermicidal cream or jelly. When placed correctly, the diaphragm blocks the entrance of the womb, and the cream or jelly immobilizes the sperm that may travel beyond the rim of the diaphragm.	It is inserted into the uterus by a clinician and left there indefinitely. IUD's generally create a condition in the uterus that hinders pregnancy from occurring. Most types can remain in place for years, if there are no problems. Some newer types, using additional copper or hormones, have to be replaced periodically. Annual check-ups are important.	Each monthly series keeps a woman's ovaries from releasing an egg and/or alters the uterine lining and the cervical mucus. The specific pill for a given woman is prescribed after a medical history and examination. The most commonly used pills are taken once a day for 21 days with 7 days off; others are taken every day in 28-day cycles. To be effective, a whole series must be taken on schedule.	It blocks the tubes which carry sperm or eggs into the reproductive system. A man continues to have ejaculations, but his semen no longer contains sperm. A woman continues to menstruate, and an egg is released each month, but cannot reach her uterus. Neither operation affects male or female characteristics, sex drive, or orgasm. The male operation is less expensive and done under local anesthesia. Female sterilization can be done several ways. Women's procedures are usually done in a hospital; but newer methods require only a few hours stay. There is a slight chance of developing some swelling, bleeding or infection.
A clinician must fit a woman for the diaphragm and show her how to insert and remove it. It must be used with a contraceptive cream or jelly and placed over the cervix. It can be put in up to six hours ahead, but if more than two hours pass before sexual relations, more cream or jelly must be inserted into the vagina. Each time intercourse is repeated, more cream or jelly must be inserted (without removing the diaphragm). Leave it in place, and do not douche for at least six hours after the last sex act. After use, wash, dry and dust the diaphragm with cornstarch.	A clinician makes a complete pelvic examination to decide if a women should use an IUD and discusses which types are possible for her. There may be some pain during the insertion. The uterus in some women expels an IUD. The time this is most likely to happen is during a menstrual period. A woman should check after each menstrual period by feeling for the nylon thread which extends down from the IUD in her uterus about ½ inch into her vagina. If the string can be felt, and it is not much longer than usual, the device is in place.	Ask your clinician, Planned Parenthood or other family planning clinic.	Consult a doctor, Planned Parenthood or other family planning clinic.
Method failures: 3 per 100 women in a year. User failures: 20-25 per 100 women in a year.*	Method failures: 1 to 4 per 100 women in a year. User failures: 6 to 10 per 100 women in a year.*	Method failures: less than 1 per 100 women in a year. User failures: 5 to 10 per 100 women in a year.*	Method failures: less than 1 per 100 men or women in a year. User failures: none.*
Insertion can be a routine part of bedtime preparation. Properly fitted and inserted, it will not be felt by either partner. No side effects except rare cases of allergic reaction.	Spontaneity. Nothing to do before intercourse. IUD's cannot be felt during intercourse. No daily routine.	Pills are the most effective of the temporary methods of birth control. As long as no pills are forgotten, protection is there all the time. There is nothing to do just before intercourse. Women taking pills usually have more regular periods with less cramping. Periods also tend to be shorter and lighter.	Sterilization is the most effective method of birth control. No need to use temporary methods (*except* that some method *must* be used after vasectomy until the semen has been tested by the doctor to be sure sperm are no longer present). Then, no need to worry about pregnancy.
A check up for size is needed every two years or following pregnancy. More cream or jelly must be inserted into the vagina every time intercourse is repeated.	Some women experience cramps, longer and heavier menstrual bleeding, and spotting between periods. There is a greater risk of infection in the uterus and tubes in women wearing IUD's. In rare instances, the IUD may perforate the wall of the uterus and surgery may be required to remove it. If pregnancy occurs, the IUD must be removed. Removal reduces the chances of miscarriage and infection. If a woman can't find the string of her IUD, or thinks she may be pregnant, she should contact her doctor or clinic at once. She should never try to remove an IUD herself.	Women with certain health conditons (explained by a clinician) should not use the pill. Risk of serious blood clotting (that in rare cases presents life-threatening problems, including heart attack) is slightly greater in pill users, especially for women over 40. Severe headaches, loss of vision, sudden chest or leg pains may be signals of serious problems, and should be reported to your clinician immediately. Some women also experience weight gain, nausea, spotting, and sore breasts, but these symptoms usually disappear after a few months of pill use.	The operation is permanent. Fertility can very seldom be restored, even if an operation is performed to rejoin the tubes. Both partners should be absolutely sure they want no more children before they decide on sterilization. There is a very slight risk of complications, as with any operation.
At a drug store, diaphragms range from $7.50 to $10.00, which does not include the clinician's fee for fitting. Lower cost or no cost at Planned Parenthood or other family planning clinic.	Since the clinician inserts the IUD in his/her office at the time of the examination, he or she charges for the examination, the device and a follow-up visit. The cost varies from $20.00 to $50.00 for all three. Lower cost or no cost at Planned Parenthood or other family planning clinic.	An examination from a private doctor ranges from $20.00 to $45.00. Pills cost $2.00 to $3.00 per monthly package at a drug store. Both the examination and the pills are lower cost or no cost at Planned Parenthood or other family planning clinic.	Vasectomy: $75.00-$150.00 Tubal ligation: Right after childbirth, $125.00. Otherwise up to $500.00 for doctor and hospital charges. Reduced fees can sometimes be arranged for low income families through Planned Parenthood.
Visit a clinician or family planning clinic for an examination and a prescription, which can be filled at the clinic or at a drug store.	From a clinician, Planned Parenthood or other family planning clinic.	Visit a clinician, Planned Parenthood or other family planning clinic for an examination and a prescription, which can be filled either at the clinic or at a drug store.	A vasectomy can be done in a doctor's office. Tubal ligations at present are done in a hospital, although newer methods require only a few hours stay.

80 Percent of Americans Believe Abortion Should Be Legal; 70 Percent Approve Medicaid Funding

The large majority of Americans who support legal abortion has continued to grow despite the intensified political efforts of antiabortion forces, according to recent opinion surveys by the two major polling organizations. A substantial majority of Americans are also in favor of Medicaid funding for abortion, according to one of the polls. A survey commissioned by *Redbook* magazine and conducted by the Gallup Organization in January showed that 80 percent of Americans think abortion should be legal in all or some circumstances, up from 77 percent in 1977.[1] Seventy percent said Medicaid should pay for at least some abortions, despite the elimination of virtually all federal funding of abortions since enforcement of the Hyde amendment in 1977. By a 60-to-37 percent majority, Americans support the 1973 Supreme Court decisions which made abortion legal, an increase over the 53-to-40 percent majority of 1977, according to a Harris Survey conducted in February.[2]

The Gallup survey, appearing in the June 1979 issue of *Redbook* magazine, was based on a nationally representative sample of approximately 1,500 persons aged 18 or older. They were asked, "Do you think abortion should be legal under any circumstances, legal only under certain circumstances, or illegal under all circumstances?" The same question was asked in Gallup Polls in 1975 and again in 1977. In the *Redbook* survey, 26 percent said they believed abortion should be legal under all circumstances, an increase of four percentage points over the 1977 Gallup Poll.[3] Fifty-four percent said abortions should be legal under some circumstances, compared with 55 percent in 1977. Seventeen percent said abortion should be illegal under all circumstances, compared with 19 percent two years earlier. (The remainder were unsure.)

A total of 34 percent said abortions should be legal without restrictions during the first trimester of pregnancy. Some 80 percent said abortion should be legal during the first trimester if the woman's life is in danger; 75 percent, if the woman is a victim of rape or incest; 63 percent, if the baby would be born deformed; 61 percent, if the mother's physical health is endangered; 59 percent, if the woman's mental health is threatened; and 42 percent, if the woman cannot afford to raise the child.

Although the so-called Hyde amendment to the DHEW-Department of Labor Appropriations Act has virtually eliminated federal funding of abortions for very poor women, 70 percent of those polled in the *Redbook* survey said they believed federal funds should pay for abortions in all or some circumstances. Of these, 23 percent said Medicaid funds should pay for abortions under all circumstances, and 47 percent said Medicaid funds should be available under various circumstances. The levels of support for funding in each circumstance were similar to the levels of support for legal abortion in that circumstance. Only 28 percent said Medicaid funds should not be used to pay for abortions under any circumstances. (In the year prior to enforcement of the Hyde amendment, some 295,000 U.S. women obtained abortions paid for by Medicaid; since that time, DHEW reports, the number of federally funded Medicaid abortions has declined by 99 percent, and 40 states have enacted laws or policies similar to the Hyde amendment.[4])

An NBC News-Associated Press national poll conducted in October 1978 produced slightly different results on the question of whether or not Medicaid funds should be used to pay for abortions.[5] In that poll, 1,600 adults were asked, "Do you think that the federal government should help a poor woman with her medical bills if she wants an abortion?" Forty-eight percent said yes, and 44 percent, no; eight percent were undecided. The major difference between that poll and the *Redbook* survey was that the Associated Press poll offered only the options of approving or disapproving of Medicaid funding, without offering the third possibility—approval under limited circumstances.

The *Redbook* survey indicates that abortion is both a highly charged political issue and one on which attitudes are in flux. Asked whether they felt strongly about abortion, 63 percent replied that they did; only about 35 percent said they did not. In addition, 35 percent said their attitudes had changed over the past several years. Of those whose attitudes had changed, 74 percent said they were more accepting of legal abortion than they had been several years ago; 19 percent were less accepting.

Among Protestants, increases in approval of abortion were slightly greater than those in the general population. Twenty-three percent of Protestants now believe abortion should be legal under all circumstances, and 60 percent, in some circumstances. Among Catholics, 21 percent believe abortion should be legal in all circumstances, and 52 percent believe it should be legal in certain circumstances.

The Harris Survey

The Harris Survey on abortion, which was conducted in February and involved a representative sample of 1,199 adults, was the most recent in the series of Harris Surveys on abortion which began in 1973. The 60 percent reported support for legal abortion is the highest level recorded in the series of polls. Support had dipped to 53 percent in 1977 from a previous high of 59 percent, possibly as an aftereffect of the political campaign by antiabortion forces that produced the Hyde amendment and subsequent restrictions on federal financial support of abortion in the Peace Corps and military. Opposition to the Supreme Court decisions was 37 percent—down from 40 percent in 1977, but still higher than the 28 percent reported in 1976.

Seventy-three percent of those questioned in the Harris Survey said any decision about an abortion in the first trimester of pregnancy should be made by a woman and her doctor without outside interference; 25 percent disagreed.

Among those in the Harris Survey, both blacks and white Catholics opposed the Supreme Court decisions legalizing abortion by a narrow margin (50 percent to 48 percent). However, an array of other groups strongly favored legal abortions: Easterners, by 65 percent to 33 percent; Westerners, by 70 percent to 27 percent; those under age 30, by 66 to 33 percent; those 30–49, by 66 to 32 percent; the college-educated, by 69 to 29 percent; and political moderates, by 61 to 37 percent.

About four out of 10 Americans (39 percent) would vote against a candidate they otherwise agreed with if they opposed his stand on the abortion issue. That proportion is about equally divided between those who favor and those who oppose legal abortion, even though proponents outnumber opponents in the general population. This is because the abortion issue is more salient politically to those who oppose the Supreme Court decisions.

References

1. E. R. Dobell, "Abortion: The Controversy We Can't Seem to Solve," *Redbook*, June 1979.

2. L. Harris, ABC News–Harris Survey release, New York, Mar. 6, 1979.

3. G. Gallup, "Despite Bitter Debate Attitudes Toward Abortion Have Changed Little Since '75," *The Gallup Poll*, news release, Princeton, N.J., Apr. 22, 1979.

4. The Alan Guttmacher Institute, *Abortions and the Poor: Private Morality, Public Responsibility*, New York, 1979.

5. NBC News–The Associated Press, news release, Washington, D.C., Jan. 11, 1979.

The Abortion Repeaters

Who are these women who do not "learn from their mistakes," who go back for a second abortion, or even a third? Why do they do it, and what can be done to keep their number from growing?

Alice Lake

Close to 1,400,000 American women had abortions in 1978. For more than one out of four of these, it was the second or third time around. Ever since abortion became legal, the percentage of repeaters has been skyrocketing—15 percent of all abortions in 1974, 23 percent in 1976, 27 percent in 1978.

These figures shock all of us, the majority who accept abortion as a woman's free choice, as well as the minority who do not. They disturb those who operate birth-control clinics and view abortion as a necessary backup to contraceptive failure, and those who counsel abortion patients on how to avoid coming back again. Perhaps most poignantly, they disturb the woman who is herself having a second or third abortion. "Intellectually, I know there's no difference between the first and the second," one of them told me. "Yet there's a part of me, a little corner of my mind, that whispers, There's something wrong with a woman who has two abortions."

No one likes abortion; most of us accept it in our flawed society as an occasionally necessary last resort. Perhaps this is why we concentrate on the repeater many of our traditional prejudices—whether against premarital sex or promiscuity or merely fecklessness.

Our strongest reaction, however, is that we have been betrayed. We have made available this way to avoid unwanted birth, and the abortion repeater is abusing the privilege. We are convinced that she deliberately chooses to ignore contraception, although it is effective and available, in favor of using abortion itself as her method of birth control. We assume that she will continue on her irresponsible path, returning again and again to the abortion clinic until she finally reaches menopause.

Before McCALL'S asked me to investigate repeat abortion, I held this viewpoint myself. But I have learned that it is not true. I have talked with a wide variety of experts in this field, and I have read most of the scientific studies made in recent years. The consensus is overwhelming: There is *no* "abortion mentality," no "typical" woman who repeatedly has abortions because she turns her back on birth control. "Women who undergo abortion are not a special subset of the population that is somehow different from women who have babies," says Patricia Steinhoff, a University of Hawaii sociologist who has done extensive research on abortion. "They are the same women, observed at a different point in their lives."

These are the facts I learned about the woman who becomes an abortion repeater:

Statistically, she is no different from those who have only one abortion, who currently number one out of every eight female Americans of fertile age (15 to 44).

She is young. Two out of three are under 25.

She is unmarried. Three out of four are single.

She is just as likely to be a mother as she is to be childless; there are 50 percent in each category.

The typical repeater stops at two abortions. In 1977, of the women who had repeat abortions, three out of four were having their second. About 16 percent were having a third, and less than 8 percent, a fourth. Only four out of every 100 women who had abortions in 1977 were having number three. (These figures would probably be even lower if they did not include immigrants from eastern Europe and Japan, countries where multiple abortion as a means of birth control is more acceptable than it is here. Dr. Christopher Tietze of the Population Council, a leading statistician in the birth-control field, points out that if young and fertile American women *did* choose abortion as their only way to limit births, they would each average more than one a year.)

Paradoxical as it may seem, the repeater usually practices better contraception than the woman having her first abortion. Teenagers particularly—one out of every three aborters—are likely to get their first introduction to contraception, and instruction on how to use it, at the abortion clinic. Few younger teens practice any form of birth control when they are first initiated into sex, and without it two out of three of them become pregnant within two years.

Dr. Michael Bracken, Yale epidemiologist and abortion expert, estimates that at most, only 5 percent of repeaters fail repeatedly to use birth control when they are having sex. Of the remaining 95 percent, his studies suggest that about half are erratic users and the other half are victims of contraceptive failure.

In general, despite popular belief to the contrary, there is no common personality defect or neurotic strain that binds together these erratic users of contraception and those few who are nonusers. "We have searched for social and emotional patterns that separate the repeater from the woman who has one abortion," says Carole Dornblaser, director of the Meadowbrook Women's Clinic in Minneapolis, one of the largest in the upper Midwest. "We just couldn't find any."

Yet abortion counselors do make some cautious observations about the repeater. Some suggest that she is less likely than others to be involved in a stable relationship with a man. Others picture her as somewhat unsure of her identity, not highly motivated to take control of her life. Dr. Colin Brewer, a British psychiatrist who studied women having a third abortion, uses the word, "instability" to describe those who use birth control erratically, then criticizes this as a "vague" concept, adding that erratic users are not necessarily neurotic. (In my own talks with women getting a second or third abortion, each personality, each account was different.)

Sometimes the current circumstances of her life appear, perhaps unconsciously, to influence a woman's actions, which is what Patricia Steinhoff meant by her statement that these are "the same women [as those who have babies] . . . at a different time in their lives." Some get pregnant just at the point when they are breaking up with a boyfriend or experiencing some other loss. In one case, a young woman tearfully said goodbye to her closest female friend, who was moving far away. That night she had spur-of-the-moment sexual relations with a casual acquaintance, an occurrence quite untypical of her, and promptly got pregnant.

Terry Beresford, president of the National Abortion Federation, the organization that sets standards in the field, describes the repeater as "a person who for a time just can't get her act together. She may temporarily be so be-

From the September 1980 *McCall's*. Reprinted by permission of the author.

set with life's problems that she can't cope." Director of counseling at Planned Parenthood of Maryland in Baltimore, Ms. Beresford stresses the temporary nature of the problem. "A woman's ability to come to terms with her sexuality and its responsibilities changes. She has kids. She accepts a contraceptive method. Eventually she may get sterilized. There aren't many abortions after thirty." (Less than 16 percent of all abortions are performed on women older than 30, although fertility usually continues for at least 15 more years.)

Even though there is no single answer, there are a number of explanations as to why the rate of repeat abortions keeps rising, each of which helps to illuminate one facet of this complex human problem. There is the *statistical explanation,* first advanced by Dr. Christopher Tietze. He marshals evidence to show that the nature of the population at risk makes multiple abortion all but inevitable. For one thing, six million women have already had one legal abortion, and this pool keeps growing. These six million are more likely to have another unwanted pregnancy, and to end it by abortion, than are the remaining forty-five million women in the reproductive age span—for these reasons:

Since they are predominantly in their late teens and early 20s, they are at the height of fertility. In 1977 teenagers had 31 percent of all abortions, and women of 20 to 24 had 34 percent.

Their ability to conceive has been proved. Indeed, they may be more fertile than most. Among other women of reproductive age, some are infertile, have had a hysterectomy or have been sterilized.

They tend to be, because of their age, more sexually active than older women.

Finally, they have shown by the initial abortion that they are willing to use this solution for unwanted pregnancy.

Another explanation for repeated abortions is the inadequacy of *birth-control methods.* Some may scoff that contraceptives fail because women fail to use them, but that is only part of the truth. Among all American women, the use of contraception is higher than ever, but *only about half of the pregnancies that occur are intended.* Even the Pill has a 2-percent failure rate, thus causing 200,000 unwanted pregnancies a year among the ten million American women who use it. After the Pill, failure rates keep rising among other contraceptives, reaching about 15 percent with over-the-counter foam.

The only methods separated in time from the sex act and thus not subject to human forgetfulness in the heat of passion are the Pill and the IUD. Both have well-publicized hazards that keep millions of women from choosing them. According to a study at Michael Reese Hospital and Medical Center in Chicago, a group of teenagers there appeared more afraid of the Pill than of pregnancy. They also seemed unaware that other methods existed. "They had no sense of alternatives to it," said Dr. Mary Rogel, who conducted the study. On an average, the hundred girls in the study started sex at 15 and were pregnant by 16.

Sometimes a doctor shares the blame for unwanted pregnancy, taking a patient off the Pill but failing to provide an effective alternative. One California gynecologist did not know that a 21-year-old, who asked him to renew her Pill prescription, had already had one abortion. "Why don't you just skip the Pill for a few months," he suggested, "just to make sure you're still ovulating? You can always use foam." She did, and she became pregnant. A second abortion followed.

Other doctors are careless about refitting a diaphragm after pregnancy and about teaching a novice how to use it properly. Instead of visiting a clinic that might have spent an hour guiding her in the use of a diaphragm, one young woman, a bit sentimental about getting engaged, went back to the family doctor who delivered her. He wanted to prescribe the Pill and became impatient and angry when she insisted on a diaphragm. With ill grace, he fitted her and gave her a prescription to take to the pharmacy. "But how do I put it in and take it out?" she asked. "Oh, they'll give you a pamphlet at the drugstore," he told her.

The way she happens to live may provide another clue to the picture of the abortion repeater. A young woman may know the facts about birth control but still use her contraceptive erratically, because it doesn't fit her style of living *at that time.* It could be simply that her tight blue jeans have no pocket big enough to hold a diaphragm or foam without an embarrassing bulge.

Most teens—and many older women—are distinctly uncomfortable about planning in advance for the possibility of having intercourse, which is of course necessary for those who do not use the Pill or IUD. They want to be swept off their feet rather than seeming to be available. "During my marriage separation," a woman in her 30s explains, "I went out to lunch with another man. I thought of taking along my diaphragm, but rejected the idea. In fact, it half-shocked me. I just wasn't ready to admit the thoughts that were titillating me."

Many workers in the abortion field believe that the most compelling explanation of why women who know better fail to use contraception faithfully is the *risk-taking theory* advanced by Kristin Luker, a California sociologist, in her book *Taking Chances: Abortion and the Decision Not to Contracept.* "Women are not either risk takers or nonrisk takers," Dr. Luker observes, "but simply persons engaged in a dynamic human process in which not using contraception sometimes becomes more rational than using it."

Dr. Luker believes that the whole process of living is a series of calculated risks, and chancing pregnancy is no different from others, such as smoking cigarettes or ignoring a seat belt. In fact, she says, "we suspect few women will have reached menopause without at least one incident of contraceptive risk-taking."

Although some are more willing to gamble than others, the process of tacit self-bargaining is the same for all, says Dr. Luker; the immediate human cost of using contraception is weighed against the remote and uncertain cost of unwanted pregnancy. A woman may think: It's really a bother to get up and put more jelly on the diaphragm, and it's right before my period so I probably can't conceive, and if I did, maybe we'd get married, and I'd like that.

But doesn't the reality of a first abortion chill the game of risk taking? Not necessarily, says Dr. Luker. It may merely give a woman more information to feed into the decision-making process. If she dismisses that first abortion as bad luck or reaps some benefit from it (becoming the center of attention, for example), if she fails to understand the dynamics of the gamble, then she may well be fated to repeat it.

Sally (not her name), 24, still doesn't quite understand how she came to have two abortions in only four months. "I'm still so angry at myself," she says. "I should walk around with a sign on my chest saying 'Fool!' "

Sally started sex at 18, but had relations only intermittently until last year when she moved in with a young man. She had used the Pill at first, "because I wanted the best and easiest method." But she gained ten pounds, a development that few teenagers are willing to tolerate. With her widowed mother's agreement, she went to the family doctor, who inserted an IUD. After Sally started to bleed heavily during her periods, the doctor removed it and fitted her with a diaphragm.

Sally and her boyfriend had been dating for four months before they decided to share an apartment. "When we used to go out on a date," she told me, "I always put in the diaphragm in advance. I was very careful." But after they began living together, "I started to get lax." Sometimes when they had relations, "I was just too lazy. And he didn't encourage me to use it. Instead he would often withdraw before orgasm." For the first four months, they had sex at least four times a week without mishap. "I guess unconsciously I said to myself, Everything's fine. Withdrawal works. We never talked much about it, although neither of us is really an irresponsible person."

Then Sally became pregnant. Her boyfriend suggested marriage, but she said no. "I love children, but I just didn't want to start marriage that way." Apparently no wiser after the abortion, the two went back to withdrawal as their excuse for not using birth control. Sally had one period. Then she became pregnant again.

"I was so angry I just wanted to punish myself," she says. "He was very loving, but I just didn't want him to come near me. It's as if I didn't want to gain any profit from the experience." Deeply ashamed, she called the abortion clinic.

Soon after the second abortion, Sally said that she was trying to figure out what made her keep playing Russian roulette. I mentioned the risk-taking theory, and when we spoke later, she said she thought she understood herself a little better. When she and the young man started to live together, she explained, he still had not completely recovered from an earlier love affair. "I guess I wanted to be the one and only." The abortion brought them closer and even elicited a marriage proposal. Did the first pregnancy thus lead to a second? Maybe, Sally says. "We've come a long way in our relationship since then," she adds. "You simply don't take chances like that with yourself and your body. I'll never have another abortion. If I got pregnant again, I would certainly bear the child."

According to Dr. Luker, women can "forget" the contraceptive because they unconsciously judge either the cost of using it as high or the likelihood of pregnancy as low. "Magical thinking" is the term some counselors use to describe a teenager's self-delusion about her chances of pregnancy. It can't happen to me, she persuades herself; I'm too young; it was my first time; I've just had an abortion. Sometimes it's her mother who indulges in magical thinking: "You won't have to tell my daughter about contraception," she assures the staff at the abortion clinic. "I'm going to have a talk with her, and she's not going to have sex any more." The result is a second pregnancy.

Young adults also use magical thinking to minimize the risk they're assuming. "I can't get pregnant because I'm sterile. The doctor told me so," is a frequent comment. More likely, the doctor made a chance remark that she might have trouble conceiving. Some young partners, unwilling to bother with birth control, help along the delusion of minimal risk by asserting that *they* are sterile. Some may even lie, claiming a vasectomy that was never performed. Others may cite childhood mumps or even diabetes as the "reason" no contraceptive is necessary.

The longer a couple avoids pregnancy with inadequate contraception (or none at all), the more tempting it is to keep on gambling. At the suburban clinic where she was awaiting her second abortion, Rhonda, a college junior, told me about a friend who "used nothing for years and never got pregnant. Lots of other people take chances and get away with it," she said bitterly.

According to the risk-taking concept, some young women flirt with pregnancy because some of its aspects appear positive: I'll be on center stage; everyone will know I'm grown up and feminine. "When I had the abortion," says one teenager, "I felt closer to my parents than I had in years." Others who are engaged, or wish they were, gamble that, if pregnancy occurs, marriage will follow. "I thought that he would want to get married," said one young woman. "I never ever thought I'd go through an abortion."

When I asked abortion counselors about married women who have more than one abortion, I heard dozens of anecdotes, but without a common thread running through them. Obviously, married women are more reliable about using birth control: They represent less than one out of four who have abortions. In some cases, they may abort a wanted pregnancy that has been threatened because of German measles or inadvertent X-ray exposure; or there may be financial reverses or unexpected marital dissension that make the pregnancy less desirable. Sometimes the woman may be having an affair and is shamed by her uncertainty about paternity.

Do repeat abortions harm a woman physically? This is another widespread concern. The answer, according to the experts, is no, but there is a "maybe" about one aspect.

Legal abortion is among the safest of all surgical procedures. If it is performed during the first 12 weeks of pregnancy (a period in which over 90 percent of U.S. abortions occur), the woman's risk of dying is no greater than from receiving a penicillin shot at the doctor's office. Bearing a child is 11 times riskier.

Possible damage to reproductive capacity is what frightens most repeaters: "I'm afraid of what may happen later when I want to have a baby." Many doctors believe that abortion may raise the chances of miscarriage, premature birth or delivery complications in a later pregnancy. Of the dozens of studies that have been made here and abroad, some confirm these fears while others refute them. "My advice," says Dr. Willard Cates, Jr., chief of the Abortion Surveillance Branch of the National Center for Disease Control, "is to tell [a patient] that we currently do not know the answer."

Dr. Cates adds a warning: *If* abortion is dangerous for future pregnancy, he and other experts believe that it will become more so with each abortion. And a newly published study indicates that a woman's chance of miscarriage increases two- or threefold after she has had two or more induced abortions —though not, apparently, after a single abortion.

In the early days of legal abortion, it was popularly assumed that the procedure might be devastating emotionally for the patient. Recent studies show, however, that the rate of hospitalization for emotional problems after childbirth is almost six times as high as after abortion.

This does *not* mean that women take the procedure lightly. "These women suffer," says Jeanine Michael, director of counseling for the Eastern Women Center, a large abortion clinic in New York City. "No one can get through it without ambivalent feelings. Once the abortion has taken place, a woman's overwhelming emotion is relief that she is no longer pregnant, but there is distress as well."

Nor do women appear to become emotionally callous when abortion is repeated. If anything, the opposite is true. Carol, 25, was highly distraught when I talked with her just after her third abortion. Typically, the circumstances of each were different: The first abortion resulted from rape when, as a college student, she had too much to drink at a party; the second time, a diaphragm that she had used effectively for four years failed; and the last, after six months without sex, followed a sudden, spontaneous burst of passion involving an old platonic friend.

As she talked with me, Carol wept. "You know you're not promiscuous, but it looks that way. That's the hardest thing for me to get used to." She wept for her parents, to whom she could not talk. They had helped her through the first abortion, although her mother is Catholic. The second time she told her father but not her mother. Now "I can't go to them," she says. "It bothers me what they would think and feel about the third time round." And she wept for herself. "It makes me feel very self-destructive."

Carol wept, too, for a baby that might have been; she wants to have children someday. When the second pregnancy occurred, she was breaking up with a man whom she had loved deeply for four years. "I wanted to bear the child," she says. "I cared about its father. But we were splitting, and it was unrealistic. The feeling still keeps coming back—it could have been our child."

Everyone wants to reduce the number of abortions, particularly repeat abortions. Yet it is unrealistic to believe this goal will be attained quickly. It requires more research for safe, effective contraceptives; fuller explanation of contraception given to girls earlier in their lives—perhaps even before menstruation starts—and to boys as well; and more assumption of responsibility by male partners.

But the essential responsibility still rests with ourselves. When we become more comfortable with our bodies and with ourselves as sexual beings, as we are in the process of doing, we will be able to use contraception with more skill and less guilt. We will find it easier to talk with the man in our life about the shared problem. And we will take better care of our bodies and enhance our respect for woman's unique gift of bearing children.

The husband's rights in abortion

Amitai Etzioni

Amitai Etzioni is professor of sociology at Columbia University and Director of the Center for Policy Research.

When a married woman seeks an abortion, does her husband have any rights regarding the decision?

The Supreme Court ruled on this question on June 30, 1976. The particular case before the Court (*Planned Parenthood v. Danforth)* involved a challenge to a requirement for spousal consent to abortion (under all but life-threatening circumstances) enacted by Missouri in 1974. (Other provisions of the same statute also challenged, such as the requirement for parental consent for unmarried women under 18, do not concern us here.) Eleven other states, including Massachusetts, Florida, and Pennsylvania, had also passed legislation mandating the husband's consent to abortion. In some cases, lower courts had struck down or stayed enforcement of these provisions chiefly on the grounds that they were incompatible with the Supreme Court's 1973 decision holding abortion during the first trimester of pregnancy (and the second trimester as well unless the mother's health is at issue) to be a private matter between a woman and her doctor, in which the state cannot intervene. The federal court that considered Missouri's statute, however, allowed it to stand. Thus, the matter reached the Supreme Court on appeal by Planned Parenthood.

At first consideration one might easily be inclined to dismiss the spousal consent requirement as simply one more attempt on the part of anti-abortion forces to reintroduce the power of the state on the side of curbing abortion. Yet, whatever the role anti-abortion groups have played in sponsoring these provisions, the question of spousal consent involves legitimate new issues that are quite different and readily separable from those issues surrounding the moral-legal status of abortion per se.

WHO MAKES THE DECISION?

The chief question is this: assuming that goverment is to have little say over first and second trimester abortion decisions, who *is* to make them — the pregnant woman alone, or the married couple, when she is married? Do we recognize only two entities — the state and the individual — or is the family also a viable and relevant entity? Does decision-making authority which has been relinquished by government automàtically fall to the individual, or may it, in some instances, be more properly assigned to some other sociological unit? Where government is prohibited a direct role may it nonetheless intervene to the extent of fixing the nongovernmental unit (e.g., either the individual or the family) which is to have the right to make the decisions in question?

When two persons marry, the state interjects itself to the extent of rendering legally binding the voluntary acquiescence by each of some individual "sovereignty" to the union they have now formed. Do the rights surrendered include that of sole decision-making with regard to a fetus?

The Supreme Court, in its landmark ruling on abortion, *Roe v. Wade* (1973), made clear that it was *not* addressing these questions, stating:

> "Neither in this opinion nor in *Doe v. Bolton,* post, do we discuss the father's rights, if any exist in the constitutional context, in the abortion decision . . . We are aware that some statutes recognize the father under certain circumstances . . . We need not decide whether provisions of this kind are constitutional. 410 U.S. at 165, N.67."

In 1976, it seemed, the time for the Court to decide had come.

The questions the justices asked as this recent case was being argued suggest that a side issue may have been very much on their minds: Is the spousal consent provision discriminatory, "sexist?" Justice Marshall, for instance, asked whether there were other Missouri statutes requiring spousal consent for any other medical procedures. According to a report prepared by Judith Mears of the Women's Rights Project of the American Civil Liberties Union, Mr. Danforth, representing Missouri's side of the case, replied that there were not. Similarly, when Danforth argued that spousal consent for abortion is constitutional because an abortion fundamentally changes family relations, Justice Blackmun, according to Mears, inquired whether Missouri required spousal consent for a hysterectomy; again the answer was no. Chief Justice Burger then asked about sterilization — to which the answer was yes.

The Court, of course, is basically limited to "reacting" rather than "legislating" but in principle either of two remedies could be applied to the implied inconsistency: Have *no* spousal consent requirement for *any* such procedures, or apply *one* uniformly to *all* such procedures, including sterilization and vasectomy and abortion. (Whether one ought in fact to consider hysterectomy and even therapeutic abortion as falling into the same category as the more purely elective interventions is a question we shall return to later.)

After all the deliberations were completed the Supreme Court ruled 6 to 3 that the states may not require a woman to get the consent of her husband before she has an abortion.

EFFECT ON THE FAMILY

Although the views expressed seem not to have affected the final decision, both lower court judges and those of the Supreme Court commented on this key question: what is the effect on the marital bond of establishment of the locus for this decision-making author-

Reprinted by permission from TRIAL magazine, November 1976, the Association of Trial Lawyers of America.

ity? Does granting the woman sole rights over the fetus further weaken what many see as our society's already too fragile family ties? The following cases illustrate the views expressed and the issues raised.

In *Jones v. Smith* 278 So. 2d 339 (1973) *cert. den.* 415 U.S. 958 (1974), characterized by the court as a case of first impression on the right of a "potential putative father" to participate in the decision to terminate a pregnancy, a Florida court affirmed a lower court denial of an injunction against the mother's abortion — but in this case the father had never been married to the mother. The court rejected the notion that by consenting to have sex with the man involved without a contraceptive, an implied contract was made to bear a child if conception were to result, or that the mother gave up her right to privacy (the legal mainstay of the 1973 decision upholding a woman's right to choose abortion.)

The Supreme Judicial Court of Massachusetts ruled similarly in the case of an estranged husband, though the grounds were different and came closer to affirming a view of the two members of a marital union as fully sovereign individuals. Stated the court: "We would not order either a husband or a wife to do what is necessary to conceive a child or to prevent conception . . . We think the same considerations prevent us from forbidding the wife to do what is necessary to bring about or prevent birth."

In striking down Florida's spousal consent requirement, a federal court rejected the notion that since the recent judicial trend has been to give greater weight to the rights of fathers in respect to existing children (e.g., in custody cases), this ought also apply to the fetus. And the court clinched its arguments by positing " . . . inescapably that the State may not statutorily delegate to husbands and parents an authority the State does not possess."

But the courts have not entirely disregarded the other, family-oriented side of the sociological coin. The Massachusetts court wrote: "Surely, if the family life is to prosper he [the husband-father] should participate with his wife in the decision." The court was not willing, however, to allow the Commonwealth to "enforce" his "*veto.*" Similarly, a federal court reviewing Florida's spousal consent statute recognized the husband's interest in the fetus but added that his interest was insufficient "to *force* upon the woman the mental and physical dangers of childbirth." [Italics mine.]

Some dissenting judges in these cases referred to the need to protect the family union and the interest of the husband, father-to-be, in the child. Citing child-care literature, Judge Reardon of the Supreme Judicial Court of Massachusetts put it best: "Furthermore, it would be absurd to posit that this interest [between father and child] springs into existence full grown on the day of birth. As in the case of the mother, the gestation is for the father one of anxiety, anticipation, and growth in feeling for the unborn child."

As I see it, there exists a reasonable middle course between forcing a woman to bear a child she does not want on the one hand and utterly disregarding the wishes of the father on the other. The husband's *consent* ought not be required; evidence that he has been notified and consulted, should be. And this should hold not just for the issue at hand but all parallel issues. (In keeping with the notion of family decision-making we would also favor, for example, a requirement that both parents be informed and consulted prior to a child's non-emergency surgery.) Concretely, with respect to abortion this would mean that before the procedure could be performed, a married woman would be expected to file with her physician, hospital, or clinic a form signed by her husband indicating that he had been informed and consulted. The purpose of this form would be, on the one hand, to hinder abortion by a married

Evidence that the husband has been consulted should be required.

woman who has not first informed her husband, while at the same time leaving the ultimate decision to her; so if the husband has had his say and is opposed, but she is not convinced, she can still proceed. (If the couple is separated or the husband not reachable — say he is at war — a statement to this effect would void the requirement to inform and consult.)

In the event that a woman claimed her husband was trying to exercise veto power by refusing to sign the form acknowledging consultation, official means of assuring notification — e.g., a registered letter from the physician or clinic to the husband — would satisfy the notification requirement. The same would hold for sterilization of the wife and, with the husband's and wife's roles reversed, vasectomy. While it would seem at first that hysterectomies and therapeutic abortions might be excluded as they are generally performed for health, rather than birth control, purposes, nonetheless, as these two procedures deeply affect the family, no immediate reason comes to mind why the husband should not be informed or consulted in a nonemergency situation.

Feelings should be aired before irreversible action is taken.

The principal sociological rationale for requiring consultation with the spouse is to encourage an airing of feelings between the couple *before* any irreversible action is taken. Husband and wife may not necessarily end up with the same views, but alienation resulting from one person taking a unilateral and clandestine step will be avoided.

Some family planning advocates would undoubtedly counter my suggestion by calling it a middle class luxury. They would argue that a minority or lower-class woman might not be able to "work this out with her husband" and thus be left with only the options of obeying his wishes or acting surreptitiously. As I see it, firstly, many lower class women are far from the spineless types implied. Second, in those instances where the woman feels thus intimidated, she could still seek an abortion following a temporary separation (e.g., she might stay with her parents) or through some other such circumvention.

Our main point is that the law does not merely regulate our lives, it articulates and symbolizes our values and mores. In an era when the family has been rendered increasingly vulnerable to dissolution, we should not gratuitously add to the stress by enshrining in law the starkly individualistic view that a child in the making, a future shared project of the family, is wholly and completely a "private" matter for the woman to determine, with no concern at all for the wishes of the father — when he is her husband. Concretely, this may mean that when the next occasion arises, the Supreme Court, which really ruled against the husband's right to *veto* his wife's abortion, may yet rule that he has a right to be informed and consulted.

Interpersonal Relationships

3

Most people have used, or are at least familiar with the term "sexual relationship." It denotes an important dimension of sexuality to which this section focuses attention: interpersonal sexuality, that is, sexual interactions that occur between two (and sometimes more) individuals.

No man or woman is an island. Interpersonal contact forms the basis for self-esteem and meaningful living; conversely, isolation generally spells loneliness and depression for most human beings. Friendship is of great importance. Qualities often sought in a friend are warmth, affection, supportiveness, and the ability to keep confidences. These qualities are often secured in an atmosphere of trust and loyalty.

Long-term friendships may develop into intimate relationships. The qualifying word in the previous sentence is "may." Today many people, single as well as married, yearn for close or intimate interpersonal relationships but fail to find them. Fear of rejection causes some to present a "false front" or illusory self that is supposedly acceptable or socially desirable. This sets the stage for a "game of intimacy" that is counterfeit to genuine intimacy. For others a major enigma may exist: the problem of balancing closeness with preservation of individual identity in a manner that at once satisfies the need for personal as well as interpersonal growth and integrity. According to one article presented in this section, the solution calls for in-depth sharing (self-disclosure) and mutual recognition. In so doing we get to know each other as we really are. Such interpersonal awareness is an indispensible foundation for genuine intimacy.

Self-awareness, sharing that awareness with a partner, and accepting a partner's state of awareness are three important bases for achieving meaningful and satisfying sexual relationships. Taken together, they constitute sexual responsibility. Throughout several articles in this section this notion is restated. Without interpersonal awareness, sexual interactions may cause misunderstanding or resentment. For example, many virgins cannot admit that they're not ready or that they have "anxious reservations." This is often especially true for the male who is culturally ascribed the status of "sexual expert." The absence of basic self-honesty and disclosure often paves the way for a traumatic first experience. Also, in long-standing sexual relationships it is not unusual for partners to have different levels of sexual interest and energy at different times. Again it is important to share this awareness with the partner rather than to expect or insist on a perfect synchronization of desire.

As might already be apparent, there is much more to quality sexual relations than our popular culture recognizes. Such relationships are not established on penis size, beautiful figures, or correct techniques. Rather, penetration of interpersonal barriers which may contain anger, resentment, frustration, or anxiety is a positive step in the direction of quality sexual relations. A person-oriented (as opposed to genitally oriented) sexual awareness, coupled with a leisurely, whole body/mind sensuality makes for quality sexual expression.

Looking Ahead: Challenge Questions

What are the most important ingredients to a satisfying sexual relationship?

How does sexism and sexual inequality influence the quality of interpersonal relationships?

Why is communication of such great importance in establishing and maintaining a quality relationship?

Who is responsible for what in interpersonal relationships?

How can sexual spoilers be avoided in intimate relationships?

PT's Survey Report on Friendship in America

THE FRIENDSHIP BOND

More than 40,000 readers told us what they looked for in close friendships, what they expected of friends, what they were willing to give in return, and how satisfied they were with the quality of their friendships. The results give cold comfort to social critics.

MARY BROWN PARLEE AND THE EDITORS OF *PSYCHOLOGY TODAY*

Mary Brown Parlee, a psychologist, is director of the Center for the Study of Women and Sex Roles at the Graduate Center of the City University of New York.

☐ Loyalty, warmth, and the ability to keep confidences are the qualities most valued in a friend; age, income, and occupation are less important.

☐ People who have frequently moved have fewer casual friends than people who have stayed put.

☐ Feeling betrayed by a friend is one of the most important reasons for ending a friendship.

☐ In a crisis, 51 percent of our sample say they would turn first to friends, not family.

☐ Thirty percent of women and 32 percent of men say they had sexual intercourse with a friend in the past month.

☐ Twenty-nine percent say they have a close friendship with someone who is a homosexual.

☐ Thirty-eight percent say they have close friends of a different racial group.

☐ Only 26 percent think career success interferes with friendship opportunities.

☐ Seventy-three percent agree that friendships with the opposite sex are different from those with the same sex.

☐ Thirteen percent would lie for a friend in a divorce proceeding.

Friendship appears to be a unique form of human bonding. Unlike marriage or the ties that bind parents and children, it is not defined or regulated by law. Unlike other social roles that we are expected to play—as citizens, employees, members of professional societies and other organizations—it has its own subjective rationale, which is to enhance feelings of warmth, trust, love, and affection between two people.

Feelings of friendship can develop within other roles, of course, as when coworkers begin to feel and act like friends, but such relationships grow more out of free choice than necessity. Because friendship lies outside—or transcends—the structured roles and institutions of society, it is a topic that allows an exploration of the ways that people relate to others at the times when they are most free.

The questionnaire on friendship that appeared in the March issue of *Psychology Today* presented such an opportunity. As far as we know, the survey is the first large-scale descriptive study of friendship completed in the 1970s; indeed, relatively few studies of friendship were done before then. The response was enthusiastic. We received more than 40,000 questionnaires from readers, one of the largest returns of all *Psychology Today* surveys. With the questionnaire forms, many readers offered comments on friendship, poems, and (at our invitation) descriptions of a single cherished friendship.

The findings—highlighted above—confirm that issues of trust and betrayal are central to friendship. They also suggest that our readers do not look for friends only among those who are most like them, but find many who differ in race, sexual preference, religion, and ethnic background. Arguably the most important conclusion that emerges from the data, however, is not something that we found—but what we did not find.

In books such as Vance Packard's *A Nation of Strangers*, social critics have pointed to the dislocation and isolation that they think grows out of the high mobility rate among Americans and a loss of community supports. Ever since the work of sociologist Émile Durkheim, they have described the impersonality and anomie of life in modern cities, where increasing numbers of people choose to live alone. They have written a good deal about a trend toward self-indulgence and lack of commitment in our society, which could very well lead to tensions in friendships just as it may be contributing to the divorce rate among married couples.

In the questionnaire responses, we looked for signs of dissatisfaction with the quality of people's friendships, but we found few. Do people confide in their friends these days? Do they tend to turn to them in times of emotional crises? Do friends become more important as one gets older? Turned around, all of these questions provide clues as to whether people today find deficits in their friendships. Most of the responses to our survey strongly

FRIENDS IN OUR SURVEY

The number of people answering the *PT* friendship questionnaire was too large for us to analyze every reply. We chose a random subsample by withdrawing every 10th response, in the order received. Here is a breakdown of that sample:

WOMEN 72%
MEN 28%

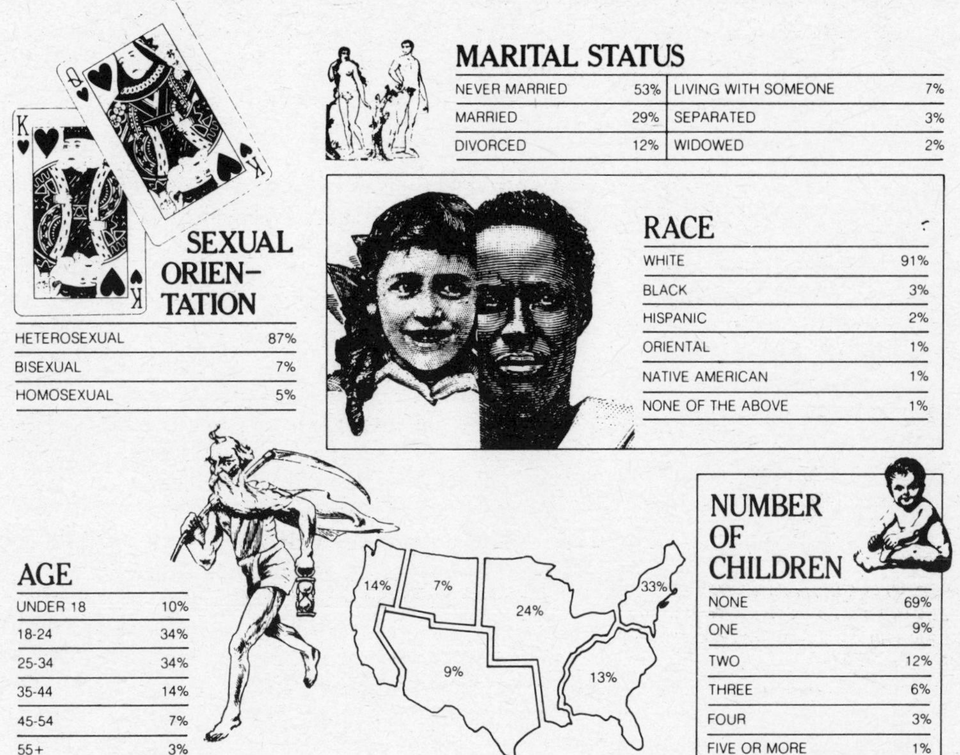

MARITAL STATUS

NEVER MARRIED	53%	LIVING WITH SOMEONE	7%
MARRIED	29%	SEPARATED	3%
DIVORCED	12%	WIDOWED	2%

SEXUAL ORIENTATION

HETEROSEXUAL	87%
BISEXUAL	7%
HOMOSEXUAL	5%

RACE

WHITE	91%
BLACK	3%
HISPANIC	2%
ORIENTAL	1%
NATIVE AMERICAN	1%
NONE OF THE ABOVE	1%

AGE

UNDER 18	10%
18-24	34%
25-34	34%
35-44	14%
45-54	7%
55+	3%

NUMBER OF CHILDREN

NONE	69%
ONE	9%
TWO	12%
THREE	6%
FOUR	3%
FIVE OR MORE	1%

EDUCATION

SOME HIGH SCHOOL	8%
HIGH SCHOOL DIPLOMA OR HIGH SCHOOL-EQUIVALENCY DIPLOMA	14%
SOME COLLEGE	31%
COLLEGE DEGREE	19%
SOME GRADUATE OR PROFESSIONAL SCHOOL	11%
GRADUATE OR PROFESSIONAL DEGREE	18%

OCCUPATION

PROFESSIONAL	31%
STUDENT	25%
CLERICAL WORKER	9%
EXECUTIVE OR MANAGER	8%
HOUSEWIFE	7%
FOREMAN OR SKILLED WORKER	4%
SALESPERSON	4%
SEMISKILLED OR UNSKILLED WORKER	3%
OTHER	9%

POLITICAL VIEWS

	FOR	AGAINST
CAPITAL PUNISHMENT	53%	47%
ABORTION	70%	30%
THE EQUAL RIGHTS AMENDMENT	82%	18%
LEGALIZATION OF MARIJUANA	67%	33%
AFFIRMATIVE-ACTION PROGRAMS FOR MINORITIES AND WOMEN	82%	18%
PROPOSITION 13	59%	41%
NATIONAL HEALTH INSURANCE	72%	28%
GAY RIGHTS	71%	29%

ATTITUDE TOWARD THE WOMEN'S LIBERATION MOVEMENT

VERY POSITIVE	31%
SOMEWHAT POSITIVE	40%
NEITHER POSITIVE NOR NEGATIVE	17%
SOMEWHAT NEGATIVE	10%
VERY NEGATIVE	3%

INCOME

LESS THAN $5,000	14%	$20,000-$29,999	18%
$5,000-$9,999	13%	$30,000-$49,999	15%
$10,000-$14,999	18%	$50,000-$99,999	6%
$15,000-$19,999	16%	$100,000+	1%

(Because the percentages are rounded off, they do not always add up to 100 percent.)

suggest they do not. When asked, for example, whether they felt that many of their friendships are not completely reciprocal, almost 60 percent answered no. At least among our readers and others like them, friendship in America appears to be in sound health.

In general, those who responded to the survey (for a breakdown of the survey sample, see box page 101) are representative of *Psychology Today* readers on every dimension but sex: women made up approximately 70 percent of the survey sample, while the sex ratio of our readers is closer to 50:50. Unfortunately, we cannot tell from survey data alone why proportionately more women responded; it is possible that either women are more likely in general to answer questionnaires, or there is something about the topic of friendship that is of greater interest to women than to men.

The respondents represent a range of educational, occupational, and income levels; they hold fairly liberal views on political issues. The majority (68 percent) are between the ages of 18 and 34, and over half are unmarried and as yet have no children.

The difficulty of capturing the essence of friendship in a survey was of particular concern to several readers. One wrote: "I don't think it can be taken apart, labeled, studied, and stuffed back together." Undoubtedly, there is something inexpressible about the feelings on which friendships are often based.

Art and poetry surely convey some of these feelings much more adequately than does scientific research. What science—and science alone—can do is allow us to find out in a systematic way what people expect from a friend, how they behave with friends, and what they think about friendship.

Qualities of Friends

The diversity among friends is revealed in the letters people wrote describing a close friendship. A partial list of people whom readers described as their best friends includes: a cousin, sister, fiancé, wife, husband, mother, boyfriend, college roommate, 83-year-old godmother, husband's grandmother, "a gay guy," "a person I took a total dislike to at first," and "a reflection of myself."

In the survey, people said they find it easy to distinguish between close and casual friends, and reported they have more close friends than casual ones. The majority of the respondents (68 percent) have between one and five close friends: those with more than 15 casual or work friends form a slightly smaller group, although still a majority (55 percent). Those with larger numbers of close friends than average also have larger numbers of casual friends, and were less likely to say they feel lonely.

A full 92 percent believe friendship is a form of love, and 77 percent say they would tell a friend that they love him or her. (Would the percentage have been that high if we had asked how many had actually received declarations of love from a friend?) Comparing friendship with love, slightly more respondents agree you can form friendships at first sight than say you can fall in love at first sight (52 percent compared with 39 percent), but the majority of the respondents (62 percent) believe that friendships end more gradually than love affairs.

Similarity—at least on the outside—is not what attracts friends to each other and keeps them together. About 38 percent of our sample report having close friends of a different racial group, while about 47 percent have close friends from a different ethnic or religious background. A slight majority of 55 percent say most of their close friends are of the same sex. Overall, the questionnaire responses are consistent with the letters describing actual friends, letters that indicate the ease and frequency with which friendships cut across social categories and boundaries.

Judging by the survey replies, readers believe that possible candidates for friendship are virtually limitless. Almost everyone seems to think it is possible to be friends with one's parents, children, bosses, or employees, someone one is romantically involved with, and (though there is less agreement here) former spouses or lovers. Many readers may know from their own experience that such friendships are not only possible but very satisfying as well.

Other people may think that such friendships ought to be possible, even if they don't know it from their own experience. One of the limitations of all questionnaire data, of course, is that there is no way of knowing whether people's responses reflect their true opinions, or are to some extent influenced by what they believe is socially desirable.

In their letters, readers were divided on the importance of similarity in friendship. Some said they think opposites attract, others said that at least some similarities of experience are important (going through the same life crises, for example). For one reader, the issue of similarity and friendship was a major concern: "My greatest disappointment in seeking friends . . . is that the groups I have been exposed to are made up of carbon-copy people. They don't share [just] one or two common interests, but *all* the same interests. Acceptance into a group depends on similarity in schedules, sports, crafts, home decor, children, religion, etc. I enjoy doing different things with different people . . . . I like to become more involved with a person than the social habits they identify with. I like to know how they feel about a lot of things."

When we asked our readers to tell us what qualities they believe to be important in a friend, they valued, above all, loyalty and the ability to keep confidences. Warmth, affection, and supportiveness were also high on the list, while external characteristics, such as age, income, and occupation, were not (see box page 103). Again, in the letters commenting on friendship in general, similar themes recurred: typical words and phrases were "trust," "honesty," "accepts me even when he doesn't totally approve," "supportive," and "understanding."

When we designed the survey, we decided to compare the qualities people thought important in a friend with their own estimate of how much they had those same qualities. We wanted to see whether people who regard themselves as independent, for example, value independence (or perhaps dependence) in their friends. People's descriptions of themselves, though, were uniformly positive.

For positive qualities, the majority of respondents rated themselves as "two's" on a scale of one (very) to five (not at all). Because of the impressive two-ness of our readership (or perhaps the very human tendency to put one's best foot forward even on an anonymous questionnaire), we could not reach conclusions about the relationship between the respondents' personalities and the qualities they value in their friends.

Some insight into what holds friendships together can be gained from looking at what drives them apart. When asked about reasons for a friendship's cooling off or ending, readers gave as the two most important reasons (aside from "One of us moved") feeling betrayed by a friend, and discovering that a friend had very different views on issues the respondent felt were important (see box page 104). The questionnaire answers thus confirm what many readers said explicitly in their comments: in a satisfying friendship, trust and feeling accepted are two of the most essential components.

Activities of Friendship

Given the importance of trust, it is not surprising that "Had an intimate talk" is the activity most or second-most frequently mentioned by both men and women as something they have done with friends in the past month. Two other items high on the list of activities also presuppose a certain amount of trust and involvement: helping out a friend and turning to a friend for help.

Social psychologists have proposed a link between trust and liking that seems to fit these friendship data. The theory suggests that trust encourages

INGREDIENTS OF FRIENDSHIP

"How important to you is each of these qualities in a friend?"

Numbers represent percentage of respondents who said a quality was "important" or "very important."

Quality	%
KEEPS CONFIDENCES	89%
LOYALTY	88%
WARMTH, AFFECTION	82%
SUPPORTIVENESS	76%
FRANKNESS	75%

Quality	%
SENSE OF HUMOR	74%
WILLINGNESS TO MAKE TIME FOR ME	62%
INDEPENDENCE	61%
GOOD CONVERSATIONALIST	59%
INTELLIGENCE	57%
SOCIAL CONSCIENCE	49%

Quality	%
SHARES LEISURE (NONCULTURAL) INTERESTS	48%
SHARES CULTURAL INTERESTS	30%
SIMILAR EDUCATIONAL BACKGROUND	17%

Quality	%
ABOUT MY AGE	10%
PHYSICAL ATTRACTIVENESS	9%
SIMILAR POLITICAL VIEWS	8%

Quality	%
PROFESSIONAL ACCOMPLISHMENT	8%
ABILITIES AND BACKGROUND DIFFERENT FROM MINE	8%
ABILITY TO HELP ME PROFESSIONALLY	7%
SIMILAR INCOME	4%
SIMILAR OCCUPATION	3%

self-disclosure (revealing aspects of yourself that are both precious and vulnerable). If self-disclosure meets with continued acceptance (not necessarily the same as approval of the feelings or actions), liking and affection deepen—as well as trust. In this theory, self-disclosure and trust must be reciprocated in order for the relationship to deepen.

Two letters from readers illustrate different facets of this trust/self-disclosure/liking cycle. One noted: "The definite and observable switch from a casual to a close friendship came about when my friend told me something about herself she felt I would disapprove of. After leaving the safe ground of constant agreement, our true feelings and thoughts flowed without the normal hesitancy one has with a casual friend or acquaintance." Another reported: "My closest friend asked for advice, which I gave and which turned out to be good. However, the friendship is not the same, because it bothers her that I know about the problem and its resolution. . . . The problem was due to a course of action she took that I can understand and sympathize with but cannot condone. It bothers me that she took that course . . . and the bother always nags at the back of my mind when I think of her or when I see her. [Now] I think less of her."

One might expect that men engage in quite different activities with friends than women do; for example, men might fit the stereotype of drinking buddies. Likewise, women might fit the cliché of indulging in gossip. Judging from our readers' answers, however, sex-role stereotypes are not a good way to predict men's and women's behavior with friends. With the notable exception of "Gone shopping with a friend" (which women say they do more than men), men's and women's reports of what they did with friends in the past month are surprisingly similar—both in actual percentages, and when the activities are ranked by the percentages of men or of women who say they engaged in them (see box, page 105).

For all that, 73 percent agree that friendships with someone of the opposite sex are different from same-sex friendships. A major reason given for the difference is that sexual tensions complicate the relationship; other reasons included having less in common with the opposite sex and the fact that society does not encourage such friendships. Almost half the respondents (49 percent) have had a friendship turn into a sexual relationship, and nearly a third (31 percent) reported having had sexual intercourse with a friend in the past month.

Rules of Friendship

In addition to inquiring about actual activities, we asked some specific questions about what people would or would not do with friends, both in general and in certain hypothetical situations. (For some respondents, of course, the "hypothetical" may actually have occurred.) We wanted our survey to give us an idea of some of the "rules" that govern, or perhaps define, behavior between friends.

As both theory and the data suggest, one rule of friendship is that friends confide in each other, sharing intimate aspects of their personal lives and feelings. Perhaps most significantly, bad as well as good news can be shared. Even though in our society, one's success is often equated with success at work, 89 percent of our sample said they would tell a close friend about a failure at work. Furthermore, over two-thirds (68 percent) said that if they had a terminal illness, they would tell a friend. Eighty-seven percent of the respondents say they talk with friends about sexual activities (60 percent discussing activities in general, 27 percent in detail). Completely inexplicably, respondents from Jewish backgrounds were more likely to talk about sexual activities in detail (35 percent) than were respondents from Catholic or Protestant backgrounds (25 and 26 percent).

According to the rules of friendship, friends confide more than facts about their personal lives. They also share their intimate feelings about each other. For example, 54 percent say they sometimes talk with friends about the quality of the friendship. Another 19 percent say they do so often, compared with 44 percent who reported they have such discussions with spouses and lovers often. It is impossible to tell from these responses whether the difference means that relations with a spouse or lover are more important than relations between friends—or that they are more problematic.

Our respondents clearly indicated that in some situations, the rules of friendship involve the right to ask for help (presumably the obligation to help a friend is also implicitly acknowledged). When asked who they would turn to first in a crisis, over half (51 percent) said they would turn to friends before family. This was true for all subgroups, even though older people in the sample said they tend to rely more on family and professional counselors in a crisis than do the younger age groups, and a higher proportion of men than women said they go it alone.

Yet friendship has limits. Only 10 percent of the sample said they thought a friend should help another commit suicide if the friend wanted to but was too feeble to do it alone (41 percent said no and 36 percent were opposed to suicide).

In short, there are no striking contradictions between people's descriptions of actual friendships, their beliefs about friendship in general, and their perception of the rules that apply to these relationships. This consistency, and the glowing descriptions of friends and friendship we received, suggest that our readers are satisfied with their friendships, even though 67 percent of the respondents also acknowledge feeling lonely "sometimes" or "often" (see box page 106).

Lasting Friendships

Asked how and when they had met most of their close friends, readers reported most frequently that such friendships began in childhood. Next in order of frequency were close friendships that originated in college, and through friends of friends.

Only slightly more than one-fourth of our sample (26 percent) agree that professional success reduces the opportunities for friendship. Life at the top (at least as it is measured by income) seems to promote an even more optimistic view of friendship opportunities: people with incomes of over $100,000 generally disagree more than others that it's lonely at the top.

Friendships do not end because one friend becomes more successful at

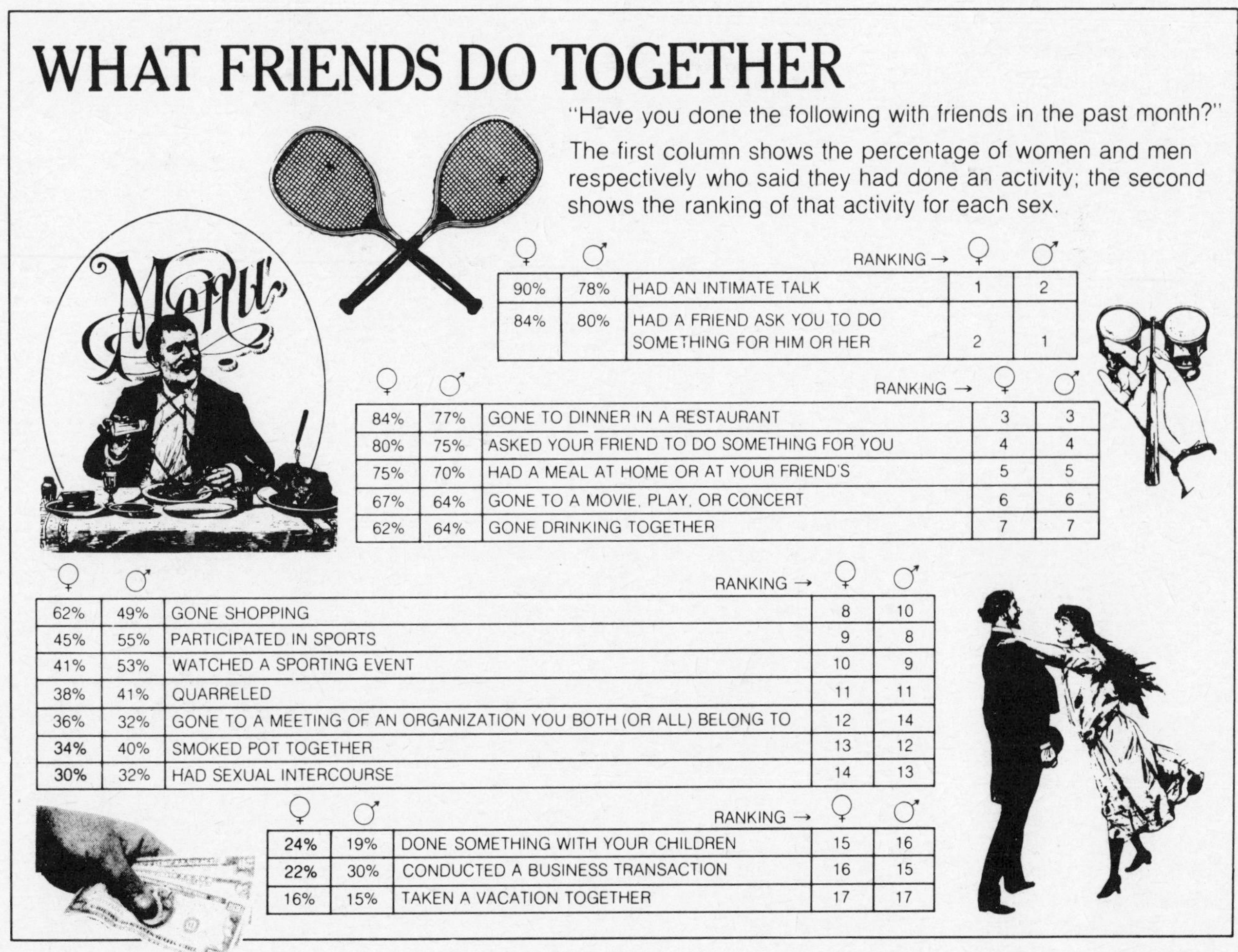

WHAT FRIENDS DO TOGETHER

"Have you done the following with friends in the past month?"

The first column shows the percentage of women and men respectively who said they had done an activity; the second shows the ranking of that activity for each sex.

♀	♂		RANKING → ♀	♂
90%	78%	HAD AN INTIMATE TALK	1	2
84%	80%	HAD A FRIEND ASK YOU TO DO SOMETHING FOR HIM OR HER	2	1
84%	77%	GONE TO DINNER IN A RESTAURANT	3	3
80%	75%	ASKED YOUR FRIEND TO DO SOMETHING FOR YOU	4	4
75%	70%	HAD A MEAL AT HOME OR AT YOUR FRIEND'S	5	5
67%	64%	GONE TO A MOVIE, PLAY, OR CONCERT	6	6
62%	64%	GONE DRINKING TOGETHER	7	7
62%	49%	GONE SHOPPING	8	10
45%	55%	PARTICIPATED IN SPORTS	9	8
41%	53%	WATCHED A SPORTING EVENT	10	9
38%	41%	QUARRELED	11	11
36%	32%	GONE TO A MEETING OF AN ORGANIZATION YOU BOTH (OR ALL) BELONG TO	12	14
34%	40%	SMOKED POT TOGETHER	13	12
30%	32%	HAD SEXUAL INTERCOURSE	14	13
24%	19%	DONE SOMETHING WITH YOUR CHILDREN	15	16
22%	30%	CONDUCTED A BUSINESS TRANSACTION	16	15
16%	15%	TAKEN A VACATION TOGETHER	17	17

work, say 90 percent of the sample. We might speculate that time at work interferes with time for friends ("Willingness to make time for me" is considered an important quality in a friend), but otherwise work and friendship do not seem to conflict. The fact that "Ability to help me professionally" is not believed to be an important quality in a friend suggests that any positive connection between work and friends is not simply a matter of mutual back-scratching.

The stability of childhood friendships seems somewhat surprising, given the geographic mobility of the respondents. Forty-six percent of them have moved two or more times in the past five years, and 48 percent of them moved at least that often before they were 16 years old.

Other data support the suggestion that networks of friends develop from psychological rather than physical closeness, a suggestion that is getting increasing confirmation in the research of sociologist Claude Fischer. Although in TV-land, the neighborhood has traditionally been portrayed as a source of close friends, in real life our readers ranked the neighborhood fifth in importance as a place where friendships start. Fewer than half as many people cite neighborhood than cite childhood as a source.

Close friendships can transcend geographic distance and persist over time with impressive robustness. A full 97 percent of our respondents say they have friends they don't see often. Seventy-two percent of them keep in touch by phone and 33 percent by means of regular reunions once or twice a year. (Many respondents indicated they keep in touch by more than one means, so these percentages do not add up to 100.) Future historians will be pleased to note that the epistolary tradition is far from dead: 70 percent of our sample say they keep in touch with absent friends by letter.

Although people take active steps to stay in touch with their friends, friendship is clearly a relationship that is valued for its special quality rather than frequency or mode of contact. A full third of the sample have friends they don't keep in touch with at all. One unusually optimistic reader put it this way: "When we meet again 100 years from now, we are certain to feel close and be able to pick up where we left off as though no separation had occurred."

The majority of our respondents (82 percent) report that their oldest close friendship is one they've had for more than six years, with a hefty 22 percent reporting close friendships of longer

WHO FEELS LONELY

Percentage of respondents who said they feel lonely "sometimes" or "often."

WOMEN 67%
MEN 67%

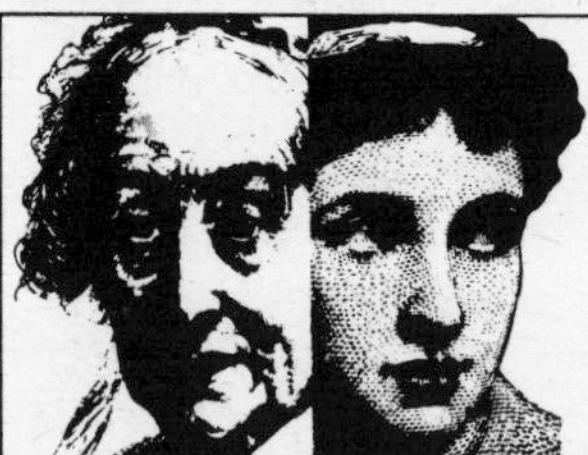

AGE

UNDER 18	79%	35-44	60%
18-24	71%	45-54	53%
25-34	69%	55+	37%

SEXUAL ORIENTATION

HETEROSEXUAL	66%
BISEXUAL	73%
HOMOSEXUAL	72%

INCOME

LESS THAN $5,000	70%	$20,000-$29,999	60%
$5,000-$9,999	73%	$30,000-$49,999	57%
$10,000-$14,999	74%	$50,000-$99,999	54%
$15,000-$19,999	69%	$100,000+	55%

MARITAL STATUS

NEVER MARRIED	72%	LIVING WITH SOMEONE	62%
SEPARATED	70%	WIDOWED	59%
DIVORCED	68%	MARRIED	56%

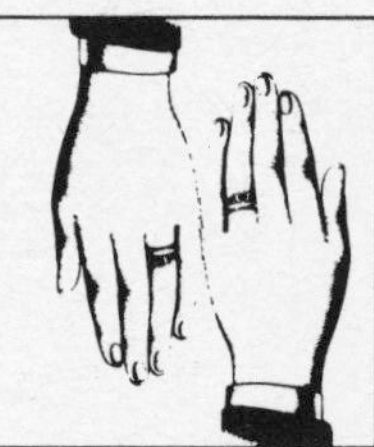

OCCUPATION

SEMISKILLED OR UNSKILLED WORKER	80%
STUDENT	69%
CLERICAL WORKER	69%
SALESPERSON	67%
HOUSEWIFE	65%
PROFESSIONAL	64%
FOREMAN OR SKILLED WORKER	62%
EXECUTIVE OR MANAGER	61%
OTHER	70%

than 20 years. About 66 percent of our sample say that friendship has become more important to them as they grow older, but this sentiment is less common among people with incomes over $100,000 and among those with high educational levels.

Cutting Across Cultures

The picture of friendship that emerges from our survey is surprisingly consistent, holding true almost regardless of the respondents' sex, race, or geographic location. A very different finding might have been predicted. Sociologists and historians, not to mention common sense and everyday observation, tell us that the experiences a person has are in many ways determined by that person's sex, race, religion, and the region of the country where he or she lives. Such differences could very well lead to differences in the way people think about all of the important aspects of living, including friendship.

In our survey, however, friendship—what it is like, the rules governing behavior among friends, and beliefs about it—seems to be a common denominator of experience that cuts across major social categories. This consistency could, of course, mean that we simply didn't ask the "right" questions—assuming there are questions that would have been answered differently by different groups. We think, however, that the questions were varied enough so that major differences would have been found if they exist. Although psychologists are generally reluctant to conclude that no differences exist (since real ones may not have been tapped by the questions), readers' responses to our survey do suggest that in many ways, friendship is not only a deeply satisfying experience, but a universal one as well.

For further information, read:

Brain, Robert. *Friends and Lovers*, Basic Books, 1976, $10.95.

Brenton, Myron. *Friendship*, Stein & Day, 1974, $6.95; paper, $2.45.

Fischer, Claude, et al. *Networks and Places: Social Relations in the Urban Setting*, The Free Press, 1977, $14.95.

Kahn, Robert L. and Toni Antonucci. "Convoys Over the Life Course: Attachment, Roles and Social Support," Institute for Social Research, University of Michigan, Ann Arbor, Mich.

Intimacy Is Not for Amateurs

A lasting relationship requires in-depth sharing that can be risky and painful — the frivolous or faint-hearted need not apply.

James J. Neutens

James Neutens is a health science fellowship professor at Western Illinois University and author of the forthcoming book Sexuality, Illness, and the Health Care Professional.

Today, we find many lonely men and women yearning eagerly for a close interpersonal relationship—an authentic relationship that will fill the emptiness in their lives. Many prowl the bars night after night; others attend social functions; while others haunt the ski slopes or fly to Europe via charter. Each searches relentlessly for love and intimacy. For most, these are exercises in futility as they return to their homes alone and hollowhearted.

Concomitantly, there are those whose lives are devoted to one special person with whom they eat, sleep and live. Yet, many of them, too, have a frustrated craving for authentic intimacy. For some this inner isolation becomes too great a burden and not knowing how to alleviate the encumbrance they seek separation or divorce. When you ask them to explain their frustration, they are very likely to say, "I'm not sure, we've just grown apart," or "I feel smothered and trapped," or "He doesn't meet my new needs, I'm unfulfilled," or "We have explored each other to the 'nth' degree and the mystery is gone."

For both these groups a major enigma exists: how to obtain love and make it grow without generating possessiveness or remoteness. In an attempt to resolve this mystery most have resorted to seductive tricks, games, tactics and manipulations. This is not surprising since deception, deceit and threats are as American as apple pie and motherhood.[1] That is, these skills are learned from parents, friends and teachers who never lived, practiced or fostered enlargement of self-respect, respect for others, or growing competence in the skills that make life and love livable. They are amateurs practicing intimacy; they are attempting to practice an art without mastering the essentials.

Prior to learning the essentials of intimacy, it is best to come to grips with the term itself. This is a difficult task since intimacy is actually a by-product obtained only after gradual progression into deep self-disclosure. In other words, authentic intimacy is an intense personal relationship developed when you share the "real" you with someone else. There are no shortcuts; it can be achieved only as continuous dialogue through life. A dialogue that engenders life and growth as the conversation unfolds.

In the amateur approach toward intimacy, many men and women fall into the trap of physical stimuli solely. Erroneously, they base their relationship on coital expression only to find it wane when the magnetism of their bodies loses much of its force. For a while they may struggle to revive the intense feelings that once existed, but, unfortunately, find they have been replaced by stale and unrewarding routine. They fail to realize that sexual intimacy, the simplest and lowest form, when not related to other types of intimacy is like a diploma without an education.

Other young people respond to love by establishing cognitive intimacy—one in which each explores the other's thoughts and motives, but only in a positive vein. Herein a couple may talk freely with great breadth but with very little depth. They are loquacious but only in nonintimate areas. Subsequently, they project an idealized image of each other by inflating strengths and concealing weaknesses. Neither partner presents the reality of his own self, nor explores the reality of his partner.

The facade commences when the courter acts in ways that he thinks are attracting to others. His objective is to create a smoothness, to capture by

"Intimacy is Not for Amateurs," by James J. Neutens, *Sexology Today,* June 1980. From CONTEMPORARY ISSUES IN HUMAN SEXUALITY

pleasing. Once he has begun this self-assigned role, he dares not leave it for dreaded fear that he will lose his partner's love. He dare not be real, for being real in this love system is to be endangered.

Similarly, his partner is laboring under the same misconception: that there is a "right" way to act to ensure peace and happiness. As a result, each plays into the hands of the other only to be deceived and manipulated. It is readily apparent that each wanted to be seen in a certain way. Concomitantly, each wanted his or her partner to be seen in a certain way. More often than not, in an attempt to please, partners oblige one another by acting just that way. In essence, they act the way they think their partner thinks he or she wants them to act. That is, each tries to become the kind of person he thinks his partner would like.

If, for example, a man believes that women are sexually naive, he is not surprised to discover his partner acting in a sexually naive manner. Infrequently, he may attempt to enlighten her and alter her outlook, but persuaded as he is that her naivete is characteristic of the female sex, he soon abandons the task. Once again a woman—this time his girlfriend, or, if married, his wife—substantiates his assumptions about females and sexuality.

Of course, he may be correct about his girlfriend or wife. However, her apparent naivete about sexual matters may have a different explanation altogether. Perhaps she is reacting to cues that her partner is giving unknowingly, cues that he does not expect her to be knowledgeable and in fact might feel uncomfortable if she did display sexual knowledge and interest. Subsequently, she assumes a role that she believes her partner will like so that he will be pleased and their relationship strengthened.

It is precisely here that trouble begins. Roles, by their very nature, are rigid and confining. All too often our masked actions fail to correspond to our real feelings. Rather than being expressed, they are smothered to conform to the wishes of those close to us or to meet societal expectations. The results are two-fold. First, we base our relationship on an idealized, lethal image which in the long run serves to divide, not unite. Second, we are establishing cognitive dissonance and eventual self-alienation and isolation. In marital therapy, the author has seen numerous individuals who have lost themselves in order to maintain the marriage.

For example, Sue D. sacrificed herself to her marriage to make it workable. She assumed the role that she believed her husband desired and played it well for many years. The role was non-lifegiving in that it did not engender life and growth. She began to identify solely with her role rather than her real self, eventually losing her real self to the created image. In the eyes of her husband and her friends, she was a "good" wife—a Stepford wife. However, beneath this graven image existed a woman in turmoil with feelings of loneliness and isolation. Her anxiety and frustration were exemplified through that familiar knot in the stomach felt by so many of us when we compromise our real selves.

The longer she was manipulated and the more she deceived, the greater was the withdrawal of her real self. She began to develop self-images of being cold, unfeeling and incapable of mature love. Like most self-assumptions, they risk being turned into a self-fulfilling prophecy: what a person assumes to be true, she unknowingly proves to herself to be true. Consequently, she did become cold, unfeeling and incapable of mature love, especially in the marital bed. Her sexual aversion brought her and her husband to therapy. Through counseling and training in dialogue the couple realized the falsity of their current relationship and through self-disclosure they helped each other grow in the directions which they agreed they needed to grow to achieve intimacy.

As noted previously, another negative aspect of cognitive intimacy is when a couple project and idealize an image of a good relationship—one that fails to engender the divine discontent which leads to questing and authentic intimacy. According to psychologists George Bach and Ronald Deutsch[2] the ideal relationship might be expressed by the formula: "one plus one equals one." The couple sees one another receding into one heart, one flesh, united forever and known as "We." In this model as the individuals disappear, each partner becomes cautious and self-conscious, afraid to be assertive for fear of what the other will think. Any meaningful dialogue degenerates to "We" conversations. For example, Julie asks Nick about a test yourself quiz she found in a magazine.[3]

Julie: Do we like to use four-letter words during sex?

Nick: (Looks up warily, uncertain about what to say.) Well, we have used them sometimes, I guess. I mean, what kind of four-letter words?

Julie: Well, I suppose words like—(she becomes uneasy and watches him.)
Like for—doing things, and body parts, I guess. I don't know. Do you think we like to?

Nick: (He does sometimes like to be blunt. But he is being asked what "we" like, so he maneuvers to please.) You've used them sometimes, haven't you?

Julie: Yes. But I think only after you do.

Nick: Hmm.

Even though both Julie and Nick may like to use explicit words during sex, this conversation has

Sex: The 3 Levels of Intimacy

NORMAN M. LOBSENZ

It's not unusual for partners to have different stages of sexual interest and energy at different times. The trick is to recognize the differences and not to allow fear of rejection to destroy an otherwise loving relationship.

"My husband and I were married four months ago. Most of the time when he wants to make love I'm very responsive. But occasionally there are times when I'm just not interested in sex as much as he is. I'm certainly not bored by his lovemaking, which leaves me wondering if there is something wrong with me?"

Marriage counselors frequently hear questions like this. "Young couples, especially," one therapist says, "seem to feel that they should be equally interested in sex at the same time, and that if they aren't it's a sign of trouble. What they don't realize is that every marriage encompasses several different levels of intimacy — and that each level has its own special rewards.

LEVEL ONE

Many couples expect (particularly in the early stages of their relationship) that sex will invariably be a peak experience — that both partners will desire it at the same time and with the same degree of ardor, and that their lovemaking will be intensely satisfying for both of them. Happily, it often is just that. Let us call this Level One of emotional and sexual intimacy. When a couple achieves this level it is a remarkably rewarding feeling.

But, counselors caution, it is hardly realistic for a couple to expect that they can reach this level of intimacy every time. The odds against two people responding simultaneously with the same degree of interest and arousal are so high that Level One sex is bound to occur far less often than we hope.

The threat to intimacy, however, is that a young wife and husband may believe that anything less than Level One is symptomatic of some lack in their sexual relationship. But what about those times when one partner is quite aroused and the other is only mildly interested? Or when the time, the place, or other circumstances are not conducive to "perfect" lovemaking, and it does not look as if the "right" moment is likely to occur soon?

LEVEL TWO

It is still possible to have a wholly satisfying sexual experience at what may be called Level Two of intimacy. As one woman put it: "My husband has a far stronger sexual drive than I do, and I'm not always able to respond to him as passionately as I would like. Sometimes I simply let myself go along quietly and gently with his desires — and sometimes I find that following his lead that way makes me more aroused than I thought I could be."

It's not unusual for partners to have different stages of sexual interest and energy at different times. There can be many reasons for the fluctuation: work stresses, financial worries, physical problems, distracting anxieties. The solution lies in finding a compromise based on what each partner says he or she would find sexually satisfactory. One such compromise is a Level Two response. It might be labeled the "I'm not all that eager but, why not?" category of sexual intimacy.

This may not be the ideal attitude one would wish for from a partner, but neither is it a rejection. Yet, in many instances, when one person reacts at Level Two, the other feels turned off. "He or she takes the attitude," one therapist points out, "that 'if you can't be as emotionally or physically involved as I am, forget it!'" But if Level Two opportunities are passed over because of their less-than-enthusiastic beginnings, many rewarding intimate moments may be lost.

LEVEL THREE

There is still another level of sexual intimacy: Level Three. At the outset, a partner who is not at all interested in lovemaking may not wish to respond at all to the other's advances. But rather than refusing sex entirely, the reluctant partner—sensing her husband's need or his wife's desire—will accommodate the other person. The unspoken (or sometimes declared) reaction is: "I don't feel like it, but I will if you really want to."

All too frequently the well-meaning offer is rejected—turned down not so much out of consideration as out of anger: "Don't do me any favors!" Yet a Level Three response is actually a special gift of love. One reason for our failure to recognize it as such may be due to the way the gift is offered. If it is put forward in a hostile way, or with overtones of self-sacrifice, or the suggestion of long-suffering submission, then it makes sex seem like a chore, a duty, or (perhaps the worst!) an act of charity. But for husbands and wives who can express their feelings tactfully, who can willingly give and freely accept this loving gesture, Level Three can be another opportunity for a special intimacy.

"Sex: The 3 Levels of Intimacy," by Norman M. Lobsenz, *Modern Bride*, August/September 1980. Copyright ©Norman M. Lobsenz.

Some newlyweds, unaware of the intimate potential in these different levels, are often confused or hurt by what they see as disinterest or outright rejection. "When I want to make love and my wife says she isn't very interested," one man complained to a counselor, "she doesn't think she owes me any explanation. But I say that it is only fair for her to give me a reason." The counselor asked the man to imagine that the situation was reversed, and that his wife wanted sex and he didn't: "Would you think you had the right to say no without giving a reason?" This question often strikes men as strange, since even in these liberated times they are more often than not the sexual aggressor. But is is not the initiator of sex who controls the decision, rather it is the partner who is in the position of being able to accept or to decline.

Most therapists agree that every person has a basic right to decline sexual intimacy without having to give reasons for doing so. "Anything else," says one expert, "verges on sexual exploitation." But because a flat "No" can be a terrible weapon of hostility or anger, it's wise for young couples to establish some ground rules. For example, husband and wife can mutually agree that when one or the other is not interested in sex, each has the right to decline lovingly, and the other person promises to honor that response without feeling hurt. (If this happens frequently, a couple may agree to seek professional help to discover if their avoidance of intimacy is masking deeper conflicts.) Another alternative is for a couple to agree to share — as equally as possible — in initiating sex, so that no one partner has the responsibility of saying "yes" or "no" all the time. Incidentally, it is easier to accept an occasional "no" if you know that a partner is likely to suggest making love at some other time.

The fact is that sexual responsiveness covers a broad spectrum of feelings, attitudes and actions. It is important for young couples to realize that each one can, in his or her own special way, contribute to a fulfilling intimacy. Anyone who insists on the perfect time, the ideal circumstances, or the synchronized meshing of desire is placing unnecessarily destructive conditions on the search for intimacy. If a couple is locked into the idea that nothing but a Level One response is worthwhile, they are depriving themselves of a considerable range of mutually gratifying sexual experiences.

"Researchers have learned," says the noted sex researcher Dr. Wardell Pomeroy, "that the most significant fact about human sexual activity is its almost infinite variety. . . . To force ourselves into a given mode of intimacy because we think we should is to abuse our sexuality, not to enhance it. All we have to do is to give sex a chance to fit naturally into our lives, experiencing it . . . in as many ways as give pleasure without creating a burden or fear or guilt."

The Games Teen-Agers Play

Mary, a 15-year-old sophomore from Newton, Mass., recalls how she was swept up into the brave, sometimes bewildering, new world of adolescent hedonism. "I wasn't able to handle the pressure," she says. "I was part of a group in junior high that was into partying, hanging out and drinking. I started to have sex with my boyfriend and it was a real downer. It was totally against what I was, but it was important to be part of a group. Everybody was having sex."

Something has happened to those endearing young charmers who used to wobble around playing grownup in Mom's high heels. They are reaching puberty earlier, finding new freedom from parental restraints, taking cues from a pleasure-bent culture and playing precocious sex games in the bedroom—often while Mom and Dad are at work. The sexual revolution, spawned as a social protest on college campuses of the '60s, has filtered down to high schools and junior high schools.

For adolescent boys, sex has always been regarded as a rite of passage, like getting permission to drive the family car. In the past decade it appears to have become a ceremonial of young womanhood as well. While statistics on teen-age dating habits are still sketchy, they suggest that sexual adventurism among young girls has risen to an astonishing degree. The latest figures in a highly respected new study by Johns Hopkins University professors Melvin Zelnik and John F. Kantner indicate that nearly 50 per cent of the nation's 10.3 million young women age 15 to 19 have had premarital sex. The percentage has nearly doubled since Zelnik and Kantner began their surveys in 1971. "Things that supported remaining a virgin in the past—the fear of getting pregnant, being labeled the 'town pump,' or whatever—have disappeared," observes Zelnik.

And teen-agers themselves report that the age of initiation is dropping. "I'd say half the girls in my graduating class are virgins," says 18-year-old Sharon Bernard, a high-school senior in New Iberia, La. "But you wouldn't believe those freshmen and sophomores. By the time they graduate there aren't going to be any virgins left."

One disturbing consequence of this advanced sexuality is that teen-age pregnancies are epidemic: 1 million teen-age girls—one out of every ten—get pregnant each year. Statistics in a 1977 study show that 600,000 unwed teen-agers were giving birth each year, with the sharpest increase among those under 14. Venereal disease is rampant among adolescents, accounting for 25 per cent of the 1 million reported gonorrhea cases every year.

For all their carnal knowledge, in fact, teen-agers are surprisingly ignorant about the hazards of freebooting sex. Many girls find it less troubling to get into bed with a boy than to prepare for the act with a contraceptive. "If you come prepared, it appears that you're easy and available," observes Dr. Jackie Boles, a Georgia State University sociologist. An estimated 80 per cent of the country's 5 million sexually active teen-agers fail to use birth control because of unwillingness, ignorance or the unavailability of contraceptive devices. Meanwhile, sex-education programs (page 115) remain controversial and inadequate. "Fewer than 10 per cent of all teen-agers are exposed to any valid sex education in the schools," says Syracuse University professor Sol Gordon, whose book, "You Would If You Loved Me," advises teenage girls on how to say no. "Most plans for sex education are pathetic."

Though parents, educators and sociologists may be aghast at the reckless sybaritism of the young, some see it in retrospect as fallout from the decade's great social upheavals: women's liberation, the exploding divorce rate, the decline of parental and institutional authority, the widespread acceptance of "living together"—and the swift media reflection of those trends. The sexual revolution, they note, has also provided an unwitting new role model for teens. "There are a lot of divorced and single parents who are dating," says Judith Gorbach, director of family planning for Massachusetts' Department of Public Health. "The message everywhere is sex."

Guideposts: The media have been quick to relay that message. Sexual precocity is being packaged and promoted—and taken as the norm—throughout the popular culture. The Jordache jean company, for example, hypes its contour-explicit pants by picturing scantily clad teen-agers astride each other in such proper media as The New York Times Magazine. In teen music, such back-to-basics disco tunes as "Take Your Time (Do It Right)" and "Do That to Me One More Time" climb high on the charts. Provocative films like "Foxes," about four Los Angeles teen-agers blundering through a sexual initiation, and "Little Darlings," about two 15-year-old girls competing to lose their virginity at summer camp, pack movie theaters with agog adults and kids. TV has been no less exploitive of the trend. According to one group of Boston teen-agers, the only place where being "hard to get" is really admired these days is on "Laverne & Shirley."

In the absence of moral guideposts, teen-agers have developed their own rules of the love game. They no longer frown on their peers if they're sexually active, though they disapprove of promiscuity. They assert it is important that there be mutual "caring" between young sex partners and preferable that they are going "steady." "It's fine as long as you don't abuse it," says Lynn Vecchio, a 15-year-old Mineola, N.Y., sophomore. "It's not something you do with anyone just for the hell of it."

But beneath the worldly veneer there are adolescent doubts and conflicts. Many teen-agers are having sex as much because it is available and fashionable as because it is desirable. Once chastity was something to be guarded—or lied about when lost. Now an uncommonly virtuous teen-ager lies to protect the dirty little secret that she is still a virgin. There is more pressure than ever for a girl to "get it over with," as one teen-ager puts it. But for every girl who can carry it off with instinctual ease, there are many who cannot. For them the experience may turn out to be "a real downer"—something less than the lyrical, erotic awakening they had been led to expect by such soft-core film fantasies as "The Blue Lagoon," the story of two teen-agers on a desert island who gradually awaken to the joys of adolescent sex. And few can handle the emotional complications of the morning after. "I never expected the guy to marry me, but I never expected he would avoid me in school," says 14-year-old Susan of San Francisco, who lost her virginity—and her boyfriend—a few months ago and wound up in a deep depression.

Some experts worry about the potentially damaging effects of such sexual disillusionments—especially at tender ages when defense mechanisms are still fragile. "Sex before 16 or 17 is counterproductive emotionally," says Claudette Kunkes, a clinical psychologist at The Door, an adolescent treatment center in New York. "Younger kids haven't developed the ego functions which are crucial in making their own choices about sex. The younger girls I've interviewed never really enjoyed it."

Sex Ed 101 for Kids—and Parents

It was the sort of steamy dialogue whispered in the back seat of a car, but the two teen-agers spoke openly before 30 classmates. "Billy, I'm pregnant," she said. "Are you sure it's me?" he blurted. "How could you say that?" she replied, hurt that he would question her fidelity. "I'm sorry," he quickly apologized.

That bit of role playing is part of an innovative yearlong course in sex education in suburban Washington, D.C. Considered one of the nation's best, the program has been a beacon of enlightenment in a country where, until recently, most sex-education classes could not even discuss such subjects as abortion, contraception, masturbation and homosexuality—what educators have dubbed the "Big Four." "Our culture is sex-saturated and sex-silent," says Mary Lee Tatum, teacher of the Falls Church, Va., course. "It puts kids under tremendous pressure."

Roughly twenty years after the sexual revolution, American educators are still uncertain about how, what or even whether they should teach teen-agers about sex. According to one estimate, only 10 per cent of U.S. teens have ever adequately studied the subject. The majority take courses of ten hours or less. Most educators acknowledge that sex education should be taught at home, but the unhappy fact is that most families fail to give children the barest facts of life. A recent study of 1,400 parents of adolescent girls in Cleveland, for example, found that 60 per cent of the mothers had never explained menstruation and 92 per cent never discussed sex. The topic is so highly charged and the taboos so deep that sex education is still seen as too controversial for many school districts even to consider teaching. "We're at the stage now where Darwinism was before the Scopes trial," says Judith Gorbach, director of family planning for Massachusetts.

Too Late: The irony is that, when questioned, both parents and children say they would like better sex instruction. According to a 1978 Gallup poll, 77 per cent of adults and 84 per cent of teen-agers favored such classes. Given that demand and the alarming rise of teen pregnancy and abortion, there are some signs of change. Until last year only the state of Maryland required that sex education be taught in public schools; now New Jersey, Kentucky and Washington, D.C., mandate such courses and several other states are considering doing so. But what most schools teach is too little too late. And anything beyond basic anatomy runs into opposition—usually from small but vocal parent groups and conservative school boards. "It's safe to teach the mechanics of reproduction but threatening to talk about values and responsibilities," says sociologist Frank F. Furstenberg Jr. of the University of Pennsylvania.

Without state or Federal guidelines, sex-education courses vary widely. But for the most part, instruction is limited to brief sessions on menstruation and puberty in the sixth grade (girls and boys separated), and high-school electives that sketch the reproductive system and the perils of venereal disease. In many schools, any mention of morality or emotion is forbidden. Rick Hawkins, a health-education teacher at Waltham (Mass.) High School, asks his students to carry around an egg for one week without letting it out of sight, as an object lesson in parenthood. But when he showed his students a chart depicting displays of affection ranging from a handshake to intercourse, he was reprimanded. "Our course stops just where it ought to begin," complains Hawkins.

Rap Sessions: Many teens, pressured by friends and unsure how to decide how far they really want to go, are simply looking for straightforward answers. "They taught me about all the body parts," said one disgusted Seattle boy. "I *knew* all the body parts; I grew up with four girls. But what is sex?" In response, some progressive programs are including discussions of ethics and responsibility. Groton School in Groton, Mass., offers off-the-record rap sessions beginning in eighth grade; kids meet weekly with faculty to discuss sexuality, exploitation, morality and love as well as the facts of sex.

The most advanced programs start long before puberty; in Palatine, a Chicago suburb, first graders learn plant reproduction; by sixth grade, pupils have studied animal and human reproduction, anatomy, puberty and body changes. Several high schools in St. Paul, Minn., even opened on-site clinics for instruction in health and birth control; the pregnancy rate has decreased 40 per cent in three years.

But the new courses worry and anger many parents. Some fear that talking about sex will encourage experimentation while others doubt that schoolteachers can handle such a complicated subject ("They have enough trouble teaching reading and math," sniffs a New Jersey mother). Still others object to what they perceive as an intrusion on the family role or a threat to religious beliefs. "These aren't neutral subjects," says Mary K. Smith, head of New Jersey's Coalition of Concerned Parents, which lobbied against required sex education. "I feel the state is stepping on my toes as a parent and placing a wedge between my child and myself." For example, if one of her nine children should ask about homosexuality, Mrs. Smith says she would reply, "We go along with the Bible: the homosexual act is sinful." In contrast, she notes, teachers might call it "a variant life-style."

Some parent groups have successfully fought attempts to liberalize courses. California recently scrapped a new sex-ed teachers' guide after parents complained; among other things, the guide proposed a preschoolers' tour of restrooms to teach 3-year-olds about physical differences. In New Jersey, parental and political objections forced the school board to rescind curricular recommendations and to raise the age for mandatory sex education from kindergarten to sixth grade.

Change: There are growing indications that many parents know they need help, and increasingly, communities are involving them in the curriculum. In Falls Church, Va., teacher Tatum spent a year conferring with the PTA, local clergy, doctors and students about her family-life course. An advisory committee still meets annually to review the program, and its success has finally inspired change in surrounding Fairfax County. After a poll last spring showed that 88 per cent of the parents who responded wanted the "Big Four" discussed, the school board decided to revamp its lesson plans for the fall. "This subject cannot be mandated from the top," says Tatum. "You're dealing with other people's kids, and you have to listen to what parents have to say."

A handful of schools are even taking the next logical step and teaching parents. The Roman Catholic schools of St. Paul and Minneapolis, for instance, now put adults through each session of their sex-education course before their ninth-graders take it; the kids are assigned to grill their folks as part of their homework. "Perhaps we will raise a generation of parents who will be comfortable talking about sex with their children," says New Jersey pediatrician Robert Bierman. "Then sex education in schools will no longer be necessary." And that, he suggests, is truly a consummation devoutly to be wished.

LYNN LANGWAY with MARY LORD in Washington, SUSAN AGREST in New Jersey and LISA WHITMAN in New York

'Bunnies': In spite of the pubescent emancipation, clearly not all teen-agers are tumbling into the nearest bed or back seat with one another. And many independent-minded adolescents insist the current licentious atmosphere is not stampeding them into sin. "I have the feeling that adults think we're out there screwing like bunnies," says 15-year-old Richard of Berkeley, Calif. "That's simply not the case. It's not something you have to get out of the way because it's on the developmental agenda. It's a choice, and some kids choose to have sex a lot, some have sex infrequently and others don't have sex at all."

Yet if the drift toward sexual precocity continues, the virginal adolescent will soon be an anachronism. Among teen-age girls, part of the explanation for the trend is biological. In the past century, the age of menarche, or first menstruation, has dropped from about 17 years to 12.5. (For boys, puberty usually begins at 13.) Young people's sexual awareness thus runs breathlessly ahead of their emotional development—particularly now that the period of adolescent dependency has grown longer.

At the same time, the vast increase of working mothers has provided a convenient sexual setting: according to some researchers, the empty house after school has become the favorite trysting spot. "Parents used to worry when their kids stayed out late at night," notes Ruth MacDonald, who designed a sex-education curriculum in Newton, Mass. "Well—surprise—it's happening in the afternoon." (MacDonald's research suggests love in the afternoon is nevertheless a furtive affair; fearful of discovery, most of the couples keep some of their clothes on.)

'Motto': Beyond biology and demography, experts believe any explanation of teen sex must take into account the emergence, beginning in the late '60s, of adolescence as a world unto itself—a generational realm bounded by its own music, its own recreational drugs and, as it turned out, its own illicit parlor games. The prevailing ethos of this new subculture has been summed up as "no waiting," an ardent belief that any pleasures available to adults should be—in fact, are—available to the young. "Adolescents notoriously have difficulty in deferring instant gratification," says University of Maryland pediatrician Murray Kappelman. "In the '60s, when the whole authority picture changed, this was extended to the area of sexuality. It was 'Everything for us right away,' which became an adolescent societal motto."

Childhood-development authorities also note the paradox that while adolescents are traditionally rebellious, within their own circles they tend to be fiercely conformist. Perhaps at no other stage of life is the behavior of one's peers so strong an influence. Experts believe that among teen-agers peer pressure is one of the most important reasons for taking the sexual plunge. Some girls manage to resist going over the brink. "A guy will say, 'Everybody's doing it, what's the matter with you?' " reports Dana, a 16-year-old San Francisco high-school junior. "You just tell him, 'Well, if everybody's doing it, find someone else to do it with.' " But not every girl will risk a flippant reply. "Think of a girl at 14 facing the pressures of rejecting her boyfriend," sighs Virginia Ghattas, a Newton, Mass., biology teacher, who says her younger students face sexual decisions today that older generations never had to contend with. And one 14-year-old at suburban Atlanta's Roswell High School has little doubt about the outcome. "All they think about is that they really want this guy to like them," she says, "and so they're going to do it."

Swagger: Girls may find themselves caught in the classic double bind imposed by male chauvinism—scorned if they don't and damned if they do. "If you say no, you're a tease and if you say yes, you're a slut," complains a 17-year-old Atlantan. Yet in many instances, girls themselves are putting the heat on. Taking a misread leaf from women's lib, they are becoming sexually aggressive and strutting a kind of locker-room swagger about their conquests. In her set, notes 17-year-old Victoria Sanchez, "Bragging is rampant; they'll brag about which jock laid them where. It's as if now that we can be equal, we're going to be equally tacky." Debbie, a 14-year-old Berkeley, Calif., freshman, recalls a sexually accomplished girlfriend whom she idolized until "she began telling me I better get my butt moving or I'd be missing out on the best thing in life. It got on my nerves. I wasn't ready."

Boys are feeling harassed, not only by the newly demanding girls but by their own macho-posturing peers—and even, at times, by their parents. "A lot of people are scared of sex and pressured by the people that are into it, so they pressure themselves," says 15-year-old Andrew Ellenberg of Hollywood, Calif. "They say, 'What's the matter with me?' And there's pressure from the parents in an abstract way. They have a way of saying, 'Don't do anything I wouldn't do,' and you think, 'What do they *expect* me to do?' "

The Pill: Sex educators say young men of the women's-lib era are, in fact, more sensitive and responsible in sexual matters than their elders were. Many are taking a more active role in birth control, for example. "We see more teen-age girls coming in with their partners than we see adults coming in with theirs," says Lori Saltzman of Planned Parenthood's San Francisco teen clinic, the first in the country to target programs for 12-to-18-year-olds. But experts concede that with the availability of the Pill and the diaphragm, responsibility for contraception falls more squarely on the girl than ever.

And that presents yet another double bind. "Many boys will respect a girl less if they find out she is on the Pill," explains Michael, a Milton, Mass., senior. "It's like she is expecting sex." Such inhibitions help to produce two startling statistics: 20 per cent of teen-age pregnancies occur after the first month of sexual activity, and 50 per cent within the first six months.

Just what is the proper form of birth control for adolescents is a problem modern medicine has yet to resolve. Doctors are reluctant to insert intrauterine devices in teen-age girls because of the hazard of inflammatory pelvic disease that could leave them sterile. The Pill, which bears a sobering legacy of multiple side effects, carries added dangers for the teen-ager, though it is the most popular form of birth control. On the other hand, the rhythm system, particularly when a young girl's periods are still irregular, is a high-risk method. Instead, many teen-agers are avoiding the risks of pregnancy by turning to oral sex as the least chancy form of gratification.

Denial: Birth control remains the greatest area of sexual ignorance. "Teen-agers commonly think they won't get pregnant the first time, or if the man doesn't ejaculate, or if they don't have an orgasm," notes Joe Friedman, of the Los Angeles Sex Information Help Line. But a knottier problem is teen-agers' refusal—or inability—to relate their conduct to its possible consequences. "It seems so improbable that they would get pregnant because they cannot imagine themselves as women," says Harvard psychologist Carol Gilligan. Adds Claudette Kunkes, of New York's The Door: "It's the 'It won't happen to me' syndrome. They even deny to themselves they're having sex. Even after abortions they deny they were pregnant."

Unfortunately, sex-education courses often do little to address such confusion. The typical course in the schools is not much more than a protracted anatomy lesson, or what some teen-agers consider overly graphic depictions of the ravages of venereal disease ("The Chiller Theater of Sex," one Sun Belt sophomore wryly calls them). Young people clearly want more information, especially on the "why" of sexual relationships rather than the "how."

Parents are equally confused about how to handle their adolescents' unseemly sexual stirrings; they vacillate between an enlightened view and viewing with alarm. Most parents are notoriously remiss in talking to their children about sex. Raised more restrictively, too many of them still suffer their own sexual hangups and are likely to transmit their conflicts when they do air the issue. Beyond that there is an Oedipal squeamishness: talking sex invades their last refuge of privacy from the children. "For a girl to talk to her mother about sex is to talk about the husband and father," says Sylvia Rose, a consultant to the Massachusetts family planning service. "It's a very difficult situation for mother and daughter."

'Old School': Adolescents find it no less awkward. "I'd rather pick a name out of a phone book and talk to a stranger than talk to my mother about sex," says Janice, a 13-year-old from Pleasant Hill, Calif. "It's too embarrassing." Many sons have just as much difficulty approaching their fathers. "I can't talk to my dad about sex," says James Williams, 18, of Los Angeles. "He's from the old school. I think he was a lady's man, but I also think he has a fear of talking about it with me. I think he fears I might get a girl pregnant. He was even hesitant about me taking sex ed in high school."

Like many school officials who oppose sex-education courses, parents also have trouble overcoming the notion that to discuss sex openly with children is to endorse it for them. "I feel sorry for the parents today as much as I do for the youths," says Mary, a sexually active senior at Chicago's Metropolitan High School, an alternative school for the gifted. "A mother really can't comfortably take her daughter by the hand to get birth-control pills. It's like writing her daughter a ticket and telling her to have a good time." Sometimes, indeed, that is the effect. In Knoxville, Tenn., 15-year-old Martha's friends were impressed when her enlightened mother got her the Pill. For her own part, the daughter expresses uneasiness about having started such an early—if protected—sex life. "I wish I had waited until I met someone I really cared for," says Martha, who lost her virginity at 14.

Even so, some experts think parents must take those chances because they remain the single most stabilizing force for their children. Sex-education specialist Ruth MacDonald, a member of the school committee in Wayland, Mass., urges that parents learn to talk more comfortably about the subject, because their children are surrounded by it. "Parents can't stop kids from listening to music or watching television," she says. "But they have to realize they are still the most important force in their children's lives—and that they have to get equal time with the other influences. This is a whole new society." Other authorities are not sure parents are up to the task. Says Dr. Donald A. Bloch, a New York psychiatrist and director of the Ackerman Institute for Family Therapy: "Families' attitudes have to change, not just adolescents'. Most parents give a real double-standard message to their kids—'Do it, but not here, and I don't want to know about it'."

The adult world seems to be sending a mixed message: it accords teen-agers new freedom without quite the approval they seek. "There's a deep ambivalence among teens about being able to enjoy the fruits of a more permissive situation," says sociologist Frank F. Furstenberg Jr. of the University of Pennsylvania, originator of a family sex-education program. "Society is always that third party looking over its shoulder and saying, 'It's up to you, but don't expect me to help you out'."

Exploits: Despite such confusions, few teen-agers would turn the clock back to a more chaste era. They believe the new openness has made them more tolerant of their friends' sexual proclivities and more healthily disposed toward their own. Many are convinced their early sexual exploits will leave them better prepared for the vicissitudes of modern marriage, and some authorities bear them out. "There's a less frantic attitude toward sex because it's so available," says the Ackerman Institute's Bloch. "There's an opportunity for friendship to blossom, and it can open up a world of relationships, not just a prelude to genital sexuality. And that may well be a foundation for better marriages."

There is also a "cool" school of opinion among teen-agers that adults exaggerate the whole phenomenon of adolescent sexuality. "We're no different than they were when they were young," says 17-year-old Mary, of Chicago's Metropolitan High School, "except the media and society in general showed us sex at an earlier age. Who wouldn't be curious?" That view accords with the findings of the Los Angeles Help Line's Joe Friedman. "Teen-agers are more active sexually but not universally," he asserts. "Now we have some incredibly sophisticated teen-agers along with some surprisingly naïve ones."

But there is a midrange of some sadly troubled ones. Tender young things are sampling sex before its season—before they are out of dental braces—and then feeling the anguish of remorse. Many are less sexually liberated than they would like to think. "There's a danger of a kind of precocious sexuality that can lead to emptiness if there's no ongoing relationship," says Bloch. "I think the biggest emotional problem these teens have is loneliness—sex without connectedness instead of sex with significance." Adds University of Maryland's Dr. Kappelman: "A major part of sex education for teens must be that they have a right to say yes or no, based upon their own perceptions of self-identity. What's different from an earlier generation is that most kids today are straightforward with each other but not as honest with themselves. Too many of them can't say to themselves, 'I'm not ready'."

Society's mixed message to the young has left them with a mixed blessing. They have more choices than their elders ever had, but no guarantees that they will choose wisely. And that has left many of them with an equivocal appreciation of the benefits of sexual emancipation. As one reflective 16-year-old from Palo Alto, Calif., summed it up: "It must have been a lot easier when society set the standards for you. It can get awfully complicated. I guess that's the price we have to pay for freedom."

DAVID GELMAN with DIANE WEATHERS and LISA WHITMAN in New York, PAMELA ABRAMSON in San Francisco, TERRENCE MAITLAND in Boston, JEFF B. COPELAND in Los Angeles and bureau reports

First Night Disasters

Dr. William Masters

There are millions of sexually dysfunctional men in this country, and a significant percentage of them have been crippled by traumatic episodes during their first attempts at lovemaking. The three major sexual dysfunctions—impotence, aversion to women and premature ejaculation—stand in the wings whenever an inexperienced boy attempts to lose his virginity. If something goes wrong, it is likely to go wrong again and again. The virgin bed should have a sign: TONIGHT IS THE FIRST NIGHT OF THE REST OF YOUR LIFE.

I became aware of first-night disasters while counseling. Time and again, husbands and wives who come to me for help proudly report that they married as virgins. When they are questioned in detail, a tragic pattern emerges. Husbands more often than not assume full responsibility for the sexual fiasco that has almost destroyed the marriage. Ironically, the wives at first reaffirm their delight in the husband's virginal state at marriage but then, without hesitation, castigate him because he didn't know what to do or when to do it. "He should have known. He's a man," is a chorus sung by many a virgin bride as she points an accusatory finger at her equally ignorant groom. It is a travesty but too true. Virginal marriages frequently are doomed to continuing dissatisfaction simply because the male member couldn't simultaneously be virginal and experienced. When the blind leads the blind, both frequently stumble, but the responsibility for this fall is inevitably laid at the husband's door. Our culture has assigned the man the role of sex expert—a role that the anxious neophyte simply can't play, because it creates unacceptable levels of performance pressure. It is a role unfair and unrealistic in the context of today's human values.

PITY THE POOR VIRGIN

Obviously, not all first-night disasters are associated with wedding bells. Any sexual encounter involving an inexperienced partner is potentially traumatic: and especially so if the inexperienced partner is male. It is one of the least desirable side effects of the double standard. In our society, a virgin female is culturally treasured, socially protected. The virgin male is culturally pressured, socially suspect and sexually anxious. He is a second-class citizen, an outcast on fraternity row. He cannot confess to his status or seek information from his peers. He must become a man—at whatever the cost.

The how-to-do-it sex books, usually written by men for men about women, are replete with directions for relieving the female of her treasure without inflicting undue trauma. The initiation of a young woman into sexual maturity is a well-scripted ceremony, with support and protection of the initiate an integral part of the scenario. After reading about foreplay, correct positions, gentleness and understanding, a male virgin is likely to be told, "This, perhaps, is most important of all and should be constantly carried in mind by the groom: All initiative, all control lies completely within his hands. The bride does only one thing of importance, and that is to relax. Even so, the husband must repeatedly remind her of this and assist her in it." (From *Modern Sex Techniques,* by Robert Street.) Why shouldn't the virginal male receive similar consideration? We have been told repeatedly that if the ceremonial script of gentleness and consideration isn't followed with reasonable care, an unfortunate first experience may render a woman nonorgasmic in perpetuity. But what of the male first-nighter who ends up as primarily impotent, sexually aversive or as a virulent premature ejaculation? It is time to state his case.

Fear is the major deterrent to any uninitiated man's sexual facility. Fear comes in many guises—nebulous, gripping, multidimensional. Fear of being caught by his or her family when the friendly living-room sofa has beckoned. Fear of intrusion by the police or any other invader in an isolated lover's lane. Fear of pregnancy. Fear of venereal disease. Fear of being trapped in an unwanted commitment. All things considered, it might be best for a young man to put off losing his virginity until he is safely ensconced in a bank vault, with a woman he loves, who has just been given a clean bill of health by the local V.D. clinic, as well as a supply of birth-control pills. But even then, the young man would have to face the most fearful questions of sexual ignorance: "What do I do now?" "How do I do it?" "Will she think I'm good?" For most men, these basic fears are spontaneously resolved. But by its very existence, fear can distract from the stimulation of the sexual opportunity. The distracted man, particularly the distracted novice, may be slow to erect. When there is slowed erection, or if only a partial erection develops, terror strikes. What will she think? Who will she tell? What will the boys say when they hear? And so it goes. Fear builds upon fear, and confidence in having an erection may never develop. The novice who doesn't know this may be devastated by his failure to perform on order.

During the next few days, when reflecting on his personal disaster, a novice may think of little else. Fear of performance increases geometrically. In his ignorance, he isn't sure what went wrong, but he is fully aware that nothing seemed to go right.

Next time he will do better, but, of course, the next time, as he strains to force an erection, he fails again. With a second failure, there is a high probability that he may never function adequately unless professional help is available. Any man, regardless of age or prior sexual experience, who has occasion to seriously question his sexual ability is well on his way to impotence. If you fail to get it up the first and second times, you may begin to think it's your fault. Nothing could be further from the truth. All it takes is a kind woman.

Unfortunately, the inexperienced woman inevitably plays the role of waiting for the man to make it happen. In doing so, she inadvertently applies more performance pressure to the anxious male. The female beginner usually does all the wrong things for the right reasons. "I didn't want to pressure him, so I *let him* set the pace." "*Let him* come to me." "*Let him* lead." "*Let him* take the responsibility." The virginal *he* is drowning in a sea of "let hims" while his inexperienced partner carefully plays out her socially assigned role of passive mate.

If a young man doesn't get lucky during his first sexual encounter, if he fumbles and bumbles, if he needs help and his partner doesn't know how to give it—or chooses not to help and afterward is quick to criticize—or even if he reaches his goal but finds getting there was a job, not fun, he frequently falls into the protective state of sexual aversion. If he becomes convinced that he doesn't feel a thing, that no woman can turn him on, or if he knows he won't like it even if it happens, how can he be faulted for avoiding the issue? He's safe, but he's also an inadequate human being.

Of course, most virginal males, despite the high probability that they will experience apprehension and pressures to perform, do function during their initial opportunities. They at least consummate the act (intromission plus ejaculation), but they may still end up sexually distressed or dysfunctional. When pressures of performance overwhelm during the initial opportunity for intercourse, many inexperienced men become sexually aversive in self-protection. They develop a hundred excuses for avoiding sexual activity that may lead to intercourse and at times actually withdraw from any form of physical contact. Headaches no longer remain the woman's province. "She doesn't turn me on"; "It was an awful day"; "I'm too tired." How many times have these old standards been verbalized? But this time they are expressed by men. If not married when aversion develops, many men even tend to avoid women in social situations so that they won't have to be put to the test.

PREMATURE EJACULATION

More often than not, things go well the first night, but they go quickly. Almost before the young man knows what has happened, he is finished. He may think of his completed sexual performance in the most positive terms of success. At last he has scored. He has proved himself a man. He can answer the locker-room question "Getting any?" with a resounding yes. Well, almost, he is not home free. If his virginal experience has been marked by haste and overexcitement (almost impossible to avoid), he may have taken the initial step toward the most frequently encountered of all male sexual dysfunctions: premature ejaculation. Almost all men who come too quickly to satisfy their partners first experience the problem on the virgin bed. The so-called minuteman establishes a pattern of sexual response in his first few sexual encounters that he cannot alter himself, regardless of how hard he tries, in later life. His body has become conditioned to one pattern. Insertion is almost immediately followed by orgasm—the two become the same act. The novice never learns to separate the many impulses that signal the impending climax. He is swept along in the rush.

Several factors can contribute to speediness. If the lovers are in a high-risk situation—such as a lovers' lane or a basement playroom—then haste becomes equated with safety. Take the money and run. If a young man has resorted to a prostitute, he may sense the meter running. Haste is equated with good business. (The prostitute may reassure the novice, commending him on his ability.)

Sometimes a beginner can't believe his partner can change her mind. It takes only a few sexual encounters to establish the groove. Or perhaps the rut.

Many sexually cripped men have no idea that they're not the most popular of sexual partners. If a man isn't married, his partners on one-night stands usually don't let him know he isn't getting the job done to their satisfaction. No one bothers to correct the situation—instead, they move on to new partners. If he is married, it is frequently several years before an unbelievably frustrated partner angrily upsets his apple cart one night by accusing him of being totally selfish, interested only in his own pleasure and never thinking of her needs. Such a disclosure usually comes as a shock, for the male who has become conditioned to speedy sex has no frame of reference. He has always aimed to please and until now has had no complaints.

Premature ejaculation can be corrected—but not by amateur effort. Distractions don't work. Biting your lip doesn't work. Thinking of the office doesn't work. Most men try to put on the brakes after they've hit the ice—by then, it's too late. Learning self-control takes a cooperative, understanding partner. In *Human Sexual Inadequacy,* I describe the squeeze technique: A woman brings her partner to the edge of orgasm, then, before he can ejaculate, squeezes the head of the penis between her fingers. The overwhelming urge to ejaculate will diminish and the process can be repeated. Gradually, the man becomes familiar with the sensations leading to orgasm and can learn to slow down and regain control.

In the past, small elements of our society have tried to attack the problem of first-night disasters. For example, at the turn of the century, the Oneida Community in Upstate New York was teaching young men ejaculatory control as a conception-control mechansim. The young men were initiated into sexual activity and taught control by post-menopausal women, and older, well-controlled men performed similar services for the young women in the colony. As a contraceptive measure, the techniques reportedly worked well, but we have no knowledge of whether or not controlled "sexual induction" by experienced partners reasonably guaranteed effective sexual performances when the young people were allowed to mate.

Ideally, we should develop adequate educational programs for the sexually inexperienced. Not the birds-and-bees thing but programs conducted by competent professionals discussing social responsibilities, underscoring sexual values and suggesting ways and means of admitting sexual ignorance with comfort. After all, if men and women had the self-confidence to acknowledge their virginal states and *ask for help* before they plunged, half the battle would be won. While there would still be distressful failures after identifying a neophyte status, the level of distress would be of little moment compared with the degree of trauma that developes when pretending an expertise we don't have or assuming or assigning a responsibility we can't meet. We must accept the facts that men as well as women can be sexually inexperienced without loss of face and that one cannot accept responsibility for a partner's facility in sexual response.

Although we have emphasized the negative in this discussion of virginal traumas, and we certainly haven't been optimistic about the possibility of altering culturally established sexual value systems, a positive note is in order for those tens of thousands of men who will have read this article and identified with one or another of the situations described. For those who have been caught in the ego grinder of sexual ignorance and who remain severely handicapped by failed first experiences, all is not lost. The sexual inadequacies that arise from virginal matings are reversible in a high percentage of cases. There is even brighter portent in the fact that our society finally has recognized the continued sexual ignorance in our young will lead them to repeat our sexual mistakes and to suffer our sexual disasters. Happily, they are learning to avoid these pitfalls, sometimes even with our help. Obviously, it's far better to avoid problems then to have to treat them: but if they exist, how much better it is to treat than to live a half life.

The Semantics of Sex
What Did You Do Last Night?

Did you (and/or your partner)

. . . . *have sex?*
. . . . *make love?*
. . . . *screw?*
. . . . *go to bed together?*
. . . . *perform coitus?*
. . . . *sleep together?*
. . . . *ball?*
. . . . *know each other (in the Biblical sense)?*
. . . . *none, some, or all of the above?*

Lester A. Kirkendall, Ph.D.

Lester A. Kirkendall, Ph.D. is co-founder of SIECUS, author of Premarital Intercourse and Interpersonal Relationships, *and a member of the* Sexology Today *Board of Consultants.*

Recently I attended a lecture in which the audience paid close attention to the speaker, who was discussing many aspects of female/male relationships. He was emphasizing the importance of equality and freedom from political and economic discrimination. There should be equal pay for equivalent work. But then he began talking about ways in which men and women relate sexually. Discussing a young married couple he knew casually, he referred to the way in which intercourse was initiated between them. "She let him at her" is the way he put it.

He had no sooner said this than a young woman in the audience waved her hand excitedly. When he recognized her, she said angrily, "I think that comment is just terrible! What you said doesn't say what you have said you were saying." After the laughter had died down, the young woman explained: "You are standing for equality between men and women, but your language about the couple's sexual relationship certainly doesn't say that. The way you phrased it, it seems that the man has the right to manipulate or overpower the woman so he can have intercourse. The woman should not permit it; in fact, her job is to fend him off."

She was right. The speaker's language did imply that the couple's relationship was an unequal one. The young woman could have gone further. She might have added that our sexual language has words and phrases that we should have examined long ago, and then perhaps rejected. We have in English words suggesting a double standard of sexual conduct: freedom for men, restrictions for women. We have evasive words that we use to avoid speaking openly and honestly about sex. We have slang words that some people use with certain persons or groups but not with others. And, finally, we have words that fix our attention on sex when sex is not the issue at all.

Currently, there are efforts being made to improve our sexual semantics, but we still have a long way to go. It might be helpful to examine both the past and present state of our sexual vocabulary, and to do this, let us return to our previously mentioned speaker.

There are other expressions he could have used that reflect our sexual double standard. For example: "She gave in to him"; "she got screwed." As in the first example, these sentences also imply that the woman was passive, the situation was dominated by the male, and that the woman might or should have prevented the sexual episode. If the lecturer had wanted to convey the idea of male aggressiveness, he might have said,"He screwed her"; "he put it to her"; or "he scored." But all these expressions still suggest male control and domination and the subordination and manipulation of the woman. Certainly, they do not suggest equality.

The double-standard approach to sexual conduct is conveyed by other expressions as well. We disapprove of prostitution, and so there is no doubt about our attitude when we call the female in a commercial-sex situation a "prostitute." But the male in this transaction is only called the woman's "patron." Even the legal world has buttressed this discrimination, for the prostitute has always been the one to be arrested and fined —not the male patron. Furthermore, a woman who is a prostitute is commonly described as a "tramp," a "slut" or a "pig." The male customer, however, is viewed much more tolerantly. Often, he is described as simply "sowing his wild oats." Were he to have intercourse with a number of women—especially nonprostitutes—he might be referred to rather admiringly or enviously as a "Don Juan," a "Casanova" or a "high scorer." Not too long ago women who had intercourse outside of marriage or even sexual activity short of intercourse, were referred to as "fallen women," as persons who had gone "astray." By the same token, today an unmarried female who refuses to become sexually involved with a man is still said to be a "nice girl" or a "pure woman."

The double-standard view of life has traditionally called for females to marry and rear a family. Those who did not do so were labeled "old maids," to be cast aside in time as unmarriageable. Understandably, some unmarried women have tried to enhance their eligibility and their social position by replacing the "old maid" label with the tag, "bachelor girls."

The unmarried man, however, has always been regarded as an "eligible bachelor," and his desirability has been signaled by invitations to dinners and parties. At these functions he often found himself paired with an unmarried woman, whose mother, more often than not, would stand in the shadows, hoping that the "eligible bachelor" would succumb to the charms of her "old maid" daughter. And if the male bachelor has money or property, his eligibility increases as he gets older.

Today there is much less of this kind of labeling. And yet today, as before, in legal terms the woman is subordinate to the man. True, the tradition was much more vigorous in the past. A woman's identity was established by the man she married. He was the head of the house and made all important decisions. She was his wife: Mrs. John Smith—not Mrs. Alice Jones. I have yet to see a male choosing the name of the person he marries. I am not, for example, Mr. Laura Williams. I do know a man who took his wife's maiden name as his middle name. That is as close as I have seen a man come to adopting the identity of his spouse. Happily, all these worn ways are changing; we are moving toward more equality in feminine/masculine relations.

Some married women are making great headway in forging past age-old restrictions. Some are deciding in favor of pursuing a career and against marriage, against being "housewives." And, of course, there are now "househusbands." The other day I came across the title of a publication which, I suppose was selected with conscious humor: *The Kitchen Sink Papers: The Diary of a Househusband.*

Another small, telling change should be noted. Did you notice that in the past, the masculine designation always came first when both sexes were mentioned? "He or She" was the standard usage, and often "he" alone was used when both sexes were implied. A pioneer in changing this situation was an author, Amram Scheinfeld.

Our sexual language also creates problems for us because of the evasive words it contains. We use these words and expressions so that we will be sure not to offend people. Or perhaps it is that we simply don't want to hear ourselves uttering the direct sexual words. This indirectness can make sexual communication extremely difficult—sometimes even impossible. We may think we are using expressions that hedge on our sexual meaning in order to display a delicate diffidence; what we, in fact, accomplish is to sow confusion or nothing at all.

Usually, evasion is most practical when sexual intercourse is the topic being discussed. They "slept together," "they went to bed," "they made love," "they were intimate": these are some typical examples of evasion. Certainly these expressions suggest many activities or situations other than sexual intercourse. One can sleep with other persons with no genital involvement, and one can have intercourse without experiencing love. And as for intimacy, there are several ways to achieve intimacy that do not involve any genital contact. Furthermore, many instances of intercourse are not intimate; bodies coming close together does not necessarily result in intimacy. As a matter of fact, the genital parts are sometimes brought together to express hostility and anger. Our understanding of sexual behavior would become clearer if we used clear language in discussing sex.

Of course, we have made some advances in that direction. We are now able to use the word "pregnant" openly, whereas in the days of my childhood a pregnant woman was said to be "in the family way" or in "a delicate condition." During the latter months of pregnancy, when the abdomen began to swell, the mother-to-be was expected to keep out of sight as much as possible; this example of nonverbal evasiveness shows how clearly custom is reflected by language.

Menstruation is another word that for a long time we hesitated to use openly. The sidestepping terms had frightening overtones. Menstruation was known as "the curse," "being sick" or "the bleeding." The words "period" or "monthlies" are less frightening but still evasive.

There are evasive words to describe men's sexual concerns, as well. Not too long ago males were warned against masturbation by being told of "dangers of self-pollution." Such alarmist language has been toned down quite a bit, yet boys are still chided for "playing with themselves." I know of a writer who admonished males against dangers coming from "impure movements of the flesh." Evidently, he was referring to erections, or "hard-ons," which males might experience while dating, fantasizing or under other circumstances.

Even today the genital organs are still referred to as the "private parts." I remember a Little League baseball coach telling me about a small boy who was joining the team and had been told by his mother that he should wear something to protect his "private parts." Not knowing for sure what she meant, but wanting to be protected, he asked an older male on the team what was involved. The older boy clarified things quickly: "Oh, wear your jock strap! It won't hurt so much if you get kicked in the balls."

Here is an instance of the use of slang to convey meaning. As this anecdote shows, we associate slang with the locker room and often refrain from using it in any but the most private, safe circumstances. The mother could not use the slang with her son, nor even the more technical term "testicles." Evidently, her son had had enough experience to know that he had to get a clarification of her meaning from someone else. One wonders what would have been the mother's response if her son's "private parts" had been injured. Would she have examined his body? Would she have shunned the more direct terms even then?

To a great extent we are overcoming the diffidence we formerly felt about using sexual slang. This timidity once made us brand any nonscientific reference to sex a "dirty word." In printed material this attitude resulted in such peculiar typographical notations as "f--- you." Actually, of course, this practice only served to highlight the truncated word even more than if it had been printed intact.

Today, because of our more liberal attitudes toward sex and sexual expressions, such words as "fuck," "cunt" or "prick" are used more openly. Now the question is the purpose of using these words. Do people sometimes use them simply to show how liberal, how free from restraints, they are? That's all right, if the people using them in this way are aware of their purpose and know that the words fit the situation. In counseling I occasionally find persons who do not like to use the formal sexual terminology. They use slang terms freely, without regarding them as "dirty words," and are more relaxed, more at ease, if I use the slang vocabulary that is familiar to both of us.

We have been discussing language habits resulting from timidity and diffidence. On the other hand, sometimes we are so focused on sex that we have genital associations to behavior that is not sexual at all, or only minimally so. In discussing sexual matters with college students in their late teens or early twenties I have often wanted to enlarge their sexual concepts, so I have asked them, "Are you sexually experienced?" If they had had intercourse, the answer was invariably yes; if they had not, it was no. Yet if sex extends beyond the genitals as it does, to many kinds of relationships, nobody can say he/she is sexually inexperienced, even if one has never engaged in intercourse. As males or females, most people try to fulfill the sex roles they have been taught to fulfill. They are aware of their genital organs and have responded to them, often through masturbation. Yet many of these people still regard themselves as sexually inexperienced.

Another instance of the way we focus on sex without regard to its meaning in a relationship can been seen in our description of rape. We talk about rape as a "sex crime," when it is really an assault, a crime of violence. It is "hostile" behavior. To think of a rape as a "sex crime" has about the same meaning as labeling a situation in which there is an angry exchange of blows between persons and someone is knocked out as a "fist crime."

If we looked closely and sensitively at every situation, our language might change noticeably. For example, the slang term I have heard used for an adolescent girl who is unpopular and unable to make friends and accepts sexual advances from almost anyone who makes them is that "she puts out." Knowing her particular circumstances from certain counseling situations, however, I have come to think that her behavior might be more accurately described as "friendless," or "foresaken behavior."

I would be pleased if, as a result of reading this article, readers would examine their own sexual vocabulary to see whether they are using inaccurate, evasive or cover-up terms. Other situations and circumstances than those discussed here can lead to such usage: homosexuality, other social customs affecting male/female relations, communicating with children. If you the reader do spot a suspect term then the next step is to think of ways to improve your sexual communication.

Our final, logical goal should be to make our language reflect what we actually have in mind. There will never be unanimous agreement about the best way to express something, but certainly there is much room for improvement. First, new words and expressions will evolve to express emerging ideas and concepts. My expectation is that our sexual vocabulary will be broadened and sharpened to bring out the existing subtleties in sexual behavior. Finally, we will have to rid our sexual language of words and terms and expressions that reflect the sexual double standard and other biases, for all of these rob sexual communication of its effectiveness. A broader and a more relaxed view that regards sex and sexuality as integral parts of life will need an improved vocabulary. It will take time to achieve this goal, but the rewards in better communication and greater understanding in the area of relationships make the effort worth our while.

What Is Your Sexual Responsibility To Your Mate?

Judith E. Steinhart, D.A.

Judith Steinhart has a doctoral degree in human sexuality. She is on the faculty in the Department of Health Science at Brooklyn College and a clinical assistant professor at the State University of New York at Stony Brook.

It was not thought, before the 1940's, women were capable of enjoying sex. As a result, men did not see their responsibility as extending beyond themselves and their own pleasure, although they might perhaps hurry the act so that their wives would not have to endure it for very long. As for the women, they felt it was their responsibility to have sex with their husbands—in fact, that it was their duty.

In the fifties, the Kinsey studies made up one of the important factors that led to the discovery that women were indeed capable of orgasmic response. Evidently this made a man feel that it was his responsibility to "satisfy" his lover/wife. If he didn't satisfy her—that is, provide her with the orgasm she was now capable of having—he felt like a failure as a man.

When Masters and Johnson learned, in the sixties, that not only were women orgasmic, but that they were physiologically capable of having multiple orgasms, men assumed the additional responsibility of providing their partners with these, too. Women also felt a pressure: They wanted to have an orgasm to prove to their partners that they were indeed sexual women, a reward to them for working so hard to produce the orgasm. To protect the male ego, women even learned to fake orgasms. Unfortunately, the effect of each partner feeling responsible for the other's pleasure and satisfaction resulted in a widening communication gap between men and women.

Today men still place enormous pressure on themselves to have and maintain powerful erections. They feel that they should be ready for sex any time, any place, whether or not they happen to be in the mood for it. (For, according to the popular view, what kind of a man wouldn't want to have sex, given the opportunity?) Similarly, women are very concerned about their partners' "performance." When a man does not have an erection in any sexual encounter, the woman feels that it is her fault, that something is wrong with her if she cannot produce an erection in her partner. She is sure if only she were thinner, bustier, blonder, softer, younger or sexier, he would get an erection, and then everything would be all right.

Even people involved in relationships are subject to such ideas. Instead of realizing that it is all right not to feel sexual all the time like clockwork, they assume they are not sexy, thin, strong, macho or sensitive enough to turn their partner on.

What is your responsibility to your mate? Who is responsible for turning on whom? The answer is, of course, that *you* are responsible for your own sexuality. It is no one's responsibility to turn you on, just as it is no one's fault if you happen to feel unaroused or disinterested in having sex. You are in control of your own sexuality, and you decide when you want it to flow. By the same token, on those occasions when the body is not willing, you should be open enough with your partner to admit it. It is no sin. Sexuality is not a gift you get from someone, nor is it a present for you to give. It is a subtle, intricate part of the entire relationship.

Your sexual responsibility to your mate comes in two parts. The first requirement is that you be in tune with yourself—with who you are and what you want. The second is that you *share* that information rather than wait for your partner to read your mind. The main focus of sexuality is the sharing with and pleasing of one's lover, not the doing of a favor for someone or "doing it right." There is no right or wrong when it comes to lovemaking.

When you feel aroused, it should not be your partner's responsibility to respond with unfailing enthusiasm. We all should be allowed to exercise some choice. Sometimes our partner will be more willing to meet our needs than at other times. And when we feel sexual we ourselves have a number of options we should be aware of. We could have sex with our partners unless they are unwilling, unable or unavailable. If they are not available, we then could have sex with someone else, by ourselves or could simply acknowledge our sexual energy without doing anything about it. The point is to have respect for a partner's decision, even if it does not match ours—to realize that people must be true to themselves, and that no one is responsible for our sexual energy or for doing something to relieve it.

So the key is to be true to yourself. Sexual responsibility means being aware of your own feelings as well as being sensitive to and acknowledging the feelings of your partner. By being responsible for yourself, you learn to share in a mature way rather than to force or manipulate your partner into doing what he/she may not really feel like doing. Consequently, you build a relationship on the solid foundation of caring rather than on the shaky one of power and control. In this sense, being responsible for your own sexual fulfillment is truly an expression of sexual health.

New Rules in The Mating Game

Judy Jarvis

Judy Jarvis is a free-lance journalist who sometimes works for Boston's The Real Paper, *where an early version of this article first appeared.*

Testimony from a thirty-one-year-old woman, a Boston television producer: "You invite him to a work-session dinner. He asks how you can advance his career. Then he asks you to sleep with him. No commitment. Then he washes the dishes."

There is no question that this is a modern scene, one that would never have taken place before the women's movement took hold. No self-respecting man on the make in 1958 would have risked a sissy image by dipping his hands in Lux liquid, no matter how tempting the woman or the job. Nor would he have offered casual sex and asked for career help. How skillful of today's man to treat her as part of the old boy network. Just like one of the guys. How can she resist?

Today's woman isn't likely to respond to "Hey, come on, baby. Let's go make it back at my place. I'm on fire for you." No, today's woman expects a more fashionable ballet dance. Remember what Erica threw back at swinger Charlie, the overtly sexual artist in *An Unmarried Woman*, when he suggested that her sex life was deficient and that he could fill the bill? "Hey, Charlie," she said. "You're out of style."

Today's new hustle is to convince her that you are not only sympathetic to her drive for equality and fairness, but that you are even more of a feminist than she is. Feminist hustlers use new buzz words. Instead of "Your eyes are so beautiful" it's "I really like strong women." But the bottom line is still the same.

"It's still the same game," says Moses, a bearded drummer for a popular jazz group. Brooklyn-born and street-wise, thirty-nine-year-old Moses isn't impressed with the new jargon. He says, "The veneer's changed, but nothing's really changed in terms of that courting stage. It was always double-talk. Only now the words are different."

The new come-ons are slick and deceptive. Even the most dedicated feminist gets stuck now and then—some because they want to, and some because they're sucked in.

"The act is so seductive," says Elaine, a twenty-four-year-old whose sexual battle scars belie her age. "I want to buy it, but that's what is so insidious about it. Men who pretend they are feminists just to get laid are really evil."

Evil or just plain confused about what they should say to a "liberated" woman, men have created these feminist hustles:

The Wordsmith

This man has carefully combed his entire working vocabulary for anti-feminist words and has systematically exorcised every last one. These guys learn the hard way which words scare away "now" women, and then they practice to get it right. A Boston finance attorney explains the gig:

"If you want to seduce the average feminist woman, you avoid key political words like 'chick,' 'baby,' 'honey,' or 'sweetheart.' And you avoid saying things that mean 'I'll take care of you,' 'I'll make your decisions,' or 'I'll plan the night's events.' You don't say, 'I'll get you a job' or 'You like this sweater? I'll buy it for you.' " You stop acting like her father, in other words.

Wordsmiths never, never call women who stay home with their children "housewives." They are "homemakers." They're compulsive about never letting the word "girl" slip through their lips, which presents a problem when they're entertaining an eleven-year-old niece in the presence of a feminist friend. Not for nothing did Joanie Caucus's student in *Doonesbury* announce that her mother had just given birth to a "baby woman." Wordsmiths also avoid talking about "sex appeal." Today it's "energy."

A nationally prominent attorney, known for his legal one-liners and his facile tongue, is new at the feminist wordsmith game, having recently divorced his wife of ten years. But now that he is back in the dating market, he's successfully transferred his courtroom skills. "Men are more attracted to women's minds and sexual energies than to their faces," he says. "When I'm thinking about a sexual partner, I look for someone who's energetic. The line I use goes something like, 'I like your energy level. I like what you're putting across.' "

An executive who puts across plenty of energy in her Detroit office recently chaired a two-hour meeting for in-house and visiting manufacturing types. "Instead of telling me I have nice legs or that the color of my dress is great for my eyes, one of the guys approached me after the meeting and said, 'Hey, you really ran a great meeting. Your company must be very proud of you. You handle yourself so well.' He dropped by my office later to see what I was doing for dinner."

The Flaming Feminist

This guy is everywhere. He's easy to identify because he's always campaigning. He's appalled that women still earn only fifty-nine percent of what men earn for a similar job. He wears a red, white, and blue "Men for ERA" T-shirt, and on any given day he can recite the number of states that are lined up behind the Equal Rights Amendment. He religiously contributes to the National Organization for Women (NOW). He is often one of the few men in the audience when prominent woman speakers come to town. He loves to pontificate on the plight of women in today's society and is most articulate when there are a few good-looking feminists within earshot. The Washington-based Flaming Feminist has a few special tools in his bag of tricks. A White House press aide reports that staffers for representatives and senators woo

"New Rules in The Mating Game," by Judy Jarvis, *Esquire*, July 4, 1978. Reprinted by permission.

women by telling them they'll get their bosses to vote right on women's issues (the "Hustle on the Hill").

A Washington lobbyist for the Equal Rights Amendment who describes herself as "stacked" spent an evening with a male member of NOW last month. When another man began to argue against the embattled legislation, this Mr. F.F. "jumped all over him. He pulled out all of his legal ammunition, told him he was a sexist, and screamed that if we all thought the way he did we'd be back in the eighteenth century. He was the knight in shining armor coming to the defense of my political views."

One Monday night not long ago there was standing room only at Friday's, a dating bar in downtown Boston frequented by city hall employees, lawyers, and mid-level executives—men and women on their way up. A small, dark-haired, hourglass-figured woman was identified to two inquiring male martini sippers by a friend as a high official in Boston mayor Kevin White's administration, his adviser on women's issues. As if on cue, the two men began to battle back and forth about women's rights, each growing more and more insistent that he was more of a supporter than the other.

"Instead of showing off their muscles, they were showing off their feminism," she recalls.

The Independence Man

He says, "I like you because you're so independent. So strong." But as soon as the woman has other plans or runs into some other man when she's out with him, he gets nervous. Then he's on the telephone the next day trying to line her up for the next seven weekends. The independence is what grabs him, but he really wants her to be more dependent, more submissive. He can't understand why she must stay in Sunday night to finish work she carted home from the office on Friday, or why she might ever want to return to her place—alone—after an evening at his place. He would be much better off with a "girl," but his eagerness to be trendy forces him to be an Independence Lover.

Some men go after the independence and don't really want it. Others pursue it because they need it.

A thirty-year-old political adviser says that men often lust after her independence as a way to keep themselves unhooked. The new variation on "I don't want to get involved" is "I like a successful, independent woman."

Another woman fell for the "you're so independent" line from a married man. "He said I was different from his wife, who stayed home all day with a maid. But all he really liked about my independence was that he didn't have to make any commitment."

Mr. Androgynous

Who can distrust a man whose game is to reveal his feminine side? Says he: "I'm no longer afraid of letting my feelings show. I want to get more in touch with my emotions. I want us to be close friends. Sometimes I'm not sure I should be this open and honest, but somehow it feels right. I'm not afraid to admit that I need to cuddle and be cuddled. Just holding each other like this is more important to me than making love. You know, recently I've begun to relate to women in a new way." The jargon is easy enough for these guys to pick up from women's books. And women aren't shy about laying it out.

A leading television cameraman thought his sensitivity to women was one-hundred-percent pure until he was exposed to the feminist hustle theory.

"Now, I can see that some of my own actions take the form of hustles. Although we are more and more open and sensitive to women's problems, we can be phonies, too."

He used to wear one gold loop earring. "I am aware now that it was an effective ploy for allowing women not to feel threatened by me or by some macho trip. I've talked to other friends who wear earrings and they say the same thing—women are more likely to be relaxed around men with earrings. It's a little bit of a problem, however, to straighten out all the gay men who come on to you thinking you're gay. But once you're past that, it really pays off with the women."

One man confesses, not without a certain amount of guilt, that he has figured out a way to show off his masculine and feminine sides at the same time. "Sometimes I use my daughter to attract women. It's a way of broadcasting that there's more to me than the public persona. I use her to show women that I'm not afraid of touching and of showing affection."

The trouble with playing Mr. Androgynous is that women are beginning to catch on to this one. They say that under the guise of liberation, these men get out of doing their share of putting up bookshelves, paying the dinner check, carrying wood for the fire, and digging out the car after a blizzard. Women also report that these men fail to walk them home even though they've had the luxury of making love in their own beds and even when their apartments are located in the worst parts of town. Women say it's the lazy man, the cheap man, who really goes for this liberated stuff because it's a good excuse for him to get out of his adult responsibilities.

The Male Groupie

This is the kind that makes a specialty of seducing successful women. With women in more and better jobs these days, men and women now come on to each other in courthouses, museums, conference rooms, and campaign headquarters more often than ever before. Many women love nothing better than to talk about their jobs (a little more role reversal) and are thus easy targets for the professional predator who feigns interest in her work just to get her into bed. A Boston businessman agrees. "Don't tell her how important you are. Let her tell you how important she is."

A Chicago law student gives himself a big head start by eavesdropping on the women he wants to meet. "Men who think they can tell a feminist by what she's wearing are crazy. I stand close by and listen to a woman's conversation before I introduce myself. Then I say, 'Oh, you're a lawyer. How do you think the Court will vote on *Bakke*?' for example."

According to a thirty-one-year-old Republican political consultant, "An inordinate number of relationships start on a semi-professional basis even if you know damn well you want it at a socio-sexual level. You say to her, 'You're involved in this campaign. I'm involved in this campaign. Let's go out and talk about it.' "

Sometimes the work-oriented hustle gives a woman time in which to decide whether she wants an affair with a man.

A young lawyer who appeared as a guest on a public affairs television show was quite taken with the show's producer, a woman who had recently separated from her longtime lover. The lawyer did not know about her painful past, but he sensed that she was most easily accessible through her work.

"He was fascinated by my job. He asked me if I like working in television; what happens when I do a show, et cetera. All the time, however, I knew what he really wanted." At the time, she was ready for a distraction and bought his "verbal foreplay," as she puts it.

"I know that I would have been very put out if this particular man had approached me in a blatantly sexual manner. What professions have allowed us to do is be coy. We can hide behind the professions. Under the guise of talking about work, we can do some assessing. Work gives us an out from confrontations which are too brazen."

The Grabby Gourmet

A thirty-year-old Hollywood film producer—six foot two, with the kind of confident good looks that cause women to approach him in restaurants—has found great success in cooking his way into a woman's heart (actually, heart's the wrong word).

"Women find the fact that I cook well an attractive quality," he says. His five-course Italian dinner—including fresh mozzarella cheese, veal, and pasta with four different kinds of cheese—"has never failed. It's particularly effective," he relates, "if I do it at a woman's home. There's something about a man in her kitchen that's very seductive. You know, taking care of her in her own space."

Washington, D.C., is a hotbed of Grabby Gourmets. Lots of dinner parties. Lots of men who cook. Kathleen, an attorney who is a top aide to an assistant cabinet secretary, was invited to eat dinner at a new man's apartment after meeting him at a cocktail party. His collection of kitchen paraphernalia was startling, she remembers: a Cuisinart food-slicing gizmo; a shiny brass Italian espresso machine; and a collection of spices and foodstuffs that would make Julia Child respectful. For each course, he had another fine wine from his "cave," as he calls it, although he stores his wines in the lower half of his coat closet.

"Yes, it worked," said Kathleen. "But I didn't see much of him after that. He knew lots about wines and foods, but he turned out to be very old-fashioned. He was impressed by my job but bewildered by it, too. He was never completely comfortable dealing with me."

The Devilish Domestic

The "I'll help with the housework just to prove how liberated I am" hustle can often be a real winner. A man met a new woman who invited him to her house, She prepared a big dinner, and he spent the night. In the morning, she got up early to make her first appointment. He climbed out of bed around eleven, washed the previous night's dishes, and tidied up the entire apartment. When she returned, she told him later, she was so undone that she sat down and cried.

"There's no question in my mind that my motives were not pure," he says. "The object of my motivation was for her to think I'm really a neat guy. Whether this translates into 'If I'm a neat guy she'll want to go to bed with me,' well, I don't always know the answer to that."

Another Devilish Domestic had less of a problem with his conscience. He asked a woman to move in with him to help share his apartment costs, or so he said. He suggested that they split household chores "right down the middle." She moved in, and before long it was obvious to her that "right down the middle" meant something different to him than it did to her. He didn't want to share the work; just the bed.

The Passive Aggressor

Many, many men say that the real change in male-female interaction since the start of the women's movement has nothing to do with them at all. "Women are so much more aggressive," they say. "They want to meet men as much as we want to meet women. Everyone's hat is in the ring now."

This new outspoken and sexual woman has elicited in men perhaps the most complex move of all. The new way men hustle women now is not to hustle at all. The ideal way, men say, is to be passive.

A White House correspondent who's a pro at this hustle reports great success in playing coy. "I asked out a woman reporter who was new to the White House beat, but she wasn't interested. I remembered my big brother's cardinal rule—Treat them like junk—and I politely ignored her for six months. Then one night we were together with a group of people, and apparently my coolness was getting to her. She asked me to have a drink with her. We went out and I sent her home in a cab. No kiss. I started to see her occasionally in more formal situations—dinners, lunches, et cetera—but I always let her make the moves. She finally asked me why I never asked her out on a Saturday night. And that was the beginning of a long and mutually satisfying relationship." (All this from a man who says it always pays to keep a woman's raincoat in your closet for unexpected sleep-over guests. Long gowns don't look so great at nine o'clock in the morning on her way home.)

Another true believer in the passively aggressive route says, "I'm lusting in my mind every bit as much now as ten years ago, only now things are much more subtle." He suggests this technique: "Spend a long evening alone with a woman. Kiss her good-night and leave. On the way out the door, turn to her and earnestly say, 'I'm not doing this because I'm not attracted to you, but I don't want to hassle you. I know you're the kind of woman who does what she wants to do.' Sure, it's calculated, but it's not inhuman and it usually works."

The new West Coast version of the Passive Aggressor gives out his business cards to women and tells them, "Call me if you're interested."

A fashion saleswoman in Los Angeles had dinner recently with an old friend who was visiting from New York. He brought two of his California buddies with him, each of whom gave her his business card (while the other was in the bathroom) and asked her to call.

Says she, "Men are afraid of being turned down, so they don't even try anymore. They want us to make all the moves."

To be sure, men have adopted this new range of come-ons in response to a new breed of womankind. We are asking, begging, in fact, to be treated differently from the way our mothers were treated. So why shouldn't men be smart enough to pick up on the changes?

"There's no reason why men wouldn't be fast enough to alter their delivery to suit the times. Hustling has been going on for thousands of years. It's bound to keep changing styles," observes a national political pollster.

And also, to be sure, no one gets hustled unless she wants to get hustled.

One man, who looked as if he'd been caught with his hand in the cookie jar while listening to an explanation of the feminist hustle, slowly shook his head.

"We're damned if we do and damned if we don't, I guess. These are not easy times for knowing what to say."

No, they're not. And bravo to the men trying to loosen up enough to try some new lines. Maybe they'll start believing them if they use them often enough.

But for some men, there may always be a fine line between sincerity and fine lines. One told me that lines weren't necessary because "I and many of my friends are genuinely far more interested in the kind of energy a woman projects and far less in mannequin beauty."

I said, "That sure sounds like a line to me." To which he responded, "A great many men really are looking for qualities that make someone a good equal friend rather than a sexual subordinate."

And then, with great feeling, he added: "Any good line will always bear a very close relationship to what people really think."

Article 33

THE PERFECT LOVER

Michael Castleman

If large groups of men and women were asked to compare their own vision of a perfect lover with what they believed to be the vision of the opposite sex, many would reply without hesitation that men's and women's images of the ideal lover were worlds apart.

The perception is not surprising. The central metaphor used today to describe relations between men and women is "The Battle of the Sexes." The Battle seems to rage incessantly with men and women huddled in sexually segregated trenches on opposite sides of a wide, crater-pocked free-fire zone. The men tell each other, in trenches decorated with *Penthouse* pinups, that women never want to "do it" as much or as often as men do. Women are considered "naturally" moody, irritable and difficult. They are thought to be so generally prudish that men must first wine and dine them (emphasis on the wine), then cajole them into bed, where they exhibit the sexual enthusiasm of corpses. If only women realized, as men do, that what they really need is a good fuck . . .

Meanwhile, behind their own emotional fortifications, adorned with the covers of Gothic romances, women agree that men are vulgar, ill-mannered, sexually insatiable beasts generally inclined toward rape, who, in the words of novelist Tom Robbins in *Even Cowgirls Get the Blues,* don't know the difference between a clitoris and a carburetor.

Like most human hostilities, however, The Battle of the Sexes is based on perceived differences more imaginary than real. The fact is, men and women share remarkable *similarities* in their tastes in both lovers and lovemaking.

WHO SAID WHAT?

Two recent surveys asked large numbers of men and women which personal attributes were most important to them in a lover. Bernie Zilbergeld compiled women's descriptions in his book *Male Sexuality* and Anthony Pietropinto and Jacqueline Simenauer catalogued men's opinions in *Beyond the Male Myth* (see Resources). Sample desired attributes from both surveys are listed below. Can you distinguish the traits desired by the men from those desired by the women?

Mature	Sensitive
Honest	A listener
Kind	Fun
Cares	Intelligent
Really listens	Supportive
Good body	Tender
Outgoing	Playful
Intelligent	Sensual
Sense of humor	Enjoys our bodies
Needs me	Sexually communicative
Friendly	Tolerates imperfections
Affectionate	Willing to experiment
Warm	Encouraging
Dresses well	Sharing
Emotional	Caring

Notice how similar the lists are. The column on the left came from the men, the one on the right from the women, but the two are basically interchangeable.

Men often believe that women judge their desirability as lovers by the size of their penises and how long they can last during intercourse. A survey of 1000 men published in Penthouse *Forum* (March 1976) showed that "all respondents, with the exception of the most extraordinarily endowed, expressed doubts about their sexuality based on their penile size." Significantly, however, of the hundreds of women who answered Zilbergeld's survey, *not one* mentioned penis size or ability to prolong intercourse as factors in choosing a lover.

Women often believe that men judge them by their figures, or in the subtle parlance of the men's magazines, by their "tits and ass." It's no coincidence that books on flattening the stomach and enlarging the bust pepper the Bestseller List. A few of the thousands of men Pietropinto and Simenauer surveyed said a woman's figure was a consideration in their selection of lovers, but it was almost always a minor consideration compared to the attributes listed above.

In the words of one respondent: "Time spent in bed is only a small part of total time together. The sexiest part of the body is the mind." Who do you think wrote that—a man or a woman?

WOMEN'S CHIEF COMPLAINTS ABOUT MEN AS LOVERS

Too fast. Too mechanical. Too genital. Women say men are so preoccupied with their penises and the mechanics of intercourse that they ignore what really turns women on—leisurely, playful, whole-body sensuality. Every square inch of the body is capable of sensual arousal, particularly through massage. The body is a limitless sensual playground. Women say they like to explore all of it and have difficulty understanding why men seem to focus all their interest on a few small corners. As one woman remarked: "I often wonder who men make love to—me or my boobs."

MEN'S CHIEF COMPLAINTS ABOUT WOMEN AS LOVERS

Too passive. Too cold. Not responsive enough. The main reason for women's aloofness is that the genital focus and "wham, bam, thank you, ma'am" lovestyle that characterizes the Playboy Philosophy preclude the leisurely pace and whole-body sensuality necessary for most women to begin to become aroused and responsive. Sexuality counselors typically tell men: Slow down, then slow down some more.

"The Perfect Lover," by Michael Castleman. Reprinted from *Medical Self-Care,* P.O. Box 717, Inverness, California 94937. *Medical Self-Care* is published quarterly, $15.00 per year.

THE SOLUTION

Unhurried, whole-body caressing is the solution to both men's and women's complaints about each other's lovestyles. Extended sensuality, especially massage (see Resources) helps lovers *relax*, which is the most important ingredient in problem-free lovemaking. Relaxation is crucial to the alleviation of both men's and women's most common sex problems, for women: lack of arousal and orgasm, for men: involuntary ejaculation, non-erection and non-ejaculation.

To facilitate whole-body sensuality, try not to separate your lovemaking into "foreplay" and "the main event." There is no such thing as "foreplay." There is only "loveplay."

Extended sensual loveplay means more time to become aroused, adventurous and experimental. It means less chance of slipping into a boring routine. A relaxed pace also allows plenty of time to discuss birth control or any other stresses that might interfere with the undivided attention lovemaking deserves. Touchy subjects feel less threatening when lovers are sensually in touch.

SIMILAR

It will take a long time to declare a general truce in The Battle of the Sexes, but couples can begin to negotiate individual cease-fire agreements right now. Men and women want the same things in their lovers, and an emphasis on sensuality eliminates each sex's lovemaking problems with the other. We're a lot more similar than we think.

Resources

The Massage Book
George Downing
1972; 184 pages
$4.95 from
Random House/Bookworks
210 East 50th Street
New York, New York 10022
The best book on massage.

Male Sexuality
Bernie Zilbergeld, Ph.D.
1978; 411 pages
$2.95 from
Bantam Books
666 Fifth Avenue
New York, New York 10019
A provocative book about men and sex.

Beyond the Male Myth
Anthony Pietropinto and Jacqueline Simenauer
1977; 467 pages
$2.50 from
Signet Books
1301 Avenue of the Americas
New York, New York 10019

This article is an excerpt from Problem-Free Lovemaking: Creative Sexuality for Men and the Women Who Love Them, *by Michael Castleman, scheduled for publication in early 1981 by Simon and Schuster.*

The 10 Common Sexual Spoilers for Women—and How to Outgrow Them

Jane Heil

"A large percentage of relationships—short- and long-term, married and unmarried—are troubled by sexual problems," according to Dr. Alice K. Ladas, marriage counselor and bioenergetic analyst, "possibly as many as half." The more psychiatrists, psychologists and sex therapists discuss and probe these problems, the more they seem to overlap and flow into larger definitions: fear, poor communication, ignorance, plus the overall problem of trying to be a sexually healthy woman in America: It isn't easy, even today. Masters and Johnson point out that, although the sexual responses of men and women are potentially very similar, the American female often develops a sexual value system that is quite different from a man's. (A sexual value system refers to the sensory experiences between birth and adolescence and how they fit with the values imposed by church, parents, community and friends. Negative values, which tend to predominate, would include taboos against masturbating or premarital sex.) We still learn, overtly and covertly, that bodily sexual pleasure is wrong, that sex is dirty and that we should repress, distort and deny our feelings. So we do. Romance and true love are held out as worthwhile goals, yet the sensory means for achieving them are systematically inhibited. Later on in life, when the body would like to say yes, the mind says no, just as it was taught to do as a child.

But beyond these general problems, there are clear categories of common sexual spoilers. And there are also simple, common-sense ways of overcoming them.

1. Poor communication. "As far as I'm concerned there's only one spoiler: lack of communication," says Don Sloan, M.D., a sex therapist and director of sex therapy and psychosomatics at the New York Medical College. "Sex *is* communication, and when patients say to me, 'We don't have sex in a satisfactory way,' all I'm looking for, to myself, is, how did that communication break down? What are they trying to say sexually that they have not been able to say with their words, with their eyes, with their hands?

"Even with as simple a problem as one partner having dirty hands, for instance, why didn't somebody say, 'I feel repulsed.' 'From what?' 'From your dirty hands,' 'Oh, then I'll wash my hands.' But it's difficult to say that: What if the other person said: 'Well, those are my hands; so long,' "

Bruce Vogel, Ph.D., Elayne Kahn, Ph.D., and Barbara Schwerin, M.S.W., directors of the New York Center for Sexual and Marital Guidance, refer to the problem as "mind reading": trying to figure out, "What does he want?" "What is he doing?" "Does he like it when I do this?" "Is this turning him on or off?" You try to read your partner's every nonverbal reaction—and that keeps you from tapping into your own feelings.

Leon Zussman, M.D., formerly co-director of the Human Sexuality Center for Long Island Jewish-Hillside Medical Center and a sex therapist in Manhattan, gave a concrete example. "You might call this poor technique, but it's really poor communication: We had a couple come to us recently; he is a little rough and gives her a real massage when he caresses her. That turns her off. She wants him to touch her very gently and delicately, in a way that he's fully incapable of doing right now. He sees himself as a pretty tough guy. She says, constantly, 'If only he would touch me the way I touch myself—and I've tried to show him.'

"The possibility for cure is very good," Dr. Zussman says. "We started off by suggesting an experience in touching: gentle, no-demand, no-pressure, no-performance touch exercises such as hand, foot and face massages, designed to promote sensual response and communication. We discussed each partner's reaction: what they liked, how they felt.

"Then we suggested that they teach each other what each one liked, needed and wanted, by guiding each other's hands all over the body including the genitals. We feel this method of nonverbal communication is easier for most people; words often come across as clinical. We encourage people to take responsibility for their own sexuality: to really share what it is they want. No one can assume that the other person can read his or her mind."

2. Anxiety. Lawrence Jackman, M.D., director of the Division of Human Sexuality at New York's Albert Einstein College of Medicine, feels that anxiety is very often linked to body-image problems. "Men's sexual anxiety seems to focus on penis size," he says. "We once did an anonymous survey and found that ninety-five out of one hundred men thought that their penis was smaller than average. Think about that for a minute! Women tend to focus on, "Wow, if he sees my little breasts he won't be turned on,' or 'If he sees my big labia or small clitoris or big hips . . .' or whatever it is you are uncomfortable about. Then you have an experience that is focused on what you think is wrong with your body—rather than on enjoyment of the sexual interaction. Women who worry about 'my small breasts' have an experience about their small breasts, rather than a sexual interaction."

"There is also performance anxiety," Dr. Vogel says. "A man feels that he is not going to be able to function as well as he would like to in bed, for whatever reason—premature ejaculation, various other dysfunctions.

"A woman can cause herself anxiety by evaluating her own performance; she may feel she should be having orgasms and she is not having them, or she is not having them often enough. Or it may reflect the relationship: She doesn't trust him, doesn't really know him. So she tends to avoid intimate kinds of relating because there really isn't intimate relating going on outside of bed. That's a good formula for a bad sex life.

"Boredom, too, is often an expression of anxiety. We do the same thing each time and this is security—but then it becomes boring because we were too anxious to introduce some novelty.

"Sex should be a creative expression," Dr. Vogel continues. "It should be an expression of our personality and of how we feel—about ourselves, our partner, about the weather. Ideally, it would be different each time. But it rarely is that, for any of us, due to anxiety."

"People are afraid, sometimes, to challenge each other with different parts of themselves," says John Bellis, M.D., director of the Connecticut Society for Bioenergetic Analysis and senior trainer for the International Institute for Bioenergetic Analysis. "It's like a dance that you do over and over. That dance symbolizes for me the need of both the man and the woman to be able to challenge the other. If the other one begins to take you for granted, you can throw in a little something to shake them up. That keeps the relationship as well as the sex alive."

3. Inhibition. Dr. Jackman links boredom to inhibition, cautioning that a couple may be bored only with their sexual pattern and not with each other. "You do the same thing the same way every Wednesday and Saturday night right after the eleven o'clock news in the dark, and you keep on doing that for ten or fifteen years—it's going to be boring. You may be too inhibited and afraid of being rejected to do anything else."

"Many people, particularly women, share the kind of family background and early conditioning that has a very pervasive effect," says Shirley Zussman, Ed.D., formerly co-director of the Human Sexuality Center of Long Island Jewish-Hillside Medical Center and, like her husband Leon, a Manhattan sex therapist. "Inhibitions persist long after the *intellectual* acceptance of new thinking. Our patients tell us either that sex was never discussed in their families or was presented in a purely biological or negative way. In many instances, there was punishment, especially in very religious households. That is the real spoiler of pleasure; however, it does yield to change. In the therapeutic situation, a kind of permission-giving by others can reduce some of the negative aspects.

"There really hasn't been a generation raised with a positive attitude toward sexuality in the early years," Shirley Zussman concludes. "Even a young woman now twenty or twenty-two-years-old heard a lot of 'Don't touch, don't look, don't talk about it.' This does persist, particularly in the way many women feel about their genitals. It is hard to allow yourself to feel pleasure there. Very often we hear this in relation to oral sex."

4. Fear of intimacy. Dr. Joseph Zucker, clinical psychologist in private practice in Manhattan, says "the fear of intimacy and closeness, of being vulnerable and open" is the sexual spoiler he sees most.

"Intimacy means allowing someone else to know you sexually and emotionally, and that can be as frightening as confronting yourself. Out of the fear of exposure, we create facades to present to the world. That's why some people are able to have terrific superficial, one-night-only sex. But soon the sex sours because, as you get to know somebody and allow that person to know you, whatever questions you have about yourself and your self-worth begin to come up. You worry that the person will see your flaws and be turned off, so you withdraw and eventually seek other strangers. That's the story of the singles scene.

"Simply being aware that you're afraid of intimacy can help. Opening up to the person you're with becomes easier, and you begin to feel more confident that he or she will accept you. Letting someone know you, even rather quickly, can make sex more meaningful and pleasurable."

5. Shyness. Dr. Bellis calls shyness a big killjoy: especially shyness about one's own body, a feeling of not liking one's body and of being afraid to face that. "Shyness in sex, just as in life, keeps you from feeling playful, and I think the lack of playfulness is a big killer.

"Shyness is based on an unsureness about one's own feelings—especially the tender feelings, those close to our heart. If those have been laughed at, if one's body and feelings haven't really been accepted enough, the natural shyness becomes intensified.

"Sometimes shyness is covered up by adults; people who are really shy seem prudish or distant or awkward, even loud. If a partner recognizes this behavior as coming from shyness, he or she can be of help. But if they are just put off by it, as they very well might be, that would be a spoiler in the relationship as well as in bed. I think that what can spoil your life can spoil sex for you.

"One of the things I've found most successful in overcoming shyness is play. And I really mean childlike play—being able to get down on the floor and make faces and being able to do this in a setting where it's accepted. Along with laughter and play, things that help people move gracefully, such as dancing, or to use their voice in a pleasant way, such as singing, can also help overcome shyness. Or skating or painting. If you can somehow use your talents creatively, it helps to expose some of your feelings in the process, and then you begin to have a good feeling about yourself. Even if you can't do one thing, you have a sense that you can do another; you can show your feelings," says Dr. Bellis.

"Another way of dealing with this shyness, insofar as it relates to a lover, is to give him an opportunity to be more accepting of us *apart* from sex—by taking baths together, say," he says.

6. Inability to be sexually assertive. "I don't see women taking as much responsibility for what happens to them sexually as do single men," says Ms. Schwerin. "Most women still feel that if they met the right man, they wouldn't have any problems.

"Many single women walk around feeling they must be in a relationship before they can allow themselves to experience their own sexuality. They think, 'If I were in a relationship, then my problem would be solved.' So they wait for that right man to come along, and if the relationship isn't the right one, the problem remains. Men, on the other hand, seem more willing to deal with their problems alone."

"Assertiveness is so important for today's woman that it deserves a big star," says New York psychiatrist, sex therapist and author (*The Sexual Self*) Dr. Avodah K. Offit. "Young women are unable, still, to ask for what they want in order to achieve simple physical arousal. They have extraordinary difficulty describing and responding to their feelings rather than to a pattern.

"Women have so little vocabulary for expressing their sexual needs. As women, we still suffer from the old mystique of expecting our mind to be read: the old belief that men must understand what we want, and if we speak, if we tell, if we request, romance is destroyed. Another verbal handicap is that women, in general, do not express themselves easily in sexual language.

"It helps to practice. Say sexual words out loud. Practice reading aloud from books that deal with sexuality. Get comfortable with either the more latinized words or, if you prefer them, the simpler four-letter ones. It sounds silly. But we simply don't learn to speak in sexual language, and often we are unable to do it in the bedroom.

"Sexual assertiveness—not aggressiveness—is also necessary: knowing and saying and doing what you want—and, especially, asking for what you want to receive. Start with the smallest, easiest possible action. Let's say you know that you want your hair and body stroked. You want your partner's hand to move slowly over your breasts rather than grabbing them. You know that you like at least ten minutes of gentle stimulation, then five minutes of more vigorous stimulation, and so on.

"You begin by saying what gives you the least anxiety: For instance, 'I would like it if you would stroke my hair.' That's usually less anxiety-provoking than to suggest that a man move his finger quickly with a circular motion. The next time, you request something that is a little bit harder to ask for.

"Of course, if you receive a negative response to, 'Would you please stroke my hair?' such as, 'No, I haven't the patience for it,' well, then, you've tested, and found a man with whom you probably shouldn't be having a relationship. But some people would prefer not to find out.

"A practical tip in terms of asking for sexual stimulation is to try to think of it as similar to asking someone to scratch your back: 'Up a little higher, down a little lower.' "

7. Having preconceived notions of what you ought to do. "I think particularly of young women," says Dr. Ladas, "and of the common notion that the only way to have an orgasm is through intercourse. Sometimes young women go for years of their lives without having an orgasm because they haven't found out how to help themselves get to that point.

"A concomitant of that is believing that you have to have simultaneous orgasms," continues Dr. Ladas. "You've 'got' to come at the same time, or it doesn't count.

"One patient, a man, told me that when he was with a young woman he cared about, she occasionally cried after she came. That is not an infrequent occurrence, because one of the things that happens when you really let go is that as muscles loosen up, a lot of sadness and longing comes to the fore. But crying is not just sadness and longing; it is also a way of relieving tension, and a way of coming back to life. Well, he was petrified and he fled. It wasn't until years later that he realized that he was making a judgment about how things ought to be, and fleeing from somebody he really cared about.

"A lot of sexual behavior has to be learned in our culture, because we don't live in a culture where we're trained to express our love sexually. There *are* some primitive cultures—Margaret Mead talks about them—where you're really trained.

"So you can be young and very much in love, and when the earth doesn't shake that first time, it can be shattering."

Dr. Jackman adds: "If you think it is your duty as a good wife to be available to your husband three times a week, then sex is your responsibility instead of your pleasure. It is just another job you have to do before you can go to sleep. Somewhat related to that is trying to live up to some norm. 'I read that the normal young couple makes love X number of times a week, therefore we must try to adjust our frequency to the norm.' Or, 'Normal people have oral sex, therefore we should.'

"Many people attempt to feel sexual when they don't, but think they should. But you can't make yourself feel turned on; it is an involuntary experience. Couples ought to do what they like to do, assuming nobody gets hurt by that. I saw a couple who have sex only twice a year, and that's just right for them. So it's a nonproblem."

8. Repressed anger. "One of the ten commandments of psychiatry," says Dr. Offit, "is that thou shalt express thine anger—in order to get it out, and be understood, and change behavior, and make up and feel better—because sex, like good digestion, usually goes on under peaceful circumstances.

"But I also think that the commitment this generation has to *expressing* anger might, for some people, be a sexual spoiler. Some people are so committed to doing that, they don't express their good feelings, too.

"It's also important to know what a psychiatrist means by 'anger.' It's an all-encompassing word, and there are other words that begin with the same syllable and are very much related, such as 'anxiety' and 'anguish,' so that expressing anger is not necessarily confined in our lexicon to 'I'm mad at you because. . . .' It's also, 'I'm disturbed and I feel distant from you because. . . .' When psychiatrists say it's important to express your anger, we don't mean, 'I'm mad at you and I want to beat you up'; it's simply important to try to reflect on, and discuss, and come to an understanding of what is disturbing."

Dr. Bellis thinks that the power struggle can also kill spontaneity and pleasure. "When there's a struggle regarding who's going to be the initiator, and who's going to be the passive one—if that can't be tossed back and forth—ultimately you lose the joy."

"There can be a withholding problem," Dr. Jackman adds. "Your partner knows what you like but won't do it for you because he's angry at you. A sexual problem can easily develop out of an interpersonal one."

"If you don't express anger in a direct way," say Ms. Schwerin and Dr. Vogel, "it is going to come out indirectly in some way—as manipulation, as a weapon. We help the person to communicate the anger directly, by stating it, or slamming a foot down or just getting it out. So she won't go to bed with the feeling of being angry; instead, she can say, 'No, I don't want to make love right now because there is something else happening that needs to come out of me before I get into that.' We give her permission to say no."

9. Spectatoring. In their book *Human Sexual Inadequacy*, Masters and Johnson identified sexual problems that seemed to respond to direct physical therapy, and they developed techniques for dealing with these dysfunctions.

Male dysfunctions include impotence and premature ejaculation; female dysfunctions include failure to achieve orgasm, dyspareunia (painful orgasm) and vaginismus (a spastic vaginal response that prevents intercourse).

One of the most common causes of dysfunction for both men and women is called spectatoring, and it often develops out of another problem: performing.

"We have a performance-oriented society," says Dr. Jackman, "in which the idea is that somehow you can perform sex better. Well, whenever you perform, you then have to ask, 'How am I doing in my performance?' and to answer that, you must begin watching yourself.

"Then, especially if there has been some problem, you are apt to think, 'Hey, I'm not getting excited fast enough,' or 'I'm not climaxing strongly enough,' or 'I'm not lasting long enough,' or whatever. The worse you do, the more you watch yourself, and the more you watch yourself, the worse you do."

Dr. Sloan says, "The same 'judge' that keeps us from stealing and engaging in other criminal acts also has been conditioned to judge certain sex acts as evil and bad, and so this spectator—your conscience—watches and ruins a natural function. I have couples carrying out specific sexual exercises at home, in private, as part of sex therapy, and during an exercise, I'll direct them to stop, look around the room: Are they being watched? And they see that no one is really there besides themselves. It relieves a lot rather quickly."

10. Physical turn-offs. Physical turn-offs come in two categories: personal hygiene and setting. Regarding physical turn-offs, Dr. Leon Zussman lists "body odor, bad mouth odor, dirt of one kind or another, such as fingernails that are dirty, belching, objectionable physical habits. Or the man might be unshaven, and that might turn a woman off; we hear that again and again. Of course, everything is subject to personal preference; some women *love* their men with a growth of beard."

"Dirty fingernails certainly play a role," agrees Dr. Sloan. "More than one 'dysfunctional' couple has been cured with just a single consultation. In one case it was dirty underwear; the guy owned a gas station and didn't change his underwear when he came to bed. It was a symbol to his wife."

"Then there are the conditions in the room," Dr. Leon Zussman continues. "Perfume, candles, lighting, music, clean satin sheets may be exciting for some, but other people don't *like* the light on or the brand of perfume, or the brand of candle scent, or the music. Rock 'n' roll has turned off just as many millions as it has turned on. The temperature, the humidity, open doors, the danger that the children may come in. . . ."

The list of prospective spoilers goes on and on. Birth control methods can turn people off, just plain ignorance about basic sexuality (especially common, oddly enough, among highly-educated types such as doctors, lawyers, scientists, professors), guilt about fantasizing, unconscious fears. . . . Some problems respond to treatment quickly, some require time and effort. But most sexual spoilers can at least be identified by improving communication, reading books and articles, taking courses in human sexuality—all of these help one, in a variety of ways, to become comfortable with one's own sexuality.

We want your advice.

Any anthology can be improved. This one will be—annually. But we need your help.

Annual Editions revisions depend on two major opinion sources: one is the academic advisers who work with us in scanning the thousands of articles published in the public press each year; the other is you—the person actually using the book.

Please help us and the users of the next edition by completing the prepaid article rating form on the last page of this book and returning it to us. Thank you.

Sexuality Through the Life Cycle

Individual sexual development is a life-long process that begins at conception and terminates at death. Contrary to our popular notions of this process, there are no latent periods during which the individual is nonsexual or non-cognizant of sexuality. The growing process of a sexual being does, however, reveal qualitative differences through various life-stages. It is with respect to these stages of the life-cycle and their relation to sexuality that this section devotes its attention.

Children, as they gain self-awareness, naturally explore their own bodies, masturbate, display curiosity for the bodies of the opposite sex, and show interest in the bodies of mature individuals such as their parents. Such exploration and curiosity is an important and healthy part of human development. Yet, it is often difficult for adults (who live in a society that is not comfortable with sexuality in general) to avoid making their children ashamed of being sexual or showing interest in sexuality. Adults often impose their "adult conceptualization" and ambivalence upon the children's innocuous explorations into sexuality. Thus, distortion of an indispensable and formative stage of development occurs which often precludes a full acceptance of sexuality later in life.

Adolescence, the social status accompanying puberty, proves for many individuals to be a considerably stressful period in life as they attempt to forge an adult identity and relationships with others. Because of the newly gained physiological capacity for reproduction, sexuality tends to be heavily censured by parents and society at this stage of life. This is especially true for the female. Standard injunctions that all sex is evil or that all adolescents are sexually irresponsible fail to contribute toward a healthy sexuality. The benefit of experience and knowledge of the older generation needs to be honestly and constructively mobilized. For this knowledge and experience to be useful though, trust across the generations must be established.

Finally, sexuality in adulthood, at least within marriage, becomes socially acceptable. Yet, for some, routine and boredom exact a heavy toll on the quality of sexual interaction. Extramarital sexual encounters are often sought and established despite the fact that such activity is conventionally stigmatized as infidelity. The problem of infidelity is not an easy one to solve. Current scholarly opinion maintains that infidelity and extramarital relations are two separate phenomena. Some individuals taking this viewpoint experiment with "swinging" and describe their activities as a way of life that improves their capacities for love and trust.

Sexuality in the later years of life is socially and culturally stigmatized by the prevailing misconception that sex is for the young. Such an attitude is primarily responsible for the apparent decline in sexual interest as one grows older. Physiological changes in the aging process are not in-and-of themselves detrimental to sexual expression or drive. As one elderly gentleman has commented, "Just because there is snow on the rooftop, doesn't mean that there isn't a fire in the chimney!" A life-history of experience, health, and growth can make sexual expression in the later years a most rewarding and fulfilling experience.

Looking Ahead: Challenge Questions

To what extent does social conditioning affect our psychosexual development?

Are there generational gaps of awareness that affect sexual development? If so, how can they be bridged?

How do our cultural expectations of marital sexuality compare with reality? What central issues emerge?

What identifiable "crises" characterize the life-stages? How can we solve them?

How much sexuality is left for the later years of life? How is sexuality in the later years typically treated by our society?

Kids and Sex

Starting Off Free to Feel

Anne C. Bernstein

Anne C. Bernstein, Ph.D., is a clinical psychologist practicing in Berkeley, California.

During the past four years, I have talked about children's ideas about how people get babies with many groups of parents and teachers. Everywhere I found attentive adult audiences, eager to learn more about how children think so that they might better communicate with the children in their lives. Early in each discussion, however, the topic shifted to another active issue for these adults: How should they respond to children's sexual behavior at school or at home? Not wanting to create guilt or feelings of unworthiness in the children, they were left with their own discomfort and the nagging feeling that some limits were appropriate. They knew that they did not want to repeat the negative messages about sexuality that they themselves had received in childhood, but, lacking positive examples, they felt unsure as to where to draw the line. And they didn't know what to do with their own feelings of discomfort, distaste, or avoidance.

So I found myself leading discussions on a subject about which I felt like a journeyman carpenter trying to construct a house from three sets of sketchy plans. I had done some thinking about childhood sexuality, but I felt less than expert on the subject. In speaking to these groups and learning from the experience of those most actively concerned with what to do on a daily basis, my own thoughts and feelings became clearer.

I'd like to discuss here some of the questions that kept popping up again and again as I reported on my research. For a more extensive discussion of how to feel more confident in your response to childhood sexuality, I recommend Sol Gordon's *Let's Make Sex a Household Word* and Wardell Pomeroy's *Your Child and Sex.*

Masturbation

Attitudes toward masturbation have changed drastically since World War I. Even Margaret Sanger, the noted birth control pioneer, wrote at that time that masturbation should be discouraged as causing permanent bodily harm. Blindness, sterility, warts, madness, and the waste of needed sperm were all blamed on that ubiquitous demon, masturbation. Given the prevalence of the activity so maligned, the only question is how our forebears explained how so many people remained sighted and sane.

Gradually medical science acknowledged that these dire allegations were unfounded, as many had already discovered from personal experience. Until recently, informed opinion on the subject was that masturbation was not harmful. But recent evidence goes further, to assert that it is a sign of healthy normality with long-term benefits as well as short-term pleasures.

As early as 1905, Freud wrote that the sexual instinct is aroused by maternal affection as well as by direct excitation of the genitals. He asked mothers not to blame themselves for the sexual impact of their tender nurturance: "She is only fulfilling her task in teaching the child to love. After all, he is meant to grow up into a strong and capable person with vigorous sexual needs and to accomplish during his life all the things that human beings are urged to do by their instincts."

Later research supported this connection between overt genital sexuality in infants and the quality of the mothering they receive. Rene Spitz observed infants throughout their first year of life. His findings were impressive. Of the babies who received virtually no nurturance, none displayed any genital masturbation, even though they received all the usual stimulation involved in ordinary diapering and bathing. Those whose mothers had personal problems that hindered the quality of the care they offered showed some self-stimulation but no genital masturbation. The babies given the best maternal care all began to masturbate by their first birthday, even without unusual genital stimulation. The study concludes that infantile sexuality develops spontaneously in the presence of quality nurturance, clearly demonstrating that it is both normal and healthy (see Gadpaille, *The Cycles of Sex*).

Masturbation provides very necessary learning about one's own body, what it's like and how it works. Familiarity with how one's body functions sexually is important to adult sexual pleasure. The Kinsey studies of sexual behavior found that women are more likely to have orgasms during intercourse after marriage if they have had orgasms, by whatever means, before. Most of the sex therapists I know who work with preorgasmic women have also noted that most of the women coming

"Kids and Sex," by Anne C. Bernstein, *New Age,* August 1978. From THE FLIGHT OF THE STORK by Anne C. Bernstein, Ph.D., (Delacorte Press).

for treatment report little or no masturbatory experience.

It is important not to discourage children from this very necessary exploration of their own bodies. Even if you are unconvinced that it has a positive role in the child's developing sexuality, trying to stop it does no good. A study by Landis and others revealed that prohibitions and threats against masturbation produced guilt but did not lessen the frequency of the behavior they were designed to eliminate.

For most parents the question is how to deal with their own old conflicts so that they don't pass on restrictive, inhibiting messages to their children. Parents, too, have feelings that they need to respect. If you are merely paying lip service to a more enlightened standard than you can actually embrace, your child will mirror your conflict. Commenting on the gap between what you know to be right and your own feelings can help children be clear with themselves.

Knowing they don't want to repeat the often well-intentioned mistakes of their own fathers and mothers, many parents today are trying to be more responsive to their children's needs. They learn that frowning or saying "Don't" leaves the shamed child feeling "I'm bad." Trying to distract the masturbating child with a toy or the suggestion of another activity does not avoid the implied criticism.

This does not mean that parents cannot or should not put limits on their children's masturbation or other sexual activity. By the time children are three or four, they can be taught that it is not good manners to masturbate in public. Preschool children, even toddlers, have already learned that there are appropriate times and places for many of their activities: Eating is done at the table, sleeping in the bedroom, elimination in the toilet, painting in a special part of the nursery. Masturbation need not be treated differently. A parent can tell a child, as did a woman quoted by Lonnie Barbach, "I know it feels good to play with your penis and it's OK, but it makes me uncomfortable when you do it here in the living room. I would feel much better if you would go in your bedroom, where you can have privacy." In this way, this mother acknowledges that the child's good feeling is appropriate and respected, but she also takes care of her own feelings of discomfort. Because she takes responsibility for what she feels, requesting that he move to another room for her benefit, she does not lead him to confuse her needs with his own. When space is more limited, parents and children will need more ingenuity to assure that each person has some time to be alone.

Children need confirmation that touching one's genitals is supposed to feel good, that pleasure is one aspect of having sexual organs, and that others have had the same experience. People usually begin to masturbate in infancy and may continue throughout their lives. It is not "babyish" to masturbate, although with children who are no longer babies some discretion about time and place and respect for the feelings and values of others is expected. Boys need to know that their erections are a normal part of male sexuality, and both sexes would be better prepared to understand their own bodies if they were told that "sometimes a special feeling called orgasm can occur" (Barbach). Kinsey found that 21 percent of the males and 12 percent of the females he interviewed had masturbated to orgasm by age twelve, figures that were elevated to 82 percent and 20 percent, respectively, by age fifteen.

Until recently, parents erred by being overly restrictive toward children's masturbation. Although still in the minority, some parents today are swinging too far with the proverbial pendulum, exhorting their children to masturbate. The problem with this approach is that masturbation is something children should do for their own pleasure, not to please their parents. What is a delight if discovered by themselves can become a duty if done at their parents' direction. It is important for children to feel that their bodies belong to themselves alone. To try to program a child to masturbate intrudes on her self-control and self-direction. According to Pomeroy, "the best a parent can do is to give the child privacy, refrain from embarrassing him or instilling him with guilt and fear, and answer his questions when and if he asks them."

One further question remains: How much masturbation is "too much"? In this context, "too much" usually means "more than I do." But compulsive masturbation can begin as early as toddlerhood. Like any other compulsive behavior, such as involuntary overeating, oversleeping, incessant talking or hitting, compulsive masturbation is a sign of emotional conflict. If it is short-lived and the only symptom of distress, it is seldom serious.

How can you tell if masturbation is excessive or compulsive? Warren Gadpaille defines a compulsive activity as one that occurs "so repetitively and incessantly as to interfere with other normal activities. One example is the child who might normally be expected to be fascinated by a new toy, playing with a friend, or enjoying a birthday party, but who seems totally preoccupied with manipulating his genitals. By focusing on the feeling in his penis, this child can withdraw his attention from the real world, giving himself the pleasure and comfort he requires without having to look outside himself toward a reality that feels frustrating." Gadpaille endorses parents' concern in such cases, pointing out that the compulsive masturbation that produces more tension than it relieves "is a symptom (not a cause) of some emotional difficulty. The difficulty can be discovered only by study of the particular child, but parents might generally try to be alert to whatever could be overtaxing the youngster's limited ego capacity to cope, such as the arrival of a new sibling, the loss of someone or something important, or a new environmental demand, such as toilet training or nursery school for which the child is not quite ready or which may be presented too forcefully." Often parents can determine what is distressing the child and either change the situation or give the child new skills with which to cope.

Sex Play

Ellen is sitting at the kitchen table finishing her coffee and reading the newspaper. From the bathroom she hears the voices of her six-year-old son and five-year-old daughter, who are sharing a tub. "Let's play sex," one proposes. "Now let's try penis to butt." Ellen is bewildered. Should she go in there and get them out of the tub quickly? Or is this harmless fun she can afford to ignore?

Jeanne is playing with her four-year-old daughter, Amy. Amy bounces on Jeanne's knee and slides down her leg, climbing back on mother's lap for more. Jeanne realizes that Amy's pleasure is sexual and becomes uncomfortable and embarrassed. She wants to stop the game without giving Amy the impression she is doing something wrong.

Peter and Jenny are four. They lie down in the corner of the nursery school, hug each other, and thrust their pelvises together. The teachers look at each other, each hoping the other will do something to stop the children, but neither wanting to have to handle the situation herself.

"What on earth am I supposed to do now?" is the feeling many adults have upon seeing children's play take an explicitly sexual turn. Profoundly aware of their own embarrassment and discomfort, and not wanting to handicap their children with anxious, angry or punitive prohibitions, they waver at the starting line, acting uncertainly, hesitating to intervene, or impulsively jumping in to let off their own steam.

Ellen allowed her children to finish their bath uninterrupted, but she was left with lingering doubts about whether this was a dereliction of maternal duty. Jeanne told Amy that she was uncomfortable playing the leg-sliding game and wanted to stop. After a brief hesitation, one of the nursery-school teachers told Peter and Jenny that their play was not a game to be played at school and attempted to divert their attention to a new activity.

You may have handled each of these situations differently from the adults described. There is no one right way to respond that rules out the alternatives. What you choose to do will have to take into account both the child's welfare and your own sensibilities. Parents who discount their own feelings, acting as they think they "should" without acknowledging some of their own conflicts, can give double messages that trap their children in pitfalls they had hoped to avoid.

The beginning journalists' instruction to find out who, what, where, when, and why, can also be of service to the parent trying to assess when and how to respond to children's sexual play. Who is participating, what they are doing, where and when and why they have chosen to do it all enter into determining the appropriate adult response.

Who

California recently passed legislation decriminalizing the private sexual activities of consenting adults. The principle behind this relaxation of legal restrictions is that people should be able to determine how they wish to behave so long as they neither exploit another person nor inflict their own standards of behavior on an unwilling audience. Although not directly applicable to children, the same philosophy can inform our judgments about children's sexual play.

Who is playing with whom? Are they equals, peers whose interests and capacities are developmentally matched? Or is one older, bigger, stronger, and able to use these advantages to intimidate or coerce the other? Is the activity something they are doing *with* each other, sharing the initiative and direction of the play, or is one doing something *to* the other, making up all the rules and leaving the other to feel acted upon rather than fully participant?

Gadpaille writes: "Children playing freely within groups of peers will interact, whether sexually or in any other way, at the level of their own spontaneous readiness. With the exception of older bullies ganging up on one or more younger children—a situation akin to child-adult sexuality—little children will express interest according to their own levels of ego and erotic development. Those who are not ready will not participate."

According to researchers permissiveness toward sexual play in childhood leads to more enjoyment of sexuality and fewer sexual problems as adults. "Many people reared in our culture," writes Gadpaille, "pay a high personal price for the supposed rewards of sexual repression, the price being alienation from one's sexual self, diminished capacity for tenderness and human closeness, a high incidence of sexual conflicts and disordered function, and perhaps the inability to think and feel like a whole person or to relate to others wholly." He concludes that "the evidence available to date is balanced in favor of relaxing the strictures against childhood sex play, both privately and with other children."

This does not extend to direct sexual activity with adults or older children, which is most often emotionally detrimental. While experts do differ about when to restrict children's sex play, clinical evidence and informed professional opinion are strongly opposed to adult-child sexual activity. There is no way for adults and children to partake in sexual activity that is respectful of the child's immature level of development. There can be no mutuality when the difference in power is so substantial. Children are in no position to freely give their informed consent to an activity determined by the more urgent sexual needs of an adult. Having learned that adults are to be obeyed, and aware of their own puny strength, they cannot be the ones to set the limits. When what is happening is more stimulating than children can handle, they typically regress to earlier, less conflict-filled times in their own lives, behaving in age-inappropriate, immature ways.

Most adults want to protect children from premature overstimulation. Parents, especially, want to make their homes safe places in which children can grow, supported by adult guidance but directed by their own development needs. When parents begin to experience sexual feelings for their own children, they react with alarm and shame. Because people seldom talk about these very secret feelings, they do not realize that sexual fantasies about one's children are common. It is normal to feel turned on by warm, affectionate, sensual little people. Acting out the fantasies could hurt the children, but having them is both normal and harmless.

Typically, parents having sexual feelings or fantasies about their children will do something to put more distance between them and the child. Picking a fight with the child reassures the parent that his feared and shameful thoughts will stay just thoughts. In *Games People Play,* Eric Berne called this maneuver "Uproar." It is marked by mutual faultfinding and raised voices. The anger of this game helps players avoid their sexual feelings, slamming bedroom doors to emphasize the limits to their intimacy. It is especially popular between fathers and their teenage daughters, but can take place between parent and child of either sex from preschool on. While this way of retreating from sexual feelings may reduce the possibility of acting them out, there are less destructive ways of assuring the same result. Even when children are their most seductive, adults can set limits without either rejecting them or mystifying the issues to produce distance.

In limiting children's sexual play, adults are called upon to exercise discretion, delicacy, and compassion. Emotional outbursts and threats may scare children into submission, but the guilt, shame, and fear left in their wake are often more disturbing than the events that occasioned such responses. Most parents want to teach their children to respect other people's wishes, rejecting coercion or exploitation as means of getting your own way. Overwhelming children with explosive tirades works against this important value. We may say "Do as I say, not as I do," but our practice is more convincing than our theory.

Who is involved is not the only issue in determining whether parental restrictions are in the child's best interests. What is going on is another criterion.

What

Mutual exploration is an important part of early-childhood learning. Curiosity about the sexual equipment of the other half of the world is both natural and normal, and many nursery schools now have open bathrooms so that children can find out more about sexual differences in an uncontrived, everyday way. Even play that involves direct genital stimulation, if it occurs between peers whose parents have similarly permissive values, can be harmless. But parents do need to be alert to whether children are being overstimulated in sex play.

Typically, children who are overstimulated will regress, acting more "babyish" when they have ventured beyond their developmental depth. Nursery-school teachers, who may expect and encourage comments and observations on sex differences by children, know that when the remarks get too silly, it's time to turn their attention to another topic.

Where and When

Where and when the play is taking place is another issue to consider in deciding when to discourage children's sex play. Wandering into a child's room and observing a game of "Doctor" in progress, a mother may choose to say "Excuse me" and close the door, teaching the children that their privacy is respected. The same mother might tell them to put on some clothes and find another game to play if she encountered the same behavior on the sidewalk or at Grandma's house. As with masturbation, and so many other things, children can easily learn that there are different times and places for different activities.

Sometimes children choose times and places for sexual play that they know adults will find unacceptable. While they may enjoy testing the limits of the adults "in charge," children are usually reassured to find that adults can assert those limits. In the dominant American culture, direct sexual activity usually takes place in private. Even when this is not wholly possible, some attempt is made to maximize the privacy of the setting for sexual encounter. Children whose play is explicitly sexual while they are in the company of adults are usually testing how those adults will respond, aware that they may be making the grown-ups uncomfortable. Their choice of a public place is frequently an invitation for intervention. You can be sure that they are begging for limits if they appear more attentive to adult reactions than engrossed in their own exploration.

It is difficult to avoid making children feel ashamed of being sexual when the society in which we live is not comfortable with sexuality in general and childhood sexuality in particular. Parents can be an important source of reassurance that it is okay to enjoy the pleasures of the body, but they cannot maintain for their children the illusion that the greater society thinks as they do. Children will also learn, from opening their senses to the content of the cultural media (language, television, advertising, radio, films, and literature to name a few) and by playing and sharing ideas with other children, that there is something embarrassing and taboo about sex. Not until there is greater agreement that childhood sexuality is a natural part of children's developing knowledge of themselves and human experience will shame and furtiveness be replaced by unselfconscious expression.

Parents can help children deal with confusing and contradictory messages about sexuality from different sources by commenting on the differences. Articulating the unsaid reduces confusion. It is preferable to tell children that other people may disapprove of children's sex play than for them to sense that there is something wrong without knowing what. Their embarrassment and giggles in talking about sex or being observed in sex play by adults shows that they have picked up on adult discomfort, whether from their parents or the larger community. They need to hear that the discomfort is real but the activity that arouses it is not bad.

Many parents who would like to be more permissive about sex play between child peers worry about their children's playmates' going home to tell Mom or Dad that Jimmy's parents let them do what their own parents forbid. Children don't usually go home and tell. If sex play is forbidden at home, they're too afraid that their parents would be angry that they've transgressed. But the problem remains a delicate one. When playmates come from homes with different values, some discussion of these differences will help them navigate the confusion of diverging paths. Parents are usually called upon to explain why they feel differently from Jane's parents about television viewing, homework, good nutrition, spanking, fights, or politics. Differences about sex play can also be explained, simply in terms of values. In a heterogeneous culture, children need to know the distinctions among fact, opinion, and value.

Nudity

To cover up or not to cover up in front of one's children is a question that makes many parents wonder. Some parents who enjoy and are used to being nude around the house worry that it might not be good for the children. Others, who are more comfortable when clothed, think that perhaps they should disrobe in front of their children as a laboratory session in sex education.

Parents' attitudes toward their own bodies have an important impact on their children's sexuality. If parents hide their bodies and are embarrassed upon being discovered unclothed, children will learn that there is something shameful about the human body. Casual and unaffected parental nudity conveys the message that parents are "at home" in their bodies, comfortable and self-accepting in being incarnate. Natural, matter-of-fact nudity in the home is beneficial to children, who will follow these models of comfortable self-acceptance. Not for them the shock at puberty reported to me by a young woman: "When I first got pubic hair, I thought I was turning into a monkey, 'cause I'd never seen an adult nude."

Parental nudity is sometimes thought to be overstimulating to children. I think it is the attitude of the adults, how they feel when they are undressed, and not the nudity itself that can be distressing. A look at other cultures shows us that nudity is not necessarily damaging to children. It is the emotional message the parent is broadcasting, not how many clothes he or she is wearing, that influences how children will feel. If parents are self-conscious about being undressed, they will transmit anxiety and doubt rather than comfortable self-assurance. If this is the case, parents can quietly request privacy, avoiding a show of distress.

Seductiveness, not nudity, is what overstimulates children. Parents can be seductive without being nude, and nude without being seductive. Nudity is not automatically seductive. It is natural and appropriate to be nude when dressing, in the bathroom, or when the family is relaxing at home. If family members are unselfconscious and matter-of-fact in their nudity, the sexual charge and excitement of exhibitionism that can be seductive and overstimulating to children will not be present. Children can tell whether parents are comfortably being themselves or making a big deal out of showing off.

No matter how comfortable parents are about being nude, they cannot create a Trobriand Island in one household. One eight-year-old boy questioned his mother about her nude sunbathing in the back yard: "What are you going to do when I bring a friend over?" When she replied, "Lie here," he protested, "In front of my *friend?*" The choice before her was clear. She could either continue her sunbathing *au naturel,* exiling her son and his friends from the house, or set up a distant-early-warning system for him to alert her that the outside world was at the door, so that some agreed-upon accommodation could be put in effect. Only the second choice conveys to a child that his needs, too, are respected.

Witnessing Adult Sexuality

Children need to know that sex is for pleasure and emotional intimacy as well as for making babies. It is important that they see that their parents' love for each other has a physical side, too. Kissing, hugging, cuddling, and being generally affectionate with each other teaches children about love. Experts agree, however, that "in our culture this doesn't mean making love with the children as spectators or participants." In talking to mothers, Barbach put it this way: "It might be good to let your child know that you and Daddy make love in the privacy of your bedroom; that during that time you don't like to be disturbed and any questions and problems can generally wait until afterward. To treat sex with dignity and love rather than to shroud it in awkward and unspeakable mystery is an excellent way of instilling a child with a healthy attitude toward sex."

There is no hard evidence that witnessing parental intercourse harms children, but most writers on the subject advocate caution. For most people the world over, during most historical periods, children have been exposed to adult sexual activity. It cannot, then, be inherently damaging. But what works in other times and places may not be optimal here and now. Gadpaille suggests that the criterion for whether this or any other practice as "benevolent" or "harmful" rests on whether early sexual stimulation influences development in a direction that is harmonious or divergent from later cultural expectations. While other cultures may provide ways for children to express their sexuality within the family, at this point in our history seeing adult intercourse may stimulate children without giving them an opportunity for discharging their excitement.

Overstimulation is a frequently given reason for parents to "take gentle pains to prevent children from intruding into their own intimacy or forcing their sexuality on them" (Gadpaille). Equally important is the tendency of young children to misperceive adult sexuality as involving violence and mutilation. Children who "accidentally" open the bedroom door when parents are making love can easily conclude that Daddy is hurting Mommy. They have no anchor in their own experience to hold them to the idea that these are two people who love each other enjoying themselves.

Opportunities for repeated, unconflicted observation of adult sex are rare in Western culture, in which the concept of sexual privacy is well established. Even when children can see and hear what is going on in their parents' bed, families frequently maintain the myth that this is not so. Parents convince themselves that the children are "too young to understand," asleep, or disinterested. Children know that they are not supposed to be witnesses to the furtive acts left unshielded by the circumstances of necessity. Secrecy and prohibition, whether successful or not, add fuel to the flames of frightening sexual fantasies.

Without either the opportunity for unlimited observation or the possibility of socially acceptable sexual outlets for children, witnessing adult sex can be both overstimulating for children and evocative of scary misconceptions. But this is not always and necessarily the case. While parents usually prefer to avoid these times, children may sometimes wander in unannounced. These occasions are best handled without panic or guilt about wounded young psyches. Telling the child that you want to be left alone and that you will be available in a short time is usually sufficient for the time being. Later you can explain what you were doing and ask if the child has any questions. Hearing you speak of the love and pleasure of sex will help counteract any impression of violence. Clear, simple, and forthright answers to questions can give them the information they seek without compromising your own intimacy and comfort or overstimulating them.

Bibliography

Barbach, Lonnie Garfield. *For Yourself: The Fulfillment of Female Sexuality,* New York: Doubleday and Company, 1975.

Gadpaille, Warren J., *The Cycles of Sex.* Edited by Lucy Freeman. New York: Charles Scribner's Sons, 1975.

Gordon, Sol. *Let's Make Sex a Household Word: A Guide for Parents and Children.* New York: John Day Company, 1975.

Pomeroy, Wardell B. *Your Child and Sex: A Guide for Parents.* New York: Dell Publishing Company, 1974.

Adolescent Sexuality

James N. Sussex, M.D.

Dr. Sussex is Professor and Chairman, Department of Psychiatry, University of Miami School of Medicine, Miami, and Director of the Mental Health Services Division of Jackson Memorial Hospital in Miami.

After I accepted an invitation to speak to this group on the subject of adolescent sexuality, I considered what to say and decided that I had a choice of presenting a theoretical discussion of sex and adolescence, with the usual emphasis on the nature of adolescence from physiologic and emotional viewpoints, or an editorial on the apparently changing sexual mores at this point in time in our culture, or a discussion of the subject in a way related to the parents of adolescents and the psychiatrist or other physician who deals with adolescents in his day-to-day work.

I can't avoid at least mentioning some of the theoretical aspects of the problem, and I don't want to pass up all opportunity to editorialize a bit as long as I've got the floor, but I'll try to keep what I say mostly in the area of the problems that any psychiatrist, or indeed any other physician, treating adolescents inevitably has to think about. My remarks will pertain to attitudes more than what to do's and how to's. They are in no way intended to be a definitive discussion of the subject and are really intended as much to stimulate thought and discussion as anything else.

Many of the taboos we regard in the Judeo-Christian cultural setting as matters of religious good and evil are really based on practical matters involving family solidarity as a means of providing safety and security for and acculturation of the children — and even more basically, perhaps, of title to them. Pride of fatherhood may indeed originate in pride of possession and ownership — and the demand for female premarital chastity and marital fidelity the logical way to assure this. Some adolescents — most boys, perhaps, but a few girls too — have always risked the wrath of the father and broken the taboos. Probably the kinds of things that adolescents do sexually have changed little over the years, but degrees of indulgence in various aspects of sexual practice have apparently changed considerably. Premarital intercourse, for example, has always occurred among adolescents in our culture, but there seems little doubt that there is more of it now than even a generation ago. Some people maintain that there is no change in the frequency at all — that it has just emerged into open discussion. Perhaps this is true for total amount of indulgence — the total number of individual premarital sex acts — but there is undoubtedly also a significant increase in the number of people who are not virgins at marriage — some increase among boys, a much greater increase among girls.

Why this increase? Some people attribute it to the availability of relatively easy and relatively certain means of avoiding pregnancy. Surely it isn't this simple. As a matter of fact, the number of girls engaging in sexual intercourse who do not use any contraceptive measure whatsoever is great enough to require us to look for other explanations.

I regard this increase as the product of at least two sets of factors, interwoven perhaps but essentially discrete. The first set of factors is represented by our shift from a culture in which work and productivity, and the self-restraint necessary to assure it, were highly regarded to a culture in which production as such requires less and less of the time and commitment of the people, and the laudable way of life is conspicuous consumption. In our culture nowadays, restraining one's impulses is actually discouraged. Instead the pressure is on the individual to act on his impulses — not to wait — since continual impulse satisfaction leads to continual consumption and this leads to prosperity in our technological society. In this context the pleasure principle is no longer incompatible with the reality principle. Hedonism is no longer anti-American. Fun is no longer wicked.

The second set of factors is embodied generally in the civil rights movement — or at least in that portion of the civil rights movement that has fought for equal rights

This address was presented at the annual meeting of the Florida Psychiatric Society in Pensacola, October 15, 1977.

for women, a battle not yet won but with significant victories in various areas. The TV commercial that has said to the women folk of our nation over the last few years, "You've come a long way, baby" — although this comment is made with reference to women having won the dubious privilege of smoking — applies as well to many other aspects of the lives of women in our culture — manner of dress, use of alcohol, choice of occupation, the vote, and, almost surely, sexual behavior as well. Regardless of whether contraception were possible or not, I feel sure we would have seen essentially the same things we are seeing now in the breaking down of the so-called "double standard" of sexual morality.

I might point out in passing that the concept of a single standard doesn't necessarily imply equal freedom of sexual behavior for both sexes. It could just as easily imply equal restriction of sexual activity for both sexes. The fact is that the single sexual standard toward which the trend seems pointed is that which the male of our society has always used as a guideline for his sexual behavior, although perhaps with some significant differences. The male has always regarded freedom of sexual activity, even to the point of frank promiscuity, as right and natural, even commendable, proving his prowess as a male and asserting his right to the admiration and envy of other males. The hunt was the name of the game, and he won who could carve the most notches in his gun, speaking in an obvious phallic symbolic sense.

We still raise our sons this way. We still believe that indulging in sexual activity, at least premaritally and maybe a bit extramaritally, is a natural, normal, and not particularly undesirable way for males to be — as long, that is, as they indulge these natural and normal appetites with someone's daughters other than our own.

Almost Single Standard

Two things seem to me to be happening. First, the girls have been saying with increasing insistence that they won't tolerate being discriminated against any longer with respect to the privilege of sexual pleasure. They have not only demanded more freedom of sexual activity but have insisted they not be regarded as bad girls if they exercise this freedom — that they be subjected to social ostracism no more than are their brothers for comparable conduct. The second thing that is happening though, is that the girls are bringing to this era of increased sexual freedom for themselves their tendency to want sexual activity only when some meaningful emotional tie exists between themselves and their partners — not always, to be sure, the desire for marriage or engagement or even for falling in love but at least some feeling of regard and affection for the partner.

This brings in the difference I referred to earlier. The girls, in their shift in sexual behavior, haven't gone all the way to the male end of the double standard because at that end lay essentially physical sex acts with partners who meant little or nothing as people. The girls have gone from the era of sexual imprisonment through a period that might be characterized as a sexual parole almost to complete sexual freedom, but seldom to what males have long engaged in — sexual license. The girls have introduced an element of interpersonal responsibility in premarital sexual relationships that all too frequently has not existed for the male of our culture at an earlier period. His view then was that good girls didn't — only bad girls did. And since they were bad girls, there was no need to regard them as people — but simply as sluts, whores, pigs. The girls themselves are now demonstrating to boys that good girls do do it with the right boy under certain circumstances. And the girls themselves — not we adults — are teaching our sons something of responsibility in sexual relationships. The girls are teaching the boys that sex with a girl he likes and who likes him is better than sex with someone for whom he's been taught to have only contempt.

And boys, perhaps for these very reasons, are beginning to think more like girls in this respect. Boys these days aren't impressed when dear old dad with a smirk tells them he knows boys will be boys but don't ever take advantage of a nice girl of our own social class — go with one of those little sluts from some other cultural group. Our sons no longer go to the other side of the tracks for their adolescent sex. They do it with the daughters of our best friends — obviously the best people in town!

Boys are restricting most of their sex activity more and more to girls they grew up with, know well, like and respect. Sex appears as part of a broader relationship and, however important it may be or how often it occurs, it is seldom the only reason the relationship exists. Even as recently as when most of us here grew up, it was common for boys to date two kinds of girls, one for sex and another for the other things boys did with girls. Today there is little reason for a boy to do this.

So the double standard is disappearing and the almost single standard that is evolving is probably a considerably more ethical one, in terms of the consideration the sexual partners have for each other, than that by which American males have lived in the past. In this sense, I can see the so-called "sexual revolution" as a move in a healthy direction. It frees girls and women from the chains of sexual slavery and it is having a civilizing effect on boys and men.

But, aside from the good that might be in such changes of sexual behavior, it would be idiotic to argue that grave dangers don't exist. Since the girl is still the one most vulnerable to really serious consequences of premarital sexual activity, it is to her situation that I would direct most of the remainder of my remarks.

Physicians Obligated

Let me say here that I recognize fully the degree of difference of opinion that may exist in this room about the desirability of premarital sexual freedom for girls. Let me urge, though, that we accept the reality of such freedom, whether or not we approve of it, and that as physicians who take care of adolescent girls in our practices we see ourselves as obligated to help them avoid undesirable consequences of their actions — or, when undesirable consequences do occur, as they inevitably must on occasion, to help them recover from them as quickly and with as little residual damage as possible.

At the outset I will say that I think physicians are not generally, as many seem to regard them, the best people to be the sex educators of our adolescents. Neither, in my experience, are many psychiatrists. For this role we are seldom well-trained. But in our favor is the fact that we are generally regarded as wise, objective, and nonjudgmental, and so we are granted an authoritative role regardless of how little of all of these qualities we may actually possess. Since schools, churches, and parents all abdicate responsibility for conveying valid, realistic sex information to our youngsters, we psychiatrists and other physicians are frequently cast in the role of sex educator even when we would prefer not to be. Discussion of the details of sex behavior with adolescent patients then, as they must face these issues in their lives, becomes not only reasonable but essential. To perform this function adequately, we must have a fair idea of the answers to such questions as these: What is normal? What is abnormal or "perverted"? What is dangerous? And under what circumstances is it more or less so?

Most of us, I presume, would regard sexual intercourse in adolescence as natural and normal even though some would argue that it is immoral or even illegal. The fact is that a great deal of adolescent sexual intercourse is occurring and that some adolescents, while doing what comes naturally, aren't so sure that it is natural. Brainwashed by their — usually — well-meaning parents and clergymen, many adolescents are not at all sure they are normal when they have sex thoughts and impulses to say nothing about acting on them. In the first half of adolescence especially, girls can have grave doubts of their normality when they find themselves growing sexually excited or strongly desiring to move from casual touching or "horsing around" with boys to more specifically sexual interplay. I knew one girl of 14 who developed an actual dread of going into situations in which a boy might touch her — even brush her — because of her embarrassment at the sudden dampness in her genital area. Her parents first became concerned about her because of sudden shyness and social withdrawal, then angry at her when they became convinced she was just being contrary, then concerned again as she began having nightmares, started to lose weight, and began having trouble with her school work. This girl wasn't phobic in the usual sense, although she did have a crippling dread of certain situations. She knew exactly why the dread existed but she was ashamed to discuss it with her mother or any other adult until finally the wise physician who was her family's doctor suspected it might be connected with sexual feelings. He opened up the subject when the girl's guard was down because of his obvious sympathy and desire to understand her, then heard her blurt out her fear of embarrassing herself in public. Reassurance of her normality, coupled with the practical suggestion that she shouldn't hesitate to use a sanitary napkin if she felt particularly vulnerable, were sufficient to meet the immediate crisis. He recognized, however, that her concern was probably overdone and suspected the existence of sexual hangups at a deeper level. He offered her the opportunity for further discussion, not on the basis of her need for psychological help as such but because of her need and desire for more information about her own sexual functions and feelings. In performing this service for her, he may have helped her avert any of several consequences that may follow an adolescent's conviction that she is sexually abnormal.

Possible Consequences

What are some of these possible consequences? This girl was already showing one consequence — an anxiety reaction with phobic features leading to increasing social withdrawal and inability to concentrate on her school work. Other girls might have developed compulsive studiousness and intellectualization, or psychosomatic symptoms, or a depressive reaction, or behavioral symptoms such as suicidal gestures or running away from home, over-eating or self-starvation, or sometimes even delusions or other psychotic symptoms. Once in a while a girl doubting her sexual normality will plunge into sexual activity in a desperate attempt to prove she's normal — not out of any real desire for sex as such.

What about masturbation? Most boys, even in this day and age, are somewhat embarrassed to acknowledge their indulgence in such activity but they don't usually feel terribly guilty or abnormal about it. Those who do need strong and direct reassurance. The occasional one who develops obsessions, compulsions, or schizophrenic symptoms obviously needs psychiatric treatment.

Girls too, though, have conflicts about masturbation. Whereas boys have usually become aware of the near universality of this activity and are in a position to pooh-pooh some of the old wives' tales about it, many girls may still never have heard anyone mention the possibility that they might do it. The result is that the masturbating girl often feels that she surely is the only girl in the world who ever did it. She isn't as likely as a boy to wonder about its having a deleterious effect on her mental or physical capacities, but she will wonder if she's sexually normal. She deserves to be told she is. Since masturbation must surely be the world's most effective means of preventing precocious or dangerous sexual intercourse, perhaps it should actually be encouraged. The frequency of masturbation in a boy or girl who is worried about masturbating is likely to go down when he or she isn't worried about it so much. The worry itself and the tension it produces lead to masturbation as a means of relief, to be followed surely by the vicious circle of guilt, more worry, more tension, and more masturbation. I doubt that encouragement would increase frequency of masturbation at all. Instead I would predict a decrease in frequency and much less likelihood that crippling anxiety and guilt will develop.

How about petting? Such activity has been known by a variety of different terms at various times, but essentially what we're talking about are those activities characterized by the sexologists as "foreplay" because they presumably are precursors to intercourse. In adolescence, however, they frequently constitute the end itself. Again, let's not argue the morality or immorality of such activity. Let's give a nod toward reality and acknowledge that it's here, close around us, all the time. A good many adolescents who have consciously decided not to engage in intercourse pet to orgasm as readily and regularly as people of our generation would once have engaged in a good night kiss. Such behavior is no longer the hallmark of the class tease, nor does the boy who participates expect, or frequently even want, the girl to participate in intercourse.

Petting has always occurred. Nowadays it's just more honest and straightforward and the ground rules better understood and accepted by both parties. Is it normal? Obviously it is not abnormal, but some people do think that using petting to orgasm as a regular substitute for intercourse, instead of foreplay per se, leads to a tendency after marriage to prefer these activities to intercourse. This view has overtones of fixation and conditioning theories and in some cases I'm sure that happens. In most, however, I am just as sure it does not. The Kinsey group reported that women who had achieved orgasm through petting prior to marriage were more likely to achieve orgasm in intercourse after marriage than those women who had not had such experience. Furthermore, it may be that a girl who has known and enjoyed premarital petting to orgasm as a fairly regular part of her sexual behavior is likely to enjoy her married sex life more in general simply because she is a more experienced and versatile sex partner.

More than anything else except masturbation, perhaps, petting to orgasm has prevented indulgence in sexual intercourse when such indulgence would have been dangerous or unacceptable to either participant. Is there any reason to try to talk adolescents out of this practice? Indeed, there may be merit in encouraging it. The argument that such encouragement will lead to increased intercourse may be nonsense. The intercourse such activity leads to would probably occur anyway. The difference is that with an approving attitude on the part of parents and physician, the adolescent girl wouldn't need to feel guilty and wouldn't need to defend herself against those guilt feeling by developing neurotic, psychosomatic, behavioral, or even psychotic symptoms.

One might argue that simply to look the other way is sufficient. I have doubts about that. When an adult looks the other way the adolescent assumes that he, the adult, is either stupid, a hypocrite, or afraid to face the issue. Any of these impressions is unfortunate and adds to the generation gap. Isn't it far more honest, and indeed safer, to take a definite stand on the matter and tell the adolescent we feel her actions are normal and good, not something to be ashamed of and guilty about?

The subject of petting to orgasm leads logically into the matter of oral sex. Although our culture has always had its advocates of such activity, their inclinations were usually acted upon only with the greatest of secrecy and usually with partners other than their spouses, fiances, or "steadies." Perhaps World War II, in its exposure of American young men to a variety of sexual experience with girls of other countries usually obtainable in this country only in a brothel, is responsible for the great increase of such behavior among adolescents. Somehow this group of young Americans apparently felt free enough to come back and teach their wives and girl friends these other forms of sex activity. This, coupled with or perhaps manifested by the more open description of such activity in even the most acceptable of recent novels, suddenly opened the eyes of America's younger generation of both sexes. In my judgment, premarital oral sex is now nearly as common among adolescents as manual petting to orgasm and possibly more common than intercourse since many adolescents use it as a substitute for the potentially more dangerous act. Boys no longer seem to regard cunnilingus as disgusting or unmanly nor are they nearly so likely as even a dozen years ago to regard a girl who will engage in fellatio as a slut. I have no idea what proportion of oral activity goes to orgasm but it does occur and with amazingly little anxiety, probably less than for masturbation.

What about group sex? I have had reported to me what I would regard as an increasing tendency to engage in various sexual acts, to and including intercourse, in the presence of others. This apparent lessening of concern about privacy is perhaps a natural outcome of the combination of increasing freedom of sexual activity and the traditional pattern of double dating. The practice seems to have begun well before the present group of adolescents came on the scene, and there are those who believe this phenomenon will increase rather than decrease in the future. Once adolescents begin engaging in sexual activity, they seem to have amazingly little reticence about it among their own peer group. They're all doing the same thing. Exchange of partners sometimes occurs but this appears to me to be rare. Even more rare are sex orgies and the multiple groupings referred to by such terms as "gang bang." The latter kind of phenomenon has occurred all through history, I'm sure, and still does, although I'll wager at no greater frequency than in the past. The girl who engages in such pastimes may well be heading for trouble and in need of help. At the very least she deserves a careful psychiatric evaluation.

This brings us to the matter of constancy and fidelity. Adolescent girls have traditionally been characterized as fickle and inconstant. Well, they are, in the sense that they are engaged in comparison shopping. And now, since sexual activity is accepted as being as much the prerogative of a girl as of a boy, at least in a meaningful relationship, it stands to reason that a girl may well have sexual intercourse with more than one boy, perhaps several, before she marries. But I would argue strongly that most of these girls are not promiscuous — that they are, rather, for the most part amazingly faithful, although serially so. In this their serial monogamy isn't a great deal different from that practiced so freely by their parental generation — except that the parental group is far more likely, in my opinion, to be unfaithful during each marriage than the adolescent girl is likely to be during the time she's going steady with a particular boy. Furthermore, and I think this is important, the boy is also more likely than not to be constant and faithful within the steady relationship.

Does age have anything to do with these things? Of course it does. We can hardly meaningfully bracket 13-year-olds and 18-year-olds in the same discussion. Although fewer girls reach marriage with their virginity and although sexual activity is more accepted generally in adolescence, I am not sure that the age of initial sexual intercourse is going down significantly. However, since our girls are reaching puberty earlier than their mothers and grandmothers, and since maternal pressure on girls for early heterosexual social popularity seems to increase year by year, I wouldn't bet that the trend won't be toward earlier intercourse.

Alternative Paths

If young adolescents are going to engage in sexual activity when they are free to do so — and they are free to do so the moment they first walk out the front door unchaperoned — we have at least three alternative paths to follow: (1) We could decide they can't be allowed any freedom at all and deny it to them — in which case all early adolescent unsupervised and unchaperoned activities would, logically, have to be banned; or (2) we could arm them with as much information as we can and provide them a sound basis on which to make what, to them, are reasonable and supportable decisions, and we could make sure that the decisions we leave to them are backed up by every reasonable measure to prevent them from getting into trouble as a result of those decisions; or (3) we could go on as we have in the past trying to scare them into conformity and making them suffer the horrible consequences if they choose to do their own thing. I am out of sympathy with the third approach not only because it's almost always a miserable failure but also because it perpetuates hypocrisy, dishonesty, insincerity, intolerance, prejudice, and bigotry — all in the name of morality — and with the consequence of many ruined young lives. The only cause for joy among the elders when an adolescent gets into trouble in the context of this kind of teaching could only come out of an essentially punitive attitude toward adolescents which says, in effect, "I told you so — it serves you right."

The first alternative may have merit — restricting unsupervised activities for the younger teenaged group — but it is difficult to convince some parents, especially the mothers but frequently with father's concurrence, who see their daughter's whole future resting on whether she is popular at 13 years of age. These are the same parents who are frantic when they find their sub-debutante making out with a neighbor boy at the poolside party and come running to a psychiatrist with fears that she is on her way to sexual deliquency. As a matter of fact, she may well be, and the parents need help in getting their messages straight.

The second alternative is the only one that makes sense to me at this point in time. If we let our 13 and 14-year-olds out alone, unsupervised, we've got to equip them with whatever information they need to make the right decisions and to protect them against the undesirable consequences of any wrong ones they may make. We don't send a daughter out in the car alone without driving lessons. Why should we send her out ignorant about sex and unprotected against a possible accident. It is amazing to me that in this day and age, when contraceptive information and materials are so easily and generally available, that so many girls of even college age seem to have no idea how to protect themselves against unwanted pregnancy. One could argue that such girls are unconsciously seeking pregnancy or are exhibiting a rebellious "I don't care" attitude and certainly this is true in some instances. For the most part, though, I am convinced that the girls just don't know what to get, where to get it or, if they do get it, how to use it properly. And they are too self-conscious and embarrassed to go to anyone for help. A girl's peers aren't a good source of contraceptive information even if she could risk showing her ignorance by asking them for it. The results of this amazing ignorance are all too often tragic.

You hope a soldier going into combat never has to use a knife to kill an enemy soldier coming at him at close range — and most soldiers don't have to face such a situation. But you prepare all soldiers for such an eventuality. By the same token a girl going into combat zones with boys should be prepared for anything that can happen to her — not that you expect it to happen but just because it might happen. She should know about her impulses and the emotional and physical signs that tell her they are operating. She should know what sex acts of various kinds are like and how they can be of possible advantage or possible danger to her. She should be given all the information she needs to make sound decisions for herself — because they will be decisions for herself made in circumstances in which a mistaken one could be tragic.

I know one girl who had been using what she called the "rhythm method," a schedule she had been given by a girl friend. How she had avoided pregnancy up to that time was a miracle because it was 180° backward. At any rate, that girl, in my judgment, deserved to know the correct information, as nearly as we can know it medically, about "rhythm." I explained it to her — including the risks. She was horrified and wondered how any girl could trust it, even if she had the sequence correctly. I said I didn't know either how any girl could trust it.

Obviously some girls can be provided with reasons that are compellingly on the side of not engaging in intercourse — but not on the basis of scare tactics. Most adolescent girls aren't stupid. Neither are they neurotic. Most of them want to make decisions that will lead toward happiness and self-fulfillment, not toward misery and self-destruction. Most of them are capable of considerable self-restraint and have a very acceptable value system built up inside themselves already. Most really don't want to become pregnant, or compromise their reputations, or make themselves available for exploitation. Most are perfectly capable of coming to decisions that are reasonable for them if they are helped to look at the real issues involved. I have had good success with quite a few girls who were contemplating possible sexual intercourse with boy friends. Not all were virgins, so loss of virginity as such was not an issue with many of them. Yet they considered carefully four questions I suggested they ask themselves.

Four Questions

Here they are. First, I tell the girl, ask yourself if there's any chance you'll get pregnant. If the answer is yes, you'd probably better say, "No," to the boy because the consequences, should you become pregnant, aren't pleasant ones. If the answer is "No, there's no chance of my getting pregnant," it may be okay to have intercourse. Move on to the next question.

Question 2: Will I lose my reputation? If the answer's "Yes" or even "Possibly," then intercourse could be a pretty dangerous proposition. If the answer's "No, my reputation's absolutely safe," then it may be safe to go ahead. Move on to question 3. I might add that girls are more concerned about their reputations these days than many adults think. Virginity as such has little to do with reputation, but who the girl does it with, why she does it, and under what circumstances do have bearing on her reputation, and few girls are willing even today to be considered promiscuous or to have the boy talk about them.

Question 3: Will I be humiliated? Here the going gets tough for the girl. To the first two questions she can answer "No" pretty easily, almost off-handedly, but this one requires her to examine the nature of her relationship with the boy, what she expects of him, and how she will feel if he doesn't come up to these expectations. I recall one girl who was excitedly contemplating intercourse with a particularly status-conferring boy, but this question brought her up short as she realized his idea of status rested apparently entirely on his love 'em and leave 'em reputation. She decided she didn't want to feel the humiliation of acknowledging to herself that he had no use for her as a person but only as a "piece." If the answer to question 3 is "Yes" or "Probably" then intercourse is an invitation to the kind of hurt that most girls dread deeply. If the answer is "No" then intercourse might be a safe and gratifying experience. Try the last question.

Question 4: Will I feel guilty? This requires the girl to examine her own standards of sexual behavior, her religious convictions, her relations with her parents, her feelings about herself and her ideals. If the answer to this question is "Yes" or even "Possibly," going on to intercourse will create some problem for the girl and she knows it. She may be willing to take the risk but by this time she has at least done a lot of thinking about it, and engaging in intercourse can never again be wholly on the basis of impulse.

If she decides intercourse is safe for her, or that she's going to do it anyway despite the risks, then I would do everything I could to make sure that bad consequences would not occur — physically, emotionally, or socially. I would provide the chance for her to discuss the matter at any time before or after her decision was implemented. I would try to assure myself that the risk of pregnancy was the least possible, including giving her whatever information she needed to get effective contraception.

What I advocate may sound to you like contributing to the delinquency of a minor. I don't think it is. No girl is going to engage in intercourse because a contraceptive is available. No girl who plans to engage in intercourse is going to change her mind because of the unavailability of one. The physician who takes a holier-than-thou attitude at that point and refuses to give a girl the information she needs to prevent catastrophe is party to the act, in my judgment, if she becomes pregnant. I wouldn't know how he could sleep very well after he heard the news. To act in the best interest of the girl seems to me the essence of being a good physician to her. How the physician who harms a girl by denying her what she needs to prevent disaster can justify his action is beyond me. Yet there are many who take such a view and condemn those who maintain that a girl who is going to have sexual intercourse premaritally should be provided with appropriate and effective contraceptive measures.

I think today's adolescents are going to come up ultimately with a new code of sexual morality based not on fear of parental or divine retribution because sexual pleasure is inherently evil but based instead on woman's right to sexual pleasure and on the ethics of interpersonal responsibility and commitment. Whether they do come up with a new code of this sort remains to be seen. Perhaps the ambivalences and conflicts and ambiguities our adolescents still haven't managed to work out for themselves will be transmitted to their children and create even more havoc in the next generation of adolescents. Certainly our generation has done little to help them resolve their conflicts since our own are so continually apparent. We, as a generation, don't know whether we want to adopt the "new morality" or not. Or perhaps it would be more accurate to say we would like to adopt it for ourselves while still totally committed to the old morality for adolescents.

At any rate, our own confusion leads us to present ambiguous cues to our adolescents — and the adolescents interpret this as insincerity, hypocrisy, and dishonesty. Quite clearly parents talk out of both sides of their mouths as they expound traditional moral values to their children and obviously espouse the different set being beamed into the house electronically. What teenager can believe his parents? The generation gap is at least partly explainable and understandable as a credibility gap.

Yet teenagers do need the benefit of the experience and knowledge of the older generation. Everything we know or believe isn't necessarily outdated. To make this experience and knowledge usefully available to an adolescent, though, we must win her trust. We must see things as they are — and tell it like it is — which includes, obviously, a multitude of potential dangers as well as a wealth of potential pleasure.

The family doctor, pediatrician or psychiatrist may be the only adults able to elicit this trust in the adolescent — and he has the obligation, in my view, to make himself available for the role of sexual advisor. He should not, of course, enter into a kind of mutual sex fantasy with the adolescent, but neither can he afford to live in his own fantasies if he is to be of service to the adolescent — either the fantasy that all sex is evil or the fantasy that all adolescents are sexually irresponsible. First and foremost, he is obligated to help his adolescent patient make the best possible decisions for herself, with the best information available, and to help her avoid harmful or undesirable consequences of her decisions, even if those decisions are not the ones he would have made for her.

A Major Problem for Minors

Cynthia P. Green and Kate Potteiger

Cynthia P. Green and Kate Potteiger were on the staff of Zero Population Growth, Inc. when this article was written. Green is now a writer for the Population Information Program of George Washington University. Potteiger is now in-house educator for Planned Parenthood of Metropolitan Washington, D.C.

Teenage pregnancy has reached epidemic proportions in the United States. Each year, more than one million teenagers become pregnant. In comparison, 54,847 Americans contracted measles and 20,123 had mumps in 1977, the most recent year for which statistics are available. By the age of 20, three in 10 American women have borne at least one child.

Early childbearing poses serious health, social, and economic consequences for teenage mothers and their children. In addition to facing higher health risks both for themselves and their children, teenage mothers are often forced to leave school and to forego job training and other opportunities for economic advancement. Unmarried mothers face social disapproval, financial hardship, and difficulty in finding work and child care facilities. If they marry, teenage mothers are more likely to have unstable marriages and financial problems than others of the same age and socioeconomic status. Women who have their first child in their teen years tend to have more children in quicker succession than their peers.

In the past, pregnant teenagers were pressured to get married or have their babies secretly and put them up for adoption. In addition, they were routinely expelled from school. Today teen mothers are asserting their right to an education, and special classes and programs have been started in many communities.

While older women's fertility has been declining during the past five years, teenagers aged 14 and younger have had increasing numbers of children, and the fertility rate of teens aged 15–16 has remained about the same. The proportion of U.S. births attributed to teenagers has been increasing; one in five U.S. births is to a teenager. Also, the number of out-of-wedlock births to teenagers is rising; teenagers account for half of all out-of-wedlock births in the United States. Most teenage pregnancies are unwanted, as is indicated by the fact that one in three U.S. abortions is to a teenager.

Experts attribute the epidemic of teenage pregnancies to increased sexual activity, nonuse or ineffective use of contraceptives, and lack of contraceptive information and services for teenagers. More than four million teenage women aged 15–19 are sexually active and at risk of unwanted pregnancy. Only half of them are currently receiving contraceptive services. Of the estimated 420,000 to 630,000 teenage females under 15 who are sexually active, only 7 percent are receiving contraceptive services even though this age group is most vulnerable to health risks if they become pregnant.

Studies show that most teenagers seek contraceptive services after they have become sexually active; many of them come to clinics initially for pregnancy tests. Traditional sanctions against premarital sex have not kept teenagers celibate but rather appear to have contributed to the nonuse and sporadic use of contraceptives as well as the tendency to select unreliable contraceptive methods.

Increasing Sexual Activity

More than half of the 21 million young people aged 15–19 are estimated to be sexually experienced—almost seven million young men and four million women. In addition, about one-fifth of the eight million 13–14-year-olds have had sex. A 1976 national survey confirmed that a growing proportion of teenagers are sexually active and that they are beginning their sexual activity at earlier ages. The study found that 35 percent of the single female teenagers had experienced intercourse in 1976 compared with 27 percent in 1971—a 30 percent increase. The proportion of sexually experienced females rises from 18 percent at age 15 to 55 percent at age 19.

Most studies indicate that teenage sexual activity is sporadic. The 1976 study found that nearly half of the sexually experienced teenagers surveyed had not had intercourse in the month prior to the survey. The proportion of sexually experienced blacks (63 percent) is twice that of whites (31 percent), the survey found, but the rate of increase for whites from 1971 to 1976 is more than twice the rate for blacks.

Along with increasing sexual experience, teenagers are also contracting venereal diseases in growing numbers. Teenagers aged 15–19 are three times more likely to contract gonorrhea than people over 20, while the risk of syphilis is 61 percent greater for teenagers.

Risking Pregnancy

Few teenagers begin to use contraception at the same time that they begin having sexual intercourse, and their contraceptive use is typically sporadic. A 1975 study in four cities found that almost half of the sexually active females and nearly 70 percent of the males surveyed risked pregnancy at least once. A national survey of teenage contraceptive practice revealed that the sexually active teenage women who had never used contraception had increased from 17 percent in 1971 to 26 percent in 1976.

Nevertheless, the 1976 survey also found that those teenagers who do use contraceptives select more effective methods today than in 1971. The study found that nearly two-thirds (64 percent) of the single teenage women interviewed had used birth control at last intercourse, and one-third of them had used the Pill or IUD. Three in 10 said they "always" used contraception. The Pill was named the "most recently used" method by 47 percent of the teenage women using contraception, while 21 percent used the condom, 17 percent used withdrawal, 8 percent used foam, cream, diaphragm, or rhythm, 4 percent used douche, and 3 percent had an IUD.

Research studies have found no evidence that the availability of abortion would weaken the motivation to use contraception

Many teenagers who do not use birth control are poorly informed about the risks of pregnancy. According to a 1971 national survey, seven in 10 of the single teenage women who did not use birth control explained that they thought they had sex too infrequently or that they had intercourse at the "safe time of the month." Ironically, only 38 percent of the teenagers surveyed could identify the time of the menstrual cycle when pregnancy is most likely to occur.

Citing other reasons for contraceptive nonuse, 31 percent of the respondents said that they could not obtain contraceptive services, 24 percent explained that contraceptives interfered with the pleasure of spontaneity of sex, and 13 percent mentioned moral or medical objections to contraceptives (Respondents gave more than one answer.) Nevertheless, eight out of 10 (84 percent) of the nonusers said that they did not wish to become pregnant.

Research studies have found no evidence that the availability of abortion would weaken the motivation to use contraception. In a 1971 study, sexually experienced teenage women were asked what they thought a young unmarried girl should do if she found herself pregnant by a boy she did not love; only one in five chose the option of abortion.

Inadequate Clinic Services

Between 1971 and 1975 the number of teenagers on family planning clinic rosters more than doubled. Nevertheless, many teenagers are still unable to obtain clinic services and many programs fail to reach teenagers early enough. One study of 40 family planning clinics found that 94 percent of the teenage patients had had sexual intercourse before seeking contraceptive services, and 75 percent had been sexually active for at least a year. Thirty percent of the teenagers had been pregnant previously.

In 1975 there were 1.1 million teenage women enrolled in organized family planning programs, constituting 30 percent of the national clinic caseload. Nearly half of the adolescent patients had never used contraception prior to enrollment. After enrollment 84 percent used the most effect methods—the Pill or the IUD. An additional 850,000–1,000,000 teenage women receive contraception from private physicians. However, about half of the four million sexually active females aged 15–19 are still not receiving family planning help from any source. A meager 7 percent of the sexually active teens younger than 15 are currently receiving family planning services.

Pregnancy among Teenagers

Planned Parenthood's Alan Guttmacher Institute (AGI) estimates that each year more than one million teenagers aged 15–19 become pregnant—one in 10 of the females in this age group. In addition, 30,000 girls younger than 15 get pregnant annually. More than two-thirds of all teenage pregnancies are believed to be unintended.

Of the million pregnancies which occurred in 1974, 28 percent resulted in marital births that were conceived following marriage, 27 percent were terminated by abortion, 21 percent resulted in out-of-wedlock births, 14 percent ended in miscarriage, and 10 percent resulted in marital births that were conceived prior to marriage.

Among pregnant adolescents 14 and younger, 45 percent have abortions, about 36 percent give birth out of wedlock, and 13 percent miscarry. Only 6 percent of these young teenage pregnancies end in marital births.

One-third of U.S. Abortions

Teenagers account for about one-third of all legal abortions—an estimated 325,000 abortions in 1975. In 1974, three in 10 teenage pregnancies were terminated by abortion. About half of all teenage abortions were obtained by 18- and 19-year-olds; 45 percent by 15–17-year-olds; and 5 percent by girls 14 and younger. Between 1972 and 1975 the abortion rate rose from 19 to 31 procedures per 1,000 women under age 20. Increased availability of abortion has slowed the rise in out-of-wedlock births which began in the late 1960s, but it has not reversed the trend.

Legal abortion is still not equally available throughout the country. Abortion services tend to be concentrated in one or two metropolitan areas in each state. The need to travel outside one's community is a hardship for young and poor women who often can't afford such a trip. The unequal distribution of abortion services is evident in the varying abortion ratios for teenagers in different states, ranging from three abortions per 1,000 live births in Mississippi to 130 per 1,000 births in New York. The Alan Guttmacher Institute estimates that a minimum of 125,000 teenagers were unable to obtain needed abortion services in 1975.

Childbearing among Teenagers

In 1975 nearly one in five (19 percent) of all births in the United States was to a teenager—12,642 births to women under 15 and 582,238 to women aged 15–19. Fertility rates for older teenagers have fallen slightly in recent years, though not as sharply as the declines among women aged 20 and older. Births to girls younger than 14 have increased, while fertility among young women aged 14–17 has remained at approximately the same level. Between 1974 and 1975 the fertility rate for girls aged 10–15 increased by 8 percent.

Half of the four million sexually active females aged 15-19 are still not receiving family planning help

The proportion of teenagers giving birth rises rapidly with age. The National Center for Health Statistics calculated that in 1975 nearly 1 percent of the 15-year-olds had had at least one child, 3 percent of the 16-year-olds, 6 percent of the 17-year-olds, 12 percent of the 18-year-olds, 20 percent of the 19-year-olds, and 30 percent of the 20-year-olds. Teenagers tend to have their children in quick succession. In 1975 nearly one-fourth (24 percent) of mothers aged 20 had had more than one child; 21 percent of all births to teenagers were second or higher order births.

Nearly two in five (39 percent) of all births to teenagers are out-of-wedlock, and the proportion of births to unmarried teens is increasing. With the decline in marital fertility there has been a corresponding increase in childbearing outside of marriage for both white and black teenagers. In 1975 one in five babies born to white teenagers and three in four babies born to black teenagers were out of wedlock. Over half (52 percent) of the out-of-wedlock births in 1975 were to teenagers—11,000 to women under 15 and 222,500 to women aged 15–19, a 5 percent increase over the previous year. Among those teenagers who give birth out of wedlock, 87 percent keep the child, 5 percent send the baby to live with others, and 8 percent give the baby up for adoption.

Mothers' Health Risk

Both the adolescent who gives birth and her infant face greater risk of death, illness, or injury than do women in their 20s. The maternal death rate is 60 percent higher for teenagers aged 14 or younger and 13 percent greater for 15–19-year-olds than for women in their early 20s. Women giving birth at ages 15–19 are twice as likely to die from hemorrhage and miscarriage and 1.5 times more likely to die from toxemia (blood poisoning) than mothers in their early 20s. The risks increase dramatically for women under 15 giving birth; they are 3.5 times more likely to die from toxemia. Although the health risks for younger teenagers are considerably higher than those for women aged 18–19, the risks generally increase with parity, so that an 18-year-old experiencing a second pregnancy may have dramatically increased health risks.

The most common complications of teenage pregnancy are toxemia, prolonged labor and iron-deficiency anemia. Poor nutrition, inadequate prenatal care, and physical immaturity contribute to the risk of complications.

Children born to teenage mothers are two to three times more likely to die in their first year than babies born to women in their 20s. About 6 percent of first babies born to girls under 15 die in their first year. The incidence of prematurity and low birth weight is higher among teenage pregnancies, increasing the risk of such conditions as epilepsy, cerebral palsy, and mental retardation.

Life Options for Young Parents

Pregnancy and motherhood are the major causes of young women leaving school. Eight out of 10 women who become pregnant at 17 or younger never complete high school. Among teenage mothers 15 and younger, nine in 10 never complete high school and four in 10 fail to complete even the eighth grade. Despite legislation and court decisions upholding the right of school-age parents to education, the dropout statistics suggest that many schools' policies and personnel may discourage pregnant students from continuing their schooling.

Because many young mothers do not complete high school and the vast majority (79 percent in a New York City study) have no work experience, adolescent mothers are doubly disadvantaged in competing for jobs. Childcare responsibilities often further restrict employment opportunities. Teenage mothers are more likely to be unemployed and to receive welfare than mothers who postpone their childbearing until their 20s. The New York City study of teenage mothers found that 91 percent of the women who gave birth at ages 15–17 were unemployed a year and a half after the birth and 72 percent were receiving welfare assistance. Even 18- and 19-year-old mothers were slightly more likely than older mothers to be unemployed and two and a half times more likely to be on public assistance.

Teenage marriages are two to three times more likely to break up, compared with those who marry in their 20s. Teenage couples who marry as a result of pregnancy are more likely to be economically disadvantaged in terms of occupation, income, and assets than are couples of similar socioeconomic status. Such marriages are also more vulnerable to divorce and separation. A Baltimore study of premaritally pregnant teenage couples (17 or younger) found that one-fifth of the marriages broke up within one year and nearly one-third dissolved within two years. Within six years, three in five of the couples were divorced or separated.

Women who give birth as teenagers tend to have a larger completed family size and tend to have their children closer together. Married women who have their first child at age 17 or younger expect a completed family of four, while wives whose first birth comes at the ages of 20–24 expect fewer than three children. Women who have their first child at age 17 or younger will have 30 percent more children than women who begin childbearing at ages 20–24, and women aged 18–19 at first birth will have 10 percent larger families.

Laws Regarding Minors

During the last five years there has been a clear trend toward liberalizing laws regarding the right of minors to consent to their own medical care. Currently 26 states and the District of Columbia specifically affirm the right of minors to consent to contraceptive care, and all 50 states allow minors to consent to venereal disease treatment. In July 1976 the U.S. Supreme Court overruled a Missouri law which required a minor to have parental consent to obtain an abortion, thus invalidating similar laws in 26 states. Earlier in 1976 the

Supreme Court ruled that federally funded family planning programs must serve eligible minors on their own consent.

Many agencies and physicians still refuse fertility control services to minors without written parental permission

---

Despite this liberal trend and despite the fact that no physician has been held liable for providing contraceptive services to minors of any age, many agencies and physicians still refuse fertility control services to minors without written parental permission.

The right of minors to purchase nonprescription contraceptives was upheld by the U.S. Supreme Court in a June 1977 decision. The Supreme Court invalidated a New York law which banned the sale of nonprescription contraceptives to persons under 16.

Teens Denied Information

Despite evidence from several studies that one of the major causes of unwanted teenage pregnancy is ignorance about human reproduction and the risk of pregnancy, young people continue to be denied the information they need to make responsible decisions related to their sexuality.

Research suggests that mass media, especially television and radio, are an important source of family planning information for teenagers. A 1974 family planning communication study found that mass media contributed more to teenagers' family planning knowledge than other sources, including parents, peers, or schools. However, the researchers' analysis of media coverage revealed that television and radio provided very little contraceptive information: television contained an average of only eight minutes of family planning-related programming in an entire month, while radio broadcast an average of 14 minutes monthly. Newspapers contained only 19 items during the month.

Contraceptive advertising on television and radio is banned by the Code Authority of the National Association of Broadcasters, thereby eliminating another potential source of information about contraceptives.

At present only 29 states and the District of Columbia require the teaching of health education in public high schools, and only six of these states and the District mandate family life or sex education as part of the curriculum. Louisiana is the only state which outlaws sex education altogether.

Many states officially "encourage" the teaching of these subjects in their education policies but allow for local options. Consequently, hundreds of school districts have ignored, restricted, or prohibited sex education.

Even where sex education is provided in schools, contraception is often not discussed. A 1970 survey of U.S. school districts revealed that only two in five sex education teachers included contraception in their curricula. Human reproduction, adolescent development, and venereal disease were the most commonly covered topics. A recent national survey of high school teachers in population-related subject areas found that only one-third taught anything about human reproduction, sexuality, or abortion. Even fewer taught about birth control.

Job to Be Done

A report submitted in 1976 to the Department of Health, Education, and Welfare by Urban and Rural Systems Associates recommends that sexually active teenagers be designated a high-priority target population for family planning services and that federal and state funding for family planning services be increased. To increase clinic attendance, the report encourages the establishment of separate teen clinics with sensitive staffs and low-cost, confidential treatment. State laws and policies which restrict teenage patients in consenting to their own contraceptive care should be modified, the report notes.

Additional recommendations for a national program to deal with the problems of adolescent childbearing were issued by the Alan Guttmacher Institute in 1976. Its recommendations include:

- Realistic sex education via school, churches, and mass media, including information about pregnancy risks, contraception, and abortion, and places where teenagers can obtain health services.
- For pregnant teens, adequate pregnancy counseling with nonjudgmental information on all available options, including abortion referral.
- Adequate prenatal, obstetrical, and pediatric care for teenagers who carry their pregnancy to term in order to minimize the hazards of early childbearing for both mother and child.
- Educational, employment, and social services for adolescent parents and day care for their infants to help teenagers realize their educational and career goals.
- National health insurance coverage for all health services related to adolescent pregnancy and childbearing with provisions to protect the privacy of minors.
- Expansion of biomedical research to discover new, safe, and effective methods of contraception more suited to the needs of young men and women.

Much more work needs to be done to educate teenagers and their parents on the problems related to teenage pregnancy and the availability of contraceptive information, counseling, and services. In addition, school authorities, social workers, and health personnel, especially physicians, must be made aware of the special needs of teenagers.

Teenage pregnancy is a complicated problem which will be with us for some time to come. Failing to act today only compounds the high human, social, and economic costs to be borne by teenage mothers, their children, and society in general.

Public Savings

Pregnancy prevention programs are highly cost-effective

in saving future government expenditures to support out-of-wedlock children and their mothers. The Planned Parenthood Federation of America estimates that every dollar spent in one year on family planning saves two dollars in the following year alone and many times the original expenditure in the long term. The California Department of Public Health calculated that if only 20 percent of eligible minors used contraceptive services and only 10 percent of teenage pregnancies were prevented, the net savings to the state would be $2.3 million in the first year.

READINGS SUGGESTED BY THE AUTHORS:

Alan Guttmacher Institute. *11 Million Teenagers: What Can Be Done about the Epidemic of Adolescent Pregnancies in the United States?* New York: Planned Parenthood Federation of America, 1976.

Baldwin, Wendy H. "Adolescent Pregnancy and Childbearing: Growing Concerns for Americans." *Population Bulletin* 31, no. 2. Washington, D.C.: Population Reference Bureau.

Gordon, Sol, and Conant, Roger. *You*. New York: *New York Times* Book Company, Quadrangle Books, 1975.

Lieberman, E. James, and Peck, Ellen. *Sex and Birth Control: A Guide for the Young*. New York: Schocken Books, 1975.

Population Institute. "Sex Education Action/Resource Bulletin." Washington, D.C..

Urban and Rural Systems Associates. *Improving Family Planning for Teenagers*. Washington, D.C.: Department of Health, Education, and Welfare, Office of Planning and Evaluation.

A Pregnant Pause in The Sexual Revolution

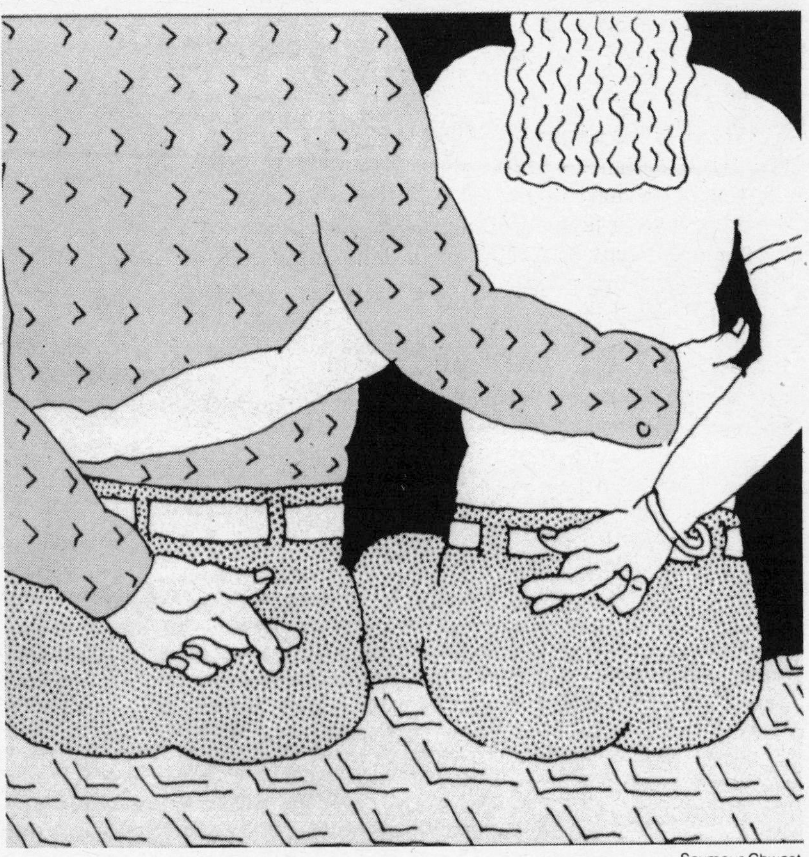

Seymour Chwast

Unwanted pregnancy may result as much from attitudes toward sex as from ignorance or carelessness about contraception.

Donn Byrne

Donn Byrne is professor of psychological sciences and Chairman of the social-personality program at Purdue University. He received his Ph.D. from Stanford University. His current research interest is human sexual behavior, especially over-population and unwanted conception. His recent books include the second edition of *Social Psychology* (coauthored with Robert A. Baron) and *Psychology: Understanding Behavior* (coauthored with Robert A. Baron and Barry Kantowitz). He and his wife, Lois, have completed a book, *Exploring Human Sexuality* (Thomas Y. Cromwell), which deals with many aspects of sexual expression.

THERE ARE 11 MILLION TEEN-AGERS in America today who have sexual intercourse from time to time. No more than 20 percent of them use contraceptives regularly. The result is almost 700,000 unwanted adolescent pregnancies a year, followed soon after by 300,000 abortions, 200,000 out-of-wedlock births, 100,000 hasty and often short-lived marriages, and nearly 100,000 miscarriages.

One might think that increased availability of contraceptives, together with competent sex education programs, would reduce these figures substantially. But according to our research, there is much more involved.

We conducted a survey at Indiana University, an institution that has an enlightened, active contraceptive program as part of the University Student Health Service. There are dormitory lectures about birth control, an educational movie for those who are interested, and freely available pills, diaphragms, and IUDs.

We asked 149 undergraduate women (most of them 18 and 19 years old) to answer an anonymous questionnaire about their sex lives. Of the 91 who were sexually active, less than a third said they *always* used contraceptives, and more than a third *never* did. This was true even though half of them, contraceptive users and nonusers alike, had undergone the frightening experience of believing they were pregnant.

We found that these undergraduates were knowledgeable about the techniques of contraception and aware of the Health Service program to provide birth control. Why, then, the inconsistency between information and behavior? The answer goes beyond sex education to sexual attitudes.

Dangerous fun. As we grow up, most of us acquire a mixture of positive and negative feelings about sexual cues. Even though sexual matters may be interesting and pleasurable, we learn that emotional dangers lie in nudity, in masturbation, in undue curiosity about the bodies of others, and even in words used to describe certain parts of the body and their functions. This mix of positive and negative feelings, different for each person, produces individual patterns of sexual attitudes that have been labeled erotophilia-erotophobia.

In research with more than a hundred Purdue University undergraduates, we have measured this sexual dimension by getting reactions to a sexually explicit movie. Volunteers who know the kind of movie they will see are shown a film in which a couple undress, engage in manual foreplay, and then perform cunnilingus and fellatio until they reach orgasm. We identify erotophobes as those who most strongly rate the film as pornographic, shocking, and more explicit than expected; erotophiles as those who react in the opposite way.

The two groups have somewhat different backgrounds and sexual attitudes. Typically erotophobes attend church frequently, don't discuss sex at home, rate themselves as sexually conservative, have inadequate sexual knowledge, live a sex life influenced by guilt, religious belief, and fear of social disapproval, and have intercourse infrequently and with few partners. Erotophiles are different in all these areas. They attend church infrequently, are sexually liberated, discuss sex at home, and so on.

Their attitudes toward sex are equally different. Erotophobes disapprove of premarital sex, feel sex is unimportant, believe it should always be linked to love, feel that erotica is potentially harmful, dislike oral-genital sex, and disapprove of birth-control clinics and abortion. Erotophiles hold different views on these matters.

Paradoxical pregnancy. Our research shows that these strong differences affect contraceptive practices, and that erotophobes are less likely to use contraceptives. That is, the more negative and anxious individuals are about sex, the more likely they are to risk an unwanted pregnancy. This seems like a paradox, but the explanation is relatively straightforward. Negative feelings about sex are rarely strong enough to inhibit sexual behavior completely, but they do inhibit the use of contraceptives by affecting each of four steps needed for contraception. First, an individual must know that intercourse is likely to occur. The sexually negative individual avoids that expectation, and sex becomes a spontaneous event.

Second, once someone admits that sex is likely to occur, he or she must procure the necessary paraphernalia by going to a doctor and/or drugstore clerk and, in effect, giving public notice of sexual activity. This can be embarrassing for anyone, but it's even more of a trial for erotophobes.

As an experiment, we had male students purchase a package of lubricated condoms in a drugstore. In describing their reactions afterward, the men who felt most uncomfortable and nervous believed that the pharmacist reacted to them as immoral persons; they also felt that condoms were unsatisfactory and unreliable. Such reactions and evaluations, typical of erotophobes, would very likely interfere with their actually obtaining condoms when the need arose.

Third, sexual partners need to communicate about one another's contraceptive plans and practices to make sure somebody has done something. In a study of young married couples, we found that erotophobic spouses were less likely than erotophiles to talk to one another about either sex or contraception.

Finally, the contraceptive must actually be used. Pills require at least one daily thought about sex, and mechanical devices require some direct contact with the genitals: inserting a diaphragm, slipping on a condom, or checking the presence of an IUD thread. Research indicates that erotophobic individuals are especially upset when they are asked to view slides depicting someone of their own sex masturbating, and that they disapprove of masturbation for themselves and for their future children. Students who respond in this way dislike contraceptive techniques that require them to touch their genitals.

Summing up. When sexual cues elicit negative feelings in an individual, that person is less likely to anticipate future sexual encounters, to endure the embarrassment of acquiring contraceptives, to communicate accurately about contraception with the sex partner, or to utilize mechanical forms of contraception.

One question remains. How do erotophobes justify this seemingly irrational behavior to themselves? They engage in sexual intercourse and yet they don't use contraceptives. They justify their inactions, we've found, by convincing themselves that contraception is sinful, unnatural, dangerous, etc., and that it is immoral for contraceptives to be made easily available to the unmarried.

These feelings persist into marriage. A Purdue study showed that married couples who want three or more children are the ones most likely to dislike erotica, to indicate that their sex lives are beset by problems, and to respond negatively to contraception and abortion. Erotophobic couples who described themselves as unhappily married were often planning to conceive and raise the largest families.

It is clear that imagination is a vital element in sexual responsiveness. People regularly create fantasies to accompany and enhance sexual activities, from masturbation to intercourse. We know that erotic images cause sexual arousal. Nonerotic thoughts, in contrast, can dampen or completely eliminate arousal.

Significantly (if unsurprisingly), our own studies of students' erotic fantasies show that the ideas of contraception or unwanted pregnancies are almost never included. Nor are they considered in hardcore pornography.

So if imagination serves as a prelude to behavior, as we've found, it's not surprising that most people don't use contraceptives when they first engage in sexual intercourse. They have no role models and no imaginative cues to make them think of contraception as a part of sexuality.

How, then, can we reduce the number of unwanted pregnancies? A simple call to celibacy is not likely to help much; effective contraception seems more promising. And since information, emotion, and imagination all influence the use of contraceptives, we should use all three in our educational efforts.

Explicit details. Accurate, complete information about contraceptives should be a part of everyone's education before and during adolescence. The information should be specific and include considerations of the problems of unwanted pregnancy and explicit details about obtaining and using each type of contraceptive.

Any child-rearing, educational, or therapeutic practices that lessen guilt and anxiety about natural sexual functions should be encouraged. This can be done without advocating any particular lifestyle. The assumption should be simply that human beings would be healthier and happier if they could react to sex without fear and self-blame.

But we also need to bring conception and its prevention into our fantasy lives. (The condom manufacturers have tried to do this, for their own purposes, with ads promoting "sensuous contraceptives.") At any rate, people who want to enjoy sexual intercourse without fear of parenthood need more than simple facts. Since rationality does not always guide our actions, we need the appropriate cues intermeshed in the fabric of our erotic thoughts.

For more information, read:

Byrne, Donn. "The Imagery of Sex" in *Handbook of Sexology*, J. Money and H. Musaph, eds., Excerpta Medica, 1977, $79.95.

Byrne, Donn. "Social Psychology and the Study of Sexual Behavior" in *Personality and Social Psychology Bulletin*, in press.

Byrne, Donn, Jeffrey D. Fisher, John Lamberth and Herman E. Mitchell. "Evaluations of Erotica: Facts or Feelings?" in *Journal of Personality and Social Psychology*, Vol. 29, 1974, pp. 111-116.

Fisher, William A., Jeffrey D. Fisher, and Donn Byrne. "Consumer Reactions to Contraceptive Purchasing" in *Personality and Social Psychology Bulletin*, in press.

MARITAL RELATIONS How Much? How Often?

Frequency of sexual intercourse varies widely from couple to couple—the "right" amount is whatever is right for you.

Howard R. and Martha E. Lewis

Howard R. and Martha E. Lewis are medical writers specializing in the field of human sexuality.

At one time or another, almost every couple differs over how often they should have sex. You and your partner are unlikely to share indentical levels of sexual desire, just as you're not likely to respond in exactly the same manner to hunger, thirst, fatigue, joy or frustration.

The imbalance is "rarely crucial," comments psychiatrist Leon Salzman of the Albert Einstein College of Medicine. "Partners who are interested in each other and who find each other sexually acceptable adjust to each other." Generally, partners will "be available to each other even if sometimes their interest is not strong."

But you can expect conflicts if you want sex significantly more or less often than your partner. Generally it's the husband who wants intercourse more frequently than his wife. He determines the minimum frequency, she the maximum.

Why do many happily married women want sex less often than their husbands? Psychiatrist Alfred Auerback of the University of California School of Medicine in San Francisco suggests: "Most men tend to rush foreplay." This leaves the wife too unstimulated to be within reach of orgasm.

Further, many men ejaculate within two minutes of penetration. "As a result," notes Dr. Auerback, "many women find their sex life unsatisfying or only partially satisfying. Recurrent dissatisfaction leads to less sexual interest for the woman."

This rarely occurs on a conscious level, so a husband is unlikely to realize that he contributes to the diminished frequency. The wife, too, may be aware only of wanting sex less. Dr. Thomas E. Clark of the Bowman Gray School of Medicine: "If the wife frequently finds herself excited but is left frustrated, then decline in level of desire becomes a functional defense."

To avoid frustration, a woman unconsciously avoids becoming sexually excited—which she may chalk up to being too tired, too busy, etc. Her husband may resent her for being "cold" and "unresponsive."

Conversely, if the wife finds intercourse a pleasurable experience, frequency is likely to be satisfactory for both partners. One barometer of a couple's frequency is how the woman feels about her own sexuality. Is she comfortable in the nude? Does she communicate her sexual needs? The more positive her attitude, the more often she's likely to make love, report psychiatrist Gordon D. Jensen of the University of California at Davis and Professor Mina Robbins of the California State University School of Nursing in Sacramento.

Fully 25 percent of the surveyed women told Dr. Jensen and Professor Robbins they wished they had intercourse more often. Family physicians are reporting more and more women complaining about insufficient frequency. Formerly, wives complained chiefly about lack of affection. This change is widely attributed to women's increasing awareness of their rights to sexual satisfaction. Now when wives are dissatisfied with the frequency of intercourse they are more likely than husbands to seek help.

Proper perspective. A high frequency of sexual activity is generally healthful. It develops your capacity for remaining sexually active in later life. It improves the functioning of the prostate gland. Intercourse is never physically harmful as long as it occurs between accepting partners and is not associated with injury or irritation.

Even so, keep sex in its proper perspective. Dr. David R. Mace, family sociologist at Bowman Gray School of Medicine, and his wife-coworker Vera observe: "The idea that it is the joy of sex that sustains a good marriage is putting the cart before the horse. It is more appropriate to say that it is the good marriage that sustains the joy of sex."

The Maces estimate that the average married couple spends the equivalent in hours of one weekend a year having sexual intercourse. Therefore, they conclude, it is unrealistic to suggest that sex is the major force sustaining the relationship.

Many happily married couples have what sex therapists consider serious sexual dysfunctions, such as potency problems or inability to reach orgasm. A survey of ninety married couples by Ellen Frank, a doctoral candidate in psychology at the University of Pittsburgh, revealed that although 42 percent of the husbands and 62 percent of the wives complained of having a serious sexual problem, fully 85 percent described their marriages as "happy" or "very happy."

Resolving conflicts. "In any intimate relationship (married or unmarried) the key issue is not frequency of intercourse but the dovetailing of needs," remarks psychiatrist Peter A. Martin of the University of Michigan and Wayne State University medical schools. Some suggestions that may help you and your partner find a frequency suited to you both:

Talk turkey. Be frank about your needs and wishes and encourage your partner to do the same. It's especially important for you to express your preferences if you avoid sex because you're chronically unsatisfied.

You and your partner may be surprised at how each perceives the other's sex life. In one study of couples married about 10 years, the typical wife reported having intercourse an average of eight times a month. This frequency matched her own desire. She estimated that her husband's preference would be eleven times a month, considerably more than her own.

The typical husband reported he had intercourse seven times a month, about one time less than his wife's report. He estimated his wife would prefer some six times a month, less than she actually would. His own preference would be nine, less than she believed he wanted.

Explore the desirability of alternate forms of sexual release. If you and your partner have a great disparity in sex drive, consider types of sexual activity besides intercourse, such as masturbation or oral sex. If a man has difficulty sustaining an erection, he can nevertheless give his partner considerable sexual pleasure by engaging in breast stroking and clitoral and vaginal stimulation.

Search out areas of marital discord. If your marriage is going through a bumpy period, there's likely to be less sex. Sexual interest may be restored if you resolve lingering resentment, anger, guilt, frustration.

In a frank discussion, you may uncover conflicts arising from early sexual training. Notes psychiatrist David S. Burgoyne of Phoenix, Arizona: "Many people are trained and educated during their developmental years to view sex as something evil, bad and dirty....This may be the cause of impaired or late development of the usual or normal sexual feelings. This later decreases frequency of sexual relations."

So can being brought up in a home with too much permissiveness. In such homes, says Dr. Burgoyne, young people may have intercourse before they are ready or with partners who exploit them. These bad experiences can sour them on sex.

Share your concern over situations causing you anxiety. Job worries, financial problems, serious problems with a child—all can contribute to a decrease in sexual relations. So can lack of bedroom privacy, with the anxiety that small children may overhear or witness lovemaking.

"The intrusion of a child may begin during pregnancy," says Dr. Diane Brashear of Purdue University. Intercourse may become less frequent during pregnancy because of fear, myth or lack of desire. After the baby is born, interrupted sleep, fatigue, anxiety about parenthood, may contribute to a pattern of less frequent sex.

Seek counseling if you're unable to resolve problems on your own. Underlying marital discord or psychological problems that account for sexual disinterest may respond to professional therapy, either for one partner or for the couple.

Competent sex therapy may help alleviate the problem if avoidance of intercourse is the result of sexual dysfunction. Premature ejaculation, impotence, difficulty in achieving orgasm—all can lead to feelings of humiliation and anxiety over performance. A couple may prefer to avoid sex altogether rather than risk failure.

Schedule time for sex. Some couples have such cluttered, exhausting lives that a good sex life is a virtual impossibility. There's little opportunity or energy for sex when both partners are chronically overworked and preoccupied. Dr. John F. Cuber, a sociologist at Ohio State University, estimates that because of the pressures and obstacles of their lifestyle fewer than one in five upper-middle-class couples manages to have an active and satisfying sex life.

Therefore, set aside uninterrupted hours for making love. Make an appointment with your partner, free of outside commitments and household worries. Hold the time inviolable—even if it means turning down invitations and withdrawing from activities.

Improve the quality of such occasions. One good sexual experience a week can be more satisfying than three disappointing ones. Comments Dr. Thomas E. Clark of the Bowman Gray School of Medicine: "Creativity, planning and preparation are as vital to continuing good sex as they are to a week at the beach or a Sunday picnic."

Discover items such as lotions, new techniques and erotic literature that enhance sensual pleasure. When the quality of sex rises, the quantity usually will also.

By contrast, boredom and routine are major reasons for sexual activity tapering off. As Dr. Donald W. Burnap, a psychiatrist in Rapid City, South Dakota, put it, "Year after year a wife may wear the same type of nightgown, and her husband may climb into bed and kiss her in exactly the same way. They may touch each other in the same places for the same length of time. They may say the same thing and climax in the same way. They know what to expect. No wonder they lose interest!"

You may be most likely to ring bells if you have intercourse at times most suited to your natural cycle. In general for a woman the rate of intercourse is highest just after menstruation ceases, possibly as a release from her abstinence during menstruation. Thereafter, frequency declines, with possibly a minor peak around the time of ovulation. It is lowest just before menstruation begins.

On which days of the week is intercourse most frequent? In a University of North Carolina Medical School study, married, middle-class women reported having intercourse most often on Sunday, with Saturday the next highest day. Unmarried women reported intercourse most often on Sunday, with Wednesday the next most popular day. Married black men reported the greatest sexual activity on Tuesday, with another peak on Friday or Saturday.

The optimum temperature for intercourse is about 70°F, concludes Dr. William H. James of University College, London. "At much higher temperatures, coitus is unattractively and clammily exhausting; at lower temperatures, bedclothes (blankets, etc.) become necessary and restrict the variety of coital techniques."

In temperate climates, birth statistics suggest that intercourse is most frequent in summer. In tropical climates it occurs most often in the cool season. In places where summers are very hot and winters very cold, intercourse rates are highest in spring and fall.

Check for physical causes. A thorough examination by your doctor can rule out physical problems that may be responsible for your lowered sex drive.

Aging may cause a natural decline troubling to a man. In general, men reach a peak of sexual feelings in early adulthood, with a gradual falling off thereafter. A man's rate often increases once he's convinced that he can enjoy a high level of sexual activity well into old age.

Women generally reach a peak in their thirties. Their sexual interest then remains relatively stable into the sixties or beyond.

Get good contraception. Reliable birth control can help alleviate fear of pregnancy, which may be causing lowered sexual interest.

Consider if you need to improve your personal hygiene. Notes Dr. David Burgoyne: "Body or breath odors that are undesirable or offensive decrease desire and thus sexual frequency. Occasionally a wife will complain that her husband's hands being unclean, rough or calloused detracts from his lovemaking."

Make hygeine part of your foreplay. You and your partner can shower together and apply fragrances and oils to each other.

A new diet and exercise program can contribute to revitalizing your sex life. Says Dr. Martin Feit of Richmond Memorial Hospital in New York: "Obesity undoubtedly...affects the frequency of sexual relations." Obese women are generally unattractive to men and have less sexual experience than other women. In Dr. Feit's experience, fat women may turn to food in part to compensate for the sexual gratification they are deprived of—which only exacerbates the problem.

Forget yardsticks. Have intercourse no more or less often than is comfortable for *you.* Don't try to meet statistical "norms." Kinsey found the average frequency of marital intercourse to be 3.9 times a week for husbands under 20, ranging down to 1.3 times a week for husbands between 51 and 55. But the couples Kinsey interviewed had intercourse varying from "twenty-five times a week" to "hardly ever."

"There is no statement about coital frequency that can fit all cases," comments psychiatrist Paul Jay Fink of the Eastern Virginia Medical School. To illustrate the range of sex drives, Dr. Fink describes a man who'd had his first intercourse when he married at age twenty-eight. Thereafter he was satisfied with sex less than once a month. Another man, by contrast, had intercourse with his wife four times a week and masturbated daily.

Your frequency of intercourse may also vary considerably with different partners. Dr. Fink tells of a man who usually had intercourse with his wife about twice a week. But when he went out with other women, he had intercourse at least three times a *night*—because "the women usually expected it."

Accept ebbs and flows as inevitable. A couple's sexual frequency may fall off drastically or virtually cease for weeks or months at a time. A study of husbands and wives, most below the age of forty and married for an average of eleven years, showed that fully one-third experienced long periods with no sex. For half, sexual activity had ceased for periods of eight weeks or more.

By contrast, couples can find themselves having intercourse more frequently than either really would like. Concludes psychiatrist Gordon Jensen and his associate Mina Robbins: "When patients engage in intercourse more often than desired, the problem may be unrealistic goals, myths or one partner's need to prove sexual attractiveness."

If you're like some couples, you may be pushing your frequency in an effort to achieve the unrealistic goal of simultaneous orgasm. So may a woman who feels that having multiple orgasms is the greatest sign of female sexual achievement.

So, too, may a man who strains at having intercourse several times a night to demonstrate his masculinity. Mulitple ejaculations for a man are relatively rare. Dr. Robert Athanasiou of the Albany Medical College estimates that intercourse on the average of once or more a day is experienced by merely 6 percent of men under the age of thirty-five and 2 percent of men over thirty-five.

Such pressure to achieve can produce greater frequency—but less enjoyment. In any event, take with a grain of salt reports of very high sexual track records. Claims of extreme sexual potency are often wishful thinking.

The best documented high-scorers? Dr. Wardell B. Pomeroy who worked with Kinsey at the Institute for Sex Research and the University of Indiana, reports that the highest rate of ejaculation among 10,000 males was about six times per day every day over a period of several years. "For short periods of time," he reports, "the rate would be higher." It is not unusual for adolescent males to report masturbating to orgasm ten to fifteen times a day.

But such sexual marathoners are not necessarily to be envied. Some males who had very frequent orgasms were "compulsive and actually derived very little pleasure from their sexual activity," reports Dr. Pomeroy "We feel that some high-rating males were so constituted physiologically that a failure to ejaculate at least once a day would leave them tense, nervous and very uneasy. Dr. Martin L. Kurkland of the Palm Springs Mental Health Clinic in California came across a forty-one-year-old married man who kept a "sexual track record." He normally had intercourse four to five times daily, sometimes more. During one twenty-four hour period he had seventeen orgasms, all during intercourse with the same woman. He'd had sexual experiences with 377 women. He finally came to Dr. Kurkland because he was afraid he was "going queer." After some counseling, he was down to having intercourse only one or twice a day and enjoying it more.

The most important message here is that everybody is different in his or her sexual needs, and the important thing is to satisfy your *own* needs, without comparing yourself to others. That's what sexual pleasure is all about.

IS THERE SEX AFTER MARRIAGE?

Sex therapists are encountering increased numbers of married patients suffering from inhibited sexual desire. The leading reason that marital sex dies: underlying rage toward one's spouse.

Carol Botwin

Carol Botwin is the author with Jerome Fine, Ph.D. of THE LOVE CRISIS which is published by Doubleday.

At a sex clinic recently, a man in his mid-20's explained that he was there at the insistence of his wife. After the honeymoon, his sexual desire for her had stopped.

Another man was there because he found his wife sexually repugnant since the birth of their first baby.

A 36-year-old woman told a psychiatrist there that she wanted to revive her sexual interest in her husband—an interest that had dissipated when she fell in love with her tennis pro.

A middle-aged woman said that she had never experienced much desire for her husband in the 15 years of their marriage, but now she felt she had been missing out on something.

These husbands and wives, typical of many being seen in sex clinics, are suffering from what psychiatrists and sex therapists have dubbed "inhibited sexual desire." It is now listed, for the first time, under sexual dysfunctions in the newly revised edition of The Diagnostic and Statistical Manual of Mental Disorders of the American Psychiatric Association.

The fact of husbands turning off to wives, and vice versa, is, of course, nothing new. Still, it wasn't until very recently that serious scientific attention began being paid. Previously, the focus in sex research, from Kinsey to Masters and Johnson, had largely been on activity, rather than inactivity.

Two articles in important medical journals in the last three years called attention to the fact that there was a lot less sex in a lot more marriages than previously assumed. A study of 100 couples, published in The New England Journal of Medicine last year in July, found that 33 percent of the husbands and wives were having intercourse two or three times a month or less.

A previous study of 365 husbands and wives by two Ph.D.'s, John Edwards and Alan Booth, published in The American Journal of Psychiatry, revealed that one-third of them had ceased having intercourse for long periods of time. The median period of abstinence was eight weeks, but some husbands and wives had gone without sex for three months or longer. More than three-quarters of those studied were under 38 years of age, a time in life when most healthy couples generally have intercourse two or three times a week.

How prevalent is lack of desire in marriage? Dr. Harold Lief, professor of psychiatry at the University of Pennsylvania School of Medicine and director of the Marriage Council of Philadelphia, over a period of three months monitored 115 consecutive cases of patients with sexual problems. He found inhibited sexual desire to be the No. 1 complaint.

At Mount Sinai Medical Center in New York, although lack of desire trails behind impotence, premature ejaculation and inability to achieve orgasm, Dr. Raul Schiavi, director of the human-sexuality program and professor of psychiatry, reports that although both married and single people suffer from other sexual dysfunctions, *every* male patient who has sought treatment for lack of desire has been married.

Is inhibited sexual desire increasing? Is there something in our culture that feeds this inhibition? Or is the destruction of passion built into marriage itself? "We are not sure whether lack of desire is increasing or not," says Dr. Lief. "Doctors are more aware of it than in the past. We can't be certain whether our awareness is just uncovering more cases that always existed. It seems to me, though, that more people are complaining about it."

"Doctors hear more complaints," says Dr. Helen Singer Kaplan, head of the human-sexuality program at New York Hospital-Cornell Medical Center, "because people now know that help is available and they are asking for it. There is no upsurge in lack of desire. People just called it something else—impotence, lack of orgasm, or they would simply say, 'I have a sex problem.' Naturally, if you don't feel much desire, you aren't going to enjoy sex."

There is agreement among experts that rising sexual expectations created by our culture, which Dr. Lief terms "sex obsessed," account, in part, for the large numbers of husbands and wives seeking treatment. Everybody wants a better sex life these days, but women, in particular, according to Dr. Schiavi, have changed significantly.

"For many years the sexual experience in marriage was controlled by the husband," he says. "The wife was passive, acquiescent. She was not expected to enjoy sex. Also, women were expected to stay in marriage no

"Is There Sex After Marriage," by Carol Botwin, *The New York Times Magazine*, September 16, 1979. Reprinted by permission of the author and the Barbara Lowenstein Literary Agency.

matter what went on, so they put up with a husband who ignored them."

Dr. Lief finds the number of women complaining about their husbands today "striking" and he agrees that a great reversal has occurred: It used to be husbands who complained that their wives weren't interested enough in sex; now it is the wives complaining about their husbands.

Dr. Kaplan, author of a forthcoming book called "Disorders of Sexual Desire," feels this to be particularly true about women in middle age, when sexual desire often increases. "The woman wakes up suddenly at a time in life when the man is 'tired'—his desire is decreasing," she says. "But among young couples in their 20's, it is more often the husband who is unhappy. He wants more sex than his wife does."

Most men and women being treated for inhibited sexual desire are in their 30's and 40's, but there are people of all ages. Both Dr. Lief and Dr. Kaplan have noticed an increase in the number of husbands and wives under 30. This doesn't necessarily mean that more young people are suffering from the dysfunction. Rather, according to Dr. Kaplan, there is more openness about sex these days and young people don't let the problem linger. The quicker the problem is caught, the better the chances for successful treatment.

There is no one answer to why husbands and wives lose interest in sex. A joke Dr. Lief tells is part of a large body of humor on the subject: A man recovering from illness is told not to get too excited about sex. "That's easy," he says. "I'll make love to my wife." Many men feel that making love to the same woman inevitably becomes boring.

Not so, says Dr. Otto Kernberg, medical director of the New York Hospital-Cornell Medical Center, Westchester Division, a psychiatric hospital: "A couple with a deep, stable relationship maintains sexual interest. Interest can go up or down according to tensions or irritations between the couple or according to whether one feels closer or more distant to a partner at different times, but the sexual interest never disappears." He continues, "Boredom sets in when there is a great deal of unconscious hostility. There is boredom when one is trying to avoid awareness that one is very angry or disappointed with the other person. Boredom is a coverup for feelings that are not recognized or expressed openly. Generally, 'bored' husbands and wives don't understand that hatred is as much a part of a relationship as love. Each must be able to tolerate both love and hatred toward a marriage partner. If a person can't, then he or she is unable to have an emotional relationship of depth, and sex becomes more and more mechanical and unfulfilling. It is then that one begins to think about change and variety and another man or woman as the answer to the boring, mechanical lovemaking."

Dr. Lief disagrees somewhat. He feels that boredom most often is a symptom of other troubles in a relationship, but once in a while, he says, he does find couples with basically good, stable relationships who have simply fallen into a rut—sex in the same old way, at the same old time.

Dr. Kaplan says that occasionally she sees husbands and wives with good relationships who have only mild, superficial problems that cause sexual boredom. Often such minor problems are due to a simple failure to communicate what one does or doesn't want. An example of this is a husband who loved his wife but lost interest in her sexually because their lovemaking lacked variety. He felt he couldn't suggest innovations because she would realize he had different and better experiences with other women and would become jealous. In another instance, a wife liked her husband in other ways but was turned off only because he always touched her in a clumsy, rough manner. She was unable to tell him this directly.

Treatment and cure are simple when boredom occurs because of mild problems like those above or when husbands and wives have fallen into the kind of rut Dr. Lief describes.

Couples are taught to speak openly about their likes and dislikes and they are assigned specific behavioral sex-therapy exercises designed to make them more sensual, uninhibited, imaginative or effective with each other in lovemaking. For instance, the wife who was turned off by her husband's rough touch was told by the therapist to place her hand on her husband's and gently guide him. In this way, she was able to show him the pressure, rhythms and places that pleased her most during love-making.

Such easy cures for inhibited sexual desire are rare, however. The standard sex therapy used in most respected sex clinics today—structured sexual exercises often coupled with brief psychotherapy—works well for other sexual dysfunctions, such as orgasmic difficulties, but fails with most people who suffer from lack of desire. Cure rates, until recently, were a dismal 10 percent—much lower than for other dysfunctions, which have success rates of 60 to 80 percent.

Interestingly, it was by studying failures for *other* problems that Dr. Kaplan found that the functional difficulties that brought patients into treatment were not always the problem. They were really secondary symptoms. Many of those who did not respond to standard sex therapy were trying to have sex without really wanting to. They lacked desire.

She reached the same conclusion that Dr. Lief and others were also coming to: There was a missing link in the sex act as it had been conceptualized previously. Until very recently, sex experts had worked on the Masters-Johnson theory that there were four major stages of human sexual response where dysfunctions occur—the excitement, plateau, orgasm and resolution phases. Now, thanks largely to Dr. Kaplan and Dr. Lief who began writing and speaking at professional meetings about it, there is general recognition of a fifth crucial phase—desire, a separate, distinct initial stage of lovemaking. If a person does not feel desire, he is suffering from a sexual problem like any other.

Once the desire phase was distinguished, experts could zero in on what interfered with it. What they found was a set of problems that were most often deeper, more complex and more resistant to treatment than the generally mild sexual anxieties and conflicts behind other dysfunctions.

To begin with, sex therapists today recognize the existence of two major categories of people who lack desire. There are those whose lack of appetite is general—they can't get interested in anyone. Then there are those who turn off selectively—they are unresponsive only to their spouses. Many who suffer from selective inhibited desire find, in affairs, the sexual excitement missing at home.

Although men have traditionally turned to affairs as a solution to lost desire for their wives, experts today are seeing more and more women willing to travel the same route. Illicit sex is indeed on the rise among wives.

Psychiatrists point out that the affair itself may be what causes desire to die in certain instances. Many husbands and wives unconsciously turn themselves off to their mates when they want to have an affair. Then, when they can't work up any excitement at home, they feel justified in finding a good sex life elsewhere. The reverse can also be true. Some men and women start an affair and then begin to feel guilty about it. Their guilt makes them lose all desire for the "wronged" mate.

Very often sexual appetite disappears because of long-standing personal psychological problems brought into the marriage by a husband or wife. A good example of this is a young woman who was able to have passionate sex with her husband during their courtship. Once married, however, the same man who had excited her suddenly left her cold. During therapy she said: "My mother never dreamed I would have sex before marriage, so I felt free to have it. After I was married, she knew I was having sex. She was in the bedroom with me, and I turned off."

Parents can enter bedrooms in other ways, too, extinguishing desire. Dr. Kaplan explains: "When a woman, no matter what her age, gains a lot of weight and begins to look matronly, or even if she just starts to act matronly, often her husband will begin to identify her with his own mother. He is, in effect, looking at his mother in bed, and, of course, he can't get excited. This can cause a man great despair because he still likes his wife. He thinks she is a lovely person but he can't feel anything sexually for her." The same, she adds, can be true for women. "When a man starts to get a pot belly, be careless about his appearance, or act like her father, the woman can get turned off, too."

For many men, unconscious identification of a wife as a "good" woman is what destroys passion. Men like this suffer from the madonna-prostitute syndrome, which therapists often find lurking in the male psyche. In this, women get divided into two camps—good (madonna), and bad (prostitute); the bad women are for sex, the good ones are not to be touched. The man mentioned at the beginning of this article, the one who lost interest in his wife after the honeymoon, exemplifies this syndrome.

Among women, the sense of a mission accomplished sometimes snuffs out sex. These victims of inhibited sexual desire feel that their only role in life is to become a wife and/or mother. One business executive complained bitterly: "My wife couldn't get enough sex all through our engagement and right up until the birth of our child. Then, all of a sudden, she didn't want any sex any more." Dr. Lief explains: "Certain women have a lifelong inhibition about sex but they cloak it. They can act and even feel sexual because it is a way of getting a man or having their children. But after getting what they want, their job is done."

Other men and women are reacting to the fear of intimacy. "In our society," says Dr. Kaplan, "intimacy is more frightening than sex. This is somewhat more of a problem for men, but it is also true for women." Losing interest in sex is a way of loosening the bonds of closeness that some people view as a snare. The same is true of those with anxieties about commitment, fear of which, according to Dr. Lief, makes large numbers of men start affairs when a wife is pregnant or gives birth. Children tighten the commitment knot.

Still others, says Dr. Kaplan, fear success, and they use sex as a trade-off. These are generally people with a poor sense of self-esteem. They don't feel worthy of the good things in life, and so, for instance, when a big promotion comes their way, they are compelled to create disaster in another area. Losing desire for a mate is a devious way of compensating for their good fortune.

The wrong attitude toward aging contributes to the waning of desire in some men. They feel they *should* be losing interest in sex as they grow older and so they do.

The prevalence of narcissism in our times also plays into the lack-of-desire syndrome. Dr. Kernberg, a leading authority on narcissistic personalities, explains: "Once the narcissistic man possesses his mate he devalues her and sex becomes mechanical, unfulfilling. He also places a great deal of value on physical attractiveness and he may lose interest in a woman as she ages. For some narcissistic women, sex is used as merchandise to obtain a man's favors. They aren't much interested in sex to begin with."

Two other motifs in our society—stress and depression—are leading causes of a generalized lack of desire that makes one immune to the charms not only of a mate, but of everyone. For a smaller number of people, desire is gradually killed off by the persistence of some other sexual dysfunction that makes them wish to avoid further failures in bed.

Illnesses, such as hepatitis, and certain drugs, such as those used to treat hypertension, alcoholism and a low hormonal level, in a very few cases have been implicated in causing lack of desire. But by far, say the experts, the leading reason why sex dies in marriage is the relationship itself. "Fifty percent of the cases I see are caused by marital interaction," says Dr. Lief.

Underlying rage is generally so strong that it even outweighs the pleasure principle—the psychological theory that holds that human beings tend to want to repeat gratifying experiences. Apparently, no pleasure is strong enough to overcome the overt or covert battle that exists between certain husbands and wives. Experts have found that when those who suffer from lack of desire somehow get inveigled into sex they find it enjoyable, but they are so subliminally hostile to their partners that they are not easily tempted to repeat the pleasurable experience.

What makes the new treatment of lack of desire different from therapy for other sexual problems? For one thing, time. For orgasmic difficulties, treatment lasts about 14 sessions. It is not unusual to rack up 30 sessions in the treatment of inhibited sexual desire.

Techniques differ markedly as well. The usual sex therapy relies heavily on sexual exercises and tasks that the patient is asked to perform in private. Although these are sometimes used as well, the emphasis in the treatment of blocked desire is on psychotherapy of one kind or another.

The actual treatment chosen depends upon the cause. Physical illnesses or drugs that inhibit sexuality are ruled out first. If depression is found, that is what gets treated rather than the dysfunction. Antidepressant drugs work in most cases and, once the depression lifts, sexual interest generally returns automatically.

When conflicts in the marriage are at the heart of the matter, marital therapy is recommended. If the problem turns out to be mostly a personal one, individual psychotherapy is chosen. Sometimes specific sexual exercises are recommended in conjunction with other treatments. Recently, Dr. Lief has been experimenting with group therapy for desire disorders. In all forms of treatment, what is stressed is the fact that a patient is able to control whether he turns off or not much more than he realizes. He is taught to recognize whatever it is that switches off desire in him.

In one recent therapy session with Dr. Kaplan, a husband was asked to tell her what had happened the previous night when he had felt like making love but suddenly turned off.

The patient answered, "Well, I went into the bathroom to wash up and I saw her hair on the sink. Why does she always have to be a pig? I felt disgusted with her. Who wants to make love to such a slob?"

A few sessions later, this patient complained that, the night before, his wife had left dishes piled up in the kitchen and it had made him so angry that he didn't feel like sex.

After listening to similar excuses on several more occasions, Dr. Kaplan asked: "Why do you suppose you always manage to have negative thoughts about your wife whenever lovemaking is imminent?"

"What do you mean?" the patient exclaimed. "That's not what happens." But after further discussion and introspection in therapy, he began to realize that, indeed, there was a hidden pattern and purpose to his actions. Armed with new knowledge that he was, in fact, turning himself off, the patient was able to ignore or banish his antierotic thoughts when they occurred and flow with his sexual feelings instead.

As important as what is being treated is what is *not* being treated—specifically, Dr. Kaplan emphasizes, impossible situations. These might include a husband whose wife is obese and crippled by arthritis, or a wife in love with her tennis instructor. "The husband's lack of attraction has a basis in reality," Dr. Kaplan says, and, as far as the wife is concerned, "there is no way you can train someone to desire a spouse if they are in love with someone else."

If a husband or wife is having an affair, treatment has such a poor chance of success that it will not be attempted unless the other person is given up.

Dr. Kaplan also points to a third kind of impossible situation. People often marry for a variety of reasons that have nothing to do with attraction—financial security, status, the desire for a stable life. "If a wife married her physician-husband because he was a 'good catch,' but he is staid, compulsive, unathletic and short, and she really goes for tall, hip-looking, active, emotional men, nothing is going to make him sexually attractive to her," she says.

The chances of being cured of sexual ennui have improved tremendously in the last three or four years. Although official figures aren't available yet, one source estimates that the success rate has more than tripled. The husbands and wives who stand the greatest chance of being helped are those whose anger doesn't run too deep, who haven't let the sexual moratorium go on for too many years, and who still would find a partner attractive if marital or neurotic problems were overcome.

There is another, final bit of good news about sex in marriage from the world of sex research. The thrill really *can* last forever, says Dr. Kaplan. Sex may calm down after the first two years, as it does in every marriage. Desire may occasionally dim due to stresses and strains in a couple's life, but passion per se need not die. In her current study of happy, long-term relationships, Dr. Kaplan has found men and women whose eyes still light up when one sees the other enter a room, even after decades of marriage. And the sex? After 20, 30 or 40 years, they still find it terrific.

Infidelity And Extramarital Relations Are Not The Same Thing

Dr. Wardell B. Pomeroy

Dr. Wardell B. Pomeroy, world famous sex researcher, is co-author of the Kinsey Reports. He is the academic dean of the Institute for Advanced Study of Human Sexuality in Los Angeles. He is also a practicing sexologist, psychologist and marriage counselor.

In my years of practice, many couples have come to me for counsel on the issue of infidelity. Two recent cases clearly illustrate the right and the wrong way to handle this potential marital crisis.

Fred and Joanne are a conventional married couple. He is a young computer expert, she is a well-educated woman who manages a department store. They live very comfortably, sharing domestic responsibilities as well as their joint income. At work, they inevitably met other people who attracted them. Fred eventually began an affair with one of his office secretaries and grew to feel terribly guilty about it.

Joanne had no idea of his involvement until she accidentally discovered it. She was shattered by the knowledge, then furious. She had been faithful and unsuspecting. She felt terribly betrayed. Fred was full of guilt, anxiety, and remorse. He didn't want to leave Joanne, whom he really loved, and she was eventually willing to give him another chance if they went to a therapist together. I tried hard to make her see the difference between extramarital intercourse and fidelity, but her strict upbringing forbade her acceptance of the idea. The only way she would stay married to Fred was if he renounced any sexual life outside marriage. But already the breach of trust was so great that their future looked very doubtful. The past could not be erased: this was no longer a happy marriage.

Here, on the other hand, are Peter and Lynn, a comparable case in both incomes and lifestyle. But when Lynn felt compelled to confess that she had sex with someone else, Peter admitted that he had, too. Talking it over, they agreed that their marriage was vital to both of them, that they loved each other, and that maybe they should take a different view of their marriage contract.

Our consultation helped set the guidelines for their new open marriage agreement. We also discussed what problems might arise, and how they could deal with them. Peter called me up six months later to say that he and Lynn had never been happier, and that they feel more fulfilled—sexually and personally—than they had ever felt before.

Fred and Joanne found themselves at the mercy of the anxiety, fear, and anger that often destroy marriages when clandestine affairs are discovered. Peter and Lynn however, have forged a new and healthy understanding through which their natural sexual urges are satisfied, with no damage to their deep love for one another. Fidelity—trust—is still the bedrock of their marriage.

Infidelity. Hundreds of songs have been written about it, from "Lipstick on Your Collar" to "Me and Mrs. Jones." But what does it *really* mean?

Webster's dictionary tells us that infidelity means "marital unfaithfulness," a definition which most people understand as *sexual* unfaithfulness. After all, marriage has usually implied the promise to "cleave only to one another." But Webster also gives a second, more vital definition: "breach of trust." *Trust* is the real cornerstone of marriage. It is the issue of trust we must tackle if we are to understand what fidelity means today.

Reprinted from *Forum Magazine,* April 1980, by permission.

Relationships between men and women have changed dramatically over the past thirty years. We raised an entire generation of young men and women who do not "cleave" to a single individual *before* marriage, and who balk at "cleaving" *afterwards*. For these young people, the promise to "cleave only" went out the window with the promise to "obey."

Sex therapists today are giving serious attention to this phenomenon. It is apparent that we are now, in fact, a widely polygamous society. Many of us have sexual relations outside marriage even though monogamy is still the accepted norm.

We've taken a long time to confront this situation. Kinsey was the first to disclose the prevalence of extramarital intercourse back in 1943. His figures showed that 50 percent of males and 25 percent of females had sex outside their marriages. The increased sexual freedom of the 1980's has raised these figures to a possible 60 percent for males and 40 percent for females. Defying the traditional marriage contract today seems almost commonplace, even though there are civil, religious and emotional penalties for such "violations." Obviously, many people still think it's worth the risk.

The real issue in this matter is not extramarital sex at all, but the terms of the marriage contract. For most religious people, of course, terms are clear. But even the sincerely devout may face circumstances in their lives which lead them to break that promise, causing great guilt and unhappiness.

Several different kinds of marital contracts are acknowledged today. Married swingers mark one end of the spectrum—those couples who enjoy extramarital intercourse with the clear understanding that each is permitted to do so. Then there are the unions in which one partner has so little interest in sex that the other is free to do whatever he or she likes. But most common, it seems, is the "unspecified contract," in which both parties profess monogamy but both have extramarital sex in secrecy.

Unfortunately, today's marriage contracts are more often implied than genuinely contracted. Rule number one for any happy marriage is a clear understanding of what the real contract between the partners entails.

In the beginning, the question of extramarital affairs may seem remote. But in time, one or both partners may be faced with the realization that there are other desirable people in the world. Then one person in particular becomes sexually appealing to one of the partners. If such a desire is satisfied, and then concealed, the contract has been violated. And if the other partner discovers the affair, a variety of unpleasant consequences may follow, including the trauma of divorce.

Oddly enough, other infractions of the marriage contract regularly occur *without* the danger of divorce. Conflict may result over work, scheduling, children or in-laws, but the parties in most cases are able to argue it out. When the breach is extramarital intercourse, however, the marriage is often threatened with utter collapse.

Where does the difference lie? Somehow the physical act of inserting the penis in the vagina is equated with deep emotional and psychological betrayal. It is assumed that the new sexual partner is getting all the love and trust and support once reserved solely for the mate. Because this assumption is so commonplace, most people decide against telling their mates about even a one-night stand. And in spite of the subterfuges, the lying, and all the other complications of any ongoing clandestine affair, the first instinct in most cases is to conceal it.

For some people, of course, concealing an affair is part of the excitement. But is this outside sexual involvement a real case of infidelity? If all the love, trust and support of one partner is going to someone new, why hide it? Why not say forthrightly, "I've fallen in love with somebody else and I want a divorce." That is the consequence of *real* infidelity. The contract is voluntarily broken.

But what if one partner has extramarital intercourse for its own sake? Although other factors, such as friendship and affection, may be involved, there may be no intent to break up the marriage, but simply the need to enjoy another person sexually. Conventionally, this is considered infidelity. But has real infidelity occurred?

In most cases, the reaction of the "betrayed" wife or husband is predictable. Since the promise of monogamy is implicit in a conventional marriage, the violated party assumes the worst. For the transgressor to ask the transgressed to accept what has happened as a physical matter, and not infidelity, is usually to ask the impossible. Humiliation, fear, and confusion cancel out any explanation made after the fact. It's too late to discuss the terms of the contract: they've already been broken.

Is all this pain really necessary? Perhaps it's time to view the marriage relationship in a different light. I suggest that the first step in this process is the realization that, in most cases, infidelity and extramarital relations are two very separate phenomena.

People easily overlook the fact that infidelity often occurs *without* sexual relations. A man may dutifully sleep only with his wife and maintain a stable atmosphere at home, when he really cares more about his relationship with his boss or his colleagues than he does about her. Conversely, a woman may be a model housewife and mother in the old sense, but may in fact care more about her social club, or even another man, though guilt prevents her from consummating this other relationship sexually. Could anyone honestly call either of these two "faithful"?

The problem of infidelity is not an easy one. In recent years, we have been hearing a great deal about "open" marriage, and it is estimated that about 5 percent of Americans now practice it. The basic premise is that both partners agree they are free to have sexual relations with other people. Whether they discuss each particular relationship or keep it private is a matter also agreed upon.

Those who argue against open marriage say that it destroys the bond of faith and trust between two people, and that with unlimited opportunities for sex elsewhere, there will be less sexual expression between partners. But the reverse is true. Recent studies of such unions show that the sexual side of the marriage is often *enhanced.*

Of course open marriage is not the ideal solution for everyone. Jealousy is a powerful, prevalent and highly destructive emotion for both men and women. It may be difficult for many people to understand that the *emotional involvement* between two people is what is important.

An open marriage contract can, however, alleviate the strain felt in any marriage when either or both partners meet someone to whom they are sexually attracted. And what is the place of that other "someone" in the open marriage arrangement? Here the same kind of honesty must be applied. The open marriage partner must make clear that no type of exclusive arrangement can result from this second relationship. Naturally, not everyone will accept such limited terms, but complete honesty is essential.

Open marriage requires great courage and effort on the part of each spouse. Marriage is a complex relationship, and shifting the dynamics of it is always a delicate process. But any couple facing the crisis of extramarital sex must think twice. Is *sex* the real issue, or is it *breach of trust?* The key to any successful marriage is honesty and faith. If you can accept all of the other's desires, no extramarital affair will destroy your love.

SWINGERS: The Conservative Hedonists

Swinging is not simply casual group sex as many believe, but a complex lifestyle with a unique set of rules and regulations of its own.

Arno Karlen

Arno Karlen is a writer and researcher in the field of sexology. He is the author of Sexuality and Homosexuality.

I first heard of organized swinging twenty years ago. The couple were, like my wife and me, in their mid-twenties. They were physically more attractive than average, more intelligent and charming. Sitting in their living room, I realized that for weeks they had been dropping hints, testing me and my wife for disapproval of unconventional sex behavior.

They described their activities as a way of life that had improved their relationship and expanded their capacities for love and trust. They had risen above selfish jealousy and possessiveness, learned to give love to more than one person at a time—and, through doing this together, to love each other more than ever. They glowed. They might have been describing a religion. And, clearly, they were making a pitch to potential converts.

My wife and I, without disapproving, accepted the description and ignored the implied invitation. Later we talked about the couple a lot. They did seem much in love. They weren't fools, and one doesn't want to think good friends are liars. My wife and I concluded that for some couples swinging might work, and we each allowed that we were not beyond fantasies of other partners. But, we both concluded, "I'm not so enlightened that I can agree to watch somebody else between *your* legs." In fact, we could not really imagine that swinging made a marriage better.

I wasn't involved in sexology then. Later I took detailed sexual histories from many swingers and even had a chance to revisit that first couple. Eventually I had to conclude that swinging is indeed a solution for some marriages. But a solution for what, and for which people?

Before getting to that, I must make clear what swinging is and who does it, for it remains a subject of many myths and tangled ideas. And I should remind readers under forty that while the word swinging is a rather recent creation of the media, the reality is older. Kinsey, in 1953, mentioned "wife swapping," though only to dismiss it as a male device for finding extramarital partners. In that decade one occasionally heard rumors of suburban, middle-class couples swapping partners at parties. And in 1960, when my friends revealed that they were involved in swapping, I wasn't personally shocked.

As a young musician in the fifties, I had often heard of and occasionally seen group sex, though it was never an organized activity in those circles. Older people had told me of orgy, sadomasochistic, and homosexual networks they had seen back in the twenties and thirties. But to their knowledge and mine, group sex occurred largely in certain show-business and Bohemian circles and in cafe society (what was later renamed the jet set).

Only in the late sixties and seventies did a few people begin to study and report on a national underground of middle-class couples who met to

Published by permission from *Sexology Today* Magazine, May 1980.

switch partners. Like that first couple I talked to in 1960, they met each other through letters accompanied by nude or seminude photos, using private mailing lists. Today they use classified ads in underground papers, and there are even publications put out by and for swingers.

In the middle and late sixties, the media began popularizing the idea of a sexual revolution, and the new term swinging was applied to everything from sex behavior to fashions. When the word started to fade from general use, it was adopted by the swappers. The word is still sometimes used to include the orgy network and the big commercial sex clubs (for singles as well as couples) that exist in many large cities. But swinging is best used to describe couples, married or at least living together, who meet and mate in an organized way.

This distinction is very important. After all, a married person who wants outside partners can do so alone, secretly or discreetly. The point of swinging is that husband and wife both do it and do it together. My first reaction was that this seemed to be courting trouble. Obviously not in swingers' eyes. But they are aware of potential problems and have provided two kinds of swinging parties, open and closed. In open swinging, nonmarital sex acts take place whenever people like, often with husbands and wives watching or even involved. In closed swinging, each man and woman who have paired off go to a separate room for privacy. Obviously the latter is less likely to provoke jealous rage.

Another distinction has been made, between "recreational" and "utopian" swingers. The latter, like the first swingers I met, see swinging as a way to improve a marriage, a way of life. The recreational swingers see it as a way to obtain or increase sexual pleasure. It is fun, not a philosophy.

How many people practice various forms of swinging no one can say. In large and even small cities in every state, swingers from networks through acquaintance, passing on names, ads and letters (those who travel use names from friends and publications wherever they go). And involvement in swinging varies from once in a lifetime to frequently over many decades, from small private parties to big clubs and weekend bashes at camps and motels. Various writers have estimated that 1 to 5 percent of Americans have tried swinging (however defined) once in their lives, and that perhaps 1 to 2 percent have done so regularly at some period.

Swinging is hardly the national pasttime, but it continues to hold the public imagination, and for good reasons. It raises basic questions about love, fidelity, monogamy, sexual variety and male-female differences in relationships and sex. Men and women who haven't been around swinging or other forms of group sex wonder about many things. Why do it if you have someone you love? Could I handle the jealousy? Without privacy, could I have an erection? What if no one wanted me? What if I ended up with someone repulsive? Would I feel inadequate because of my body or my sexual performance?

Most of these things turn out not to be problems. Swinging can continue only if people become regulars, and for that they must feel as comfortable and as safe as possible. Therefore swinging follows unwritten rules: scrupulous personal hygiene; great care about contraception and VD; low-pressure sexual invitations that can easily be avoided; the right to decline any partner or activity (menstruation and fatigue are handy universal excuses). Although swingers take oral sex for granted, the less common sex acts are usually avoided. Female homosexual acts may occur, but male homosexual contact not at all or only by special agreement and usually in private.

Some individuals and groups don't adhere to these rules, especially some big groups in the largest cities. But rule-breakers run the risk of not being invited back, so swingers as a group probably display less halitosis and more tact than the majority of sexual partners one might meet at random. Of course good looks and good erotic technique don't go unnoticed, so a person with either will be much desired and much invited.

The biggest rule, of course, is not to make jealous displays. Most people have some awkwardness and ambivalence in their first swinging experiences, and the veterans usually make allowances for that. They also do all they can to minimize jealousy among themselves. After a party, most spouses don't give each other many details about what they did and are careful to add that of course the spouse is more skilled, exciting and attractive than any other partner of the evening.

In fact, the least debated result of swinging is the opportunity it gives to learn from watching and to gain reassurance and confidence from a variety of partners. The man afraid that his penis is too small, the woman afraid her thighs are too skinny or too fat, may soon find that he or she is not only acceptable but desired, exciting. New partners stimulate their responsiveness and increase their erotic skills. Some, especially women, find that they can give and receive more pleasure than ever imagined. And they learn what swinging ultimately requires most of all, sensitivity to the needs and feelings of others.

The loss of sexual anxieties and heightened self-confidence account for much of swingers' enthusiasm. That change is sometimes carried back to the marital relationship. This can happen because the cardinal rule of swinging is that no emotional intimacy occur. The husband and wife meet after the party, saying to themselves and each other, "I may have fucked someone else, pushed and tickled the flesh, but it wasn't personal. It's you I love and care about."

This is where some people's credulity fails. This depends somewhat on whether one is male or female. To most men, as Kinsey said, one of the strongest proofs that men and women are different is that women would even question whether sexual variety is appealing. The harem fantasy is probably universal among males, based in their biosocial nature; and the female tendency to be more conservative about variety and about choice of partners probably also has evolutionary roots. These tendencies are not polar opposites, but leanings greater in one sex than in the other. How people enter swinging is a good example of how it operates.

The great majority of couples enter swinging because the husband cajoled, convinced or threatened his partner. Some men spend months or years preparing their wives psychologically, maneuvering them toward group activity. Many of the women go along reluctantly, even out of fear that failing to do so will cause their mates to leave them. The reluctance and resentment remains within many outwardly compliant wives even after several years of regular swinging. I have heard very few swinger wives admit it themselves, but almost all said that many other women they'd met in swinging confessed bitterly to doing it only to keep their mates.

But once in swinging, quite a number of the women change their minds. In fact, the men and women sometimes reverse their original attitudes. The women become orgasmic or multiorgasmic for the first time or finally shed lifelong inhibitions; the men, surprised to see their wives respond as they never did in the past, become insecure and possessive. Now it may be the wives who want to go on swinging, and the husbands who are negative or ambivalent.

Another element is involved in whether people take to swinging—how conventional they are. Again, some metropolitan swinging circles are unconventional and varied, but the classic portrait of the suburban or small-city swinger (and some big-city ones as well), is superconventional. One kind and likeable group who allowed me extensive interviews could be the mold for many others. They ranged from stockbrokers to physicians to electronics repairmen, from housewives to shop owners. Meeting them outside the swinging situation, I learned that many were conservative Republicans, hard working, little given to using drugs or to heavy drinking (both are *verboten* at most swinging parties). Their chief topic of conversation even outside swinging parties was swinging. And although they were only mildly utopian about swinging—they stressed the fun as much as the marital and emotional benefits—they glowed enthusiastically when they talked of their hobby.

Actually, swinging was more than a hobby for them, it was one of the few unconventional things they had ever done—one of the few things they had done not because they thought they should but because they wanted to. Their swinging companions filled most of their social world, because they shared a genuine sense of adventure. There was, for instance, a woman who had been dragged into swinging by her husband a year or so before; now, quite aside from her relationship with her husband, which had long been deteriorating, she felt free to explore and enjoy her own sexuality for the first time.

Meeting such people makes one understand better why the extramarital sex is done together rather than separately. These are people who consider themselves conventional in many ways and take satisfaction in it; they are committed to their marriages, to the idea of marriage, or to both, and they turn "cheating" into a shared venture. For some uncommunicative couples, it is the first unpredictable thing they ever shared, either with husbands or with friends.

I do not mean to glamorize swinging or to gloss over its problems. The stress on presenting a cosmetic self—attractive, not too old, without political or religious views, and in many places preferably white and middle class—makes it difficult to expand in any area but sexuality. Sex, though varied and skillful, is often a conscientious performance. Commitment and intimacy are landmines. Very fat people need not apply. Those who cannot work out most conflicts or jealousy need not return to do so on others' time. Many people find that swinging drives them apart; even some couples with years of swinging behind them live with smothered jealousy and dissatisfaction. Sometimes bonds develop with extramarital partners, sometimes frustration grows that such bonds don't develop.

And there is some truth in Kinsey's comment that often swinging is—or at least begins with—men's desire for extramarital partners. Swinging can be quite a convenience; extramarital affairs can be very time-consuming and emotionally and socially dangerous. But there is another reason for swinging, I think, and I have never seen it mentioned. It is so simple that it may have eluded attention.

Just as men tend to want a variety of partners, they also tend to have clocklike orgasmic desire, more urgent and more regular than in most women. A man who craves, say, three orgasms a week is likely to get them one way or another, if not through coitus with his wife then with another partner, by masturbation or even involuntarily, through wet dreams. Many men deny this to their partners because they know a lot of women feel it sounds impersonal. A surprising number of men involved in swinging are very far up in the scale of sexual activity. Some, in their forties or fifties, want and can reach orgasm at least once a day; some, I have on the independent accounts of themselves, their wives, and their other partners, regularly reach two or three orgasms a night four nights in a row. Some women will accept sex this often but few want it that often. There is only one study, to my knowledge, comparing the sex behavior of swingers and non-swingers, and it supports strongly my impression that sexually, as a group, men swingers are geared high above average. Many, constantly more vigorous than other men, have gone through life feeling deviant.

Very simply, these men are in some way like erotically undeveloped women. If they have limited their sexuality largely to one partner, they have spent most of their time wanting more than almost any partner can enthusiastically give. In swinging they find high frequency and variety. Although many swing only once a week or once a month, they feel liberated by the experience of acting out their full erotic potential and being appreciated for it.

Various experts have ascribed different reasons for swinging to those involved in it. As often as not, the motives are allegedly neurotic or reflect inability to make one lasting, intimate relationship. I think this is true of some people. When I met again the first swinging couple I'd ever talked to, I could see that after two decades of marriage, their lives were joined more in appearance than in spirit. I learned that their marital and sexual lives had never really been good and had kept drifting farther apart with the years. My first impression of hollow rhetoric about the benefits of swinging had, I think, been right.

But I am no longer sure that one should generalize from those reservations. I now mistrust not only those who claim, as one writer has, that those who swing together stay together, but also those who say swinging is always neurotic and destructive. To begin with, some people simply are not capable of deep or sustained intimacy, and there is no point in admonishing them to be other than who they are. I have seen people whose sexuality and, to some extent, emotionality have blossomed through swinging; perhaps it isn't because of the sexual activity itself, but because swinging is the first commitment to joint risk they have made. It has given a sense of self-acceptance to many highly sexual men and erotically unrealized women. For some people, it is just plain fun. One can say what might be misleading about their convictions and perceptions, but I have found convincing some couples' statement that swinging did indeed preserve or improve their marriage. I must conclude that aside from starting life over as different people, it was the best choice they had. Many are in swinging for only a few months or years; having exhausted it, they return to a monogamous life. I should add that some people whose marriages split through swinging might have split anyway. If swinging didn't save their marriages, at least it saved them.

I asked before, what does swinging save people from, and for what? At best, from being less than they were capable of, for expanding their own lives as best they could, in their own ways. Clearly I don't advocate swinging to anyone. In interviewing swingers, one is talking only to those who could adapt to it. There are all the others—we don't know how many—who quarrelled badly at the very suggestion, quit in recriminations half way to the first try, or broke up in rage or resentment after trying once or twice. Anyone considering such a step should be convinced without anyone's urging.

Swinging would not be an easy or safe decision for me. Other things aside, the very organized quality of it is alien to much in my behavior and emotions. Because of that, I have felt obliged to look for good in it, and I have seen some for certain people. If the study of sexuality teaches anything, it is respect for people whose decisions wouldn't come easily to oneself.

Is There Sex after 40?

Not much, if you believe these college students. Mom and Dad are still in love, of course, but sex has little to do with it.

OLLIE POCS, ANNETTE GODOW, WILLIAM L. TOLONE, AND ROBERT H. WALSH

Ollie Pocs was born in Latvia and came to Texas as a cowboy in 1950. Educated at the University of Illinois and Purdue, he has been teaching at Illinois State University since 1960 and is in charge of the Family Life Resources Center. He has received specialized training from Masters and Johnson and Hartman and Fithian in sex therapy.

Annette Godow, a licensed clinical psychologist and certified sex therapist, received her doctorate in psychology from the University of Illinois. She is now teaching at the College of Charleston and is engaged in private practice.

William L. Tolone is an associate professor of sociology at Illinois State University. He received a Ph.D. from the University of Tennessee in 1970. He has published in the areas of deviance and sex and specializes in the design of social research.

Robert H. Walsh received his M.A. and Ph.D. from the University of Iowa. Since 1968 he has been engaged in intergenerational and longitudinal research on sexual attitudes and behavior. He teaches on marriage and the family at Illinois State University.

ONCE UPON A TIME, most college students believed that their parents:

☐ had intercourse once a month or less,

☐ never had intercourse before they were married,

☐ never had oral-genital sex.

How far have we progressed since the much heralded sexual revolution? Not very far, on the evidence. The students who held these naive beliefs didn't go to the school in the Gay '90s, the depressed '30s, or the grey-flannel '50s. They attended a large Midwestern state university in the 1970s.

We've heard for years how parents don't understand the sex lives or sex attitudes of their children. It appears the misunderstanding runs both ways. As one college student, a young woman, told us: "When I was 16, my 40-year-old mother shocked me one day by announcing that she was pregnant. I knew the facts of life and all, but somehow I just didn't think of my mother as doing *that*."

The young woman was one of 646 Illinois State University students who took part in a study we made of what students whose parents were still married believed about their sex lives. The 239 men and 407 women presented an idyllic picture of their parents, at least in the nonsexual part of the questionnaire. More than 90 percent said their parents were happily married and nearly that many felt they were still in love. The parents were white, predominately middle-class and middle-aged.

We felt from the start that the students would have some trouble recognizing and dealing with their parents as sexual beings, but we were surprised how much trouble. Some had a hard time even getting through the questionnaire. Six percent of them refused to answer most of the items, which dealt with premarital petting; premarital, marital, and extramarital intercourse; masturbation; and oral-genital sex.

No recreational sex. Some students felt it was wrong even to think about these things. They had the most trouble with questions about recreational sex, sex purely for pleasure. Nearly 20 percent, for example, ignored the questions about past and present parental masturbation. A few students expressed their feelings bluntly: "This questionnaire stinks." "Whoever thinks about their parents' sexual relations, except perverts?" "What stupid-ass person made up these questions?" The mere thought of their parents' sexuality was obviously banned for some young men and women.

These emotional reactions reflect the strong taboo our society, and most others, have against incest. Since family members usually share limited space, they're bound to see each other occasionally at least partially undressed. The incest taboo defuses a sight that might be a sexual stimulus in another situation, and permits family members to maintain intimate but nonsexual relationships. The taboo thus encourages young people to repress any image of their parents as sexual creatures.

Since we had no direct measure of the parents' actual sex lives, we used the figures Alfred C. Kinsey reported in his 1948 and 1953 books on the sexual behavior of American men and women. If sex in the 1970s is more frequent and varied than it was 30 years ago, as seems likely, then Kinsey's figures probably underestimate the parents' real sex activity.

We compared our students' estimates with Kinsey's data in 20 different areas. In every one, the estimates were low, usually very low. The tables on the next page sum up these comparisons.

One reason for this misunderstanding is our youth-oriented culture. The things that are fun, including sex, are the province of youth. People who are middle-aged or older supposedly do not care much about sex, and cannot do much about it if they do.

The widest spread between fact and fancy showed up in estimates of premarital and extramarital sex. Only 10 percent of the women, for example, thought their mothers had intercourse before they were married, compared to Kinsey's figure of 50 percent, and only a third thought their fathers had, compared to Kinsey's 92 percent. The male students came closer but their guesses were still less than half the reality.

Not my mother. Students were even further off when it came to extramarital activity. Only two percent of the sons and daughters thought their mother did such a thing, while Kinsey found that 13 times that many did. The estimates of dad's straying were again closer but still much too low.

The students missed almost as badly with good old-fashioned married coitus, the most widely accepted type of sexual behavior. Kinsey said that parents in this age range (41 through 45 for the mothers, 46 through 50 for the fathers) had intercourse about seven times a month. Our students' estimates averaged three times a month, less than once a week.

About one-fourth of the sons and daughters believed their parents never had intercourse any more, or had it less than once a year. More than half thought the figure was once a month or less. Only four percent thought three to four times a week was about right, and none of the 646 students could see it happening more than four times a week.

This raises a curious point. Apparently most of the 90 percent of students who felt their parents were happily married and still in love believed they maintained this happy state without the help of sex, or at least not much of it.

Students came closest to the truth about the most innocuous item on the list, premarital petting by their fathers. Perhaps this was a grudging admission that even their parents "must have done something." And since the students knew the double standard flowered in the early days when their parents were young, they figured the old man probably played around with someone, if not with mom.

Marriage didn't help. The biggest surprise to us was how inaccurate the married students were in their perception of their parents' sex lives. We felt that as students got closer to marriage, their parents would consider them more adult and would probably be more open in discussing sex with them. This apparently didn't happen. The married students did little better than the rest in understanding the reality of their parents' sex lives.

Many families head off discussions of sexual matters through a conspiracy of silence. Neither adults nor offspring really want to know what the other is doing. The parents, particularly, may suspect the worst, but they'd rather hope for the best.

Since marriage didn't seem to increase the students' accuracy much, we looked at other differences: sex, religious feeling, sexual experience, social class, home-town background, etc., all without much success. The students whose estimates came closest to reality were the ones with the most sexual experience themselves. Those who believed sex was important for everyone also did better, as did older students. But even those groups consistently and considerably underestimated the real level of parental sexuality.

We've already suggested several reasons for this consistent misreading. There is the stereotype of sex as a youthful activity, in which older people have little interest and less capacity; the incest taboo, which discourages any thought of parents as sexual beings; and the conspiracy of silence, which keeps parents and children blissfully unaware of the other's activities.

A pat on the rump. These all contribute to the gap in sexual understanding, but the biggest reason is more basic. As good parents, adults are expected to pass on our society's generally nonpermissive attitudes toward sex. They do this with words and deeds. Sex-researcher and therapist William Masters noted that one of the best kinds of sexual education children can get is seeing Dad pat Mom on the rump while they're doing the dishes. Parents usually hide such demonstrations of affection, thus conditioning their children to think of them as asexual.

Many parents not only avoid showing physical affection around the kids but avoid mentioning pleasure when they talk about the facts of life. They usually explain matters when Mommy is obviously pregnant, saying, "You'll be getting a baby brother or sister soon." Children are seldom told that most of the time their parents have sex for pleasure, not procreation. As a result, even adolescents who know about sex don't think of their parents as sexual.

Parents who don't talk about sex at all create an even more sexless image. It would be interesting to learn whether failure to talk about sex is an isolated phenomenon in families that otherwise communicate freely. Many parents may discuss politics, money, religion, and other interesting issues openly but freeze up on sex.

We usually hear about peer pressure in relation to young people, but parents feel pressure from their peers, too. If they believe that their friends and neighbors don't approve of adolescent sexuality—certainly the case in most communities—parents will try harder to control their children. The result is that even men and women who were sexually active in their own youth become strict about sex as parents. Some even avoid the topic completely for fear that talking about it will increase the child's interest in sex and encourage experimentation. This is something like trying to stop a riot with a popgun. It's quiet but not very effective.

It's clear that sexual misunderstanding runs both ways. Parents are afraid their children will become promiscuous, pregnant, syphilitic, or all three. Young people think their parents are sexless old fuds. Are things likely to change?

Daughters' Beliefs vs. Kinsey's Findings

Type of Activity	Thought mother did	According to Kinsey	Thought father did	According to Kinsey
premarital petting	63%	99%	80%	89%
premarital coitus	10%	50%	33%	92%
extramarital coitus	2%	26%	7%	50%
oral-genital sex	25%	49%	29%	59%
masturbation	31%	62%	62%	93%

Sons' Beliefs vs. Kinsey's Findings

Type of Activity	Thought mother did	According to Kinsey	Thought father did	According to Kinsey
premarital petting	69%	99%	81%	89%
premarital coitus	22%	50%	45%	92%
extramarital coitus	2%	26%	12%	50%
oral-genital sex	30%	49%	34%	59%
masturbation	49%	62%	73%	93%

We can imagine two opposing scenarios. In one, society learns to accept the sexuality of both parents and children. Shame and hypocrisy are banished. Young people benefit from adult experience and wisdom, while adults learn new, alternative views. People generally admit that sex is primarily for recreation, make proper use of contraceptives, and are prepared to reduce illegitimacy, abortion, and venereal disease. With the taboo on sexual communication between the generations broken, communication improves in all areas. In the second scenario, the basic facts are the same, but the results are much less satisfying. The new sexual openness creates as many problems as it solves. For those who see themselves as sexually unattractive, uninterested, or incompetent, the openness makes matters worse. They suffer about sexual deficiencies the way today's teen-agers worry about their weight, their hair, acne, or the latest dance steps.

Both old and young find themselves trapped, the former in living up to the new expectations of nonstop sexual bliss, the latter in handling the responsibilities that go with the new privileges. Sex, instead of becoming more "natural," is more misused, exploited, and commercialized.

The real future, we suspect, will be lived somewhere between these extremes. There will be more sexual openness between generations, which will improve communications. But marriage, the family, and parent-child roles will still be with us, carrying with them misunderstandings between the generations, sexual and otherwise. When our children become parents, and have our grandchildren, they will likely agree with what Socrates said 2,500 years ago: "Our youth now loves luxury. They have bad manners, contempt for authority, disrespect for older people. Children nowadays are tyrants."

For more information, read:

De Beauvoir, Simone. *The Coming of Age*, Putnam, 1972, $10.00; Warner, 1973, paper, $2.25.

Pocs, Ollie and Annette Godow. "Can students view parents as sexual beings?" in *The Family Coordinator*, Vol. 26, No. 1.

Walsh, Robert H. "The Generation Gap in Sexual Beliefs" in *Sexual Behavior*, Vol. 2, pp. 4-10.

The New Sex Education and the Aging

Mary Ann P. Sviland

There is an increasing awareness that sexual discrimination against the elderly persists, even in this era of expanding sexual understanding and liberalization of attitudes and behavior. To date, little effort has been directed toward assisting older persons to attain the same sexual expression and growth which is afforded the young. Rather, within many segments of this county, society still forces mandatory retirement from sexual activity in the elderly. Imposed social barriers to sexual expression range from psychologically subtle family nonacceptance of the elderly person's social companions to physical segregation of husbands and wives in retirement facilities and nursing care homes.

The topic of old people and sex is a comedian's stock-in-trade for predictably getting a laugh out of the audience. For example, in a recent television program, Edgar Bergen reinforced the myth of declining male sexuality with this typical joke: "I started out the other night to paint the town red, but then I found I had run out of paint."

Who are the elderly whose sexual needs society has found amusing or insignificant? Today, over 20 million people in the United States are over 65 years of age, comprising 10 percent of the population.[1] The elderly are now the fastest-growing age group in the United States. Average life expectancy has increased from 47 years in 1900 to 66.8 years for a male, and 74.3 years for a female born today. Every day 1,000 people reach age 65. With new drugs and medical techniques and the presently declining birth rate, the elderly could well comprise 25 percent of our total population by the year 2000.

SEXUALITY AMONG THE AGED

Sexuality in the aged is a meritorious area for sex education focus. The general belief that sexuality is the domain of the young has resigned many senior citizens to premature impotency, frustration, self-depreciation, loneliness, and depression.[2] Helping older persons improve their sexual function and adjustment is not an end in itself but is a means of fulfilling a deeper one—the timeless need of all humans for intimacy and love. Furthermore, thwarted sexuality may contribute more to depression in the elderly than previously assumed. The lack of an intimate and empathetic relationship, with concomitant feelings of loneliness and unattractiveness, may account for much clinical depression currently diagnosed as involutional. The positive value of companionship to general physical health is evidenced in the lower morbidity and mortality rates of older married persons compared to older single persons.

Primary opposition to sexuality in the aged arises from adult children who view their aged parents' normal urges for intimacy and romance as a threat leading to social disgrace and as signs of second childhood.[3] The contrast of positive reactions versus negative reactions to rebudding parental sexuality was clearly depicted in the teleplay "Queen of the Stardust Ballroom." The married daughter of an elderly widow expressed shocked disgust when her mother cast off her drab widow's weeds for attractive clothing, tinted hair, and makeup after she had met a man she liked. In clear contrast the widow's son, through his quiet, comfortable approval, encouraged her romance. His encouragement was a major factor in the widow's full enjoyment of her romance. Greater denial of parental sexuality is apt to be expressed toward the mother than toward the father, and generalizes to unacceptance of sexuality in all elderly females. Mateless parents who express loneliness are told to take up a hobby or are pressed into household service instead of being encouraged to reenter the mainstream of life through reenactment of romantic involvement. Often repression of parental sexuality stems from children's disillusionment and hidden resentment. Some adult children who inhibited their own sexuality for many years in deference to their parents' restrictive sexual values simply cannot tolerate the feeling of betrayal and wastedness at their parents' newly liberalized sexual values and behaviors. The aversion to parental sexual acting out is readily observed in the strict nursing home sexual prohibitions designed to please the billpaying adult children, despite the fact that free acceptance of sexuality in homes for the aged has been advocated as humanistic.[4]

To provide an adequate context for the objectives of the sex educator in the field of aging, awareness is needed for the psychosocial issues influencing sexuality in the elderly. These issues include cultural stereotyping and myths on aging; research shortcomings; research findings on elderly sexuality; and restrictive cultural and physiological factors.

CULTURAL STEREOTYPING AND MYTHS ABOUT AGING

The word "agism" (or "ageism") was recently coined to signify the profound prejudice against the elderly and biased stereotyping that is as bad as or worse than racism or sexism.[1,5] Misunderstandings, inaccurate assumptions, and stereotypes that abound in the public mind include the following: most elderly are infirm and live in rest homes; older people think and move slowly; they are emotionally disengaged and bored with life; senility is inevitable; the aged are inflexible, unproductive, and in essence lonely, poor, bedridden, incompetent. Yet in fact, only 4 percent of the elderly are institutionalized. A cross-sectional study of emeritus college professors showed most memory and cognitive variables functioning well, equivalent to an average younger group.[6] In essence, age magnifies but does not radically alter character and personality traits evolved earlier in life. A sociable, energetic, flexible young person with many pursuits will become a sociable, energetic, flexible, involved old person.

Similarly, common myths and stereotypes about elderly sexuality include: aging inevitably leads to impotence; many women lose sexual interest following menopause; the frequency of sexual response lessens with age. Again, only approximately 5 percent of impotence seen in previously well-functioning males is of a nonreversible physical origin. Much impotency diagnosed as organic attributable to aging is actually attributable to such psychological and environmental variables as performance anxiety, loss of interest, or partner unavailability. Many women demonstrate an increased sex drive after menopause.[7] Finally, one longitudinal ten-year study conducted in 1969 on people over 60 years found that over 15 percent of the subjects showed increased patterns of sexual activity as they grew older.[8,9]

Growth of sexuality in the elderly was more recently confirmed by the author of this chapter in a medical-setting program designed to help elderly couples become sexually liberated.[10] This program was established for couples over 60 with a basically sound marital relationship and no sexual dysfunction who wanted to decrease their sexual inhibitions and expand their repertoire of sexual behaviors to conform to recently liberated mores. Raised in a more inhibited era, they wanted to erase still prevalent internal taboos toward such activities as oral-genital sex or sex for pleasure. An interesting phenomenon occurred during the course of therapy in approximately 20 percent of the couples, which involved an increase of sexuality that exceeded their earlier activity. For example, in one couple with the male aged 62, the man developed a pattern of three erections and two orgasms per sexual session, when his prior lifelong pattern involved only one orgasm per session.[11] It had simply never occurred to him that satisfactory sex could be followed by even more satisfactory sex. Sexual decline in the elderly may more accurately reflect variables highly correlated with age rather than with the aging per se.

RESEARCH SHORTCOMINGS ON ELDERLY SEXUALITY

What is actually known about elderly sexuality? Probably little. And there is good reason to believe that earlier findings do not reflect the sexual pattern of today's elderly.

Discrimination in terms of the agism stereotype of the sexless older years is reflected in sexual research. Since publication of the Kinsey reports on male and female sexuality over two decades ago fewer than a dozen studies of elderly sexual behavior, which attempt to sample an elderly population, have been reported. Kinsey devoted only 3 out of 1,700 total pages to older people and included only 162 subjects over 60 years of age in a total population of 20,024.[12,13] Similarly, the Masters and Johnson study of sexual response done with the last decade included only 31 male and female subjects beyond age 60 in a total population of 694 subjects.[14] Therefore only 4.5 percent of their samples were over 60 years of age, yet people over 60 comprise 26.7 percent of the total population aged 18 or older.

An additional shortcoming of research on aged sexuality is that the reports are essentially sociological. Without psychological information there is no way to differentiate functional from physiological bases of cessation of sexuality. Age offers many elderly men and women with sexual conflicts an acceptable alibi to remove themselves from anxiety connected with sexual behavior.[15] Variables which might negatively influence sexuality, such as poor health, low sexual interest of the spouse, prohibitive group mores, sexually impairing medications, or unwillingness to risk aggravation of minor physical disability through sex are not controlled. Furthermore, the studies glaringly omit exploration of the emotional aspects of the relationship. Obviously life with a nagging, critical mate could deflate sexual expansiveness, which clarifies the fact that sex behavior does not necessarily correlate with sex drive alone.

Finally, even if previous studies accurately reflected sexual behavior in the elderly, the data on which these studies were based may now be outdated. Liberalization of sexual values occurring in the 1950s has resulted in the sanctioning of sexual behaviors previously viewed as pathological. With new social acceptance, greater frequency of these behaviors could be expected to be found in the elderly as well as in the young, which would make all prior normative data outmoded.

The important message of this section is that prior normative data which may now be invalid and obsolescent should not be used as a basis for restricting sexuality in the elderly. The phenomenon of regression to the norm indeed exists. If a 70-year-old man is told that the average orgasm frequency for his age group is 0.9 per week, he would probably never attempt more even if 3 ogasms per week is his actual functioning capacity. The supernormal frequencies found in some elderly males may more accurately reflect innate capacity and could become the average expectation in a more guiltless, biologically natural culture.[16]

RESEARCH FINDINGS ON PHYSICAL AND ENVIRONMENTAL EFFECTS ON ELDERLY SEXUALITY

Contrary to popular mythology, the greater the sexual interest, activity, and capacity in earlier life, the greater the interest, activity, and capacity in later years.[17] Early termination of sexual activity occurs where sex was not important in early life.[18] Although continued elderly male sexuality is related to prior frequency and interest, continued elderly female sexuality is related only to past enjoyment.[19]

Male sexual function reaches peak responsiveness around age 18 and then shows a steady decline while female sexuality in our culture reaches peak responsiveness in the late thirties and early forties and can maintain this level into the sixties.[20] Sometime in the fifties, the male shows declining frequency of orgasm and increasing length of refractory period (time between orgasm and next possible erection). In sharp contrast to men, elderly women remain capable of enjoying multiple orgasms.[21] Between 50 and 60 years the wife may want sex more than the husband is able to give.[22,23] However, frequency of morning erections, a sign of physical and sexual vigor, does not significantly decline until the male is 66 years or older.[24]

Partner availability and good health are critical to continued sexuality. Illness, whether acute or chronic, lowers male sexual responsiveness and an ill wife restricts the aging male's sexual opportunity. Seven out of ten healthy married couples over 60 years are sexually active, some into their late eighties.[25] In constrast, only 7 percent of the single, divorced, or widowed persons over 60 years are sexually active.[26]

Surveys conducted at the Kinsey Institute and at Duke University found that 70 percent of married males aged 70 remain sexually active, with mean intercourse frequency of 0.9 per week and with some males maintaining a frequency of 3.0 per week.[27,28] By age 75, 50 percent of married males still engage in intercourse.[29]

There is less research on elderly female sexuality than on the elderly male. However, 70 percent of the married females and 12 percent of widowed and divorced females aged 60 engage in intercourse.[30] Masturbation incidence was higher for widowed and divorced females with 25 percent of single females aged 70 still masturbating. Sexual abstinence in the elderly female is not primarily biological but the result of social and psychological factors since widowed or divorced elderly women do not typically seek partner replacements unless the female is unusually attractive and secure.[31]

Worry over sexual failure can create secondary impotence in the male. Orgasmic dysfunction in elderly females and lack of erection, erectile loss, and retarded ejaculation problems in the elderly male have been successfully eliminated when their common basis, performance anxiety, was systematically removed.[32] The effects of endocrine replacement therapy or drugs on loss of sex is debatable; it has not been established if libido, cosmetic appearance, or general state of well-being is affected.[33] There is mounting evidence that estrogen replacement following menopause increases medical risks, including cancer.[34] There is no scientific evidence that procaine preparations (Gerovital H3) enhance libido or arrest the aging process, although procaine may be an effective anti-depressant which in turn could enhance playfulness.[35]

RESTRICTIVE CULTURAL AND PHYSIOLOGICAL FACTORS

Although the culture imposes some restrictions on the elderly male, his sexuality is primarily limited by physical factors. In contrast, the elderly female, where physical capabilities and responsiveness have not depreciated, is primarily limited from sexual expression by cultural factors. Understanding of this distinction is necessary for a more rational approach to sexuality in the aged.[36]

The elderly male experiences reduced sexual stamina which adversely affects his sex life. Biological changes may include decreased orgasm frequency, longer refractory periods following orgasm, loss of awareness of pending orgasm, and greater need for direct stimulation for arousal.[37] Sexual adjustment and satisfaction in the elderly male may require shifts in the sexual pattern. The female may need to take a more active role in sexual situations and both partners may need to learn new behaviors to increase compatibility and minimize the functional effects of aging on male sexuality.[38]

Since aging does not substantially affect sexual capacity of elderly females, compared to elderly males, cultural factors such as the double standard impede sexual actualization in elderly females. Women are faced with approximately eleven years of matelessness since they tend to marry males four years older and the life expectancy for males is seven years shorter. Females outnumber males 138.5 to 100 at age 65 and 156.2 to 100 at age 75.[39] Thus, elderly females glut the marketplace, which makes it easier for widowed males to remarry.

Various solutions have been proposed to eliminate the elderly widow's sexual dilemma, but it appears that the most logical solution would be to allow elderly females access to younger males, without social censure.

There is no need to view sexual contact with an older person as physically repugnant—this stems from our cult of youth as beauty. Many of the physical signs of aging, the paunch and the wrinkles, are due to poor body caretaking, not the aging process. Many elderly people who lived prudently are remarkably attractive without the physical signs we attribute to old age. People, both male and female, must be allowed to pick their partners solely on the basis of compatibility. This would make acceptable the relationship of the younger male with an older female. Age-discrepant relationships do not necessarily indicate psychopathology in either party. In dealing with the sexual needs of the expanding geriatric population, society will have to take a more liberalized view regarding alternate life-styles. People should be encouraged to choose their mates on the basis of psychological needs, not preconceived standards of propriety or normalcy.[40]

NOTES AND REFERENCES

1. Robert N. Butler, *Why Survive? Being Old in America* (New York: Harper & Row, 1975).

2. Mary Ann P. Sviland, "Helping Elderly Couples Become Sexually Liberated: Psycho-Social Issues," *Journal of Counseling Psychology* Vol. 1, no. 5 (1975), pp. 67-72. Reprinted as "Sexual Liberation Therapy for Elderly Couples" in Robert Kastenbaum, ed., *Old Age on the New Scene* (New York: Springer, in press).

3. S.R. Dean, "Sin and Senior Citizens," *Journal of the American Geriatric Society* Vol. 14 (1966), pp. 935-938.

4. Victor Kassel, "You Never Outgrow Your Need for Sex." Presented at 53rd Annual Meeting New England Hospital Assembly, Boston (March 27, 1974).

5. *Los Angeles Times*. "Aging: A Time Bomb." A Complex Psychosocial Process: Part V, page 13 (January 18, 1976).

6. K. Werner Schaie and C.R. Strother, "Cognitive and Personality Variables in College Graduates of Advanced Age" in G.A. Tallend, ed., *Human Behavior and Aging* (New York: Academic Press, 1968).

7. William H. Masters and Virginia E. Johnson, *Human Sexual Response* (Boston: Little, Brown & Co., 1966).

8. Eric Pfeiffer, A. Verwoerdt and H.S. Wang, "Sexual Behavior in Aged Men and Women. 1. Observation on 254 Community Volunteers," *Archives of General Psychiatry* Vol. 19 (1968), pp. 753-758.

9. Eric Pfeiffer, A. Verwoerdt and H.S. Wang, "The Natural History of Sexual Behavior in a Biologically Advantaged Group of Aged Individuals," *Journal of Gerontology* Vol. 24 (1969), pp. 193-198.

10. Mary Ann P. Sviland, "Helping Elderly Couples Become Sexually Liberated."

11. Mary Ann P. Sviland, "Sexual Rejuvenation in Men Over 60—and Women Too" Paper presented at Society for Scientific Study of Sex, Western Region, Los Angeles (June 1975).

12. Alfred Kinsey, W.B. Pomeroy and C.I. Martin, *Sexual Behavior in the Human Male* (Philadelphia: W.B. Saunders, 1948).

13. Alfred C. Kinsey, W.B. Pomeroy, C.I. Martin and Paul H. Gebbard, *Sexual Behavior in the Human Female* (Philadelphia: W.B. Saunders, 1953).

14. Masters and Johnson, *Human Sexual Response.*

15. Martin S. Berezin, "Sex and Old Age: A Review of the Literature," *Journal of Geriatric Psychiatry* Vol. 2 (1969), pp. 131-149.

16. W.R.Stokes, "Sexual Functioning in the Aging Male," *Geriatrics* Vol. 6 (1951), pp. 304-308.

17. A.D. Clamon, "Introduction" to panel discussion: Sexual Difficulties After 50, *Canadian Medical Association Journal* Vol. 94 (1966), p. 207.

18. Eric Pfeiffer and G.C. Davis, "Determinants of Sexual Behavior in Middle and Old Age," *Journal of the American Geriatric Society* Vol. 20 (1972), pp. 151-158.
19. Ibid.
20. Helen S. Kaplan, *The New Sex Therapy* (New York: Brunner/Mazel, 1974).
21. Ibid.
22. Alfred Kinsey et al., *Sexual Behavior in the Human Male.*
23. Alfred Kinsey et al., *Sexual Behavior in the Human Female.*
24. Alfred Kinsey et al., *Sexual Behavior in the Human Male.*
25. D. Swartz, "The Urologist's View," panel discussion: Sexual Difficulties After 50, *Canadian Medical Association Journal* Vol. 94 (1966), pp. 213-214.
26. A.D. Clamon, "Introduction" to panel discussion: Sexual Difficulties After 50.
27. Eric Pfeiffer et al., "The Natural History of Sexual Behavior in a Biologically Advantaged Group of Aged Individuals."
28. Alfred Kinsey et al., *Sexual Behavior in the Human Male.*
29. A.D. Clamon, "Introduction" to panel discussion: Sexual Difficulties After 50.
30. C.V. Christenson and John H. Gagnon, "Sexual Behavior in a Group of Older Women," *Journal of Gerontology* Vol. 20, no. 3 (1966), pp. 351-356.
31. Helen S. Kaplan, *The New Sex Therapy.*
32. Mary Ann P. Sviland, "Sexual Rejuvenation in Men Over 60—and Women, Too: Sexual Therapy Techniques." Workshop, Third Annual Western Region Meeting, The Society for the Scientific Study of Sex, Los Angeles, CA, September, 1975.
33. Martin S. Berezin, "Sex and Old Age: A Review of the Literature."
34. Sheldon H. Cherry, *The Menopause Myth* (New York: Ballantine Books, 1975).
35. Arthur Cherkin and Mary Ann P. Sviland, "Procaine and Related Geropharmacologic Agents—The Current State-of-the-Art." Proceedings of the First Workshop of the Veterans Administration Geriatric Research, Education and Clinical Centers, VA GRECC Monograph No. 1, October 1975.
36. Mary Ann P. Sviland, "Helping Elderly Couples Become Sexually Liberated."
37. Helen S. Kaplan, *The New Sex Therapy.*
38. Mary Ann P. Sviland, "Helping Elderly Couples Become Sexually Liberated."
39. K.M. Bowman, "The Sex Life of the Aging Individual" (editorial), *Geriatrics* Vol. 9 (1954), pp. 83-84.
40. Mary Ann P. Sviland, "Helping Elderly Couples Become Sexually Liberated."

Sexual Wisdom for the Later Years

Lester A. Kirkendall, Ph.D

Dr. Lester A. Kirkendall is a co-founder of SIECUS (Sex Information and Education Council of the U.S.), author of "Premarital Intercourse and Interpersonal Relationships," and a member of Sexology Today's Board of Consultants.

Though seventy-six years old, I am still learning about human sexuality, particularly as I have experienced it myself throughout life. Had I known earlier some things I know now, life would have been more joyful. I realize that this may sound peculiar coming from someone who has counseled people in regard to sexual problems, and has taught courses on human sexuality for many years. However, even we professionals in the field have been affected by the prevailing cultural misguided views about sex and have much to learn.

I used to think my sexual education began when I went to college and started reading about and studying sexuality. I know now that it goes back much further. When I entered college, I was already burdened with ideas that would make a great difference in my later life, even though I wasn't aware then of their existence.

I was reared in a very forbidding sexual environment. As I was growing up, and particularly when I entered adolescence, sex attracted me like a magnet. During this time the strict silence (and believe me, silence can be strict) of the adults around me said plainly that sexuality was to be foregone until marriage. For some of them to say this was hypocritical; I now know this. For years, however, I was throwing off contradictions I had learned as a youth, while at the same time looking for a rational, yet caring, approach to sexuality.

Also, my friends and I learned a number of things which we should have discarded when they came to our attention. They complicated my life throughout my youth and middle age, in later years I have pretty well abandoned them, and am better off for throwing them overboard. Unfortunately many people,including the young, still believe these things.

I am referring to the myths my friends and I learned, erroneous ideas passed on from one generation of young people to the next. We received no straightforward sex education from anyone. For one thing, we learned that *sexual matters could not be discussed with older persons.* We thought of anyone who was more than seven or eight years older than ourselves as aged, as someone we could not talk with concerning sexual matters. And if that person was a teacher or religious in any sense, he was particularly to be avoided. It was even worse if the person was a female. Males of the same age might compare notes, swap stories, but talking seriously with females was taboo.

I now know that this inability to communicate is carried over into marriage and makes all kind of adjustments more difficult for a couple but is especially hard on the sexual relationship. Since one is a sexual being throughout life (though I didn't know this as I was growing up), the inability to communicate also causes difficulties among older couples. That is why I am a strong advocate of sex education, particularly the kind that stresses relationships and has as its goal the breaking down of communication barriers. Parents should strive for openness in sexual communication in the home and they should include their children. The schools, the mass media, the churches and leaders in other groups should all broaden and expand sexual learning. For sex education is a lifelong process that can have a meaningful impact on human development; it is not just facts about reproduction.

Another thing my friends and I learned was that *sex was penile-vaginal penetration*—nothing else. Among the males with whom I grew up there was quite a bit of openness about masturbation, but somehow this practice was not regarded as sexual: It was just something we did as males. Group masturbation provided us with opportunities to find out who could "come first and shoot the farthest." It also prepared us to be inadequate in male-female sexual relationships, since it taught the male how to ejaculate far ahead of his partner's orgasm or to concentrate on his own performance to the exclusion of everything else. Sex was not regarded as a mutual relationship that involved you with a partner.

The decline in male performance power is a complication that comes with aging, but in our youth we didn't even know it existed. We prided ourselves on a performance capacity that would be quite lost to us in later years. What we were at eighteen, physically, we thought we would be at sixty, if we thought of it at all.

Yet at age seventy and eighty erections do not come so easily, and when they do they are not so firm nor so long-lasting as before. It's easy to lose an erection, and once it is lost it's not easy to bring it back. Neither are orgasms as pleasurable as formerly, though they do release tension.

People can maintain sexual activity well into their eighties or nineties—there is no question about that. We are assured of it by many writers. But a couple's enjoyment would be much greater if they had learned to appreciate prolonged body closeness, to express affection and feeling through touching all parts of the body. They might then enjoy genital touch and caressing without the male feeling that he had failed if he did not get a strong erection or effect a complete penetration and ejaculate. But this de-emphasis of the penile-vaginal approach to sex, if it is to be successful, must be begun before one is eighty. Throughout life sexuality should be considered a part of caring and reaching out to others to be expressed through touching, hugging, embracing and body caressing. This pattern of relating can begin with birth, while sexual play and intercourse only become possible with maturation.

Part of the sexual problems associated with aging are actually the result of self-fulfilling prophecies. If you expect that you will be unable to perform sexually, then failure becomes even more likely for you. But one safeguard against the fear of failing sexual performance is to be more concerned with caressing and reaching out to others than with mere genital performance.

This approach challenges another myth that my friends and I batted among ourselves, namely, that *sex is an overpowering physical urge.* A common expression of ours was that "it's in your glands," and of course it (sex) being in your glands made any kind of control impossible.

I came across an interesting instance in counseling of how quickly this myth can be shattered. A young man who had assumed that his sexual desires were based on an uncontrollable physical drive told me of a visit he had paid his girl. They were alone in the house; her parents had left for the evening. In the girl's bedroom they undressed for intercourse and he was just ready to insert his penis when suddenly they heard a car in the driveway, a car they knew to be her parents'. "I didn't have a bit of trouble controlling my sex drive!" the young man told me.

His capacity to exercise control resulted from a sudden change in the existing situation. What his experience tells all of us, whether we are twenty or sixty (but especially if we are twenty), is that sexual desires can be controlled by the way we think. If we realize our sexual patterns are not the wisest or most appropriate behavior for later years, they can be altered. Communication can be improved; we can engage in touch and caressing with those we care for and thereby increase our enjoyment.

Some of the things my friends and I learned were contradictory and when acted upon, resulted in conflict. For example, we thought of *sexual experience in heterosexual terms,* yet at the same time we were expected to prove our *masculinity to each other largely through sexual performance.* This meant that the male always needed to control the situation, to be dominant; the female was essentially a sex object.

The way men seek out intercourse with pickups illustrates how unimportant women can be in males' drive to compete sexually. When I was doing research on male sex patterns, I talked with a number of young men who had had sexual relations with pickups. The circumstances surrounding such occurrences soon made it clear that this type of experience served as an opportunity for male bragging rather than really being a sexual experience. So far as the sex part of them was concerned, some of the men would have been quite satisfied to omit these episodes, particularly if later they could have still had stories to tell their male friends. They needed a female in order to have something to talk about; she was simply an accomplice to the deed.

The males prepared for these boasting experiences by telling friends that they were planning to pick up a female. If they had done so, they would describe what the experience had been like and how effective their performance had been. Usually, they wanted their male friends to feel they had more sexual experience than was actually the case. There was not much listening to others; each male was too busy boasting about his own achievements. Several times I asked the male I was interviewing what kind of experiences his associates had had. The replies I got could be summed up by what one male said: "I didn't hear what they said. I was telling about mine."

The sexual problems older women face are different from those of males, but they are nevertheless quite serious. By the time they are around seventy, many older women have no partners. Generally, women marry older men who in the natural course of things, lose their physical capacities before the women. Furthermore, a woman's life span is normally several years longer than that of a man. Thus, many women are certain to be without male partners during the last few years of their lives unless they are able to draw younger men into a sexual relationship or can engage in casual affairs.

As a result of this situation, many older women are left without males to love them. They may find other women to serve as companions, or possibly even earlier in their lives, sexual partners, but the sad thing is that when they had male partners, many women were sex objects rather than loved persons. Given this fact, they, like men, are likely to blossom into sexual beings in their later years.

Men, who are much more responsible for this conditioning than women, are similarly deprived. As I said above, for most males sexual behavior means penile-vaginal relations with females. They are so fearful of homosexuality that any kind of genital—or even affectional—response toward another male is often regarded as evidence of homosexuality, and completely rejected.

A former counselee, a young man of about twenty, told me of a very close and very caring relationship he had had with another male during their teens. (To have called it a "loving" relationship would have been unacceptable to either one of them.) Both went into the armed services, and this young man's friend was sent to Vietnam. There he was often in the thick of battle, and his friend, my counselee, feared that any time he would hear that his friend had been killed. Then he received word: His friend was being sent home and in a few days they would be reunited. They met at the air terminal, and when they came together engaged in a long, loving hug. Suddenly my counselee was aware that he had a strong erection. "God, I was scared," he told me. "Does this mean that I'm a homosexual?"

Feeling that it did, he reacted coldly toward his friend, keeping his distance from him. He became fearful that if he extended himself to other men he might respond sexually again and that this would be further proof of homosexuality. He was aware that erections are sometimes the result of exciting and unusual experiences. The experience activates the neural system and in this matter causes an erection.

The fear of homosexuality and the need to prove masculinity by heterosexual conquest cut some men off from close relations with both male and female friends. By using women as sex objects, they turn them into nonpersons. They find affectional attachments to males frightening. Consequently, by the time they arrive at old age, they have reached out to people only casually, and are unable to express any deep, heartfelt affection for anyone. Their sexuality has been so subdued, repressed and misdirected that, for all intents and purposes, it no longer exists. Personally, I no longer need to express my masculinity through sexuality. This misconceived idea of masculinity is one of the things I gladly threw overboard. I can express my affectional feelings for both women and men, and I receive similar expressions of affection from them. However, the affectional expressions I receive from males come almost entirely from men who are younger than I. I am hopeful that these men's later years will be more joyful than the declining years of some of the older men I know.

A satisfying and enjoyable life in the later years will be more likely for us as soon as we realize that, whatever our years, we are all aged, in some sense, and aging. Certainly, a twenty-year-old is aged in comparison to the time he or she was a babe in arms. Each of us is a day older today than we were yesterday. Putting into practice a philosophy of reaching out—in the area of sexuality as well as other areas—will make all the rest of life better for us.

Zero
Population
Growth
orts ERA
YOU HAVE
NOT
COME A
LONG WAY
BABY

Continuing Sexual Concerns

5

This final section deals with some ongoing concerns that surround sexuality. Sexually transmitted diseases, sexual inequality, rape, pornography, bisexuality, homosexuality, and special populations merit special consideration here because of the widespread social stigmatization, misconceptions, and dysfunctional consequences that attend these issues.

Sexually transmitted diseases are inappropriately labelled "social diseases." This stigmatization is a reflection of the general negative aura that surrounds sexuality in our traditional culture. Such diseases would be much less a "social problem" if individuals could forget their embarrassment over having contracted them through sexual activity and seek immediate medical treatment for themselves and their sexual contacts.

Social misunderstandings create undue stress and anxiety for many who face this life passage. An article about menopause, for example, discusses four of the most common menopause myths in an effort to distinguish between misconceptions and real stresses of menopause and the very real potential for fulfillment and freedom it offers. Health concerns surrounding heart disease are similarly grounded in fiction as opposed to fact. If proper care is taken, heart disease should not interfere with one's sex life. Another instance of misunderstanding creating undue anxiety evolves from the notion that sexual activity demands the presence of an erection. Under the influence of this belief, much self-esteem and relational quality has been sacrificed in the event of erectile "failure." It should come as reassurance to many that this need not be the case. Closely related to this pernicious notion is the equally misplaced belief in the power of certain "magical" substances (aphrodisiacs) to stimulate flagging sexual excitement. The truth is, none of them work and some of them can be lethal!

Some of the most devastating and flagrant of violations to individual sexual integrity arise from the misuse of sexuality as a means of power, control, or humiliation. Such is the case with sexual harassment at work, rape, and some pornography. Equally onerous to individual integrity is the negative stigmatization that our society imposes on bisexuals and homosexuals. Numerous myths and stereotypes abound that create for these persons a status of "abnormal." Tragically, these individuals are ostracized from society and often from their own families. A similar fate is often suffered by those special populations who have physical and/or mental disabilities. In our society, these persons score no points for being handicapped and are erroneously perceived as "inferior" and asexual. Against this tendency, several articles are presented proclaiming that everyone is entitled to love and to the opportunity for sexual expression.

Finally, this section concludes with a discussion of prison populations, and charges that prisons are institutionally approved arenas of sexual traumatization, brutality, and offense. A system of conjugal visitation is proposed as a potential solution to the present policy of punishment by sex segregation.

Looking Ahead: Challenge Questions

If sexually transmitted diseases are curable, why are they continually being spread?

What is the closest thing to an aphrodisiac?

What cultural values are revealed by the ways in which our society regards special populations?

Are there better ways of dealing with sexual violence? Can the rape laws be made more effective?

Can we make a distinction between "different" and "deviant" behavior?

STDs

The old list of venereal diseases has been expanded and renamed. The new list of *Sexually Transmitted Diseases* requires vigilance on the part of researchers, physicians and patients.

Sandee Gregg

Nietzsche, Henry VIII, Al Capone, Van Gogh. The famous and the infamous. These individuals are believed to have suffered nervous system damage, insanity and eventually death due to syphilis. Today they probably would not die of the ravages of that disease, but it is likely they would be exposed to one or more venereal diseases that may bear unrecognizable names quite different from syphilis or gonorrhea. Venereal diseases are growing in number; what was once quitely referred to as VD has become the not-so-quiet collection of sexually transmitted diseases (STDs)—a collection that eludes and confuses patient and physician alike.

This club includes not only the age-old gonorrhea, syphilis and pubic lice, but also, alarmingly often, nongonococcal urethritis, as well as genital herpes, vaginitis infections, Group B streptococcus and hepatitis. The soaring incidence of these diseases is so great that public health specialists and venereologists are calling the increase an epidemic more widespread than the flu. It is estimated that one in 20 Americans is affected by an STD each year. These diseases cross all barriers of sex, age, race and socioeconomic status.

In these sophisticated times of modern medicine, why are these diseases on the rise? Three factors are at work. First, baby-boom-era children are now adults, and sexual mores have changed in this country, so there are more people engaging in more sex. Secondly, there is still a great deal of ignorance on the part of the public as well as among physicians about what a sexually transmitted disease is and how it should be handled. Because sex is involved, there is a reluctance on everyone's part to discuss these illnesses. The increase can also be attributed to better reporting of disease in some communities and more scientific research that has identified and named new pathogens.

A/E Editor's note: Views expressed are those of the author and do not necessarily represent the official position of the American Chemical Society.

"STDS," by Sandee Gregg, *SciQuest*, Vol. 53, No. 9, pages 11-15, November 1980.

The problems with these diseases are both immediate and far reaching. Besides causing discomfort and embarrassment, they are easily passed on to unsuspecting people, and—if left untreated—can lead to serious infections and sterility. Of particular concern in recent years are newborns. Pregnant women who harbor gonorrhea, strep, herpes or *Chlamydia* in their vaginas can transmit them to their babies as they pass through the birth canal. These infections can cause blindness, retardation, pneumonia or meningitis in newborns.

There are approximately 24 pathogens that cause STDs, but the most common are *Neisseria gonorrhoeae, Treponema pallidum* (causes syphilis), herpes virus, *Trichomonas vaginalis* and *Chlamydia trachomatis.* Today the most worrisome diseases are those caused by the latter three organisms; they are the ones least understood by the general public as well as the medical profession. These diseases can be devastating when they attack without recognizable symptoms and therefore go untreated. Of greatest concern are *Chlamydia trachomatis* and herpes simplex virus 2 (genital herpes).

Chlamydia trachomatis is a bacterium that causes nongonococcal urethritis (NGU) in men, pelvic inflammatory disease (PID) in women and conjunctivitis, an eye infection, and pneumonia in newborns. According to Dr. King K. Holmes at the University of Washington in Seattle, *Chlamydia* infections will soon outdistance gonorrhea (G.C.) as the number one sexually transmitted disease. On many college campuses it is already more common than gonorrhea.

In the future, a common complication of *Chlamydia* infection may make it much more infamous than G.C. *Chlamydia* infections are the leading cause of pelvic inflammatory disease, which often leads to infertility in women, particularly teens. This complication led Donald R. Hopkins, assistant director for international health at the Center for Disease Control (CDC) in Atlanta, to open an international symposium on the subject this past spring with the comment, "Today's epidemic of pelvic inflammatory disease is tomorrow's epidemic of infertility."

Compared with other STDs, *Chlamydia* is a fairly new discovery and scientists are just beginning to understand it. It is a bacterium that behaves like a virus. As with a virus it only multiplies in the cytoplasm of the host cell, but unlike a virus it contains two types of genetic material, both RNA and DNA.

Because of its complicated construction, *Chlamydia* is difficult to culture. Simple gram-staining techniques available to most doctors easily detect *N. gonorrhoeae* and yeast, but *Chlamydia* must be cultured in standard cell cultures like a virus. This requires sophisticated and expensive lab equipment not readily available to many doctors. For this reason phy-

	Pathogen	Symptoms	Possible Complications	Treatment
***Gonorrhea**	Bacterium: *Neisseria gonorrhoeae*	Painful urination; discharge from penis and vagina (many women have no symptoms)	Pelvic inflammatory disease in women; infection of testes.	Penicillin; tetracycline; ampicillin
***Syphilis**	Bacterium: *Treponema pallidum*	First stage: sores and lesions on the mouth or genitals	If untreated, can lead to serious disease in many organs; death	Penicillin; erythromycin; tetracycline
NGU (nongonococcal urethritis)	Bacterium: usually *N. gonorrhoeae* or *Chlamydia trachomatis*	Painful urination; sometimes a discharge from penis	Epididymitis; infections in newborns	Tetracycline; erythromycin
PID (pelvic inflammatory disease)	Closely related to NGU in men, same pathogens	Affects cervix and fallopian tubes; fever; severe abdominal pain	Ectopic pregnancy; sterility	Penicillin; tetracycline; sometimes surgery to unblock or remove tubes
Trichomoniasis	Protozoan: *Trichomonas vaginalis*	Foamy, itchy discharge with odor (men have no symptoms)	Annoying and recurrent	Metronidazole (Flagyl)

*These diseases are reportable to the Center for Disease Control in Atlanta.

sicians often misdiagnose or miss chlamydial infections altogether. To complicate matters, explains Dr. A. Eugene Washington, a researcher for the VD unit at the CDC, *Chlamydia* is fastidious—sometimes it can be grown easily in the lab, and other times not, even under the same conditions. Until better tests are widely available, most doctors will have to rely on diagnosis by elimination, namely ruling out G.C., says Dr. Washington.

At least 55 percent of nongonococcal urethritis is caused by *Chlamydia*. The rest is probably due to ureaplasma, a tiny bacterium, or to miscellaneous infectious agents like *Trichomonas* (a protozoan) or *Candida albicans* (a yeast). NGU produces many of the same symptoms as gonorrhea—burning during urination and a discharge. If treated improperly or not at all, it can lead to epididymitis, an infection of the tube carrying sperm to the scrotum, prostatic infection and sterility. It's estimated that NGU affects three million Americans annually, but that's only a guess because it is not a disease that must be reported to the Center for Disease Control as gonorrhea and syphilis are.

The variation of NGU that strikes women is infection of the cervix, which can quickly become pelvic inflammatory disease (PID). Often this condition isn't diagnosed until a woman experiences severe abdominal pain, fever, and elevated white blood count. PID affects some 850,000 women every year. If untreated, or if a woman experiences repeated bouts with the infection, the scar tissue that forms in the tubes will cause ectopic pregnancies or will damage the tubes beyond repair. An ectopic, or tubal, pregnancy is when conception takes place in a fallopian tube and the fetus begins growing there instead of moving into the uterus. Such a pregnancy can rupture the tube and be deadly to the mother. Also, a bout of PID causes infertility in some 20 percent of all cases. These tragic complications underscore the importance of treating female contacts of men with NGU.

If *Chlamydia* from the mother's cervix is passed on to a newborn during vaginal delivery, it can cause a serious eye infection. If the pathogen gets into the respiratory system, it can infect delicate lung tissue causing life-threatening pneumonia. The costs of treating infected newborns added to the costs due to primary infections raise the total direct and indirect cost of PID in the U.S. to more than $2 billion.

Luckily chlamydial infections can be treated. The road to that discovery was rather intriguing. It began in Vietnam when many troops began showing up in overseas hospitals with some type of venereal disease that did not respond to conventional penicillin treatment. At first doctors thought they were dealing with a new strain of penicillin-resistant gonorrhea. To investigate the problem, in 1965 a young navy lieutenant, Dr. King Holmes, was flown to an aircraft carrier in the Philippines. He worked out a super-penicillin treatment for the mysterious urethritis. However, lab cultures showed

	Pathogen	Symptoms	Possible Complications	Treatment
Genital Herpes	Herpes virus	Genital sores and blisters that come and go, often with fever	Cannot be cured; can be transmitted to newborns causing death	No proven treatment to date
Pubic Lice ("crabs")	Parasite: *Phithirus pubis*	Itching in the hairy parts of the body	Easily transmitted by sexual contact, clothing or linen	Gamma benzene hexachoride shampoo or lotion
***GI** *(granuloma inguinale)*	Bacterium: *Donovania granulomatis*	Painless red, fleshy sores on genitals or mouth	If untreated, can damage genitalia	Tetracycline; streptomycin
***LGV** *(lymphogranuloma venereum)*	Bacterium: *Chlamydia trachomatis*	Hard-to-see pimples on genitals; urethral discharge; diarrhea; cramps	Can become full-blown disease of lymphatic system; conjunctivitis in newborns	Tetracyline or sulfisoxazole
***Venereal Warts**	Virus: varies	Skin-colored, cauliflower-shaped warts on genitals	Warts may grow and spread	Topical medications
***Chancroid** ("soft chancre")	Bacterium: *Hemophilus ducreyi*	Painful genital ulcers	May spread	Tetracycline or sulfisoxazole

Comparison of the Occurrence of STDs for 1979

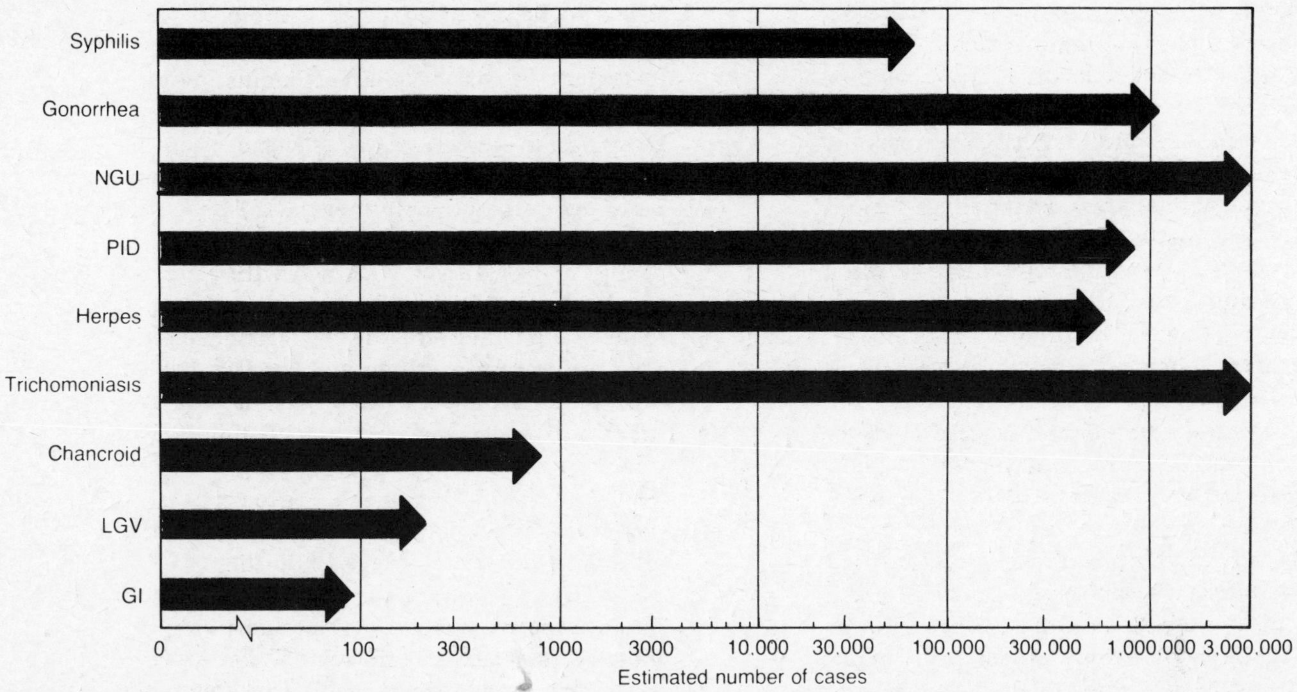

Estimates from Center for Disease Control and American Social Health Association

that 60 percent of the cases weren't gonorrhea, but *Chlamydia*, and it hadn't responded to the penicillin. So Dr. Holmes and his colleague, Dr. David W. Johnson, began treating the infections with another antibiotic, tetracycline, which took care of the problem quite well.

In fact, the Center for Disease Control's Dr. Washington points out that proper treatment, seven to 14 days with tetracycline, will cure both G.C. and NGU. He suggests that treating all cases of G.C. with tetracycline automatically prevents complications. G.C. and NGU often occur simultaneously in patients, and if a clinician cultures for G.C. the second infection is likely to be missed. Then a week or so later, the patient still has complaints, especially men who exhibit discharge. This is called PGU (postgonococcal urethritis) and is almost always NGU, which means the patient must be treated with another antibiotic. Tetracycline also is given to clear up chlamydial infections in newborns.

Perhaps the most frightening venereal disease is the one that is least understood—herpes simplex virus 2 (HSV 2 or genital herpes). Subtle biochemical differences in this virus differentiate it from type 1 herpes that produces common cold sores. HSV 2 is a more serious disease and has received a great deal of attention in the past seven years as the number of its victims climbs steadily. The American Social Health Association estimates there are half a million new cases of herpes each year, and over five million Americans already have it. Medical officials estimate that the percentage of sexually active Americans who have been in contact with herpes has increased from five percent to 30 percent in the past decade. The frightening thing about genital herpes is there is no cure and it can infect infants during birth.

Of particular concern for pregnant women is the fact that the disease can be active without the visible sign of sores. Kathleen Johnston, a Washington D.C. area journalist, described the realization that she had herpes and the implications it held for her newly conceived child in the Aug. 17 *Washington Post*:

"I didn't know I had it for some time. My first gynecologist here in Washington finally diagnosed it, but didn't warn me that it could pop up at any time, that it was now 'latent' in my body, probably forever. He also didn't know or bother to tell me that herpes could complicate any future pregnancy. My husband and I had just recovered from a mild outbreak of sores last October when we discovered I was pregnant. My obstetrician for the pregnancy, Stanley Marinoff, had confirmed the herpes with a culture. During our first prenatal chat, he flatly told me we might not be able to avoid a Cesarean section, despite our strong desires for natural childbirth. His ground rules were that if I came up with a positive culture, visible sores or no, within a week or two of my due date, we'd have to set a date for surgery. The consequences of an undetected infection, transmitted during birth to our baby, Dr. Marinoff made clear, could be death or permanent damage."

Herpes is a viral infection that causes periodic fever and aches similar to the flu, plus painful sores in the genital area. During these periods the disease is highly contagious. The infectious periods are recurrent and unpredictable, often disappearing for months at a time. Virologists hypothesize that the virus hides in nerve endings during the periods when the disease seems to be in remission.

Determining whether the disease is in remission is crucial for pregnant women. Johnston described the stress associated with the uncertainties as traumatic.

"Toward my 30th week," she said, "I went to see Grossman to begin a series of herpes culture tests—the prelude to finding out whether I was 'clean' enough for a vaginal delivery. Finally after having been very apprehensive, we felt we were getting a handle on the situation. Grossman has been conducting the tests with 100 percent success—when cultures are positive in the last week or so of a pregnancy, he has generally performed C-sections. He hasn't lost a baby yet to herpes infection and 'I don't want to,' he says. 'That's why I do what I do.'"

Another danger of herpes is that it is suspected as a cause of cervical cancer in women. It is recommended that exposed women have a Pap smear to test for the cancer twice a year.

In the case of both *Chlamydia* and herpes, scientists agree they only know about half of what they wish to know. The process of learning how these pathogens operate, and what it takes to control them is tedious. VD experts have been working with the National Institute of Allergy and Infectious Diseases devising a priority list for research and development.

Near the top of the list is to develop a simple and inexpensive test for *Chlamydia*, and a more sensitive test for gonorrhea in men and women who, for some unknown reason, exhibit no symptoms. Understandably, herpes is also high on the priority list. Interferon, a naturally occurring antiviral protein, is causing a great deal of excitement these days—particularly in cancer research. However, it was tried a few years ago in herpes patients, with disappointing results. Currently there are several researchers conducting a cooperative study with zovirax. This drug belongs to a class of agents known as DNA analogs; it contains a synthetic DNA that fools the virus into thinking it belongs there and then destroys the virus. It is a topical ointment that seems to be absorbed by cells infected with herpes, though there is still some question as to its toxicity in normal cells. Dr. Samuel Thompson, another CDC researcher, says the Food and Drug Administration may soon approve clinical trials of an oral version of the drug that may work better than the ointment.

Possibly the most promising antiviral agent against herpes is acyclovir, another DNA analog. It has shown considerable success in animal models, and clinical trials using it in humans are now underway in Britain and the U.S. Babies born with herpes are treated with ARA-A, another antiviral cream, but most children still develop mental and motor problems, says Dr. Thompson.

Methods of stopping STDs before they strike are still in embryonic stages. In the case of G.C., preventive antibiotics have been discouraged because there is some concern this would promote resistant strains of the bacteria. Perhaps the most intriguing idea now being considered is a vaccine for G.C. Recent studies suggest humans may respond immunologically to gonococcal antigens, a necessary factor in making a vaccine. Bacterial vaccines are most likely to be effective if the antibodies they elicit inactivate the mechanisms by which the bacterium causes disease. So as soon as it can be determined which type of human cells gonococci attack first, scientists will be well on their way to developing a vaccine that will elicit the correct protective response.

Development of a G.C. vaccine may be the first step toward the lofty goal of preparing vaccines for a host of STDs. Until that day when all STDs are either curable or preventable, Kathleen Johnston, the new mother of a healthy child, summed up the hopes and fears of many:

"I look in on [my baby]. I know she's long past the dangerous period. She'll remain safe from us and our disease as long as we take reasonable sanitary precautions. Meanwhile, we'll hope for something more reliable, like a cure."

Suggested Readings

(1) Gregg, S., and Ismach, J., "Beyond VD," *Medical World News*, March 31, 1980, page 49.

(2) Hollinshead, A., and Knaus, W., "Herpesvirus—A Link in the Cancer Chain?" *Chemistry*, **50**, (4) 17 (May 1977).

(3) Keith, L., and Brittain, J., "Sexually Transmitted Diseases," Creative Informatics, Aspen, CO, 1978.

(4) Lasagna, L., "The VD Epidemic: How it Started, Where It's Going and What To do About It," Temple University Press, Philadelphia, PA, 1975.

MENOPAUSE COUNSELING: COPING WITH REALITIES AND MYTHS

Kathie Beckman Smallwood, Ph.D.
Therapist,
Adjunct Professor, Family Life and Sex Education
North Texas State University
Denton, Texas

Dorothy G. VanDyck
Counselor,
Life Planning/Health Services Inc.
Denton, Texas

An Abstract

The purpose of this article is to bring together and summarize selected, realistic, available information on the menopause. It is an attempt to separate myth from reality for the benefit of professionals who will be called upon to help women and their families realistically understand, cope with, and pass through the menopause.

Introduction

In the structure of today's society, a young female woman/child in the beginning stages of puberty is usually surrounded by a host of adults who are willing to inform, guide and support her through the new experience of "growing into womanhood." It can be a very exciting time of life for her! Mother, (hopefully father), older sisters, peers, counselors, teachers and health educators are available as a strong support system. Society tends to see her beginning of menstruation as the beginning of sexuality, the development of female beauty and attractiveness, and the transition to adult life. By contrast, the middle-aged woman facing menopause may not have any support system at all. In our increasingly mobile society, parents and sisters may be far away, while nearby friends and colleagues may be closemouthed about what is happening. As a result, today's woman typically faces the ending of menstruation pretty much alone. She may have one confidante in her husband or primary sex partner, but often he knows less about the realities of menopause than she does. Thus the ending of menstruation is usually a very confusing, frightening and sad experience in comparison to the celebration of its' beginning. Since most of the facts of menopause are not fully known and understood by the woman, the old myths usually take over. The biggest myth is the very idea that menopause is "*the* change of life." It is as if a woman will suddenly and mysteriously become a different person once her ovaries reduce their level of estrogen production; or, worse yet, that the cessation of menstruation is the "beginning of the end." Even Gail Sheehy (1976), in her brilliant best seller *Passages*, labels the climacteric as a "mystery". She describes other "passages" with words such as "change" "merge", "pattern', "crisis", or "problem". Only the climacteric gets the "mystery" label in her work.

Definition of Menopause and Climateric

Menopause is defined as the point of cessation of menstruation. It is brought on by the gradual decline in estrogen level production by the ovaries over several years, to the point where menstrual bleeding actually ceases. The symptoms may include a gradual decrease in mentrual flow, a decrease in predictability of the cycle, or, in a few women, an abrupt cessation of menstruation. For most women, the onset of menopause occurs between the ages of forty-five and fifty, but it can begin earlier or later. When a woman has had no period for twelve months she is considered to be "through menopause".

The term climacteric refers to the whole process of transition in ovarian and hormonal function, while the term menopause refers to the cessation of menstruation (Lanson, 1975; Weideger, 1976). Sometimes the two terms are incorrectly used interchangeably. This can create confusion. The climacteric is marked not only by a reduction in estrogen level production, but also by a substantial and often irratic increase in the production of FSH by the pituitary in an effort to stimulate the ovaries. The hypothalamus is also affected since it is ultimately responsible for the smooth functioning of the pituitary. The end result is a temporary imbalance in the hormonal system, which can take many years to be completely resolved by the body.

The climacteric is the whole transition process, while the menopause is the actual point in time when menstrual flow has ceased.

This article deals primarily with the menopausal years, rather than the climacteric.

From *The Journal of Sex Education and Therapy,* Vol. 1, No. 6, Winter 1979. Reprinted by permission of the American Association of Sex Educators, Counselors & Therapists.

5. CONTINUING SEXUAL CONCERNS

Realities of Menstruation and the Climacteric

Related Physical Symptoms

About 40% of the women experiencing menopause report hot flashes, or flushes, accompanied by sweating (Boston, 1973; Green, 1965; Mckinlay, 1974). A typical hot flash is experienced as a sudden rush of fiery heat from the waist up, increased reddening of the skin surface, and a drenching perspiration. Following the hot flash there may be a very cold chill, whitening of the skin surface, and sudden shivers. When hot flashes occur at night, which is not uncommon, insomnia is often the result. The cause of these flashes is vasomotor instability due to the transition of hormonal balance.

The same transition in hormnal balance can be responsible for other less often reported symptoms. These include heart palpitations, sensations of cold in the hands and feet, dizziness, fainting, headaches, weight gain, constipation, fatigue, tension, irritability and depression. No one woman experiences all of these symptoms, but reports indicate that about 15% of women experiencing menopause will suffer one or more of these related effects (Lanson, 1975; McKinlay, 1974).

Still another related symptom is low backache. This can be the result of reduced levels of mineral in the bones. The long range result in postmenopausal years can be ostioporosis (porous, brittle bones) or spinal compression which is evidenced in loss of height or a "dowager's hump' in the spine.

Changes in the Sex Organs

Researchers, including Masters and Johnson, have concluded that women are fully capable of enjoying sexual intercourse and orgasm an entire lifetime, if they have had good sexual relations before menopause and continue to be sexually active through the menopause and into the years of postmenopause (Kaplan, 1974; Masters and Johnson, 1966). It is well recognized by prefessionals in the field of sex therapy that absence of sexual activity is the quickest route to sexual dysfunctioning (Kaplan, 1974; Masters and Johnson, 1966). Research also clearly points out that the estrogen hormone transition does produce certain changes in the sex organs. These changes, if not understood by the woman and her sex partner, may discourage the woman from wanting to participate with joy and enthusiasm in the sexual experience. The professional working with the woman should help her and her partner to be alert to these changes and encourage the woman to see a physician if dyspareunia (painful intercourse) develops.

Breasts: Although the breast tissue may loosen some and sag a little, the nipples still have erectile capacity during sexual excitement. The breasts still increase in size if stimulated sexually, and engorgement of the areolae still occurs. This indicates that the breasts are every bit as receptive to sexual arousal as before the menopause.

Vagina: The lining of the vagina thins out somewhat, vaginal lubrication declines, and the capacity for vaginal expansion and enlargement during intercouse is reduced somewhat. As a result, some women who previously experienced no pain during intercourse may indeed feel some vaginal discomfort. Pressure and irritation of the urethra or bladder during or immediately after intercourse may occur. The application of vaginal jelly (KY, non-prescription) or the use of prescription preparations containing estrogen may help alleviate the problem. Reducing sexual activity is not the solution to these problems, although it may be the natural tendency, since the vaginal muscles lose even more elasticity if not stimulated regularly through intercouse or masturbation.

The large outer folds of the vagina (major labia) also show reduced elasticity during intercourse. There is less flattening, separation and elevation of these folds than before menopause. Likewise, the small inner folds (minor labia) show less thickening and engorgement. As a result, the opening of the vagina may be somewhat smaller in size and lighter in color during sexual excitement. Some discomfort during penetration may result, which could be relieved by the use of vaginal lubricants.

Clitoris: In the post menopausal woman, the clitoris *may* become more exposed because of labial atrophy. Should this happen, very direct and prolonged stimulation of the clitoris may become an unpleasant and distressing irritation. It would be essential that the woman communicate with her sex partner about this so they could use less direct and intense stimulation of the clitoris.

Skin: Some sex therapists consider the skin to be the largest sex organ of the body. The skin is also affected by the reduction of estrogen production in the woman's body. It loses much of it's elasticity and softness. Wrinkles begin to develop which many women find to be distressing evidence of aging. Probably the best way to keep aging skin as healthy as possible is a combination of physical exercise and healthy eating habits.

Contraception During Menopause

The whole question of birth control during the menopausal years can cause many tensions if the woman or her partner has not been sterilized and does not want a pregnancy. Since periods become unpredictable, the missed periods cause much anxiety for the couple not confident of their contraceptive method. Feelings about abortion on the part of both the woman and her partner may need to be explored to determine whether or not this may be a viable back-up to contraceptive failure.

For many couples sterilization is the most satisfying and effective form of contraception. Since the menopausal process usually extends over a period of several years, it would not be unreasonable for a couple to consider this form of contraception as a possibility. A very thoughtful decision must be made concerning who will be sterilized. For the male, the procedure is a vasectomy; for the female a laparoscopy (popularly known as "bandaid surgery".) Neither person should be made to feel pressure; rather, there must be agreement, understanding and emotional support for the decision.

Even though the use of birth control pills can prolong menstrual regularity and cycles beyond the natural point of menopause, a woman using the pill may experience some of the other symptoms of menopause. It is very important to note that oral contraceptives are not recommended for women over the age of forty, because of the greatly increased risk of complication.

If a woman is using an IUD, she could continue until her menstrual periods have been absent for one year, without any greater risk than before menopause.

To use the "natural family planning" (rhythm) method during the menopausal years is quite unreliable and becomes extremely anxiety producing as periods become more erratic. Unfortunately, this method of birth control is one of the main reasons women refuse intercourse in the beginning phases of menopause. After a prolonged period of being "off sex" both male and female may find it difficult if not impossible to resume satisfactory activity at a later date. Where the male is concerned, temporary impotency may be the result of a short (6 months) period of abstinence. The longer the abstinence, the more serious the problem of impotency may become.

If a woman in the menopausal years does not choose sterilization as her birth control method, she should be encouraged to consider the diaphragm or foam and condoms. These forms of contraception are without side effects and they do not interfere with the normal progression of reduced ovarian function. They can be used effectively if the couple understands the method thoroughly and uses the method correctly. It is always recommended that foam and condoms be used together so as to increase effectiveness.

Estrogen Replacement Therapy

Because so many of the physical discomforts of menopause are caused by reduction in estrogen level and the subsequent hormonal imbalance, many physicians and researchers have advocated estrogen replacement therapy (ERT). Yet, because of certain possible side effects and the fact that the long range results of extra estrogen intake on the body are not fully known, ERT is currently an open controversy in the medical field. It is therefore crucial that a woman very carefully consider all the pros and cons of ERT and that she have expert medical advice concerning her specific case.

The pros of ERT are that it can relieve the hot flashes and revitalize the vaginal tissue. The psychological benefits may be reduction in tension and depression and a revitalization of a sagging self image.

Possible negative side effects from too much estrogen include fluid retention, gastrointestinal disturbances, weight gain, vaginal bleeding and skin pigmentation. Most important is the fact that increased incidence of cancer of the endometrial lining has not been disproved.

The recommendation to use ERT is one that only a qualified physician can make after considering the patient's complaints and completing a thorough examination. However, after a review of the pros and cons with the physician, the woman will be the one to make the final decision whether or not to use ERT. If this is her decision, she needs to remain under close supervision of her physician for proper regulation of dosage and monitoring of physical symptoms.

Myths About Menopause

Four of the most common and most devastating myths about menopause are discussed below.

Myth One: *"Menopause, being the change of life, is the beginning of the end."* It is true that menopause is a transition in a woman's life and that certain physical changes will occur. But it is just one transition in a lifetime of changes. Although a major passage, it is not the only change in a woman's life and it is certainly not the end! At the turn of the century, when the average life expectancy was forty-eight years, the menopause may indeed have signaled the beginning of the end of an average life. Today the average life expectancy for women is 73 years. Therefore the average woman has at least 25 to 30 years of life to look forward to after the menopause. Probably this myth is rooted in history's reality. Fortunately, it is not true today.

Myth Two: "A woman is no longer sexually attractive after her "change". In a society like ours where sexual attractiveness has traditionally been equated with youth and reproductive capacity, a woman indeed has feared the aging process. Couple this fear with the specific sexual changes that are predictable at menopause and it is poignantly clear why women can feel less sexually attractive with the onset of menopause. Several realities are very important in dispelling this myth. One is the knowledge and awareness that, although a woman is indeed changing sexually, she is still fully capable of sexual pleasure, intercourse and orgasm. A second reality is that her male sex partner, if he is about her age or older, is also experiencing normal sexual changes, the most obvious being a reduced capacity for erections. The danger is that the woman (or the man himself) may interpret his less frequent erections as a reduction of sexual interest in her because of her age. The healthy solution is for both partners to understand that they are going through a normal sexual transition and that coping will probably take a lot of communication, re-evaluation, and willingness to work through the passage together. A third reality is that the end of child bearing capacity does not mean the end of the capacity for sexual pleasure. For some women, the relief from fear of pregnancy can mean even greater freedom to enjoy sexuality. Fourth, and probably the greatest challenge, is for a woman to be brave enough to believe that sexual attractiveness is not categorically equated with youth, that each person has a unique capacity for healthy sexuality as long as she or he maintains a self image that permits sexuality to function as an integral part of personality.

Myth Three: "A woman just falls apart at menopause." Given all the physical symptoms possible at menopause and during the climacteric, it is no wonder that women feel as if they are falling apart physically, sexually and emotionally. Just imagine experiencing hot flashes, discomfort during intercourse, insomnia, heart palpitations and depression. Any normal person would of course fear she was falling apart! The main way to counteract this myth is with supportive, accurate and detailed knowledge that it is normal to experience these symptoms, however difficult they truly are, that professional help is available and that the symptoms will subside in time.

Myth Four: "A woman is useless after her 'change' ". If a woman values herself or is valued by others primarily for her youth and reproductive capacity, this myth may indeed become reality. In addition, if her whole life has revolved around being needed by her children who are now approaching maturity and eager to be independent, the myth may become an even more depressing reality. It may indeed seem the "beginning of the end" in terms of being needed. All human beings have a healthy need to be worthwhile, productive and needed. What may be triggered by the onset of menopause can therefore be a very real crisis of the middle age passage. Gail Sheehy (1976) describes the crisis of middle aged women as one of daring to choose a new career once the children are gone or "Mother's Release from the Nest". Pauline Bart (1972), in her research on depression in middle aged women, found depression to be greatest in overprotective, overly child-oriented, middle class housewives as compared with working women. From these indications, it seems clear that one major way to work through this myth is for a woman to become aware of other ways and significant opportunities ahead of her for continuing to be productive. The range of possibilities is wide and needs very careful exploration by each woman. Possibilities include further education, returning to a career interrupted by the motherhood career, choosing a new job or career, individualized artistic creativity, political involvement, volunteer work and travel. Although the range of possibilities is great, the choice may not be easy. No passage in life is easy, but the potential for healthy growth and fulfillment is very exciting.

Implications For Counseling

Women bring their own uniqueness to bear in coping with the inevitability of menopause. At one extreme of behavior there is the woman who defies her body to change. She is determined not to experience one twinge of discomfort, not one single hot flash. She will not be running to anyone for hormone therapy. At the other extreme, one finds the nervous, irritable, depressive, sickly woman who has been blaming every ache or pain, every up or down, on "that time of life," since she passed age thirty. In between these extremes are the majority of women who are waiting, wondering and fearing what will come. In the past, only about 10% of the women experiencing menopause have sought medical help, much less personal counseling (Bart, 1972; Davis, 1977; Weideger, 1976). With the growing acceptance today of seeking counseling for personal and sexual problems, professionals will have the opportunity and challenge of helping women and their families cope with the menopause. (This certainly has been the writers' recent experience and was the impetus for searching out the material that eventually was included in this article.)

There are several approaches counselors can incorporate in dealing with the menopausal client or her family. One is to be aware that the physical symptoms may be accompanied by a wide range of psychological and emotional reactions, which in turn may tend to magnify or intensify the physical symptoms. Such reactions may be in response to either the realities or the myths of menopause. In either case, it is essential for the counselor to understand and communicate to the client that though the menopause may be a difficult time, it is a normal life passage which can be worked through.

Secondly, it is crucial that the counselor help the client sort out and separate the realities of menopause from the myths. In the process, it is wise to recommend that the client have a thorough medical examination. Once the facts and myths are separated, the next step is to help the client accept and deal with the physical realities. This may include working through her self image, helping her evaluate sexual values and establish sexual priorities and encouraging an informed decision about ERT and contraception.

A major part of counseling will be to deal with the psychological realities. This may include working through new career and life decisions as well as counteracting irrational myths and fears about life after menopause. It is very important for the woman to realize that she is understood, cared for and supported in her passage through menopause. This support can be found not only in counseling, but also hopefully in her family configuration and friendship system. It is surely the counselor's task to facilitiate the development of any possible support in the woman's life outside the counseling situation.

The crisis of menopause may also uncover old, unresolved psychological problems. Individual, family or marital conflicts that may have been previously denied, blocked or repressed may suddenly surface under the pressure of menopause. In such cases, the counselor's responsibility is to help the client work through the older, more deeply rooted problems.

In summary, the challenge to the counselor is to help the woman realistically integrate the menopause transition into her life by separating reality from myth, by coping with the physical and psychological impact on her current existance, and by evaluating and establishing priorities for the future. The whole counseling process, like the passage through menopause itself, will be an intricate combination and interplay between the very real stresses that are typical of menopause and the very real potential for finding new freedom and fulfillment beyond menopause.

REFERENCES

Bart, P. B. Depression in middle-aged women, in V. Gornick & B. Moran, (Eds.). *Women in sexist society*, New York: New American Library, 1972.

Boston Womens Health Collective (Ed.). *Our bodies, ourselves*. New York: Simon & Schuster, 1973.

Davis, M.E. *A doctor discusses menopause and estrogens*. Chicago: Budlong Press, 1977.

Glass, R.H. & Case, N.G. *Woman's choice: A guide to contraception, fertility, abortion and menopause*. New York: Basic Books, 1970

Green, T.H. *Gynecology: Essentials of clinical practice. Boston: Little, Brown & Co., 1965.*

Kantor, H.I. Sexual effects of estrogen replacement. Medical Aspects of Human Sexuality, 1977, ll, 85-86.

Kaplan, H.S. *The new sex therapy. New York: Brunner/Mazel, 1974.*

Kupperman, H.I. The climateric syndrome. The Medical Folio, 1962,5.

Lanson, L. *From woman to woman.* New York: A. A. Knopf, 1975.

Levine, L. & Doherty, B. *The menopause.* New York: Random House, 1952.

Masters, W. H. & Johnson, V.E. *Human sexual response.* Boston: Little, Brown & Co., 1966.

Masters, W. H. & Johnson, V. E. *Human sexual inadequacy.* Boston: Little, Brown & Co., 1970

McKinlay, S. M. & Jefferys, M. The menopausal syndrome. *British Journal of Preventive and Social Medicine,* 1974, 28, 108.

Mortality risk associated with pill. Editorial. *Family Planning Perspectives,* 1977, 9, 278-280.

Mozley, P.D. Woman's capacity for orgasm after menopause. *Medical Aspects of Human Sexuality,* 1975, 9, 104-110.

Neugarten, B.L. & Kraines, R.J. Menopause symptoms in women of various ages. *Psychomatic Medicine,* 1965, 27, 266.

Nowak, C.A. Does youthfulness equal attractiveness? in L. Troll, J. & K. Israel (Eds.). *Looking ahead: A woman's guide to the problems and joys of growing older.* Englewood Cliffs: Prentice Hall, Inc., 1977.

Pakter, J., Nelson, F. & Savigir, M. Legal abortion: A half-decade of experience. *Family Planning Perspectives, 1975, 7, 248-255.*

Rhoades, F.P. Continuous cyclic hormone therapy. Journal of the American Geriatric Society, 1974, 22, 183-185.

Sheehy, G. *Passages: Predictable crises of adult life.* New York: Bantam Books, 1976.

Stone, S.C. Discontinuing contraception at menopause. *Medical Aspects of Human Sexuality,* 1976, 10, 177-178.

Tietze, C. new estimates of mortality associated with fertility control. *Family Planning Perspectives, 1977. 9. 74-76.*

Weideger, P. Menstruation and menopause: The physiology, psychology, the myth and the reality. New York: A. A. Knopf, 1976.

Wilson, R.A. & T.A. The fate of the nontreated postmenopausal woman: A plea for the maintenance of adequate estrogen from puberty to the grave. *Journal of American Geriatric Society,* 1963, 11, 347.

Ziel, H.K. & Finkle, W.D. Increased risk of endometrial carcinoma among users of conjugated estrogens. *New England Journal of Medicine,* 1975, 292, 1167-1170.

Footnotes

[1]Women over 40 years old account for the smallest percentage of legal abortions, but the ration of abortions per 1,000 live births is highest for this age group according to Pakter, Nelson and Svigir (1975).

Sex and Heart Disease

If proper care is taken, a heart condition need not interfere with your sex life.

Howard R. and Martha E. Lewis

Howard R. and Martha E. Lewis are medical writers and co-authors of The Parent's Guide to Teenage Sex and Pregnancy *(St. Martin's Press).*

Heart disease need not be a reason for abstaining from sexual activity. You generally can resume less physically demanding forms, such as masturbation and oral sex, within a month or so after heart surgery or a heart attack. Intercourse can usually resume after two to three months. Indeed, after heart surgery you may enjoy sex more, since the operation generally reduces pain and shortness of breath.

If you're a heart patient, your resuming sexual activity depends on how well you've recovered. Only a physician familiar with your condition can give you specific advice. But to get it you may need to ask.

Don't be reluctant to initiate a sexual discussion with your doctor. He may be uneasy about sexuality. If he fails to bring the subject up, you may mistakenly assume that he believes such activity is beyond your limit.

Sexual intercourse increases your heart rate, blood pressure and breathing. Thereby sex increases the stress on your heart. This added burden is about the same as from briskly walking a few blocks or climbing two flights of stairs. When you can do those tasks, you usually can also have intercourse.

The actual physical burden of intercourse is actually less than widely thought. One major study found that the maximum heart response was a fairly moderate 120 beats per minute—for only ten to fifteen seconds for most subjects. Often the heart rate rose less from intercourse than from driving a car or experiencing anger.

Heart patients, however, often doubt their ability to resume normal physical activities, especially sexual intercourse. Fear of death and symptoms such as chest pain and shortness of breath may prevent you from enjoying sex.

You can closely assess how much sexual activity you can tolerate. Undergo a standard series of stress tests followed by electrocardiograms. From the ECG's your doctor can tell what your maximum heart rate can safely be. He can then estimate if your heart rate during intercourse falls within safe limits.

For an even more precise determination of how sex affects your heart, you can get a Hellerstein Sexercise Tolerance Test, using a form of tape recorder at home while making love. Such objective measurements can help give worried patients the confidence to return quickly to their former level of sexual activity.

Chances are your doctor will recommend an exercise program to improve your cardiovascular condition. Any increase in your tolerance for exercise speeds your resumption of sex.

Dying during intercourse? Many heart patients fear they'll have an attack and die during intercourse. That's very rare, reports cardiologist Herman K. Hellerstein of Case Western Reserve University. Sexual activity was associated with sudden death in only three of 500 heart patients he studied.

You may suffer sexual impediments from loss of self-esteem. A heart condition can make you weak and dependent, unable to do productive work. Insomnia, anxiety and depression often follow. These states may result in sexual dysfunction.

Impotence may follow a heart attack or heart surgery. In most cases, the impotence is of psychological origin. "This should not be surprising in view of the enormous physical and psychological stress they've been subjected to," comments psychiatrist Stanley S. Heller of the Columbia University College of Physicians and Surgeons. A woman's fears about sexual activity may make her inhibited and unresponsive, with difficulties achieving orgasm.

Sexual problems can be caused by your medication. Some drugs used to treat heart disease or hypertension interfere with sexual activity. Impotence is an especially common side effect and often can be remedied by a change of drugs.

Some heart patients unconsciously use their medical condition as an excuse to retire from an active sex life, in which case professional counseling may be required.

Call your doctor's attention to any sexual difficulties that persist. Include your mate in discussions about resuming sexual activity. Take the opportunity to talk out sexual problems that may obstruct your recovery. Your doctor can advise you—or refer you for information—about increasing sexual activity by stages.

Speeding your sexual recovery. At least at first, take it easy in bed. Sex doesn't have to be athletic to be pleasurable. By using restraint, you can ordinarily remain within your exercise tolerance. Psychiatrist Benjamin H. Glover, Jr. of the University of Wisconsin Medical Center urges his heart patients to take time to enjoy each other "rather than race to orgasm."

To reduce the strain on your heart, resume intercourse in a lying-on-your-side position. This saves you from having to support your body weight.

There is some evidence, though, that coital position may not make much difference. The woman-on-top position is often thought to be excellent for the man with coronary heart disease. Yet in a study of normal males, heart rate and blood pressure were the same in man-on-top and woman-on-top positions.

Medication just before intercourse may help you avoid heart problems. If you experience chest pain during lovemaking, your doctor may prescribe propranolol (Inderal) or nitroglycerin to be taken immediately prior to intercourse. These drugs decrease heart rate and blood pressure.

Beware of self-prescribing. Many tranquilizers and antidepressants decrease sexual responsiveness. Some impair a man's ability to maintain an erection or to ejaculate.

Marital sex is safer. Many doctors warn their heart patients that extramarital sex poses particular problems. Some eight out of ten men who die during intercourse do so while engaging in sex with partners other than their wives.

The circumstances in which extramarital sex often occurs can add to the risks of intercourse. About a third of the victims had been drinking heavily. A date is also likely to involve a heavy meal. Surroundings may be unfamiliar. All these stresses increase demands on the heart.

Further, the fear and guilt associated with adultery make it more stressful than the simple act of intercourse alone.

When to avoid sex. In general, it's best for a heart patient to avoid intercourse in the following circumstances:

If you've had a full meal. Food, especially an elaborate dinner, increases the workload on your heart.

If you've drunk a lot. Alcohol makes increased demands on the heart. Moreover, even a small amount can dull sexual responsiveness—and so bring about frantic activity.

If you're tired or sick. Try to have intercourse in the morning, when you're well rested and feeling fine.

If you're very cold or hot. During periods of extreme weather, the temperature regulatory mechanisms of your body impose additional strain on your heart. If your home is adequately heated or cooled, the outdoor temperature need present no problem. During hot, humid weather where there's no air conditioning, make love during the cool hours of evening or early morning.

If you're new to a high altitude. Cardiologist William Likoff of Hahnemann Medical College discourages his patients from having intercourse at altitudes above 5,000 feet, particularly if they've just arrived there. On the other hand, if you've lived at high altitude for a long time, you can probably have sexual relations "without unusual consequences."

Sexual Harassment On the Job:

Why more and more women are fighting back

Nancy Josephson

In the three years she worked for him, Mary Heelan says, her boss's overtures went from lighthearted flirtation to an outright demand that she sleep with him or find another job. Heelan, a $15,000-a-year project manager, refused, was fired, and for the next six months sat at home and cried. "Then suddenly I got angry," she remembers. "I decided somebody had to do something." So Mary Heelan fought back. She sued.

What made Mary Heelan so angry was that the company didn't believe her when she told them she was fired for not sleeping with her boss. "After I was fired, somebody called my boss and asked him if it was true. He denied it and they believed him instead of me," she says.

The judge in the suit, however, agreed with her. The company was found guilty of sexual discrimination under Title VII of the 1964 Civil Rights Act. Heelan settled with her employer, reportedly for close to $100,000.

Until recently, there were only two ways to handle sexual harassment on the job: either suffer it silently or quit. Now, women are fighting back. One Manhattan secretary received a $10,000 settlement after she filed charges claiming she was fired for refusing to sleep with her boss. In upstate New York, a city school district awarded a woman $10,000 after she filed sexual harassment charges with the New York State Division of Human Rights. Another young woman who took a job as a lobby attendant in a large New York City office building filed suit against her employer, claiming she was forced to wear a revealing outfit on the job.

Most experts agree that the real issue in sexual harassment is power, not sex at all. A man may think he's being friendly when he gives a woman a playful little hug. But it's nothing to joke about when he's in a position to fire her for rejecting his advances.

Heelan, now thirty-five and living in Colorado Springs, Colorado, with her husband and children, maintains that fear of a confrontation that would jeopardize her job kept her from reporting her boss's behavior each time he suggested that they have an affair. She even remained silent when he retaliated by filing damaging memos in her personnel folder, calling her "childish," "ungrateful" and "disobedient." Their fragile working relationship began to disintegrate. When Heelan continued to refuse, her boss began sabotaging her work, she says. Finally, she complained to company officials. They told her, Heelan says, "it will pass, it's a phase, it will go away." "One afternoon my boss came into my office," she remembers. "He said, 'This is the day you're going to stop this childish disobedience.' That's the term he used for my refusal to go to bed with him. He said, 'This is the day you're going to abide.' I said 'No,' and he said 'You can consider yourself fired.' "

About the same time, a New Jersey woman, Adrienne Tomkins, claims she was having similar trouble with her boss. Tomkins, a stenographer, was about to be promoted to private secretary, and her boss invited her for lunch to discuss her future with the firm. The way Tomkins recalls it: After two hours, he suddenly began talking about people involved in office relationships. She grew uneasy; she told him she wanted to return to work. When she got up to leave, he grabbed her arm, pulling her back to her chair. Then, Tomkins says, he told her he wanted to sleep with her. "It's the only way we can have a working relationship," she recalls him saying.

Tomkins called in sick the following morning. She wanted to quit. But when she learned that she couldn't get unemployment benefits without a full-scale investigation, Tomkins requested a transfer to another job.

Tomkins didn't get the comparable position she says she was promised. Instead, she was bounced to another department, stripped of all her responsibilities and given no work to do except filing and occasional bits of typing. Irritation turned to anger. Under the daily harassment, Tomkins became ill and lost time at work. Her company retaliated with disciplinary layoffs. She complained and was labeled a troublemaker. Finally, she was fired.

Tomkins, like Heelan, fought back. The suit she filed reportedly brought her a $20,000 out-of-court settlement. Although the company, a large public utility, denied the sex discrimination charges, it paid Tomkin's legal fees and, as part of the settlement, agreed to set up a review board to investigate future sexual harassment complaints. Tomkins's boss still denies that he propositioned her and that he demanded sex in exchange for the job.

Recently, a sexual harassment scandal rocked the city of Austin, Texas, where three state health department employees charged that they were sexually harassed by their boss. The women claimed that their supervisor repeatedly badgered them, even grabbed their breasts and pinched them. One woman claimed that she was constantly hounded with questions about sex while she was seeking a divorce. The situation grew so unbearable, the women said, that one employee had to have her doctor prescribe sleeping pills for her.

Clearly, women needn't put up with sexual harassment. "Making someone's employment contingent on responding to sexual advances is sexual discrimination and is therefore illegal," says Karen Sauvigne, program director of Working Women's Institute, a New York based group that counsels sexual harassment victims and has a backup center for attorneys litigating in this new area. "The courts now say that if a boss asks, 'Will you go to bed with me?' and a woman says, 'No,' and as a result is fired, she may have a case."

Ironically, there is no textbook definition of sexual harassment. Therefore, many of those things that make a woman uncomfortable—a pinch, a look, even locker room talk—may not be illegal under sex discrimination laws. To claim sexual harassment under the sex discrimination statute, there must be a direct relationship between the abuse and, say, loss of a job, a pay raise or a promotion. "The next step," Sauvigné says, "is to get the courts to recognize that it is also sexual harassment when the working conditions are made so unbearable that a woman can't do her job."

Not surprisingly, women list the commonplace pat on the fanny as one of the most frequent forms of sexual harassment on the job. They also say that being touched—supposedly by accident—and being forced to listen while a man describes his sexual conquests are both common at work.

Working Women's Institute found that 70 percent of the women they surveyed had encountered some form of sexual harassment in the workplace. Peggy Crull, Ph.D., the Institute's research director says the group receives several hundred letters and calls a week from women requesting help. Most of the victims report symptoms of stress—headaches, sleeplessness, weight loss or gain—"things you'd experience in a negative work environment," Dr. Crull says.

For one young woman, an assistant professor of comparative literature at a leading state university, trouble with the department chairman cost her her job. In this case there was not an outright demand for sex; instead, the chairman repeatedly insinuated that her friendships with her male colleagues weren't strictly professional. On several occasions, she remembers, the department head interrupted her conversations with men in the department to warn the men to "watch out" for her. Once, the department chairman stopped to remind her that she was walking across campus with a happily married man. On another occasion, she and a married male colleague were called into the chairman's office for a forty-five minute lecture on married life. The department chairman, she says, was careful not to make any specific allegations. But he succeeded in embarrassing the two young academicians. When her tenure was denied, the literature instructor filed sexual discrimination charges with the state division of human rights. She was awarded $5,000.

For some women, the period of adjustment afterward is as difficult as the incident itself. Diane Williams, a serious and soft-spoken young black woman, remembers how embarrassed she felt telling her father that she had lost her job. He had worked at the same company for more than thirty years. She held on to her public relations job at the Justice Department for just nine months.

"The worst thing was that I was dismissed with twenty-five minutes notice on a Friday," says Williams. She claims that her boss was pressuring her to see him socially. He even sent her a note saying, "Seldom a day goes by without a loving thought of you." Williams refused her boss's advances and she claims he retaliated by attacking her work.

Some women believe incorrectly that the only way to escape sexual harassment on the job is to quit. A Cleveland, Ohio, woman whose boss told her to report to work one Saturday, did so only to find her boss standing there naked. She left and never went back. "Women quit to get away from sexual harassment," says Lucille E. Wright, Ph.D., a Cleveland State University education professor who recently completed a local study of sexual harassment on the job. "Women believe that even if they do report sexual harassment, little can be done because it's so hard to prove."

Women who don't quit often remain silent, blaming themselves for their boss's actions. Other women, too frightened or embarrassed to seek advice from a sympathetic friend or colleague, accept their boss's passes as just another part of the job.

There are ways to cope with sexual harassment in the office, short of quitting or bringing suit. One thing a woman should do is let the offender know—in the clearest language possible—that she isn't interested in his offer. With this, she puts her objection on the record. "You can't just sit there silently," Dr. Crull says. "The way we're socialized, if you aren't direct about it, a man may think you like it, or he'll think you're playing coy or hard to get." Be firm—in a polite way.

If this doesn't work, Dr. Crull suggests seeking a sympathetic colleague to take the offender aside and ask him to stop. She also suggests reporting the incident to company officials, either in the personnel department or in another department that is empowered to handle staff complaints. This may stop the problem. If not, Dr. Crull says, at least the complaint is on record.

5. CONTINUING SEXUAL CONCERNS

Because women are becoming more and more aware of their rights in the workplace, management is improving procedures to deal with sexual-harassment complaints. In New Jersey, Public Service Electric and Gas Company issued a flyer after the Tomkins incident, stating that it would not tolerate sexual harassment by any supervisors on the staff. Washington, D.C., Mayor Marion S. Barry, Jr., issued an order prohibiting sexual harassment in any form and establishing procedures for filing complaints. Democratic Congressman James M. Hanley recently called for hearings to investigate sexual harassment in the federal government, after hearing of complaints at the Department of Housing and Urban Development.

The next step, women's groups say, is convincing the public that there are subtle—but still upsetting and discriminatory—forms of harassment on the job. One New York woman, for example, filed suit against her boss because he insisted that she wear, as a uniform, a poncho that was open at the sides. The woman claims that her boss threatened to fire her if she refused to wear the outfit. In Detroit, thirty airport waitresses joined a class action suit against their employer, claiming they were required to wear scanty outfits. The group said the airport waiters were allowed to dress modestly, while the female employees' costumes were revealing. No one was fired and no one quit during the dispute, and the women received new uniforms. But to protect themselves from future problems, they refused to drop the suit.

In a case against Yale University, an undergraduate said she received a "C" in a course because she refused to sleep with the instructor. She sued the university, claiming that the school failed to provide adequate channels for students to file such complaints. After a seven-day trial in U.S. District Court, the judge handed down a decision that, to some, was the greatest setback so far. The judge ruled that there had been no proposition, that the student's grade reflected her academic performance and that Yale was not remiss in its handling of the case.

The suit was the first of its kind, according to Catharine MacKinnon, now teaching at Yale Law School and author of *Sexual Harassment of Working Women.* Although MacKinnon found the decision inadequate, she says, "The people at Yale have taken sexual harassment somewhat more seriously since the suit, but this does not mean they have solved the problem."

In a recent study, Al Louis Ripskis, an employee in the Department of Housing and Urban Development, discovered widespread sexual harassment in the federal bureaucracy. He also found that nearly one-third of the women who responded to the survey admitted to having gone along with the demands. And, some claimed that it had paid off. Only a few women who said they had turned down their bosses reported the incidents to any official. The victims, the survey showed, were mostly clerical workers earning less than $15,000 a year. Ripskis, who published the results of his survey, maintains that sexual harassment is "much more pervasive than we ever thought," and has "seriously affected" performance on the job.

For some, sexual harassment is still difficult to discuss. Helen Lewis, executive director of the District of Columbia's Commission for women, says that although there's increased awareness of the problem, some people still don't believe sexual harassment is a serious problem. "When you begin to discuss it with people who haven't thought about it before," Lewis says, "an immediate response is that the people who are complaining don't have a sense of humor."

For the victim, it's no joke.

8 steps to take to fight back

Sexual harassment on the job is illegal. It runs the gamut from unwanted sexual advances to a demand for sexual favors if you want to keep your job or advance in your company. But be forewarned: Fighting back isn't easy. Going to court can be costly, and sexual harassment is often hard to prove. But if you decide to fight back, here's what to do:

- At the first sign of trouble, tell the harasser you aren't interested in his offer. Be firm but be polite. Don't give him ammunition to use later.
- If he continues to harass you, complain to your union, a grievance committee or personnel department. It's in the company's interest to rectify the problem. A lawsuit is costly for them, too.
- Keep a diary. Mark the time, date and place of each incident. List witnesses. Note any physical or emotional stress you have related to the incidents. If you see a doctor due to stress, record that, too.
- Look for support among your colleagues. Other women he has pressured may be willing to corroborate your charges.
- If you quit because the situation is intolerable, detail your charges in a letter to the head of personnel. That way, your complaint is on record should you file for unemployment benefits.
- If you are fired for turning down your boss's advances, talk to an attorney. You may have to prove your charges before you can collect unemployment benefits.
- Consult local feminist organizations for the names of attorneys familiar with sexual harassment cases. In San Francisco, call Women Organized for Employment, 415-982-8963; in Washington, the Women's Legal Defense Fund, 202-638-1123; in Chicago, Women Employed, 312-782-3902; in New York, Working Women's Institute, 212-838-4420; and in Boston, the Alliance Against Sexual Coercion, 617-482-0329.
- If you plan to sue the company under the sexual discrimination statute, Title VII of the 1964 Civil Rights Act, file a complaint with the local Equal Employment Opportunity Commission within 180 days of leaving the company. To get compensatory and punitive damages, you must sue the company, the harasser, or both.

INCEST

SEXUAL ABUSE BEGINS AT HOME

ELLEN WEBER

Ellen Weber, a free-lance writer living in Berkeley, California, has researched and written for films on child abuse.

One girl out of every four in the United States will be sexually abused in some way before she reaches the age of 18. Although it is widely assumed that her assailant will be a mysterious pervert, according to a 1967 survey conducted in New York City by the American Humane Association, only one quarter of all sexual molestations are committed by strangers. Only 2 percent take place in cars; only 5 percent in abandoned buildings. In a full 75 percent of the cases, the victim knows her assailant. In 34 percent, the molestation takes place in her own home.

Molestations by a stranger are generally one-time occurrences, but in the case of incest or sexual abuse by a known assailant, the victim may be trapped in a relationship for years. And while the guilt and shock of a sexual encounter with a stranger are often defused by supportive parental reaction, the family of a sexual abuse victim often fails to intervene on her behalf.

Sexual abuse occurs in families of every social, economic, and ethnic background and runs the gamut from "fondling" to fellatio, cunnilingus, sodomy, and, ultimately, full intercourse. Little girls as young as four or five may be shown dirty pictures in magazines, or forced to pose nude in seductive poses. The average age of sexual abuse victims is 11 years, and victims have been as young as eight months.

Since sexual abuse often begins before a child understands its significance, force is rarely involved; the perpetrator uses his position of authority or trust to convince the naïve child that their relationship is "for her own good," or a normal part of growing up. According to several psychiatrists, when the victim learns the truth, she may feel both betrayed by the offender, and guilty and ashamed about her own cooperation. At this point, the victim will usually resist the relationship, only to be frightened with stronger and stronger threats; but her own sense of complicity may prevent her from asking anyone else for help.

Even when help is sought, the family may close its eyes to the charge out of a sense of loyalty to the offender, the fear of public embarrassment, or perhaps the loss of a father's income. The mother may not want to believe her husband capable of such atrocious behavior, or she may simply feel powerless to do anything about it. Dorothy Ross, coordinator of a sexual abuse treatment center in California, explains "Sometimes mothers are afraid of being beaten or of their family's being broken up or of the loss of financial support. Often it's a vague fear of not knowing what to do, where to go, what's going to happen." Sometimes the girl is actually blamed.

Some experts have found a correlation between sexual abuse and later antisocial behavior. Dr. Richard Burnstine, a Chicago pediatrician, has found that nearly all the girls at Chapin Hall, a home for disturbed and homeless children, had been sexually abused. A large portion of adolescent runaways are children trying to escape from a sexually abusive relationship. When physical escape proves impossible, they may embark on long careers of drug use. John Siverson, a family therapist in Minneapolis who has treated more than 500 cases of adolescent drug addiction, reports that some 70 percent of his clients were caught in some form of family sexual abuse. The same is true of 44 percent of the female population at Odyssey House—a residential drug treatment program with centers in seven states—and out of the 52 cases only two had ever been reported to the authorities.

Women who have been sexually abused as children [the ratio of girls to boys in reported cases is 10 to 1] report adult sexual problems, ranging from an inability to achieve orgasm to a total revulsion for heterosexual relations. Many of the victims interviewed for this article strongly believe that the only thing any man is after is sex, and that all they (the victims) are good for is sex. Not surprisingly then, many sexual abuse victims turn to promiscuity or prostitution at some time in their lives. In a recent study of adolescent prostitutes in the Minneapolis area, it was found that 75 percent of them were victims of incest. It is also suspected by several clinical psychologists that the victim's feelings of low self-worth, and distaste for sex, make victims prone to marrying men who will sexually abuse their daughters.

The National Center on Child Abuse and Neglect estimates that there are at least 100,000 cases of sexual abuse each year, though it is the most unreported category of criminal activity. Other professionals, such as Hank Giarretto, director of the Santa Clara Child Abuse Treatment Program in San Jose, consider a quarter of a million cases a conservative estimate.

Vincent De Francis, director of the Children's Division of the American Humane Association in Denver, Colorado, says that the incidence of sexual abuse is "many times greater" than that of physical abuse. Yet in comparison with society's efforts for the battered child, the sexual abuse victim has been virtually ignored. For instance, while every state specifically requires the reporting of physical abuse, nearly half of the states do not specifically mention sexual abuse in their mandatory reporting laws.

"People can more easily identify with the physically abusive parent," says Dorothy Ross, a California probation officer and the coordinator of the Child Sexual Abuse Treatment Program in San Jose, California. "But the idea of a father having sex with his own daughter is so horrible, so abhorrent, we don't want to believe it goes on."

In a study of 20 families involved in incest, the American Humane Association noted that 10 of these families had had contact with several public agencies "without revealing that the violation of society's most fundamental taboo was a feature of their home life."

As Dr. Jacob Lebsack, associate director of the National Study on Child Neglect and Abuse Reporting in Denver, explains, "Many social workers will report and talk about bruises but are unwilling to press further to determine if this is a case of sexual abuse in which the bruise is only a secondary characteristic."

"I think you're sort of embarrassed to ask the question," says Dr. David Friedman, a pediatrician at USC Medical Center where child abuse has become a central concern. He admits having missed a good deal of sexual abuse when he was in private practice. "You're afraid you will lose the patient by implying that it's possible."

On the average, sexual abuse reports are not made until the victim can't stand it any more and tells someone, or becomes pregnant. Even then, the victim herself is usually removed from her home and placed in protective custody or a foster home, a procedure which unfortunately reinforces her conviction that she is the offending party. She is then asked to repeat the embarrassing details of the abuse to police, investigators, protective service workers, the district attorney, and, if she qualifies as a witness, to the defense attorney under cross-examination in open court.

Usually, however, the abuser is never brought to court because there is not enough evidence to prosecute. The Los Angeles Police Department, for example, receives about 100 reports of sexual abuse by a parent or guardian each year, but no more than 30 percent of these ever reach the stage of a formal complaint; and only a very small percent ever get to court. Corroborating evidence is difficult to obtain in any sex crime, but in a case reported weeks, months, or years after the offense, it is practically impossible. Other members of the family may refuse to testify, even after they have brought charges, and the victim herself may not make a credible witness if she's fallen into the predictable pattern of promiscuity or drug use. The result is often a one-on-one situation which most D.A. offices—interested in a good conviction rate—are reluctant to take to court. The offender is released, but for her own protection, the victim resumes her "sentence" in the foster home.

Many professionals find it hard to say whether the abuse, or its aftermath, is more traumatic for the victim. Often the victim's mother is forced to go on welfare, her sisters and brothers are also placed in foster homes; her parents—usually at the court's urging—are permanently separated or divorced.

Certainly, says Dorothy Ross, "If the abuse hadn't made an impact, then by the time the system gets through with her it has become the most important thing that ever happened in her life." While law enforcement officials would like to see more cases prosecuted, so that the offender—and not the victim—is punished, others feel that the child's welfare is often sacrificed in the massive onslaught against the perpetrator. De Francis of the Humane Association feels that if a child is involved in legal proceedings, she should be surrounded by social services that will cushion the impact. As a preventive measure, he also stresses the need for schools to give children some understanding of parenting roles, responsibility, and behavior so that they will recognize when they are being mistreated by adults.

At present the only comprehensive program designed to meet the needs of both victims and offenders is the Santa Clara Child Sexual Abuse Treatment Program in San Jose, California (CSATP). Started five years ago CSATP provides therapy and counseling for daughters, fathers, and mothers, as well as practical assistance and emotional support through the maze of courtroom procedures. Therapy for the victim is aimed at relieving her own feelings of guilt over the abuse and family breakup, and helping her deal with her anger and resentment toward both parents. For the offender, the program emphasizes "taking responsibility for what [he has] done," says Director Giarretto. Offenders and their wives are helped to recognize the marital (not just sexual) problems which, according to Giarretto, are often a primary cause of sexual abuse.

Some of the families in the program are referred by the courts—as an alternative to the father's imprisonment or as a condition for probation. Many of the cases police formerly had to drop for lack of evidence are now referred to CSATP. The program lasts for an average of six months to a year, although many of the graduates continue to attend Daughters United or Parents United—the two self-help groups generated by CSATP. About 400 families have completed treatment in the past five years, and only two repeat cases of sexual abuse have been reported.

CSATP is being looked to as a model for other state programs in California. Last year Governor Jerry Brown signed into law a measure that would create statewide treatment centers for abused children and their families. Elsewhere in the country, police departments and district attorneys' offices now have special units trained to handle sexual abuse problems with greater sensitivity. In some places, child-abuse hotlines, rape crisis centers, and hospital sexual assault services are expanding their facilities to recognize and treat sexual abuse. In California the National Organization for Women has set up a Task Force on Sexual Abuse; it hopes to establish a national task force during the April NOW convention to coordinate local efforts to help victims.

The magnitude of the problem of incest is perhaps only matched by the degree of secrecy which surrounds it. As more assistance becomes available, more of the hidden victims are reaching out for help. For example, in 1974, the number of cases referred to CSATP increased from 31 to 145. In 1975, there were 169 referrals, and in 1976, 269 cases were referred—all from the vicinity of Santa Clara County. (In Los Angeles, there were only 107 cases reported last year.)

The taboo against family sex, far from preventing it, only keeps us from recognizing and treating those who violate it. If society is going to help the victim of sexual abuse, it is going to have to become less terrified of it. And then we will see just how big the problem really is.

Rape: 'Not a sex act—a violent crime'

AN INTERVIEW WITH DR. DOROTHY J. HICKS

"Rape is not a sex act. It is a violent crime that has nothing to do with sex except that sex organs are involved. Rape is an attempt to humiliate a victim who happens to be vulnerable and handy at the time. It's really the ultimate invasion of privacy and terribly misunderstood."

The views are those of Dorothy J. Hicks, MD, who, as medical director of the Rape Treatment Center at Dade County's Jackson Memorial Hospital in Miami, has had ample opportunity to analyze the crime and its victims. Since the Rape Treatment Center opened in January 1974—the first rape victim walked in for treatment during the ribbon-cutting ceremony—the center has treated an average of 65 rape victims a month, ranging in age from two months to 91 years. Most have been female victims, but about 4% are male. The degree of violence inflicted on these patients has varied from victims who were assaulted, mauled, and "almost" raped to women who were brutally beaten, mutilated, and left for dead.

In 1975, some 2,986 rapes were reported in the state of Florida, and 56,093 such crimes were logged nationwide, according to the Uniform Crime Report. And without question the number committed far exceeds the number reported to authorities; on this, police, social workers, physicians, and women activists all agree. They differ only on the question of how great the disparity is; estimates of actual rape range from twice to 10 times the reported figures. Earlier this year, the National Institute of Mental Health established a National Center for the Prevention and Control of Rape to support research into causes of rape, laws dealing with the crime, treatment of rape victims, and effectiveness of existing programs to prevent and control rape.

"Yet," comments Dr. Hicks, "I have trouble convincing many people that there really is such a thing as forcible rape." The problem boils down to the fact that many people think rape is sex perpetrated on a woman who really was asking for it by being seductively dressed or behaving provocatively toward an oversexed man.

According to Dr. Hicks, a normal man usually cannot imagine forcibly raping someone; if a woman said no to his overtures for sex and then started screaming and crying when he pressed his point, the man would become disgusted and turned off. Since such a man can't imagine himself raping a woman, it's difficult for him to believe another man would be able to do so.

Similarly, some women—particularly professional women, such as policewomen, physicians, or nurses—cannot imagine getting into a situation they could not handle; they, too, sometimes have trouble believing that forcible rape is not the result of seduction. Even victims have difficulty understanding that they are not in some way responsible for provoking a sex act: As one victim told Dr. Hicks, "I can't believe it. He didn't even kiss me first."

"Too many people think that if women wore longer skirts and looser clothing everything would be OK," says Dr. Hicks. "They should know that one year the majority of rape victims in Chicago wore turtlenecks and slacks—hardly seductive. And how can one say that a two-month-old baby or seven-month-old baby or a seven-year-old boy or an 86-year-old lady are particularly 'sexy'?

"Furthermore, our knowledge of rapists substantiates that this is not sex. More than half of convicted rapists are married, and it is not uncommon for a convicted rapist to admit that he raped a woman shortly after having sexual intercourse with his girlfriend or wife. These are hostile people who think about rape when they are not raping someone and who plan their crimes carefully.

"This is not hanky-panky," Dr. Hicks stresses. "If a woman 'paints herself into a corner' and can't get out, if she finally says, 'OK—do your thing and leave,' this woman probably is not going to be crushed by the experience. However, women who are forcibly raped often are destroyed by the psychologic trauma of the experience."

Unfortunately, widespread misunderstanding about rape as a crime has made the likes of police officers, juries, spouses, and other family members look askance at the rape victim as somehow a guilty participant in the crime. All too often women are not believed when they report a rape. Until recently, New York state law required a woman to have a witness to a rape. In certain parts of the country women still are required to take lie detector tests before a public defender will consider prosecuting, whereas if a house is burglarized, the owner is not required to submit to polygraph testing. Rape is the only crime in which a victim becomes the accused.

"As if it's not enough that a victim is assaulted and humiliated! Often no one believes her or treats her as if she were an innocent party," says Dr. Hicks. "And then, when she seeks medical and legal help, the victim often is treated insensitively. People—including physicians—have not understood how rape can ruin a life, because sometimes the trauma does not show for three to four years. Some victims never get over it and entire families are affected drastically." She gives a few examples:

- One woman has moved four times since she was raped two years ago and does not feel safe anywhere.
- A Latin woman, raped in her home six years ago, now will not enter her house unless a brother or nephew goes in and completely searches it; a search must be conducted whether she has gone to the grocery store or has been away from the house several days.
- A high-school class secretary who was raped has never finished school and has been in and out of psychiatric institutions for the past 10 years.
- A middle-aged woman had great marital difficulty after being raped; after the couple divorced, the husband shot himself in the head.
- A boy who was repeatedly molested by his two sisters began raping women at the age of 15; he raped frequently and violently, until he was caught at age 23.

These are not isolated instances. Dr. Hicks estimates that after being raped, 60% of victims change their life-style. Within two years of the assault more than half of rape victims divorce their husbands or break off with boyfriends. Sometimes personality problems develop or the woman becomes sexually unresponsive after the experience.

Other times, the men are responsible for the break. A man who would think nothing of marrying a divorcee may "come unglued" over the idea that his wife has been raped by another man. One woman treated at the rape center had been raped and seriously beaten; her nipples were bitten off, and a shoe was forced into her vagina. When she returned home after four days in the hospital, the man with whom she had been living had moved out, taking every stitch of his clothing and belongings.

Psychologic aftermath

"We know that women will have problems as they deal with their own psychologic aftermath of a rape," says Dr. Hicks. "And we tell the patient that the rape will no doubt affect her. Nevertheless, we want to help the person come out stronger rather than weaker after the rape trauma."

Dr. Hicks became involved in the Rape Treatment Center shortly after a group of Miami feminists decided that something needed to be done about the hundreds of rape victims in Dade County. Under the leadership of feminist Roxy Bolton, the women marched down Miami's Flagler Street in 1972 to "advertise" the problem of rape and the need for action. Eventually, the Metro Commission gave the go-ahead for a task force to be set up. Meetings were held with the chiefs of police, hospital administrators, physicians, and nurses.

"Because they were feminists, the women wanted a woman gynecologist on the task force," Dr Hicks recalls. "There aren't too many of us around, so my department chairman asked me if I'd sit in on an organizing meeting. I did—and at that meeting, they concluded we needed a rape treatment center.

Dr. Hicks is medical director of the Rape Treatment Center, presently housed in a converted mobile home parked next to the hospital's emergency room.

"The day after the meeting the newspaper came out with the story that was a surprise to me: 'Dr. Dorothy Hicks: Head of Rape Treatment Center.'"

All this was decided about December 8 or 9, 1973; the center opened during the first week of January 1974 and, as already mentioned, the first patient came in during the opening ceremony.

The Rape Treatment Center is housed in a converted double-sized mobile home parked adjacent to the Jackson Memorial Hospital emergency room. Although it is carpeted and paneled, it is not elaborate: just a few offices, an examining room, a conference room, a quiet lounge area for rape victims who await treatment, and a tiny laboratory area.

The center operates as a fiscal appendage of the emergency room and the hospital. Nursing staff is siphoned off from the emergency room. Charlotte R. Platt, RN, is director of the emergency department nursing services and of nursing for the Rape Treatment Center. She is responsible for assigning to each emergency room shift at least two nurses—one man and one woman—who have had on-the-job training to work in the Rape Treatment Center.

Six physicians from the hospital's department of obstetrics and gynecology rotate through the treatment center as needed. They are not the physician-on-call for the rest of the service, and they are specially trained to be sensitive to the problems of rape victims. (Some have purchased or rented their own long-distance pagers or "beepers," because the center has no money to buy any.) During the day, however, Dr. Hicks handles most of the cases that come in. In addition, the psychiatry department provides counselors—psychologists, psychiatric nurses, or psychiatric social workers—to talk to rape victims who need help.

One function of the center is totally autonomous: All medical files on rape cases are completely confidential, separate from the hospital, and the center does not send copies to the central records department. In fact, only Dr. Hicks and Mrs. Platt have keys to the locked files next to Dr. Hicks' desk, so that even when a medical record is subpoenaed by a public defender, the rape center directors know.

What is an emergency?

"I believe rape treatment centers are necessary because rape victims do not receive optimal treatment in hospital emergency rooms," states Dr. Hicks. "They do not, chiefly because they do not constitute an emergency in general.

"Rape victims are not surgical emergencies," she continues. "In fact, only 1 to 1.5% of victims at our center require major surgery. These women are not gynecologic emergencies, as is a patient with a ruptured tubal pregnancy. Nor are the victims psychiatric emergencies; usually they are deceptively calm, dazed by the experience. Their symptoms may not appear for several days, months, or even years.

"On the other hand, rape cases are rape emergencies and the treatment should be prompt," says Dr. Hicks. "Rape emergencies should not be kept off in a corner until all other emergencies are treated. Their problems are serious and need attention.

"In addition, a rape treatment center is important because it makes a victim realize that her or his experience is not an isolated occurrence," continues Dr. Hicks. "Victims then realize that it happens all the time to other people." Usually only one victim is in the center at a time; however, once three victims of three different rapists were brought in for treatment at the same time.

The treatment for rape victims that has evolved at the Rape Treatment Center starts the minute the person comes in for treatment and lasts as long as he or she seeks follow-up counseling.

After arriving at the emergency room, a victim is taken to the center by one of the trained nurses or by the police. After the victim states that she or he has been raped, the word "rape" is not used; the case is referred to as a "medical examiner's case." Before the Rape Treatment Center was organized, all victims in Dade County who reported a rape to the police were examined by the medical examiner or by one of three physicians who worked for him. Rape victims taken to Jackson Memorial Hospital were examined in Ward D, the old prison ward. ("Hardly a place conducive to rapport with a patient," notes Dr. Hicks.)

Now each victim is examined by one of the six physicians on the panel and offered medical treatment, including prophylaxis for gonorrhea or syphilis and DES to prevent pregnancy. In addition, the doctors do qualitative alkaline phosphatase testing and a microscopic examination for sperm to detect the presence of semen. Then they give the aspirate of the material—and any other physical evidence—to a police officer to be taken immediately to the crime laboratory where more precise tests are done. After the examination an appointment is made, if the victim chooses, for a follow-up medical examination in six weeks. Then a counselor from the hospital's crisis intervention center talks with the rape victim. The assault itself may not be the immediate crisis: Perhaps a woman is most upset that her husband will not believe her—or that her child saw the rape take place. Husbands and "significant others" also are eligible for counseling at the center. The counselor makes an appointment for another counseling session to determine if the patient will need extensive follow-up.

Contrary to what some might think, a woman who is treated at the center is not necessarily dealt with exclusively by women professionals.

"It is a fallacy to think that only another woman can be an effective counselor for a woman rape victim," says Dr. Hicks. "A sympathetic person who understands the problems is not necessarily female. In fact, some of our greatest difficulties have been encountered with women, such as a few nurses and a detective or two, who did not like rape and did not like rape victims. On the other hand, one of our best counselors is a man, and one of the kindest, most gentle detectives is a big, tall man." Dr. Hicks noted that the center does try to make certain that the nurse is a woman if the victim is a woman. For male rape victims, a male nurse is involved.

Is rape worse for men?

"We usually call in a male physician to examine and treat a male victim of sexual assault, even if I'm sitting right in the next room not doing anything," says Dr. Hicks. "We want to make our patients as comfortable as possible throughout, and the very last person a man—such as the 28-year-old who was brought here the other day—wants to see for examination and treatment is a woman physician. Sexual assault is much more difficult for a man to accept."

The victims are encouraged by the people at the center to report the rape even if they do not wish to prosecute. Each victim also is told about the Victims Advocates Program, an association set up to help someone get through the local legal maze if she or he wishes to prosecute.

"The chief reason the center works so well is cooperation," says Dr. Hicks. "I cannot stress this enough. We have great cooperation with the police department, the nursing staff, the hospital administration, and the medical school. We have had this right from the start, once the police realized that the doctors did not want to run the police department and once the doctors got over the false idea that the detectives wanted to run our departments.

"We are all interested in treating victims and catching rapists," she continues. "As far as I'm concerned, every woman who walks in that door who says she has been raped should be treated as if she were. It is not up to MDs to decide who has been raped—that's up to the courts.

"When I talk about rape I mean 'alleged rape.' If a woman even thinks she's been raped, we treat her as such, for she'll have all the psychologic trauma of someone who has been beaten up and raped," says Dr. Hicks.

As she sees it, a rape treatment center helps physicians and police officers as well as victims. A doctor practicing alone would see perhaps one or two rape victims in a year and would have trouble keeping the necessary chemicals fresh to run the simple laboratory tests, whereas the Miami center sees hundreds of women annually. The personnel know how to present physical evidence optimally to police detectives, who in turn hand it over to prosecuting attorneys. The center benefits police, because they know that they have one place to take a rape victim who reports the crime and that the physicians who treat the patient will know what to do to preserve the evidence.

Conviction rate up

Since the center opened, the conviction rate for rapists in Dade County has increased from 7 to 27%—in less than two years.

Who is the rapist?

Although she has been treating rape victims, Dr. Hicks also has found out quite a bit about who rapists are and how they operate. A study of 120 convicted rapists—under treatment at South Florida State Hospital in a sex offender program directed by psychologist D. Geraldine Boozer—reveals a number of interesting facts about men who rape.

Many started out as "peeping Toms" and then progressed to rape; a few began as exhibitionists. More than half of the group had been married while they were out raping women, and most had children. Usually, the man's wife was the last to suspect he was a rapist. Rapists tend to rape women at least once a week, although some raped three and four times a week. Convicted rapists said when they weren't raping a woman they were thinking about it. These men tended to become increasingly more violent with time, since it took progressively more violence to turn them on. Also, they tended to take weapons along with them as they kept on raping; a rapist often becomes more violent until he eventually kills someone.

Many of these men came from female-dominated homes where no males were present. A good many of them had been sexually assaulted themselves as children.

"Psychotherapy is helpful for these men," says Dr. Hicks. "Often they are fairly normal and productive except in this one serious area. Of the 120 men who volunteered or were assigned to the two- to three-year sex offender program, only seven were arrested again after parole—compared with a 57% recidivism rate for other convicted rapists."

However, Dr. Hicks is not against jailing rapists, even if it does not "cure" him. "If a rapist is incarcerated one year, that's saved some 50 women from being assaulted that year; a two-year term means that perhaps 100 women were spared. So we do need to get these people out of circulation."

Dr. Hicks does not spend all of her time in the Rape Treatment Center. She also is associate professor in the department of obstetrics and gynecology at the University of Miami School of Medicine, teaches medical students, sees patients, and directs the obstetrics and gynecology service in the emergency room. She joined the faculty in 1967, moving south and leaving her home state of Ohio. Born in Cleveland, Dr. Hicks received her MD in 1944 from Temple University School of Medicine in Philadelphia and returned to her home town for her internship. She spent four years in general practice in Cleveland before deciding she wanted a residency. After a few thoughts about ophthalmology, anesthesia, and radiology, she settled on obstetrics and was accepted at (Case) Western Reserve University Hospitals. She is a diplomate of the American Board of Obstetrics and Gynecology. At present she lives on one of the islands along Miami Beach with her three Belgian griffons and one 80-lb German shepherd who accompanies her on her evening walks.

Dr. Hicks and her colleagues want to see the Rape Treatment Center's services improved in time. "If we had some of our own money, we could hire counselors exclusively for the center. Rather than sending rape victims over to the crisis counseling center for follow-up work, all talking and counseling could be done right here," she says. She'd also like to set up a few rooms where victims could stay as long as they want, rather than having to return home shortly after treatment.

"At this time, education is one of our most important tasks," states Dr. Hicks. "Since our center has opened, I can see a difference in Dade County. Cases against rapists are tighter, conviction rates are up. Now judges are determining degrees of rape and sentencing accordingly. Also, judges are giving out sequential sentences to convicted rapists who have assaulted many women, so that it's a significant number of years before such a man is ready for parole.

"We must keep educating people about the fact that rape is a crime. Victims should not be treated as guilty, and victims should report the crimes, not hide them," she concludes.

The Marital Rape Exemption

Should rape be defined without reference to marital status? Should sex on demand be a marital obligation, enforcible by might? A recent law review article suggests that state legislatures should act promptly to eliminate or at least modify the general rule of law that a husband cannot be prosecuted in the case of forceful sex with his wife. The author condemns this "marital rape exemption" as supported by only outmoded rationales and a contradiction to the principle of equality in marriage.[1] If the exemption were indeed entirely abrogated, a wife would be entitled in the case of unpermitted sex to file a criminal complaint against her husband. Under the proposed recodification of federal criminal law (dealing with federal jurisdiction), forceful sexual intercourse committed by a spouse would constitute rape. The question remains, however, whether this proposed change is as desirable as its proponents, largely feminist and women's rights groups, claim or if other types of changes in the law governing rape prosecutions are more appropriate.

Formal recognition of the rape exemption in the common law dates from the seventeenth century. It has its genesis in a statement in Sir Matthew Hale's famous work, *The History of the Pleas of the Crown,* wherein it is stated:

> The husband cannot be guilty of a rape committed by himself upon his lawful wife, for by their mutual matrimonial consent and contract the wife hath given up herself in this kind unto her husband, which she cannot retract.[2]

On the strength of Lord Hale's statement, the husband's immunity from prosecution was recognized in the United States as early as 1857 in a Massachusetts case.[3] In most states, the rule remains unquestioned today.[4] The only way to convict a husband of raping his wife is if he forces her to have sexual relations with a third person.[5]

Much of what has been said so far depends, as is so often the case in the law, upon definitions of terms. "Husband" could include anyone legally married to the victim or only those legal spouses who are not the subject of a legal (court decree) separation or only those who are cohabitating with the woman at the time, whether they are legally married or not. In Michigan, Minnesota, and Nevada, to exclude the exemption, the husband and wife must not only be living apart, but also one of them must have filed for divorce or separate maintenance.[6]

Delaware and South Dakota recently eliminated the husband's exemption altogether. In Delaware, rape is classified in two degrees. Rape is in the first degree if the victim is not the defendant's voluntary social companion on the occasion of the offense and had not previously permitted him sexual contact. Marriage or previous sexual contact, however, does not negate a charge of rape in the second degree.[7] A husband has no defense to a charge of second-degree rape other than those accorded to any stranger charged with the same offense. For that matter, the husband is given no special priority over other men known to the wife. One would assume, however, that the fact of the couple's marital relation would be a relevant factor considered by a judge or jury when weighing, among other issues, an accused husband's proffered defense of consent. On the other hand, that is only a relevant factor after the husband has been charged with the crime and hauled into court to answer the charges.

There is in the Delaware statutory scheme an explicit inclusion of "persons living as man and wife, regardless of the legal status of their relationship" in the definition of husband and wife for purposes of other sexual offenses where the marital exemption is not eliminated.[8] Thus, any man living with the woman he attacks is protected from prosecution for "sexual assault," a class A misdemeanor, and "sexual misconduct," a class E felony,[9] as well as for first-degree rape; but the husband can be convicted of the "middle" offense of second-degree rape, a class B felony (which is punishable by from 3 to 30 years imprisonment). The logic of such a scheme is far from clear.

In South Dakota, the 1975 revision of its code on sex offenses includes a redefinition of the term "rape" which omits the earlier definition which had excluded husband–wife intercourse.[10] The notes to the revised law make it clear that the legislature did not intend to retain the exemption for husbands. Some have hailed this change in definition, like the Delaware change, as a welcome abrogation of the common law defense of marital status.[11]

In the thirteen or so states where the husband's immunity from prosecution is only judicially implied from the common law history growing out of Lord Hale's famous declaration, there is at least the possibility that the courts in those states will reevaluate the husband's exemption and remove it as a judicial revision of the common law. Such a change could be justified as a judicial revision of law originally written by judges in earlier cases.

That was argued in the recent case of *State v. Smith,*[12] where the state prosecutor uged that the New Jersey statute (which had no express provision for the exemption)[13] be judicially construed to prohibit all forcible sexual intercourse with a woman against her will regardless of the marital relation of the parties. The Essex County court concluded that the marital exemption must be judicially implied, since the court lacks authority to depart from the common law rule and create criminal responsibility where none had previously existed. The court devotes several pages of its lengthy opinion, however, to condemning the injustices of the exemption.

The court addressed the policy arguments that allowing husbands to be prosecuted would increase the risk of fabricated accusations, unduly invade the sanctity of the marriage relationship, increase the wife's ability to gain an advantage over an estranged husband with respect to property settlements, become a weapon of vengeance for the spurned wife, and lessen the likelihood of reconciliation, rejecting them all. The court first noted that the criminal justice system is well accustomed to dealing with false or fabricated charges, summarily dismissing as a "naked assertion" Lord Hale's statement that "It is an accusation easily to be made and hard to be proved and harder to be defended by the party accused, tho never so innocent."[14]

The court seems to have overlooked the logic behind Lord Hale's assertion. There will seldom be a witness to the sexual relations of a man and his wife, be they forcible or consensual. It will simply be his word against hers. The criminal law is accustomed to dealing with crimes with no witnesses but not with crimes with no evidence of a crime nor witnesses, as will be the case in any marital rape where there are no visible bruises. In fact, the response of the criminal law in such a situation has often been to deny the occurrence of a crime until some objective evidence can be found other than the allegations of a single aggrieved person.

The court also notes that there are false charges other than rape which a vengeful wife can allege against her husband, citing assault and battery, larceny, and fraud as specific offenses. It should be apparent, however, that none of these charges is as severely penalized by the law.

Lord Hale's statement that an allegation of rape by a husband is "easily to be made" points out the special position the wife holds with respect to her husband. If anyone knows the husband's darkest secrets, it is she. For that reason, the law of evidence as a general rule refuses to admit as evidence the testimony of a wife against her husband or vice versa. There is too great a chance for perjury, either way, depending on the feelings of the moment. It would allow the wife to hold a sword of Damocles over her husband.

The New Jersey court also belittles the proposition that allowing criminal prosecution of rape lessens the likelihood of reconciliation, stating that reconciliation is already highly unlikely where a relationship has deteriorated to the point of forcible sexual advances by the husband. The court fails to recognize, however, that it is not the case where there truly was a forcible rape that is objected to but those cases where an allegation of marital rape would be a spiteful part of a domestic quarrel. Lord Hale, noting that the allegation was "easily made," appreciated the likelihood that angry wives would recognize that as well.

Notes

(The research assistance of S. Lee Terry, Jr., third-year law student at Wayne State University, is gratefully acknowledged.)

1. Note, "The Marital Rape Exemption," 52 *N.Y.U. L. Rev.* 306, 322 (1977). See also Comment, "Rape and Rape Laws: Sexism in Society and Law," 61 *Calif. L. Rev.* 919, 925 (1973); Susan Brownmiller, *Against Our Will* (New York: Simon & Schuster, 1975), p. 428.
2. Matthew Hale, *The History of the Pleas of the Crown*, vol. 1, p. 629 (S. Emlyn ed. 1778).
3. *Commonwealth v. Fogarty*, 74 Mass. 489, 490 (1857).
4. Today, 27 states provide in their rape statutes for the husband's immunity. Of these states, 19 include this immunity in their definition of rape or sexual assault. Eight other states have separate statutory exemptions. In the states that do not provide for the exemption by statute, some 13 states, the courts have uniformly applied the common law rule.
5. *See* Annot., 84 *A.L.R.* 1017 (1962).
6. *Mich. Comp. Laws Ann.* § 750.520 (Supp. 1976); *Minn. Stat. Ann.* § 609.349 (Supp. 1976); *Nev. Rev. Stat.* § 200.373 (1975).
7. *Del. Code*, tit. 11, §§ 763, 764 (Supp. 1977).
8. *Del. Code*, tit. 11, § 772 (Supp. 1977).
9. *Del. Code*, tit. 11, §§ 761, 762 (1975).
10. *S.D. Compiled Laws Ann.* § 22-22-1 (Supp. 1976).
11. Note, "The Marital Rape Exemption," 52 *N.Y.U. L. Rev.* 306 at 317 (1977).
12. 148 N.J. Super. 219, 372 A.2d 386 (1977).
13. *N.J. Stat. Ann.* § 2A:138-1 (West 1969).
14. Hale, op. cit. at 634.

EROTICA and PORNOGRAPHY

A Clear and Present Difference

Gloria Steinem

Human beings are the only animals that experience the same sex drive at times when we can—and cannot—conceive.

Just as we developed uniquely human capacities for language, planning, memory, and invention along our evolutionary path, we also developed sexuality as a form of expression; a way of communicating that is separable from our need for sex as a way of perpetuating ourselves. For humans alone, sexuality can be and often is primarily a way of bonding, of giving and receiving pleasure, bridging differentness, discovering sameness, and communicating emotion.

We developed this and other human gifts through our ability to change our environment, adapt physically, and in the long run, to affect our own evolution. But as an emotional result of this spiraling path away from other animals, we seem to alternate between periods of exploring our unique abilities to forge new boundaries, and feelings of loneliness in the unknown that we ourselves have created; a fear that sometimes sends us back to the comfort of the animal world by encouraging us to exaggerate our sameness.

The separation of "play" from "work," for instance, is a problem only in the human world. So is the difference between art and nature, or an intellectual accomplishment and a physical one. As a result, we celebrate play, art, and invention as leaps into the unknown; but any imbalance can send us back to nostalgia for our primate past and the conviction that the basics of work, nature, and physical labor are somehow more worthwhile or even moral.

In the same way, we have explored our sexuality as separable from conception: a pleasurable, empathetic bridge to strangers of the same species. We have even invented contraception—a skill that has probably existed in some form since our ancestors figured out the process of birth—in order to extend this uniquely human difference. Yet we also have times of atavistic suspicion that sex is not complete—or even legal or intended-by-god—if it cannot end in conception.

No wonder the concepts of "erotica" and "pornography" can be so crucially different, and yet so confused. Both assume that sexuality can be separated from conception, and therefore can be used to carry a personal message. That's a major reason why, even in our current culture, both may be called equally "shocking" or legally "obscene," a word whose Latin derivative means "dirty, containing filth." This gross condemnation of all sexuality that isn't harnessed to childbirth and marriage has been increased by the current backlash against women's progress. Out of fear that the whole patriarchal structure might be upset if women really had the autonomous power to decide our reproductive futures (that is, if we controlled the most basic means of production), right-wing groups are not only denouncing prochoice abortion literature as "pornographic," but are trying to stop the sending of all contraceptive information through the mails by invoking obscenity laws. In fact, Phyllis Schlafly recently denounced the entire Women's Movement as "obscene."

Not surprisingly, this religious, visceral backlash has a secular, intellectual counterpart that relies heavily on applying the "natural" behavior of the animal world to humans. That is questionable in itself, but these Lionel Tiger-ish studies make their political purpose even more clear in the particular animals they select and the habits they choose to emphasize.* The message is that females should accept their "destiny" of being sexually dependent and devote themselves to bearing and rearing their young.

*See "The Law of the Jungle (Revised)," by Cynthia Moss, *Ms.*, January, 1978.

porn-, por'no-. From Greek *pornē*, prostitute (prob. from *pernemi*, sell, as captives) . . . **por-nog'ra-phy,** *n.* **1.** Description of prostitutes and of prostitution . . . **2.** The expression or suggestion of the obscene in speaking, writing, etc.; licentious art or literature. **e-rot'ic,** *a.* Of or pertaining to passionate love or sexual desire; suggested by or treating of love; amorous; amatory. . . . *n.* **1.** *Lit.* An amatory composition, especially in poetry. **2.** *sing.* or *pl.* A theory or science of love. —*from "Funk & Wagnalls New Standard Dictionary of the English Language."*

Defending against such reaction in turn leads to another temptation: to merely reverse the terms, and declare that *all* nonprocreative sex is good. In fact, however, this human activity can be as constructive or destructive, moral or immoral, as any other. Sex as communication can send messages as different as life and death; even the origins of "erotica" and "pornography" reflect that fact. After all, "erotica" is rooted in *eros* or passionate love, and thus in the idea of positive choice, free will, the yearning for a particular person. (Interestingly, the definition of erotica leaves open the question of gender.) "Pornography" begins with a root meaning "prostitution" or "female captives," thus letting us know that the subject is not mutual love, or love at all, but domination and violence against women. (Though, of course, homosexual pornography may imitate this violence by putting a man in the "feminine" role of victim.) It ends with a root meaning "writing about" or "description of" which puts still more distance between subject and object, and replaces a spontaneous yearning for closeness with objectification and a voyeur.

The difference is clear in the words. It becomes even more so by example.

Look at any photo or film of people making love; really making love. The images may be diverse, but there is usually a sensuality and touch and warmth, an acceptance of bodies and nerve endings. There is always a spontaneous sense of people who are there because they *want* to be, out of shared pleasure.

Now look at any depiction of sex in which there is clear force, or an unequal power that spells coercion. It may be very blatant, with weapons of torture or bondage, wounds and bruises, some clear humiliation, or an adult's sexual power being used over a child. It may be much more subtle: a physical attitude of conqueror and victim, the use of race or class difference to imply the same thing, perhaps a very unequal nudity, with one person exposed and vulnerable while the other is clothed. In either case, there is no sense of equal choice or equal power.

The first is erotic: a mutually pleasurable, sexual expression between people who have enough power to be there by positive choice. It may or may not strike a sense-memory in the viewer, or be creative enough to make the unknown seem real; but it doesn't require us to identify with a conqueror or a victim. It is truly sensuous, and may give us a contagion of pleasure.

The second is pornographic: its message is violence, dominance, and conquest. It is sex being used to reinforce some inequality, or to create one, or to tell us the lie that pain and humiliation (ours or someone else's) are really the same as pleasure. If we are to feel anything, we must identify with conqueror or victim. That means we can only experience pleasure through the adoption of some degree of sadism or masochism. It also means that we may feel diminished by the role of conqueror, or enraged, humiliated, and vengeful by sharing identity with the victim.

Perhaps one could simply say that erotica is about sexuality, but pornography is about power and sex-as-weapon—in the same way we have come to understand that rape is about violence, and not really about sexuality at all.

Yes, it's true that there are women who have been forced by violent families and dominating men to confuse love with pain; so much so that they have become masochists. (A fact that in no way excuses those who administer such pain.) But the truth is that, for most women—and for men with enough humanity to imagine themselves into the predicament of women—true pornography could serve as aversion therapy for sex.

Of course, there will always be personal differences about what is and is not erotic, and there may be cultural differences for a long time to come. Many women feel that sex makes them vulnerable and therefore may continue to need more sense of personal connection and safety before allowing any erotic feelings. We now find competence and expertise erotic in men, but that may pass as we develop those qualities in ourselves. Men, on the other hand, may continue to feel less vulnerable, and therefore more open to such potential danger as sex with strangers. As some men replace the need for submission from childlike women with the pleasure of cooperation from equals, they may find a partner's competence to be erotic, too.

Such group changes plus individual differences will continue to be reflected in sexual love between people of the same gender, as well as between women and men. The point is not to dictate sameness, but to discover ourselves and each other through sexuality that is an exploring, pleasurable, empathetic part of our lives; a human sexuality that is unchained both from unwanted pregnancies and from violence.

But that is a hope, not a reality. At the moment, fear of change is increasing both the indiscriminate repression of all nonprocreative sex in the religious and "conservative" male world, and the pornographic vengeance against women's sexuality in the secular world of "liberal" or "radical" men. It's almost futuristic to debate what is and is not truly erotic, when many women are again being forced into compulsory motherhood, and the number of pornographic murders, tortures, and woman-hating images are on the increase in both popular culture and real life.

It's a familiar division: wife or whore, "good" woman who is constantly vulnerable to pregnancy or "bad" woman who is unprotected from violence. *Both* roles would be upset if we were to control our own sexuality. And that's exactly what we must do.

In spite of all our atavistic suspicions and training for the "natural" role of motherhood, we took up the complicated battle for reproductive freedom. Our bodies had borne the health burden of endless births and poor abortions, and we had a greater motive for separating sexuality and conception.

Now we have to take up the equally complex burden of explaining that all nonprocreative sex is *not* alike. We have a motive: our right to a uniquely human sexuality, and sometimes even to survival. As it is, our bodies have too rarely been enough our own to develop erotica in our own lives, much less in art and literature. And our bodies have too often been the objects of pornography and the woman-hating, violent practice that it preaches. Consider also our spirits that break a little each time we see ourselves in chains or full labial display for the conquering male viewer, bruised or on our knees, screaming a real or pretended pain to delight the sadist, pretending to enjoy what we don't enjoy, to be blind to the images of our sisters that really haunt us—humiliated often enough ourselves by the truly obscene idea that sex and the domination of women must be combined.

Sexuality *is* human, free, separate —and so are we.

But until we untangle the lethal confusion of sex with violence, there will be more pornography and less erotica. There will be little murders in our beds—and very little love.

BISEXUALITY: A CHOICE NOT AN ECHO?

A Very Personal Confession by "Orlando"

I used to be hopelessly heterosexual.

It wasn't that I didn't love women—my closest, most comfortable friendships were with other women; and while I often wished I could share that same intimacy with a man, I wasn't even sure if it was possible, much less how to make it happen. In practice I judged men by an entirely different yardstick, giving them lavish credit and gratitude for things I would almost take for granted in women. But I had undeniably fallen in love with several men, even married one. And I loved their bodies. Even after I no longer needed men for social affirmation, economic support, or children, I still loved to look at them, and to touch them.

As for women's bodies, the possibility barely crossed my consciousness until I joined the Feminist Movement in 1969 and for the first time began dealing with lesbians, and with lesbianism as a political issue. I remember having terribly sincere discussions with the other heterosexual women in my consciousness-raising group, in which we'd gamely acknowledge that if we ever got truly fed up with men, we might be able to close our eyes and let a lesbian make love to us. But actively delighting in another woman's body? Flirting with a woman? Falling in *love* with a woman? It was the dark side of the moon.

Years later, at a particularly restless and lonely point in my life, a woman I liked propositioned me. My response—if I can reduce a complex swirl of emotions to two words—was, *why not*? I couldn't imagine sleeping with her, but the idea of having sex with a person who was already a friend was overwhelmingly appealing to me.

Since then, I've come to think of myself as bisexual—although let me say right up front that I dislike sexual labels. Worse, "bisexual" has always sounded to me like a description of someone who has sex either twice a week or every other week. "Ambisexual" would probably be a better label, but I'll use the conventional term here for shorthand clarity.

A friend of mine who's into astrology claims that bisexuality was predestined for me by Gemini rising and lots of exotic goings-on in the fifth house, but when I look back at the particular twists of circumstance that eventually led to my bisexual identity, I can imagine it happening differently or not at all.

By the time I met the woman with whom I had the most intense sexual experiences of my life, I had been having perfectly satisfying sex with men for 15 years. I had also already had an affair with a woman which, while important to me in many ways, was far less physically charged than any of my heterosexual relationships. If I'd never hooked up so passionately with the second woman, I might consider myself a confirmed heterosexual today. Had I met her earlier, I might have danced off to join the Amazon Nation. And while I didn't start sleeping with women to be "politically correct" as a radical feminist, it's obvious that without the context of the Women's Movement, the option of lesbian relationships probably never would have been something I could slide into so positively. Then again I could fall madly, monogamously, in love with someone (male or female) tomorrow. My dreams and fantasies could remain bisexual; I could continue to be sometimes equally attracted to the male and female star at the movies; still, the world would define me not by my own sexuality, but by my lover's gender.

While the sexual case histories of bisexuals vary wildly in almost every other respect, this same quirk-of-fate, right-person-at-the-right-time pattern is common, and I suspect that it's the source of a great many negative stereotypes. Plenty of people, both homosexual and heterosexual, have a strong investment in believing that sexual preference is immutably fixed at an early age—which may be true in many cases but is demonstrably not in others. It's far less threatening to view bisexuals as warped in childhood than as adults who *choose* to act on pleasurable opportunities available to all of us. (Several heterosexual friends of mine who comfortably support "gay rights" from a distance were nonetheless thrown into personal turmoil by my bisexuality. "If you're so much like me as a *heterosexual*" said one, "it makes me wonder if maybe I could have this whole other side, too—and I don't want to.")

New York psychoanalyst Robert E. Gould, from his own practice and workshops, estimates that about 10 percent of all women and 15 percent of all men in this country behave bisexually for at least part of their lives, and the percentages may be increasing. According to a wide-ranging 1977 survey of women of all ages and backgrounds at the outpatient Gynecological Unit of the University of California Medical Center in San Francisco, bisexuality may also be an increasingly attractive lifestyle: while only 3 percent of those interviewed considered themselves bisexual, 28 percent "envisioned bisexuality as a future possibility." Almost all of these were heterosexuals who saw lesbian relationships as "potentially more loving, more satisfying, and, especially, more intimate."

Bisexuality has also recently become a television talk-show staple and the subject of numerous books, some of them of the schlock Swingers-Who-Lead-Double-Lives variety and others quite well meaning. Even the supportive literature frequently collapses, however, under the weight of attempts to pinpoint "the bisexual personality" or "the bisexual experience." (Can you imagine a book defining "the heterosexual personality"?) Unlike homosexuals, bisexuals have no discernible subculture, no developed political position, and *less* in common with each other sexually than homosexuals or heterosexuals. (Two researchers who do recognize this diversity are Drs. Pepper Schwartz and Philip Blumstein of the University of Washington, who write that "the most fundamental conclusion" from their studies has been that "the data defy organization.") This article, in fact, doesn't pretend to speak for anyone's feelings but mine.

Still, the stereotypes persist: bisexuals are faddishly shallow—and sick. "They don't know where they're at, like Jell-O that has never set," according to New York psychologist Natalie Shainess, "because they're too immature in their sense of gender."

We are also seen as promiscuous, decadent, kinky. While homosexuals may consider us cop-outs in the gay struggle, heterosexuals tend to see any nonheterosexual's sex life as the definitive aspect about her or him, just as whites are too often obsessed with someone's blackness. By this logic, bisexuals are presumably twice as sexual, especially if we're women—who are traditionally viewed primarily in carnal terms anyway. I sometimes find it jarring if not painful to realize that some people assume I spend most of my time in bed, doing anything and everything with anyone and everyone. (It happens that the majority of my affairs have been long-term relationships, sometimes simultaneously with a few people I cared about, other times monogamously. Still other times I've had periods of celibacy.)

Above all, bisexuals supposedly do not really exist. We are considered either closet lesbians who can't martial sufficient loyalty to our own sex, or adventuristic "straights" out to prove how liberated we are. (I think that as a feminist I find this accusation the most infuriating of all, since it implies either way that I use and trivialize women.) Those of us who *do* refuse to be labeled as "gay" or "straight" are expected to lead precisely balanced lives resembling a sexual Chinese banquet, with equal selections from Column A and Column B.

My own life is predominantly heterosexual, a circumstance I attribute not to some innate straightness (or some concomitant fear of lesbianism), but to the fact that 90 percent of the people I meet who are attracted to *me* are heterosexual men. I led a predominantly lesbian existence for more than six months a few years ago, most of which time I was involved with one woman. Although I recognize that it's unusual and hard for many people to accept, I feel I have no sexual preference.

I have known, or know of, other male and female bisexuals who may have a distinct sexual preference but are committed to a specific person of the nonpreferred gender; who have no sexual preference but feel a social or political pull toward either the "gay" or "straight" world; who derive very different sexual and/or emotional satisfaction from men and women, and need both; who have a definite sexual preference but "make do" with the nonpreferred gender; who like sleeping with both sexes but only fall in love with one; who are fundamentally homosexual or heterosexual but enamored of the idea of bisexuality; whose sexual preference seems to go in cycles at different times of their lives; or whose only bisexual experience is within group sex.

Not all of these people would call themselves bisexual. I've also known "lesbians" who are strongly attracted to men but are held back by social pressure and by fears of vulnerability. And I've known "heterosexual" women who are drawn toward lesbianism but fail to act on their feelings for exactly the same reasons.

Homosexuals and heterosexuals alike often distrust bisexuals, but some of that feeling stems from their stereotypes about each *other*. At the extreme end of the lesbian spectrum, we have the folk wisdom that "only a woman can really understand another woman's body," and that all male-female sex is inherently a form of rape. The parallel heterosexual line presupposes that the "natural" penis-vagina combination is unbeatable, and that lesbian sex amounts to no more than kissy-face snuggling.

My heterosexual friends, both male and female, have almost all assumed at first that my bisexuality springs from political conviction at best, masochism at worst. (After all, if one can "choose," who wouldn't choose the most socially acceptable kind of sex?) It is hard to convince them that I do not need an ulterior motive to sleep with a woman. One male lover of mine was dazzled by the concept of dating such a groovy lady until I persuaded him that my lesbian affairs were serious, and not engaged in to score Groovy Lady points—and then he didn't see me for two months. Similarly, I think that one of the reasons bisexuals are so disdained in sections of the lesbian feminist community is that we challenge the cherished myth that heterosexual women just don't know what they're missing.

Often layered on top of this homosexual-heterosexual rivalry is the taboo of male-female competition. Even people who are totally comfortable with nonmonogamy can get frantic at the idea of sharing a bisexual lover with the opposite gender. For instance, a common opinion among lesbian feminists is that bisexual women are quick to use other women for sexual pleasure, but that they will never ultimately choose a woman over that powerful ticket to respectability—a man.

Heterosexual men, at the same time, have been brainwashed all their lives into seeing women as the objectified "sexy" sex and even the most arrogant of men often have little inner sense of male physical beauty, at least not beyond the penis. Nor have they been socialized to deal with "losing" to a woman. Probably all of us, male and female, are programmed to believe at some level that men are the winners in the world and women are the beauties and these "opposites" will forever attract. A bisexual lover may make a nonbisexual feel inadequate about her or his "lack" of the "opposite" quality.

A man involved with a heterosexual woman, for example, never suffers anxiety that his own supposed lack of beauty will cause him to lose her to a woman; he only fears other "winners," but he knows how to compete with them. As a bisexual woman, I find it difficult to convince heterosexual men (or lesbian women) that I am capable of loving anyone totally, since I must always be theoretically longing for what only the other gender can give me. (Some bisexuals, indeed, only sleep with other bisexuals.)

I tend to look for the same personality traits in both men and women, and the same sexual qualities as well. In my own less-than-encyclopedic experience, I've found more sexual variation between people than between genders: I've had lovers of both sexes who were intuitive, experimental, sensual, multiorgasmic, intimate, passionate, aggressive, gentle, passive, klutzy, egomaniacal, prudish, and inconsiderate. Obviously, male and female bodies are different—but so are large and small bodies within the same sex, and I don't know too many people who consider that an identity-shattering dichotomy. When you love, you don't care deeply whether someone's short or tall; it's the person *inside* the body that counts, and for me gender—like size for other people—is a relatively minor adjustment.

Dr. Fred Klein, author of *The Bisexual Option* (Arbor House), claims that "the bisexual sees potential sex partners first as human beings and then as sexual objects," and that virtually all of his interview subjects have reported a "feeling of wholeness" about themselves. I strongly identify with Klein's concept, but I would add that such "wholeness" must also be predicated on feminism, without which bisexuals can't hope to relate to their lovers as equally-valued individuals. The duality implicit in the very word "bisexual" (not to mention such gems as "a.c. / d.c." and "switch-hitter") is the antithesis of what I experience. If anything, I personally felt bifurcated when I was a feminist with exclusively heterosexual love affairs: all of my sexual energies were zooming off in one direction and my friendships in the other.

More than anything else, I've come to cherish the *vantage point* of bisexuality. For one thing, it keeps me honest. While I certainly bring the requisite number of neuroses into any affair, when things get sticky I often have only to ask myself, "would I accept this kind of behavior from a woman (or a man)?" as the litmus test for tolerable misery. (For example, I've tended to be more accepting of coldness from men and manipulativeness from women.) Bisexuality has also forced me to confront—and change—some close-to-the-bone assumptions about virtually everything: love, friendship, men, women, feminism, and myself.

For years I was married to a painfully self-controlled, self-absorbed man. I loved him desperately, in the truest martyred sense of the word, and I spent a lot of time feeling inadequate for not being Superwoman enough to inspire him to meet my own apparently voracious emotional needs. Because he hadn't been the only such man in my life, I concluded—with a boost from the Women's Movement—that maybe men were just "like that." In fact, too many of them *are*—and if a shrink had told me I was neurotically drawn to ungiving men, I would have dismissed her out of hand for bad politics.

The first woman I slept with was superficially very different from my ex-husband: she cried, and she talked about her feelings. And yet within weeks we were living-out a lesbian-cloned version of my marriage, with me speaking all my old reliable script lines. This time I was turbulently thrown back on myself, minus any convenient feminist truisms about Men Out Of Touch With Their Emotions. That experience galvanized me in a way that no heterosexual relationship ever could have, and the psychological digging that followed literally changed my life.

I was also to learn that certain problems I had always attributed to male-female relationships were simply perils of sexual relationships, period (*i.e.*, jealousy, lack of communication, sexual pressure, and controlling behavior) and that some (by no means all) of the easy sisterhood between heterosexual women stems from the fact that we lack the power to hurt each other that sexual relationships uniquely provide.

Probably the keynote emotion of my early lesbian experiences was vulnerability. Women who recognize their lesbian feelings at a young age no doubt gradually learn to integrate their sexual impulses with all of the usual clothes-borrowing, secret-sharing, late-night-giggling comforts associated with female friendship. In my case, it was a crash course. I was suddenly having rotten affairs with women I might ordinarily confide in about some rotten affair with a man. And I was incredibly naïve.

I have never, for instance, been particularly moved by men whose wives don't understand them, but one woman I cared for, who was always on the verge of leaving the imperfect man she lived with, had me on a hook for months. And while being treated like a "cunt" by a man doesn't exactly brighten the day, I was absolutely devastated by a woman who seduced me once and then refused even to have lunch with me. Not to mention another woman who was extremely confused about lesbianism, frequently wished out loud that I was a man, and once told me that she sometimes had to repress vomit at the thought of my body and What We Did. I thought I was a failure with women. But after a rotten heterosexual encounter, I had always refused to write off "men" in general, and it was probably only my feminist sense that I owed women the same benefit of the doubt that prevented me from giving up on lesbianism completely after these experiences.

Sex with women, on the other hand, was surprisingly natural. The only part that seemed to me to take forever to learn was responding to women *outside* of bed. That was another matter. After years as a more-flirtatious-than-average heterosexual, I didn't have the faintest idea how to behave seductively with a woman. A man might think I was "accidentally" touching his thigh or just happening to bend over provocatively, but another woman would see right through me. Surely she would hoot with laughter? I was also so focused on *who* I was sleeping with that I was slow to see my early lesbian experience in purely sexual terms or to extrapolate it to women in general.

I remember my second woman lover idly asking me one day if I didn't love the fact that women were soft. As idiotic as it sounds to me now, I had never really noticed it before. Today the softness of women, their smoothness and wetness and smallness, and the intense identification that one can sometimes feel with another woman's body are as erotically powerful for me as any quality of a male body has ever been. But it *was* a learned response.

I suspect that there's an analogy between bisexuality and bilingualism: if you learn a second language as an adult, even if you come to think and dream in it, the learning process is still going to be different from the one you experienced as a one-year-old. To pursue the analogy, a bilingual person has a different perspective on her native language than a person who's never spoken anything else. When I have sex with a man now, the experience is no longer what it was when I was heterosexual. I approach it as a bisexual—*because I know what he's responding to.* Because I have loved women, I know what it feels like for him to love me. Sometimes this double vision can be dizzyingly erotic; always it gives me feelings of empathy for men that were never there before.

On the other hand, bisexuality has made me less stereotypically "sexy" with men. As a heterosexual, I was supremely confident in bed, but only because I knew I had all the poses and moves down pat. No matter how loving the man was, he (or some *Playboy* consortium of "men") was still the authority between us on what constituted appropriate female sexual behavior. Feminism certainly made a dent in all of that for me, but only up to a point. As a bisexual, I *know*, beyond hearsay or rhetoric, that a woman doesn't have to have a perfect body to be sexy to me, that menstrual blood isn't revolting, and that I don't die if a woman tells me what she likes in bed. That knowledge equalizes the authority and gives me a very different kind of confidence with men—to be myself.

In fact, one of the most dramatic side effects of bisexuality for me has been the way it's revolutionized my dealings with men. I didn't plan it that way, certainly. (Even as I write this, I can hear thousands of lesbian readers groaning: *oh, no—she's telling us to sleep with women to improve our sex lives with men.*) But it's important to acknowledge that once men were deprived of the monopoly on the commodity I seemed to be addicted to, *i.e.*, S-E-X, a whole layer of resentment toward them vanished.

I also remember having a hideous anxiety attack within hours after I first slept with a woman: now that sexual tension was theoretically possible with all of my women friends, I wondered, would I start feeling the same painful emotional distance from them that I'd associated with men? I swore to myself that the answer was going to be no. But as I consciously worked to integrate my feelings for women, I gradually began having very different kinds of relationships with men as well, both lovers and nonlovers. Three of my most valued friends today are men I had long sexual involvements with. Those sexual friendships in turn helped give me the inspiration to get over my negative early lesbian experiences and to open myself up to the possibility of falling in love with a woman again. With both sexes, I seem to have come full circle.

All of which is not to suggest a touchy-feely attitude that men and women are just identical human folks. I am a feminist. Men have caste privileges and socialized expectations that enrage me. In any relationship that I have with a man, there is going to be a certain focus of tension around the way he responds to the demands of feminism and the way *I* deal with the fury I feel for the options available even to a feminist man—a fury that wouldn't enter the equation with a nonfeminist woman who, at bottom, at least shares my oppression. And while I've never experienced any homophobic self-hatred myself, in any relationship I have with a woman, the pressures of homophobia from the outside world are bound to be lurking there.

The point is that I have my choice of fighting other people's homophobia or sexism, even at the most mundane level, whether in the form of a man on the street gawking at me holding hands with a woman (*is she flinching? should we do this? how can I ignore him?*) or a waiter automatically proffering the wine to the man I'm with (*doesn't he know this isn't trivial? will he say something? should I?*). With men, it's also a matter of breaking down barriers of difference to get to what is common between us; whereas, with women, it's a question of seeing that our sameness is partly an illusion, and that we have to go deeper. They are simply two very different arenas. And I sometimes think that if I ever decide to be exclusively "gay" or "straight," it will have more to do with my choice of arenas than my choice of body types.

I am also not one of those trendy people who believes that "we are all bisexual," or that bisexuality is the only (or the best) way to achieve that fabled humanist wholeness. There *is*, for most adults, such a thing as sexual preference. (Most of us, for that matter, have sexual tastes totally apart from gender. A friend of mine once noted—not without a grain of accuracy—that everybody I like, male or female, looks a little like Al Pacino.) Occasionally I do find myself guilty of the sexual chauvinism I deplore in homosexuals and heterosexuals. It usually takes the form of imagining that I am some advanced, evolved, postrevolutionary sexual being. The crash comes within about 20 minutes when something happens to remind me that I'm living in prerevolutionary times.

Bisexuality can be fatiguingly *complicated*. I hate the fact that some heterosexual women feel uncomfortable being alone with me, and that some heterosexual men find me titillating for all the wrong reasons. I resent the fact that while I'm vulnerable to all the antigay bigotry in the world today, I can expect very little support from most of the "gay community." Most of all, I am troubled by the way that bisexuality can be used against me as an instant lavender herring—especially by my lovers.

Several years ago, not long after a decidedly unamicable separation from my ex-husband, I got involved with a delicious and intelligent woman who was exactly the kind of person I wanted to fall in love with someday—after I played out the usual postmarital nonmonogamous phase I was going through. I was also terrified about my bisexuality being discovered before the separation wounds had healed and turned into the focus of a gory child-custody case, for which I then had zero money and even less emotional energy.

My lover had more experience with women than I, and we fought constantly about what she deemed my insufficient commitment to lesbianism. Totally obscured in the bickering was any discussion of whether either of us was strong enough and so fully committed to each other to withstand a relationship that could potentially shake up both our lives. The answer was no—and when, at her prodding, I let myself fall in love with her, the results were disastrous.

Months later, still in shock, I began seeing a man who was every bit as delicious and intelligent as the woman had been. The man was interested in a serious, long-term relationship. I had just emerged from several, thank you. As soon as I told him that my recent lover had been a woman—mainly in the interests of not having to fudge my pronouns any longer—everything changed. All problems, sexual and emotional, became proof positive that I was a Lesbian Who Couldn't Love Men. Even when he didn't say it, I knew he was thinking it. Totally obscured *this* time around was any dialogue about the best way for me to give him some commitment and for him to give me some space. I finally refused to sleep with him any more. The man at least has since become a very dear friend (the woman has not), but for a long time, looking back on both of those relationships made me ache all over.

At various points in the writing of this article, I've found myself wondering what difference it would have made If I'd Known Then What I Know Now. The truth is that despite some erroneous preconceptions and some dumb mistakes along the way, I'm happy with my bisexuality, for reasons having to do with much more than sexual options.

Given the choice I'd do it all over again. I would readily concede that heterosexuality is more socially acceptable and less complicated—but so are a lot of other things I have no regrets about not pursuing. As a state of mind for me, bisexuality somehow *fits*. Like feminism or motherhood or work, it also happens to have been a conduit for changes I never planned on but which are now so much a part of me that I can't imagine life otherwise. More than that, it's been a way (not *the* way, but my way) to begin to transcend barriers of human difference and reach for the androgynous inner selves in me and in others that exist in and beyond sexual ecstasy.

"Orlando" is a pseudonym used by the writer to protect the privacy of people described in her article.

The Meaning of Gay

An interview with Dr. C. A. Tripp by Philip Nobile

Philip Nobile is a contributing editor of New York *Magazine.*

n the whole, Freud preferred shipping homosexuals off to South America. The Roman church would send them even farther south and for all eternity. And while homosexuality is no longer classed as a mental disorder by the American Psychiatric Association, even now, ten years after the Stonewall riot, which sparked the gay activist movement, homosexuals are still in trouble in our society. Many folk, including neo-conservatives, Right-to-Lifers, and born-again Christians, to mention but a few, continue to regard homosexuality as a threat to the harmony between the sexes.

Kinsey had intended to meet the homosexual scare head-on in a sequel to his landmark male and female volumes. He reported in *Sexual Behavior in the Human Male* that a third of American men had at least one homosexual experience to orgasm, but he died before he could spell out in his painstaking inductive fashion the significance of same-sex activity. Had Kinsey lived a few more years, the "homosexual question" might not be as muddled today.

The publication four years ago of *The Homosexual Matrix,* an exceedingly controversial study by psychologist Dr. C. A. Tripp, owed much to Kinsey. Tripp was a protégé of Kinsey's and rather than allow many of Kinsey's original ideas to remain unpublished he decided to carry out the project himself. Tripp feels Kinsey and he are compatible on all the major issues. "He thought, and I agree, that the potential for homosexual behavior is consistent in every society, but its expression is determined by specific cultural supports or restrictions."

Tripp's view of homosexuality is bold and unsettling. It is supported by natural history and anthropology and is replete with startling insights into heterosexuality as well as homosexuality. He argues that friendship and compatibility eventually kill zestful sex and; conversely, that only some sort of resistance, barrier, or distance keeps partners revved up for each other. He also notes that homosexuality, like heterosexuality, originates in a positive attraction rather than in a fear of something else (e.g., a dominating mother, castration anxiety, identity problems, *vagina dentata,* etc.). He points out for the first time that homosexuality is even higher in competitive and macho societies than in societies where there are no taboos against it.

Dr. Tripp's career is impressive if somewhat unusual. He left his small hometown of Corsicana, Texas, at eighteen to study photography at the Rochester Institute of Technology in 1938. He subsequently joined the Kodak Research Laboratories. After enlisting in the navy in 1942, he was purportedly discharged on medical grounds but was in fact transferred undercover to Twentieth Century–Fox laboratories in New York City, where he assisted in the production of confidential films for the army and navy.

After the war, Tripp opened up a photo studio in Greenwich Village. But his interests were turning toward human behavior, and he began to immerse himself in psychiatric literature. Under the tutelage of the prominent Freud disciple Theodor Reik, he prepared to become a lay analyst. Reik, impressed by his initiate's intuitive grasp of the subject, recommended him to a publisher to prepare a cross-index of psychoanalysis. (Tripp has a photographic memory, or at least an instant recall of stored data; one evening a friend of his interrupted our interview to inquire about extramarital intercourse in young men. "You'll find a chart on that on page 586 in Kinsey," he told his friend immediately. I checked the reference, and Tripp was right.)

In 1948, Tripp read Kinsey's male volume and called him with a long list of questions. Kinsey kindly invited this inquisitive stranger for a weekend visit to his Institute for Sex Research in Bloomington, Indiana. Kinsey admired Tripp's roving curiosity and critical mind and promptly began to disabuse him of Freudian dogma. The conversion went smoothly, and thus began a working partnership that lasted until Kinsey's death in 1956.

At Kinsey's urging, Tripp returned to school in 1951. Six years later he had his B.A. and Ph.D. In 1960, Tripp went into private practice on Central Park West. He reduced his predominantly heterosexual patient load to one day a week in order to complete *The Homosexual Matrix.*

His research was extensive: Tripp

duplicated Kinsey's European tour, made eleven trips to Puerto Rico to compare and contrast Spanish and American sexual mores; he interviewed over 700 homosexuals; he debriefed scores of field anthropologists for cross-cultural information; he used much of Kinsey's unpublished data, and during the last two decades has closely observed homosexuals in many occupations and at every social level.

Whether or not one assents to the theories of Dr. Tripp, he brilliantly advances the discussion of homosexuality beyond the anathemas of psychiatry, the manifestos of gay lib, and the ignorance of common supposition.

In this interview for *New York* Magazine I asked Dr. Tripp to go beyond the ideas in his book and to define the meaning of gay.

Nobile: *Does homosexuality threaten the survival of the species?*

Tripp: Hardly. Its consequences are too trivial for that, and anyway societies with the highest homosexual rates invariably have high birth rates. We know why too; the moral strictures of a society where homosexuality is constrained usually also restrict heterosexuality. Thus where anti-sexual edicts are relaxed, in Moslem countries, for example, both forms of sex tend to increase, with a consequent rise in the birth rate.

Q. Is homosexuality a biological aberration?

A. Years ago when it was thought that some instinct produces heterosexuality, homosexual variations were ipso facto "deviant." But we now know that due to certain evolutionary changes in the brain of man and other anthropoids, sexual preferences (and the value systems that control them) have to be learned. And they're learned in response to the lure of real or imagined advantages, not, as psychiatry has thought, in response to dominant mothers, neglectful fathers, or fears of something else. You don't like blondes because you hate brunettes.

We can thoroughly discount heredity. As Kinsey noted, even if homosexuals were wiped out of today's population, the incidence of homosexuality in the next generation would not necessarily be reduced. Moreover, if hormones, genes, and other biological influences had any significant effect, then homosexuality, like left-handedness, would be quite stable cross-culturally—instead of varying as it does from nearly zero in some societies to pervasive in others.

Q. In the forties Kinsey found that 4 percent of American men and about a third as many women were predominantly homosexual. Do these statistics still hold?

A. According to recent studies by the Institute for Sex Research they do, and it's a double surprise. Many laymen have thought the sexual revolution with its endless talk of homosexuality must surely have increased it. Sex researchers half-expected the same "loosening" of the mores to *reduce* homosexuality, mainly by permitting easier and earlier heterosexual experience. Both theories proved wrong. A greater readiness to talk about sexual variations doesn't mean people are quickly ready to adopt them. And while it is true that the younger generation's age-at-first-intercourse has been dropping in recent years, the stability of the homosexual figures suggests that the die is cast at much younger ages.

Q. Can one always spot a homosexual?

A. Absolutely not. Even expert sex researchers such as the original Kinsey group could only manage to detect some 15 percent of homosexual males and about 5 percent of homosexual females. And they were relying on several cues—dress, circumstance, referral, and so on. By the way, effeminacy was not an important cue in these observations since only a fraction of homosexuals are effeminate, and, besides, heterosexuals often show such signs. Furthermore, a great many people involved in homosexuality are the opposite of what the layman would expect, meaning that they are macho males of the truck driver–cowboy–lumberjack variety.

Q. Although effeminacy cannot be equated with homosexuality, is it not true that the greater number of effeminate men are indeed homosexual?

A. I would guess more than 85 percent of the overtly effeminate males are homosexual. But at the same time certainly more than 90 percent of homosexuals show no effeminacy.

Q. What is the connection between supermacho types and homosexuality?

A. Those he-man types place great emphasis on maleness and male values —and thus have an extraordinary tendency to eroticize male attributes, which is, after all, what most male homosexuality is all about.

Q. Why should certain professions —hairdressing, interior decorating, dance, and fashion—attract more than their share of the homosexual population?

A. For a couple of reasons. In this culture, certain jobs are thought to be effete, and heterosexuals are reticent to take them. Homosexuals, on the other hand, are not inhibited by this connotation and feel free to fill these openings. The other factor is more elusive—a question of disposition. Take music, for example. I checked the Eastman School of Music in the forties and the Juilliard in the fifties and found that homosexuality is relatively frequent among pianists and organists and yet notably rare among violinists. And in certain branches of foreign service—the British foreign service, for example—there has been a predominance of homosexuals. Here there are many interlocking correlations, such as the homosexual's frequent talent for linguistics and often his special interest in foreign lands.

Q. Speaking of foreign lands, how would a geographic survey of homosexuality look?

A. Like a crazy quilt of incidences. Among small tribal societies, as Margaret Mead has noted, homosexuality is sometimes so rare that you only see it in their language or in some institutionalized puberty rite. While in others such as the Tanganyikan Nyakyusa or Algerian Kabyles, one has to look carefully to find a single male who is not extensively involved in it. Part of this wide variation is well understood. Homosexuality hovers near zero in societies that bolster heterosexuality with child marriage (e.g., nearly all the African Gold Coast tribes). And it doesn't rise much above zero in societies that eschew heroics and thus take the glory out of maleness (e.g., Pygmy tribes in which special credit is denied to the successful hunter; his feats are credited instead to luck or to some god). But wherever a society lauds bravery, courage, and an individualized derring-do, homosexuality can be high to very high; such attitudes encourage an idealization and thus the easy eroticization of male attributes. In our society this vigorous homosexual potential is held down to moderate levels by specific taboos against it and by a variety of heterosexual expectations and encouragements. Turn the clock back to when these heterosexual encouragements were weaker and you'll glimpse the much more prevalent homosexuality of our Greek and Roman forefathers—or if you prefer a modern example, the Arab scene will do, as will the Greco-Roman holdover in today's Southern Italy.

Q. Why is it so difficult to isolate the causes of homosexuality?

A. While we know scores of major influences in detail, nobody can weight each of these accurately enough to explain exactly why Bill turns out to be heterosexual and Andy homosexual. A close analogy is weather prediction: All the variables are known, yet advance forecasts regress to levels hardly better than seasonal chance owing to myriad combinations that can end up in either rain or sunshine. Dozens of experience factors combine to support heterosexuality, while many of the same and similar experiences in a slightly different shuffle can lend their weight to a homosexual result.

Q. Kinsey found that 50 percent of young boys eroticize male attributes, so why do only 4 percent wind up exclusively homosexual?

A. Because most of them also come to eroticize female attributes, a taste which is more strongly reinforced by social expectancy and demand.

If one wants to look a bit closer at the matter and ask how many men ever practice homosexuality, the answer would be a third of the male population. If one wants to discount this high figure on the grounds that a single tryout doesn't necessarily "mean" anything and ask the question, How many people extensively repeat homosexual experiences, let's say for at least three years? the 33 percent would drop to something like 25 percent. If you add still another requirement and ask, How many people retain a definite homosexual response for life? the statistic is near the 13 percent that Kinsey estimated. It's only when you add the proviso of exclusivity that the homosexual ratio drops to 4 percent.

Q. How does the 4 percent develop an exclusive homosexuality despite all the social barriers against it?

A. A powerful homosexual conditioning usually begins at such an early age the child is hardly aware of social pressures against it—and is often more aware of pressures against heterosexuality. (Sex researchers have consistently found that pre-pubertal youngsters are more ready to discuss their homosexual play than they are their heterosexual.) Furthermore, in all clear-cut cases of sexual conditioning, a person tends to build up strong aversions to the polar opposites of what his tastes are. Thus, once a male is turned on by the muscularity and angularity of males, he tends to build up a distaste for the softness and roundness of the female form. Similarly, the male who has come to respond to the roundness and softness of some women is already turned off by women who lack these qualities—so, for him, the very thought of an intimate sexual contact with a hard, angular male is a symphony of horrors. All exclusive tastes are alike in these respects.

Q. Is bisexuality increasing?

A. It appears to be decidedly up with women but not with men. Males are much more firmly locked into their sexual directions. But women—with the enormous pliancy that characterizes female sexuality throughout the mammalian species—have become able to respond quickly to certain changes in our mores. We have some tangible data for this. Among swingers, far less than 1 percent of the men ever reach over for even a momentary male-male contact—while according to G. Bartell's *Group Sex* some 64 percent of the women readily do so.

Q. How does bisexuality affect sex between men and women?

A. At low or moderate levels of demand, a touch of homosexuality often strengthens a person's heterosexual commitment. It's as if the homosexual element is too weak to offer any real competition to the marriage and yet is strong enough to both satisfy a person's need for diversity and cut down on one's roving eye toward other heterosexual partners—which is the real enemy of most marriages.

Incidentally, one sees the same thing in reverse too. The ongoing homosexual relationship is often stabilized by a touch of heterosexuality in one or both partners.

Q. Does most of what you have said about male homosexuality apply to lesbians as well?

A. Much of it does apply, but there are startling differences between males and females on several levels. Males tend to eroticize such things as the specific body shapes of their partners, while the eroticization women achieve tends to be much more conceptual, often more emotional in tone and content, and otherwise less visual and much less related to specific body cues.

Q. Does the prevalence of homosexual activity in prisons produce converts?

A. Not many. Seventy-one percent of long-term prisoners are involved in overt homosexuality, but only 4 percent of these first practiced it in prison.

Q. Does this mean that the confirmed heterosexual—no matter how long he is deprived of women and has access to men—generally will not dabble in homosexuality?

A. That is one of the findings of a secret United States Army sex-research study conducted during World War II and still locked up in the Pentagon. And from other sources, too, it seems that among large groups of men isolated on various South Pacific islands during the war, homosexuality did not increase. Nor did it develop among our prisoners in Vietnam. To a large extent such evidence means what it seems to mean: that firmly conditioned sexual patterns tend to stay put. And yet, this remarkable stability, which stems from each individual's past conditioning, is not the only thing that determines a person's sexual behavior; the prevailing group mores of the moment can also play an important role. Thus in most prisons and on an occasional ship at sea where the implicitly agreed-upon mores become "homosexuality is okay here," the floodgates are opened and even a trace of homosexuality in people may balloon into a major, highly motivated activity.

Q. What determines the way homosexuals perform in bed?

A. As in heterosexuality, that depends on individual tastes, what social level is involved, how well the partners know each other, and how much affection there is. Lower-social-level males tend to rely on anal intercourse and simple fellatio more than do persons at middle and upper social levels. In fact, an unpublished Kinsey tabulation shows anal intercourse to be "preferred" by only 11 percent of middle- and upper-level males; they engage in much more fellatio and myriad other oral and masturbatory techniques. It's not that the lower-level male tends to be more simplistic and less imaginative. Whether heterosexual or homosexual, he is more inclined to see variations in sexual technique as "unnatural," sometimes even as a risk to his macho—for example, when he "lands on the bottom." And he not infrequently interprets anything that smacks of masturbation—including femoral, that is, between-thigh, intercourse—as both trivial and "a perversion." Lower-level homosexual males tend to engage in more kissing and other oral techniques than do their heterosexual equivalents—a difference which Kinsey attributed to more interaction between social levels in the homosexual population.

Lesbian techniques are remarkable. In the first place, they often involve a degree of drawn-out continuous affectionate exchanges—sometimes extending over several hours—which is beyond the comprehension of most males. And while some of the physical techniques used by a woman to bring her female partner to orgasm are sometimes very elaborate, other techniques are so bland-looking as to seem hardly effective. Yet they are very effective indeed because they zero in on a woman's requirements with "intuitive precision," an intimately accurate knowledge of what really works. Both the Kinsey and recent Masters and Johnson studies have rated lesbian techniques as far more effective for women than ordinary heterosexual intercourse.

Q. In a male or female homosexual pair, is the relative "toughness" or "softness" of the partners an indication of which one is dominant in bed?

A. No, it isn't. In fact, dominance in bed is notoriously unpredictable. However, when one partner is clearly dominant in bed, which is often not the case, there is a tendency for the roles to be the opposite of what one might have expected. The socially dominant lesbian often leans back in bed and expects to be made love to, which is an almost classical complaint among lesbians. And not only is the relatively soft male notably inclined to land on top, the very aggressive male is remarkably inclined to *want* to be on the bottom in anal intercourse. These reversals of role are not a surprise. Far down in the mammalian pattern, there's a tendency for the most aggressive and sexually vigorous individuals to be the ones most inclined to reverse their roles.

Q. You make the remarkable statement in your book that homosexual techniques are more varied than those of heterosexuality.

A. That's because the need for heterosexual variety is reduced—in part by the very excellence of its male-female genital union. In addition, its clear-cut role expectancies tend to conventionalize it. And of course the use of stereotypes in heterosexuality is socially recommended, and extreme variations are widely regarded as "abnormal." By contrast, no forms of homosexuality have the head start of being approved, let alone demanded. Thus the whole matter of what the partners do together is left more to individual invention—an invention that, with the aid of the high rapport between same-sex partners, often does come up with exceptional variety.

Q. Are homosexual males more promiscuous than heterosexuals?

A. Yes, but there's nothing to suggest that promiscuity is any higher for homosexual than for heterosexual males when they're faced with equal opportunity.

Q. Are fetishism, S&M, and the other paraphilias more common among homosexual males than others?

A. Undoubtedly so. It's much easier for males to find these interests among males than among females. This situation is well shown in prostitution: A call girl who charges $100 expects several times this amount for mildly kinky sex; the rate may reach $800 an hour for less mild participations. Not so with the call boy. His rate is less than $100 and it is unusual for "special requests" to cost much if anything extra. Remember that these differences reflect the contrast between the sexes rather than whether the sex itself is homosexual or heterosexual.

Q. Are homosexual couples less inclined than heterosexuals to insist on sexual "fidelity"?

A. Not usually. Like everybody else, they tend to start off with the heterosexual model of monogamy, which is one of their problems. Of course sexual exclusivity is always easy for anybody to maintain during a period of high romance, but since the duration of "romance" is only a year or so, homosexual males soon face what heterosexuals face, the waywardness of males. It is interesting that the lesbian relationship often survives a total loss of sexual interest between the partners—a mixed blessing, since these can continue far past both their sexual and emotional usefulness. Apparently this is because for so many women there's a "nest building" tendency that can far exceed their interest in sex, which seems to bear out the ancient claim that women supply more of the cohesiveness in ordinary marriages than men do.

Q. Do friendship and intimacy kill good sex, and is some form of barrier or resistance needed to keep erotic zest alive in a long-term partnership?

A. Yes to both parts of the question. The resistance theory makes sense to many people. But others are shocked to the core, particularly if they are in the midst of a situation where they are not being very honest with themselves. No doubt most people want and need compatibility with their partners, but a smooth personal closeness requires the comfortable, worn-in quality of an old shoe—comforts that are utterly lacking in the newness and surprise that characterize every aspect of titillating sex and a new romance. Of course, the illusion of new lovers is that they will eventually have all the joys of sex along with the comforts of compatibility. But in practice, intense sexual interest can never survive the familiarity and predictability that are implicit in the high compatibility of a "good" marriage.

Q. Are you saying that good marriages don't hold up, or at least that good sex in them doesn't?

A. That's not it. In the first place, it would be presumptuous of me, or of anybody, to say exactly what a good marriage is for other people. Some couples who have many fights and quarrels rate their marriage as "good" or even "very good." They are particularly likely to maintain a lively, intense bedroom scene, by the way. Invariably a couple's sexual motivation is only aroused when something in the situation is resistant to it. This resistance can be in a partner's partial standoffishness, in one's fear and fascination with an attractive but "dangerous" person, or mixed into the feelings of both partners as they physically invade each other's privacy. Or the resistance may appear in neither partner but in something that intrudes between them—an unavoidable delay or some bittersweet separation.

The most poignant romantic situations invariably involve such things as the displacements of wartime, a threat of losing each other, or the interference of disapproving others. The attraction of Romeo and Juliet was incited by the distance of the balcony, the feuding of their families, and the impending marriage of Juliet to another man. Likewise, the appeal of a Lolita, the fascination with a virgin bride, and the excitements of surreptitiousness in a hundred forms are all examples of particular kinds of resistances that act as stimulators. In a nutshell: Sexual zest does not arise from the comforts of a smooth compatibility, nor can it survive them; it is put to sleep by the music of high accord.

Q. Does the resistance factor, like most sexual activities in man, have its analogue among lower animals?

A. Yes. There are numerous examples of animals that, like dogs, do a good deal of running away from, as well as running toward, their mates during a teasing courtship. Then there are other species in which a sharper resistance is apparent, where the male has to fight his way through a crowd of competing males to reach a female. Among a great many of these species the absence of a fight or of some other impediment to easy access results in impotence or sterility. (Before this was understood, zoo keepers were quite perplexed that they could not breed most of their animals in captivity, or even get a male to "be interested" in a ripe female. They now solve the problem by putting some barrier between the mates and then suddenly raising it.) These are not isolated examples. In not a single known species of any animal or insect is sex a sweet and gentle business from start to finish; usually it's a fairly violent affair full to overflowing with tension and torment.

Q. But how universal is the resistance factor in man?

A. You might as well ask how universal is the law of gravity. Even in the numerous permissive societies, where there is hardly a social barrier to sex, the tension and resistance is moved into the sex act itself. In central South America, for instance, Choroti women spit in a lover's face during coitus; Apinaye women bite off bits of a man's eyebrows, loudly spitting them aside. Ponapean men of the South Pacific do the same to their female partners, pulling their eyebrows out by the roots. Turkese women poke their fingers into a man's ears. Siriono couples of Bolivia poke fingers into each other's eyes along with much scratching and pinching of necks and chests. And Trobriand Islanders, who are particularly free in permitting sexual liaisons, bite each other on the cheek and lips till blood flows, snap the nose and chin, tear each other's hair, and otherwise lacerate their lovers during coitus. It's worth remembering that these styles of sex predominate only in sexually permissive societies. Conversely, societies which expect sexual expressions to be gentle and affectionate are, across the board, highly restrictive in sex, especially in terms of partner accessibility.

Q. Why is the question of curing homosexuality so controversial? Surely you can either change homosexuals or you can't.

A. Not quite. The "cure" issue is seldom raised these days. Nobody could possibly cure homosexuality because the phenomena it comprises are not illnesses in the first place. A number of moralists and psychiatrists still claim to be able to *change* homosexuality, but whether that is ever possible depends entirely on your criteria. If stopping the action is all that's meant, then joining a monastery or a nunnery might do it, or listening to Billy Graham and swearing off in the name of Jesus might work for a while. Or if "making a commitment to heterosexuality" is the criterion—Masters and Johnson demand this of their patients—then this sometimes "works" but only with people who have a degree of heterosexual response and who, by dint of will under the eyes of kindly authority figures, push their homosexual tastes aside. It all amounts to a brittle, desperate, tenuous hold on a forced heterosexuality.

But if by change you mean getting a person to not want what he does want, and at the same time make him sexually want what he has never wanted, then forget it; there's never been a validated case on record, and I predict never will be. Just think how hard it would be to get the average heterosexual guy to be turned off by women *and* revved up by men—the same goes for the homosexual male in reverse. Hell, we can't even change a breast man into a leg man, let alone hurdle the heterosexual-homosexual divide. Sexual preferences of all kinds tend to be as stable as they are sharp, especially in males.

Q. Can you foresee a time when homosexuality will be fully accepted in the United States?

A. If you mean accepted openly and generally, certainly not. In the first place we know from cross-cultural studies that minority sexual practices are never fully accepted. Homosexuality has been fully sanctioned only in those times and places where it has predominated. Examples of predominantly homosexual cultures are found in 64 percent of the tribes cataloged by Ford and Beach in *Patterns of Sexual Behavior* and in ancient Greece, recently shown in K. J. Dover's *Greek Homosexuality.* Our society will probably go only a small distance toward accepting homosexuality. The great middle class will gradually adopt the attitudes that now prevail at the upper social levels—a tacit acceptance of homosexuality and an embarrassment in appearing prudish about it, yet a disdain for it whenever disdain is socially useful. Even this will take time. Remember, Judeo-Christian mores are fundamentally ascetic and still don't approve even heterosexual sex without love and "responsibility."

A Message To Parents Of Gays

Charlotte Spitzer

Charlotte Spitzer is a licensed marriage, family and child counselor and founder of Los Angeles Parents and Friends of Gays.

One of the most profound shocks a parent can receive is to discover that his or her son or daughter is a homosexual. The repercussions of this discovery can wreck or permanently damage the lives of both parents and child—but it doesn't have to. Charlotte Spitzer, founder of Los Angeles Parents and Friends of Gays, outlines the methods she has pioneered to help families pull through this crisis with understanding and love.

When a child comes home after getting battered and rejected out in the world, he can look forward to getting the love and comfort he needs and the reassurance that he is a worthwhile human being. Unfortunately, this is not true for the homosexual. Not only does society reject him, but his own family does, too.

Probably the most painful rejection one can experience is rejection by one's own parents. Every child needs to feel good about himself as he grows up. He gets this feeling from his family, the source of his first experiences. It is by his family that he needs to feel accepted and secure.

Adolescence is a particularly difficult time for most children. When a child does not have those closest to him—presumably the ones who care—helping him to deal with his worst fears, he can be beset with self-doubts.

For homosexual children, adolescence is a nightmare. Even if they haven't put that label on themselves, they are aware that they are different from other children, and yet they are terrified to share their feelings and fears with their parents. They have heard the same negative remarks about homosexuality that we are all exposed to and are, as a result, often filled with self-loathing. Afraid to communicate, they suffer from overwhelming feelings of isolation and despair.

My own daughter waited until she was twenty-one before coming to me and telling me she was a lesbian, and even then I was shocked. I had never suspected anything of the sort, having never noticed any tell-tale signs that I was aware of. She had dated throughout high school and had even had an intense relationship with a young man during her first two years in college.

I could not understand it. What had gone wrong? More specifically, where had I gone wrong? I felt an enormous sense of guilt. Since I felt that there was something wrong with homosexuality, I blamed myself for her "abnormality," as I blamed myself for everything that went wrong with my kids.

In addition to feelings of guilt, I was terribly ashamed and afraid of what people would think. I couldn't imagine how I could tell my aged mother, my relatives and my friends. I didn't want them to reject my child, to feel sorry for me or treat her like a pariah. I also realized I would be deprived of grandchildren and would never know the happiness of being a grandparent. I was overwhelmed with sadness.

For a while I denied reality. I hoped that perhaps she was only going through a phase. After all, she had been disappointed in love. Out of her hurt, I thought, she was turning away from relationships with men. She might get over it soon, especially if "Mr. Right" came along. Another vain hope I had was that she had been temporarily influenced by some person or other to experiment with someone of the same sex. Sooner or later she would return to "normal." I went through the gamut of all feelings, experiencing anger, too. Why me, I wanted to know. I hadn't been such a bad parent. It was only later, in retrospect, that I realized my child must have trusted me enough to tell me and that I was grateful she had done so.

Eventually, I calmed down and became more objective. I knew my daughter was a fine person. She was loving, talented, caring, and seemed to function well. None of that had really changed since she had made her revelation. I began to see that maybe it was I who needed to change my attitude—to reconcile what I had been conditioned to believe about homosexuality with this young woman, my daughter. Obviously, there was more I could learn on the subject.

I was greatly concerned about the kind of life my daughter might live as a lesbian, having picked up the idea that all homosexuals were unhappy people who lead a furtive, dismal existence. But when I began to read the available literature on homosexuality, much to my surprise and relief, I found that those popular notions had no basis in fact. Furthermore, homosexuals were not "sick," I learned.

I read that homosexuality was the sexual preference of at least ten percent of the population. Delving deeper, I came up with the information that sexual orientation is a complex matter, determined in very early childhood, according to most of the basic researchers, and that it was simplistic and inaccurate to hold parents responsible for making their children homosexual. As to what homosexuals are like, they are not distinguishable from heterosexuals. Only a tiny portion fit the stereotypes of the masculine "butchy" lesbian and the feminine "swishy" gay male. Like all of us, they have the potential for leading a full, productive, happy life. The main difference is in the rejection and oppression they face from society.

Greatly relieved, I could now pose the only important question in this situation. "What do I really want for my child?" The answer: I wanted her to fulfill herself in the way that was best and most satisfying for her.

It was around this time that I attended a panel discussion in my community sponsored by a Nurses' Association. One of the panelists was a young lesbian who reminded me of my daughter. She was bright, lovely, gentle. She talked about the fact that as a writer she was doing what she wanted, that she led a very full life, and felt good about herself. The only saddening part of her life was her mother's refusal to accept the fact that she was a lesbian. Her mother chose to believe that she was going through a phase and would "come to her senses" someday. Because of this attitude, the young woman could not share herself fully with her mother.

I wept, intensely aware now of the pain I would be likely to cause my daughter if I did not fully accept her. I vowed I would not allow that to happen.

I had some support during my search for answers from a very close friend and from my loving husband, but I wished I could have talked to other parents in the same situation. It occurred to me that other parents might feel the same way—I decided that there might be a need for a help line for parents of homosexual children. I offered my services to the Gay Community Services Center, which responded enthusiastically to the idea and soon set up the phone service.

When the calls started coming, I heard from all sorts of people, but they all had a similiar story. They were all going through what I had gone through: guilt, shame, worry about their children's welfare, puzzlement, anger.

I listened sympathetically and let them know I understood what they were experiencing, because I had experienced the same turmoil and pain. Most of what they heard in the past about homosexuality was probably untrue, I assured them, and I tried to help them sort out facts from fiction and urged them to read some of the material I had found helpful.

I also urged them to continue communicating with their gay children, advising them to be honest in sharing their feelings with them. "Let your children know that you are having a hard time, but that you are trying to come to terms with the issue," I said. It would be as much a mistake, I cautioned, to pretend that the problem didn't exist as to refuse to acknowledge the child's lifestyle.

I encouraged the parents who called to allow their gay children to bring their friends and lovers to meet them, suspecting that the stereotypes would break down once the parents met other gay people. Parents often have the idea that their child is special, not really "queer," but has simply been corrupted by the real gays. However, when they come face to face with other gays, they usually can't hold on to such rationalizations.

I soon sensed that the time had come to form a support group. I had gathered a significant number of names of parents from all the calls, and I asked a parent I had counseled to help me send out the announcements of a meeting to them. I envisioned providing a place where parents could come together and comfortably talk about their feelings and concerns. They could help one another by comparing notes and getting feedback from other people who were in the same boat as they. The hoped-for result was that they would feel free to love and relate to their children, even though they were gay and society frowned upon homosexuality.

Of the thirty or so people who showed up for the

meeting, most of them were parents, but there were a few friends of gays who came to lend support, and some curious gays, delighted by what was happening. It was evident that everyone was glad about the idea of getting together, and we were launched. We met in each other's homes for the first few times and then moved into a church that has since become the permanent home of the group. After three years, it is still in operation.

The transformations that have occurred through these meetings have been remarkable. In a relatively short time parents have not only learned to accept their children, but have even begun to feel good about them. It was dramatically demonstrated over and over again that in an environment where they could feel safe, comfortable and understood, parents were able to unburden themselves and begin the process of reeducation and adjustment.

I don't want to give the impression that it was easy and smooth. It wasn't. Often one spouse blamed the other, sometimes both blamed each other. The accusations ranged from, "You were too critical, too permissive, too cold, mollycoddling," to "You were not there enough," and on and on. Sometimes one parent expressed a sense of betrayal that the spouse had accepted the child before he/she was willing to do so. There is no question but that the process was painful and difficult. I knew it had to be, having gone through it myself.

I'll never forget one of the examples of change that occurred a few months after we had started the meeting. One day I got a telephone call from a desperate twenty-six-year-old man who identified himself as Chris. For nine years he had been trying vainly to get his mother to accept him. His mother—a very kind, very religious woman who was in a terrible conflict over his homosexuality—had consulted her priest, who admonished her to stand firm and not accept her son's sexual orientation. Although agonized about it, she had obeyed the priest's counsel and insisted that her son must change.

As a result of this long-lasting situation, Chris had stopped functioning. He quit school, gave up his job and sat at home, lonely, isolated and depressed to the point of considering suicide. Nothing mattered so much to him as that his mother accept him as a homosexual. When he asked if I would call her, I explained that I could not do that, because it would be an invasion of her privacy. She might resent the intrusion, and the call would be useless. However, I said that if he could prevail upon her to call me, I would do whatever I could to persuade her to come to a meeting.

I don't know what he said to her to get her to call, but call she did. Perhaps she was so worried about him, fearful he might do something desperate, that she had forced herself to make the contact. I informed her that in all probability Chris could not change who he was, and that if she really did not want to lose him—either literally or figuratively—she would have to reexamine her attitude. After we had exchanged experiences, I urged her to attend the next parents' meeting, assuring her that she could get more help there than I could give her over the phone. She agreed to come.

A few days after we had spoken, Chris called, excited and encouraged that his mother had made the call, and especially elated that she had agreed to come to the next meeting.

On the evening of the meeting a sweet little lady arrived, introduced herself to me and proceeded to share her pain, her conflict and her concerns about Chris with the group. We all felt for her when she cried and wrung her hands. We gave her as much support as we could, but remained firm in our conviction that she could change her attitude if she was really concerned about her son's well-being. She vowed she would work at it, and, at the end of the meeting, admitted that unburdening herself had already been a great source of relief to her.

A day or two after the meeting I got another call from Chris, who was now virtually bubbling over with enthusiasm and gratitude. Buoyed by what had happened, he had gone out and gotten a job.

At the next month's meeting Chris' mother proudly announced that her son seemed to be snapping out of his depression. As for her, she was finding it easier each day to change the way she felt toward Chris. It was a slow process, but as long as he saw her progress, Chris was willing to let her take as much time as she needed. The group applauded her courage and gave her the support she needed to continue.

Later, when another parent who was there for the first time wept as she told of her, took her hand and explained comfortingly that she had gone through the same process at the last meeting. I wanted to hug her for reaching out to the other parent and for sharing herself, and at the end of the meeting I did just that.

In many ways, and in many forms, this gratifying experience has been repeated. Joy has replaced pain after parents have come to the group meetings.

However, it is the parents who don't call and don't come forward who make me feel concerned. For the loss is on both sides. No parent wants to give up a child, and no child wants to be rejected by his parents. Each needs the other. And I believe that a heavy price is paid in mental and physical health by parents who reject their gay children.

The saddest part of it is that this kind of suffering is unnecessary. Help is available. Change is possible. There are parent groups in almost every city in the United States. There are books and articles in most book stores that can help broaden one's perspective and put a great deal of uneasiness to rest.

The courage to be honest is never easy, but it is possibly the only viable choice for both parents *and* their gay children. I spoke to a group of gays a while back, and months later, one of them called me. He admitted that he hadn't been particularly interested or involved in my talk, feeling that it meant very little to him at the time. His parents lived a great distance from him, and he had decided it didn't matter that they were ignorant of his lifestyle.

But not long after my talk his parents had informed him that they would stop off to visit him on their way elsewhere. The young man got panicky at first. He was living with his lover, and his parents were sure to notice. What should he do? Summoning up all his courage, he decided to tell them about himself. He couldn't hide this part of himself—it didn't feel right. He would just have to risk their rejection.

He was calling me to tell me the outcome of the encounter and to thank me, because what I had said at the meeting had helped him to be open with his parents. When they assured him that they still loved him, whatever his sexual orientation, he broke down and wept with relief. He said that he felt free for the first time in his life. Since this incident, he has gone on to do many important things for the gay liberation movement, partly because of the strength he derives from his parents' acceptance.

This experience is not an isolated one. And yet sometimes the results are not joyful; in fact, sometimes they are tragic. Among these, occasionally there is an individual who cannot stand the pain of rejection by those whom he loves, and so he chooses to end his life rather than go on.

What a waste of human life and loss of human potential when this happens. It is impossible to describe how devastating it is for a parent to lose a child. The sense of remorse and finality is overwhelming. What saddens me most when I hear about such a case is that I know, from personal experience, how avoidable such a tragedy is.

I also know how great a part preconceived notions play in parents' refusal to accept their gay

Recommended Books on Homosexuality

These books can be ordered from the publisher or through any book store.

Howard Brown, M.D., *Familiar Faces, Hidden Lives,* Harcourt, Brace, Jovanovich, New York, 1977.

Don Clark, Ph.D., *Loving Someone Gay, What Every Parent Should Know About Homosexuality,* Signet Paperback, New York, 1977.

Betty Fairchild and Nancy Hayward, *Now That You Know,* Harcourt, Brace, Jovanovich, New York, 1979.

Laura Hobson, *Consenting Adult,* Warner Paperback Books, New York, 1976.

John J. McNeill, S.J., *The Church and The Homosexual,* Sheed, Andrews, McNeill, New York, 1976.

Del Martin and Phyllis Lyon, *Lesbian Woman,* Bantam Books, New York, 1972.

N. Pittenger, *Time for Consent,* SCM Press, 1976.

Dr. Charles Silverstein. *A Family Matter,* McGraw Hill, New York, 1977.

Scanzoni and Mollenkott, *Is The Homosexual My Neighbor?,* Harper and Row, New York, 1979.

C.A. Tripp, *The Homosexual Matrix,* Signet Paperback, New York, 1977.

Ginny Vida, Ed., *Our Right To Live: A Lesbian Sourcebook,* Prentice-Hall Paperback, New Jersey, 1979.

Dr. George Weinberg, *Society and the Healthy Homosexual,* Doubleday.

children, as it is very hard for parents to ignore attitudes inculcated by society. That is why I have committed myself to changing the attitudes of society toward homosexuals. It is important that all the misinformation about homosexuality that is disseminated in our society be dispelled.

There is still so much misunderstanding about the nature of homosexuality. Many people think that a homosexual decides, as an adult, to love members of his own sex. In fact, most homosexuals insist that they knew they were different from their heterosexual peers from very early on. Researchers for the most part agree that sexual preference is established at a very early age, usually by the time a child is five.

Parents need to know these facts and many, many more. Armed with information, they can stop blaming themselves and concentrate on giving their gay children the support they crave. They can help them lead the kind of full, healthy life that is every individual's birthright. Finally, they can use their influence as taxpayers, as citizens who vote and as respected members of their communities to demand that the society give all gays the human rights it has so long denied them. Our gay children need and deserve our love and support.

To contact a parents of gays group in your area, write to: Parents and Friends of Gays, P.O. Box 24528, Los Angeles, CA. 90024 or Parents of Lesbians and Gay Men, Box 553, Lenox Hill Station, New York, N.Y. 10021.

Love, Sex and Marriage for People Who Have Disabilities

Sol Gordon

Sol Gordon received his Ph.D. in psychology from the University of London' in 1953. He is currently Professor of Child and Family Studies at Syracuse University's College for Human Development. He is also Director of the Institute for Family Research and Education which is dedicat ed to strengthening the family by encouraging honest communication between parent and child.

Everyone is entitled to love, to the opportunity for sexual expression and to be considered marriageable.

What a sweeping statement to make especially when writing about people who have disabilities severe enough to have a dramatic impact on their day-to-day lives. And yet I am convinced that the statement is true and can have a liberating impact on hundreds of thousands of people with severe physical disabilities who believe they are not only unloved but, more poignantly, unloveable.

This article is addressed to disabled people (and their parents) who have average intelligence* but who, for one reason or another, are not making it. By making it I mean having friends and leisure time interests and working toward, or at, a satisfying job; to put it another way, to feel loved, loveable, sexual and marriageable.

For those people who are blind or deaf or physically incapacitated or paraplegic and who are doing well, you have our blessings and you are a source of inspiration. This article is not for you.

Let me begin by suggesting that there are two critical problems that many, if not most, severely disabled people have.

*See the October, 1976, issue for "Sex Education for People Who Are Mentally Retarded."

First, in our society you score no points for being disabled. Every person who is disabled has to struggle to make it.

Second, many people with disabilities feel inferior. If I am going to make my point clear and influence you in a special way, I would declare that no one can make you feel inferior without your consent.

Not too long ago I made this statement at a meeting of several hundred severely disabled people, their parents and teachers. There was an emotional outburst from a workshop leader. She shouted, "How can you say things like that when you see before you people who need only look at themselves in the mirror to know that what you say represents empty promises of a future that is not possible for any of them!"

The answer came from a woman confined to a wheelchair. She said, "You know, when I look only at myself, I feel depressed. When I take in the world I live in, I'm impressed. And when I allow God to touch me, I feel blessed."

Pandemonium broke out. What was an unreceptive, silent, almost sullen audience became a group of people wanting desperately to talk about their hidden aspirations — mainly in terms of their strong desire for love, companionship and sexual expression.

This meeting inspired me as nothing else ever has to declare far and wide that there are very few limitations that people with handicaps, their parents, their teachers and the general public cannot overcome. The opening statement of this article can ring true for everybody.

Here are some messages I would like to offer:

5. CONTINUING SEXUAL CONCERNS

1. Nobody can make you feel inferior without your consent.
2. If you have an interest (hobbies, work, talents, passions) someone will be interested in you.
3. If you are bored, you are boring to be with.
4. If you do not have a sense of humor, develop one. If you cannot develop a sense of humor, you can always become a supervisor.
5. Organize. Join an advocacy group for the handicapped and their parents.
6. Work toward being a realist (remember, everybody is a hero in somebody else's situation).
7. Do not dwell on the meaning of life. Life is not a meaning. Life is an opportunity for any number of meaningful experiences.
8. All thoughts, all desires, all impulses are normal. Behavior can be immoral or abnormal, but not thoughts. If you are preoccupied with thoughts that are unenjoyable to you, it is only because you feel guilty. These thoughts then become obsessive (involuntary). Guilt is the source of energy behind the repetition of thoughts that are unacceptable to us. We all must realize that whatever thoughts we have — whether they be sexual, sado-masochistic, lustful (even the ones that Jimmy Carter and, would you believe, Jerry Ford have) — are completely normal. Only what we do counts, not what we think about.
9. Read. Discover as much as you can about yourself and the world. For heaven's sake, do not watch more than an hour or so of television each day. Haven't you noticed that the more television you watch, the more exhausted you are?
10. Operate on the assumption that the so-called general public is uncomfortable with you. Most people are uncomfortable in the presence of severely disabled people. And, if you announce that they do not have to feel guilty about being uncomfortable, then they will not have to respond by withdrawing from you or having pity. Take the initiative and tell people what you would like them to do. And somehow convey to them that it is okay to feel uncomfortable.

I feel that these "rules" are the basic steps toward realizing your own goals in the area of sexual expression and marriage.

Nothing I have suggested is easy. In fact, all really meaningful experiences in life involve risk, hard work and the ability to postpone momentary gratification for long range satisfaction.

If you have not gotten the message, let me say it another way. Socialization skills and opportunities are more important than anything else. If you feel good about yourself, someone will feel good about you. If you feel friendly, someone will be friendly to you. If you are open to sexual expression, someone will want to be sexual with you.

The ethical and moral rules of society apply to everyone — certainly including disabled people. This means, of course, that we are opposed to any form of exploitation and any behavior that is not agreed to by both partners.

And now for a revolutionary suggestion. I have been troubled by seeing so many disabled people alone, lonely and frustrated. Many are confined (should we say imprisoned) to their own homes, cared for mostly by caring and loving parents who are also, in some way, imprisoned in their own homes. What about organizing a national network of friendship and marriage brokers — organizations that would "match" disabled people who would not otherwise meet? Start by telephoning each other — in some prearranged way so that a person is not to make more than one or two unreciprocated calls as an example — and then for example, arrange for wheelchair bound people to be together in a home for a week or two. There are many things that could be done, especially during summer vacations, giving parents as well as disabled people a break.

Lest this be interpreted to mean that I am opposed to integration, or what people call "mainstreaming," let it be understood that anybody who can arrange their own friends and marital partners, fine. I am talking about people whose opportunities are limited for one reason or another.

Here are some important publications and ideas that supplement what I have written.

Books for Disabled People to Read That Are Consciousness Raising

Living Fully – A Guide for Young People with a Handicap, Their Parents, Their Teachers, and Professionals by Sol Gordon et al. Available from THE EXCEPTIONAL PARENT **Bookstore (S-44).**

YOU – The Psychology of Surviving and Enhancing Your Social Life, Love Life, Sex Life, School Life, Work Life, Home Life, Emotional Life, Creative Life, Spiritual Life, Style of Life, by Sol Gordon with Roger Conant. Available from THE EXCEPTIONAL PARENT **Bookstore (G-17).**

Books for Teenagers

But I'm Ready to Go, a novel by Louise Albert about a 15-year old who has serious learning disabilities. Available from Bradbury Press, Dept. EP, 2 Overhill Road, Scarsdale, New York 10583. $7.95.

Books Primarily for Professionals

The very best book I have read about sexuality and the disabled is Wendy Greengross' *Entitled to Love – The Sexual and Emotional Needs of the*

Handicapped. National Fund for Research into Crippling Diseases, Vincent House, 1 Springfield Road, Horsham, Sussex, England RH12 2PN. Write for price and ordering information.

Life Together – The Situation of the Handicapped compiled by Inger Nordqvist. Available from The Swedish Central Committee for Rehabilitation, Fack, S-161 25, Bromma 1, Sweden. Write for price and purchasing information.

Integration of Handicapped Children in Society, edited by James Loring and Graham Gurn. Routledge and Kegan Paul, 9 Park Street, Boston, Massachusetts 02108. $10.95.

Sex Education and Counseling of Special Groups: The Mentally and Physically Handicapped by Warren R. Johnson. Available from Charles C Thomas, Publisher, 301-327 East Lawrence Avenue, Springfield, Illinois 62717. $12.50.

The Disabled and Their Parents: A Counseling Challenge by Leo Buscaglia, Available from THE EXCEPTIONAL PARENT **Bookstore (S-63).**

Sexual Options for Paraplegics and Quadriplegics by Thomas O. Mooney, Theodore M. Cole and Richard A. Chilgren. Available from THE EXCEPTIONAL PARENT **Bookstore (S-64).**

Sex Education for the Visually Handicapped in Schools and Agencies . . . Selected Papers. American Foundation for the Blind, New York, New York. 1975. $3.50.

Booklets

Sexual Rights for the People . . . Who Happen to be Handicapped by Sol Gordon. Available from Ed-U Press, 760 Ostrom Avenue, Syracuse, New York 13210. $.50.

Sex Education for Disabled Persons by Irving R. Dickman. Available from Public Affairs Pamphlets, 381 Park Avenue South, New York, New York 10016. $.35.

No Place Like Home – Alternate Living Arrangements for Teenagers and Adults with Cerebral Palsy by Irving R. Dickman. Available from United Cerebral Palsy Association, 66 East 34th Street, New York, New York 10016. $2.25.

Accent on Living: Reprint Series #1, "The Disabled Person and Family Dynamics," "Sex and the Disabled Female," "Sex and the Spinal Cord Injured Male." Available from Accent on Living, P.O. Box 700, Bloomington, Illinois 61701. $1.95.

Film

The best film I have ever seen on the subject of sexuality and marriage for handicapped people is *Like Other People,* Perennial Education, Inc., 1825 Willow Road, Northfield, Illinois 60093. Rental — $37.50; purchase price — $375.

Bibliography

The best bibliography on the handicapped and sexual health is the SIECUS Report, *The Handicapped and Sexual Health.* Available from Ed-U Press, 760 Ostrom Avenue, Syracuse, New York 13210. $1.00.

Slide Show

A very special color slide show entitled *Handicapism,* which exposes personal, social and professional forms of dehumanization is available for $45 from the Human Policy Press, P.O. Box 127, University Station, Syracuse, New York 13210. Write for its complete publication list as it has many books, slide shows, posters and children's stories.

Directory and Preparation for Educational Opportunities

A National Directory of Four Year Colleges, Two Year Colleges and Post High School Training Programs for Young People with Learning Disabilities. Available from Partners in Publishing Co., P.O. Box 50347, Tulsa, Oklahoma. $7.00.

A preparation for college program for learning disabled people with a focus on socialization skills is available from Diana Bander, Goddard College, Summer School Center, Plainview, Vermont 05667.

Newsletter

Get on the mailing list of *Options,* a free, monthly newsletter published by Association for Sexual Adjustment in Disability. Printed and mailed through the courtesy of Easter Seal Society, P.O. Box 3579, Downey, California 90242.

Of course, there are many other books and resources available. If you have had a good experience with them, write to us and we will list them as a supplement in a forthcoming article.

How the Handicapped Make Love

In the area of sexuality, many handicapped persons seem to be ahead of the game.

Earl G. Pepmiller, M.Ed.

Earl G. Pepmiller is an Instructor and Assistant Professor, Occupational Therapy Curriculum, at the University of Missouri.

Recently at a dinner party two couples stood out. Sally is married to Joe, who is paralyzed from the midchest to his toes. Mary and Tom were the center of attention, because people at the party had not been socially acquainted before with a woman who has only one leg.

There was light conversation, good food and drink. Sex became a topic of conversation, as so often happens. Sally insisted that she was deeply in love with Joe, who she said, "satisfies my every need."

It was obvious Tom and Mary were very much at ease with each other. As the evening wore on, these two couples revealed much about their sex lives that plainly astonished everyone.

It is easy to see that a great many individuals in our society are not at ease with the handicapped; moreover, many people who would like to become emotionally involved with someone who happens to be handicapped have a fear of doing so. There is little to be concerned about if the relationship is built on honest trust and genuine, mutual attraction.

Coming to Grips With A Handicap

We are all handicapped in some sense. Each of us is deficient in one respect or another. The handicapped, however, have suffered traumatic insults to the body, which has resulted in the amputation or paralysis of a part of the body. People who have had an injury or disease—which created these dysfunctions—are very much aware of how people respond to them. They are also aware of the sensory loss of a large segment of their body.

Not all handicapped people have come to grips with their loss and adapted to a different body image. Those who have not made this adjustment are generally not interested in sex or sensual stimulation in general. They are not the group of people whom this article is discussing.

Those among the handicapped who *have* made the necessary adjustments to their condition and have accepted themselves as they are, know and understand the loss of sensation and its effect on their lives. These people feel good enough about themselves to be interested in, and enjoy, a wide range of sensuous experiences, which helps them feel as they suspect "normal" people feel.

One important part of this sensuous experience is sex. Many of the handicapped people we are talking about lead a much fuller sex life than the average person because of a couple of factors. First, the mere knowledge that they are alive and able to enjoy the company of others exhilarates them. Second, the fact that their physical dysfunction prevents them from receiving stimulus in the usual manner has driven them to learn adaptive ways of giving their sex partners pleasure and creating freedom from fear in the sex act.

Amputees

Amputees are perhaps more like the "normal" population than any other handicapped people. The rest of their body feels and responds to stimuli in the same way as does the "normal" person's. Interestingly, the loss of a limb, or a part of a limb, seems to give them added sexual appeal, as far as their sex partners are concerned. A woman with a short leg stump is regarded by many men as having an extra erogenous area, with some men considering a stump to be as exciting to fondle as a breast. Many women report that their sex partners give unusual attention to this feature of their anatomy. It is also apparent that some women are very attracted to men who have lost part of their leg, although the loss of an arm does not hold the same attraction for male or female. The loss of any limb, however, does tend to get much attention from the sexual partner. Such things as choosing a position during presexual arousal to insure that the handicapped partner is comfortable and is able to respond to caresses then becomes a heightening point in the arousal for both partners. The same conditions are exhibited during intercourse and afterplay.

Amputees have the same problems, difficulties and concerns as the general public in regard to pregnancy, frigidity, impotence and premature ejaculation. Yet, among handicapped people, partners seem to have a higher level of awareness of these matters than the population at large.

Paralysis With Sensory Loss

The paraplegic or quadriplegic female responds to sexual arousal, and participates in sexual activities, in an entirely different manner from the female amputee. She has lost not only the use of all or part of her body, but also lost any sensation in that area. She cannot, therefore, respond to nor feel caresses in that part of the body, and so, to that extent, does not participate in the "normal" sexual responses and activities.

The paralyzed woman may be capable of becoming pregnant and bearing a healthy child. Her menstrual cycle may remain unchanged, but she cannot feel changes in her condition or tell the location of her legs in space without looking.

Her responses in intercourse are those of a passive partner as far as her lower extremities are concerned. She is unable to control the muscles in and around the vagina, and also unable to lift her legs and place them around her sex partner or to move her hips during intercourse. However, this lack of physical motion or sensation does not deter the well-adjusted handicapped woman from enjoying sexual acts.

She is extremely sensitive to caresses and oral stimulation of the face, neck, and breast. She develops verbal and nonverbal responses to this stimulation, which further arouse her sex partner. During this period of penetration she is extremely aware of his breathing, the aroma of sexual discharge, and his heartbeat—and she lets him know how all these things make her feel. Her partner's sexual enjoyment is her goal, and if he is fully satisfied, she does appear to experience a release of emotion that approaches the responses of orgasm in a non-paralyzed woman.

The paralyzed woman may develop a technique of bringing her partner to orgasm orally as well as participation in the usual erogenous-zone caresses generally associated with preintercourse and postintercourse activities. Usually more willing to enter into and develop alternate methods of sexual satisfaction than her "normal" sister, she has learned that no sexual position or response is abnormal or kinky. Her absorption in the sensual feelings of her partner makes her feel useful and gives her a sense of satisfaction—both of which provide the gratification that is necessary for everybody's life.

In spite of the apparent full paralysis of his lower body, the paralyzed male may have sustained one of the various types of incomplete spinal-cord lesions. He may have one of several types of penile responses. He may have a totally flaccid penis, which will never become erect. Or he may have a penile response which creates an erection that is not relieved by discharge. Or, again, he may have a psychogenic erection that responds to caressses or sensuous thoughts.

Some paralyzed men have a normal sperm count and are capable of ejaculating and of fathering a child. On the other hand, others do not have an adequate sperm count and never have a discharge.

The paralyzed male usually participates in the sort of intercourse in which his sexual partner is totally responsible for inducing an erection in him. She must become the active one, since he cannot lift his legs or buttocks or move the muscles in and around his penis. The position such a couple most often uses for intercourse is with the female astride the male, who lies on his back.

The man may be capable of one of two types of erection, in which the length of intercourse is determined by something other than the onset of ejaculation. If he has the capacity for flexogenic erection, activated by stimulating another part of the body, no amount of sexual stimulation, whether mental or physical, will cause him to lose that erection. Only upon the deactivation of the reflex that created it is it lost, and so the length of time that the penis is erect becomes highly unpredictable. Some women are extremely grateful for this condition, since it can result in long bouts of intercourse. However, this type of erection also presents some problems. It can happen that once the female has achieved orgasm, the male may still be erect. And, instead of long sessions of intercourse, an erection may suddenly vanish, and it may not be possible to start another reflex action. Thus, since flexogenic erections are quite erratic, couples must often enjoy sexual acts when and if the opportunities arise rather than be able to plan them.

The man who has flexogenic responses requires a partner who can find the reflexive motion that will create the erection and also release it. This takes understanding and cooperation on the part of both partners. Many women report a degree of anxiety and guilt associated with creating an extended erection.

With the other erection that permits penetration—the psychogenic erection—the length of time of the erection is controlled by the ejaculation or the emotions. The penis cannot feel the folds of the vagina nor the sensation and friction that would normally be caused by the penetration and withdrawal during the thrusting of the sexual partner. As a result, the discharge is brought on by other means. Usually, however, once achieved, erection is maintained longer than in the intact male who feels the friction, warmth and muscle tone of his partner's vagina.

The third condition that has been mentioned is that of a flaccid penis, which can never achieve erection, even when the bladder is relatively full. In such an instance, sex by penetration can only be achieved with some kind of penile prosthesis. Many sexual partners with this condition still like to position themselves on top, with the flaccid penis laying pointed towards the navel. In this position, the penis provides a type of appendage upon which the clitoris can be massaged to create the sensation of pleasure leading to orgasm.

As with the paralyzed female, the male does not feel the friction of intercourse or the spasm of ejaculation. However, he is made aware of the sex act through his partner's verbal and nonverbal behavior—her breathing, the eye contact and, of course, the odors that accompany sexual excitement.

During intercourse he is able to see his sex partner, and to caress her face, neck and breasts. (Many paralyzed men report that the female breast moving in rhythm with their lover's thrusting is extremely exciting to them.) He is able to observe the changes in the nipple as his partner approaches her orgasm. All of these things tend to create a sexual situation in which both partners reach satisfaction. From her position on top, the female is able to observe and feel the satisfaction her partner derives from her response.

Like the female paralyzed individual, therefore, the male is able to provide his partner with an enjoyable sexual experience. He may develop caressing techniques that meet the needs of the female who does not choose to massage herself on a flaccid penis. Often the female will develop fellatio techniques she can practice on the male even if he cannot feel her oral stimulation; the primary reason for this appears to be that the male gets real satisfaction from seeing and hearing his partner enjoying the oral caressing of his penis. The woman's enjoyment is in part due to her awareness of the male's enjoyment and the verbal feedback she gets from him during their act (she is of course aware that he will not discharge during the oral stimulation), in addition to the sensation she receives in itself.

The male may develop techniques of cunnilingus that will permit his sexual partner to experience release of tension without any penile contact. Among handicapped people in general, oral sex is far more accepted than among other people.

Hemiplegia

Another group of paralyzed persons are hemiplegics, who are afflicted with paralysis of the right or left half of the body. Not unlike those with paralysis of the lower extremities, they suffer loss of sensation and motion on their affected side, but can participate fully in sexual activities with understanding partners.

Since the primary sex organs are situated at a point that is equivalent to the midline of the body, hemiplegics retain partial sensation and function in them. Usually the penis is capable of erection and ejaculation. On the unaffected side the breast will respond and the vagina be capable of excitement.

To consider the subject of sex and the handicapped is to realize that all people are sexual beings. Just because certain persons have a handicap that limits or reduces motion and feeling does not mean that they cannot, and do not, enjoy sex. The attainment of sexual satisfaction and the enjoyment of a long, healthy marriage is just as possible among the handicapped as it is among "normal" people. All that is required between two people is concern and openness. And in this respect many handicapped people seem to be ahead of the game. They already know what most of us spend most of our lives trying to learn—that sex has to do with concern for your partner's feelings and needs. When these needs are met, sex is just the way it is supposed to be: beautiful.

Enjoying Sex During Pregnancy

Here are the facts you need to know to make sex safe and pleasurable all through your pregnancy.

Linda Reich Rosen, Ph.D.

Linda Reich Rosen has a Ph.D. in experimental psychology.

"Sexual intercourse during pregnancy, as a general rule, robs the child in the uterus, reduces its constitutional vigor, and predisposes it to various debilitating diseases; and, in some instances, quite extinguishes the flame of life." (1866)

That's how our ancestors felt about sex during pregnancy, and, indeed, about sex at almost any time in the life cycle. Sex was thought to be physically and morally dangerous, to be avoided whenever possible and certainly inappropriate for the pregnant woman. Even the most passionate of nineteenth-century lovers must have thought twice before risking "debilitating disease" in their unborn children, and so it seems likely that for many couples, sexual intercourse stopped soon after a pregnancy was confirmed.

Concern about the sex life of the pregnant woman is certainly not limited to the United States—almost all societies have developed rules for how often, when and in what positions the pregnant woman can have sex. These rules vary tremendously. For example, among many Polynesian tribes sex is permitted right up to the day of delivery. In contrast, a number of African and Indian tribes insist that sex stop as soon as a woman has missed a single menstrual period. Between these extremes are cultures that permit sex until the expectant mother can feel her child moving, or until the last months or weeks of pregnancy.

In the past, the sex life of the pregnant woman was regulated more by superstition than by scientific fact. Fortunately, the "sexual revolution" of the last decades has cleared up many myths and misconceptions about sex during pregnancy, a growing body of research has shown that sex can be a safe and pleasurable experience for the pregnant woman. But old attitudes and fears do not die easily, and most pregnant women—and their mates—still have serious questions about sex during pregnancy.

"Is Sex Safe During Pregnancy?"

Probably the single greatest concern of expectant parents is whether having sex can harm their unborn child. Although we've come a long way from fears of "debilitating disease," we do tend to worry that sex during pregnancy might lead to either a miscarriage or a premature birth.

Let's talk about miscarriage first. To date, there is no evidence that sexual intercourse can cause a miscarriage in a normal pregnancy. After all, if it were possible to terminate an unwanted pregnancy simply by having sex, there would be no need for the millions of abortions performed around the world every year. So, for the vast majority of women, even the most vigorous sexual activities present no threat to pregnancy. There is, however, one exception: women who have already had two or more miscarriages are often advised not to have sex, particularly during the first three months of pregnancy. This advice is a way of "playing it safe"—since we cannot be completely sure that sex is safe for such women, it seems better to abstain than to take any chances.

What about sex during the last months of pregnancy? Here, doctors have also played it safe by asking women to abstain, especially in the last six weeks before delivery. This advice is based on several concerns: that orgasm may start the delivery process too soon, that intercourse can cause infection, and that sex will be uncomfortable at this time.

Actually, most women have little to fear from sex during the last weeks of pregnancy. For instance, sexual intercourse positions can be varied so that the woman is comfortable. Many couples find that while the "man on top" position places too much weight on the woman, the "side-by-side" position is both comfortable and satisfying. Others switch from intercourse to oral or manual stimulation.

There may be increased possibility of infection during the last month of pregnancy, according to a recent study published in the *New England Journal of Medicine,* but with the discovery of antibiotic drugs, infections can be medically controlled at any time during pregnancy, even when the infection occurs just before delivery.

5. CONTINUING SEXUAL CONCERNS

Can orgasm cause a baby to be born too soon? Orgasm certainly does produce strong contractions, but these may actually be helpful in strengthening the muscles used during delivery. No one knows precisely what starts the delivery process, but there is evidence that in some women, orgasm can trigger delivery very late in pregnancy. In fact, certain cultures believe that orgasm is a good way to start labor for a woman whose time has come, and also advise intercourse when a birth is overdue. Remember, it is orgasm, and not intercourse, that seems to start delivery for some women. (Masturbation, which usually produces an orgasm more intense than that of intercourse, should be avoided by women who have a history of premature delivery.)

With a few exceptions, sex can be a safe and healthy part of pregnancy. Of course, the exceptions are important, and difficult pregnancies may require special rules. When there is any sign of trouble—for example, pain or bleeding—it is better to "play it safe" and avoid sex. But for the majority of women who have normal pregnancies, there are no medical reasons to give up the intimacy and pleasure of sex.

"Will I Be Sexually Attractive?"

Many women worry about their attractiveness during pregnancy, and no wonder—the sex symbols of our culture are slim and flat-bellied, a very different "look" from the rounded shape of the pregnant woman. Although we have all heard of men who are especially "turned on" by pregnant women, we tend to think of this as the exception rather than the rule. For example, Masters and Johnson found that many pregnant women blamed their physical appearance for their husbands' lack of interest. When the husbands were questioned, however, very few were troubled by their wives' appearance; instead, they expressed concern that sex might harm the unborn child. Every couple will react differently to changes in the pregnant woman's body, but it seems likely that a loving husband who is pleased and excited by his wife's pregnancy will continue to find her attractive.

"Will I Feel Sexy?"

That depends. If you enjoyed an active sex life before pregnancy, you probably won't suddenly lose interest as soon as your test comes back positive. On the other hand, if sex was never that much fun, then pregnancy may be a convenient and acceptable excuse to abstain.

No matter how sexy you were, however, your pregnancy means that you will have to contend with some important physical and emotional changes: your growing body, your feelings about being a mother, and so on. The later the stage of pregnancy, the more intense these changes will be. And, in general, the later the stage of pregnancy, the less sex there will be. Research from a number of countries—the United States, France, Germany, Denmark, Thailand—all shows the same basic pattern: as the pregnancy progresses, a greater number of couples limit or stop their sexual activity. By the ninth month, a majority of couples abstain. When asked why they stop having sex, pregnant women report a variety of reasons: fear of harming the baby, physical discomfort or awkwardness, fatique or simply lack of sexual interest.

Not every pregnant woman loses interest in sex. In fact, some women find that pregnancy actually heightens their sexual desire and pleasure. It is not uncommon for a woman to experience her first orgasm, or her first multiple orgasm, during pregnancy. This is probably due, in part, to the physical changes that take place in the pelvic area. Masters and Johnson have shown that sexual response is related to the flow of blood into and out of the genitals, and, since pregnancy increases genital blood supply, it is not surprising that some women feel very sexy during pregnancy.

"Is Sex Important During Pregnancy?"

Let's return, for a moment, to the nineteenth century. In a society where sex was valued as a means of producing children, sexuality had little or no importance for the pregnant woman. Indeed, the nineteenth-century woman was not supposed to feel sexy at any time. But things have changed, and nowadays we accept the idea that sex is important to women, with one exception—the pregnant woman. Until very recently, her sexuality was ignored by most medical scientists, and even so prominent a sex researcher as Alfred Kinsey had nothing to say about sex during pregnancy.

The fact is that sex can be an important and satisfying part of the pregnancy experience. With a few medical exceptions, most women are capable of enjoying sex right through pregnancy. Sex is important as a way of giving and receiving love, of sharing intimacy, and of feeling attractive and desirable. And the need to be loved, intimate and attractive does not disappear simply because a woman becomes pregnant.

Of course, not every woman feels sexy during pregnancy. Every woman is unique, and, in the same way, each pregnancy is a unique and special experience. It would be wrong to insist that the pregnant woman "should" or "should not" be sexually active. Instead, we should be sure that each pregnant woman is provided with medical information about the safety of sex, and then give her the freedom to make her own sexual choices.

Prison Sexology: Two Personal Accounts of Masturbation, Homosexuality, and Rape

John Money and Carol Bohmer

John Money, PhD, is Professor of Medical Psychology and Associate Professor of Pediatrics at The Johns Hopkins University School of Medicine and The Johns Hopkins Hospital. Carol Bohmer, LLM, PhD, is an Assistant Professor of Medical Psychology at the same institutions.

Abstract

As revealed in two unrelated reports from prison inmates, the sexology of all-male incarceration subdivides into masturbation, wet dreams, and partner contacts in association with heterosexual imagery; consenting homosexual pairing with one partner exclusively androphilic and the other bisexual; coercive partnerships with one partner dominating but not injuring the other and neither being permanently and exclusively androphilic; and violent homosexual rape. The long-term outcomes of prison celibacy and homosexuality are not presently known. These outcomes need to be studied systematically and prospectively. It is suggested that it is illogical to punish sex offenders by incarcerating them in an environment that breeds sex offending. A system of conjugal visitation, and possibly of family living in prison, is a more logical, and probably the only alternative to institutionalized sexual brutality and homosexuality that is situationally evoked.

Over the last decade a few reports of sexuality, including assaults in prison, have filtered out through prison walls. However, these reports have gone largely unnoticed in the sex-research community and elsewhere. In a society which feels greatly dedicated to punishment, and also greatly ambivalent toward prisons and the treatment of prison inmates, it is perilously easy to ignore evidence of the rape of society's outcasts.

This paper describes what goes on in prisons in the words of two prisoners. The first report was sent to us, unsolicited, by a nonviolent sex offender sentenced on an ephebophilic charge and incarcerated in the Illinois prison system. It has been abridged and edited to produce a more parsimonious and clearer presentation. The second request is a condensation of a tape-recorded interview, given at our request, by a young man known to us since age ten as heterosexual. He served time for an offence of assault while drinking. We have no evidence to suggest that the authenticity of either report need be questioned.

Preparation of the article was partially supported by U.S. Public Health Service Grants #HD00325 and HD07111. This paper would have been multiauthored, with the names of the two informants included, except that self-disclosure might endanger their welfare and recivilizanization.

Illinois Report

The philosophy of the federal courts, which also applies to Illinois, recently has been that men are sent to prison *as* punishment not *for* punishment. Since growing awareness has retired such practices as the "bat" at Huntsville, Texas, the "grave-digger's shovel" in the Arkansas Prison system, and the "hole" in practically all prisons, the "*as* punishment" has come to mean taking a few years of a productive man's life and depriving him of his ordinary mode of sexual expression. However, for the homosexual placed among hundreds or thousands of randy, sexually deprived men, there is very little deprivation of his ordinary mode of sexual expression. And, although the system officially penalizes sex acts in prison, the administration would probably lose a case in court in a state where consenting adults are allowed to perform homosexual acts. But since the administration has such a poor record of prosecuting even the most flagrant rape case, the consensual cases ordinarily result in no more than a short time in segregation, which allows the homosexual to practice his art with even greater impunity and appreciation.

The rape of an inmate in prison is of little consequence to the administration because they have far greater things to worry about, such as rape of guards, suicides, and killing of inmates and guards. Among prisoners, the lowest man in the pecking order is the man who gives up his body with a minimum of fight. Those who willingly and cheerfully submit are viewed as sissies, sometimes to be protected, often to be considered suitable cell partners. But the "punk," the unwilling guy who lets himself get raped without a fight, is scorned.

To my certain knowledge two officers were raped in the two years I spent in "Jailtown." Naturally none of the perpetrators was found, for to be forced to testify to a man-to-man rape requires more fortitude than in the case of male-female rape. During an uprising in Jailtown, one officer was repeatedly raped as he was held hostage. He is still on duty at Jailtown, is respected, and is known as a man "not to be crossed" because he does not take his troubles to the captain or the warden. The other was a young, rather handsome guard. He reported only his wallet stolen, but the possessor of that wallet told me of the rape of the guard by four inmates. He's not around any more.

Some cellmates have become more intimate than comrades, through the very real necessity for sexual expression. The relationship is not an aggressive-passive one, but rather a mutuality of taking care of one another's needs. This only comes after months, and sometimes years, of celling together because it takes that long before a trust can be established. I remember one case in Jailtown where a man who appeared to be quite young was celling with a much older man. I was invited to share a small cake that the kitchen had baked for the younger man's birthday. It had one candle, a ordinary storm-emergency candle. The younger man, to my amazement, told me he was celebrating his 40th birthday and his 20th anniversary of celling with the same man. Both had wives on the outside, and both took care of each other—the older being dominant and taking his enjoyment in anal intercourse and giving oral copulation to the younger. Later, the younger was paroled and the team broken up, but the one who remained told me he was getting up to where it didn't matter much any more, after his 70th birthday and 35 years behind the walls.

In that same house was "Ruby," the queen, black, crippled, and an expert in judo and way-out sex. He/she reputedly had made 40 customers in one day. Hormones had created a little something in the chest, enough for the cellhouse sergeant to make him/her wear a shirt at all times, even when in the cell.

In another cellhouse there was "Betty Lou," a most regal type who chose her lovers nightly. All other cells were required to be without drapes or obstructions in the front, but Betty Lou's had been decorated with blue pile lining intended for jackets. Betty Lou entertained her lovers in privacy.

On one occasion, "Controlled Segregation" took in "Bill,"[1] one of the most flagrant street queens ever to cruise the streets of Chicago. Surely the judge had hoped he/she would drop dead or perhaps make an unlawful flight, for even after conviction there was no bond required. Bill was instructed simply to surrender to the warden on a certain day. Bill did surrender, in a blue and white antebellum dress with hoops, parasol, and beaded purse—not through the back door, like most prisoners who come from Chicago by bus, but in a limousine at the front door. Immediately, Bill went into "East Segregation," a place where contact with the prison population is theoretically at a minimum. Bill did not go to be fingerprinted, to be issued clothes, nor to be physically examined. All that was done in Bill's cell. It was comical to watch Bill, for in seconds the shirttail was tied up and toilet paper mammaries appeared. This drives guards up a wall, for there is no effective rule against swishing while you walk, or making toilet paper mammary glands, or smiling provocatively at a well-hung prisoner.

Along the gallery where I currently live, a Queens' Row has recently been established. Here the obvious homosexuals of the prison are concentrated, and as a result the overtly macho inmates gather outside their cells, flex their muscles, adjust their crotches, and generally put on as good a show as the drag queens themselves.

Jailtown has a unit known as "Safekeeping." Like so much in the Illinois Prison System, the title is grossly misleading. Safekeeping in Jailtown is very possibly the most dangerous housing a man can have in that prison. Many younger inmates choose to be locked up 24 hours a day on the 4th floor of Safekeeping rather than take their chances among the general prison population. In this cellhouse, the cellhouse clerk had a very fine hustle in which he would sell the young inmates as they came through the doors, for a fee from $25 to $100. One inmate I came to know was sold for $250. He had just come from the county jail for murder. Aged 17, he had a slight build, long blond hair, blue eyes, and a little girl posterior. The inmate who bought him told him that he must either choose to submit or die. He did later douse himself with inflammables and became a torch, having written letters to the media which never got through the mail room. He didn't know that the mail room keeps a record of each letter coming or going from an inmate and, if there is a suicide, his letters of the last days are stopped.

If a young inmate who is sold can afford it, he can usually buy his way out by reimbursing his master. The administration is aware of such transactions and knows details—dates, prices paid, the clerks involved. Noth-

[1]Also known as "Trigger" and "Trig."

ing is done. Who cares what murderers, rapists and armed robbers do to each other?

A lot of kidding, serious joking, and innuendo is bantered back and forth in prison about masturbation. I quite frankly tell my cellmates not to be disturbed if the bed shakes at night. Now that my present cellmate knows at night when I freely masturbate, the bed above also often starts shaking. It is true that some of the fantasy has become shopworn, and some of it has become perverted to an almost unrecognizable degree, but I have an advantage over my prison mates of having had 40 years of a very good sex life before I came to prison. They must vicariously depend on clippings from magazines, whereas my experiences are as vivid as the day they happened, in some instances almost 30 years ago.

Governors and legislatures can build walls, correctional authorities can write prohibitions until the world is indeed as level as a Kansas wheatfield, but they cannot stop men from thinking about sex, from masturbating, nor from other avenues of sexual expression.

Maryland Report

I was in jail for eighteen months. At first I never tried to indulge in sex with another male companion. As time went on without a woman, I had desires for a woman, and sometimes I used to watch a man shower and, you know, I actually got a hard-on. It wasn't like I intentionally done it. It was just that I would be in the shower and soaping myself down and my penis would get, you know, harder and harder, and I'd just start masturbating right there . . . Some guys, I don't know how to describe them, you know, have more a woman's physique, perfect curves from the back, big cheeks. I don't know . . . it's like a flash when you see it, and all. You can see a guy with a figure and it's just that quick . . . But if you're in the shower masturbating, a guy next to you would actually get offended because he'd think you'd be jerking off on him, and that's where your trouble lies.

The first time that I had sex with a male companion was in the cell block. I knew it was this guy's first time in there and he wasn't aware of all that was going on. So I was teaching him how to play cards, and so forth. And this one particular night he was sitting on my bunk. He was, like, rubbing his feet against mine, you know, and automatically, you know, I got a hard-on. I just asked him—I had to do it in a bully type way and heavy voice and, you know, whatever. And the guy just gave in and the next thing I know we indulged in sex, anal sex . . . Being gay must have been in him because I didn't have that much resistance, though I guess it never showed . . . I did it again a couple of times, but not with the same guy . . . I always just picture him as a woman, a woman I wanted to be with when I was on the outside. Even when I masturbated I actually put myself into seeing, you know, my penis emptying into a woman . . . It happened the same in wet dreams. It seemed as though I was right there, you know, happening in real life. I could actually feel it, you know, my penis inside of a woman's womb, you know, the steady thrusting. And immediately afterwards I'd wake up, looking for the female companion.

It never really affected me, thinking of myself as homosexual, because when I left the institution, you know, I left all my habits that I had there. I didn't have to indulge in that no more, and so I just left it all behind me. I don't even know how to say it, you know. I was just in there for a certain length of time and my sex desire just crept up so great. I just had to be around sex.

I've seen a lot of sex in prison. I used to be a tier runner, giving out mail and, at night, I would take around a window key so the guys could open their windows, and I'd actually see guys, you know, humping, one in the position of a woman.

There was a homosexual guy who used to bring down these magazines of different, you know, men having sex with men, and she—you know, I call him she—would say: Look at all my sisters . . . I actually seen him get married. Up in the chapel, you know. I mean it's unbelievable, you know, to get the okay from the warden. Some of them homosexuals in there, you couldn't tell that they wasn't a woman. The only difference would be that they would be hanging, their penis would be hanging.

I never had a guy force sex on me, maybe because of the way I carry myself, you know. I guess, if a guy would come to me personally, I'd probably get in a fight. But some guys, nice looking guys—and say he has some features of a woman—of course some other guy will come up to him and approach him.

Like this guy in "Receiving," waiting for transfer to "Population;" damn nice looking guy, you know, and it don't take too much for it to get around. There's this other guy in Population doing life and twenty years. He's got nothing to lose. He comes over and he say, hey, when you get here in Population, I want you to be my wife. It was as though he was talking to a woman. The guy was shocked, but the other one took the weakness of it right there. What is supposed to be done, if a guy come approach you in that type of manner inside an institution like that, is to automatically defend yourself right then and there. If not, the guy's going to figure you're weak and start to get you into trouble. And he's telling the next inmate he'll fight over this man—he's mine.

I've never seen a guard get into that, but I have seen the guards set someone up. I mean, by setting up, unlocking an inmate's cell door and letting other inmates go in and, actually what you call rape. Maybe the inmate gave the guard a hard way to go and he gets back at him . . . I seen it three times. And, you know, it's unbelievable. You can hear the guy hollering and no one doing nothing about it. And you know it could have been you as well as anybody else. You figure, you know, five guys up in the cell—six feet, two-hundred and some pounds, you know. It's a hell of an experience, knowing they rape like that . . . Inmates call them ass-hole bandits. Like a guy likes to drink, you know, or a guy likes to take drugs.

I know two cases of a guy getting raped and committing suicide. Let me say it's one hell of an experience, if you actually hear a guy being raped, and nothing can be done about it, and then the guy kills himself . . . one was transferred to a cell next to me. I could actually hear the guy crying. Then he hung himself.

The other guy slashed his wrists. The guy told me he was going to kill his self. And I was saying: Is it really worth it? You know, he was telling me how they would hold him down, and he was going to kill his self because he couldn't let his girlfriend know that . . . And then the guy was dead. He'd sliced his wrists. This guy was only about 17-years-old. The other one was maybe 19 or 20.

Discussion

These two reports, obtained totally independently of one another, disclose an all-male prison sexology of remarkable similarity in two separate institutions. There may be some diffusion of prison sexology from one institution to another within the United States, but it is also likely that the sexual stimulus conditions of all-male prison life anywhere produce similar sexual reactions. These reactions create a community sexologically characterized by overt masturbation and by homosexual couplings that may be either consensual, coercive or assaultive (rape).

Overt acts of masturbation and homosexual coupling are accompanied by covert imagery. The stories of both inmates indicate that their masturbation fantasies in prison were composed of imagery evoked from past, preprison memories. For the Illinois inmate, these would have been fantasies of eroticism with adolescent youths. For the Maryland inmate, they were fantasies of eroticism and copulation with same-age girl friends.

In the latter inmate's case, heterosexual imagery was so prepotent that it could be released not only in a masturbation fantasy or sleep dream, but also in a shower room by the actual visual stimulation of some males who, in rear view, had female-reminiscent curves. A touch stimulus could produce a similar reaction with sufficient strength to result in coercive sex with anal penetration as a substitute for vaginal penetration. In this case, coercive sex with a male as a substitute for a woman did not progress to assaultive rape of a man. In prison argot it required a special kind of inmate, an "ass-hole bandit," to rape a male. The masturbation imagery of such an inmate needs to be ascertained. They may have been sadistic with their women on the outside, but such men are not known in prison as having had an outside history as rapists.

In the absence of continuous sexological follow-up of long-term prisoners, it is not possible to decide the degree to which long incarceration might chronically change the imagery of a man's erotosexual arousal. The Maryland inmate was quite sure that, when he left the institution, he left his inmate habits there. His subsequent sexual life on the outside attests to the accuracy of that claim. Thus his case appears to be a genuine one of situation-specific homosexuality which is, more precisely, situation-specific bisexuality. He left prison relatively untraumatized.

In both reports, the ultimate in being traumatized was to be gang-raped and then to commit suicide. One suspects that the personal outcome of being sexually traumatized is, in its severity, a function of the personal intensity of the traumatic insult. This is a hypothesis that remains to be tested. Not only the intensity, but the longevity of the insult may be implicated. There are anecdotes, but no systematic body of knowledge, regarding the outcome of either consensual, coercive, or violent long-term homosexual encounters in prison.

These two personal accounts of prison sexology demonstrate the illogic of punishing sex offenders by incarcerating them in an environment that breeds sex offending, and of punishing violent offenders in an environment of assault which includes violent rape, some of it augmented by the guards. Further evidence of this illogic and further support of the accuracy of these two independent reports is to be found in Davis (1975), Buffum (1972), and Scacco (1975). The information in these references, and in Gagnon and William (1968) and Kirkham (1971) is in accord with that put on record by journalists who have investigated prison sexuality.

It is not sufficient to recommend more guards or new buildings (Davis, 1969; Scacco, 1975). The problem of sexuality in prison can be solved only if it is attacked where it begins, namely in sex segregation as a condition of punishment. A system of conjugal visitation, or even family living in prison, is a potential first answer to institutionalized sexual brutality and situational homosexuality (Davis, 1975).

Two reports do not, of course, constitute a sufficient source of data. But within the prison system, there is granitic resistance against sex research.

It is possible that the recent spate of suits by raped prisoners against prison authorities will do much to improve the sexual climate in prison (Burke, 1979). The prospect of heavy financial loss for failing to protect an inmate against sexual assault may force the authorities to reexamine their organization and staffing methods in ways that no negative publicity seems to have been able to do.

References

Buffum, P. *Homosexuality in prisons.* Washington, D.C.: United States Government Printing Office, 1972.

Burke, T. A prolonged sentence of fear. *Research in action of Virginia Commonwealth University, Richmond, Virginia, 4*, 3-6, 1979.

Davis, A.J. Sexual assaults in the Philadelphia prison system. In D.M. Peterson and C.W. Thomas, Eds. *Corrections—problems and prospects.* Englewood Cliffs, N.J.: Prentice-Hall, 1975.

Gagnon, J.H., & Simon, W.S. The social meaning of prison homosexuality. *Federal Probation,* 32, *1,*1968.

Hopper, C.B. Conjugal visiting. In N. Johnston and L.D. Savitz, Eds. *Justice and corrections.* Somerset, N.J.: John Wiley and Sons, Inc. 1978.

Kirkham, G.L. Homosexuality in prison. In J.M. Henslin (Ed.) *Studies in the sociology of sex.* New York: Appleton-Century-Crofts, 1971.

Scacco, A. *Rape in prison.* Springfield, Ill: Charles C. Thomas, 1975.

Additional Source Material

Davis, A. *Report on sexual assaults in the Philadelphia prison system and sheriff's vans.* Submitted to The Honorable Alexander F. Barbieri, conducted jointly by the Philadelphia District Attorney's Office and Police Department. Typescript, 1969.

Sagarin, E. Prison homosexuality and its effect on post-prison sexual behavior. *Psychiatry,* 1976, *39,* 245-257.

Smykla, J.O. *Cocorrections—a case study of a coed federal prison.* Washington, D.C.: University Press of America, 1979.

Weiss, C. *Terror in the prisons—homosexual rape and why society condones it.* New York, Bobbs-Merrill, 1974.

Accepted for publication June 1, 1980

WHO'S WRITING AND WRITTEN ABOUT

INDEX

Credits/Acknowledgments

Cover design by Charles Vitelli.
Cover photo: EPA Documerica

1. Sexuality and Society
Facing overview—EPA Documerica.

2. Sexual Biology and Health
Facing overview—EPA Documerica. 71—Katrina Taylor, *Psychology Today,* May 1979.

3. Interpersonal Relationships
Facing overview—WHO photos by L. Almsay/E. Mandelmann.

4. Sexuality Through the Life Cycle.
Facing overview—EPA Documerica.

5. Continuing Sexual Concerns
Facing overview—EPA Documerica.

WE WANT YOUR ADVICE

ANNUAL EDITIONS: HUMAN SEXUALITY 81/82

Article Rating Form

Here is an opportunity for you to have direct input into the next revision of this reader. We would like you to rate each of the 60 articles listed below, using the following scale:

1. **Excellent: should definitely be retained**
2. **Above average: should probably be retained**
3. **Below average: should probably be deleted**
4. **Poor: should definitely be deleted**

Your ratings will play a vital part in the next revision. So please mail this prepaid form to us just as soon as you complete it.
Thanks for your help!

Rating	Article
	1. The Pleasure Bond: Reversing the Antisex Ethic
	2. Alfred C. Kinsey: Man and Method
	3. Learning to Talk About Sex
	4. Sexuality and College Life
	5. What Every Woman Should Know About Men
	6. What You Tell Your Child About Sex (Without Saying a Word)
	7. Putting Sex Education Back in the Home
	8. Reflections of a Dean Who Is "Into Sex"
	9. The Battle over Sex Education in New Jersey
	10. The Most Erotic Part of Your Body
	11. All About the Clitoris
	12. Women's Most Versatile Muscle: The PC
	13. The Male Orgasm: What Every Girl Should Know
	14. Four Teens Tell Why They're Young, Single and Pregnant
	15. Warning: Cigarette Smoking Is Dangerous to Reproductive Health
	16. Genetic Counseling: Is It Right for You?
	17. Barren Couples
	18. Fetal Adoption
	19. Margaret Sanger: Rebel in the Midst of Victorian Moralism
	20. Rating the Latest Methods of Birth Control
	21. Birth Control Methods
	22. 80% of Americans Believe Abortion Should Be Legal; 70% Approve Medical Funding
	23. The Abortion Repeaters
	24. The Husband's Rights in Abortion
	25. The Friendship Bond
	26. Intimacy Is Not for Amateurs
	27. Sex: The 3 Levels of Intimacy
	28. The Games Teen-Agers Play
	29. First Night Disasters
	30. The Semantics of Sex
	31. What Is Your Sexual Responsibility to Your Mate?
	32. New Rules in the Mating Game
	33. The Perfect Lover
	34. The 10 Common Sexual Spoilers for Women and How to Outgrow Them
	35. Kids and Sex
	36. Adolescent Sexuality
	37. A Major Problem for Minors
	38. A Pregnant Pause in the Sexual Revolution
	39. Marital Relations: How Much? How Often?
	40. Is There Sex After Marriage?
	41. Infidelity and Extramarital Relations Are Not the Same Thing
	42. Swingers: The Conservative Hedonists
	43. Is There Sex After 40?
	44. The New Sex Education and the Aging
	45. Sexual Wisdom for the Later Years
	46. STDs
	47. Menopause Counseling: Coping with Realities and Myths
	48. Sex and Heart Disease
	49. Sexual Harassment on the Job: Why More and More Women Are Fighting Back
	50. Incest: Sexual Abuse Begins at Home
	51. Rape: "Not a Sex Act—A Violent Crime"
	52. The Marital Rape Exemption
	53. Erotica and Pornography: A Clear and Present Difference
	54. Bisexuality: A Choice Not an Echo?
	55. The Meaning of Gay
	56. A Message to Parents of Gays
	57. Love, Sex and Marriage for People Who Have Disabilities
	58. How the Handicapped Make Love
	59. Enjoying Sex During Pregnancy
	60. Prison Sexology: Two Personal Accounts of Masturbation, Homosexuality, and Rape

(continued on back)

About you

Name ______________________ Date ______________________

Address ____

City ______________________ State ____________ Zip ________

Telephone ______________________

1. What do you think of the Annual Editions concept?

2. Have you read any articles lately that you think should be included in the next edition?

3. Which articles do you feel should be replaced in the next edition? Why?

4. In what other areas would you like to see an Annual Edition? Why?

NO POSTAGE NECESSARY IF MAILED IN THE UNITED STATES

HUMAN SEXUALITY 81/82

BUSINESS REPLY MAIL

First Class Permit No. 84 Guilford, Ct.

Postage Will Be Paid by Addressee

Attention: Annual Editions Service
The Dushkin Publishing Group, Inc.
Sluice Dock
Guilford, Connecticut 06437